MANGA
IMPACT!

# MANGA IMPACT!

## THE WORLD OF JAPANESE ANIMATION

EDITED BY
CARLO CHATRIAN
& GRAZIA PAGANELLI

Φ

# CAST OF CHARACTERS

## 008 - 257

**E S S A Y S**

FROM DOGA EIGA TO ANIME...*260*
CHILDISH PERCEPTIONS...*261*
ERO-ANIME: MANGA COMES ALIVE...*262*
TAKING A LONGER AND DEEPER LOOK...*263*
HOW MANGA REINVENTED COMICS...*264*
COMPUTER GRAPHICS OR BACK TO GOOD OLD
ORIGINALS?...*265*
'THE POWER OF GOD'...*266*
ENTERTAINMENT FOR THE EYES...*267*
MANN(G)A FROM HEAVEN...*268*
RELATIONSHIPS BETWEEN MANGA AND ANIME...*269*
VIDEOGAMES + MANGA + ANIME...*270*
TROUBLES OF THE HUMAN HEART...*271*
FROM CITY TO NETWORK...*272*

GLOSSARY...*274*
INDEX OF TITLES...*279*
INDEX OF DIRECTORS
& CREATORS...*285*
INDEX OF CHARACTERS...*289*
BIBLIOGRAPHY...*292*

# PREFACE

People often have the impression that the world of *JAPANESE ANIMATION* is just too vast to be contained in a single book: there are too many stories, too many films, too many circumstances, too many authors and too many market implications to be able to explain all the interlocking connections between them. It is a universe in constant ferment, forever changing and evolving, while nevertheless remaining linked to a tradition intrinsic to Japanese culture and perspective. ● This ever-changing world has, on occasion, hurtled into our Western lives like a meteorite, blasting an impact crater into our collective consciousness — and it has immediately been stigmatized by the press and the cultural world. Yet the language and culture underlying

the manga phenomenon have left their mark on generations now. The genre has evolved from a homely, innocuous and peaceful vision to a more complex outlook in which the blows of the real world are not hidden or, worse, suppressed altogether. It has taken some time to digest this change of perspective, and its implications are not wholly clear even today. ● This book is an adventurous and fascinating exploration of the complexities of the world of manga, but it does not aim to be either a comprehensive study or a scholarly treatise. As with any journey, it sometimes diverges from its own broadly mapped path to follow the personal interests of the book's editors and authors — over twenty in number, from five different countries. Seeking, perhaps, to replicate the heterogeneity of the subject,

we have preferred to retain individual nuances in writing, style and culture, so that each text becomes the account of an experience, the chronicle of an impact — the author's personal encounter with a character, film or director. ● The model we have used here is that of a *GRAND PORTRAIT GALLERY*, one designed on the comic-book form, in honour of Japanese animation's "big brother". Quoted in the title and immediately denied in the subtitle, manga permeates this book. Here and there it surfaces, sometimes in the form of an entry dedicated to a particular artist whom we consider truly fundamental within the universe of animation, sometimes in the form of a more structured reflection, before submerging once more into the body of that phenomenon – animation – that has at different times plundered manga, denied it, exalted it or fostered it. ● *MANGA IMPACT!* should be read, then, as a fascinating journey that starts with the current scene in Japanese animation as a whole and then embarks on illuminating detours into its history, not only by way of its most famous protagonists but also by means of surprising discoveries and unpredictable propositions. Rejecting hierarchies, we have opted for the most democratic

structure possible: over 300 entries of approximately the same length. Into this flood of names and images are interleaved essays in which authors have expanded on particular subjects. These thirteen texts are more substantial reflections that augment the information in individual entries, highlighting connections between past and present, underlining the significance of certain themes, or focusing on social, cultural or economic aspects of Japanese animation. ● The entries are organized in *ALPHABETICAL ORDER*, thus avoiding the pitfalls of categories. Remaining true to our subject, we have followed the convention of writing Japanese names

with the surname first (e.g. Miyazaki Hayao rather than Hayao Miyazaki), but using the Latin alphabet. We have sought to reproduce in the images the richness of a universe not only inhabited by characters drawn using both pencil and computer graphics but also populated by three-dimensional models in vinyl and die-cast metal – images whose contours seem to move, forming a poster-picture of amazing iconographic power. ● *THE APPENDICES* place at the reader's disposal the means of navigating this vast subject, providing keys to disentangle the labyrinth of possible routes on the journey. The glossary and the indices of titles, characters and creators cannot be considered exhaustive, but they will help to clarify for the reader the technical aspects of animation and will assist in the mastering of the terminology, an important first step towards becoming familiar with the complex world to which this book is dedicated.

*CARLO CHATRIAN & GRAZIA PAGANELLI*

# .HACK

VIDEOGAME

TV SERIES

.HACK//SIGN, 2002 ● DIR: MASHIMO KOICHI ●
SCR: ITO KAZUNORI ET AL ●
MUS: KAJIURA YUKI ● PRD: BANDAI VISUAL,
BEE TRAIN, YOMIKO ADVERTISING ●
TV SERIES ● EPS: 26

RIGHT: SCENES FROM .HACK//LEGEND OF
THE TWILIGHT, THE SECOND .HACK SERIES
FROM 2003, FEATURING KUNISAKI SHUGO
AND HIS SISTER RENA

.hack is an unusual franchise. At first, it is not particularly surprising that the same title is used for television series, DVDs, videogames and comics. However the original .hack (pronounced 'dot hack') project, started in 2002 and still growing, has little to do with the classical spin-off. The various components were created in parallel, like tiles belonging to the same mosaic. The manga, the first .hack animated TV series – .hack//Sign – and the games all offer different views of the same reality, or, to be more exact, the same 'virtuality'. All the pieces of this ambitious puzzle come together in a vast Matrix-like world of online role-playing, a cross between the virtual world of Second Life and multiplayer gaming of World of Warcraft. Two further TV series, four OAVs and a feature film followed. ● By incorporating some of the typical features of videogames in the anime series, the .hack saga invents new relationships with space and time, as well as rewriting the normal rules of conduct, to create a peculiar area of fiction, like an Alice's Adventures in Wonderland for the digital age. As well as exploring many contemporary issues such as flight into imaginary worlds, life as a game and reliance on technology, .hack also owes its appeal to the care lavished on the development of its characters. They are rarely what they seem and when gaming, the adventures of their alter egos take centre stage. Beneath the guise of a heroic fantasy epic, .hack is about an identity crisis, which underlines the modernity of this project. ● E.H.

SCENES FROM GENIUS PARTY (2007),
GENIUS PARTY BEYOND (2008) AND MIND
GAME (2004, DIR. YUASA MASAAKI)

# 4°C

STUDIO

In 1986, a group of former Studio Ghibli workers got together to launch production company Studio 4°C, taking their name from the temperature at which water is most dense but still fluid. Among them was Eiko Tanaka, a line producer on Miyazaki's My Neighbour Totoro and Kiki's Delivery Service. She is now an internationally respected producer and one of the few women to lead an anime studio. In 1995 the studio's first proprietary project, two segments of Katsuhiro Otomo's three-part film Memories, created a sensation using computer technology to support artistic excellence. Studio 4°C works on advertisements, music videos, computer games and more, but is especially noted for both theatrical features and short films. Morimoto Koji's 1996 music video Extra was just the beginning of a spectacular stream of short films from individual directors working at the studio. The seven-part video anthology Genius Party (2007) was followed in 2008 by a further five-part anthology, Genius Party Beyond, featuring gifted directors such as Maeda Mahiro and Nakazawa Kazuto. The studio also works on feature films such as Mind Game (2004), directed by Yuasa Masaaki, and Tekkonkinkreet (2006), directed by Michael Arias. Its innovative approach allows individual creativity to blossom and gives directors a chance to make their mark in the crowded anime industry. ● H.M.

SEE ALSO: ANIMATRIX; KURO & SHIRO; MEMORIES; MIND GAME; MORIMOTO KOJI

# ABE NORIYUKI

DIRECTOR

Born in 1961, Abe Noriyuki graduated from the Department of Science and Engineering at Waseda University, Tokyo. He majored in Architecture, a discipline that provided him with a real-world perspective on the design of fictional places and objects in anime. Ironically, many of his most famous works have been ficticious stories that oblige him to break the real world's laws of physics. ● He joined Studio Pierrot in 1986, and gained his first visible credit two years later on the television series *Norakuro-kun* (1987) as a storyboarder and episode director. He soon moved on to direct episodes alongside storyboarding and left Pierrot in 1990 to become a freelance director. His first credit as executive director was for *Yu Yu Hakusho* (*Yu Yu Hakusho: Ghost Files*, 1992), a television series that went on to win the coveted *Animage* Grand Prix award in 1993 and 1994. At that time, the award was an acknowledgement of quality bestowed by fans with a long memory of precedents and high-points in the anime business. ● Abe is primarily a television director but he often — whether through luck, talent or design — seems to select projects whose success on television is so great that a movie spin-off inevitably follows, thereby securing him feature credits on his resume. The popularity of *Yu Yu Hakusho* led him to an impregnable position as executive director, producing many TV animation series based on popular manga publications in *Shonen Jump* as well as other popular comic magazines. His standing today is largely based on his directorship of another popular television show the long-running *Bleach* (2004). ● J.Cl.

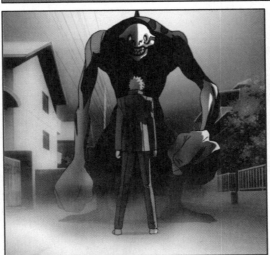

RIGHT: SCENES FROM THE TV SERIES BLEACH (2004, DIR. ABE NORIYUKI, 53 EPS), FEATURING THE CHARACTERS KUROSAKI ICHIGO AND RUKIA

SEE ALSO: GTO; KUROSAKI ICHIGO

---

# ADACHI MITSURU

MANGAKA

Adachi Mitsuru (born in 1951 in Isezaki) is not easily pigeonholed, but if one had to choose the most perceptive and acute interpreter of adolescence in manga, his name would surely be on the short-list. In artistic terms, his manga are neither definitively *shonen* nor *shojo*, but his love stories sit well in all kinds of teenage magazine. Adachi's position in the world of manga is unique, as demonstrated by the millions of copies he has sold and the incessant interest taken in his work by cinema and television, not only as anime but also as live-action dramas. ● The young Adachi moved from the provinces to Tokyo in order to fulfil his dream of becoming a mangaka. Tezuka Osamu's historic magazine *Com* was the first to publish his stories, and he quickly rose through the ranks, doing duty as an assistant to other artists until his editor partnered him with scriptwriter Yamasaki Juzo. They began focusing on sport, particularly baseball, and age-old teenage stories in which a competitive spirit invariably leads straight to a student championship. ● Having won his creative independence with *Nine* (1978), Adachi — still flying the flag for baseball — turned out one manga after another, from *Hiatari Ryoko* (1980), *Miyuki* (1980), the long-running masterpiece *Touch* (1981) and the wonderful *Rough* (1987) right up to the recent *Cross Game* (2005). While television continues to court him for films and anime, Adachi pursues his chosen path, creating well-integrated combinations of competitive spirit and high-school comedy, his romanticism speaks to a young generation thirsty for attention and credibility among adults. Not only well drawn with an unmistakable graphic style (Adachi's trademark sticking-out ears), his characters are unique and well-rounded, while impeccable dialogue gives them a distinct voice, imbued with a poetic sense of wonder at the everyday. ● M.A.R.

SEE ALSO: UESUGI TATSUYA & KAZUYA

# AKAHORI SATORU

 MANGAKA

Akahori Satoru (born in 1965) is the creator of numerous anime series and manga. He could be described as the artist most capable of bringing the fantasies and obsessions of fans to the screen. ● Unlike the introspective figure of the typical *otaku*, Akahori is in constant contact with the world and has even created a series bearing his own name (*Akahori Gedou Hour Rabuge*, 2005). An impassioned spokesman for the genre rather than an egomaniac, Akahori delights in a technicolour universe without rules. His characters are invariably strange or sarcastic with twisted smiles, his heroes are little more than heroic, his women sexy and provocative. These figures inhabit the magical worlds of witches and wizards, and show off elaborate moves and countermoves in combat. He is equally adept in science fiction as in fantasy. ● It would be hard to tire of his work, even the less well-made examples, but it is easier to appreciate his *otaku* thinking in mischievous series such as *Saber Marionette J* (1996) – arguably his most famous title – which is a favourite among manga and anime fans. The prolific Akahori has also created hits such as *Sorceror Hunters* (1996, dir. Mashimo Koichi, Habara Nobuyoshi), *Moucolle Knights* (2000, dir. Aoki Yasunaga et al), *Lime Wars* (2003, dir. Suzuki Akira) and *Mouse* (2003, dir. Yamaguchi Yorifusa). He has written for many more hit shows, including *Dragon Ball Z* (1989, dir. Okazaki Minoru et al), *Galaxy Fraulein Yuna* (1995, dir. Yamaguchi Yoshinobu), *Princess Army* (1992, dir. Sekita Osamu) and *Sakura Wars* (2000, dir. Ishiyama Takaaki, Nakamura Ryutaro). He created the manga based on the resoundingly successful TV series *Magical Shopping Arcade Abenobashi*, made by the Gainax studio. ● M.A.R.

RIGHT & BELOW: SCENES FROM THE SERIES *SABER MARIONETTE J* (1996, DIR. SHIMODA MASAMI, MASUNARI KOJI, TV SERIES, 25 EPS), FEATURING SABER MARIONETTES LIME AND CHERRY

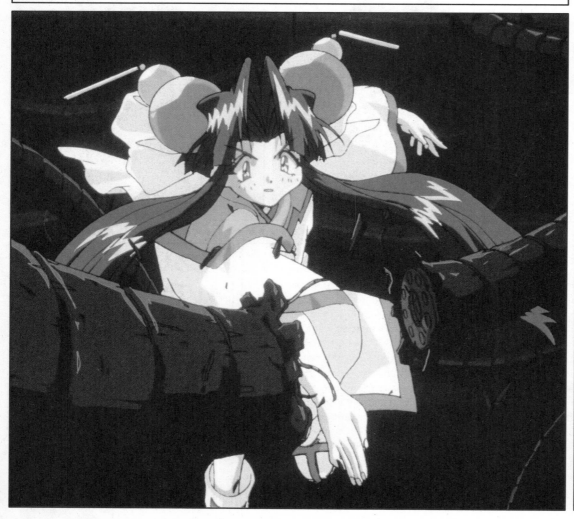

SEE ALSO: AMANO AI; GAINAX; GOKU

# AKIRA

First published in 1982, the same year that Ridley Scott's *Blade Runner* was released in cinemas, Otomo Katsuhiro's manga established the cyberpunk genre in Japan and has been highly influential in its precise draughtsmanship and cinematic style. The anti-hero Tetsuo (or 'Man of iron') encapsulates the three great obsessions of science-fiction cinema: mutation, destruction and the cult of power. However, it is the child Akira who brings an enigmatic quality to the story: it is he who punctuates the narrative with his presence or absence, appearing in Tetsuo's hallucinations and forcing him to become aware of his supernatural powers. These elements are interwoven with the themes of stolen childhood and futuristic political ideas that reflect the author's personality (Otomo was deeply affected by the Sixties protest movement) and the climate of the Cold War. ● The film version was notable for its prodigious use of manpower and resources (it required a combined effort by thirty studios). Though undoubtedly a visual feast (many of Japan's best animators were involved in the project) and pioneering in its use of computer graphics and lip-synching, the film suffers from limitations in the script and some of the characters are only sketchily delineated. Nevertheless, the Esper fight scenes, the *bosozoku*-style car races led by Kaneda and the majestic sight of skyscrapers crumbling to the ground mark it as a classic. In Japan, *Akira* is a cult work and a benchmark for anime producers, setting a technical standard that has never been surpassed. Abroad, it headed the peaceful invasion of anime and manga in the late eighties and early Nineties and remains one of the high points of modern Japanese cinema. ● S.G.

RIGHT & ABOVE: BOSOZOKU GANG-MEMBER KANEDA AND HIS MODIFIED BIKE IN SCENES FROM THE 1988 FILM *AKIRA*

AKIRA ● 1988 ● DIR: OTOMO KATSUHIRO ● SCR: OTOMO KATSUHIRO, HASHIMOTO IZO ● DES: MIZUTANI TOSHIHARU ● ANI: NAKAMURA TAKASHI ●
MUS: YAMASHIRO GEINOH ● PRD: AKIRA COMMITTEE – MASH ROOM ● FILM ● DUR: 124 MINS

# AKIYAMA KATSUHITO

**DIRECTOR**

SEE ALSO: KNIGHT SABERS

Associated with many projects from studio AIC, Akiyama Katsuhito has a preference for fantasy and science-fiction subjects, many deriving from already successful manga, such as *Bastard!!* (1992). Drawing on the skills of such brilliant animators as Onda Naoyuki and Okuda Atsushi, who can turn even the most lacklustre story into something special, Akiyama's works have carved a particular niche in the anime world. His films intended for the video market, *Gall Force* (1986), *Bubblegum Crisis* (1987) and *Sol Bianca* (1990), for example, often feature the winning combination of combat-hardened, yet seductive, female heroines. ● However, his cult OAV film *Ai no Kusabi* (*The Space Between,* 1994) is aimed at *yaoi* (a genre focusing on the homosexual encounters of beautiful young men) enthusiasts. It is an interpretation of the final episode of Yoshihara Rieko's novel of the same name, published in instalments in the magazine *June* between December 1986 and June 1987. In a science-fiction megalopolis dominated by the supercomputer Jupiter, love is forgotten and experienced only as an act of domination between the Blondies and the mongrels of the ghetto (young slaves forced to satisfy the sexual whims of the wealthy). The future envisioned by Akiyama is a glacial world of bright lights and shadows that wrap themselves, shroud-like, around the bodies of the protagonists. Redemption can come only through revolution, by overthrowing the 'Blondies' and regaining love through sacrifice. ● M.A.R.

# AMANO AI

**CHARACTER**

BELOW: AMANO AI, THE BEAUTIFUL STAR OF THE 1992 SERIES VIDEO GIRL AI. SOFT-FOCUS BACKGROUNDS EMPHASISE THE ROMANTIC CONTEXT AND KEEP ATTENTION FIXED ON THE LEADING CHARACTERS

At times sweet and kind, at others uninhibited and hot-tempered, the sixteen-year-old Amano Ai is the secret dream of every *otaku*. As her name implies, Ai is an artificial being designed for love (as well as being an abbreviation of artificial intelligence, *Ai* means love in Japanese). ● A further manifestation of the magical girlfriend genre of *Urusei Yatsura* (1981), Ai appears from a videotape played by sensitive and innocent Moteuchi Yota, the male protagonist of the story. Seemingly doomed to eternal disappointment in love – his friends nickname him 'Motenai Yoda' ('without women') – Yota attempts to cheer himself up with a 'video girl' hired from the mysterious Gokuraku (Paradise) rental shop. However a glitch in Yota's VCR causes Ai's playback to be defective, and, unlike other video girls, she emerges 'faulty' with the capacity to feel human emotions. Like Sadako in Nakata Hideo's horror film *Ringu* (2002), young Ai enters the human dimension through the television screen and turns life upside down for the incredulous viewers. Here begins a comedy of errors, setting up a love triangle between the poor wimp, the unattainable dream-girl and the girl next door. ● Conceived by mangaka Katsura Masakazu in 1990, the *Video Girl Ai* OAV series stands out for its delicate storytelling and soft, detailed drawing. The plot was perfectly suited to an animated series for the home video market, which was duly made in 1992 by the Shueisha publishing company and the animation studio I-G Tatsunoko (soon to be renamed Production I.G.). The original character designs were adapted by Goto Takayuki to suit the angular style popular in the Nineties, while director Nishikubo Mizuho used his experience of working on the *Miyuki* (1983) anime series to get the best out of the clichés of romantic comedy. ● L.D.C.

DENEI SHOJO AI ● VIDEO GIRL AI ● 1992 ● DIR: NISHIKUBO MIZUHO ● SCR: AKAHORI SATORU ● DES & ANI: GOTO TAKAYUKI ● MUS: SHIMIZU NOBOYUKI ●
PRD: I.G., JUMP VIDEO, TATSUNOKO ● VIDEO SERIES ● EPS: 6

# AMANO MASAMICHI

COMPOSER

Amano Masamichi (born in 1957 in Akita) studied at the prestigious Kunitachi College of Music, Japan's national university for composers and performers. After graduation, he found growing fame as the composer of pieces for the flute, but also became one of the first musicians in Japan to master the newly available Fairlight CMI, an early polyphonic digital-sampling synthesizer. It was this instrument, rather than his more traditional flute works, that brought him to the attention of the anime world. His most widely heard composition is arguably the soundtrack to the infamous erotic-horror series *Urotsukidoji* (*Legend of the Overfiend*, 1987), distinguished in particular by a mournful, recurring piano melody entirely at odds with the grotesque imagery. ● Later works for higher-budget anime and live-action movies saw Amano able to dispense with the synthesizer in favour of his conventional roots, conducting a full orchestra – often the Warsaw Philharmonic, with whom he seems to enjoy a special relationship. Several of his classical compositions have origins in his populist work on soundtracks, as demonstrated by his orchestral symphonies *GR* (based on the soundtrack of *Giant Robo*, 1991), *SIN* (*Sin: The Movie*, 2000), *PN* (*Princess Nine*, 1998) and *Stratos 4* (2003). Amano is notable for a singular dedication to his craft, regardless of the status or budget of the work for which he is composing. His stirring score for *Super Atragon* (1995), for example, remains the most enduring aspect of an otherwise forgotten video anime. In recent years, he has become better known outside the anime world as the composer of the soundtrack to the live-action film *Battle Royale* (2000). ● J.Cl.

LEFT: THE GIRL PILOTS OF *STRATOS 4* (2003, DIR. MORI TAKESHI, 13 EPS), SCORED BY AMANO

SEE ALSO: HISAISHI JOE; KANNO YOKO; KAWAI KENJI; KIKUCHI SHUNSUKE; SAKAMOTO RYUICHI

# AMANO YOSHITAKA

CHARACTER DESIGNER

An illustrator who is active on several fronts, Amano Yoshitaka was born in 1952 in Shizuoka. Fascinated by western comic books and their Japanese counterparts, he took up drawing in his teens. The American comic book illustrator Neal Adams was a strong influence on him, as were the Sixties and pop artists such as Peter Max. At just fifteen he joined the animation department at Tatsunoko Production. He ultimately advanced to character designer and was involved with such cult series as *Gatchaman* (*Battle of the Planets*, 1972) and *Time Bokan* (1975). His collaboration with Tatsunoko lasted until 1982 when, seeking new challenges, he decided to become freelance. ● In 1983, he illustrated the first of Hideyuki Kikuchi's *Vampire Hunter D* novels with drawings characterized by his highly refined style and androgynous figures. Experimentation and elegance are also distinctive features of his work. ● Amano published his first collection of drawings in 1984 and worked on Oshii Mamoru's visionary film *Tenshi no Tamago* (*Angel's Egg*, 1985), bringing him closer to the world of animation. He has since achieved international fame as the designer of *Final Fantasy* videogames. In 1997, he settled in New York, which he described as 'a fantastic city, where I can dream freely' and mounted his solo exhibition *Think Like Amano*. In 1998, he collaborated with the musician David Newman and the Los Angeles Philharmonic to create the animated musical *One Thousand and One Nights*. ● D.D.G.

LEFT: PUBLICITY IMAGE FOR THE TV SERIES *TIME BOKAN* (1975, DIR: SASAGAWA HIROSHI, 61 EPS)

SEE ALSO: FINAL FANTASY; GATCHAMAN; TATSUNOKO; TIME BOKAN; VAMPIRE HUNTER D

# ANIMATRIX

*The Animatrix* can be described as a homage to the Wachowski brothers, who have in turn acknowledged the debt that their *Matrix* films owe to anime. This anthology of nine animated short films expands the world of *The Matrix*, using a series of parallel stories to bridge the gap between *The Matrix* and its sequel *The Matrix Reloaded*. The project attracted some of the biggest names and most important studios in anime, evolving from Square's 3D photo-realistic first episode, the *Final Flight of the Osiris*, to the mixed animation of Maeda's two episodes (which form a prequel to the overarching storyline, combining historic reportage and video clips to retrace the origins of the empire of the robots and the end of the human race). Both segments directed by Watanabe have a consciously American gloss, they both begin halfway through the timeline but have completely different outcomes. In *Kid's Story*, the hero realizes that the power of the Matrix is an illusion and frees himself from its grip. *Detective Story* sees the main character point the gun towards the camera with a mocking smile, echoing Spike Spiegel in *Cowboy Bebop* (1998). Kawajiri's *chanbara* episode is pure virtuoso action, typical of his style. In *World Record*, Koike repeats the race metaphor from his earlier short *The Running Man* (1987) to indicate the limitations of human physicality. The subjectivity and fish-eye shots of *Beyond* by Morimoto bring a surreal visionary approach to a story about children who venture into a haunted house, while in Peter Chung's *Matriculated*, the psychedelic new-age setting makes it the most cryptic and bizarre episode of the series. ● S.G.

SCENES FROM *THE ANIMATRIX*, 2003, BASED ON THE WORLD CREATED BY THE WACHOWSKI BROTHERS IN THEIR *MATRIX* TRILOGY ● TOP: IMAGE FROM *MATRICULATED* DIRECTED BY PETER CHUNG ● ABOVE: TWO IMAGES FROM KAWAJIRI YOSHIAKI'S SEGMENT *PROGRAM*

THE ANIMATRIX ● 2003 ● DIR: PETER CHUNG, ANDY JONES, KAWAJIRI YOSHIAKI, KOIKE TAKESHI, MAEDA MAHIRO, MORIMOTO KOJI, WATANABE SHINICHIRO ● SCR: MORIMOTO KOJI, WATANABE SHINICHIRO, KAWAJIRI YOSHIAKI, LARRY & ANDY WACHOWSKI ● DES: HASHIMOTO SHINJI, MINOWA YUKATA ● MUS: DON DAVIS ● PRD: MADHOUSE, SQUARE USA, STUDIO 4°C, VILLAGE ROADSHOW PICTURES ● FILM ● DUR: 89 MINS

Anne Shirley, the little orphan girl created by the Canadian author Lucy M. Montgomery, is the poetic soul of animation for children. With her carrot-red braids, her face smothered in freckles and her unforgettable grey eyes lost in contemplation, this little girl is a veritable force of nature. Carefree and kind-hearted, and vain but insecure, Anne is a breath of fresh air that blows not only into Avonlea – the small town where she finds refuge – but also into an entire tradition of television series based on famous children's novels. ● Created by Takahata Isao, *Anne of Green Gables* is an extraordinary coming-of-age story, pervaded by a contagious sense of irony and unfailing melodrama (a quality that has imbued much of his work since *Heidi*, 1974). Great effort has been made with the realistic design of the characters – conceived by Kondo Yoshifumi – as well as generating a fantastic wealth of supporting detail in terms of set design and backgrounds (the result of meticulous attention to historical records and exhaustive research). An expressive soundtrack, solemn yet light and airy, plays its part in the success of the whole, coloured with the distinctive daydream-like tones that mark the original opening and closing theme music. Miyazaki Hayao's contribution to the layout is a defining feature, essential to the rigorous framing of each shot, the travelling shots and the formal enrichment of every scene. ● The series traces Anne's story as she grows up on Green Gables, the farm belonging to Marilla and Matthew Cuthbert, from the little orphan lost in her own fairy-tale world to an earnest and practical young woman ready to face life and reality, supported by the close ties and friendships she makes in Avonlea. ● M.A.R.

# ANNE OF GREEN GABLES

ABOVE: ANNE SHIRLEY, THE YOUNG HEROINE OF THE 1979 TV SERIES ANNE OF GREEN GABLES

AKAGE NO ANN ● ANNE OF GREEN GABLES ● 1979 ● DIR: TAKAHATA ISAO ● SCR: CHIBA SHIGEKI, ISOMURA AIKO, TAKAHAIA ISAO ●
DES & ANI: KONDO YOSHIFUMI ● MUS: MORI KURODO ● PRD: FUJI TV, NIPPON ANIMATION ● TV SERIES ● EPS: 50

# ANNO HIDEAKI

DIRECTOR

Anno Hideaki was born in 1960 in Yamaguchi. Fresh from his education at the Osaka University of the Arts, he took part in several projects during the Eighties, first under the label of Daicon Film and then Studio Gainax. His production debut was the popular video series *Top o Nerae! Gunbuster* (*Gunbuster*, 1988) and his narrative technique showed interesting signs of individuality in *The Secret of Blue Water* (1990). However it was with the television series *Neon Genesis Evangelion* (1995) that his reputation was cemented. ● Excessively creative, Anno abandoned Studio Gainax halfway through the series *Kareshi Kanojo no Jijyo* (*His and Her Circumstances*, 1998) to explore live-action cinema. His first outing was *Love & Pop* (1998), an adaptation of a novel by Murakami Ryu, followed by *Shiki-Jitsu* (a collaboration with director Iwai Shunji) in 2000, and an adaptation of Nagai Go's *Cutey Honey* in 2004. All three feature an experimentalism that clashes somewhat with the formal rigour of the best sequences of *Evangelion*. An eccentric and contradictory personality – he unites Zen suspense with a video-clip aesthetic – and an *otaku* who sets his sights on the cinema of the masters, Anno has demonstrated that it is possible to express poetry and style within the framework of the television series and free it from the bonds of the genre. In 2006, he established Studio Khara. His recent works include *Evangelion 1.0: You Are (Not) Alone* (2007) and *Evangelion 2.0: You Can (Not) Advance* (2009), both studio Khara productions. ● S.G.

SCENES FROM *NEON GENESIS EVANGELION* (1995, DIR. ANNO HIDEAKI, 26 EPS) ● ABOVE: KATSURAGI MISATO, FIELD COMMANDER FOR THE TEENAGE PILOTS OF EVANGELION AND SURROGATE 'BIG SISTER' TO SHINJI ● CENTRE & FAR LEFT: IKARI SHINJI, BOY PILOT OF EVA–01 AND ESTRANGED SON OF ITS CREATOR ● LEFT: THE EVA UNIT IN COMBAT

SEE ALSO: *CUTEY HONEY; DAICON III & IV; EVANGELION; NADIA*

016

# APPLE, SHARON

CHARACTER

Singer Sharon Apple is the a pop-sensation of planet Eden and the Macross universe. However, Apple is not a living being, but a virtual character, a hologram produced by a computer. Her character is reminiscent of Eve from the OAV *Megazone 23* (1985) and Rei Toi, the virtual idol of *Idoru*, William Gibson's 1997 novel set in Tokyo. The main antagonist of the four-episode OAV *Macross Plus*, Apple is the virtual personality of Myung Fang Lone, an unsuccessful singer endowed with a unique voice. While Myung's artistic personality begins to be erased by Sharon Apple's success, she also finds herself divided between her love for the reckless pilot Isamu Dyson and her deep affection for Dyson's nemesis Guld Bowman. This emotional triangle is unwittingly solved by Sharon Apple when, without Myung's knowledge, an illegal chip is implanted in Sharon's artificial intelligence, allowing her to have feelings and free will. At her first concert on Earth, Sharon Apple tries to dominate the computer that controls the Macross universe. Myung, with the help of her two suitors, defeats Apple, successfully preventing the world from falling prey to a deranged artificial intelligence, and makes her choice in love. ● Produced in 1994, *Macross Plus* is one of the first anime to make conspicious use of computer graphics and the first *Macross* sequel in which director Watanabe Shinichiro and his loyal character designer Kawamoto Toshihiro were involved. The story is set in 2040, twenty-eight years after the events and the battles between humans and Zentradi played out in the original *Macross*. Sharon Apple, a new character, introduces a musical element that has carved out its own independent success, thanks to the musical themes of Watanabe's loyal colleague Kanno Yoko. ● F.L.

RIGHT & BELOW: SHARON APPLE IN THE OAV *MACROSS PLUS* (1994) – THE DEVIOUS DIGITAL DIVA CAN SHAPE-SHIFT WITHOUT INPUT FROM HER PROGRAMMERS

*MACROSS PLUS* ● *1994* ● DIR: KAWAMORI SHOJI, WATANABE SHINICHIRO ● SCR: NOBUMOTO KEIKO ● DES: MASAYUKI ● ANI: AONO ATSUSHI ET AL ● MUS: KANNO YUKO ● PRD: BANDAI VISUAL, BIGWEST, STUDIO NUE, TRIANGLE STAFF ● VIDEO SERIES ● EPS: 4

# ARAKI SHINGO

CHARACTER DESIGN

Line drawing reigns supreme. This is the key to understanding Araki Shingo, a veteran of cartoons who prefers not to write original stories, but brings those of others to life. Born in 1939 in Nagoya, he burst on to the scene in the mid-Sixties at Mushi Production, presided over by Tezuka Osamu, and subsequently became an industry personality in his own right. ● It is easy to divide up the designer's career; the periods that have made him a superstar among anime fans are easily identifiable, and his greatest creative moments are surely his collaborations with the designer Himeno Michi. His handsome young men and unforgettable female figures are so influential they can be described as the Adams and Eves of anime. Araki's origins are in the typical rough line style of the Sixties, as illustrated by series such as *Tomorrow's Joe* (1970). These adaptations remained faithful to the original manga design, while *Babil II* (1973) saw figures with even greater energy. However it is in the main characters of series such as *UFO Robot Grendizer Raids* (1975), *Majokko Meg-chan* (*Megu, The Little Witch*, 1974) and the exciting *Cutey Honey* (1973) that a certain aesthetic taste prevails. Araki's animation becomes synonymous with modelling, and the characters are almost engraved on the paper or celluloid. In the hugely popular *The Rose of Versailles* (1979) his characters developed into icons, far removed from everyday gender identities. ● M.A.R.

ABOVE: ANDRÉ FROM *THE ROSE OF VERSAILLES* (1979, DIR. DEZAKI OSAMU, NAGAHAMA TADAO, 40 EPS)

SEE ALSO: CUTEY HONEY; HIMENO MICHI; JARJAYES, OSCAR FRANÇOIS DE; MUSHI; UFO ROBOT GRENDIZER RAIDS

# ARALE

CHARACTER

Before the famous series *Dragon Ball* (1986), manga artist Toriyama Akira's other great creation was *Dr Slump*. The doctor, a bungling scientist as his nickname implies, lives in Penguin Village (a world that Toriyama effectively revisits in many of his works), where humans, dinosaurs and anthropomorphic animals coexist peacefully in an idealized world combining fantasy with parody and satire. ● Enter Arale, a robot girl created by Slump and endowed with invincible strength alongside a disarming innocence and childlike naivety. Toriyama's manga, and the ensuing television series, sets up an entertaining story in which the rigid restrictions of a strictly codified society can be held up to ridicule and the impulses of the human spirit, expressed by the sunny character of Arale, can be appreciated; Arale's infectious good humour always wins over those around her. There is sex in these stories too (the scientist is an inveterate womanizer), although it is always seen through the lens of humour. ● The houses of Penguin Village are shaped like various humorous objects (the café is a giant coffee-pot for example) and the rich cast of supporting characters even has room for parodies of superheroes such as Suppaman ('Sour Salt-Prune Man'), a caricature of Superman. The whole series becomes a satire on technophobic science fiction and the symbol of a society that is learning to laugh at itself. The design of the anime series follows the elements laid down by Toriyama, who loves rounded, striking figures in bright colours that attract a young audience while at the same time reflecting the fantastical, folk-tale element of the story. The second TV series, made without Toriyama's direct involvement, was the first anime to use computer-coloured frames instead of cels. There are also 10 Dr. Slump movies. ● D.D.G.

ARALE IN VARIOUS SERIES OF DR SLUMP ● ABOVE: ARALE, 1981 SERIES ● ABOVE RIGHT: ARALE AND HER FRIEND AKANE, 1981 SERIES ● RIGHT: ARALE

DR SLUMP ● 1981 ● DIR: OKAZAKI MINORU, YAMAUCHI SHIGEYASU ● SCR: TSUJI MASAKI ET AL ● DES & ANI: KOIKE SHINJI ● MUS: WATANABE TAKEO ● PRD: TOEI ANIMATION ● TV SERIES ● EPS: 243

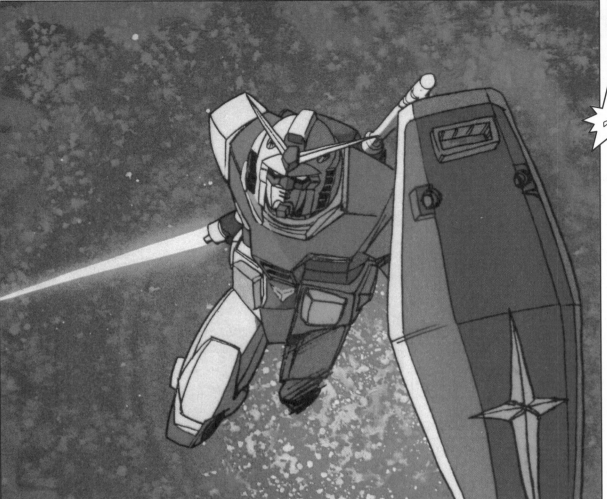

# ARAMAKI SHINJI

DIRECTOR

Some directors took their first steps in anime as designers, while others debuted as screenwriters or performed various roles in the animation process. Before directing *Appleseed* (2004), his first feature film, at the age of forty-four, Aramaki Shinji acquired extensive experience in the very specialized area of mecha design. In the twenty-five years it has taken for directors to populate their works with giant robots and bionic machines, Aramaki has become one of the most sought-after specialists in the field. ● During his long career, he has put his stamp on successes including *Mobile Suit Gundam* (1979), *Megazone 23* (1985) and *Bubblegum Crisis* (1987); worked on *Wolf's Rain* (2003) for director Okamura Teusai and *Fullmetal Alchemist* (2003) for director Mizushima Seiji; contributed to the return of *Astro Boy* (2003); and brought his masterful touch to successful videogames such as *Castlevania: Curse of Darkness* (2005) and *Sonic Unleashed* (2008). However, while these areas of his work are important, it was his move to film directing that confirmed Aramaki's fame beyond the circle of connoisseurs. ● In 2004, he chose to try his hand with a monument of the manga world: *Appleseed*, a post-apocalyptic science-fiction manga in cyberpunk style by Shirow Masamune. The film's production is particularly noteworthy and the technique of cel-shading the digital images is reminiscent of traditional, hand-drawn animation. The film was a great success, and, despite a lukewarm reception from the critics, a sequel subtitled *Ex Machina* was produced by John Woo and released in 2008. In the first *Appleseed*, Aramaki chose to focus on the film's architectural dimensions and graphics, rather than on human aspects of the story, something that he partially redresses in the second outing. ● E.H.

ABOVE: THE GIANT ROBOT GUNDAM FROM *MOBILE SUIT GUNDAM* (1979, DIR. TOMINO YOSHIYUKI, 43 EPS) ● LEFT: THE SWAT TEAM LEADER KNUTE DEUNAN IN *APPLESEED* (2004, DIR. ARAMAKI SHINJI, 107 MINS)

SEE ALSO: ELRIC, EDWARD; GUNDAM; KNIGHT SABERS; KNUTE, DEUNAN

# ARMORED CORE

The massive popularity of the mecha genre can be seen in the success of the wide range of merchandise associated with it. Similarly, the videogame industry has profited from many spin-offs of anime series. There have been countless titles – from shoot 'em ups to combat and strategy games – inspired by the *Mobile Suit Gundam* (1979) saga alone. The tide flows both ways with successful videogames such as *Sakura Taisen* (Sakura Wars, 1996) being later made into animated films. Similarly, in 2006, an OAV based on the highly successful game series *Armored Core* was announced, although the project has not yet borne fruit. Nevertheless, the game has retained a special place in mecha culture, whether played via a console or on a mobile phone. ● Since 1997, the Tokyo-based development studio From Software has released thirteen episodes of this videogame series. In a post-apocalyptic future, where multinationals vie to control the world, the player is entrusted with various missions in the role of warrior-robot pilot. The real stars of the show are the mecha themselves, which are as detailed and complex as any of their anime counterparts. To achieve this level of sophistication, the game's creators employed Kawamori Shoji, a past master in this field, as designer-in-chief of the robots deployed in almost all the *Armored Core* games. ● This is the ultimate experience for the mecha-lover, where players can take control of these incredible machines and experience the same thrill as a flight simulator. *Armored Core* is a demanding game; one can not become a great pilot without hours of practice. However, the secret of the game's success is arguably the facility to customize your robot. Some players spend as much time in the workshop swapping parts and taking care of the robot's appearance as they do actually piloting the machine. ● E.H.

RIGHT & BELOW: SCENES FROM THE 1997 VIDEOGAME *ARMORED CORE* ● TO DATE THERE ARE OVER 20 GAMES ACROSS 5 PLATFORMS, PLUS A SPIN–OFF MANGA

ARMORED CORE ● 1997 ● DIR: KOBUN SHIZUNO ● MUS: HOSHINO KOTA ● PRD: VIEWWORKS

# ARREN

 CHARACTER

Arren, the young prince of Enlad, is at the centre of the feature-length anime *Tales from Earthsea*. He is cursed with a Jekyll-and-Hyde-style split personality, and his 'Hyde' character, Lebannon, must remain a secret to avoid the effects of black magic being used upon him. In the skies above Enlad, a kingdom of scarcity and drought, dragons appear and devour one another. The sages of the kingdom confirm that this is an omen that the world's equilibrium is in danger of being thrown into turmoil. In a fantasy interpretation of the Oedipus story, Arren explodes in a sudden fit of anger and kills his beloved father. In despair, he flees the kingdom and embarks on a journey of purification. A meeting with the loving and protective arch-magician Sparrowhawk, a new father figure, is crucial in enabling him to gain mastery over his dual personality. Meanwhile, the treacherous magician Cob, Lord of the city of Hort, is turning men into his slaves and growing in power. Cob needs to discover the secret name of Arren's other identity in order to obtain the gift of immortality and eliminate Sparrowhawk. ● Freely inspired by the novels *Tehanu* and *The Farthest Shore* by the American fantasy and science-fiction writer Ursula K. Le Guin, *Tales from Earthsea* (2006) is the first work of Miyazaki Goro, son of Hayao, whose involvement in the studio thus far had been limited to planning the theme park of Studio Ghibli. The result is a well-cast film that was very successful in its own country, but it does not achieve the depth and poetry of his father's films. It is curious to note, therefore, that the film should open with a scene of patricide, which is not a feature of the original novels. ● F.L.

*GEDO SENKI ● TALES FROM EARTHSEA ● 2006 ● DIR: MIYAZAKI GORO ● SCR: MIYAZARU GORO, NIWA KEIKO ● DES: TAKESHIGE YOJI ● ANI: INAMURA TAKESHI ● MUS: TERASHIMA TAMIYA ● PRD: SUZUKI TOSHIO ET AL, STUDIO GHIBLI ● FILM ● DUR: 115 MINS*

RIGHT: HEROINE THERRU AND ARREN IN SCENES FROM *TALES FROM EARTHSEA*, 2006 ● BELOW: SCENE FROM THE FILM

---

Born in 1944, Ashida joined Tezuka Osamu's Mushi Production in the Sixties and worked on several television series as an animator. He was promoted to chief animator on *Star Blazers* (1974), the first of a brief, but concentrated, series of successes that would project his name on to the international stage. However, it was not until the mid-Eighties with the double directorial achievement of *Fist of the North Star* (1984) and *Vampire Hunter D* (1985) that his key stylistic features would be established. Ashida's adaptation of *Fist of the North Star*, already a successful manga created by Buronson and Hara Tetsuo, stayed faithful to the original story. Ashida even paid homage to the gothic style of the manga, utilizing dark atmospheres with reddish backdrops against which the main characters were silhouetted as giants, heightening the statuesque quality of the figures already present in the original manga. These features are also found in *Vampire Hunter D*, a film based on the novels of Yoshitaka Amano. Not content with easy effects, Ashida prolongs obsessive atmospheres and plunges the audience into the grip of anxiety. ● In his 1986 feature-length animation of *Fist of the North Star*, Ashida partly abandoned the distinctive features of the television series for a more popular dynamic energy. Curiously, Ashida kept a low profile in the following years, working mainly as a character designer or coordinator on projects like the recent *Batman: Gotham Knight* (2008), partly turning his back on the further developments expected of him. ● D.D.G.

# ASHIDA TOYOO

DIRECTOR

SEE ALSO: HOKUTO NO KEN; VAMPIRE HUNTER D

# ATOM
## ASTRO BOY

CHARACTER

With his disarming Betty Boop-like gaze, his helmet of spiky hair and his jet-powered legs, Tetsuwan Atom or Astro Boy, a cybernetic-age Pinocchio, is an enduring icon of anime. ● Created by Tezuka Osamu in 1951 for the pages of *Shonen Magazine*, Astro Boy is a robotic replica designed as a replacement for Tobio, the son of Doctor Tenma, who died following a car accident. Convinced that the robot child will be unable to take the place of his lost son, Tenma disowns him and sells him to the Hamegg circus. He is eventually rescued by Professor Ochanomizu, who guides him in the development of human emotions and directs his future as a hero. ● Astro Boy was the main character in a live-action television series before becoming the hero of the first anime television series with a steady character and narrative continuity. The series lasted for four seasons (1963–6), and allowed Tezuka to lay down the foundations of the animation technique that would later be established as characteristic of anime. The series also had a defined economic plan: the first episodes were undersold for 750,000 yen, and the creation of a glossary of animated expressions and movements gradually and progressively helped to reduce costs. ● In 1964, the feature-length film *Hero of Space* by Takagi Atsushi brought colour to the world of Astro Boy pictures for the first time. Tezuka recreated the character in a new series of manga between 1975 and 1980 and in 2003, the character returned to a new series of anime, combining artistic renewal with faithfulness to the original. An American-produced film, *Astro Boy*, by David Bowers saw the character rendered in digital animation. ● J.Co.

*SCENES FROM THE 1963 SERIES ASTRO BOY ● TOP: ASTRO BOY AND FAMILY (LEFT TO RIGHT: JETTO, ASTRO'S BROTHER; ASTRO GIRL, HIS SISTER; ASTRO BOY, AND HIS ROBOT MAMA AND PAPA) ● RIGHT: THE CHILD ROBOT ASTRO BOY*

*TETSUWAN ATOM ● ASTRO BOY ● 1963 ● DIR: TEZUKA OSAMU ● SCR: TEZUKA OSAMU ET AL ● DES: TEZUKA OSAMU ● ANI: SAKAMOTO DAISAKU ● MUS: TAKAI TATSUO ● PRD: MUSHI PRODUCTION ● TV SERIES ● EPS: 193*

# AYUHARA KOZUE

CHARACTER

Stubborn, determined and tireless, Ayuhara Kozue follows the path that will lead her to triumph in volleyball with single-minded fervour, her favourite activity since she was able to overcome health problems as a child through sports training. On becoming the team captain at her new school, Fujimi College, she devotes every moment and every thought to the achievement of victory. ● Drawn with big, round eyes, Kozue always wears her hair gathered in a ponytail. Her expression is serious and absorbed, focused and tenacious. Together with her friend Midori, she spends her high-school years honing her athletic skills, making many personal sacrifices in the interest of becoming champion. ● A response to the success of the Japanese women's volleyball team at the 1964 Tokyo Olympics, the tone of the series is dramatic and the mood often tense. Training and volleyball matches are imbued with pathos, as if the future of the team and the sport were at stake in every game. Attack Number One is also characterized by an intense and highly expressive style. The episodes revolve around dramatic visual descriptions of volleyball games where instilling wonder, rather than sustaining realism, is the goal. Games are unpredictable and one smash or swipe can give an improbable trajectory to the ball, which often moves so fast it becomes invisible to opponents. The severity of the central character is reflected in the simplicity of both the design and the animation. Details are, however, given great emphasis, up to the point that volleyball becomes a battle for growth and a metaphor for life. ● G.P.

SCENES FROM THE 1969 SERIES ATTACK NUMBER ONE ● TOP RIGHT: SCHOOL VOLLEYBALL STAR YOSHIMURA ● CENTRE: AYUHARA AND YOSHIMURA BECOME RIVALS ● BOTTOM RIGHT: AYUHARA UNDER ATTACK ● BELOW: A PUBLICITY IMAGE FOR THE SERIES SHOWS AYUHARA AND YOSHIMURA WITH AYUHARA'S COACH AND BOYFRIEND

ATTAKU NO. 1 ● ATTACK NUMBER ONE ● 1969 ● DIR: FUMIO KUROKAWA, OKABE EIJI ● SCR: TSUJI MASAKI ET AL ● DES: IKEDA JUN ● ANI: ARAKI SHINGO ● MUS: WATANABE TAKEO ● PRD: TMS ● TV SERIES ● EPS: 104

# BELLADONNA

Drawing inspiration from French historian Jules Michelet's *La Sorcière* (1862), *The Tragedy of Belladonna* is a erotic reinterpretation of medieval witchcraft legends that also references the sexual revolution of the Seventies. In medieval Europe, abused Jeanne becomes a witch as a reaction against the male-dominated society that imposes customs such as *ius primæ noctis* (a feudal lord's right to the virgins of his estate). The sinuous, sensual body of the witch, framed by long iridescent hair, is central to the story: constantly laid bare, it becomes a decorative feature in a combination of shapes and colours profoundly influenced by pop and psychedelic culture. In a series of increasingly explicit sexual scenes, Belladonna flirts with the devil to the point of being completely possessed. ● *Belladonna* is in fact the last of three full-length Animerama films made by Mushi Production for an adult audience. Defined as an anime romanesque, this film completes the revolutionary undertaking begun by Tezuka Osamu with his earlier *Senya Ichiya Monogatari* (*One Thousand and One Nights*, 1969) and *Cleopatra: Queen of Sex* (1970): to free the animated cartoon from its childish connotations and make it a fully adult form of expression. ● However, the project turned out to be over-ambitious and was not a commercial success. Excessive costs and the cutting of many sequences by distributor Herald ruined the Mushi studio, which was already in the red and had lost the services of Tezuka. Yamamoto Eiichi, who had directed the other two films, concentrated entirely on Fukai Kuni's fascinating illustrations, inspired by early-twentieth-century artists such as Aubrey Beardsley and Egon Schiele. He tried to compensate for the reduced animation by panning the camera over still images, achieving a curious balance between the narrative experimentation of *Ninja Bugeicho* (1967, dir. Oshima Nagisa) and the pop graphics of *Yellow Submarine* (1968). Meanwhile the compelling voice of Tachibana Mayumi, mingles with Sato Masahiko's bewitching soundtrack. ● L.D.C.

TOP & LEFT: SCENES FROM THE 1973 FILM THE TRAGEDY OF BELLADONNA. THE VISUAL EXPERIMENTATION WAS PARTLY THE RESULT OF BUDGET RESTRICTIONS WHICH MADE IT NECESSARY TO GET THE MAXIMUM SCREENTIME OUT OF EVERY IMAGE. MONOTONE AND BACKGROUND-LESS PICTURES WERE MIXED WITH STILLS AND CONVENTIONAL ANIMATION

KANASHIMI NO BELLADONNA ● THE TRAGEDY OF BELLADONNA ● 1973 ● DIR: YAMAMOTO EIICHI ● SCR: YAMAMOTO EIICHI, FUKUDA YOSHIYUKI ● DES: FUKAI KUNI ● ANI: SUGII GISABURO ET AL ● MUS: SATO NOBUHIKO ● PRD: MUSHI PRODUCTION ● FILM ● DUR: 89 MINS

# BELLDANDY

Belldandy's name derives from Verdandi, goddess of the present in Nordic mythology. She is summoned to Earth when university student Morisato Keiichi, trying to phone a take-away restaurant, accidentally calls the celestial 'Goddess Helpline' and invokes her aid. When he jokingly wishes she could live with him, he finds himself landed with a beautiful girlfriend always ready to help him. Belldandy is one of the most sunny-natured and loving characters of the *seinen* manga panorama, always ready to help her neighbour and forgive mistakes (often risking sin through her ingenuousness). ● *Oh My Goddess!* falls within the same gentle and sentimental vein of *Urusei Yatsura* (1981) and *The Kabocha Wine* (*Pumpkin Wine*, 1982, dir. Yabuki Kimio), where a couple of kids with different opinions are forced to live together with humorous results. Stopping short of the grotesque and crazy excesses of manga by Takahashi Rumiko, the work of Fujishima Kosuke nevertheless resembles it in several ways: the pessimistic and interfering nature of the supporting characters (Belldandy's two goddess sisters and Keiichi's *senpai*), who meddle in the lives of the two protagonists; indispensable action elements delivered in the form of the goddesses' powers; and the same story of paranormal love, chaste and platonic, the outcomes of which are always left to the imagination. Strangely, although he is at Belldandy's side from the very first episode, Keiichi never gets around to declaring his love for her, even with a second TV series in 2006 providing a further 25 episodes directed by Goda Hiroaki. ● S.G.

AA! MEGAMI-SAMA! ● OH MY GODDESS! ● 1993 ● DIR: GOHDA HIROAKI ● SCR: HASEGAWA NAOKO, KONDO KUNIHIKO ● DES & ANI: MATSUBARA HIDENORI ET AL ● MUS: YASUDA TAKESHI ● PRD: AIC ● TV SERIES ● EPS: 26

# BEM

Humanoid Monster Bem lives out his adventures along with two other monstrous companions who, like him, hide their true features behind a human appearance. The dynamic between the three characters is based on an ideal family model with Bem as the authoritative father, mother-figure Bera, whose garish appearance is reminiscent of the elaborate make-up of kabuki theatre, and the child Bero, who is arguably the real star of the series. ● Bero is the intermediary between monsters and people in a world where fantasy creatures carry out their evil intentions amidst the human inhabitants. Here, we encounter a classical form of horror, a long way from the science-fiction hybrids and themes of physical mutation that are so often seen in anime (although they do arise in the 2006 remake). The series contains a number of detailed references to Japanese culture, for example the use of the term *yokai*, which refers to a number of mischievous or malevolent creatures from Japanese folklore. The hybrid story also includes western elements such as gangsters and mad scientists, while backdrops alternate between urban scenes and sinister landscapes with bare trees and driving rain or isolated houses where the forces of evil roam free. The background music incorporates jazz motifs with obsessive refrains, creating a sense of unease. In this setting, Bem, Bero and Bera, clearly uneasy about the fact that they are different, attempt to find a way to become human beings whilst using their powers to defeat the enemies of a humanity that fears and scorns them. This narrative plays itself out through fantastical dramas that, in the case of Bero, take on the form of a short cautionary tale. ● D.D.G.

SCENES FROM THE 1968 TV SERIES HUMANOID MONSTER BEM ● LEFT & BELOW RIGHT: BERO, WHOSE CATCHPHRASE IS "I JUST CAN'T WAIT TO BE HUMAN!" ● BELOW CENTRE: MOTHER-FIGURE BERA, AND BELOW LEFT: HUMANOID MONSTER BEM ● THE TRIO HOPE THAT, BY BRINGING JUSTICE TO THE MONSTER REALM, THEY MAY BECOME HUMAN

YOKAI NINGEN BEM ● HUMANOID MONSTER BEM ● 1968 ● DIR: WAKABAYASHI TADAO, ISHIGURO NOBORU ● SCR: ADACHI AKIRA ● DES: MORIKAWA NOBUYOSHI ● ANI: MORIKAWA NOBUHIDE ● MUS: UNO MASAHIRO ● PRD: DAICHI DOGA, FUJI TV ● TV SERIES ● EPS: 26

# BIBLE STORIES

Three years after Tatsunoko's *Anime Oyako Gekijo* (*Superbook: Video Bible*, 1981, dir. Higuch Masakazu et al) combined Bible stories with the narrative device of time travel and several unusual characters, the Vatican and the Italian broadcasting company RAI approached Tezuka Osamu with a proposal for an animated version of the Old Testament. Not long before, Tezuka had completed his monumental fourteen-volume manga about Gautama Buddha, founder of Buddhism, and he proceeded to devote two years to making a pilot of the story of Noah's Ark for the new series. His death in 1989 meant that the project was never completed. ● Dezaki Osamu took over as director of this ambitious twenty-six-part series, starting with an episode about Genesis and the expulsion of Adam and Eve. He worked his way through the main stories of the Old Testament, ending with the birth of Jesus as his finale. The connecting thread is that it is all seen through the eyes of Roco the Fox, providing a comic leitmotif in an otherwise somewhat high-flown, edifying treatment. *In the Beginning: Bible Stories* works as an effective, didactic complement to another of Tatsunoko's biblical projects, *Taimu Kyoshitsu: Tondera Housu no Daiboken* (*Adventures of the Tondera House*, 1982, dir. Higuch Masakazu et al), a similarly childlike and somewhat playful interpretation of a selection of New Testament stories. *Bible Stories*, however, fails to deliver the complexity of approach and the humanist (rather than religious) perspective that the agnostic Tezuka brought to his manga masterpiece *Buddha*. Although this production was completed by the early Nineties, the series was only shown in Japan in 1997, after its release in Germany, Italy and the USA. ● J.Co.

TEZUKA OSAMU NO KYUYAKU SEISHO MONOGATARI ● IN THE BEGINNING: BIBLE STORIES ● 1997 ● DIR: DEZAKI OSAMU ● SCR: TEZUKA PRODUCTION ● DES: TEZUKA OSHMU, SEYA SHINJI ● ANI: YOSHIMURA MASAKI et al ● MUS: HATTORI KATSUHISA ● PRD: NIPPON TV, RAI, TEZUKA PRODUCTION ● TV SERIES ● EPS: 26

With his face disfigured by a long scar, his shock of black and white hair, and dandified outfits, Black Jack, the surgeon who can do the impossible, is one of Tezuka Osamu's most famous characters (Tezuka himself qualified as a doctor before beginning his career in manga and anime). Black Jack started life in the pages of *Shonen Champion* magazine as the hero of a five-instalment mini-series to mark Tezuka's thirty years as a mangaka and quickly became very popular. ● After barely surviving the explosion that killed his mother, Hazama Juro's life was saved by the miraculous intervention of a surgeon and he is thereafter determined to devote himself to the practice of medicine. Transformed into Black Jack, a maverick outsider whose services are for sale to the highest bidder, he can be altruistic when his sense of justice demands it. His closest friend is Pinoko, a tiny girl who Black Jack discovered living as a teratoma in the body of her twin sister (a fertile imagination is at work here). ● A live-action movie of *Black Jack* was made by Obayashi Nobuhiko in 1977, but the character's first appearance in anime was in the twenty-sixth episode of the 1980 remake of *Astro Boy*. Black Jack also made a memorable cameo appearance in the film *Phoenix 2772: Space Firebird* (1980), before Dezaki Osamu launched a ten-episode OAV series devoted to the character in 1992, which in turn led to the first full-length anime film of his adventures. Another live-action film appeared in 1995, directed by Konaka Kazuya. In 2004, Tezuka Makoto (son of Tezuka Osamu) revived the character for a new anime series, and for a full-length film in which Black Jack confronts the menace of biological warfare, *Black Jack: Futari no Kuroi Isha* (*Black Jack: The Two Doctors of Darkness*, 2005), prior to a further appearance of this legendary character in the television series *Black Jack 21* (2006). ● J.Co.

# BLACK JACK

 CHARACTER  TV SERIES

SCENES FROM THE 1993 SERIES BLACK JACK ● ABOVE LEFT: PUBLICITY IMAGE FOR THE SERIES ● TOP RIGHT: BLACK JACK, READY FOR SURGERY ● ABOVE RIGHT: BLACK JACK'S OLD ADVERSARY CROSSWORD BECOMES HIS PATIENT

B

BLACK JACK ● 1993 ● DIR: DEZAKI OSAMU ● SCR: MORI ETO, OKAMOTO KIHACHI ● DES & ANI: SUGINO AKIO ●
MUS: SHOJI OSAMU, SUZUKI KIYOSHI ● PRD: TEZUKA PRODUCTION ● VIDEO SERIES ● EPS: 10

# BONES

BONES was founded in 1998 and quickly established itself as a successful anime studio thanks to a string of hits, especially its biggest international success, the TV series based on Arakawa Hiromu's manga *Fullmetal Alchemist* (*Hagane no Renkinjutsushi*, 2003). The feature film *Fullmetal Alchemist: Conqueror of Shamballa* further enhanced their reputation. Founded by former Sunrise staffers Minami Masahiko, Osaka Hiroshi and Kawamoto Toshihiro, it's no surprise that Bones excels in the computer imaging techniques for mecha action scenes. This expertise is showcased in television series like director Izubuchi Yukata's *RahXephon* (2002) and Kyoda Tomomi's *Kokyoshihen Eureka Seven* (*Eureka 7*, 2005). ● The studio's first job was working with Sunrise on the *Cowboy Bebop: Knockin' on Heaven's Door* movie. Other works include the television series *Darker Than Black: Kuro no keiyakusha* (*Darker Than Black: The Black Contractor*, 2007) and *Soul Eater* (2008), as well as the animated feature film *Stranger Mukoh Hadan* (*Sword of the Stranger*, 2007). ● H.M.

*RIGHT & BELOW: EDWARD ELRIC IN TWO SCENES FROM FULLMETAL ALCHEMIST (2003, DIR. MIZUSHIMA SEIJI, 52 EPS)*

*SEE ALSO: ELRIC, EDWARD; SPIEGEL, SPIKE; SUNRISE*

# CALIMERO

Calimero, a little, black animated chicken created by Nino and Toni Pagot, made his first appearance in 1961 in a television advert for the detergent manufacturer Mira Lanza. Following the character's enormous success, the Pagot Studio produced a television series based on his adventures two years later. In 1974, a series of forty-seven episodes for a Japanese audience was co-produced by the Pagot Studio and Toei Animation and was remade in 1992 by a long list of collaborators including Telescreen Japan, TV Tokyo and Mitsui & Co., but the production was supervised by Toni's son, Marco Pagot. ● The popularity of the 1992 series led to the making of a further fifty-two episodes, written by celebrated screenwriters Takayama Jiro and Sekijima Mayori. Of the two series, the latter is probably the more important because it introduces interesting innovations that keep the character up to date without compromising its original nature. Calimero acquires the company of a new character, his cousin Valeriano (called Giuliano in the Japanese version). Together with their friends the 'Green Team', the two chickens amuse themselves making films, leaving their home environment and travelling the world in search of journalistic scoops. ● F.L.

ABOVE: NINO AND TONI PAGOT'S POPULAR CHICKEN, CALIMERO

CALIMERO ● 1974 ● DIR: SERIKAWA YUGO ET AL ● SCR: YOSHIDA TAKESHI ET AL ● DES: TAKAHASHI SHINYA ● ANI: NAGARI FUSAHITO ● MUS: KINOSHITA TADASHI ● PRD: PAGOT STUDIO, TOEI ANIMATION ● TV SERIES ● EPS: 47

---

Candy – Candice White – is a strong and stubborn, yet lonely and sweet girl. Having spent her childhood in a small American orphanage run by Miss Pony and Sister Maria, Candy experiences several painful and life-altering events that bring her to a better understanding of herself without losing the altruism and generosity that make her what she is. Hers is an unexpected story, made up of coincidences, friendships and devotion to life. Candy's character was created for a novel by writer Mizuki Kyoko and developed into a manga with the artist Igarashi Yumiko for *Nakayoshi* magazine in 1975. Like the novel, the television series is also set in the USA and England shortly before and during World War I. Orphaned and alone, Candy is involved in a silent struggle with the adult world. ● Candy's world is one of modernity and female emancipation. It is the world of the city set against that of the countryside, the dawning of a new, faster and multifaceted age. This is perhaps one explanation for her choice of name; by rejecting the noble surname of the Ardley family who adopted her, Candy is able to put herself first. And indeed, Candy escapes from an exclusive English boarding school not only to follow Terrence, the young man she loves, but also to fulfil her longing for change. ● The style shines with refinement: realism appears to be the prime objective, while the narrative setting is more classical than ever, following the same lines as the literary novel. Characters are described in depth and it is impossible not to identify with them. ● G.P.

# CANDY CANDY

RIGHT: CANDY IN HER ROLE AS A WARTIME NURSE IN THE 1976 SERIES CANDY CANDY

CANDY CANDY ● 1976 ● DIR: SERIKAWA YUGO ET AL ● SCR: YUKIMURO SHUNICHI, SHIROYAMA NOBORU ● DES: IGARASHI YUMIKO, SHINDO MITSURU ● ANI: MORISHITA KEISUKE, TOMIZAWA KAZUO ● MUS: WATANABE TAKEO ● PRD: TOEI ANIMATION ● TV SERIES ● EPS: 115

C

# CASSHAN

CHARACTER

Azuma Tetsuya (also known as Casshan or Casshern) is a troubled hero, a messianic cyborg warrior sworn to atone for his father's crimes by ridding the world of the robots that threaten to destroy it. His dark secret is that the robots are also his father's creation. ● *Casshan: Robot Hunter* is an apocalyptic conflict that foreshadowed the later cataclysms of *Neon Genesis Evangelion* (1995) and *Vexille 2077 Nihon Sakoku* (*Vexille*, 2007). Conceived amid Watergate, Vietnam and the seventies recession, when the oil shocks rocked the Japanese economy, Tetsuya inherited a negative, rebellious tradition from several live-action anti-heroes, particularly the newly popular *ronin* of historical dramas, and their counterparts in children's television, such as *Masked Rider* (1971), *Skullman* (1970) and *Kikaider* (1972). Fathers in anime tradition often bestow robots on their sons. However, Dr Azuma, Tetsuya's father, is the inventor of a race of violent machines that lay waste to the Earth in the brutally logical assumption that the only way to save the Earth's ecology is to destroy humanity. Similar ideas have been seen many times since in science fiction, most notably in James Cameron's *Terminator* (1984), itself a major influence on many later anime. ● The strangely prescient, doom-laden plot of the original 1973 television series was resurrected on video at the height of Japan's next recession in 1993, and again during the worldwide credit crunch with the 2008 anime reboot/remake *Casshern Sins* (2008). The new version features an amnesiac Tetsuya, unsure of his original allegiance, waking in a world many centuries after the initial catastrophe. Humanity is dying out and all but infertile, while the once victorious robots are corroding in the poisonous atmosphere. ● J.Cl.

RIGHT: CASSHAN IN A SCENE FROM THE 1993 OAV SERIES
CASSHAN: ROBOT HUNTER

SHINZO NINGEN CASSHAN ● CASSHAN: ROBOT HUNTER ● 1973 ● DIR: FUKUSHIMA HIROYUKI ● SCR: TORIUMI JUNZO ET AL ● DES: YOSHIDA TATSUO ET AL ● ANI: HAYASHI MASAYUKI, IGUCHI CHUICHI ● MUS: KIKUCHI SHUNSUKE ● PRD: TATSUNOKO PRODUCTION ● VIDEO SERIES ● EPS: 35

---

*Cat Soup* was inspired by the 1998 manga *Nekojiru Udon* created by Nekojiru (the pseudonym of Hashiguchi Chiyomi) who committed suicide later the same year. The first anime version was a mini-series of twenty-seven two-minute episodes broadcast on Asahi Television in 1999, and in 2001 producer Otsuku Toshimichi commissioned director Sato Tatsuo to make a thirty-minute OAV, which won international acclaim, the Excellence Prize at the Japan Media Arts Festival and the prize for Best Animated Short at the Fantasia Festival. ● The story, taken from Nekojiru's imaginary world, follows two anthropomorphic cats, Nyatta and Nyako. Nyako dies of an illness, but her little brother manages to recapture half her soul and restores her to a semblance of life. Determined to recover the other half, Nyatta undertakes a journey studded with surreal adventures, during which he has to deal with various divine entities and at last manages to restore his sister's spirit. Sato, made famous as director of the science-fiction series *Senkan Nadeshiko* (*Martian Successor Nadesico*, 1996), adopts a non-realist style in this surreal film, depicting a disturbing and cruel imaginary world where events bordering on violence are transformed by his visionary interpretation. The whole anime is dominated by the idea of the transformation of matter: mechanical insects, elephants made of water and scenes that change on the mere whim of the god of the moment. Flooded lands are succeeded by petrified deserts, blending reality and unbridled imagination as if in a dream. Combining stylized figures (the cats) with more outlandish characters, *Cat Soup* recalls the art of great western animators such as Bill Plympton, although the grotesque element is more contained here. There is no dialogue beyond a few speech bubbles, reaffirming the film's printed origins. ● D.D.G.

# CAT SOUP

FIL

NEKOJIRU-SO ● CAT SOUP ● 2001 ● DIR: SATO TATSUO ● SCR: YAMANO HAJIME ● DES: YUASA MASAAKI ● ANI: IWA MICHIKO, YUASA MASAAKI ● MUS: UNCREDITED ● PRD: J.C. STAFF ● DUR: 33 MINS

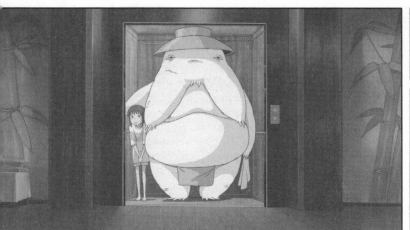

# CHIHIRO

Chihiro is a twelve-year-old girl – a rather spoilt, shy and moody only child – who is transformed by legendary director Miyazaki Hayao into a modern-day version of *Alice in Wonderland*. Her adventure starts with a car journey to a new home because her father is being transferred for his work. Trying to stay ahead of the removal van, the man loses his way and finds himself down a side street leading to a wood that ends in front of a tunnel. The entrance to the world of dreams lies in this mysterious tunnel that Chihiro enters following her parents. The tunnel opens up into a marvellous hilly landscape, crossed by a big river and towered over by an enormous building. Everything looks lived-in but there is not a soul around. Soon, Chihiro learns that she is not living a dream but a nightmare reality in which her parents are transformed into pigs and the big building is a spa centre for spirits and divinities who come to life only as darkness falls. ● The film *Spirited Away* is a splendid metaphor of Chihiro's entrance into adult life: the world that Miyazaki Hayao offers is fascinating, both in its impeccable designs and in the formalities of the story. Although the central themes are borrowed from traditional Japanese folklore and mythology, Miyazaki succeeds in creating an extraordinary melting pot of narrative in which Lewis Carroll mixes with the dark side of Grimm's fairytales. ● F.L.

LEFT & BELOW: CHIHIRO AND CHARACTERS FROM THE BEWITCHED CITY IN *SPIRITED AWAY* (2001), INCLUDING THE TRANSLUCENT SPIRIT NO FACE, THE GOOD WITCH ZENIBA AND THE SIX-ARMED BOILER ROOM KEEPER KAMAJII

SEN TO CHIHIRO NO KAMIKAKUSHI ● SPIRITED AWAY ● 2001 ● DIR & SCR & DES: MIYAZAKI HAYAO ● ANI: ANDO MASASHI ●
MUS: HISAISHI JOE ● PRD: SUZUKI TOSHIO ET AL, STUDIO GHIBLI ● FILM ● DUR: 125 MINS

# CHIRICO CUVIE

CHARACTER

Chirico Cuvie is a special forces Armored Trooper pilot, known as 'Perfect Soldier'. Born in the year 7196 in the Astragius galaxy, this blue-haired, muscled warrior is genetically engineered to be the ultimate hero. Unsurprisingly, his creators lack much of his sense of perfection or justice, and he soon becomes an unwitting pawn in a mission of interstellar espionage. Ordered to act against his own side, he is forsaken by his unit, accused of being a traitor, and forced to go on the run. In the process, he uncovers a conspiracy at the heart of a war that has raged for so long that both sides have forgotten its cause. ● Made in the Eighties, at the height of science-fiction cinema's love-affair with apocalyptic worlds and space wars, *Armored Trooper Votoms* was one of the first television anime to discard fanciful, superheroic robotics in favour of gritty, realistic technology. Creator Takahashi Ryosuke and designer Okawara Kunio pushed for technology in which the Vertical One-man Tanks for Offence and Maneuvers (Votoms) were more like tin cans with machine guns – augmented suits of armour using guns little different from those on twentieth-century Earth. Only the starships and medical technology were appreciably different from many Earth technologies – regarded by some as lazy science fiction, but by others as a deliberate move into more solid, believable speculations about far future military life. ● Over the course of the *Votoms* television series and its video sequels and prequels, Chirico would find love with Fyana, another perfect soldier. They went into cryogenic suspension, emerging thirty-two years later for the final coda, *The Heretic Saint*. ● J.Cl.

LEFT & BELOW LEFT: THE SOLDIERS OF THE 1983 TV SERIES *ARMORED TROOPER VOTOMS* ● ABOVE LEFT & BELOW: THE HERO CHIRICO CUVIE

SOKO KIHEI VOTOMS ● ARMORED TROOPER VOTOMS ● 1983 ● DIR: TAKAHASHI RYOSUKE ● SCR: GOBU FUYUNORI ● DES: SHIOYAMA NORIO ET AL ●
ANI: SHIOYAMA NORIO ● MUS: INUI HIROKI ● PRD: SUNRISE ● TV SERIES ● EPS: 52

# CHRISTOPHER, ROSETTE

CHARACTER

he scene is an alternate fantasy New York in the late 1920s and Rosette Christopher a young novice who has recently entered the Magdalene Order. Her challenge is o deal with a variety of demonic threats through exorcism with the help of her friend hrono, a rebel demon locked in the body of a boy. There is a special bond between em that could go far beyond simple friendship, even though she wears the veil. This ight seem scandalous, not to mention sacrilegious, but once the characters in this nime, drawn from Moriyama Daisuke's manga, have been established, they soon earn osolution, not only for the depth of the feelings that torment the protagonists but lso for their distinctive costumes which are very different from the black and white f real religious orders. ● Only the imaginative world of Japanese fantasy could permit self the luxury of venturing into this type of story and still satisfy the die-hard anime ns (it is worth noting that Rosette has enchanting green eyes and blond hair), while erving up an inexhaustible dose of action, irony and little dramas set into the story ong the way. Nothing is as it seems, for although the series focuses on encounters ith demons, director Kou Yu has established that the heart of *Chrono Crusade* is the ortrait of a young woman and her philosophy of life, no matter whether it is depicted a comic and outlandish manner or shot through with the thrill of terror. ● Another recious ace the series holds is the quality of the work done by the Gonzo studio nimators, always at the cutting edge when it comes to blending traditional animation nd digital techniques. ● M.A.R.

ABOVE: CHRONO (LEFT) AND ROSETTE CHRISTOPER (RIGHT) IN A PUBLICITY IMAGE FOR THE 2003 SERIES CHRONO CRUSADE

CHRNO CRUSADE ● CHRONO CRUSADE ● 2003 ● DIR: KOU YU ● SCR: TOMIOKA ATSUHIRO ● DES & ANI: KURODA KAZUYA ● MUS: NANASE HIKARU ● PRD: GONZO ● TV SERIES ● EPS: 24

ith her traditional Chinese costume and white bows in her hair, Chun-Li looks like a meek nd mild kind of girl. But she fears no one and her lightning kicks bring terror to her male dversaries in the videogame *Street Fighter*. A star of the highly popular second series of e game brought out by Capcom in 1991, the brown-haired 'wasp' with thighs of steel is not nly one of the two or three most famous heroines in all of videogame history but also, in ore general terms, a key figure in Japanese pop culture. Cosplay fanatics, who dress up as eir favourite pop culture icons, can bear witness to this: she is one of the most portrayed f all characters. ● Chun-Li joined Interpol aged eighteen to unravel the mystery of her ther's disappearance. In the feature-length animation based on *Street Fighter II*, which was stributed in Japan in 1994, she is a meticulous agent who easily handles a memorable fight cene in her own home, just as she comes out of the shower. Throughout the film, Chun-Li eems to be the most human character of the group, more rational and more sensitive than e muscle-bound Neanderthals surrounding her, while at the same time being extremely apable on the field of battle. ● In the game, as in the manga spin-offs, *Street Fighter* effects cosmopolitan fusion of all the modern myths of hand-to-hand fighting; those taking part this world challenge fight include a Bruce Lee clone, a Russian wrestler and a Hollywood-tyle soldier. Chun-Li avoids both the trophy-woman stereotype and that of the androgynous mazon but incarnates the extra spirit of costume battle. ● E.H.

# CHUN-LI

CHARACTER

GHT: CHUN LI, HE KICKBOXING EROINE OF STREET GHTER II (1994)

STREET FIGHTER II: THE ANIMATED MOVIE ● 1994 ● DIR: SUGII GISABURO ● SCR: IMAI KENICHI, SUGII GISABURO ● DES: MURABE SHUKO ET AL ● ANI: MAEDA MINORU ● MUS: KOMURO TETSUYA ● PRD: GROUP TAC ● DUR: 98 MINS

C

# CITY HUNTER

TV SERIES

CHARACTER

Saeba Ryo may be a fearless hero but he is not above reproach. Throughout Tokyo and especially Shinjuku, an area famous for its nightlife among other things, Ryo is known only as City Hunter: he is the one that people turn to when they need to deal with a problem, even if it means working on the fringes of the law and among the dregs of Japanese society. However Ryo has an improbable Achilles heel: whenever he meets an attractive woman the skilled enforcer transforms on the spot into a catastrophically thick-witted skirt-chaser. This theme continues through all 140 episodes of the four TV series. ● Ryo's dual personality is reflected in the very form of the series and OAVs adapted from Hojo Tsukasa's altogether darker and more risqué manga. In a flash, the story changes tone and flips from predominantly serious action into complete and utter buffoonery within a single sequence and without diminishing the coherence of the whole. Both *City Hunter* and its muscular protagonist are heroic and grotesque. It comes as no surprise, then, that when Ryo starred in a live-action feature-length film made in Hong Kong in 1993 the role was given to the master of kung-fu clowning, Jackie Chan, known for being equally at ease in athletic performance and in the comedic register. ● Above all, *City Hunter* glorifies a certain idea of the city as a space that favours all kinds of adventure, from police capers to love affairs. For the series, as for Ryo, there are plenty of dangers – and there is no shortage of the ridiculous and bad taste either. But such are the rules of the game in *City Hunter*: no matter what, no matter when – anything goes. ● E.H.

BELOW: RYO AND HIS PARTNER MAKIMURA KAORI IN THE OPENING CREDITS FOR THE 1987 TV SERIES *CITY HUNTER* ● RIGHT: SCENES FEATURING RYO SAEBA. THE 100-TON HAMMER IS USED TO EXPRESS KAORI'S REACTION TO RYO'S SKIRT-CHASING

*CITY HUNTER* ● 1987 ● DIR: KODAMA KENJI, IMANISHI TAKASHI ● SCR: HOSHIYAMA HIROYUKI ET AL ● DES: KAMIMURA YOSHIKO ● ANI: KITAHARA TAKEO ● MUS: KUNIYOSHI RYOICHI ● PRD: SUNRISE ● TV SERIES ● EPS: 51

MANGAKA

# CLAMP

The most surprising aspect of CLAMP's productions lies in the eclecticism and flexibility reflected both in their works and in the formation of the team. Created in 1987, the CLAMP brand, after a few changes, now has four active members: Ohkawa Nanase (screenplay), Mokona [Apapa] (designer), Nekoi Tsubaki (secondary designer) and Igarashi Satsuki (assistant and team manager). ● As school friends involved in self-produced publications, they embrace many aspects of the entertainment field, working on manga, anime, musical videos, novels and art books. Their output is dominated by an aim to marry the Baroque and affected elegance that is typical of *shojo* manga (comics intended for a female readership), with expressive energy, dynamism and spectacular efficiency – often anti-realistic – typical of male authors such as Nagai Go (*Devilman* (1973) is one of their favourite manga), and in particular Okazaki Takeshi and Hagiwara Kazushi, for whom they worked at the start of their career. This allowed their style to represent a break from the manga production of the Nineties and they reinvented the classical design models, giving way to a representation of anti-naturalistic and graphically more androgynous characters. ● Their name remains associated particularly with the saga (manga and anime) of *X* (1996), a complex and apocalyptic tale about two militant factions gifted with extrasensory powers, and the *majokko* (magical girl) genre, for which they created the two very popular series *Cardcaptor Sakura* (1998) and *Magic Knight Rayearth* (1994). *Tsubasa Chronicle* (2005) recycles the leading characters from *Cardcaptor Sakura* and *Magic Knight Rayearth* in another adventure quest story. Their most recent engagement concerns the character designs for *Code Geass: Lelouch of the Rebellion* (2006), the star of which, both a terrorist and idealist, well represents the capacity for synthesis of their works. ● D.D.G.

ABOVE: SCENE FROM *TSUBASA CHRONICLE* (2005, DIR. MASHIMO KOICHI, 26 EPS) ● ABOVE RIGHT & RIGHT: *CARDCAPTOR SAKURA* (1998, DIR. DAICHI AKITARO, ASAKA MORIO, 70 EPS)

SEE ALSO: KINOMOTO SAKURA

Beautiful, wilful and supremely convinced of her ability to rule over men with her sexual powers, the Egyptian queen Cleopatra knows that she faces her greatest trial at the approach of Roman invaders. She easily seduces Julius Caesar and Marc Antony, but is thwarted ultimately by Octavian, who turns out not to be interested in women. ● Cleopatra was the eponymous star of Tezuka Osamu's last-ditch attempt to save the spiralling debts of Mushi Production. Facing dwindling budgets and rising competition in television, he attempted to enter a new genre with adult cinema anime. A follow-up to *Senya Ichiya Monogatari* (*One Thousand and One Nights*, 1969), *Cleopatra* featured a group of twenty-first-century travellers returning to the time of the Roman Republic – one of them with the intention of seducing the legendary Cleopatra. The film was loaded with innovative experiments, including jarring anachronisms, a live-action sequence, a kabuki-style murder scene and slapstick depictions of the Roman army. However, its much-anticipated erotic component seems tame by modern standards, and it appears to have displeased all audiences equally. ● This disappointment was particularly notable in the USA, where the film was misleadingly retitled *Cleopatra: Queen of Sex* and falsely advertised as the first cartoon to receive an 'X' certificate (in fact, it was never submitted to the Motion Picture Association, probably out of fear that it would *not* receive an adult rating). Cleopatra's voice actress, Nakayama Chinatsu, would go on to play another famous anime character, *Jarinko Chie* (*Chie the Brat*, 1980) for director Takahata Isao, before switching careers and becoming a politician. Mushi Production declared bankruptcy in 1973, amid a recession that placed many other studios in similar financial difficulty. ● J.Cl.

# CLEOPATRA

CHARAC

ABOVE: TEZUKA OSAMU'S VERSION OF CLEOPATRA, QUEEN OF EGYPT, IN THE 1970 FILM *CLEOPATRA, QUEEN OF SEX*

CLEOPATRA ● CLEOPATRA: QUEEN OF SEX ● 1970 ● DIR. TEZUKA OSAMU, YAMAMOTO EIICHI ● SCR: SATOYOSHI SHIGEMI ● DES: KOJIMA KO ● ANI: NAKAMURA KAZUKO ET AL ● MUS: TOMITAISAO ● PRD: MUSHI PRODUCTION ● FILM ● DUR: 112 MINS

CHARACTER

# COBRA

Who is Cobra? In the first episode of the series, taken from Terasawa Buichi's manga, even the protagonist doesn't know, or rather, doesn't remember. Having stood down from intergalactic affairs, this twenty-fourth-century swashbuckling enforcer-cum-executioner has transformed himself into a placid office worker. The records have been wiped, his face transformed with plastic surgery and every link with his past has been lost, until one day, when he decides to go to a centre selling dreams on demand and, in a sequence redolent of the Philip K. Dick short story on which director Paul Verhoeven based the film *Total Recall* (1990), all his memories come flooding back. ● Cigar firmly lodged in his mouth and female android at his side, the brawny blond dons a red jumpsuit and launches himself into explosive adventures pitting him against the terrible space pirates guild. Fitted with his 'psychogun', a bionic arm emitting lethal delta rays, Cobra personifies the man-machine image whose hybrid nature and confused identity seem to influence the very form of the series. With animation that was extremely polished for its day and the subtle use of a varied range of music, the series alternates moments of casual comedy in a jazzy atmosphere with graphically daring action scenes broken up with stylized stills and the almost abstract trajectories of rays of light. ● The forerunner of director Watanabe Shinichiro's TV series *Cowboy Bebop* (1998), *Space Adventure Cobra* is a mature work and an unsparing view of a futuristic society. In this sense *Cobra* keeps faith with the best science-fiction traditions, depicting a society that emerges as a disturbing reflection of our own (although the series also displays a marked taste for epic grandeur). ● E.H.

ABOVE: SCENES FROM THE 1982 SERIES *SPACE ADVENTURE COBRA*, SHOWING OUR HERO AND HIS LOVE, JANE FLOWER ● RIGHT: A PUBLICITY IMAGE FOR THE SERIES

SPACE COBRA ● SPACE ADVENTURE COBRA ● 1982 ● DIR: DEZAKI OSAMU, TAKEUCHI YOSHIO ● SCR: TERADA KENJI ET AL ● DES: SUGINO AKIO, OTSUKA SHINJI ● ANI: SUGINO AKIO ET AL ● MUS: HANEDA KENTARO ● PRD: TMS ● TV SERIES ● EPS: 31

CHARACTER

# CONAN

In 1978, NHK (Japan Broadcasting Corporation) commissioned Nippon Animation to produce *Future Boy Conan*, inspired by the book *The Incredible Tide* (1970) by Alexander Key. The series was directed by Miyazaki Hayao in his debut as director, in a collaboration with Takahata Isao and Hayakawa Keiji. Miyazaki makes several changes to the novel, first and foremost the time in which it is set. The timing of the story is changed from 2222 to 2028 and the setting is a post-apocalyptic world suffering the consequences of a global conflict. With most of Earth now sunk below sea level, only Indastria, a despotic island state, and a small outpost called the 'Lost Island' survive. The survivors of a spacecraft find refuge on this small patch of ground when they fall to Earth following an abortive attempt to set off into space. ● Conan is an orphan, the only child born on the island where he lives with his grandfather. His life is turned upside down when he finds a girl lying unconscious on the beach: her name is Lana and she is being pursued by one of Indastria's aircraft. The ship's crew kidnap Lana, and as they escape they kill Conan's grandfather. This is a cult series that features numerous themes dear to Miyazaki, such as his pacifism and ecological and utopian ideals – reflected in the respect for nature and the distrust felt towards an omnipotent science – as well as his interest in the world of adolescents and in representing their journey of initiation that leads them to enter the world of adults. ● F.L.

SCENES FROM THE 1978 SERIES FUTURE BOY CONAN ● ABOVE: CONAN (CENTRE), LANA (LEFT) AND MASTER HUNTER JIMSY (RIGHT) ● RIGHT: THREE IMAGES FROM THE SERIES SHOW MIYAZAKI HAYAO'S LOVE OF AERIAL ADVENTURE AND FLYING MACHINES

MIRAI SHONEN CONAN ● FUTURE BOY CONAN ● 1978 ● DIR: MIYAZAKI HAYAO ● SCR: NAKANO TAKAAKI, YOSHIKAWA SOJI ● DES: MIYASAKI HAYAO, OTSUKA YASUO ● ANI: KAWAJIRI YOSHIAKI, KAWAUCHI HIDEO ● MUS: IKEHAMA KENICHIRO ● PRD: NIPPON ANIMATION ● TV SERIES ● EPS: 26

C

# CREAMY MAMI

CHARACTER

*Creamy Mami*, an anime series about a girl granted magical powers, shares similar themes with *Little Witch Sally* (1966) and *Himitsu no Akko-Chan* (*Secret Akko-Chan*, 1969). However these are the hedonistic Eighties and, unlike her enchanted precursors, little Morisawa Yu doesn't use her gift to help others, but to become a pop singer. The series was Studio Pierrot's debut in the *majokko* (little witches or magical girls) genre – an area that proved to be highly successful for them. *Creamy Mami* stands out as a hugely influential series and is important in understanding the evolution of the *majokko* genre where the little sorceresses of Earth are finally allowed to supersede the tradition good witches from afar, an idea first established by Yokoyama Mitsuteru in *Little Witch Sally*. ● Despite the fantasy component the series is capable of voicing reality through a star who struggles to protect her own double life – she is a dreamy little girl and an acclaimed *aidoru* (singer) at the same time. The tone is light and features comic sketches although sometimes rather introspective, inserted within a structure that successfully balances the sociological component with that of magic, all saturated with a sense of wonder that has inspired the imagination of a generation. ● Artistically, Studio Pierrot uses a soft touch, with somewhat rounded and impressive designs that reveal partiality for pastel shades – bright but never aggressive, just like the stars. The dualism between Yu and Mami gradually leads to rivalry between the two souls of the star, who is divided between the entertainment of her public and the need to live out her own life. Studio Pierrot took up this theme again and broadened it in *Maho no Star Magical Emi* (*Magical Emi*, 1985). ● D.D.G.

LEFT: A PUBLICITY IMAGE FOR THE 1983 SERIES *CREAMY MAMI* SHOWS LITTLE YU AND HER CUTE TEENAGE ALTER EGO, POP IDOL CREAMY MAMI

MAHO NO TENSHI CREAMY MAMI ● CREAMY MAMI ● 1983 ● DIR: KOBAYASHI OSAMU, MOCHIZUKI TOMOMI ● SCR: ITO KAZUNORI ET AL ● DES: TAKADA AKEMI ●
ANI: KAWAUCHI HIDEO, TAKAHASHI SHINYA ● MUS: MAIKANO KOJI ● PRD: STUDIO PIERROT ● TV SERIES ● EPS: 52

# CUTEY HONEY

...oney is a provocative, blonde android girl ...reated by Dr Kisaragi to take the place ...f his dead daughter in a clear homage ...o Tezuka Osamu's *Astro Boy* (1963). The ...ain difference from that classic character, ...owever, is Honey's strongly defined femininity ...nd curvaceous body. *Cutey Honey*, created ...1973 by Nagai Go, introduced the first ...emale protagonist in a manga for boys, ...lacing the beautiful android in a Catholic ...chool in Tokyo. Honey is oblivious to her ...therness, and only becomes aware of her ...owers when her father is killed by the ...reacherous criminal organization 'Panther ...Claw', an all-female space Mafia who want ...o kidnap every man on the planet and ...nly Honey can stop them. Able to turn ...erself into a motorcyclist (Hurricane), a ...inger (Misty), a hostess (Idol), a camera ...oman (Flash), a model (Fancy) and a skilled ...wordswoman (Cutey), Honey winks at the ...ale audience during each transformation, ...howing a glimpse of her naked body. The ...character is inspired by various superhero ...eries, in particular the *tokusatsu* (action) ...elevision series by Kawauchi Kohan, *7-Color ...Mask* (1959) and its subsequent remake ...*Rainbowman* (1972), in which the hero ...disguises himself with seven different masks ...*Rainbowman* was also animated in 1982 by ...director Okaseko Kazuhiro). The *Cutey Honey* ...elevision series, produced by Toei Animation, ...as directed by Katsumata Tomoharu who ...rings expressionist devices that he first ...xplored in the series *Mazinger Z* (1972). The ...creenplay is by Tsuji Masaki, who was already ...he author of television versions of *Attack ...Number One* (1969) and *Devilman* (1973), and ...he designs of the celebrated Araki Shingo ...soften the original manga's graphic style. ● ...*Cutey Honey* was also the first science-...iction comic to introduce two new elements ...o the genre, later used to great success: ...he enchantress-idol, as in *Creamy Mami* ...1983), and the action genre starring girls, as ...n *Sailor Moon* (1992). The original TV series ...was followed by another in 1997 plus two ...video series and two movies – one animated ...and one live action. ● L.D.C.

ABOVE RIGHT: THE POPULAR ANDROID GIRL CUTEY ...HONEY FROM THE 1973 SERIES ● RIGHT: JEWEL ...PRINCESS, ONE OF CUTEY HONEY'S EVIL FOES

CUTEY HONEY ● 1973 ● DIR: KATSUMATA TOMOHARU ● SCR: TSUJI MASAKI ET AL ● DES: ARAKI SHINGO ● ANI: ARAKI SHINGO ET AL ●
MUS: WATANABE TAKEO ● PRD: DYNAMIC PLANNING, TOEI ANIMATION ● TV SERIES ● EPS: 25

# CYBORG 009

CHARACTER

FILM

ABOVE: SHIMAMURA JOE, LEADER OF THE
CYBORGS, FROM THE 1968 TV SERIES CYBORG
009. ALTHOUGH THE EARLIER MOVIE WAS MADE
IN COLOUR, SOME TV SERIES WERE STILL MADE IN
BLACK AND WHITE

The idea of the superhero as an outsider, tormented by his condition and the great responsibility involved in managing his exceptional powers, has given rise to a striking modern genre. In 1963, Stan Lee produced one of the most complex versions of this concept with the *X-Men* saga. His group of mutant adolescents, marginalized and condemned to isolation, were models for adolescence in a state of perpetual crisis. ● A year later, although not necessarily influenced by Lee's characters, Ishinomori Shotaro created *Cyborg 009*, a series that can be regarded as the manga answer to *X-Men*. Like its forerunner, the series took as its protagonists a mixed group of reluctant superheroes in the form of nine humans kidnapped by the evil 'Black Ghost' organization and transformed into experimental cyborgs with superhuman powers. Later recruited by Dr Isaac Gilmore as members of an army of good. ● The characters of *Cyborg 009* are a multiracial group, including a Russian boy with telepathic powers and a French former ballerina with X-ray vision. All manifest the inner conflict of the tormented superhero to various degrees, and suicidal Cyborg 004, Albert Heinrich, seems to signal a future dark development of the archetype. ● *Cyborg 009* first saw life as a manga, with several narrative cycles featuring in different publications between 1964 and 1985. It was first adapted for animation in 1966, in the shape of the film of the same name by Serikawa Yugo. Two further films followed in 1967 and 1980 and three television series in 1968, 1979 and 2001. ● J.Co.

CYBORG 009 ● 1966 ● DIR: SERIKAWA YUGO ● SCR: TSUJI MASAKI, SERIKAWA YUGO ● DES: ISHINOMORI SHOTARO ● ANI: YAMADA KAZUHIRO ●
MUS: KOSUGI DAIICHIRO ● PRD: TOEI ANIMATION ● FILM ● DUR: 64 MINS

# DAICON III & IV

A taste for pastiche must have inspired Anno Hideaki, Sadamoto Yoshiyuki and a few other friends to choose 'Daicon' as a protective talisman for their debut. In 1981 the twentieth Japan Science-Fiction Convention was held in Osaka. It was nicknamed Daicon for its location (the first character of Osaka can also be read as 'dai') and was the third JNSF event held there. It was inaugurated with the short film *Daicon III*, in which a schoolgirl of about ten is transformed into a superheroine, destroying every monster, robot or spacecraft in her path. A year later, the experiment was repeated, this time in an even greater parody. In *Daicon IV*, the child has grown into an attractive pin-up and Godzilla, the spaceship Yamato, Marvel superheroes and a number of super-robots all fall victim to her strength. ● Viewed in perspective, *Daicon* (as well as maintaining its debunking power) can be seen as one of the symbols that launched *otaku* (the name given to obsessive manga and anime fans) culture. The success of this film, with its amateur budget but well-defined ideas, led to the creation of the famous production company Gainax. In itself, the short film is little more than a popular video clip, though the concept behind it reveals a new school of thought in the science-fiction universe. The frame of reference is no longer reality, no longer the cinema, no longer the comic strip, but animation itself and the levity with which the great stars of animation are treated is not intended to be disparaging. Quite the contrary, it is the mark of absolute passion, not without a certain self-irony, that characterized an entire generation of fans. ● C.C.

LEFT: SCENES FROM THE *DAICON IV* OPENING FILM (1984) ● BELOW: THE YOUNG STAR OF *DAICON III*, JUST BEFORE HER TRANSFORMATION INTO THE ADULT HEROINE OF *DAICON IV*

*DAICON III & IV* ● 1982/1984 ● DIR: YAMAGA HIROYUKI ● SCR: NOT CREDITED ● DES: SAEGUSA TORU ● ANI: ANNO HIDEAKI, AKAI TAKAMI ● MUS: KITARO, ELECTRIC LIGHT ORCHESTRA ● PRD: DAICON IV COMMITTEE ● DUR: c.4 MINS EACH

ROBOT

# DAITARN 3

TV SER

Daitarn 3, counterpart to the more tragic Zanbot 3 (the super-robot of *Muteki Choujin Zanbot 3*, directed in 1977 by Tomino Yoshiyuki for studio Sunrise), uses solar energy as opposed to the 'moon attack' weapon of its predecessor and the series as a whole has a generally sunnier feel. ● The producers were keen to cash in on the popularity of the James Bond franchise, and the personality and charms of pilot Haran Banjo and his two female assistants are showcased as much as their abilities. Idols as well as heroic figures, they won the attention of both sexes through their charisma as much as their fighting skills. Although the series does go out of its way to illustrate society's obsession with image, the crew's adventures are presented as dazzling ceremonies in which their enemies sometimes disguise themselves as film stars, or use illusion or music. The fight scenes between robots follow a stylized pattern and always culminate in a spectacular 'knock-out blow'. The more experimental episodes even use onomatopoeic effects found in comic books, creating a witty atmosphere only found elsewhere in parodies produced by the Tatsunoko studio such as *Time Bokan Series: Yattaman* (1977). ● Tomino's work has a satirical edge and a certain amount of fun is poked at the repetitive, implausible mechanisms of the robot genre and aspects of human behaviour are ridiculed. On the other hand, the series also highlights fears of science raging out of control and the younger generation's sense of obligation in remedying the mistakes of their parents. The mission of the cruel Meganoids (cyborgs bent on taking over the Earth) is inspired by a perverse plan to 'improve' the human race, decimating a civilization that seems deserving of punishment, but it was Banjo's own father who was behind the original creation of these enemies. ● D.D.G.

SCENES FROM THE 1978 TV SERIES *DAITARN 3* ● ABOVE LEFT: CLOSE-UP OF THE ROBOT DAITARN 3 ● ABOVE: THE ROBOT IN COMBAT ● CENTRE LEFT: THE PILOT OF DAITARN 3, HARAN BANJO ● LEFT: BANJO'S TWO FEMALE ASSISTANTS, SANYO REIKA AND TACHIBANA BEAUTY

MUTEKI KOJIN DAITAN 3 ● DAITARN 3 ● 1978 ● DIR: TOMINO YOSHIYUKI ● SCR: ARAKI YOSHIHISA ET AL ● DES: SHIOYAMA NORIO, KOGUNI KAZUYOSHI ● ANI: NAKAMURA KAZUO ET AL ● MUS: WATANABE TAKEO ● PRD: SUNRISE ● TV SERIES ● EPS: 40

# DALLOS

In the twenty-first century, the moon is colonized by Earth, which desperately needs raw materials for its growing population. Millions of settlers from the most marginalized sections of society live and work under the dome of a gigantic metropolis. Tired of working as slaves for the sole benefit of Earth's inhabitants, the new generation of colonists, those born on the moon, rebel against the oppressive control of the lunar military government. They organize themselves into armed groups and hide in the ancient and mysterious fortress-cum-sanctuary, Dallos. The origins of this stronghold are unknown but it is crucial to the rebels' cause as the base of their rebellion. By the end of the story, the fortress has taken on a life of its own, shooting laser rays at the enemy. ● Produced by Studio Pierrot and inspired by Robert Heinlein's *The Moon is a Harsh Mistress* (1966), *Dallos* is considered to be the first OAV ever made. It was released from 1983 to 1984 in four episodes (the first released after the second) and was later cut together as a two-hour film (which was cut to eighty-five minutes for the American market). Although aiming for higher quality than television productions, the disjointed narrative betrays the presence of more than one director. Ostensibly the direction was by the young Oshii Mamoru and some of his trademark themes are present (the guerrilla war of liberation and the relationship between man and machine) but in practice his mentor Toriumi Hisayuki was co-auteur. The battle scenes are the most successful element, with sustained pace, greater care taken with the figures' movement and an interesting variety of battle suits. *Dallos* had a great influence on the Japanese animation industry, opening up a new market and leading to a more experimental approach, as well as the development of products aimed at adult viewers. It was to be the benchmark for OAVs for years after its release. ● S.G.

SCENES FROM THE FIRST OAV *DALLOS* ● TOP LEFT: THE GIANT DOMED CITY ON THE MOON ● LEFT: TERRAN COMMANDANT ALEX RIGER AND HIS SISTER ● BELOW & BELOW LEFT: THE HERO NONOMURA SHUN IN A MOBILE SUIT, HIS SISTER AND THE HOODED PROFILE OF HIS GRANDFATHER ● BELOW RIGHT: REBEL LEADER DOG MCCOY

*DALLOS* ● 1983 ● DIR: OSHII MAMORU ● SCR: OSHII MAMORU, TORIUMI HISAYUKI ● DES: OKADA TOSHIYASU, SATO MASAHARU ● ANI: OKADA TOSHIYASU, TANEMOTO TAKEMI ● MUS: NANBA HIROYUKI ● PRD: BANDAI VISUAL, STUDIO PIERROT ● VIDEO SERIES ● EPS: 4

# DANGUARD ACE

ROBOT

After all the resources on Earth have been exhausted, scientists study the possibility of colonizing a fictional tenth planet in the solar system, sending out the rocket ship *Satellizer* in order to reach it. The ship is able to transform into the enormous anthropomorphic robot, Danguard Ace. The mission, captained by Commander Ichimonji, fails after a character called Doppler brainwashes Cosmos by using an iron mask that removes free will and makes the Commander his slave. These events have a lasting effect on the whole series, the only mecha created by Matsumoto Leiji after the end of his collaboration with Nagai Go and Toei Animation. ● To take up the mission again, Danguard requires an expert pilot able to guide him. To this end, Doctor Oedo gives the mysterious Captain Dan (a man wearing an iron mask with no memory of his past) the task of leading three young cadets. Among these is Ichimonji Takuma, the cleverest of the three, with whom Dan develops a love/hate relationship. There follows a painful conflict between the father figure, injured in body and spirit, and the impatient and restless son. ● This is the key to the series' originality: in *Planet Robot Danguard Ace* there are no aliens or empires from other galaxies. Here, man fights against man, and against his own thirst for power. In fact, the centre of the story is not the battles, but the relationships between the characters, the evolution of their mutual stories and the tensions and turbulence of those who are at the edge of the abyss. ● G.P.

*ABOVE LEFT: THE CREW OF DANGUARD ACE, 1977 (LEFT TO RIGHT: CAPTAIN DAN, ICHIMONJI TAKUMA, KIRINO LISA, DR. SADO, DR. OEDO, DR. TANUKI, TANAGA THE ROBOT AND CHIEF MECHANIC BUNTA) ● LEFT: THE GIANT ROBOT BRINGS DOWN ONE OF ITS MANY ENEMIES*

*WAKUSEI ROBO DANGUARD ACE ● PLANET ROBOT DANGUARD ACE ● 1977 ● DIR: KATSUMATA TOMOHARU, NISHIZAWA NOBUTAKA, ISHI TERUO, SUKAYA NOBUYUKI, AKEHI MASAYUKI ● SCR: YAMAZAKI HARUYA, YOSHIKAWA SOJI ● DES: ARAKI SHINGO ● ANI: ARAKI SHINGO, SAIJO AKIRA ● MUS: KIKUCHI SHUNSUKE ● PRD: TOEI ANIMATION ● EPS: 56*

One manga, two animated series and a variety of wrestlers donning his mask for real matches have cemented the character of Tiger Mask as an indomitable and technically accomplished hero. On looking into his initial adventures, however, the figure that emerges is one weighed down with conflicts, echoing those of a Japan in transition. ● Growing up in an orphanage, Date Naoto yearns to become 'as strong as a tiger' to improve the lot of his unhappy contemporaries. He trains as a wrestler with the underground 'Tigers' Den' organization, learning to become a cruel and unscrupulous demon of the ring, but his developing relationship with his audience, including children who identify with him, forces him to re-examine his behaviour and become a true hero. This betrayal earns him the undying enmity of the 'Tigers' Den'. Set in a Japan burdened with extreme social inequality, in the middle of an industrial boom that is creating deep rifts in society, the story culminates in Naoto's visit to Hiroshima. Both a media and popular hero, Naoto becomes his country's conscience and takes time to reflect on the relationship between past and present and between the media and the public. ● The 1969 television series adapted the manga scripted by Kajiwara Ikki, with its story of youth redeemed through an odyssey of self-denial and pain almost to the point of martyrdom that does not necessarily bring victory. Naoto's continuous encounters with picturesque but cruel adversaries reinforce his Christ-like persona until, in an explosive final episode, the hero is unmasked and his idealism defeated. ● The anime's design has a deliberately grubby, angular look quite unlike the softer manga, but it succeeds extremely well in rendering the strain and violence of the world of wrestling. Three features were edited from the TV series for holiday release, before a further TV series was made in 1981. ● D.D.G.

## DATE NAOTO

CHARACTER

ABOVE: POPULAR HERO DATE NAOTO WEARS THE TIGER MASK AND CAPE IN THE 1969 TV SERIES TIGER MASK

TIGER MASK ● 1969 ● DIR: TAMIYA TAKESHI ET AL ● SCR: TSUJI MASAKI ET AL ● DES: TSUJI NAOKI ● ANI: KIMURA KEIJIRO, MURATA KOICHI ● MUS: KIKUCHI SHUNSUKE ● PRD: TOEI ANIMATION ● TV SERIES ● EPS: 105

# DEEN

Production house Studio DEEN was founded in March 1975 by former members of Sunrise. It retains close links with Sunrise while working with other studios, such as Studio Gallop on the 1997 movie *Ruroni Kenshin: Requiem for Patriots*, Studio Ghibli on *Spirited Away* (2001) and BONES on *Sword of the Stranger* (2007) ● DEEN is well known for its manga-based TV series, starting in 1984 with the second part of hit TV series *Urusei Yatsura* for Kitty Films. After *Urusei Yatsura*, DEEN adapted more Takahashi Rumiko manga – *Maison Ikkoku* in 1986 and *Ranma ½* in 1989. The studio also worked on movies, some drawn from its television series. Mamoru Oshii made his early movie *Tenshi no Tamago* (*Angel's Egg*, 1985) there, followed by the *Patlabor* OAVs (1988) and movie (1989). ● DEEN animated Fujisawa Keisuke's *Taiho Shichauzo* (*You're Under Arrest!*, 1994), Group SNE and Yasuda Hitoshi's *Rokumon no Moncollé Knight* (*Moncollé Knights*, 2000), and Oyuki Konno's *Maria-sama ga Miteru* (*Maria Watches Over Us*, 2003.) More recent works include *Fruits Basket* (dir. Daichi Akitaro, 2001), *Rave Master* (dir. Watanabe Takeshi, 2001), *Jigoku Shojo* (*Hell Girl*, dir. Watanabe Hiroshi, 2005) and *Higurashi no Naku Koro Ni* (*When They Cry*, dir. Kon Chiaki, 2006). ● H.M.

IMAGES FROM TWO SERIES PRODUCED BY STUDIO DEEN ● ABOVE: AKANE AND RANMA IN *RANMA ½* (1989, DIR. SHIBAYAMA TSUTOMU ET AL, 161 EPS) ● LEFT: LUM AND ATARU IN *URUSEI YATSURA* (1981, DIR. OSHII MAMORU ET AL, 218 EPS)

SEE ALSO: MAISON IKKOKU; OSHII MAMORU; SAOTOME RANMA; SUNRISE; TAKAHASHI RUMIKO; URUSEI YATSURA

# DEVILMAN

CHARACTER

Graphic violence, a profound reflection on youthful rebellion and the repression perpetrated by fearful adults are the distinctive features of *Devilman* (1972), Nagai Go's finest manga, in which he reworks a number of ideas from his unfinished *Ma-O Dante* (*Demon Lord Dante*, 1971). Although the man/devil dualism is integral to every incarnation of *Devilman*, there are striking differences between Nagai's original manga and the anime series shown the same year. In the manga, the central character, Fudo Akira, agrees to merge his personality with that of the demon Amon in order to free humanity from the scourge of demons who are about to conquer the Earth. The television version, however, uses an outline already seen in series such as *Tiger Mask* (1969): Akira dies while travelling in the Himalayas and his body is taken over by a demon that has come to Earth to conquer it. The demon soon after discovers love and decides to rebel against his own kind. ● Although the series does not hesitate to show graphic violence and demonstrates the most untrammelled fantasy in its imaginary creatures, the anime is essentially a superhero story; the protagonist, with his double identity, undergoes spectacular transformations to combat the demons sent to kill him. His story is told in thirty-nine episodes, alongside comic supporting roles and the little amorous skirmishes typical of contemporary formats, leading up to a finale that does not resolve the conflict between Devilman and his enemies. Instead, it is mainly concerned with squaring the circle of the star-crossed love story between the protagonist and his beloved Miki. To see the 'real' Devilman on screen, audiences had to wait until 1987 when the first chapters of the manga were translated into animation for the OAV market. This much darker, more sexually oriented version of the character was developed further in *Amon: The Apocalypse of Devilman*, directed by Takeshita Komichi. ● D.D.G.

RIGHT: DEVILMAN FROM THE VIDEO RELEASE AMON: THE APOCALYPSE OF DEVILMAN (2000, DIR. TAKESHITA KENICHI, 50 MINS) AS DESIGNED BY NIRASAWA YASUSHI ● BELOW: DEVILMAN FROM THE 1987 OAV, DIRECTED BY IIDA TSUTOMU AND DESIGNED BY KOMATSUBARA KAZUO

DEVILMAN ● 1972 ● DIR: AKEHI MASAYUKI, KATSUMATA TOMOHARU ● SCR: TSUJI MASAKI ET AL ● DES: KATSUMARA GEKI ET AL ● ANI: KOMATSUBARA KAZUO ET AL ● MUS: MISAWA GO ● PRD: DYNAMIC PLANNING, TOEI ANIMATION ● TV SERIES ● EPS: 39

MANGAKA

# DEZAKI OSAMU

IMAGES FROM THE WORK OF DEZAKI OSAMU ● TOP: TWO IMAGES OF MASTER THIEF LUPIN III. DEZAKI OSAMU DIRECTED FIVE OF THE ANNUAL LUPIN TV SPECIALS ● ABOVE LEFT: REMÌ, ORPHAN HERO OF *NOBODY'S BOY* (1977, DIR. DEZAKI OSAMU, 51 EPS) ● ABOVE RIGHT: A MONTAGE OF CHARACTERS FROM THE TV SERIES *THE ROSE OF VERSAILLES* (1979, DIR. NAGAHAMA TADAO ET AL, 40 EPS)

Dezaki Osamu had long desired to be a manga artist like his idol Tezuka Osamu. Born in 1943 in Tokyo, he joined Mushi Production in the Sixties and quickly rose through the ranks, becoming one of the greatest directors working under Tezuka, his manager and mentor. He worked on productions for cinema, television and OAV, bringing with him a passion for Italian and European cinema and design. ● Even today, with all the young talents and pop culture that floods the anime genre, Dezaki remains the most traditional of directors and takes the greatest care when experimenting (as seen in his transformation of *Moby Dick* into a science-fiction series, for example). He formed an exceptional artistic trio with designer Sugino Akio and photographic director Takahashi Hirokata. His immense directorial back catalogue boasts a number of unbeatable television productions: the tough boxer *Tomorrow's Joe* (1970), the melodrama *Nobody's Boy* (1977), the historic *The Rose of Versailles* (1979), the dramatic *Black Jack* (1993) and the witty *Lupin III* (1989–95). ● However, Dezaki is at his most lively and striking in films such as *Space Adventure Cobra* (1982), taken from a manga by Terasawa Buichi, in which the science-fiction mould is hidden behind cinema-loving passion and figurative narcissism (the shafts of light that spread over the screen almost blind the viewer). Another example is the masterpiece *Golgo 13* (1983), based on the comic by Saito Takao, in which the protagonist descends into the internal darkness of an implacable killer with the same aplomb as that seen in the seventies films of Fukasaku Kinji or Suzuki Seijun. ● M.A.R.

SEE ALSO: BLACK JACK; COBRA; DUKE TOGO; GENJI HIKARU; JARJAYES, OSCAR FRANÇOIS DE; OKA HIROMI; REMY; YABUKI JOE

# DIGIMON

CHARACTERS

Toei Animation's response to the worldwide success of *Pokémon* was a new series of monsters with a beguiling design. Hongo Akiyoshi's approach was not based on the idea of collecting little wild monsters but instead the creatures are 'digital monsters' originating from 'Digiworld'. Therefore, the hunting and jousting aspects of *Pokémon* are lost, but the empathetic mechanism remains unchanged as the monsters are tied to young human characters and evolve to face any unexpected event or enemy. ● The outline is not so very far away from that of other robot stories (it's no coincidence that the new genre was to influence the gigantic machines of *Gear Senshi Dendo* (*Gear Fighter Dendoh*, 2000, dir. Fukuda Mitsuo)). While the humans 'guide' the monsters, the more friendly aspects of the monsters simultaneously help the children overcome the solitude of a society where parents are almost totally absent. The cohesion of the group and the appeal to positive feelings – typical of the cautionary tale – allow the young friends to defeat the threats of increasingly powerful enemies. ● The videogame setting is maintained with several 'levels' to be overcome in the evolution of the Digimon, which relate to the strength of the enemy and the fears that reign in the children's hearts. The narrative structure, in turn, demonstrates a certain leaning towards repetitiveness over the five series that compose the saga. However, the worthy professional skills of directors such as Kakudo Hitoyuki (*One Piece*, 1999) and the animation of Miyahara Naoki (*Dragon Ball Z*, 1989) combined to bring great success to the saga. The franchise continues with four further TV series and ten movies to date. There are also more than 20 video games. ● D.D.G.

RIGHT: A PUBLICITY IMAGE FEATURING CHARACTERS FROM THE DIGIMON SAVERS SERIES (2006, DIR. HOSODA MAMORU ET AL)

DIGIMON ● 1999 ● DIR: HOSODA MAMORU, KADONO HIROYUKI, IMAMURA TAKASHI, IMAZAWA TETSUO ● SCR: NISHIZONO SATORU, MASAKI HIRO ● DES: NAKATSURU KAPPEI ● ANI: SHIBATA HIROKI ● MUS: ARISAWA TAKANORI ● PRD: TOEI ANIMATION ● TV SERIES ● EPS: 253

# DORAEMON

CHARACTER

TV SERIES

Doraemon at first appears to be a blue, talking cat that lives with young Nobi Nobita and sleeps a cupboard in his small bedroom. In fact, Doraemon is a robot sent back in time from the twenty-second century by the boy's descendants, hoping to alter the course of his life and ensure better fortunes for themselves. Nobita is lazy, he does badly at school and is disrespectful to his parents so the robotic cat becomes his guardian in an attempt to better his prospects. Doraemon has a pocket in his chest, from which he can produce an astounding number of amazing gadgets to help Nobita in all sorts of situations, though the boy's wrong-headed approach to life usually sabotages his efforts. ● This cat is an icon for generations of Japanese children: an evergreen that has flourished for four decades in manga and anime. *Doraemon* can be seen as a child's equivalent of the *Tora-san* series of live-action films, with repetitive plots all based on a similar basic proposition. There has been a succession of full-length feature films, all with an underlying moral message, and all released in Japan during the school holidays. ● The series is set in a universe where time stands still; the characters do not grow old and their adventures are unconnected, sometimes even contradictory. From the original story onwards, many of the narratives exploit space–time paradoxes in highly imaginative flights of fancy. The television episodes explore an everyday fantasy world, set in the neighbourhood of the Nobi household, while the plots of the 48 full-length features and 13 TV specials are more ambitious. This is an ongoing series, although there have been several 'endings' that hint at a final separation between the boy and his famous cat. In March 2008, Doraemon was awarded the title World Anime Ambassador. ● S.G.

BELOW: AN ACTION SCENE FROM THE LONG-RUNNING TV SERIES DORAEMON, BEGUN IN 1973

DORAEMON ● 1973 ● DIR: ONUKI NOBUO, SHIBAYAMA TSUTOMU, KUSUBA KOZO ● SCR: SUZUKI RYOHEI ET AL ●
DES: FUJIKO–FUJIO, OKAWARA KUNIO ● ANI: NAGAKI FUSAHITO ET AL ● MUS: KOSHIBE NOBUYOSHI, KIKUCHI SHUNSUKE ●
PRD: SHIN–EI ANIMATION, TMS ● TV SERIES ● EPS: OVER 2000

---

Dororo, the little, round-faced orphan who is later discovered to be a girl, is not in fact the heroine of the manga and television series that bear her name. This role properly belongs to her travelling companion through the heart of feudal Japan, Hyakkimaru. As a result of a pact concluded with forty-eight demons by his power-hungry father, Hyakkimaru is born without arms, legs, eyes or a mouth. A hybrid being fitted with many prostheses, he sets out on a quest to conquer the demons and recover his missing body parts. ● Following the success of the televised versions of *Astro Boy* (1963) and *Princess Knight* (1967), Tezuka Osamu decided in 1968 to adapt a far more sinister manga for the small screen. He first made a pilot in colour, but the twenty-six-episode series released for public consumption the following year was in black and white. As well as featuring more detailed animation and drawing than earlier television series, *Dororo* was notable for its extreme violence. The populations of whole villages are decimated as heads fall, blood gushes, blades sink into soft flesh, and demonic voices infiltrate the soundtrack. ● A melancholy tale borrowing from the tradition of samurai films and Japanese ghost stories, *Dororo* marked the beginning of a more adult direction in Tezuka's animated work. It is also impregnated with a dualism that is seen more clearly in the final credits, as Hyakkimaru strides along almost mechanically, set on his quest, head in the clouds, while Dororo skips joyfully behind him with her puppy. The tragic hero's desperate courage is offset by Dororo's naive enthusiasm and *joie de vivre*, no matter how black the circumstances – a glimmer of humanity shining in the darkness. ● E.H.

# DORORO

CHARACTER

TV SERI

DORORO TO HYAKKIMARU ● DORORO ● 1969 ● DIR: SUGII GISABURO ET AL ● SCR: SUZUKI RYOHEI ET AL ● DES: TEZUKA OSAMU ● ANI: KITANO HIDEAKI ● MUS: TOMITA ISAO ● PRD: MUSHI PRODUCTION ● TV SERIES ● EPS: 26

RIGHT: DORORO, HER TRAVELLING COMPANION HYAKKIMARU, AND HER PUPPY, FROM THE 1969 TV SERIES DORORO

---

# DRAGON QUEST

VIDEOGAME

It is difficult to unravel the labyrinthine story of *Dragon Quest*, the videogame created for Enix by Horii Yuji in the Eighties, one of the best-selling role-playing games in the world. Horii's fundamental, yet simple, goal was to secure a vast audience among the general public as well as the classic core of die-hard fans. The saga usually focuses on a hero who has to face terrible adversaries in an exotic magical battle, fighting a vast army of monsters ranging from the traditional to the bizarre: apes, stone giants, blue pterodactyls and so on. ● Behind the scenes, Horii's own work has been elegantly combined with that of Toriyama Akira, whose famous graphic style can be seen here and there, presenting the main characters and the wide variety of monsters to the best of their advantage while still leaving ample scope for the imaginations of other artists when manga interpretations of the game were created. These include *Dragon Quest: Dai no Daibouken* (*Dragon Quest: Dai's Great Adventure*, 1989), drawn by Inata Koji, and *Dragon Quest Retsuden: Roto no Monsho* (*Dragon Quest: Emblem of Roto*, 1991) by Fujiwara Kamui. ● There are the inevitable anime versions too: the first *Dragon Quest* title was translated into a series directed by the veteran Nishizawa Nobutaka in 1991; the second became a film (1996) produced by Nippon Animation and directed by Sunaga Tsukasa, in which the magic of protagonist Arus is combined with the poetry of evocative and epic imagery almost as if striving to escape the restrictive confines of the videogame universe and slip away into pure fantasy. ● M.A.R.

DRAGON QUEST ● 1986 ● CREATOR: HORII YUJI ● PRD: ENIX

# DUKE TOGO

GOLGO 13 ● 1983 ● DIR: DEZAKI OSAMU ●
SCR: NAGASAKA HIDEYOSHI ● DES: KOBAYASHI
SHICHIRO ● MUS: OMORI TOSHIYUKI ● PRD: TMS ●
FILM ● DUR: 94 MINS

CHARACTER

BELOW: THE FRIGHTENING VISAGE OF DUKE TOGO IN
THE 1983 FILM GOLGO 13

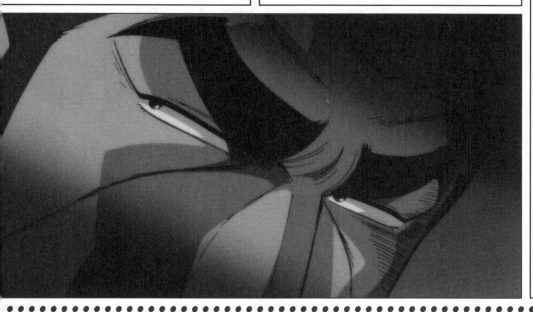

Narrow eyes, thick eyebrows, ultra-short black hair and two lines stretching his face into a sardonic grimace: these are the instantly recognizable features of Duke Togo, the cruel killer of the Rising Sun. There are few who have survived an encounter with him. ● Everything to do with this popular and historic cartoon character is a mystery; even his date and place of birth are unknown. Widely known by the pseudonym 'Golgo 13', he is an all-purpose hired assassin: modern samurai and ruthless killer. He is also renowned for amorous exploits worthy of James Bond, the novel and film character with whom Duke Togo, invented in the late Sixties by manga genius Saito Takao, has often been compared. ● Duke Togo is not, however, a pale Japanese imitation of Ian Fleming's 007. Rather, he is a fragmented mirror, reflecting inner demons and a total contempt for human life, with no apparent hope of redemption. From his first appearance in *Big Comic* to the present day, Duke Togo has been one of the most enduring of comic-strip characters, a trademark personality who has brought Saito great popularity and success. An important chapter in the history of manga, Saito's wealth of angular and geometrical shapes are poles apart from the rounded images of his predecessor Tezuka Osamu. ● The fame of Duke Togo was magnified by the 1983 film *Golgo 13*, directed by Dezaki Osamu, who reproduced Togo's criminal DNA with implacable realism. This one-off masterpiece was followed by an OAV entitled *Queen Bee* (1998) and a television series produced in 2008 to celebrate the character's fortieth anniversary. ● M.A.R.

# DYNAMIC PRODUCTION

STUDIO

When Dynamic Production, or Dynamic Pro, was founded in April 1969 by Nagai Go, he created a new kind of manga studio. Instead of simply producing work to Nagai's explicit directions and scripts, employees of Dynamic Pro are creative professionals who work closely together to generate ideas for new projects, overseen by Nagai. New works take shape through extensive discussion and development in-house, involving the artists, writers and assistants. In many cases no single author is identified, and the work is credited to 'Nagai Go and Dynamic Pro'. ● A powerhouse of ideas, Nagai has created many manga and anime classics, often releasing manga and anime television series within weeks of each other. His most famous titles includes *Devilman* (TV series 1982, OAV series 1987), *Cutey Honey* (1973), *Mazinger Z* (1972), *Getta Robot* (1974) and *UFO Robot Grendizer Raids* (1975). ● A sister company, Dynamic Planning, was established in 1974 and handles his anime rights. It is credited as producer or 'planner' of all Nagai anime since its foundation. ● H.M.

RIGHT: AKIRA FUDO IN *DEVILMAN* (1987, DIR. IIDA TSTOMU, 2 EPS)

SEE ALSO: CUTEY HONEY; GETTA ROBOT; MAZINGER Z; NAGAI GO; UFO ROBOT GRENDIZER RAIDS

# EDOGAWA CONAN

CHARACTER

When teenage detective Kudo Shinichi is transformed into a child by members of a mysterious organization, he decides to rename himself Edogawa Conan (in honour of the creator of Sherlock Holmes and the Japanese myster writer Edogawa Rampo). The result became a small revolution in manga, giving rise to one of the longest-running manga series in modern times. ● It all started in 1994 on the pages of the magazine *Shonen Sunday*, where Detective Conan made his first appearance in a work by the young *mangaka* Aoyama Gosho. The original intent was to tell a short story, but its huge success meant that *Detective Conan* has become a vehicle through which all the possible mechanisms associated with the thriller genre can be explored, including locked-room mysteries, film noir and the legal thriller. In this respect, Aoyama has shown an ability for narrative unprecedented in the history of manga, where the precision of the script is not always the most important feature of a series. ● The manga version of Conan has currently reached over 600 chapters, while the television series has already passed the 500-episode mark and annual feature films based on the series do battle in Japan with the most famous American blockbusters. Each movie is a self-contained adventure revolving around a crime, like *The Time-Bombed Skyscraper*'s theft of military explosives, *The 14th Target*'s stalkers murders and *The Last Magician of the 20th Century*'s stolen Faberge egg. The protagonist continues to have breathtaking adventures, but credit for brilliant deductions is always given to bumbling detective Goro because nobody is willing to believe the words of a child. Conan is also 'helped' by a gang of youngsters, who turn out to be something of a burden, and the thriller genre is in fact enriched by these ironic elements, making the character perfect for young audiences and helping to make him into a popular icon. A recent television special, crossing over with crime-adventure anime *Lupin III*, demonstrates the level of fame reached by this small hero, who has achieved equal billing with the giants of animation. ● D.D.G.

PUBLICITY IMAGES FROM THREE DETECTIVE CONAN SPIN–OFF MOVIES ●
RIGHT: *THE TIME BOMBED SKYSCRAPER* (1997, DIR. KODAMA KENJI, 90 MINS) ●
ABOVE RIGHT: *THE 14TH TARGET* (1998, DIR. KODAMA KENJI, 90 MINS) ●
ABOVE LEFT: *THE LAST MAGICIAN OF THE CENTURY* (1999, DIR. KODAMA KENJI, 90 MINS) ● BELOW: A JUVENILE CONAN AND HIS OLDER SELF SHINICHI

*MEITANTEI CONAN* ● *DETECTIVE CONAN* ● AKA *CASE CLOSED* ● AKA *GREAT DETECTIVE CONAN* ● 1996 ● DIR: KODAMA KENJI, YAMAMOTO YASUICHIRO ● SCR: KASHIWABARA HIROSHI ET AL ● DES: SUDO MASAAKI ● ANI: SUDO MASAAKI ET AL ● MUS: ONO KATSUO ● PRD: TMS ● TV SERIES ● EPS: 530

Eiken animation studio was formerly Tele-Cartoon Japan, the animation department of TCJ (Television Corporation of Japan) advertising studios, opened in 1952. Its name was changed in March 1969, but it had been producing its own anime for TV since 1963. Mushi Production's *Astro Boy* series was first broadcast in January that year, sparking a strong demand for TV animation. TCJ contributed three series in that year: *Sennin Buraku* (Hermit Village), *Tetsujin 28-go* (Gigantor) and *8 Man* (8th Man). ● Both *Gigantor* and *8 Man* were successful overseas, but Eiken's most famous domestic work is probably *Sazae-san* (1969). Machiko Hasegawa's story of an ordinary Japanese family in post-war Japan began as a *yon-koma manga*, or four-panel comic strip, in 1946. Eiken's TV version made its debut in October 1969, and is still on the air, making it the longest-running cartoon series in the world. As one of Japan's longest-established anime studios, Eiken has produced many titles which are almost unknown overseas, like *Oyako Club* (1994), and *Play Ball* (2005). ● Almost all film studios in Japan have now switched to digital graphics. Eiken remains one of the few to cherish and use the traditional methods of cell animation, but is looking to the future with flash animation *Kaden Kung Fu* (2009). ● H.M.

# EIKEN

STUDIO

SEE ALSO: MUSHI; TATSUNOKO; TETSUJIN 28-GO; TOEI ANIMATION; SAZAE-SAN

CHARACTER

# ELRIC, EDWARD

Born in the parallel, magically influenced world of Amestris, Edward Elric is touchy about his stature, hot tempered and fiercely protective of his brother Alphonse. He is also the youngest State Alchemist in the history of his homeland's military, a child prodigy whose incredible achievements hide a series of tragedies and a deep sense of personal guilt. ● Apparently deserted by their father, and bereaved at the loss of their mother, the two Elric boys began experimenting with alchemy at an early age. This intense focus gave Ed his great abilities, but also literally cost him an arm and a leg – he uses prosthetics made of 'automail'. Worst of all, amid the ongoing experiments to bring his mother back from the grave, an alchemical incident caused Alphonse to lose his entire body. At the beginning of the boys' anime adventures, Ed is tailed by what first appears to be a talking suit of armour – Alphonse's soul possesses the suit, and is patiently waiting for his brother to rescue his physical form. ● *Fullmetal Alchemist* (2003) was a surprise success in both Japan and abroad, drawing fans in with an initially shallow premise that soon spirals into more meaningful meditations on duty and responsibility. Ed acts like a spoilt brat, but has been left that way by a deprived and traumatic childhood – in fact, every single act he performs is a facet of true loyalty, filial piety and the desire to do right, even if the consequences are disastrous. Perhaps because of these feet of clay, he became one of the most popular anime figures of the turn of the century, voted Best Character in the 2003 *Animage* readers' poll. ● J.Cl.

SCENES FROM THE 2003 SERIES FULLMETAL ALCHEMIST ● ABOVE LEFT: FLAME ALCHEMIST COLONEL ROY MUSTANG AND HIS AIDE (BACKROUND) WITH THE BROTHERS ALPHONSE AND ED (FOREGROUND) ● ABOVE CENTRE: ED IN HIS ALCHEMIST'S UNIFORM WITH AL AND COLLEAGUES ● ABOVE RIGHT: ED WITH HIS PROSTHETIC METAL ARM ● LEFT: ALPHONSE AND ED IN COMBAT

HAGANE NO RENKINJUTSUSHI ● FULLMETAL ALCHEMIST ● 2003 ● DIR: MIZUSHIMA SEIJI ● SCR: MIZUSHIMA SEIJI, AIKAWA NOBORU ● DES: ITO YOSHIYUKI ET AL ● ANI: SUGIURA KOJI ● MUS: OSHIMA MICHIRU ● PRD: ANIPLEX, BONES, SQUARE-ENIX ● TV SERIES ● EPS: 51

# EVANGELION

The concept of mecha as a potential fantasy of power and adolescent self-affirmation had been explored by Nagai Go in *Mazinger Z* (1972), but it was the popular and controversial *Neon Genesis Evangelion* saga that took the implications of this association to their ultimate conclusion, without fear of delving into their more gloomy aspects. In a dystopian future characterized by a cataclysmic event that culminated in the extermination of half the world's population, the 'Evangelion Unit', colossal cybernetic war machines that can only be piloted by teenagers born after the tragedy, are the only hope of defence from the 'Angels', an unknown enemy that launches periodic attacks against humans with lethal biomechanical weapons. Shinji, son of the scientist Ikari Gendo, fragile Rei, restless Misato and arrogant Asuka Langley make up the fragmented group that will try to take responsibility for preventing an apocalypse. ● Anno Hideaki, creator of the saga, filled *Evangelion* with a transcendent spirit, with frequent references to the Catholic religion, Kabbalah and Buddhist symbols as well as echoes of Jungian thought, while also including references to popular television culture and games in the mecha tradition. The anticlimactic end to the TV series led to an angry reaction from many of the series' followers. Cult British TV show 'The Prisoner' (1967–8), to which *Evangelion* is often compared, had a similarly conflicting ending and provoked a similar reaction three decades earlier. ● Subsequent films revisited the whole saga and proposed alternative endings, including *Evangelion: Death and Rebirth* (1997) and *The End of Evangelion* (1997), however neither pleased the fans. The saga, which has had a parallel existence in the form of manga, has enjoyed a new cinematic comeback in a series of films that began with the hit *Evangelion 1.0: You Are (Not) Alone* (2007). ● J.Co.

IMAGES FROM THE 1995 SERIES NEON GENESIS EVANGELION AND THE FILM EVANGELION 1.0: YOU ARE (NOT) ALONE (2007) ● ABOVE: THE EVA UNIT IN COMBAT FROM EVANGELION 1.0 ● LEFT: A PUBLICITY IMAGE FOR THE TV SERIES ● BELOW: REI, THE ENIGMATIC PILOT OF THE EVA UNIT FROM EVANGELION 1.0

SHINSEIIKI EVANGELION ● NEON GENESIS EVANGELION ● 1995 ● DIR: ANNO HIDEAKI, TSURUMAKI KAZUYA ● SCR: ANNO HIDEAKI, SATSUGAWA AKIO ●
DES: SADAMOTO YOSHIYUKI, YAMASHITA IKUTO ● ANI: MASAYUKI ET AL ● MUS: SAGISU SHIRO ● PRD: GAINAX ● TV SERIES ● EPS: 26

054

# FINAL FANTASY

VIDEOGAME

FILM

In 1987, *Final Fantasy* was nothing more than a simple videogame thought up by the young Sakaguchi Hironobu, who worked for a desperate publisher named Square. Twenty-two years later, its sequels, remakes and ensuing episodes have multiplied, and the game has developed into films, manga and a television series. Today, *Final Fantasy* is both a promising hallmark of the prosperous company Square Enix – born in 2003 from the merger of Square with its boss and competitor – and an outreaching network where different works come together and sometimes fleetingly interrelate. ● *Final Fantasy* has a privileged relationship with the world of animation, if only because of the role played by the great designer Amano Yoshitaka, who created its characters. The epic saga is also distinguished by its courageous digital imaging, right up to the grandiose *Final Fantasy: The Spirits Within* (2001), a feature film with a screenplay by Sakaguchi that follows on from his narrative innovations in the videogames. Not greatly loved, the box-office flop was, nevertheless, a touching meditation on how shapes, dreams and universes come to life, enhanced by a major photographic reality show that is often disturbing. ● The other anime FFs are less audacious. *Final Fantasy: Unlimited* (2001), made by Maeda Mahiro, is a straightforward series in twenty-five episodes crammed with nods to the videogame. Another digital feature film, *Final Fantasy VII: Advent Children* by Nomura Tetsuya and Nozue Takeshi (2004), and an OAV entitled *Last Order* released in 2005, take up the story and intrigue of the highly successful videogame *Final Fantasy VII* (1997), revisting its key moments and shedding light on certain shadowy areas. Technically faultless, the result has some limitations as a creation in its own right, but the high DVD sales confirm the enduring popularity of the franchise. ● E.H.

ABOVE & RIGHT: COMBAT SCENES FROM THE FILM *FINAL FANTASY VII: ADVENT CHILDREN* (2004, DIR. NOMURA TETSUYA, NOZUE TARESHI, 101 MINS)

**F**

*FINAL FANTASY* ● 1987 ● DIR: SAKAGUCHI HIRONOBU ● MUS: UEMATSU NOBUO ET AL ● PRD: SQUARE ENIX

VIDEO SERIES

# FLCL

What is FLCL? An acronym or an unidentified object in the anime universe? Nothing is certain in this unusual six-episode OAV, which ranges from adolescent erotica to para-philosophical science fiction. The title itself reads in Japanese as *Furi Kuri*, which is not only a deconstruction of onomatopoeic expressions typical of manga, but also recalls the two American expressions 'fool' and 'cool' (the series is known in North America as *Fooly Cooly*). ● The protagonists of FLCL are all archetypes of anime and manga. The everyday life of a shy twelve-year-old named Naoto is invaded by the crazy, intergalactic detective Haruka, who is on a mission to find Atomsk, a powerful alien. A blow from Haruka's Rickenbacker guitar causes the television-headed robot Canti to emerge from a portal in Naoto's head. The series enjoys an inexhaustible mutation of styles, from detailed hyper-realism to animation on fake manga pages, although the ever-present blanket of sound from rock group The Pillows provides a sense of continuity. ● This unique collaboration between Production I.G. and Gainax, the most innovative animation studios of the Nineties, blends short stories about human emotions with wildly exaggerated events, a technique already employed in their earlier successes *Top o Nerae! Gunbuster* (*Gunbuster*, 1988) and *Kareshi Kanojo no Jijyo* (*His and Her Circumstances*, 1998). Here the irreverent parody of the anime genre that began in *Excel Saga* (1999) is accompanied by referential quotes from *South Park*, *Lupin III* (1971) and John Woo movies, as well as tributes to classic animation films such as Miyazaki's *Castle in the Sky* (1986). The directors Otsuka Masahiko, Ando Takeshi and Saeki Shoji constantly deconstruct and renew the language of animation under the general direction of the brilliant Tsurumaki Kazuya. Tsurumaki experiments with techniques and exploits the versatility of the talented animators in the studio, most notably character designer Sadamoto Yoshiyuki. ● L.D.C.

SCENES FROM THE 2000 SERIES FLCL ● ABOVE LEFT: NAOTO AND HARUKA WITH TV ROBOT CANTI ●
ABOVE RIGHT: NAOTO AND HIS BROTHER'S GIRLFRIEND MAMIMI ● CENTRE RIGHT: STRANGE AND
SURREAL CHARACTERS FROM THE SERIES ● RIGHT: HARUKA CHARGES INTO ACTION

FURI KURI ● FLCL ● 2000 ● DIR: TSURUMAKI KAZUYA ● SCR: ENOKIDO YOJI ● DES: SADAMOTO YOSHIYUKI ● ANI: HIRAMATSU TADASHI, IMAISHI HIROYUKI ●
MUS: THE PILLOWS ● PRD: GAINAX, PRODUCTION I.G. ● VIDEO SERIES ● EPS: 6

CHARACTER

The protagonists of *Around the World with Willy Fog* are all anthropomorphic animals, fully clothed and capable of doing anything, such as attending an elegant party, negotiating risky business deals or thwarting insidious plots concocted by their high-society rivals. The elegant Willy Fog is a lion who, with the refined ways of the perfect English Lord, accepts a challenge to travel the globe in just eighty days. What he does not know is that the members of the Reform Club who challenged him intend to follow him and derail his plans in order to win their bet. ● Thus begins a long journey (twenty-six episodes) visiting all the corners of the world, from England and Italy to Egypt and North America, with an elegant, if rapid, pace and a rounded style, where music invades the scenes and always affects the characters and events. ● Taken from Jules Verne's novel *Around the World in Eighty Days*, this series is extremely faithful to the original, both in keeping with its curiosity and adventurous spirit as well as the magic and wonder of travel. Willy Fog perfectly embodies the character of the nineteenth-century traveller who does not give up the comforts of modern life but also can not be easily intimidated by difficulties. Attention to small details adds to the didactic elements of the series without ever sacrificing the pleasure of the journey or the true wonder of discovery and pride of those who succeed, especially when intellect overcomes mishaps. ● The result of a co-production between BRB International and Nippon Animation, co-directed by Spanish director Luis Bellester Bustos and Kurokawo Fumio with character design by Kumata Isamu, *Around the World with Willy Fog* tells universal stories and is instantly recognizable, fun and lively. ● G.P.

ABOVE: PUBLICITY POSTER FOR THE 1985 SERIES AROUND THE WORLD WITH WILLY FOG, INSPIRED BY JULES VERNE'S NOVEL AROUND THE WORLD IN EIGHTY DAYS (1873)

F

ANIME HACHIJUNICHIKAN SEKAI ISSHUU ● AROUND THE WORLD WITH WILLY FOG ● 1985 ● DIR: LUIS BELLESTER BUSTOS, KUROKAWA FUMIO ● SCR: NAKANISHI RYUZO ● DES: KUMATA ISAMU ● ANI: ISHINO HIROKAZU ET AL ● MUS: KIKUCHI SHUNSUKE ● PRD: BRB INTERNACIONAL, NIPPON ANIMATION ● TV SERIES ● EPS: 26

# FUJIKAWA KEISUKE

Fujikawa Keisuke (born in 1934 in Nitto, near Kyoto) is a veteran of animated cinema and a pillar of the science-fiction community, with links to talents such as Matsumoto Leiji and Tezuka Osamu. The variety of his small-screen productions reveals the immense flexibility required of writers by the anime industry. Anchored in long-established themes, Fujikawa proved extremely skilful in moving from complex genres to gentler works for children such as *Donbe Monogatari* (1981). ● In his cinematic screenplays, written either alone or with assistance from Yamamoto Eiichi and Nishizaki Yoshinobu, Fujikawa found the freedom to address his subjects and themes in greater depth. However his best results are arguably his interpretations of Matsumoto's manga. In *Star Blazers* (1974), the intergalactic journeys captained by Kodai Susumu are the foundation of the 'space-opera' (a spectacular genre saturated with epics), where heroes face adversaries from other worlds who mirror human weaknesses in their diversity. *Cutey Honey* (1973) has Fujikawa scripting the action-packed adventures of Nagai Go's shape-shifting android schoolgirl. In *Shin Taketori Monogatari Sennen Joou* (*Queen Millennia*, 1981) Fujikawa seems to conceal the most important answers in space itself. Facing a civilization on the ropes, the film glances at our own past for inspiration – it's no coincidence that the queens protecting Earth have names like Cleopatra and Himiko. This nostalgia is also seen in Fujikawa's other great work, *Utsunomiko* (1989), a movie directed by Kurokawa Fumio and video series directed by Imazawa Tetsuo, based on a series of successful 'light novels' imbued with the necessity for certain writers to rethink their own cultural traditions, which are all too often overshadowed by the illusions of the exotic West. ● M.A.R.

ABOVE: THE ANDROID GIRL CUTEY HONEY FROM THE TV SERIES *CUTEY HONEY* (1973, DIR. KATSUMATRA TOMOHARU, 25 EPS), ONE OF MANY POWERFUL WOMEN WHOSE TV ADVENTURES WERE SCRIPTED BY FUJIKAWA

SEE ALSO: JEEG, THE STEEL ROBOT; KISUGI; MAETEL; MATSUMOTO LEIJI; MAZINGER Z; NISHIZAKI YOSHINOBU; TEZUKA OSAMU; UFO ROBOT GRENDIZER RAIDS; YAMATO

# FUJISHIMA KOSUKE

MANGAKA

The designer/illustrator Fujishima Kosuke (born in 1964 in Chiba) owes much of his popularity to the female characters of his works. An instant favourite in Japan his books soon became successful and much-loved publications in the West. The second of his comics, *Oh My Goddess!*, is worthy of particular mention. Designed for a young male audience, it tells the story of goddesses come down to earth to help Morisato Keiichi, a pure-hearted but nerdy character who falls in love with the goddess Belldandy. ● Faithful to a public of younger admirers, Fujishima's manga have a good mix of irony and romance, but also reflect a growing interest in action and more complex plots. The long-running *Oh My Goddess!* was first published in 1988 and, from a graphic point of view, has matured along with its author. Once an assistant of the illustrator Egawa Tetsuya, Fujishima has developed an elegant and captivating style of drawing. His stories lend themselves perfectly to animation and are a gift for devotees of the genre. Fujishima has also established himself as a highly regarded character designer in the world of anime. ● Like many of his colleagues, Fujishima sometimes indulges in passions outside his normal sphere of work. It is not uncommon to see his splendid illustrations of automobiles in a range of anime from the police cars of *Taiho Shichauzo* (*You're Under Arrest!*, 1989) to those of *éX-Driver*, a manga created in 2000, which has since become an OAV series. ● M.A.R

LEFT, ABOVE LEFT & ABOVE CENTRE: SCENES FROM THE SERIES ÉX-DRIVER (2000, DIR. KAWAGOE JUN, 6 EPS) ● ABOVE RIGHT: SCENES FROM THE SERIES OH MY GODDESS! (1993, DIR. GODA HIROAKI, EPS 41) FEATURING BELLDANDY AND KEIICHI

SEE ALSO: BELLDANDY

F

# GAINAX

STUDIO

In 1981, Anno Hideaki, Sadamoto Yoshiyuki and Yamaga Hiroyuki were part of a group of students with a passion for anime. They got together to make two acclaimed short films, and founded Gainax in December 1984. ● Their first professional project was a feature film, *Oritsu Uchugun Honneamise no Tsubasa* (*Wings of Honneamise*, 1987, dir. Yamaga Hiroyuki). As science fiction and anime fans themselves, they made works with wide fan appeal, and their dynamic, original style has made a huge impact on audiences all over the world. Even when adapting existing manga, as in *Re: Cutey Honey* (2004), Gainax bring their own unique qualities to the work. They are widely considered one of Japan's most original anime production companies. ● This originality shines in titles such as OAV series *Top o Nerae! Gunbuster* (*Gunbuster*, 1988) and TV series *Fushigi no Umi no Nadia* (*The Secret of Blue Water*, 1990). TV series *Neon Genesis Evangelion* (*Shinseiki Evangelion*, 1995) is probably their greatest success worldwide, and is often described as a turning point in anime history. Other works include TV series *Kareshi Kanojo no Jijyo* (*His and Her Circumstances*, 1998), *Abenobashi Mahoh Shotengai* (*Magical Shopping Arcade Abenobashi*, 2002), *Tengen Toppa Gurren Lagann* (*Gurren Lagann*, 2007) and the OAV *Otaku no Video* (1991). ● H.M.

ABOVE: PUBLICITY POSTER FOR ONE OF THE STUDIO'S RECENT CREATIONS, *TENGEN TOPPA GURREN LAGANN* (*GURREN LAGANN*, 2007, DIR. IMAISHI HIROYUKI, 27 EPS) ● LEFT: TWO SCENES FROM THE SERIES *GURREN LAGANN*

*SEE ALSO: ANNO HIDEAKI; DAICON III & IV; EVANGELION; LHADATT, SHIROTSUGU; MAEDA MAHIRO; NADIA; OTAKU NO VIDEO; YAMAGA HIROYUKI*

## GALLOP
STUDIO

Production company Studio Gallop was founded in December 1978, by former staffers from Mushi Production. Like many new studios, Gallop started out subcontracting for other productions, but began producing their own animated works in 1986. Since then, the studio has produced many TV series for children. Particularly noteworthy are their adaptations from the monthly manga magazine *Ribon*, aimed at a female audience. ● Their best-known works are the television series *Hime-chan no Ribon* (Hime-Chan's Ribbon, 1992), *Akazukin Chacha* (1994), *Kodocha* (1996), *Yu-Gi-Oh! Duel Monsters* (2000) and *Eyeshield 21* (2005). They have also contributed to movies such as Miyazaki Hayao's *Kiki's Delivery Service* (1989) and the 1997 film and TV versions of *Ruroni Kenshin*. ● H.M.

ABOVE: A NIGHTMARISH CHARACTER FROM THE SERIES
*RURONI KENSHIN* (1996, DIR. FURUHASHI KAZUHIRO, 94 EPS)

SEE ALSO: DEEN; GAINAX; HIMURA KENSHIN; MUSHI; NIPPON ANIMATION; PRODUCTION REED; SUNRISE; TEZUKA PRODUCTION

## GALLY
## ALITA
CHARACTER

In a world sharply divided between haves and have-nots, lower-class humans struggle to live on a giant mountain of trash beneath the utopian floating island of Zalem. Gally (named Alita in English) is a mystery, a robot girl found amid the junk and restored to life, only to display all the hallmarks of having been created for a sinister military purpose. ● This science-fiction pin-up began as a series of sketches by artist Kishiro Yukito, inspired by the modular android toys known in the West as the Micronauts. The storyline was almost an afterthought, hence Alita's 'amnesia' in the anime, which recalls a chapter of the manga when the creator had yet to work out her backstory himself. ● Released in 1993 at the height of foreign interest in science-fiction anime, *Gunnm* gained a strong following abroad as *Battle Angel Alita* in part of the post-*Akira* rush of anime on video. But where other late twentieth-century successes (*Bubblegum Crisis*, 1987, or *Lodoss-to Senki*, 1990) were soon remade for television, *Battle Angel* was not. The remake rights were sold to James Cameron, but currently this nineties icon only exists in anime form in two thirty-five-minute video episodes. ● *Battle Angel* is part of a long tradition in anime, drawing not only on the idea of a scientist who creates for himself a surrogate child, but also on the idea of a robotic love interest, childishly innocent in affairs of the heart, despite the outward appearance of sexual maturity. Such artificial girlfriends include the feminized computers of *Chobits* (2002), and the televisual companion of *Video Girl Ai* (1992). ● J.Cl.

GUNNM ● BATTLE ANGEL ALITA ● 1993 ● DIR: FUKUTOMI HIROSHI ● SCR: ENDO AKINORI ● DES: YUKI NOBUTERU ● ANI: YUKI NOBUTERU ● MUS: WADA KAORU ● PRD: ANIMATE, KSS, MOVIE MADHOUSE ● VIDEO SERIES ● EPS: 2

# GANTZ

TV SERIES

Like the monolith in *2001: A Space Odyssey* (1968), Gantz is a mysterious sphere that can bring out the evil inherent in the human soul. In the manga by Oku Hiroya, first published in 2000 by *Young Jump* magazine, the black ball does not cross time like Kubrick's monolith, but is located in an ordinary apartment in Tokyo. From there, through a strange power, it summons people snatched from the arms of death and forces them to take part in a cruel game where points are awarded to those who kill alien beings. ● The game, however, is merely the catalyst for a discussion exploring the concept of existence itself. Oku was interested in showing people returning to their everyday lives, having experienced the thrill of being heroes in a game where you kill or die for real. Thus the manga turns its pitiless gaze upon a dissatisfied and frustrated humanity. ● The television series, directed by Itano Ichiro, follows the development of the manga, while emphasizing certain elements. Although the style of the design and animation can appear almost schematic – a near-perfect reproduction of computer-generated geometry – as the episodes continue small details appear that enrich the character design. Itano also enjoyed varying the pace of the story, using temporal leaps without feeling he had to justify them. Within the game sequences, the audience's perspective moves from watching events from an external viewpoint to seeing the action through the characters' eyes, as if it were a game in which the viewer had changed player. Thanks to Itano's skill in varying points of view and Oku's narrative strength, *Gantz* is one of the high points of contemporary anime, along with science-fiction series *Kaiba* (2008). ● C.C.

SCENES FROM THE 2004 TV SERIES *GANTZ* ● TOP: THE BATH WHERE KEI DIES (LEFT), A STRANGE VISION (CENTRE) AND AN ALIEN HUNT (RIGHT) ● ABOVE: PUBLICITY IMAGE FOR THE SERIES. CHARACTERS KURONO KEI (CENTRE) AND HIS CLASSMATE KATO MASARU (RIGHT) ARE HIT BY A SUBWAY TRAIN, WHILE KISHIMOTO KEI (LEFT) SLITS HER WRISTS. ALL THREE ARE DRAWN INTO GANTZ' STRANGE GAME AS PART OF ITS TEAM OF REANIMATED ALIEN HUNTERS

GANTZ ● 2004 ● DIR: ITANO ICHIRO ● SCR: SOGO MASASHI, TOGAWA SEISHI ● DES: ONDA NAOYUKI, NAKAJIMA TOSHIHIRO ● ANI: ARAI HIDEMASA ● MUS: TOGAWA NATSUKI ● PRD: FUJI TV, GPH, SHOCHIKU, STUDIO GONZO ● TV SERIES ● EPS: 13

# GATCHAMAN

RACTERS

BELOW: A FIGHT SCENE FEATURING ·THE VALIANT WINGED HEROES OF THE 1972 SERIES *BATTLE OF THE PLANETS*. THE GATCHAMAN TEAM FIGHT BLACK-CLAD MINIONS, WITH TEAM LEADER KEN IN THE FOREGROUND

Western fans of the late-seventies series *Battle of the Planets* may not be as familiar with *Gatchaman* as they think. What was distributed outside Japan was in fact a heavily reworked version compared with the pioneering series that appeared six years earlier. Re-edited in the USA, the 105 episodes were condensed to eighty-five and a small robot vaguely reminiscent of R2-D2 was added to support the protagonists in an ill-concealed attempt to cash in on the success of the first *Star Wars* film (1977). In particular, scenes thought to be too shocking such as character deaths and cities in flames were cut so as not to offend the sensibilities of a western audience. ● The overall plot was retained but the series undoubtedly lost the dark atmosphere inherited from Japanese monster films made from the Fifties onwards, following in the footsteps of *Godzilla* (1954) where the memory of Hiroshima and Nagasaki casts its subtle but omnipresent shadow. *Gatchaman* also alludes time and again to the catastrophe at the origins of modern Japan, hinted at in the form of repeated attacks by various pitiless robots and other creatures. ● The triumphant response to these attacks, however, remains unvaried from one version to another. Five orphans, given the names of different birds, who become even more formidable when they combine forces, invariably appear out of nowhere to prevent the worst. With its band of combatants in their colourful jumpsuits, *Gatchaman* is undoubtedly the forerunner of all the *Super Sentai* (*Power Rangers*, 1975) series. With its skilful blend of youthful energy and portentous explanatory pauses, the series can surprise the viewer even today. But it does so above all because in a Japan astride two eras, this series is a remarkable transitional oeuvre. ● E.H.

KAGAKU NINJA TAI GATCHAMAN ● GATCHAMAN ● AKA: BATTLE OF THE PLANETS ● 1972 ● DIR: TORIUMI HISAYUKI ● SCR: TORIUMI JINZO ET AL ● DES: YOSHIDA TATSUO, OKAWARA KUNIO ● ANI: SADO MIYAMOTO ● MUS: SAKUMA BOB ● PRD: TATSUNOKO ● TV SERIES ● EPS: 105

# GEN

CHARACTER

In his autobiographical manga *Hadashi no Gen* (*Barefoot Gen*, 1973), Nakazawa Keiji depicts the aftermath of the bombing of Hiroshima as seen through the eyes of a child. Animating the manga posed various technical problems but these were brilliantly solved in a 1983 film by Mori Masaki and produced by Madhouse. ● The story begins with a wartime summer like any other, but the explosion of the bomb reveals a world in ruins, haunted by corpses living on borrowed time. Gen moves through this hell with his mother, who has given birth to a baby girl, and an orphan he takes under his wing. ● The daring and sensitivity of *Gen* make it a milestone in Japanese animation. Its successful blend of adult vision and child's-eye view is equalled only by Takahata's *Grave of the Fireflies* (1988). The sight of half-vaporized bodies wandering the streets of Hiroshima is unforgettable, the sketchiness of the drawing gives a power to the representation which, had it been more detailed, might have verged on obscenity. ● Unlike the manga, the film dared to represent the moment the bomb exploded. At this point the animation changes, becoming expressionistic and accompanied by the frightening sound of the blast. Black-and-white frames evoke a lightning flash before men, women, children and a dog vaporize in garish colours. The naive and childish character of these extreme images is particularly moving. ● Both film and comic insist on the courage of the child going through hell, and the brutality of the images forbids sentimentality. Neither has yet been accorded the place it deserves among the great depictions of World War II. ● S.D.

BELOW: A PUBLICITY IMAGE FOR THE 1983 FILM *BAREFOOT GEN* ● RIGHT: GEN, HIS FAMILY AND HIROSHIMA IN RUINS

HADASHI NO GEN ● BAREFOOT GEN ● 1983 ● DIR: MORI MASAKI ● SCR: NAKAZAWA KEIJI ● DES & ANI: TOMIZAWA KAZUO ● MUS: HANEDA KENTARO ● PRD: GEN PRO, MADHOUSE ● FILM ● DUR: 83 MINS

Genji Hikaru is the son of the Emperor during the Heian period. Beautiful, cultured and refined, he excels in music and poetry. Libertine and bold, polygamous but respectful of women, he flits from one love affair to the other in search of the perfect wife, affected by the trauma of the premature loss of his mother. He believes he has found his ideal woman in Lady Fujitsubo, his father's wife, with whom he begins a secretive and incestuous affair. He then meets his young niece, Murasaki, and decides to raise her in his court to make her into the perfect woman, eventually falling in love with her. ● *The Tale of Genji* is one of the masterpieces of Japanese literature, considered by many to be the first psychological novel. The work of Murasaki Shikibu, it is difficult for the modern reader to fully understand, leading to several debates on its meaning. The writing itself is predominantly phonetic and can have several interpretations, and the plot is permeated by Buddhist thought from times long gone. The tale has been animated by Sugii Gisaburo and made into a feature film. As the dialogue is impossible to recreate, the film focuses on the Zen atmosphere, using fixed settings and slow tracking shots, exploding in the final scene in which Genji learns the meaning of *mono no aware* (the inherent tragedy of things). Dezaki Osamu has also made the novel into a series, released in 2009. Here, the animation is more dynamic and the direction less minimal, discreetly echoing the style of *Rose of Versailles* (1979), with bright colours and a strong use of blurring effects. These films are targeted at adult audiences, not just because of the complexity of the subject matter, which is at times erotic, but mainly because of the absence of *chanbara* (sword fighting) that the younger audience is accustomed to expect from anime set in medieval times. ● S.G.

# GENJI HIKARU

*CHARACTER*

*MURASAKI SHIKIBU GENJI MONOGATARI ● TALE OF GENJI ● 1987 ● DIR: SUGII GISABURO ● SCR: TSUTSUI TOMOMI ● DES: NAKURA YASUHIRO ● ANI: MAEDA YASUO ET AL ● MUS: HOSONO HARUOMII ● PRD: GROUP TAC, HERALD ● FILM ● DUR: 110 MINS*

# GETTA ROBOT

*ROBOT*

*TV SERIES*

*Getta Robot* features three teenage pilots who fly three specially designed jets that fit together to form giant robots. Each mecha is suitable for fighting in different environments, in the air, on ground or underwater. Nagai Go's original idea was developed by Ishikawa Ken, who made it a life-long project and took the robot manga to new heights. Ishikawa gradually shifted the focus of the story from the robots to the Getta energy fuelling them. This energy becomes the vehicle for a further evolution of the human race, the potential source of man's rebirth or damnation and the sustenance of ever more dreadful and lethal giant machines. ● The first animated series, produced by the Toei Animation studio in 1974, imprinted the design of *Getta* on the mind of a generation, but considerably softened the brutality of the original manga, returning to the comfortable pattern of a clash between heroes and villains. It was not until the Nineties that audiences received a taste of Ishikawa's radical ideas as a new OAV series allowed the Getta to tackle even more extreme incarnations of the genre. The background was now a struggle between different evolutionary phases of life on Earth (an idea already present in germ), with a global significance transcending space, time and civilization. The three pilots are extremely diverse characters, the original team consisting of a martial arts fighter, a violent hooligan and a clumsy sumo wrestler. They are joined by new characters, some female, suggesting the basis for a new social order, the dynamics of which are yet to be explored. ● D.D.G.

BELOW: TWO SCENES FROM THE 1974 SERIES GETTA ROBOT, BASED ON THE MANGA BY NAGAI GO, FEATURING HERO NAGARE RYOMA (RIGHT) AND HIS COMRADE TOMOE MUSASHI (LEFT)

GETTA ROBOT ● GETTER ROBO ● AKA: STARVENGERS ● 1974 ● DIR: KATSUMATA TOMOHARU ET AL ● SCR: YUKIMURO SHUNICHI, MATSUORA SEIJI ● DES: KOMATSUBARA KAZUO ● ANI: KOMATSUBARA KAZUO ET AL ● MUS: KIKUCHI SHUNSUKE ● PRD: DYNAMIC PLANNING, TOEI ANIMATION STUDIO ● TV SERIES ● EPS: 51

# GHIBLI

Studio Ghibli was founded in June 1985 to produce the feature-length animations of Miyazaki Hayao and Takahata Isao. Since then, it has made some of the finest animation in the world, and become internationally synonymous with Japanese animation. Many moviegoers both inside and outside Japan have never seen any anime except for Ghibli films. ● Unusually, the studio focuses on feature-length animation for theatrical release. It also produces animated television advertisements, short films, and even music videos such as *On Your Mark* (1995, dir Miyazaki Hayao); but it has never made a TV series. The studio's uniqueness stems from its total control of every part of the creative process, from the initial idea to final photography. The Ghibli team works full-time on Ghibli movies, unlike other studios where much of the work is subcontracted. ● Miyazaki and Takahata's early films were made at other studios, but from 1986 onwards all their works have been produced and animated at Studio Ghibli. Miyazaki's subsequent films include *Spirited Away* (2001), *Howl's Moving Castle* (2004) and *Ponyo on the Cliff by the Sea* (2008). Takahata's works include *Grave of the Fireflies* (1988), *Only Yesterday* (1991) and *Pom Poko* (1994). Morita Hiroyuki directed *The Cat Returns* (2002) and Miyazaki's son Goro directed *Tales From Earthsea* (2006). Yonebayashi Hiromasa directed *Karigurashino Arriety* (*The Borrower Arriety*, 2010). ● *Spirited Away* won the American Academy Award for Best Animated Feature in 2003, becoming the first anime to win an Oscar. ● H.M.

TOP LEFT: PONYO AND SOSUKE FROM *PONYO ON THE CLIFF BY THE SEA* (2008, DIR. MIYAZAKI HAYAO, PRD. SUZUKI TOSHIO ET AL, 100 MINS) ● CENTRE LEFT: THE FAMILY IN *ONLY YESTERDAY* (1991, DIR. TAKAHATA ISAO, PRD. TOKUMA YASUYOSHI, 119 MINS) ● BOTTOM LEFT: THE HAPPY BAND FROM *POM POKO* (1994, DIR. TAKAHATA ISAO, PRD. SUZUKI TOSHIO ET AL, 119 MINS) ● ABOVE: AN ANTHROPOMORPHIC CAT FROM *THE CAT RETURNS* (2002, DIR. MORITA HIROYUKI, PRD. SUZUKI TOSHIO ET AL, 75 MINS)

SEE ALSO: CHIHIRO; KIKI; LAPUTA; MIYAZAKI HAYAO; OKAJIMA TAEKO; PORCO ROSSO; SAN; SEITA & SETSUKO; SUZUKI TOSHIO; TAKAHATA ISAO; TOTORO

# GINKO

With his white hair and fresh face, Ginko travels through Japan to search for 'Mushi', tiny creatures, invisible to the naked eye, which can nest in human bodies, causing all manner of problems. Ginko is a 'Mushishi', a Mushi hunter, but his disinfection technique is much less flashy than that of the American ghostbusters. ● Ginko, a man whose heart is as clear as his one good eye, was created by Urushibara Yuki and first appeared in 1999 in Kodansha's *Afternoon* magazine. The series has won many prestigious awards for both the peculiarity of its subject matter and the quality of its graphic design, and was adapted for animation by Artland studios in 2005. The result is a refined series, both in terms of its atmosphere and in its use of computer graphics. ● *Mushishi* is set in a verdant Japan where progress seems absent and men live in close contact with the forces of nature. In each episode, Ginko encounters a new case, and his ability to take action and free the patient from the Mushi lies in knowing how to talk to people and absorb their story, he lost his own memory after an encounter with a Mushi. ● In an industry flooded with hyper-kinetic products, the relaxed atmosphere of *Mushishi* is unique. The series is equally surprising for its abundance of dialogue and descriptions that take precedence over action. The effectiveness of the result is highly dependent on the beauty of the design, the light variations and the clarity of the colours, which are all extremely natural. ● These are gifts that *Bugmaster* (2006), the live-action feature by Otomo Katsuhiro, does not possess in equal measure. Although it may be a sincere and interesting attempt to move between animation and live action, it does not succeed in communicating the original's sense of wonder. ● C.C.

SCENES FROM THE 2005 SERIES MUSHISHI ● ABOVE RIGHT: GINKO THE MUSHI HUNTER TRAVELS THROUGH THE SNOW ● BELOW & RIGHT: GINKO ON THE HUNT FOR MUSHI. THE TINY CREATURES CAN TAKE MANY FORMS, BUT NOT EVERYONE CAN SEE THEM

MUSHISHI ● 2005 ● DIR: NAGAHAMA HIROSHI ● SCR: KUWABATA KINUKO ET AL ● DES: UMAKOSHI YOSHIHIKO ●
ANI: UMAKOSHI YOSHIHIKO ET AL ● MUS: MASUDA TOSHIO ● PRD: ARTLAND ● TV SERIES ● EPS: 26

# GOKU

A light-hearted interpretation of the legendary figure of the Monkey King, Goku is the hero of the popular saga *Dragon Ball*. Over a period lasting eleven years, Toriyama Akira produced about 8,400 pages of manga, and 519 chapters were later published in forty-two volumes. Goku first appeared in *Weekly Shonen Jump* magazine and was an immediate hit, with the collected editions of the series achieving record sales of well over 120,000 copies. ● Goku has an unmistakable pointy hairstyle, a monkey's tail, prodigious skill in martial arts and a wide range of super-powers. He begins his career as an uncontrollable child who gradually develops into his final incarnation as a mega-warrior with a subtle, almost messianic tinge to his character. As the story unfolds, his origins are revealed and traced back to the extra-terrestrial Saiyan race. ● The saga begins in a humorous vein, with a vulgarity that can be disconcerting to a western reader, but epic hyperbole gradually takes control of the story and eventually dominates its development. The huge success of this manga meant that television lost no time in turning it into three series: *Dragon Ball* (1986–9, 153 episodes), *Dragon Ball Z* (1989–96, 291 episodes) and *Dragon Ball GT* (1996–7, sixty-four episodes, with a plot that had diverged totally from the original manga). Concurrently, Toei Animation also produced two longer episodes (with more in-depth exploitation of certain aspects of the saga) and thirteen independent films, unconnected with the original story. In 1996 the world of *Dragon Ball* was the inspiration for an unauthorized live-action spin-off: the Chinese film *Xin qi longzhu Shenlong de chuanshuo* (*New Dragon Ball: the Legend of Shen Long*), but the official cinema version is the Fox super-production, directed by James Wong (2009). ● J.Co.

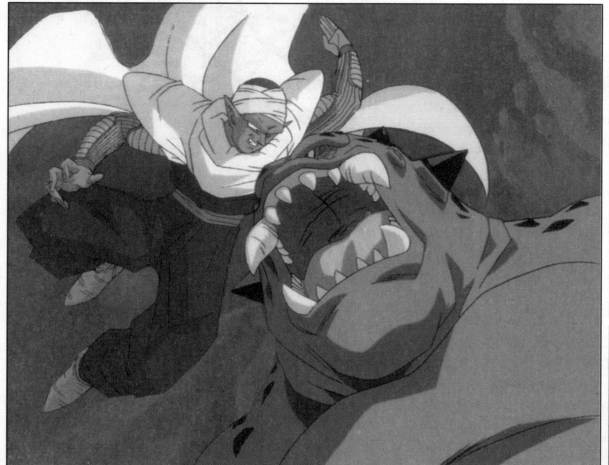

SCENES FROM THE TV SERIES *DRAGON BALL Z* (1989, DIR. NISHIO DAISUKE, 102 EPS) ● TOP: GOKU AND PICCOLO ● ABOVE: FORMER ENEMY TURNED ALLY PICCOLO FIGHTS A MONSTROUS FOE ● RIGHT: GOHAN, THE HERO GOKU'S SON, CALLS ON HIS POWERS BEFORE A BATTLE

*DRAGON BALL* ● 1986 ● DIR: OKAZAKI MINORU ET AL ● SCR: HIRANO YASUSHI ET AL ● DES: TSUJI TADAMASA, IKEDA YUJI ● ANI: MAEDA MINORU ET AL ● MUS: KIKUCHI SHUNSUKE ● PRD: FUJI TV, TOEI ANIMATION ● TV SERIES ● EPS: 153

# GONZO

STUDIO

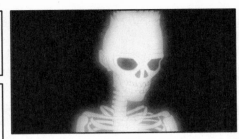

Founded in September 1992 by Shouji Murahama and three other former Gainax staffers, production company Gonzo started out subcontracting support work from established studios and helping to produce film-related video games. Their first original work, the OAV series *Ao No Rokugo* (*Blue Submarine No. 6*, 1998), used digital technology to create beautiful images of high technical quality, making Gonzo a leading name in the world of animation. ● Following this, Gonzo became known in Japan as a pioneer of digital techniques, beginning with 3D computer games. Outside its three main activity sectors – television series, full-length features and OAVs – Gonzo also works on current affairs films and online games. The studio is also a pioneer in proactively seeking opportunities and relationships to make anime aimed at the international market, such as *Afro Samurai* (2007). Given its specific style, Gonzo makes many works for adult fans of the genre, almost completely neglecting the children's market. ● Since launching *Gate Keepers* in 2000, Gonzo has made over fifty TV series, including *Full Metal Panic!* (2002), *Kaleido Star* (2003), *Last Exile* (2003), *Samurai 7* (2004), *Gantz* (2004), *Gankutsuo* (*The Count of Montecristo*, 2004), *Bakuretsu Tenshi* (*Burst Angel*, 2004), *Black Cat* (2005–6), *Bokura no* (*Ours*, 2007) and *Dragonaut: The Resonance* (2007). Its full-length feature films include *Gin iro no kami no Agito* (*Origin: Spirits of the Past*, 2006), *Brave Story* (2006) and *Kappa no Coo Natsuyasumi* (*Summer Days with Coo*, 2007). ● H.M.

IMAGES FROM TWO SERIES PRODUCED BY GONZO ● TOP: TWO SCENES FROM *GANTZ* (2004, DIR. ITANO ICHIRO, 26 EPS) ● ABOVE & LEFT: PUBLICITY IMAGES FOR *BAKURETSU TENSHI* (*BURST ANGEL*, 2004, DIR. OHATA KOICHI, URATA YASUNORI, 24 EPS)

SEE ALSO: CHRISTOPHER, ROSETTE; GAINAX; GANTZ; HARA KEIICHI; I.G.

# GOSHU
## GAUCHE

In a small country village in post-war Japan, Goshu plays the cello in the orchestra that accompanies local cinema projections. During trials for an upcoming musical contest, the conductor reproaches him for not playing with enough emotion. The young Goshu then begins to practise all the notes at great length, under the fierce gaze of a portrait of Beethoven hanging in his humble hut. Finally, it is a group of small animals, including a cat, a cuckoo, a *tanuki* and a family of mice, who teach him the deeper sense of music. ● *Gauche the Cellist* is the faithful adaptation of a famous children's tale by Miyazawa Kenji. The film took six years to make, as its director Takahata Isao was also working on other important children's series at the time. Miyazawa had imagined Goshu as an adult musician, whereas Takahata drew him as a teenager. In this way, his learning process is also his journey into adulthood. Goshu is transformed by his dialogue with nature – allegorically represented by the animals that visit him – from a solitary and awkward boy, who hides his insecurities behind his nervy and proud character, into a man who is aware of his own abilities and his place in the world. In this film Takahata is already showing a mature style, characterized by sobriety of movement, clever balance between fixed backgrounds and dynamic scenes, and an obsessive attention to detail (the animator even took cello lessons to be able to correctly draw the movement of Goshu's fingers). ● The central role of music recalls *Fantasia* and several *Silly Symphonies* by Disney, while the extremely delicate watercolours in scenes by Takamura Mukuo paint a far-away Japan, with flavours of Basho's haiku and the poetry of Jacques Prévert, much loved by Takahata. ● S.G.

SCENES FROM THE 1982 FILM *GOSHU THE CELLIST* ● ABOVE RIGHT: GOSHU WALKING IN THE TRANQUIL COUNTRYSIDE NEAR HIS HOME ● RIGHT & BELOW: GOSHU PRACTISING UNDER THE STERN GAZE OF BEETHOVEN

CELLO HIKI NO GOSHU ● GAUCHE THE CELLIST ● AKA: GOSHU THE CELLIST ● 1982 ● DIR & SCR: TAKAHATA ISAO ● DES: SAITA SHUNJI ● ANI: SAITA SHUNJI ET AL ● MUS: MAMIYA YOSHIO, LUDWIG VON BEETHOVEN ● PRD: OH PRODUCTIONS ● FILM ● DUR: 63 MINS

Goto Takayuki (born in 1960) is one of the most prolific character designers and animation directors, and also works in the field of videogames and anime for young children. He has handled the adaptations of many successful manga, and is a designer in the classical *shojo* tradition, using intense round eyes, angular tufts of hair, wide fringes that often cover the entire face, and pointed noses that can hardly be seen in frontal shots. Among his most famous works are the science-fiction *Akai Kodan Zillion* (*Red Photon Zillion*, 1987) and the romantic *Video Girl Ai* (1992), directed by his friend Nishikubo Mizuho, and the OAV fantasy *Boku no Tama wo Mamotte* (*Please Save My Earth,* 1993). He was editing director of the teenage series *Kimagure Orange Road* (1987), based on drawings by Takada Akemi that he later reinvented to produce a more adult and detailed direction for the second film. ● In 1987, Ishikawa Mitsuhisa asked Goto to be a partner in the founding of I.G. Tatsunoko (which became independent in 1993 under the name Production I.G.). Goto is still director of Studio No. 1, while also continuing to work as a character designer and personally training staff. He follows a rigorous twelve-hour daily timetable every day, in contrast to his friend Kise Kazuchika, director of Studio No. 2, who prefers to work at night. In more recent times Goto has become better known as one of the talents to give audiences the series *Ghost in the Shell: Stand Alone Complex* (2002), more faithful in its atmosphere and style to the original manga than the two Oshii films. Goto ranks as one of the most productive forces in television. His latest work is the strange *Chocolate Underground* (2008), in which he imagines an alternative reality where sweets are banned. As a director, his only OAV work is the forty-five minute, sentimental *Otohime Connection* (1991). ● S.G.

# GOTO TAKAYUKI

CHARACTER DESIGNER

ABOVE: AMANO AI, THE MAGICAL GIRLFRIEND FROM *VIDEO GIRL AI* (1992, DIR. NISHIKUBO MIZUHO, 6 EPS)

SEE ALSO: AMANO AI; I.G.; KASUGA KYOSUKE; KISE KAZUCHIKA; TAKADA AKEMI

Group TAC was established in March 1968 as an independent offshoot of Tezuka Osamu's Mushi Production by some of Mushi's sound-effects staff. At first, most of Group TAC's work was on sound effects for other studios. They did not begin producing and distributing their own titles until 1975, with TV series *Manga Nihon Mukashi Banashi* (*Japanese Folk Tales*, 1975–95, dir. Rintaro et al). This series was so popular that its sequel ran for almost twenty years, from 1976 to 1994, securing Group Tac's reputation. It is probably the studio's best-known work in Japan. ● Anime fans are likely to be more familiar with the studio's TV series based on Adachi Mitsuru's manga. Sugii Gisaburo, one of the studio's founders, directed many of these series. The first, high-school baseball romance *Touch* (1985–7), was so successful that two television specials and three full-length theatrical features followed. ● Group Tac has many full-length feature films to its credit, including *Jack to mame no ki* (*Jack and the Beanstalk*, 1974), the haunting *Ginga Tetsudo no Yoru* (*Night on the Galactic Railroad*, 1985), the elegant and evocative *Murasaki Shikibu Genji Monogatari* (*The Tale of Genji*, 1987) and an adaptation of a popular children's book, *Arashi no Yoru Ni* (*One Stormy Night*, 2005), all directed by Sugii Gisaburo. In 1987 the studio produced a restored edition of one of anime's classic treasures, *Entotsuya Pero* (*Chimney Sweep Pero*), a paper silhouette animation produced in 1930. ● It continues to make popular TV series such as *Alice Academy* (2005, dir. Omori Takahiro) and *Tokko* (2006, dir. Abe Masashi). ● H.M.

# GROUP TAC

STU

SEE ALSO: ADACHI MITSURU; GENJI HIKARU MUSHI; SUGII GISABURO; SUBASA OZORA; UESUGI TATSUYA & KATSUYA

# GTO: GREAT TEACHER ONIZUKA

With his bleached hair and a cigarette in his mouth, a bored look about him and his aggressive nature, Onizuka Eikichi at first appears to be little more than a hooligan. After leaving school, the former lout needs a job and uses his street skills to bag himself a teaching post, assuming that the role will have few responsibilities. ● He ends up at the dead-end Holy Forest Academy, where he has to look after the most difficult class in the school. He also finds himself at loggerheads with the irascible Deputy Head, Uchiyamada Hiroshi, a teacher who considers children from the wrong side of the tracks to be despicable scum. ● These are the ingredients that make up the wildly successful manga by Fujisawa Tohro, which has spawned an anime series as well as live-action television series and movies. Onizuka is in the same vein as other well-known manga and anime delinquents-made-good, such as Sakuragi Hanamichi of *Slam Dunk* (1993, dir. Matano Hiromichi et al) or Mitsuhashi Takashi of *Kyo Kara Ore Wa!!* (1992, dir. Mori Takeshi). His unconventionality grabs the attention of younger audiences and provides an attractive role model, while the series as a whole reveals a thinly veiled criticism of Japanese society and its rigid education system. Onizuka's so-called 'misconduct' allows Fujisawa to highlight the contradictions and hypocrisy of those in power; Onizuka, despite his impetuousness, is shown to be the only 'pure' character, devoid of the prejudices that conventionality instills in others, and he finds himself having to redress wrongs on more than one occasion, albeit by unorthodox means. ● D.D.G.

ABOVE & RIGHT: EIKICHI ONIZUKA, THE UNORTHODOX TEACHER AND HERO OF THE 1999 TV SERIES GTO: GREAT TEACHER ONIZUKA

GTO: GREAT TEACHER ONIZUKA ● 1999 ● DIR: HANYU NAOYASU, ABE NORIYUKI ● SCR: SOGO MASASHI, SUGA YOSHIYUKI ● DES: USAMI KOICHI, KITAYAMIA MARI ● ANI: ROKUNOHE KUMIKO ● MUS: HOMMA YUSUKE ● PRD: STUDIO PIERROT ● TV SERIES ● EPS: 43

# GUNDAM

ROBOT

KIDO SENSHI GUNDAM ● MOBILE SUIT GUNDAM ●
1979 ● DIR: TOMINO YOSHIYUKI ● SCR: HOSHIYAMA
HIROYUKI ET AL ● DES & ANI: YASUHIKO YOSHIKAZU
ET AL ● MUS: WATANABE TAKEO, MATSUYAMA YUJI
● PRD: SUNRISE ● TV SERIES ● EPS: 43

RIGHT: MOBILE SUIT GUNDAM SEED FROM *GUNDAM
SEED* (2002, DIR. FUKUDA MITSUO, 50 EPS). THE
ORIGINAL RX–78 GUNDAM HAS BEEN UPGRADED
AND REVAMPED IN EVERY SERIES AND MOVIE, AND
FACES MORE FEARSOME OPPONENTS EACH TIME

When Japanese television broadcast the very first episode of *Mobile Suit Gundam* in April 1979, Tomino Yoshiyuki can hardly have imagined the extraordinary destiny that awaited his new series. Thirty years later, it's almost impossible to keep count of the many sequels, feature-length spin-offs, manga, videogames and toys that make up the immense *Gundam* universe. Things did not run so smoothly at first, however; the success the television channel expected did not materialize immediately and the initial series was cut short. It was not until after the first airing ended that its popularity really took off. ● Although the connections between the different works appearing under the *Gundam* label may seem obscure to the layman, the saga has evolved without betraying Tomino's original intentions – the first of which was to break away from Nagai Go's fantastical super-robots in favour of a more 'realistic' approach. In particular, this is true of the mecha design, whose shapes, materials and movements are minutely scrutinized, and also the psychological as well as dramatic approach of the stories that juxtapose brutal warfare with social comedy anchored in the everyday. ● Rather than a mere machine, each Gundam robot is like a second, heavier body with super-powers that their young pilots must get used to. Tense air battles, almost resembling aerial ballet, are metaphors for the turbulence of adolescence. Set in a melancholy, violent and almost apocalyptic universe, the series manages to retain a spirit opposed to the glorification of brute strength. The Japanese cousin of *Star Trek* and the forerunner of *Evangelion*, *Gundam* is a monument of manga culture – but it is still very much a living monument. The Gundam story so far includes 14 TV series, 7 movies, 10 further movies compiled from TV episodes, 8 OAV series, over 150 novels and manga, and over 130 Gundam video games for 20 platforms. Sunrise built a life-size RX 78 Gundam in Tokyo as part of the show's 30th anniversary celebrations in 2009. ● E.H.

# GUTS

RIGHT: THE TORMENTED
WARRIOR GUTS FROM THE
1997 SERIES *BERSERK*,
DEVISED BY MIURA KENTARO

CHARACTER

Guts is the protagonist of the popular medieval fantasy *Berserk*, based on a manga of the same name by Miura Kentaro that became a best-seller in the West as well as Japan. The popularity of *Berserk* is enhanced by the factual details laced into the plotline that relate to the perpetual fall of man. With the Holy See far away and impotent, God appears to have turned his back on man in order to make way for a horde of demons and monsters. In Miura's ancient world, the solitary warrior Guts is the only offer of hope, armed with his terrifying yell of revenge and a huge sword that he uses to fend off his adversaries. His solitary existence is interrupted by the arrival of a group of mercenaries called the Band of the Hawk. They are led by Griffith, an ambitious knight who, in true messianic fashion, dreams of a better world, even at the risk of sacrificing his companions-in-arms to the demons by becoming their monarch. ● Adapted for television by director Takahashi Naohiko in 1997, the series wanders sumptuously from battle to battle, thrusting characters and personalities to the front line. Past and present merge to offer a plausible excuse for the fate that awaits Guts, and provide the public with a liberal dose of duels to the death and fierce butchery at the expense of the demons. In addition *Berserk* is supported by the excellent design of Umakoshi Yoshihiko and the splendid music of Hirasawa Susumu. ● M.A.R

KENPU DENKI BERSERK ● BERSERK ● 1997 ● DIR: TAKAHASHI NAOHITO ● SCR: IMAGAWA YASUHIRO, TOMIOKA ATSUHIRO ●
DES: UMAKOSHI YOSHIHIKO, MATSUBARA TOKUHIRO ● ANI: MATSUBARA TOKUHIRO, SENBA YURIKO ● MUS: HIRAZAWA SUSUMU ●
PRD: OLM, VAP ● TV SERIES ● EPS: 25

To celebrate its first twenty-five years of existence (or thirty-three years if the earlier period, when the studio was called Nippon Doga – or Japan Animation – is included), Toei Animation made this faithful adaptation of Tchaikovsky's ballet with his music elegantly interwoven into its fabric. The aim was to prove that Japanese anime could compete on equal terms with classic full-length Disney films. Having used traditional European fairytales as source material on previous occasions, the studio launched a new series entitled *Sekai Meisaku Dowa* (World Masterpiece Fairytales) in 1977 specifically for this type of anime, to which *Hakucho no Mizuumi* (Swan Lake) was added in 1981. ● Yabuki Kimio was appointed director as he was already closely involved with the studio, having adapted Hans Christian Andersen's tales in *Andersen Monogatari* (Fables From Hans Christian Anderson, 1968) and directed the first adventure of the studio's trademark *Puss 'n' Boots* (1969), of which some elements recur in *Swan Lake*, notably the wicked and yet somewhat ridiculous character of the wizard and the final scene in his castle. ● *Swan Lake* tells the love story of Prince Siegfried and Princess Odette: she is condemned by the sorcerer Rothbart's spell to turn into a swan during the daytime so that she cannot attract potential suitors. The tale is told from the viewpoint of some squirrels, a device that allows the film a comic dimension. Echoes of certain Disney classics such as *Cinderella* (1950) and *Sleeping Beauty* (1959) do not detract from the overall power of the film, which was hampered by the theft of 2,500 animation cels during production. ● J.Co.

# HAKUCHO NO MIZUUMI
## SWAN LAKE

HAKUCHO NO MIZUUMI ● SWAN LAKE ● 1981
DIR: YABUKI KIMIO ● SCR: FUSE HIROKAZU ●
DES: TSUJI TADANAO ● ANI: NODA TAKUO
ET AL ● MUS: PETER TCHAIKOVSKY ●
PRD: TOEI ANIMATION ● DUR: 72 MINS

# HAKUJADEN
## LEGEND OF THE WHITE SNAKE

BELOW: SCENE FROM THE 1958 FILM *LEGEND OF THE WHITE SNAKE*. THE BEAUTIFUL PRINCESS BAI–NIANG, STILL IN HER SERPENT FORM, FALLS IN LOVE WITH XU–XIAN WHEN HE IS STILL A CHILD. YEARS LATER THEY MEET AGAIN

*Hakujaden* (Legend of the White Snake, released in the USA as *Panda and the Magic Serpent*) deserves to be defined as a pioneering film. It was the first Japanese feature-length animation in colour and, coincidentally, it marked the debut of a seventeen-year-old inbetweener who was later to become famous under the name of Rintaro. But above all, it was the first feature-length animated film made by Toei Animation, a studio that represented the vanguard of Japanese animation for the next twenty years under the leadership of artists including Otsuka Yasuo, Miyazaki Hayao and Takahata Isao. ● Made by the director Yabushita Taiji and the great animator Mo Yasuji, both from the Nippon Doga (or Japan Animation) studio that Toei Animation had only just acquired, *Legend of the White Snake* characterizes all the ambitions of the studio that created it. Drawn from Chinese mythology, the film is a nod towards Asia and was intended as a gesture of reconciliation towards Japan's neighbours at a time not long after World War II. But at the same time, the choice of detailed animation and the presence of picturesque animals with human features made it a film that looked towards the West with the aim of challenging the colossal productions made by Disney. ● *Legend of the White Snake* tells the story of the star-crossed love between a man and a serpent transformed into a beautiful princess, and brings both legend and the printed story to life with great elegance. With its talking animals, metamorphoses and depictions of the most far-fetched of visions, the film is an inspired exploration of the innumerable creative possibilities of animated cinema and one that demonstrates precisely how well this medium can serve the powers of the imagination. ● E.H.

HAKUJADEN ● *LEGEND OF THE WHITE SNAKE* ● AKA: *PANDA AND THE MAGIC SERPENT* ● 1958 ● DIR: YABUSHITA TAIJI, OKABE KAZUHIKO ●
SCR: YABUSHITA TAIJI, YASHIRO SOICHI ● DES: OKUWARA AKIRA, MORI YASUJI ● ANI: OTSUKA YASUO ET AL ● MUS: IKEDA MASAYOSHI ●
PRD: TOEI ANIMATION ● DUR: 76 MINS

# HANEDA KENTARO

aneda Kentaro (born in 1949 in Tokyo, where he died in 2007) studied at the Toho akuen School of Music, and taught for many years as a professor at the Tokyo School f Music. His work as a composer and arranger on several high-profile productions has nsured recognition outside Japan as well as in his home country. ● Haneda lost his father t the age of four and was raised by his mother and grandparents. His grandfather was nvolved with a children's choir, and encouraged the young Haneda in musical activities. child piano prodigy, he was playing a grand piano by his early teens. ● Following raduation, Haneda worked as a session musician, and then as the leader of a backing and for the singer Watanabe Machiko. He made regular appearances on Japanese elevision, particularly on the programme *Pops on the Piano*. As a composer, he provided oundtracks to the computer games *Wizardry* (1981) and *Ys* (1987), although not their nime adaptations. He composed many piano-based scores for Japanese television shows nd films, and offered broader, pop- and orchestra-based themes for numerous anime, ncluding *Space Adventure Cobra* (1982), *Sherlock Hound* (1984) and *Space Pirate Captain Harlock* (1978) but is probably best remembered for the score to the original *Macross* (1982). ● Haneda's creative peak as a composer spanned the Eighties – a eriod that saw many of the video releases that would carry anime to foreign markets. hereafter, he was better known a pianist and television host, with growing fame as a erformer that left him with little time or inclination for further composition. Despite his eclining health, he performed on Senju Akira's *Shukumei* concerto in 2004, a recording hat remains the best-selling classical CD in Japanese musical history. ● J.Cl.

TOP: THE CANINE STARS OF *SHERLOCK HOUND* (1984, DIR. MIYASAKI HAYAO, 26 EPS) ● ABOVE: COBRA FROM *SPACE ADVENTURE COBRA* (1982, DIR. DEZAKI OSAMU, TAKEUCHI YOSHIO, 31 EPS)

H

SEE ALSO: AMANO MASAMICHI; COBRA; HARLOCK; HOLMES, SHERLOCK; KANNO YOKO; KIKUCHI SHUNSUKE; MACROSS

## HARA KEIICHI

WORKS BY THE VERSATILE DIRECTOR HARA KEIICHI ● TOP: THREE SCENES FROM THE SERIES CRAYON SHIN-CHAN (1992, DIR. HONMA MITSURU, HARA KEIICHI, OVER 500 EPS) SHOWING SHIN-CHAN AND HIS FAMILY ● ABOVE: DORAEMON THE ROBOT CAT FROM DORAEMON (1973, DIR. ONUKI NOBUO, SHIBAYAMA TSUTOMU, KUSUBA KOZO, OVER 2000 EPS) ● RIGHT: A PUBLICITY POSTER FOR KAPPA NO COO TO NATSUYASUMI (SUMMER DAYS WITH COO, 2007)

Hara Keiichi (born in 1959 in Tatebayashi) worked in advertising before joining the Shin-ei Animation studio. He progressed quickly, working on several projects before devoting himself to *Doraemon* (1983–6) and *ESPer Mami* (1988). In 1992, he worked on the popular series *Crayon Shin-chan*, which follows the capers of a five-year-old, becoming its director in 1996. He adapted *Crayon Shin-chan* for the cinema with great success in 2001, with a sequel in 2002. ● After these two feature-length films came Hara's 2007 masterpiece *Kappa no Coo to Natsuyasumi* (*Summer Days with Coo*). Along with Miyazaki's *Ponyo*, Coo is among the most endearing characters created for children; both are water-dwellers and both are discovered by a little boy in need of a friend. It is very possible that *Ponyo* owes as much to *Coo* as Hara does to Miyazaki's work. Coo is a *kappa*, or water-sprite, a kind of beaked turtle that walks upright and has a little hole in its head containing a reserve of water This is the creature's Achilles heel, for if the water in its head runs out, the kappa weakens and dies. ● The plot of the film is divided into three parts: the first, where Coo wins over his adoptive family, including a reluctant little sister; the second, where Koichi takes Coo to the river to try in vain to find others of his kind; and the third, where, having been discovered and clumsily exhibited by the family as a curiosity, Coo takes fright and flees the media attention. ● This film owes its great success to the comic appeal of this little mop-haired creature, waddling along with outspread arms. As with Miyazaki's work, the tale gains unexpected weight and substance from ancient mythological references, represented here by the death of Coo's father centuries before and the discovery of his mummified arm. ● S.D.

# HARLOCK
## CAPTAIN
## HARLOCK

CHARACTER

Harlock is a mysterious and tormented character. His wide, black cape and the patch covering his right eye give him the appearance of a pirate, while the scar that disfigures part of his face reveals his past as a warrior. Captain Harlock is a taciturn and idealistic hero, at times violent, and yet capable of great courage. His home is the *Arcadia* space ship and his family are the crewmembers who have sworn loyalty to his flag. A romantic outlaw, Harlock does not accept the regime of the Unified Earth Government, which has reduced the population of Earth to a state of apathy and transformed the planet into a barren place almost completely devoid of resources, yet he fights to save the Earth from alien threats. ● Conceived by Matsumoto Leiji, Harlock has become a symbol of uncompromising struggle against injustice. The atmosphere is gloomy, colours are dark, the narrative lines tense. The past weighs upon the present like a shadow, leaving our protagonist held in a state of exile, and hoping for freedom. ● With intense music composed by Yokoyama Seiji and performed by a symphonic orchestra, the tale is brought to life with exquisite mastery. Aside from the historic series, a great number of Harlock manga have also been animated, including the film *Arcadia of My Youth* (1982), the series *Captain Harlock, Endless Orbit SSX* (1982) and the OAV *Captain Harlock: The Endless Odyssey* (2002), directed by Rintaro, in which the story begins where it left off in the first series. The character of Harlock also appears in other series created by Matsumoto, namely *Galaxy Express 999* (1978, dir. Nishizawa Nobutaka et al) and *Fire Force DNA Sights 999.9* (1998, dir. Shirato Takeshi and Kojima Masayuki). ● G.P.

SCENES FROM THE 1978 SERIES *SPACE PIRATE CAPTAIN HARLOCK* ● ABOVE: THE BROODING EXPRESSION OF CAPTAIN HARLOCK ● RIGHT: HIS VESSEL THE SPACESHIP *ARCADIA*

H

UCHU KAIZOKU CAPTAIN HARLOCK ● SPACE PIRATE CAPTAIN HARLOCK ● 1978 ● DIR: RINTARO, FUKUSHIMA KAZUMI ●
SCR: UEHARA MASAMI, YAMAZARI HARUYA ● DES: MATSUMOTO LEIJI ● ANI: KOMATSUBARA KAZUO ● MUS: YOKOYAMA SEIJI ●
PRD: TOEI ANIMATION ● TV SERIES ● EPS: 42

# HARU

The 'odd one out' from Studio Ghibli, which is more usually devoted to work by Miyazaki and Takahata, Morita Hiroyuki's feature-length film does not enjoy the same reputation as those of his colleagues. Although charming, this children's tale is simpler, narrower in scope and has no philosophical ambitions. ● *Neko no Ongaeshi* (*The Cat Returns*) begins with a chance occurrence when schoolgirl Haru saves a cat from being run over. To her great surprise, the cat stands up and thanks her. She is then whisked off to the 'cat kingdom', where the Cat King intends to thank her for saving his son by forcibly marrying the two of them. ● The animation is slicker than that of the Ghibli masters and the finest work can be seen in the cat characters, who stand upright with their front paws folded, bowing and waving in an amusing imitation of human gestures. The cats are sometimes seen sprawled in positions of relaxation or awkwardness, as is the case with the prince on the pedestrian crossing when Haru sweeps him up in a net to save him from a passing car. A procession of cats is even comically flanked by bodyguards, who set about any intruder with great vigour. ● *The Cat Returns* also makes no secret of its debt to *Alice's Adventures in Wonderland*: the cat prince hurrying through the streets at the beginning of the film is a clear reference to Lewis Carroll's white rabbit and Haru shrinks like Alice before taking on the appearance of a cat. In her feline form, Morita gives his heroine an enchanting appearance, her two little pointed ears giving the impression that her human face had something missing. The film's denouement is somewhat rushed, but the absence of Miyazaki's lustre has fortunately not prevented the film from finding an audience, particularly in France. ● S.D.

ABOVE LEFT & CENTRE: THE TWO PROTAGONISTS HARU AND BARON IN THREE SCENES FROM THE 2002 FILM *THE CAT RETURNS* ● BELOW LEFT: HARU FINDS HERSELF TRANSFORMED INTO A FITTING BRIDE FOR THE PRINCE OF CATS

NEKO NO ONGAESHI ● THE CAT RETURNS ● 2002 ● DIR: MORITA HIROYUKI ● SCR: YOSHIDA REIKO ● DES: MORIKAWA SATORU ● ANI: INOUE EI, OZAKI KAZUTAKA ● MUS: NOMI YUJI ● PRD: SUZUKI TOSHIO ET AL, STUDIO GHIBLI ● FILM ● DUR: 75 MINS

Born in 1942 in what was then the Japanese colony of Taiwan, Hata Masami returned as a child to a homeland he had never seen in 1945. He briefly studied at the Tamamomo College of Arts, but dropped out to join Mushi Production where he worked on *Princess Knight* (1967) and *Cleopatra: Queen of Sex* (1970) amongst others. With the collapse of Mushi in the 1973 recession, Hata freelanced for Tokyo Movie Shinsha – where he directed *Andersen Monogatari* (*Andersen Stories*, 1968) – and Madhouse, before finding a new home at the recently established animation wing of the merchandise company Sanrio. With Sanrio's brief move into full-length features, he was able to become a feature director at the relatively young age of thirty, directing the disturbing children's parable *Chirin no Suzu* (*The Ringing Bell*, 1978), the lavish feature *Sirius no Densetsu* (*Legend of Sirius*, 1981), which he also wrote, and *Yosei Florence* (*Journey Through Fairyland*, 1981). The latter was the last full-length feature to be produced by Sanrio, which moved into smaller, lower-budget works in the late eighties. ● He returned to Tokyo Movie Shinsha in 1985 to direct *Super Mario Brothers*, one of the first anime to be based on a computer game. Despite his rôle at TMS, Hata is credited on many Sanrio productions of the Nineties as a supervising director or scenarist, notably on spin-off films featuring the merchandising icons Keroppi and Hello Kitty. His most recent work is on *Stitch!* (2008), the Japanese spin-off of Disney's *Lilo & Stitch* (2002). ● J.Cl.

LEFT: SCENES FROM TEZUKA OSAMU'S FILM *CLEOPATRA: QUEEN OF SEX* (1970, DIR. TEZUKA OSAMU, YAMAMOTO EIICHI, 122 MINS), TO WHICH HATA MASAMI CONTRIBUTED

SEE ALSO: LITTLE NEMO; MARIO

# HAYAKAWA KEIJI

Born in 1950 in Aomori Prefecture, Hayakawa Keiji has been making his mark in the anime world since the Seventies, working for important studios such as Toei Animation, Gallop, TMS and Nippon Animation. ● His fame is mainly down to his efforts as a director and designer. He joined Toei in 1969 as assistant director to Ikeda Hiroshi and his team on *Himitsu no Akko-Chan* (*Secret Akko-Chan*) and he contributed to some of the studio's other successes, such as *Sarutobi Etchan* (*E-chan the Ninja*, 1971, dir. Serikawa Yugo). In subsequent years, he worked on the *Heidi* series, for which he probably designed his first storyboard (episode 36), and on the Nippon Animation series *Sindbad no Boken* (*Arabian Nights: Sinbad's Adventure*, 1975, dir. Kurokawa Fumio). ● He debuted as a director in 1977 with *Ashita e Attack!!* (*Attack on Tomorrow*) but the turning point in his career came the following year with the *Future Boy Conan* series, for which he directed sixteen episodes, alternating with directors such as Miyazaki and Takahata. Hayakawa's path almost crossed Miyazaki's again in the mid-Eighties on the series *Meitantei Holmes* (*Sherlock Hound*, 1984), when he directed a few episodes after Miyazaki had left. He became well known as a director during the Eighties and contributed to some important science-fiction series: *Uchusen Sagittarius* (*Space Sagittarius*, 1986), taken from the *Altri Mondi* comic book by Andrea Romoli; *Maps* (1987); and the OAV parody *Kenritsu Chikyu Bogyo* (*Prefectural Earth Defense Force*, 1986). In the Nineties, Hayakawa directed several episodes of the *Digimon Adventure* series (1999). In recent years he has distinguished himself with series that have adolescence as a theme, such as *Hajime no Ippo* (*Fighting Spirit*, 2001) and *Kiba* (2006). ● F.L.

RIGHT: SCENES FROM *FUTURE BOY CONAN* (1978, DIR. MIYAZAKI HAYAO, 26 EPS) ●
BELOW: SHERLOCK HOLMES IS ON THE CASE IN *SHERLOCK HOUND* (1984, DIR. MIYAZAKI HAYAO, 26 EPS)

SEE ALSO: CONAN; DIGIMON; HOLMES, SHERLOCK

CHARACTER

# HEIDI

*Heidi, Girl of the Alps* is one of the historic successes of Japanese animation. The picture of Heidi racing across the Alpine meadows in the company of Peter, Blinky the Bluebird and her faithful goats became an iconic image of freedom. As conceived by director Takahata Isao, who backed up his reading of Johanna Spyri's source novel with extensive field research, the Heidi story became a fascinating affirmation of individual identity. Featuring everyday problems and serious dramas, the heroine's story climbs constantly towards its life-affirming peak. ● If the character design is somewhat naive, albeit effective, the scene design and layout are hugely impressive in their use of colour and detailed definition. Amid the Alpine landscape – drawn with a typically Japanese delight in the framed view, shortened perspective and detail – the grandfather's house, with the three huge pine trees that protect it, seems like an island: a safe haven and a port from which to set sail. In contrast to the view of nature offered in Disney productions (from *Snow White* to *Mulan*), the forests, gorges and mountains in *Heidi* have been there since long before the characters, which move across them without altering their appearance. The fixed camera angles, elementary and immutable, convey this vision perfectly. ● The series was split into three parts, each defined by its locations and thought out in symphonic terms as separate movements. The first part describes the arrival of the orphaned girl at her grandfather's house; the second is marked by the move to Frankfurt and the aristocratic home of Clara, under the severe gaze of Frau Rottenmeier; and lastly, the third tells of the return to the mountains. The tight narrative progression overall, together with the careful pacing of each single episode, hooked millions of children and older viewers worldwide. ● C.C.

SCENES FROM THE 1974 SERIES HEIDI, GIRL OF THE ALPS ● ABOVE & RIGHT: HEIDI AT HOME IN THE MOUNTAINS, PLAYING IN THE WOODS, WALKING WITH HER GRANDFATHER AND WITH PETER'S GRANDMOTHER

HEIDI, GIRL OF THE ALPS (ALPS NO SHOJO HEIDI) ● 1974 ● DIR: TAKAHATA ISAO ● SCR: OKAWA HISAO ET AL ● DES: KOTABE YOICHI ● ANI: OKADA TOSHIYASU ● MUS: WATANABE TAKEO ● PRD: FUJI TV, ZUIYO ENTERPRISES ● TV SERIES ● EPS: 52

H

# HI NO TORI 2772

FILM

Influenced by the music of Igor Stravinsky, Tezuka Osamu conceived what was to become one of his most ambitious manga projects: *Phoenix*, an exploration of the dreams and longings of immortal human beings. The saga, which ran to thirteen volumes between 1967 and 1988, drew on a spectacular array of stylistic and narrative resources associated with the mythological bird. The project was still unfinished when Tezuka died, but its structure – consisting of freestanding cycles that tackle different periods from the dawn of human history to man's final decline – makes it accessible, even in its fragmentary state. ● Kon Ichikawa adapted it for the cinema in 1978, with a stimulating section animated by Tezuka himself. Of the numerous anime versions, *Phoenix 2772: Space Firebird*, directed by Sugiyama Taku, contains the most striking references to the original books, drawing in particular from *Future*, *Universe*, *Resurrection* and *Nostalgia*, which focus on the story of Goto, an android pilot. After rebelling against his own dystopian society, Goto eventually sacrifices his life to save the Earth. Written in conjunction with Tezuka, *Space Firebird* opens with ten extraordinary minutes of silence, documenting the birth and early years of the hero under the gaze of Olga, a robot that can change shape at will, transforming from a maternal figure into a romantic ideal. ● All the trademarks of Tezuka's animations are present, from the appearance of stock characters to the comic counterpoint of some of the Disney-inspired musical scenes, harmonized in fluid animation in which the legacy of the Fleischer brothers coexists with the very essence of the anime genre. ● J.Co.

ABOVE: OSAMU TEZUKA'S GOLDEN PHOENIX IN A SCENE FROM THE 1980 FILM *PHOENIX 2772: SPACE FIREBIRD*

HI NO TORI 2772: AI NO KOSUMOZON ● PHOENIX 2772: SPACE FIREBIRD ● 1980 ● DIR: SUGIYAMA TAKU ● SCR: TEZUKA OSAMU, SUGIYAMA TAKI ● DES: ITO SHINJI ET AL ● ANI: NAKAMURA KAZUKO, ISHIGURO NOBORU ● MUS: HIGUCHI YASUO ● PRD: TOHO ● DUR: 116 MINS

# HIMENO MICHI

CHARACTER DESIGNER

The name of Himeno Michi is inextricably linked to that of Araki Shingo, her teacher and friend, with whom she formed a lasting artistic partnership creating dozens of character designs. As a girl, she followed many anime television productions bearing the name of Araki in the titles. She fell in love with his character *Babel II* (1973) and she finally met Araki when he visited her school. Once she graduated, she started working at his side in the new Araki Production studio. Despite the lack of a real apprenticeship, her hand was naturally fast, allowing her to create designs for series as important as *UFO Robot Grendizer Raids* (1975). ● Araki himself confesses that he learnt a great deal from his young assistant and that he owes his gradual abandonment of the aggressive style that had marked his previous productions to her. Himeno's style is sweet, soft and extremely attentive, and finally bloomed in full beauty in 1979 with the masterpiece *Rose of Versailles*. Her first designs stood out for their quality, and with the arrival of director Osamu Dezaki, the designs for the film characters became more intense, putting the original comics to shame. ● The eyes are more subtle, the features more adult, the shadows more pronounced, the glances hidden behind a perpetual melancholy. From this moment on, long, coloured hair sinuously rippling in the wind became one of Himeno's trademarks, culminating in *Saint Seiya* (1986). The faces of her men are often effeminate while their slender bodies bend easily and move in a highly suggestive manner, as though performing in the famous Hyogo ballet. Himeno is also a prolific illustrator and designer for 'light novels' and videogames. ● S.G.

ABOVE: CYGNUS HYOGA IN *SAINT SEIYA* (KNOWN IN EUROPE AND THE USA AS *KNIGHTS OF THE ZODIAC*), IS ONE OF HIMENO MICHI AND ARAKI SHINGO'S MANY CREATIONS (1986, DIR. YAMAUCHI SHIGENORI, MORISHITA KOZO, KIKUCHI KAZUHITO, AKEHI MASAYUKI ET AL, 114 EPS)

SEE ALSO: ARAKI SHINGO; DEZAKI OSAMU; JARJAYES, OSCAR FRANÇOIS DE; SAINT SEIYA; UFO ROBOT GRENDIZER RAIDS

With a distinctive cruciform scar on his face, Himura Kenshin wanders Japan in the late 1870s, a masterless samurai who was once a professional killer for a patriotic society. Swearing never to kill again, he fights with a reverse-bladed sword (used only in defence), and meets with a pretty girl, Kamiya Kaoru, whose sword-master father was killed in the last great samurai rebellion. ● *Ruroni Kenshin* ran for an impressive ninety-five episodes as an anime series, offering a compelling angle on much of the modern history that Japanese schoolchildren are obliged to study, as its protagonist encapsulates the contradictions inherent in the founding of the modern Japanese state. A former samurai and executioner, he was part of the group that overthrew the old order of the Shogun, only to find violent samurai like himself anachronistic in the modern world of the Meiji Restoration. ● Himura is constantly confronted by old friends who have become enemies, or vice versa. Allegiances in the early Meiji period are confused, and there is much disagreement over what constitutes loyalty – to the Emperor, to the Shogun, or to one's old clan. The result is a world that is tantalizingly modern, but still presents samurai conflicts and scenery that could pass for medieval. Kenshin himself embodies this ambiguity – caught between samurai ethics and modern attitudes more familiar to a twenty-first-century teenager. This constant debate over his place in the world made Kenshin a credible icon for Japanese youth. Meanwhile, foreign fans warmed to the romantic idea of the twilight of the samurai era, where, despite swift modernization, men with swords could still be found in the Japanese countryside. ● J.Cl.

# HIMURA KENSHIN

CHARACTER

*RURONI KENSHIN* ● 1996 ● DIR: KAZUHIRO FURUHASHI, TSUJI HATSUKI ● SCR: SHIMADA MICHIRU, SUGA YOSHIYUKI ● DES: HAMAZU HIDEYOSHI ET AL ● ANI: SUDA MASAMI ● MUS: ASAKURA NORIYUKI ● PRD: FUJI TV, STUDIO DEEN, STUDIO GALLOP ● TV SERIES ● EPS: 94

DIRECTOR

Born in 1956 in Tokyo, Hirano Toshihiro is one of the great figures of the manga and anime world. Artistically inseparable from his wife, the illustrator and animator Kakinouchi Narumi, whom he met in the early eighties, he began his career working on the television series *Gaiking* (1975), before moving on to *Dr Slump* (1981), *Macross* (1982), *Urusei Yatsura* (1981) and *Megazone 23* (1985). He finally achieved popularity with the robotic anime *Dangaioh* (1987), in which he developed his character design skills by drawing on the knowledge of scriptwriter Aikawa Noboru. This series of OAVs, which contains several references to Nagai Go, features some splendid heroines and was driven by a desire to get away from the realistic science-fiction approach of television series such as *Mobile Suit Gundam* (1979). ● Thanks to his new-found fame, Hirano grasped the opportunity to make his debut as a director with *Vampire Princess Miyu* (1988), relying on the writing skills of Aikawa and the perfect draughtsmanship of Kakinouchi (who later also illustrated the manga version). Despite Hirano's heroine being a mutant hero – able to suck the vital energies of human beings instead of the more traditional blood – this anime immediately became a classic of the vampire genre and was revived as a television series in 1997. ● The series contains references to the horror comics of Mizuki Shigeru and reflects Hirano's passion for places sacred to the Japanese, which influence his deliberately disturbing and supernatural settings. ● M.A.R

# HIRANO TOSHIHIRO

ABOVE: TWO CHARACTERS FROM *VAMPIRE PRINCESS MIYU* (1988, DIR. HIRANO TOSHIHIRO, 4 EPS) WITH WHICH HIRANO TOSHIHIRO MADE HIS DEBUT AS DIRECTOR

SEE ALSO: MACROSS; MIYU; URUSEI YATSURA

# HIRASAKA RYUJI

CHARACTER

Since animation can depict literally anything, without the cost of sets, locations or live actors, it often favours genres that live-action film-makers would find prohibitive. In the mainstream, this has encouraged thriving sub-genres of science fiction and fantasy, but in the pornographic sector, similar concerns have pushed anime erotica towards niches that live-action pornographers are reluctant to touch – illegality, non-consensual sex and scatology. ● *Night Shift Nurses* began in 1999 as a 'simulation' – a computer game with limited interactivity, allowing the viewer to steer the story at certain points. Like most visual novels, it used anime-style artwork for its still images. It was adapted into anime form in 2000, as part of the 'Discovery Series', a long-running selection of one- and two-part adaptations of erotic computer games, often with a sado-masochistic theme. Possibly because of its superficial similarity to the primetime television series *Leave it to the Nurses*, then at the height of its popularity, *Night Shift Nurses* was an unprecedented success, and spawned over a dozen sequels. ● The stories centre on a deviant doctor, Hirasaka Ryuji, and the mind-games he plays with the nurses at his hospital to groom them for seduction and degradation. The plots begin with psychological torment and blackmail as Hirasaka manoeuvres his victims into a submissive mindset, and follows with their torture, most of which involves bondage, bodily invasion, urine and faeces. As is often the case with transgressive porn, many stories include a framing device that shows the protagonist being punished for his actions, even though the *raison d'être* of the entire show is to titillate the viewer. The shock value of such anime often gains them far wider attention abroad than they truly merit. ● J.CI.

ABOVE: MALEVOLENT DOCTOR HIRASAKA RYUJI AND HIS DOMINATED VICTIMS FROM THE 2000 SERIES NIGHT SHIFT NURSES

YAKIN BYOUTOU ● *NIGHT SHIFT NURSES* ● 2000 ● DIR: OKEZAWA NAO ● SCR: SAGA RYO ● DES: HINO KUNIYOSHI ● ANI: IIJIMA HIROYA ● MUS: SANO HIROAKI ● PRD: AT-2 PROJECT ● VIDEO SERIES ● EPS: 12

# HIRASAWA SUSUMU

COMPOSER

When he began his musical career with the group P-MODEL in 1979, Hirasawa Susumu (born in 1954 in Tokyo) was immediately consigned by the critics to the category of techno pop. The label may have fitted well enough at the time, but now it seems much too restrictive. ● A solitary artist on stage, committed to composition and interactive live performances, Hirasawa has a predilection for thought-provoking activities: for example, he used solar energy to power his production studio while recording the album *Solar Ray* (2001). ● Many of his works have been produced with anime in mind. He wrote the music for Kon Satoshi's television series *Moso Dairinin* (*Paranoia Agent*, 2004) and the film *Paprika* (2006), the originality of which won him high praise. Inspired by the New Age movement, a scene that Hirasawa has always admired, one of his favourite pieces is the soundtrack to the series *Berserk* (1997), a composition of rare effectiveness (compared with the play-it-safe approach of most Japanese musicians) and evocative beauty. ● Hirasawa tends not to draw on pre-existing material (scripts and film clips) and often finds his inspiration on the spur of the moment or in a comic book. This approach allows him to explore his musical material with the freedom of a pilgrim (a guise in which he likes to see himself). Similarly, Hirasawa considers himself a diviner, who wanders over the score in search of a sudden flash of illumination, resulting in an irresistible outpouring of musical notes. ● M.A.R

SEE ALSO: GUTS; KON SATOSHI; PAPRIKA; SAGI TSUKIKO

# HISAISHI JOE

COMPOSER

Hisaishi Joe (born in 1950 in Nagano) is arguably the finest composer working in Japanese cinema today. His compositions are indissolubly linked with the work of two outstanding film-makers – Miyazaki Hayao and Kitano Takeshi. He began composing for anime in 1974 and his relationship with Miyazaki began with *Nausicaä of the Valley of Wind* (1984) and has continued ever since. He introduced a sweeping, solemn, symphonic form to his music that ennobles the animation and imbues it with unprecedented depth of feeling. His compositions are complex, unfolding in stages while retaining their simple and moving melodic structure. ● The chords of *Nausicaä* and *Castle in the Sky* (1986) are the ideal accompaniment to the airborne journeys featured in both films, while in the epics *Princess Mononoke* (1997) and *Spirited Away* (2001), the most accomplished moments are created by a dialogue of orchestra and piano. A drum accompanies childish steps in *My Neighbour Totoro* (1988) while sea-tossed travels in *Ponyo on the Cliff by the Sea* (2008) are a pastiche of Wagner's *Ride of the Valkyries*. Miyazaki's universe also owes much to Hisaishi's warmer compositions, such as the songs in *Totoro* and *Ponyo*. ● Hisaishi varies his work considerably from one film to another and, even within a single film, he comes up with astonishing vocal ideas: the extraordinary high-pitched voice that marks the attempt to shoot the Forest Spirit in *Princess Mononoke*, for example, or the insistent children's song in *Nausicaä*, which is reminiscent of one of Ennio Morricone's compositions for Dario Argento. ● In 1991 Hisaishi composed the music for Kitano's *Ano Natsu, Ichiban Shizukana Umi* (*A Scene at the Sea*), collaborating with him a further six times on various projects culminating in *Dolls* (2002). He has also composed for various films outside Japan and become an internationally renowned conductor. ● S.D.

LEFT: SCENES FROM *PONYO ON THE CLIFF BY THE SEA* (*GAKE NO UENO PONYO*, 2007, DIR. MIYAZAKI HAYAO, PRD. SUZUKI TOSHIO ET AL, 101 MINS)

SEE ALSO: CHIHIRO; LAPUTA; MIYAZAKI HAYAO; NAUSICAÄ; PONYO; SAN; TOTORO

# HOJO TSUKASA

Hojo Tsukasa was born in 1959 in Kokura, on the island of Kyushu. He perfected his drawing technique whilst still at school and in 1979 he entered a contest to discover new authors sponsored by the publisher Shueisha. It was with Shueisha that he began his professional career and saw his first big success, *Cat's Eye* (1981). In traditional style, Detective Toshio is an inept man paired with a far more resourceful companion, Hitomi. However, unbeknownst to Toshio, Hitomi is also the very art thief that he is hunting for, and repeatedly outsmarted by. The manga's unique blend of crime and humour, heightened by a hint of eroticism, reveals a sensitive author able to examine the scant rapport between the sexes in a changing society. ● 1985 saw the appearance of another great saga from Hojo, *City Hunter*, which, through the character of the womanizing private eye Saeba Ryo, continues to describe the relationship between men and women with humour and intelligence. His most radical title appeared in 1996 with the release of *Family Compo*, in which Hojo describes the emotional ties within a family unit where relations between the sexes are often reversed (to the extent that some characters appearing to be men are revealed as women and vice versa). This unusual plot allows Hojo to fully explore his characters' feelings and urge for universal acceptance. ● In more recent times he has contributed to the latest *Fist of the North Star* feature films, the result of a collaboration with his friend Hara Tetsuo. His creation of the character Reina allows for an unprecedented and more thorough exploration of the feelings that guide the saga's heroes ● D.D.G.

*SCENES FROM CITY HUNTER (1987, DIR. KODAMA KENJI ET AL, 51 EPS) ● ABOVE: SAEBA RYO AND HIS PARTNER MAKIMURA KAORI ON THE ROOF OF THEIR BUILDING ● LEFT: ON DUTY EVEN WHILE SLEEPING, RYO HANGS ONTO HIS GUN*

*SEE ALSO: KISUGI; CITY HUNTER*

# HOKUTO NO KEN
## FIST OF THE NORTH STAR

Originally created as a manga in 1983 by the artist Hara Tetsuo and the author Buronson (the pen name of Okamura Yoshiyuki), *Fist of the North Star* represents an aesthetic manifesto of eighties anime, particularly in its clear cinematic influences. The protagonist Kenshiro, or Ken, combines the feline agility of Bruce Lee in combat with a muscular physique reminiscent of a youthful Sylvester Stallone, while his taciturn character makes reference to Mel Gibson's *Mad Max* (1979), on which the entire story also draws for its post-nuclear holocaust setting and the styling of Ken's enemies. ● A Christ-like figure, Ken offers himself as the saviour of a world that has been thrust into chaos and must safeguard an ancient and deadly martial art (*Hokuto Shinken* or 'Divine Fist of the Great Bear'). At the same time, he must fight his own brothers who want to supplant him as heir to the tradition. Adventure is mixed with soap-opera intrigue and imbued with a tragic air of sorrow. ● Originally a manga series, the story developed into a two-season television series and a film, both enhanced by the extremely physical style adopted by director Ashida Toyoo. These have been followed more recently by multiple video mini-series and a project comprising five feature-length films produced to celebrate the story's twenty-fifth anniversary. In all of these, *Fist of the North Star* has remained true to the original manga, its tone varying through a continuous series of showdowns where the dualism between Ken and his adversaries reflects that which is ever-present in the universe, the dichotomy between yin and yang. Therefore, his exploits take on an almost cosmic value and destiny is written in the stars, enriching the epic and tragic stature of the protagonist's odyssey. ● D.D.G.

IMAGES FROM THE 1984 SERIES HOKUTO NO KEN ● ABOVE RIGHT: A MOMENT OF DESPERATION FOR KEN AS HIS BELOVED JULIA DIES ● RIGHT & BELOW: FIGHT SCENES FROM THE SERIES

HOKUTO NO KEN ● FIST OF THE NORTH STAR ● AKA: KEN THE GREAT BEAR FIST ● 1984 ● DIR: ASHIDA TOYOO ● SCR: TAKAHISA SUSUMU ● DES & ANI: SUDA MASAMI ● MUS: AOKI NOZOMI ● PRD: TOEI ANIMATION ● TV SERIES ● EPS: 152

# HOLMES, SHERLOCK

CHARAC

In 1984, the TMS studio entrusted Miyazaki Hayao with an anime reinterpretation of Arthur Conan Doyle's famous detective stories about sleuth Sherlock Holmes. The crucial iconographic element in this reinvention was to give each character the face of a type of dog – Holmes himself is a fox, while his nemesis Moriarty resembles a wolf – hence the English title, *Sherlock Hound*. The set construction combines the architecture of late-nineteenth-century England with machine technology that recalls fantasy realism à la Jules Verne. Miyazaki had great faith in the project and, with his customary care, had gone to England with colleagues to study the landscapes and architecture that the characters would have encountered. ● Work began on this reinterpretation of the famous Holmes stories in the early eighties, as a co-production between RAI and Tokyo Movie Shinsha. However, problems with the Conan Doyle estate caused delays in production and Miyazaki was diverted from the project to work on *Little Nemo* (1989), having completed only six episodes of *Sherlock*. During these long months of work, however, a friendship was forged between the director and Marco Pagot, a young but experienced director. He and his sister Gina gave their names to the two lead characters of Miyazaki's *Porco Rosso* (1992). The character design of Mrs Hudson, Holmes' housekeeper, also provides the inspiration for 'Gina' in the later film. ● F.L.

SCENES FROM THE 1984 SERIES SHERLOCK HOUND ● ABOVE LEFT: A CHASE SCENE FEATURING CONAN DOYLE'S CLASSIC HERO AS IMAGINED BY MIYAZAKI AND HIS LOYAL PARTNER WATSON ● BELOW LEFT: SHERLOCK HOUND, THE GREAT INVENTOR, WORKS IN HIS LAB

MEITANTEI HOLMES ● SHERLOCK HOUND ● AKA: GREAT DETECTIVE HOLMES ● 1984 ● DIR: MIYAZAKI HAYAO, MIKURIYA KYOSUKE ● SCR: YAMAZAKI TOSHIYUKI ET AL ● DES: KONDO YOSHIFUMI ● ANI: TANNAI TSUKASA ● MUS: HANEDA KENTARO ● PRD: RAI, REVER, TMS ● TV SERIES ● EPS: 26

CHARACTER

# HOLS

A flock of crows flies skywards from a rocky landscape. As the cawing of the birds fades into the distance, a ferocious snarling breaks out: an axe, racing legs and silver wolves flash across the screen. They hurtle by too quickly for more than a glimpse; only in the next scene does a longer shot reveal an armed boy surrounded by wolves. ● The striking images and the dynamism of the figures in the opening sequence make the first appearance of the boy warrior Hols very effective in this tale of heroic exploits. Alone, tenacious and dauntless in a hostile environment, the hero is fighting, as we soon learn, for his village. His deeds are borrowed from the Nordic sagas and the enemies he has to confront belong to a well-known tradition that sets Good against Evil on an incremental scale. The introduction of the character of Hilda, a girl with a heart of ice and a melodious voice, gives a new twist to the plot. She is spying for the dastardly Grunwald but she gradually repents when confronted by the vulnerability of the human community, and it is she who influences the course of events in Takahata Isao's first full-length film. ● Remarkable for its artistic qualities, *Little Norse Prince*, was the first important production to result from the collaboration between Otsuka Yasuo, Miyazaki Hayao and Takahata. It has great stylistic originality and resourcefulness, with still shots used for an action scene when the money had run out, and effective cinematographic references (to Soviet cinema in particular). The detail, close-up and panoramic shots are all handled with consummate skill, making the most of the camera's expressive potential. This film (shot in CinemaScope) signalled the entry of Japanese animation into the modern era. ● C.C.

LEFT & ABOVE: VARIOUS SCENES FROM THE FILM *LITTLE NORSE PRINCE*, 1968, SHOWING THE MANY ADVENTURES OF HOLS AND HILDA, THE BEAUTIFUL AND MYSTERIOUS GIRL HE LOVES

H

*TAIYO NO OJI HOLS NO DAIBOKEN* ● *LITTLE NORSE PRINCE* ● AKA: *GREAT ADVENTURE OF HOLS, PRINCE OF THE SUN* ● 1968 ● DIR & SCR: TAKAHATA ISAO ● DES: MIYAZAKI HAYAO ● ANI: OTSUKA YASUO ● MUS: MAMIYA TSUNEO ● PRD: TOEI ANIMATION ● FILM ● DUR: 82 MINS

Dark-haired pitcher Hoshi Hyuma is determined to make it in the world of baseball. He joins the Yomiuri Giants baseball team, and suffers a gruelling training regime at the hands of his father, whose own career was cut short by a war wound. First appearing in manga form in 1966, he reached television anime in 1968, and returned in several sequels and movie spin-offs, most recently in a 2002 remake. ● Hyuma's Japanese name conjures an image of wild, soaring heroism (a flying horse); his surname literally means Star. Hyuma aspires to be the best player in the team, his rise in stature tied inextricably to the 'Giants' he idolizes and emulates. ● As the first true sports anime on television, *Star of the Giants* blazed a trail for an entire sub-genre. Tropes and ideas from martial arts and adventure were adapted for the baseball games, using dramatic zooms and freeze frames of the action. Similarly, the episodic strategies and 'combats' on the sports field that lead Hyuma to face ever more powerful adversaries is a forerunner to the escalating 'boss battles' seen in computer games. Hyuma's own character is an anime archetype – the bushy-browed, hot-headed hero, striving to aspire to the legacy of a father-figure who never quite attained his own potential. ● *Star of the Giants* was also an early template for the funding and distribution of anime. The real-life Yomiuri Giants team is part of the same Yomiuri group that owned the network that broadcast the show – an early exercise in the vertical integration that dominates modern anime. The series was made in colour at a time when many viewers still had monochrome television sets, encouraging the popularity of 'movie' edits shown in cinemas. ● J.Cl.

# HOSHI HYUMA

CHARACTER

*KYOJIN NO HOSHI* ● *STAR OF THE GIANTS* ● *1968* ● DIR: NAGAHAMA TADAO ● SCR: YAMAZARI TADAAKI ET AL ● DES: KAWASAKI NOBORU ● ANI: KUSUBE DAIKICHIRO ET AL ● MUS: WATANABE TAKEO ● PRD: TMS ● TV SERIES ● EPS: 182

# HOSODA MAMORU

DIRECTOR

Hosoda Mamoru was born in 1967 in Toyama, and has since established his reputation as one of the most interesting anime directors working today. After joining Toei Animation in 1991, he debuted as a director with various episodes of the *Digimon Adventure* (1999) series and co-directed the *Digimon: The Movie* (2000). In 2003 he made a short film entitled *Superflat Monogram* inspired by the work of Louis Vuitton. He was subsequently considered as director for *Howl's Moving Castle* (2004) but was eventually replaced by Miyazaki Hayao himself. In 2005, Hosoda directed the sixth film in the *One Piece* series, *Omatsuri Danshaku to Himitsu no Shima* (*Baron Omatsuri and the Secret Island*, 2005), which was also his last for Toei. It was the most successful instalment so far, made in a style reminiscent of the epic Westerns of Sergio Leone. ● The following year, Hosoda directed his most important film, *The Girl Who Leapt Through Time* (2006). The story of Makoto, a young schoolgirl who discovers the ability to travel in time and alter things that happen to her, is a classic tale of cinema and Japanese television, and there are various preceding live-action versions. Hosoda's 2009 movie *Summer Wars* has been critically acclaimed worldwide. ● F.L.

RIGHT: NADJA OF *ASHITA NO NADJA* (2003) FOR WHICH HOSODA DIRECTED SOME EPISODES

SEE ALSO: DIGIMON; HOWL'S MOVING CASTLE; KANNO MAKOTO; LUFFY, MONKEY D

# HOWL'S MOVING CASTLE
*FILM*

Working in her late father's milliner's, Sophie meets the handsome, mysterious young wizard Howl, shortly before she is struck by a terrible curse that transforms her into a wizened old woman. Forced to run away, she meets a scarecrow who leads her to a rickety galleon-cum-fortress with smoke belching from its numerous chimneys that stomps across a mountainous landscape on four spindly legs. The moving castle is home to the notorious wizard, who is fleeing from the Witch of the Waste. Aiming to break the curse and regain her younger body, the old Sophie moves into the castle as a cleaner. ● And so the scene is set for a film brimming with subtle elements and extraordinary creatures that change appearance and transform in the blink of an eye, appearing and disappearing, moving through space and time. Clever, talking scarecrows, characters who can disguise themselves as roaring fires and cunning sorceresses inhabit this bewitching world, where the beauty of nature is threatened by war, violence and the thirst for power. Anything can happen in the places visited by the castle, a winged monster, safe-house, living creature and symbol of freedom and poetry. Based on a story by Diana Wynne Jones, Miyazaki Hayao depicts a magical city filled with sophisticated people with decadent homes and streets filled with greenery and flowers. However, in this world, the line between reality and imagination is so fine that all you really need to change scene is your imagination – it's merely a question of choice and desire. The film represents different stages of life, switching between an enchanted childhood world and violent reality. ● G.P.

SCENES FROM THE 2004 FILM HOWL'S MOVING CASTLE ● BELOW: THE WITCH OF THE WASTE AS SHE FIRST APPEARS ● BOTTOM RIGHT: TURNIPHEAD THE SCARECROW, HOWL'S APPRENTICE MARKL AND HEEN THE DOG ● BELOW LEFT: TWO IMAGES OF SOPHIE AS AN OLD WOMAN WITH THE WIZARD HOWL ● ABOVE LEFT: HOWL'S WANDERING CASTLE

HOWL NO UGOKU SHIRO ● HOWL'S MOVING CASTLE ● 2004 ● DIR & SCR & DES: MIYAZAKI HAYAO ●
ANI: YAMASHITA AKIHIRO ET AL ● MUS: HISAISHI JOE ● PRD: SUZUKI TOSHIO ET AL, STUDIO GHIBLI ● FILM ● DUR: 119 MINS

STUDIO

# I.G.

Ishikawa Mitsuhisa and Goto Takayuki, formerly of Tatsunoko Production, founded Production I.G. in December 1987. The new studio was initially known as I.G. Tatsunoko, and worked under contract to produce remakes for television, and on joint ventures with other companies. In 1993 its founders renamed the studio Production I.G. According to Ishikawa, its aim is to make anime that can stand alone, rather than simply being an extension of manga. ● In 1989 and again in 1993, I.G. worked on Oshii Mamoru's first two *Patlabor* movies. Oshii called on them again in 1995 to work with him on *Ghost in the Shell* (*Kokaku Kidotai*). The worldwide success of the movie and its sequels brought the studio to international attention and led to its collaboration with Quentin Tarantino on *Kill Bill: Vol. 1* (2003). ● The studio went on to release more theatrical feature animation, including Okiura Hiroyuki's *Jin-Roh: The Wolf Brigade* (1999), Kitakubo Hiroyuki's *Blood: The Last Vampire* (2000), *Ghost in the Shell 2: Innocence* (2004) and *The Sky Crawlers* (2008), both directed by Oshii. I.G. is also active in producing TV series, for example working on CLAMP's *XxxHOLIC* (2006, dir. Mizushima Tsutomu) and *The Prince of Tennis* (2001, dir. Hamana Takayuki.). It has established a reputation for ground-breaking technical innovation and state-of-the-art animation. ● H.M.

A SELECTION OF IMAGES FROM SOME OF I.G.'S BIGGEST SUCCESSES ● TOP: THREE IMAGES OF THE FEMALE CYBORG MAJOR KUSANAGI MOTOKO FROM *GHOST IN THE SHELL* (1995, DIR. OSHII MAMORU, 83 MINS) ● CENTRE RIGHT: FUSE KAZUKI, CONFLICTED PROTAGONIST OF *JIN-ROH: THE WOLF BRIGADE* (1999, DIR. OKIURA HIROYUKI, 98 MINS) ● RIGHT: THE INGRAM ROBOT FROM *PATLABOR THE MOVIE* (1989, DIR. OSHII MAMORU, 118 MINS)

SEE ALSO: JIN-ROH; KANNAMI YUICHI; KUSANAGI MOTOKO; MADHOUSE; NISHIKUBO MIZUHO; OSHII MAMORU; PATLABOR; SAYA

# IDEON

ROBOT

Conceived by Tomino Yoshiyuki immediately after *Mobile Suit Gundam* (1979), *Space Runaway Ideon* does not immediately seem to follow the same narrative development of the earlier series. In *Gundam*, the giant robots were a mass-produced means of combat, whereas the Ideon, the super-robot of the title, is more than a simple automaton. The modular robot is made up of three armoured vehicles that were discovered by explorers from Earth abandoned on the distant planet of Solo. Preserved within it is the secret of the mysterious source of 'Ide', a mighty energy source that powers the Ideon's unbeatable weapons. On closer inspection, however, it appears that themes introduced in *Gundam* have not been entirely abandoned. ● The mecha design seen in *Space Runaway Ideon* is of an ordinary standard, but the mature and striking characterization is unusually dramatic for a television series aimed at children. As in *Gundam*, Tomino's characters are ambiguous, short-tempered people, whose behaviour can not always be described as heroic, while the distinction between the humans and their enemies the 'Buff Clan', a humanoid people from a world similar to Earth, is progressively reduced over the course of the series, leading the viewer to reflect on the senselessness of war. Tomino's direction further emphasizes the dramatic qualities of battle through the use of split-screens and close-up shots, even showing the deaths of various characters in full. For the first time in a commercial series, the director also introduces a profound sense of mysticism – to the extent that *Space Runaway Ideon* was declared source of inspiration for director Anno Hideaki's *Neon Genesis Evangelion* (1995), a series that was to rejuvenate the whole robot genre. ● L.D.C.

SCENES FROM THE 1980 SERIES *SPACE RUNAWAY IDEON* ● ABOVE RIGHT & RIGHT: IMAGES OF IDEON'S PILOT COSMO YUKI WITH TEAM–MATE KASHA IMHOF ● BELOW: IMAGES OF THE IDEON ROBOT IN BATTLE

*I*

*DENSETSU KYOJIN IDEON* ● *SPACE RUNAWAY IDEON* ● 1980 ● DIR: TOMINO YOSHIYUKI ET AL ● SCR: TOMITA SUKEHIRO ET AL ● DES: KOGAWA YUKIEN, SUBMARINE ● ANI: KOGAWA YUKIEN ● MUS: SUGIYAMA KOICHI ● PRD: SUNRISE ● TV SERIES ● EPS: 39

# IKEDA RIYOKO

MANGAKA

Born in 1947 in Osaka, Ikeda Riyoko began her career with the short story *Bara Yashiki no Shojo* in 1967. The story, like all Ikeda's early work, reflects the influence of Tezuka Osamu. Her first major success came in 1979 with *The Rose of Versailles*, which tells the story of the French Revolution through the lives of three characters: Marie Antoinette, Queen of France; the Swedish Count Hans Axel Von Fersen; and Captain Oscar François de Jarjayes, a woman brought up as a man. Oscar is a complex character, owing much to Tezuka's *Princess Knight*, and elevates the *shojo* genre to previously unknown levels. ● The manga is different from Ikeda's previous work by virtue of its length and the stylish artwork that alternates between the simplest of drawings to grand and elegant illustrations. Her enormous success has made her the queen of *shojo* manga and stories with a historical background, a genre to which she returns several times in the course of her career. *Jotei Ekaterina* (1982) is dedicated to Empress Catherine II of Russia, while *Eiko Naporeon: Eroika!* (1987) tells the story of Napoleon's life and allows Ikeda to return to the settings of *The Rose of Versailles*. Her longest and most complex work though, was *Orpheus no Mado* (1975), set during the Russian revolution, which allowed her to sharpen and perfect her style. ● After 1991, she decided to devote herself exclusively to scriptwriting, entrusting the design work to her colleague, Miyamoto Erika. Her interest in art in its more varied forms led her, in 1995, to study singing and to record CDs as a soprano. In 2008, the French government awarded her the *Légion d'honneur* for her contributions to promoting French history throughout the world. ● D.D.G.

ABOVE: THE YOUNG CROWN PRINCESS MARIE ANTOINETTE. AN EXAMPLE OF THE REFINED DESIGN FOR *THE ROSE OF VERSAILLES* (1979, DIR. NAGAHAMA TADAO, DEZAKI OSAMU, 41 EPS), THE BEST-KNOWN OF IKEDA RIYOKO'S CREATIONS

SEE ALSO: ARAKI SHINGO; CLAMP; JARJAYES, OSCAR FRANÇOIS DE; RIBBON NO KISHI

---

# IKENO FUMIO

SCRIPTWRITER

Ikeno Fumio's name first appeared in anime credits in the late sixties for directing cheap slapstick children's cartoons like *Freckles Pooch* and *Pinch & Punch*. His work spanned the next two decades, but his great experience as an animator saw him move away from directing into a crucial but often overlooked part of the anime production process. ● Ikeno's true vocation was in drawing storyboards, a very specialized area of animation. Known as *e-konte* in Japanese (literally, 'picture continuity'), the skill calls on the artist to draw a shot-by-shot outline of how a finished work will appear – a visual, comic-style representation of the television show or film. The work requires a illustrator with the ability to combine the eye of a manga artist with an understanding of the practicalities of animation. ● Ikeno's work often has a foreign aspect. More often than not, his storyboards were called upon to grapple with the unfamiliar, exotic western locations, buildings and details to be used for such anime as *Little Women* (1987), *Little Lord Fauntleroy* (1988), *Rascal the Racoon* (1977), *Belle & Sebastian* (1981) and *Anne of Green Gables* (1979). Ikeno occasionally returned the director's role, such as in the television special that depicted the life of Helen Keller, as well as in episodes of *Hattori-kun the Ninja* (2004). ● J.Cl.

BELOW: THE EXUBERANT ANNE SHIRLEY IN *ANNE OF GREEN GABLES* (1979, DIR. TAKAHATA ISAO, 50 EPS). IKENO FUMIO COLLABORATED ON THE DEVELOPMENT OF THE STORYBOARD

SEE ALSO: ANNE OF GREEN GABLES; RASCAL; SHIRATO TAKESHI

# IKUHARA KUNIHIKO

The major difference between Ikuhara Kunihiko (born in 1964 in Kanagawa) and other directors of his generation is that while he has an affection for the milestones of anime such as *Star Blazers* (1974) and *Mobile Suit Gundam* (1979), he knows that he can not make works of that kind. This dandy among directors was instead inspired to join the anime world because of Yamamoto Eiichi's art-house animation *The Tragedy of Belladonna* (1973), a film that changed the very perception of animation. ● Ikuhara's professionalism as director of the *Sailor Moon* (1992) series and films won him considerable artistic freedom, allowing him to pick and choose his future projects as well as winning him the enthusiastic support of anime fans, who celebrate him like a pop star. ● The project that transformed his career, however, was *Revolutionary Girl Utena*, devised in 1997 by the Be-Papas creative group that he founded together with manga artist Saito Chiho, animator Hasegawa Shinya and screenwriter Enokido Yoji. Ikuhara wrote and directed both the television series and a sumptuous film made in 1999, in which he invokes such iconic anime as *The Rose of Versailles* (1979) and *Princess Knight* (1967). His tribute to these forerunners is only one of surface appearance, however, as *Utena* is a multifaceted creation that Ikuhara personally dresses, colours and moves through a maze of intersecting questions and paradoxes. ● M.A.R.

RIGHT: IKUHARA KUNIHIKO DIRECTED SEVERAL EPISODES OF THE NINETIES MAGICAL–GIRL CLASSIC *SAILOR MOON* (1992, DIR. KOBAYASHI OSAMU, SATO JUNICHI ET AL, 46 EPS). HERE, USAGI–CHAN AND HER BELOVED MAMORU ARE UNAWARE OF EACH OTHER'S SECRET IDENTITIES AS SAILOR MOON AND TUXEDO MASK

SEE ALSO: JARJAYES, OSCAR FRANÇOIS DE; RIBBON NO KISHI; SAILOR MOON; TENJO UTENA

# INITIAL D

TV SERIES

Fujiwara Takumi is an unusual hero. An exceptionally talented racing driver, he has no desire to take part in the street races that his friends are obsessed with. In fact, his mastery of the high mountain roads remains unknown to the others for some considerable time. Takumi perfected his driving technique as a young teenager – well before reaching legal driving age – delivering the tofu sold by his father, himself a former speed champion. But for Takumi this is just a job like any other.
● With this, *Initial D* sets up a curious plotline. In classic sports stories, we follow a character as they struggle to acquire the skills required for victory, but Takumi has all the talent he needs right from the start, and his success is almost a given. Shigeno Shuichi's manga, and the series derived from it, instead focuses on the way Takumi gradually acquires a taste for competitive driving. In the end, it's no longer enough just to be a virtuoso driver, as Takumi comes to love racing too.
● An exuberant celebration of Japanese street-racing culture, *Initial D* couples this with a rite-of-passage story which, although rather naive in its romanticism, gives it an emotional resonance beyond a mere collection of car-borne combat sequences. In the anime series, the car-race sequences inevitably invite comparison with the videogame (*Initial D* has also been a very popular saga in the arcades since 2001). It has also been argued that the switches between 2D and 3D animation flirt with the notion of another dimension, a fantasy world where existence becomes utterly simple, freed of all moral and physical constraints. ● E.H.

SCENES FROM THE 1998 SERIES *INITIAL D* ● TOP RIGHT: FUJIWARA TAKUMI (RIGHT) WITH TAKAHASHI KEISUKE, A FORMER RIVAL AND TEAM-MATE ● BELOW RIGHT: FEMALE RACING DRIVER, SATO MAKO ● BELOW: RACE SEQUENCES DEMONSTRATING THE INNOVATIVE MIX OF 2- AND 3-D ANIMATION IN *INITIAL D*

INITIAL D ● 1998 ● DIR: MISAWA SHIN ● SCR: ASHIDA HIROSHI, KISHIMA NOBUAKI ● DES & ANI: FURUSE NOBORU ● MUS: KATSUMATA RYUICHI ● PRD: FUJI TV, GALLOP, OB PLANNING, PRIME DIRECTION ● TV SERIES ● EPS: 26

# INTERSTELLA 5555

FILM

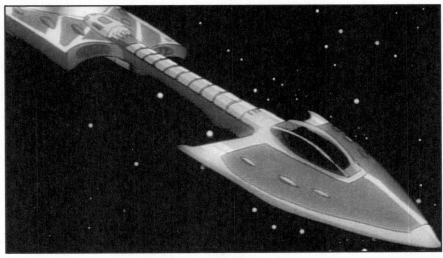

In the middle of a pop concert, somewhere on a distant planet full of blue-skinned inhabitants, a masked commando force descends from a fleet of spaceships and captures the group on stage. The four members of the band are spirited away to Earth by means of an international wormhole, their memories altered and their identities changed, as each of them is implanted with a chip that controls their will. Under the control of the mysterious kidnappers, they become the Crescendolls, a new group who shoot up the charts to global super-stardom. In the meantime, out in space, a young alien on board a spaceship in the shape of an electric guitar is following hot on the trail of the band; it is he who helps them to recover their identities.
● *Interstella 5555* is a film made in 2003, with a soundtrack entirely composed by elctro group Daft Punk and devised in collaboration with the legendary creator of Japan's most popular science-fiction cartoons, the artist Matsumoto Leiji. The film rests equally on the characters conceived by Matsumoto, a delightful compendium of his previous creations but with more modern and pronounced features, and on the direction assured by a team of artists that also includes Takenouchi Kazuhisa and veteran Nishio Daisuke, both of Toei Animation. ● Without dialogue, but with Daft Punk's songs taken from the album *Discovery* to provide Matsumoto with the necessary inspiration, the film is a courageous and successful mix of music and animation that recalls certain artistic experiments by Tezuka Osamu. In this spectacular setting, Matsumoto's reflective and steady universe is suddenly and unexpectedly imbued with the pop glamour of cult creations such as *Macross*. ● M.A.R.

INTERSTELLA 5555 — THE STORY OF THE SECRET STAR SYSTEM ● 2003 ●
DIR: MATSUMOTO LEIJI, TAKENOUCHI KAZUHISA ET AL ● SCR: DAFT PUNK ●
DES: SATO MASAKI ● ANI: TAMEGAI KATSUMI, KHIKAWA KEIICHI ● MUS: DAFT PUNK ●
PRD: TOEI ANIMATION ● FILM ● DUR: 68 MINS

ABOVE: MATSUMOTO LEIJI'S EXTRAORDINARY CREATIONS BRING THE MUSIC OF DAFT PUNK TO LIFE IN THE 2003 FILM *INTERSTELLA 5555: THE STORY OF THE SECRET 5 STAR SYSTEM*

# ISHIGURO NOBORU

DIRECTOR

Developing an interest in manga at school, Ishiguro Noburo (born in 1938 in Tokyo) studied film at Nihon University, where he also formed a Hawaiian band with several friends. After graduation, he joined TV Doga, the children's animation wing of Fuji TV, but soon left for Onishi Production before deciding to work freelance. He was a sketch artist on *Astro Boy* (1963) and moved on to projects such as *Wansa-kun* (1973) — a musical anime where Ishiguro became known as an animator who could match musical notation to storyboards. Later in his career, he would famously revisit his musical interests as director of *Ginga Eiyu Densetsu* (*Legend of Galactic Heroes*, 1988), where space battles were accompanied by stirring symphonies from classical composers. ● Ishiguro's best-known work was as the director of *Star Blazers* (1974), the long-running saga that left Ishiguro permanently associated with the science-fiction medium, despite a résumé in many other styles. In 1978, he was one of the founding members of Artland, the production house that continues to farm out his services today, on anime such as *Lupin III* (1971) and *Mushishi* (2005). He was also credited as the director, alongside Shoji Kawamori, on the *Macross* movie *Do You Remember Love?* (1984), which featured the power of music in a central role. ● Ishiguro appeared briefly as a voice actor in *Macross* in the role of the movie director Sho Blackstone, a pun on the Japanese meaning of his name. His most recent work as director is the science-fiction series *Tytania* (2008), based on novels by Tanaka Yoshiki, creator of *Legend of Galactic Heroes*. ● J.Cl.

A DEFEATED INSPECTOR ZENIGATA (ABOVE) AND THE MASTER CRIMINAL IN *LUPIN III*, (1971, DIR. OSUMU MASAAKI, MIYAZAKI HAYAO, TAKAHATA ISAO, 23 EPS); ISHIGURO NOBURO DIRECTED FIVE EPISODES OF THE SERIES

SEE ALSO: BEM; GINKO; MACROSS; TOPO GIGIO; YAHAGI SHOGO; YAMATO

# ISHII KATSUHITO

Like his older colleague Iwai Shunji, Ishii Katsuhito is the very incarnation of the modern Japanese film-maker. His first short, *The Promise of August* (1996), won the grand prize at the Yubari International Film Festival in Japan and Ishii went on to direct advertisements and music videos, notably for SMAP, Japan's biggest pop group, with whom he subsequently collaborated on several films. This success enabled Ishii to shoot his first live-action, feature-length film *Samehada Otoko to Momojiri Onna* (*Sharkskin Man and Peach Hip Girl*, 1998), based on the manga by Mochizuki Minetaro. The film stars Asano Tadanobu, who became a devotee of Ishii's work, and it topped the Japanese box office in 1999. ● Fascinated by manga and anime culture, Ishii's work leans towards science fiction and comedy and he combines the two in his collaborations with Koike Takeshi, who created animated sequences for Ishii's second film, *Party 7* (2000). They co-directed *Trava: Fist Planet* (2003) for the Grasshoppa company, for whom Ishii was a consultant. This company has produced over thirty shorts by young film-makers, as well as works by well-known artists including Anno Hideaki, who acted in Ishii's masterpiece *Cha no aji* (*The Taste of Tea*, 2004). ● In 2008 Ishii shot *Yama no anata: Tokuichi no Koi* (*My Darling of the Mountains*), a remake of a film by Shimizu Hiroshi, and its modern counterpart *Sorasoi* with his own production company, Nice Rainbow. Both are stories of escape and love triangles. Ishii also worked with Koike again on the feature-length anime *Redline* (2010) and began a parallel career in the plastic arts, another facet of his activities combining pop and tradition, from flowering cherry trees to lascivious aliens. ● S.S.

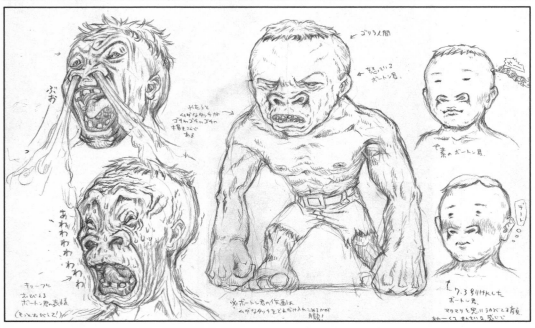

**BELOW & LEFT: A PREPARATORY WATERCOLOUR AND SKETCHES FOR THE FILM *CHA NO AJI* (*THE TASTE OF TEA*, 2004, DIR. ISHII KATSUHITO, 143 MINS) ● ABOVE LEFT: CHARACTER SKETCHES DEMONSTRATE THE ECLECTIC STYLE OF ISHII'S WORK**

SEE ALSO: I.G.; MADHOUSE

SEE ALSO: I.G.; MADHOUSE

098

# ISHINOMORI SHOTARO

MANGAKA

Born Onodera Shotaro in 1938, Ishinomori had a passion for drawing from an early age. He sent numerous samples of his work to manga publishers, and at the end of the Fifties he met Tezuka Osamu, who has great influence on his visual style and production themes. ● In 1964, after changing his last name to Ishimori (and again later to Ishinomori), he published the manga that would make his name as a great science-fiction writer: *Cyborg 009*. The series tells the story of a group of nine cyborgs fighting for their freedom against the sinister 'Black Ghost' organization, and has been transferred to animation several times. ● An innovative author who is attentive to the stimuli offered by modern life, Ishinomori shows he is also able to deal sensitively with ideas from other cultures. *Ryu the Cave Boy* (1971), for example, was inspired by *Planet of the Apes* (1968) yet in Ishinomori's hands it became an original work that explores themes such as racism and man's relationship with nature. His focus on the superhero also places Ishinomori's work in the foreground of the *tokusatsu* genre – live-action films or television adventures of superheroes featuring elaborate special effects, such as the *Kamen Rider* (*Masked Rider*, 1971) series and *Himitsu Sentai Goranger* (*Secret Squadron Five Rangers*, 1975), the first example of the *sentai* genre, made famous in recent years by the exploits of the Power Rangers. ● A charismatic but reserved figure, in his varied career Ishinomori has fostered such talents as Nagai Go and worked in various fields, creating comic strips spun off from videogames and, in 1988, a cartoon guide to Japanese economics. He died prematurely in 1997 before he was able to finish *Cyborg 009*. ● D.D.G.

IMAGES TAKEN FROM SERIES BASED ON ISHINOMORI SHOTARO'S MANGA ● ABOVE RIGHT: THE CAST OF *CYBORG 009* (1966, DIR. SERIKAWA YUGO ET AL, 64 MINS) ● RIGHT: RAN AND RYU FROM THE SERIES *RYU THE CAVE BOY* (1971, DIR. AKEHI MASAYUKI, 22 EPS)

SEE ALSO: CYBORG 009; RYU; SUPER SENTAI

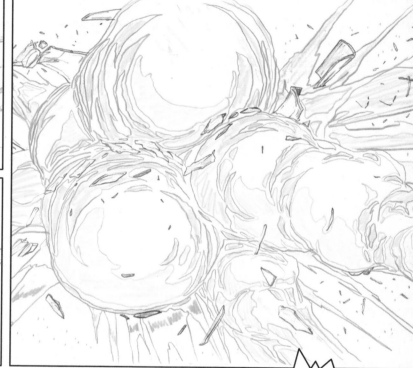

# ITANO ICHIRO

DIRECTOR

TOP: A STORYBOARD FOR A SEQUENCE FROM *BLASSREITER* (2008, DIR. ITANO ICHIRO, 24 EPS) ● ABOVE: SCENES FROM THE SERIES *GANTZ* (2004, DIR. ITANO ICHIRO, 26 EPS)

Itano Ichiro is anime's action man, a specialist in imparting visceral movement, fast motion and the illusions of speed and gravity. Born in 1959 in Yokohama, he began his career at Studio Musashi on the television series *Planet Robo Danguard Ace* (1977) shortly after finishing school. An avid fan of giant robots and military machinery in his childhood, Itano soon began specializing in their animation, most notably for the first series of *Mobile Suit Gundam* in 1979. ● In the Eighties, Itano was also a pioneer in the gaming world, credited as the director of animation sequences on many early videogames with anime tie-ins, such as *Macross Plus* (1994), *Vampire Hunter D* (1985) and *Quo Vadis 2*. ● His early directorial work in anime proper is split between robot- and machinery-heavy shows such as *Macross* (1982), and series with a greater emphasis on action, such as *Violence Jack* (1986) and the controversial *Angel Cop* (1989). As well as directing the acclaimed *Gantz* (2004), he has become part of the blurring line between animation and live action in the twenty-first century, directing the digital effects for several parts of the *Ultraman* (1966) franchise. ● Itano has become known for several distinctive film-making tropes in his anime. The 'Itano Circus' is an explosive, multiple-launch missile attack, complete with curving contrails and devastating explosions, as seen in the key frames from *Blassreiter* (2008) above. He also became known for scenes made as if the action were being filmed by characters holding hand-held cameras, buffeted and shaken by turbulence; some of his aerial combat sequences have been deliberately framed as if filmed by sky-diving cameramen in freefall. He was also an early aficionado of different lens styles, deforming images as if shot through telephoto, wide-angle or fish-eye lenses. ● J.Cl.

SEE ALSO: GANTZ; GUNDAM; MACROSS; YAHAGI SHOGO

# ITO KAZUNORI

SCRIPTWRITER

Ito Kazunori, born in 1954 in Yamagata Prefecture, is best known for his work as a screenwriter and script editor on several high-profile feature films, manga adaptations and television serials. His contributions place him at the centre of developments in anime from the mid-Eighties onward. He is also a member of Headgear, a collective of five artists and writers, including director Oshii Mamoru and character designer Takada Akemi. ● Ito came to prominence in 1986, with adaptations of Takahashi Rumiko's domestic melodrama *Maison Ikkoku* (1980) and the 'suburban space-opera' *Urusei Yatsura* (1981). He is also one of the creators of the *.hack* franchise, which employs manga, anime, videogame, television and costume media. The franchise anticipates many of the themes of contemporary cyber-crime anime such as Mitsuo Iso's *Denno Coil* (2007) and Shirow Masamune's *Real Drive* (2008), and is unique in its audacious use of mixed multimedia platforms. ● Ito is perhaps best known for his work as screenwriter for director Oshii Mamoru, the two have been long-time collaborators since working together on the prominent mecha movie *Mobile Police Patlabor* (1989) and its sequel. In 1995, the pair collaborated in the adaptation of Shirow Masamune's *Ghost in the Shell* (1995), certainly Oshii's best-known work and one of the defining anime works of the Nineties. Ito's signature intellectualism and wit added a new take on the *Ghost in the Shell* characters, and has inspired the new generation of conscientious and psychological works indicative of millennial anime. He went on to work on Oshii's 2004 live action film *Avalon*. ● D.S.

RIGHT: A FRENCH LANGUAGE PUBLICITY POSTER FOR THE FILM *AVALON* (2001, DIR. OSHII MAMORU, 107 MINS) ● BELOW: SCENES FROM *GHOST IN THE SHELL 2: INNOCENCE* (2004, DIR. OSHII MAMORU, 99 MINS)

SEE ALSO: .HACK; I.G.; KUSANAGI MOTOKO; OSHII MAMORU; PATLABOR; SHIROW MASAMUNE; TAKADA AKEMI; URUSEI YATSURA

**I**

# IZUBUCHI YUTAKA

CHARACTER DESIGNER

Izubuchi Yutaka (born in 1958 in Tokyo) is one of anime's premier designers, a draughtsman whose flights of fancy and/or sense of reality have helped shaped anime's visions of the future, the fantastic and the just plain cool. ● His first anime job was on *Tosho Daimos* (*Starbirds*, 1978). Attending the same high school as renowned illustrator Mikimoto Haruhiko and designer/director Kawamori Shoji, Izubuchi soon found himself working alongside Kawamori at Studio Nue, a design studio specializing in mecha – armour, machinery and robots. ● His contacts within Studio Nue led to design work on the *Mobile Suit Gundam* (1979) series, while his involvement with the Headgear collective, an organization of fans within the anime industry, made him one of the creators of the *Mobile Police Patlabor* (1988) series. Yuki Masami, the author of the *Mobile Police Patlabor* manga, once described Izubuchi as 'more dear to me than a wife'. Izubuchi also worked for his fellow *Patlabor* animator Oshii Mamoru, designing the armour suits seen in the *Kerberos* series (1986). ● Subsequently, Izubuchi has continued to design both machinery and characters, memorably branching out into high fantasy with *Lodoss To Senki* (*Record of Lodoss War*, 1990), a popular saga inspired by an early Japanese role-playing game in the style of *Dungeons & Dragons* (1974). He has lent his talents to live-action films as well, providing some of the machinery for the science-fiction submarine movie *Lorelei*, and also character designs for superhero shows such as *Masked Rider – The First*. ● While credited with the story, storyboards and supervising direction on the robot combat series *RahXephon* (2003), he seems to prefer to keep to his first love – design (on costumes, armour and anything else that requires a unique vision). ● J.Cl.

LEFT: A PUBLICITY IMAGE FOR *RECORD OF LODOSS WAR* (1990, DIR. NAGAOKA AKIRA, 13 EPS), ONE OF IZUBUCHI YUTAKA'S MANY COLLABORATIONS

SEE ALSO: KAWAMORI SHOJI; MIKIMOTO HARUHIKO; OSHII MAMORU; PATLABOR

# JARJAYES, OSCAR FRANÇOIS DE

CHARACTER

Oscar François de Jarjayes was born in 1755 in Orléans. Brought up as a boy by her father, a general in the French army, she became a Captain of the Royal Guard in the service of the young Marie Antoinette, while still a teenager. Devoted to duty, she suppressed her femininity in order to dedicate her life to chivalry and rejected the love of the handsome Count Fersen, the former secret lover of Marie Antoinette. With the advent of the Revolution, Oscar felt she could no longer share the queen's ideals and left to support the insurgents. She was followed by André Grandier, a childhood friend who harboured a secret love for her. ● In one of the most beautiful scenes of the series, André opines 'Even if it is the colour of blood, a rose will always be a rose, it can never be a lilac.' His words describe one of anime's most famous characters, who symbolized women's emancipation from convention but was simultaneously incapable of living her life in denial of her instincts. ● *The Rose of Versailles* is also famous for the homoerotic subtext (which was more explicit in the original manga) that has made Oscar a gay icon — she dresses as a man and attracts more than one female character. A combination of split screens of melancholy faces, slow-motion sequences with Impressionist back-lighting and highly effective music provided the public (not just enthusiastic anime fans) with many memorable moments, such as André's death at the height of the Revolution. The series ended in 1980 under the direction of Dezaki Osamu (who took over from Nagahama Tadao from the nineteenth episode). ● S.G.

ABOVE RIGHT: QUEEN MARIE ANTOINETTE ● RIGHT: SWORDSWOMAN OSCAR SURROUNDED BY THE MAIN CHARACTERS FROM THE 1979 TV SERIES THE ROSE OF VERSAILLES

J

*VERSAILLES NO BARA* ● *THE ROSE OF VERSAILLES* ● *1979* ● DIR: NAGAHAMA TADAO, DEZAKI OSAMU ● SCR: SHINOZAKI YOSHIMI ET AL ●
DES: ARAKI SHINGO ET AL ● ANI: ARAKI SHINGO, HIMENO MICHI ● MUS: MAIKANO KOJO ● PRD: TMS ● TV SERIES ● EPS: 41

When the young Shiba Hiroshi, part human, part machine, turned into the 'head' of the giant robot Jeeg,' the robot genre saw the 'pilot' disappear. Ships and controls no longer acted as intermediaries between humans and machines, and a hybrid figure was born, marrying the mecha genre to popular cyborg/superhero series such as *Casshern* (1973) and *Tekkaman* (1975). *Jeeg, The Steel Robot* gives a further nod to the masked hero tradition with the dual-identity of Hiroshi/Jeeg and it is no coincidence that Hiroshi's younger brother, Mayumi, unaware that the steel giant hides the body of his brother, comes to idolize Jeeg. ● The struggle of Hiroshi, a young rebel indifferent to the mission that his father chose for him, is that of a generation more westernized than their parents and not opposed to the loss of tradition. Car-obsessed Hiroshi wears a white jumpsuit like a then-contemporary Elvis or Evel Knievel, but must fight against ancient creatures from Japanese history and folklore: Queen Himika (based on the third-century sovereign Queen Himiko), Haniwa monsters (a reworking of funerary 'warrior' statuettes) and the Yamato no Orochi spaceship (science fiction's version of the mythological dragon defeated in Shinto tradition by the sea-god Susanoo). ● The series' depiction of extreme physical fighting, with many leaps and acrobatic moves, reflects creator Nagai Go's passion for wrestling and its dark atmosphere highlights the work of the technical cast, largely recruited from *Mazinger Z* (1972). The magnetic robot idea paved the way for imitations such as *Ga-Keen, The Magnetic Robot* (1976) and a 2007 sequel/remake, but the original series remains a cultural milestone. ● D.D.G.

# JEEG, THE STEEL ROBOT

TV SERIES

ROBOT

ABOVE: JEEG (CENTRE) ABOUT TO BATTLE TWO OTHER ROBOTS IN A SCENE FROM THE 1975 SERIES JEEG, THE STEEL ROBOT

JEEG, THE STEEL ROBOT ● 1975 ● DIR: YOSHIO NITTA, KAZUJA MIYAZAKI, MASAYUKI AKEHI, SERIKAWA YUGO, KAZUO NAKAMURA ● SCR: YAMAURA HIROYASU ET AL ●
DES: NAKAMURA KAZUO, KATSUMATA GEKI ● ANI: NAKAMURA KAZUO ET AL ● MUS: WATANABE MICHIAKI ● PRD: DYNAMIC PLANNING, TOEI ANIMATION ● TV SERIES ● EPS: 46

# JIN-ROH

FILM

Although directed by Okiura Hiroyuki, *Jin-Roh* was originally conceived by writer and film-maker Oshii Mamoru as a feature-length addition to the *Kerberos* saga that he began 1986. Before *Jin-Roh,* there was a series of radio broadcasts, manga and two live-action films, *The Red Spectacles* (1987) and *Stray Dog: Kerberos Panzer Cops* (1991), directed by Oshii himself. This fictitious universe has continued to expand ever since, and Oshii's vision has developed with rare consistency. The Kerberos world is an alternate reality in which Japan became a totalitarian society, where all rebellion is crushed by special units of heavily armed soldiers, their helmets emitting red light where their eyes should be. Although Mamoru Oshii intended to direct *Jin-Roh* himself he eventually entrusted the screenplay to Okiura Hiroyuki, an exceptionally talented animator but a novice director, with whom he had collaborated on the two *Patlabor* films (1989 and 1993) as well as on *Ghost in the Shell* (1995). The result is as rich and complex as it is visually striking. A multilayered film overflowing with evocative correlations, *Jin-Roh* is a narrative palimpsest where political metaphors, an existential journey, a love story and variations on *Little Red Riding Hood* are all superimposed one over another. ● For the film's hero, an anti-terror policeman called Fuse Kazuki, everything revolves around a single, haunting image impossible to erase: that of a girl, a suicide bomber, whom he was unable to shoot dead before she detonated a bomb in the heart of Tokyo — an insoluble moral dilemma. Examining group psychology, military order and the roles that each individual is expected to fulfil, *Jin-Roh* is a profound and fundamentally pessimistic interrogation of identity, subjectivity and otherness: an interrogation of what it is to be human. ● E.H.

SCENES FROM THE 1999 FILM *JIN-ROH: THE WOLF BRIGADE* ● ABOVE RIGHT: TEENAGE BOMBER AGAWA NANAMI ● RIGHT: FUSE KAZUKI AND AMEMIYA KEI WHO CLAIMS TO BE AGAWA'S SISTER TO ENTRAP FUSE

JINRO ● JIN-ROH: THE WOLF BRIGADE ● 1999 ● DIR: OKIURA HIROYUKI ● SCR: OSHII MAMORU ● DES: OKIURA HIROYUKI, HIRAMATSU TADASHI ● ANI: KAMIYAMA KENJI ● MUS: MIZOGUCHI HAJIME ● PRD: PRODUCTION I.G. ● FILM ● DUR: 98 MINS

J

# JIRO

CHARACTER

*The Dagger of Kamui* is a harrowing adventure story interwoven with the history of late-nineteenth-century Japan. Jiro, the son of a ninja from Yamato and an Ainu (an aboriginal people of Japan) woman, is abandoned as a baby and raised by a village woman. Unjustly accused of killing his adoptive parents, he is urged to seek revenge by the monk Tenkai, who brings him to the alleged culprit: a maimed warrior named Taroza. Years later, having grown up at the court of Tenkai under the harsh laws of *bushido* (the samurai code of honour and morals), Jiro learns that the man he killed was his father and that for his entire life, he has been the victim of Tenkai's machinations. Tenkai's purpose is to drive him to despair, convinced that, once on the trail of his ancestors, Jiro will lead him to a legendary treasure discovered many years before by Taroza. Using his formidable ninja techniques, Jiro begins a long personal struggle that ends in his defeat of the wicked Tenkai and the end of the shogunate. ● Based on a series of novels by Yano Tetsu, *The Dagger of Kamui* condenses (with sharp editing and fast-paced directing) a host of events into a brilliantly animated film, covering a period of around twenty years and a wide range of settings. In his quest for the treasure, Jiro scours Japan, Russia and America, making contact with the Native Americans and even passing the time of day with Mark Twain, who is impressed by his integrity. ● The film's wide range of characters and reference to precise historical events brings it an epic quality. First exploited by the shogunate, then converted to the Emperor's cause, the long-suffering Jiro eventually withdraws from the battlefield and chooses to live in solitude with only a wolf for company. ● S.G.

# JOJO'S BIZARRE ADVENTURE

VIDEO SERIES

JOJO NO KIMYO NA BOKEN ● JOJO'S BIZARRE ADVENTURE ● 1993 ● DIR: FUTAMURA HIDEKI, KITAKUBO HIROYUKI, NOMURA KAZUFUMI, FURUSE NOBORU ● SCR: KITAKUBO HIROYUKI ● DES: HANEYAMA JUNICHI ● ANI: HANEYAMA JUNICHI ● MUS: MARCO D'AMBROSIO ● PRD: STUDIO A.P.P.P. ● VIDEO SERIES ● EPS: 13

A manga from the imagination of Araki Hirohiko, *Jojo's Bizarre Adventure* is a tour de force – a journey through a surreal world which, on the surface, resembles Hara Tetsuo's *Fist of the North Star* (1984), but is much more in keeping with the surreal manga by Ito Junji or even, in its deliberate absurdity, Kago Shuntaro. The story follows the successive generations of the Joestar family in their long-running feud with the malevolent Dio, an aristocrat turned vampire. ● *Jojo's Bizarre Adventure* is *Shonen Magazine's* second longest-running manga series. Organized into various cycles or parts, the story unfolds in a variety of periods, with different characters taking centre stage in each. Beginning in the 1880s, the action moves to the Thirties, then to the Eighties, and finally to the Nineties. In each instance, a member of the Joestar lineage faces off against Dio or one of his many malevolent companions. ● The intensely surreal premise and fractured narrative of *Jojo* often overshadows any discussion of its art and animation. In the OAV series (1993, 2001) adapted from the manga, incredibly simple plot components contrast with finely animated and ingenious action sequences that exhibit some fine keyframe animation and shot construction. *Jojo* is second to none in its effects animation and the final conflict between Dio and Jotaro Joestar is a moment of anime action-direction at its finest. ● D.S.

# JUBEI

CHARACTER

The stories of *Ninja Scroll* unfold in a cruel world. Set in a feudal Japan beset by fantastical elements, the bloodthirsty anime, heir to the chanbara genre, is overflowing with scenes of gore and morbid eroticism. This heroic epic about the ronin Jubei (inspired by a legendary samurai) and the long-limbed female ninja Kagero, is rich in sword-fight scenes often culminating in a rain of severed limbs and gushing rivers of blood. It has been argued that director Kawajiri Yoshiaki decided to turn to animation simply because he realized it was not possible to represent these events in live-action film without exorbitant costs or terrible shock to the audience. ● Although it tests audience sensibilities severely, *Ninja Scroll* offers more than a complacent window onto a series of extreme action sequences. It unveils a whole universe of mysteries, a place dominated by false appearances, where a tattoo can suddenly turn into a real and deadly snake. Against a background of plague-decimated villages, amidst forests infested with pitiless demons, Kawajiri creates a flamboyant shadow-theatre in which myths are made flesh. In counterpoint to his harsh-featured heroes' physical prowess, Kawajiri has supporting aural and visual symbols that help give the film real consistency: a cloud of fireflies lights up the night, a spider waits patiently in its web or the current sweeps away a branch in the river. ● *Ninja Scroll* is an influential film that enjoyed unusual success for a Japanese animation at the time in US cinemas, but opinions about its aesthetic choices differ widely – the cost, perhaps, of having the nerve to take its ideas to the extreme. A second movie is mooted after a TV series was aired in 2003. ● E.H.

RIGHT: THE RONIN JUBEI, THE CENTRAL CHARACTER OF THE 1993 FILM *NINJA SCROLL*

J

JUBEI NINPUCHO ● NINJA SCROLL ● 1993 ● DIR & SCR: KAWAJIRI YOSHIAKI ● DES: KAWAJIRI YOSHIAKI, YUTAKA MINOWA ● ANI: MINOWA YUTAKA ● MUS: WADA KAORU ● PRD: MADHOUSE ● FILM ● DUR: 92 MINS

# KAIBUTSU-KUN

In late sixties anime *Little Monster*, Kaibutsu, the prince of Monster Land, comes to Earth as part of his training to become king. He lives in a decaying western-style villa in the centre of Tokyo accompanied by the Wolfman, a werewolf with a thick German accent; Dracula, who drinks tomato juice rather than blood; and the stout and easygoing Franken (a young Frankenstein's monster), who acts as butler. They meet primary-school pupil Hiroshi when his baseball lands in the villa's garden. Kaibutsu decides that he and Hiroshi should become friends and invites himself round for a visit, opening a 'dimensional door' between their two houses through the refrigerator. The Earthling is then involved in a series of madcap adventures involving an array of different monsters. Kaibutsu, who is friendly enough towards humans but obnoxious and authoritarian towards his assistants, fancies himself as an intermediary between the human and monster worlds. Although small, he has superhuman strength, taking cowardly monsters to task and opposing the bullying kind who give the humans a hard time. He can change his appearance as required and is equipped, like Luffy in *One Piece* (1999), with elastic, extendable limbs. ● Based on a manga created by the Fujiko Fujio duo, authors of *Doraemon* (1973), *Little Monster* anticipates some of the later work's peculiarities, particularly the outsider hero who, though inclined to help others, ends up causing more problems than he solves, disturbing the peace and tranquillity of his new neighbours. Although similar in origin to the celebrated *Gegege no Kitaro* (1968), *Little Monster* is more akin to *Urusei Yatsura* (1981), which shares a penchant for chaotic stories driven by, or lapsing into, nonsense. ● S.G.

RIGHT: SCENES FROM THE 1968 SERIES *LITTLE MONSTER* SHOWING KAIBUTSU AND FRIENDS IN MONSTER LAND ● BELOW: A SECOND SERIES WAS MADE IN COLOUR IN 1980

KAIBUTSU-KUN ● LITTLE MONSTER ● 1968 ● DIR: OSUMI MASAKI, YAMADA TAKASHI ● SCR: YAMAZAKI HARUYA ET AL ● DES: SHIBATA TSUTOMU ● ANI: KUBII NORIO, TOMINAGA SADAO ● MUS: OKAMOTO MICHIO, KOBAYASHI YASEI ● PRD: SHIN-EI ANIMATION, TMS ● TV SERIES ● EPS: 49

Captain Shiro Kaieda is an archetypal figure from a different age – a square-jawed, barrel-chested giant of a man. But while he resembles a Hollywood action hero, he is also a quintessentially Japanese figure from the pre-war era – a mid-ranking military officer who takes matters into his own hands, dragging his homeland to the brink of war. ● Affronted at a corrupt cover-up by Japan's American allies, Kaieda steals the *Seabat*, a secret prototype submarine, and proclaims both it and its nuclear arsenal to be a new and independent rogue state. Its new name, in reference to both Japanese folklore and the history of World War II, is *Yamato*. The remainder of the anime involves a series of encounters between the *Seabat* and the US Navy, as Kaieda relentlessly outwits his supposed superiors. ● The submarine sub-genre is theoretically ideal for anime. Movement is often linear or indistinct in the shadows and drama conveyed through tension, as officers huddle over their instruments and listen for sonar readings. Such tense visual stillness and audio-based 'action' help stretch an anime budget further than usual, particularly when a live-action adaptation would surely have required the loan of real military hardware, and hence the unlikely cooperation of the US Navy. ● Based on a 1988 manga by Kawaguchi Kaiji, *Silent Service* allegorizes a Japan that was involved in global affairs, widely recognized as an economic superpower, and yet still beholden to the USA for its defence. Even today, Japan is constitutionally forbidden from maintaining 'offensive' military forces. The character of Kaieda was a hero for an assertive Japan, ready to stand up to the nation that had defeated it in World War II and dominated its foreign policy for decades. Although infamous for attacking the USA, its true impact lay in its equally controversial challenge to Japan's post-war constitution. ● J.Cl.

# KAIEDA SHIRO
# CAPTAIN KAIEDA

CHARACTER

ABOVE: CAPTAIN KAIEDA AND HIS CREW MEMBERS OF THE SUBMARINE SEABAT IN THE 1995 SERIES SILENT SERVICE

CHINMOKU NO KANTAI ● SILENT SERVICE ● 1995 ● DIR: TAKAHASHI RYOSUKE ● SCR: YOSHIKAWA SOJI ET AL ● DES & ANI: KATO SHIGERU ET AL ● MUS: SENJU AKIRA ● PRD: SUNRISE ● VIDEO SERIES ● EPS: 3

# KAJIWARA IKKI

MANGAKA

Takamori Asaki (1936–1987) never worked directly in anime, although he established many of the archetypes of modern sports anime and his comic scripts were transferred to anime with minimal changes. A high-school dropout who returned to education later in life to get a degree, he found work on the magazine *Chuo Koron*. Despite early ambitions to become a novelist, he soon found a more lucrative trade writing the scripts for manga, at first using the pseudonym Kajiwara Ikki. ● Kajiwara specialized in manga stories for boys, including high-school conflicts and daily dramas, many of which were later adapted in other media. He found a useful blue-chip niche for himself, churning out sports stories in which a rookie in any given sport endures a harsh training regime and overcomes bad luck in order to make it to the top of their profession. Kajiwara applied this template to *A Karate-Crazy Life*, the baseball heroism of *Star of the Giants*, the wrestling drama *Tiger Mask* and the soccer tales of *Kick Fiend*, as well as several other martial arts and sports stories, many of which were similarly adapted into anime. ● Kajiwara wrote manga scripts considerably faster than his numerous collaborators could draw them, and soon, faster than his publishers could print them. As early as 1968, he was writing stories such as the boxing drama *Tomorrow's Joe* (a.k.a. *Rocky Joe*) under the second pseudonym of Takamori Asao, in order to conceal the level of his output from rival editors. His use of pen names has kept his powerful influence on the anime and manga world obscure from many foreign fans. ● Kajiwara also had a brief cameo as the voice of a journalist in *Lupin III: Mystery of Mamo*, directed by Yoshikawa Soji in 1978. ● J.Cl.

SEE ALSO: DATE NAOTO; HOSHI HYUMA; YABUKI JOE

RIGHT: SCENE FROM *TIGER MASK* (1969, DIR. TAMIYA TAKESHI ET AL, 105 EPS). HERO DATE NAOTO (LEFT) IS CAPTURED BY AN ADVERSARY

# KANNAMI YUICHI

CHARACTER

The Kildren are ruthless pilots genetically engineered to add thousands of hours of aerial combat experience to the speed of their adolescent reaction times. The most powerful of these 'gladiators' – employed by two rival companies, and destined to die in combat from the moment they are first programmed – is new arrival Kannami Yuichi. ● With his sad eyes, melancholy expression and tight-lipped mouth, Yuichi does not seem to be very different from his colleagues, but he is obsessed by his lack of memories and driven by a strange impulse towards Kusanagi, the young female commandant of the base – possibly a deliberate reference to the Major of the same name in *Ghost in the Shell* (1995). ● The silent tragedy of Oshii Mamoru's *Sky Crawlers* (2008), a film based on the novels of Mori Hiroshi, is expressed through its characters. As they wait for their inevitable encounter with the Teacher, an unbeatable fighting ace, the Kildren embody a sense of predestination characteristic of Oshii's work. The film paradoxically brings depth to the 2D characters whose tragedy it is to have been denied any depth of experience. Yuichi is an Oedipus figure – a rebellious wanderer who wants to kill and usurp his father – who finds himself reliving a story that has already been repeated countless times. ● Assisted by his usual team, the animator Nishibuko Toshihiko and composer Kawai Kenji, Oshii has produced an original and sophisticated work, with some outstanding aerial sequences. His vision of the skies is complex and fascinating: a place one longs for, especially when contrasted with the sombre hues of life on earth. This luminous backdrop is the setting for gladiatorial combat worthy of the Roman Colosseum. ● C.C.

AURORA SUKAI ● THE SKY CRAWLERS ● 2008 ● DIR: OSHII MAMORU ● SCR: ITO CHIHIRO ● DES & ANI: NISHIO TETSUYA ● MUS: KAWAI KENJI ● PRD: PRODUCTION I.G. ● FILM ● DUR: 122 MINS

# KANNO MAKOTO

Poor Makoto is anything but successful at school because of her clumsy nature and a tendency to arrive late for class. In *The Girl Who Leapt Through Time*, she discovers a mysterious power that allows her to go back in time in a single leap, but things quickly get complicated. ● Indeed, the complications of this conceit demanded that a prestigious team was mobilized for its realization. This team included director Hosoda Mamoru (first choice for *Howl's Moving Castle*, 2004, dir. Miyazaki Hayao), designer Yamamoto Nizo (formerly art director for Miyazaki), character designer Sadamoto Yoshiyuki (*Neon Genesis Evangelion*, 1995, dir. Anno Hideaki) and no less a science-fiction writer than Tsutsui Yasutaka, who wrote the original story in 1965. Rather than politically or historically motivated, Makoto's time travels are subjective and emotional. Hosoda's is primary concern is with exploring Makoto's feelings and reworking the dynamics of classic school comedies at a brisk pace that is not stifled by the constant coming and going between past and present. The animation therefore focuses on the realistic depiction of gestures and models' bodies so that each figure is able to express, in a single movement, their emotions and state of mind. It is this quality, more than the psychological aspect, however well done, which gives the film the freshness which wins audiences. Hosoda makes intelligent use of the background as a setting for 'before' and 'after' action, making time itself a co-star, the true centre of gravity for the composition. ● D.D.G.

LEFT & BELOW: SCENES ILLUSTRATING THE TIME WARPS OF THE TEENAGER MAKOTO IN *THE GIRL WHO LEAPT THROUGH TIME* (2006), THE FILM THAT LAUNCHED DIRECTOR HOSODA MAMORU

TOKI WO KAKERU SHOJO ● THE GIRL WHO LEAPT THROUGH TIME ● 2006 ● DIR: HOSODA MAMORU ● SCR: OKUDERA SATORU ● DES: SADAMOTO YOSHIYUKI ● ANI: KUBOTA CHIKASHI ET AL ● MUS: YOSHIDA KIYOSHI ● PRD: MADHOUSE ● FILM ● DUR: 98 MINS

K

# KANNO YOKO

COMPOSER

While still studying piano at Waseda University, Kanno Yoko (born in 1964 in Miyagi) became keyboard player with the group TETSU100%. Already a performer and songwriter, she sold her first tie-in composition for a computer game in 1985. Since then, Kanno has composed the soundtracks for over twenty anime works, initially in collaboration with her ex-husband, Mizoguchi Hajime, with her internationally acclaimed work on the OAV *Macross Plus* (1994) making her the darling of international anime fans. ● It is difficult to pin down a single Kanno 'style' as her work ranges from big-band and jazz sounds on the soundtrack of 1998 anime *Cowboy Bebop* (for which she formed a new group, Seatbelts), to the drum-and-bass of *Ghost in the Shell: Stand Alone Complex* (2003) and the mellow lounge music of *Mayonaka wa Betsu no Kao* (*The Other Side of Midnight*, 2002). However, her most prominent achievements are her expansive and lavish compositions that have helped to drag anime soundtracks out of the age of cheap synthesizers and into a world of full-blown orchestral epics such as those Kanno composed for *Escaflowne* (1996) and *Brain Powered* (1998). ● Kanno is in such high demand that comparatively little of her work is not associated with a commercial, television series or game. Even those works intended for independent release, such as her original album *Song to Fly*, are soon snapped up by producers in other media. ● Gabriela Robin, a singer credited on several Kanno tracks, is rumoured to be a pseudonym for Kanno herself. Kanno is also said to be the model for the hacker tomboy 'Ed' in *Cowboy Bebop*, and supplied a voice for the anime anthology *Genius Party Beyond* (2007). ● J.Cl.

TWO MAJOR SUCCESSES FEATURING MUSIC BY KANNO YOKO ● ABOVE RIGHT: *COWBOY BEBOP* (1998, DIR. WATANABE SHINICHIRO, 26 EPS) ● RIGHT: *THE VISION OF ESCAFLOWNE* (1996, DIR. AKANE KAZUKI ET AL, 26 EPS)

SEE ALSO: APPLE, SHARON; KANZAKI HITOMI; MACROSS; SPIEGEL, SPIKE

# KANZAKI HITOMI

CHARACTER

Hitomi Kanzaki is a high-school student with two passions: the hundred-metre race and tarot reading, a device that allows her to predict the future, when she finds herself transported to Gaea, a fantasy world of medieval settings and advanced technology. This is just the beginning of an adventurous journey in the company of young prince Van Fanel and his mighty 'guymelef', an anthropomorphous robot operated by magic. Initially disorientated, she soon wins the favour of Gaea's knights and the respect of its vain princesses, and learns to stand up to Merle, a very jealous cat-girl. ● However, Hitomi's presence in this world is not by chance: she unwittingly becomes one of the balancing elements that govern the 'Ideal Destination', as Emperor Dornkirk has declared war on many of the countries of Gaea. Torn emotionally between Van, of her own generation, and the charming knight Allen, Hitomi becomes a pawn of the emperor, who manipulates her from afar by means of an alchemy machine. ● With the series *The Vision of Escaflowne*, Sunrise demonstrated its aptitude for moulding new genres, in this case mixing medieval epic *shojo* sentimentalism with combat between robots. The passionate result, the fruit of a long period of screenplay work, owes little to repetition and digression. Just one year after Anno Hideaki directed *Neon Genesis Evangelion* (1995), *Escaflowne* demonstrated that television animation, while keeping within the boundaries of commercial entertainment, had changed in terms of shape and intentions. The feature film though, which trivialized the plot by altering Hitomi's cheerful nature, is insignificant. ● S.G.

RIGHT: FOUR SCENES FROM THE 1996 TV SERIES *THE VISION OF ESCAFLOWNE* FEATURING THE HEROINE HITOMI AND THE YOUNG PRINCE VAN FANEL ● BELOW: A PUBLICITY IMAGE FOR THE SERIES

*TENKU NO ESCAFLOWNE* ● *THE VISION OF ESCAFLOWNE* ● 1996 ● DIR: AKANE KAZUKI ET AL ● SCR: KAWAMORI SHOJI ET AL ● DES: YUKI NOBUTERU ET AL ● ANI: KOBARA SHIGEKI ET AL ● MUS: KANNO YOKO, MIZOGUCHI HAJIME ● PRD: SUNRISE ● TV SERIES ● EPS: 26

K

# KASUGA KYOSUKE

KIMAGURE ORANGE ROAD •
1987 • DIR: KOBAYASHI OSAMU
• SCR: TERADA KENJI ET AL
• DES: TAKADA AKEMI • ANI: GOTO
MASAKI, SUGIYAMA TOYOMI •
MUS: SAGISU SHIRO • PRD:
STUDIO PIERROT • TV SERIES •
EPS: 48

For Japanese teenagers who grew up in the Eighties, Kyosuke is the boy, torn between two girls, who can never make up his mind. We first see him in *Kimagure Orange Road* (1987) climbing a long flight of steps on the outskirts of Tokyo, where he bumps into the beautiful fifteen-year-old Madoka. After this encounter, followed by an action-packed sequence in which the girl clashes with some young hoodlums, Kyosuke realizes he is attracted to Madoka, a girl with a mysterious, contradictory personality. But every time he attempts to transform their friendship into something deeper, he is interrupted by Hikaru, a lively girl who worships Madoka but is also in love with Kyosuke. • A sentimental teen comedy, which found many admirers abroad, much of the action of *Orange Road* hinges on supernatural occurrences as Kyosuke and his family all possess secret powers. This aspect of the story drives some of the most exciting episodes, with Kyosuke the victim of hypnosis (by his jovial grandfather), self-hypnosis (when he tries to instil courage in himself while looking in the mirror) and, above all, time travel, with tragi-comic effects that resemble the films *Back to the Future* (1985, dir. Robert Zemeckis) and *Groundhog Day* (1993, dir. Harold Ramis). This theme is also central to the series finale, as Kyosuke goes back four years, seeking to recapture the identity of the boy who first kissed Madoka, and is amazed to discover that it was him. • The full-length films in this franchise, more serious in tone and with superior visuals, explore the love triangle in greater depth, bringing to an end the friendship between Hikaru and Kyosuke, who eventually chooses Madoka, and showing their subsequent reconciliation. Kyosuke's thoughts are often emphasized by a final mask-like shot of his face. Similarly, the final shot of each episode is transformed into a still photograph. • S.G.

# KATSUMATA TOMOHARU

A graduate of Nippon University's film school, Katsumata Tomoharu (born in 1938 in Shizuoka) is one of the cornerstones of the celebrated Toei Animation studio. He began his career in samurai cinema, but from the Seventies onwards, he assumed the role of director at Toei Animation and became one of the studio's first series directors, supervising the directors of individual anime episodes and ensuring stylistic uniformity across a series. • Katsumata's name is linked particularly to animated series created by Nagai Go, such as *Devilman* (1972), *Mazinger Z* (1972), *Cutey Honey* (1973), *Great Mazinger* (1974), *UFO Robot Grendizer Raids* (1975) and *Dino Mech Gaiking* (1976). The incredible success of these series can in part be attributed to his markedly filmic style of directing, which broke with the tradition of previous television productions through the use of wide-angle shots, close-ups and fast-moving editing. Katsumata's energy and dynamism are also in evidence in his first feature film *The Return of Pero* (1972), the second animated film dedicated to the character of Pero the cat, who later became the symbol of Toei Animation. The well-known story of this cute cat in boots is transposed to the American West, where Katsumata openly drew inspiration from spaghetti Westerns and depicted scenes of shooting and killing unusual in a children's film. • Always faithful to Toei, Katsumata directed 1977's *King Arthur* and is also hailed for his direction of anime versions of science-fiction manga by Matsumoto Leiji, such as *Planet Robot Danguard Ace* (1977) and the Captain Harlock movie *Waga Seishun no Arcadia* (Arcadia of My Youth, 1982). • L.D.C.

LEFT & ABOVE LEFT: KING ARTHUR (1979, DIR. AKEHI MASAYUKI ET AL, 30 EPS) • ABOVE CENTRE: THE CAST OF DANGUARD ACE (1977, DIR. KATSUMATA TOMOHARU, 56 EPS) • ABOVE RIGHT: DR HELL IN MAZINGER Z (1972, DIR. SERIKAWA YUGO ET AL, 92 EPS)

SEE ALSO: CUTEY HONEY; DANGUARD ACE; DEVILMAN; GETTA ROBOT; KITARO; UFO ROBOT GRENDIZER RAIDS

# KAWAI KENJI

COMPOSER

It is impossible to discuss the work of musician Kawai Kenji (born in 1957 in Tokyo) without discussing his scores for the films of Oshii Mamoru. The professional association of composer and director dates back to the live-action film *Jigoku no banken: akai megane* (*The Red Spectacles*, 1986), but whether in film or animation, one is the creative mirror of the other. ● In his youth, Kawai was a member of a fusion band and a keen fan of Ennio Morricone, Dave Grusin and Burt Bacharach. As a professional film composer, he has become a unique figure within the anime business: a great eclectic able to switch easily from romantic comedies, such as *Maison Ikkoku* (1986), to the explosive entertainment of *Ranma ½* (1989) and *Bakuretsu Hunter* (*Sorcerer Hunters*, 1995), via the evocative score of the thrilling *Vampire Princess Miyu* (1988). ● Kawai follows a rigorous process of research and experimentation and his talent obliterates the common conception of the soundtrack as a separate, lesser, genre within the music world. Significant innovations in the genre are apparent in the score for *Patlabor 2: The Movie* (1993) and are further developed in his fascinating soundtracks for *Ghost in the Shell* (1995) and *Ghost in the Shell 2: Innocence* (2004). Melodies create images that themselves become characters, echoes that recur in thrilling symphonic parts or sounds articulated repeatedly, at times backed up by choruses or whispering, poetic voices. Rarely repeating himself, Kawai is a courageous innovator. ● M.A.R.

ABOVE RIGHT: LARVA IN *VAMPIRE PRINCESS MIYU* (1988, DIR. HIRANO TOSHIHIRO, 4 EPS) ● RIGHT: AKANE IN *RANMA ½* (1989, DIR. SHIBAYAMA TSUTOMU ET AL, 161 EPS)

SEE ALSO: KUSANAGI MOTOKO; MAISON IKKOKU; MIYU; OSHII MAMORU; PATLABOR; SAOTOME RANMA

# KAWAJIRI YOSHIAKI

*DIRECTOR*

Kawajiri Yoshiaki (born in 1950 in Yokohama) began his career at Tezuka Osamu's Mushi Production as an animator on such titles as *Legend of the Forest* (1987) and subsequently honed his talents at Madhouse. He was initially interested in drawing manga and in an effort to improve his line-work he entered, and was quickly fascinated by, the anime industry. The author and director of numerous bloody action films, he is involved at every stage of production from screenwriting to editing, and his outstanding directorial skills have ensured that his work stands out among the more run-of-the-mill commercial products. ● Although he has dabbled in various genres, fantasy-horror is Kawajiri's chosen field. He creates dark stories that exalt physical strength and violence, reducing women to sex objects and instruments of conquest, his savage rape scenes invariably followed by the garish mutilation of the body. Although undeniably sexist in his subject matter, Kawajiri's careful attention to continuity and other aspects of live-action film-making combines unforgettably with the spectacular aesthetic of his animations. Preferring strong colours, predominantly blue and red, Kawajiri creates high-contrast scenes in which the human figure is often reduced to a back-lit silhouette and represents shots or blade-thrusts as a ballet of sparkling lightning bolts. Rather than classic textured backgrounds, he prefers frenetically alternating stroboscopic colours that emphasize the violence of the action in an almost psychedelic environment. Graphically, he uses numerous lines and pronounced shading to give maximum emphasis to the musculature of his characters. ● Kawajiri is also the author of three well-received experimental shorts in which he plays both conceptually and stylistically with the distortion of time, a trope beloved by the anime industry. ● S.G.

ABOVE: SCENE FROM *LEGEND OF THE FOREST* (1987, DIR. TEZUKA OSAMU, FILM, 23 MINS)

SEE ALSO: *ANIMATRIX*; *JUBEI*; *MANIE MANIE*; *VAMPIRE HUNTER D*

# KAWAMORI SHOJI

*DESIGNER*

*DIRECTOR*

As the popularity of anime grew, the industry was not slow in recognizing the need to recruit a new generation of artists who were the product of the popular culture it had helped to form. Kawamori Shoji (born in 1960 in Toyama) is one such recruit: a cartoonist who grew up watching television, reading manga and dreaming of a creative career in the mad world of animation. As a young engineering student, he was a great fan of the *Star Blazers* series. His mecha designs began to gain attention in the anime industry and he dropped out of college before finding work as a designer with Studio Nue, where he would make a significant contribution to the cult series *Macross* a few years later. ● Mecha design takes a revolutionary turn in Kawamori's hands. His speciality is the hyper-realistic depiction of all types of mechanical devices, from an ordinary tank to the best-equipped spacecraft. The classic expression of this style is his feature film *Macross: Do You Remember Love?* (1982), which wittily combines classic seventies science fiction with the Japanese pop-culture phenomenon of female idols. The film's action sequences are rich in detail, as if Kawamori were acting as puppet master using perfect scale models on screen. This convincing imagining of machinery and heightened spatial awareness is consistently high and evident in most other Kawamori projects, from *Macross Plus* (1994) and *The Vision of Escaflowne* (1996) to *Macross Frontier* (2008). In 1996, Kawamori directed the OAV *Ihatov Gensou: Kenji no Haru* (*Spring and Chaos*), a poetic homage to the writer Miyazawa Kenji using experimental techniques in computer animation. ● M.A.R.

ABOVE RIGHT & RIGHT: WINGED PRINCE VAN FANEL, HERO OF *THE VISION OF ESCAFLOWNE* (1996, DIR. AKANE KAZUKI ET AL, 26 EPS)

SEE ALSO: *APPLE, SHARON*; *GUNDAM*; *KANZAKI HITOMI*; *MACROSS*; *MATSUMOTO LEIJI*

# KAWAMOTO KIHACHIRO

DIRECTOR

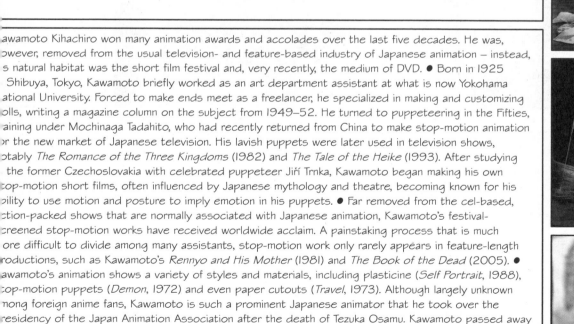

Kawamoto Kihachiro won many animation awards and accolades over the last five decades. He was, however, removed from the usual television- and feature-based industry of Japanese animation – instead, his natural habitat was the short film festival and, very recently, the medium of DVD. ● Born in 1925 in Shibuya, Tokyo, Kawamoto briefly worked as an art department assistant at what is now Yokohama National University. Forced to make ends meet as a freelancer, he specialized in making and customizing dolls, writing a magazine column on the subject from 1949–52. He turned to puppeteering in the Fifties, training under Mochinaga Tadahito, who had recently returned from China to make stop-motion animation for the new market of Japanese television. His lavish puppets were later used in television shows, notably *The Romance of the Three Kingdoms* (1982) and *The Tale of the Heike* (1993). After studying in the former Czechoslovakia with celebrated puppeteer Jiří Trnka, Kawamoto began making his own stop-motion short films, often influenced by Japanese mythology and theatre, becoming known for his ability to use motion and posture to imply emotion in his puppets. ● Far removed from the cel-based, action-packed shows that are normally associated with Japanese animation, Kawamoto's festival-screened stop-motion works have received worldwide acclaim. A painstaking process that is much more difficult to divide among many assistants, stop-motion work only rarely appears in feature-length productions, such as Kawamoto's *Rennyo and His Mother* (1981) and *The Book of the Dead* (2005). ● Kawamoto's animation shows a variety of styles and materials, including plasticine (*Self Portrait*, 1988), stop-motion puppets (*Demon*, 1972) and even paper cutouts (*Travel*, 1973). Although largely unknown among foreign anime fans, Kawamoto is such a prominent Japanese animator that he took over the presidency of the Japan Animation Association after the death of Tezuka Osamu. Kawamoto passed away in August 2010. ● J.Cl.

ABOVE & RIGHT: IMAGES SHOWING THE ECLECTIC WORK OF KAWAMOTO KIHACHIRO

K

SEE ALSO: KURI YOJI; MOCHINAGA TADAHITO; OFUJI NOBURO; TEZUKA OSAMU; TSUJI NAOYUKI

# KEI & YURI

DIRTY PAIR • 1985 • DIR: KASHIMA NORIO, TAKIZAWA TOSHIFUMI • SCR: HOSHIYAMA HIROYUKI ET AL • DES: DOKITE TSUKASA ET AL • ANI: TOMISAWA KAZUO, DOKITE TSUKASA • MUS: KIMORI TOSHIYUKI, KUNIMOTO YOSHIHIRO • PRD: STUDIO NUE, SUNRISE • TV SERIES • EPS: 24

CHARACTERS

If the West has *Charlie's Angels*, then Japan has Kei and Yuri, a twenty-second-century crime-fighting duo who jet off on missions across the galaxy as part of the World's Welfare Works Association. Heroines of a multitude of television series, cartoon films and videos since 1985, the official name of the two young adventuresses is 'Lovely Angels' but their explosive exploits have earnt them the somewhat less elegant nickname of 'Dirty Pair'. ● While the girls always achieve their objectives, systematically thwarting the mysterious projects of public enemies, it is rare for matters to be resolved without significant collateral damage. Kei and Yuri possess a considerable aptitude for clumsiness combined with reckless urges. Their taste in provocative poses is certainly not the only thing that sets them apart from more common or garden variety righters of wrongs. ● *Dirty Pair* is notable for its joyously youthful tone. Indeed its blue- and pink-haired heroines, with their huge pistols at the ready, never miss a chance for a girlie chat before storming into action. The somewhat kitsch saga of Kei and Yuri fluctuates between an almost-serious tale and pure parody. It comes close to an exploration, as sarcastic as it is affectionate, of make-believe (eroticism for the general public) and the light-hearted side of science-fiction. The clumsy twosome have a seemingly infinite capacity to stimulate the imagination and have seen many incarnations, including western comics by Adam Warren. ● E.H.

LEFT: SCENES FROM THE 1985 TV SERIES *DIRTY PAIR* FEATURING THE ACTION HEROINES KEI AND YURI

---

# KEN, THE WOLF BOY

TV SERIES

In the Sixties, *Astro Boy* (1963) was the black-and-white, small-screen hero par excellence. In an effort to undercut the dominance of this series and square up to the challenge of Tezuka Osamu's other new productions, Toei Animation and others set out to counter his boy robot with the ideal adversary, and Ken, The Wolf Boy appeared ten months after the first broadcast of *Astro Boy*. Unusually, *Ken* was not based on an existing manga, but an original story (albeit with strong echoes of *Tarzan* or *The Jungle Book*) depicting the extraordinary adventures of a wild boy raised by wolves in the wilds of Africa. Yet, despite Toei's skill in interpreting the television market, they were still far from having found an antidote to Tezuka's popularity. ● The series held a number of winning cards, including artistic performances under the guidance of its undisputed creative sovereign, director Tsukioka Sadao. Not only did he personally design the characters, aiming for simplicity and avoiding extraneous lines, but he also surrounded himself with the studio's best talents, both veterans and newcomers (Daikuhara Akira, Otsuka Yasuo, Takahata Isao and a very young Miyazaki Hayao) to seek ways of entertaining that broke with tradition. The series also set itself exceptionally high standards of quality: each episode was made using over 3,000 drawings (compared with the 1,000 of *Astro Boy*) – a very high number for the time – and Tsukioka's comic inventions are brilliantly original. ● Tsukioka later abandoned the wearisome world of serial production, preferring to narrow his field and work in the world of advertisements and shorts. ● M.A.R

OKAMI SHONEN KEN • KEN, THE WOLF BOY • AKA: KEN, THE WILD BOY • 1963 • DIR: TSUKIOKA SADAO ET AL • SCR: IIJIMA SATOSHI ET AL • DES: TSUKIOKA SADAO • ANI: KITAMASA TAKESHI • MUS: KOBAYASHI YASEI • PRD: TOEI ANIMATION • TV SERIES • EPS: 86

# KIKI

Kiki's big red bow is the young witch's only deviation from the mandatory all-black apparel when she has to leave her family home for her year's apprenticeship. Astride her broom with her familiar, a black cat named Jiji, she sets off on her journey, knowing that a twentieth-century witch has to make herself useful, not just mix potions. Awaiting her is Koriko, a city that seems to rise out of the sea. Despite some early difficulties, Kiki soon finds her niche, running a flying delivery service. ● The film by Miyazaki Hayao combined modern trends and tradition in a work as touching as his young, fresh-faced heroine with her permanently rosy cheeks. It is more than coincidence when a maternal country baker accepts Kiki as a lodger in her house: bread-making, like magic and painting, is an ancient art, as much a vocation as a profession. ● *Kiki's Delivery Service* is a straightforward tale but not at all banal. Miyazaki had no qualms in deviating from his source material, a novel by Kadono Eiko: he is more interested in exploring Kiki's influence on a society that still needs magic than in merely telling her story. People who come into contact with the young witch feel compelled to rediscover the value of what has been lost, qualities such as politeness and altruism. Kiki seems to have brought not only magic but also something of a countryside atmosphere into a town that becomes less urban through her presence. As if to emphasize this, Miyazaki made some appealing references to *Heidi* (1974): the scent of hay in the train and the scenes with the dog Jack. Most tellingly, our first sight of the young girl is in profile, stretched out on a soft, grassy slope. ● C.C.

SCENES FROM THE 1989 FILM *KIKI'S DELIVERY SERVICE* ● ABOVE LEFT: KIKI WITH TONBO, HER WOULD-BE BOYFRIEND ● CENTRE LEFT: KIKI WITH HER BLACK CAT JIJI ● WITH HER FRIEND URSULA ● BELOW: THE APPRENTICE WITCH ALONE IN THE BAKERY

*MAJO NO TAKKYUBIN ● KIKI'S DELIVERY SERVICE ● 1989 ● DIR & SCR: MIYAZAKI HAYAO ● DES: KONDO KATSUYA ● ANI: OTSUKA SHINJI, KONDO YOSHIFUMI ● MUS: HISAISHI JOE ● PRD: SUZUKI TOSHIO ET AL, STUDIO GHIBLI ● FILM ● DUR: 102 MINS*

K

# KIKUCHI MICHITAKA

MANGAKA

SEE ALSO: AKAHORI SATORU; ISHINOMORI SHOTARO; SHIROW MASAMUNE

Kikuchi Michitaka (born in 1963 in Tokyo) is better known to manga fans by his pseudonym Asamiya Kia. ● Kikuchi began the career that would make him famous by working on comics for the Kadokawa publishing company. Whilst there, he collaborated on a number of anime productions, either working on outside projects or supervising adaptations drawn by his alter ego Asamiya, ensuring that the sharp-edged but elegant design, slender bodies and wide, expressive eyes of the manga are accurately transferred to the large or small screen. Works of particular interest include *Detonator Orgun* (1991) and the television series *Sonic Soldier Borgman* (1989), both of which revitalize Kikuchi's favourite type of science fiction – a cross between cyberpunk and alien hybrids. ● Kikuchi supervised the disconcerting and ambitious two-film adaptation of his manga in *Silent Möbius* (1991) and *Silent Möbius 2* (1992), taking charge of its beautiful character design and revamping the original plot. The films' success captured the hearts of the audience and led the way to a television series in 1998, where a notable effort was made to reconstruct every detail of the manga, from the characters' wardrobe to the spectacular backgrounds. ● M.A.R

# KIKUCHI SHUNSUKE

COMPOSER

One of the finest composers for Japanese cinema and, in particular, for animated films from the Sixties onwards, is undoubtedly Kikuchi Shunsuke. He ranks alongside Ifukube Akira, who wrote the music for *Godzilla* (1954), and Watanabe Takeo, whose scores are characterized by a unique melancholy. ● Born in 1931, Kikuchi is a prolific composer of soundtracks, a professional faithful to his own style of composition, and a pillar of the Toei studio, where he has worked on both animated films and television series. The memories of a whole generation of anime fans are imprinted with the triumphal marches he wrote for robotic series such as *Mazinger Z* (1972), *Getta Robot* (1974) and *UFO Robot Grendizer Raids* (1975), all immediately recognizable musical themes loaded with pathos. ● Kikuchi has always been skilled in writing orchestral music using the brass section, ideally suited to evoking both gaiety and melancholy and his compositions sometimes suggest the powerful themes of classic cowboy movies. ● How could one forget the melancholy signature tune he wrote for *Tiger Mask* (1969), backed by strings and a male-voice choir – a meeting of powerful musical ideas, epic and frenetic, almost as if his intention were to restore the concept of personal courage? Other masterpieces of this kind are the opening song of anime series *Casshern* (1973) and the pieces he composed for *Hurricane Polymar* (1974), *Planet Robot Danguard Ace* (1977), *Dragon Ball* (1986), *King Arthur and the Knights of the Round Table* (1981) and *Kamen Rider* (1971), all products of a rich and varied career. ● M.A.R.

*LEFT: THE CAST OF **PLANET ROBOT DANGUARD ACE** (1977, DIR. KATSUMATA TOMOHARU, 56 EPS), A PUBLICITY IMAGE FOR THE SERIES*

SEE ALSO: CASSHAN; DATE NAOTO; GETTA ROBOT; GOKU; MAZINGER Z; TOEI ANIMATION; UFO ROBOT GRENDIZER RAIDS

# KINDAICHI HAJIME

CHARAC...

Kindaichi Hajime has a bad reputation – he rarely turns up for school and dabbles in conjuring tricks and sleight-of-hand. But he also swears, upon the reputation of his detective grandfather, that he can solve any murder mystery that is presented to him. This makes him a dream ticket for anime since his first on-screen appearance in 1996 – a surly youth with an old-time pedigree and a finely honed sense of justice, turning teenage self-righteousness to a good cause. The parents like him because he fights crime; the kids like him because he catches adults who do wrong, and often gets to do it in exotic locations. ● With a popularity that made one of his creators one of the highest artist taxpayers in nineties Japan, Kindaichi is a rare franchise indeed, a murder-mystery that regularly makes it into cinemas, and whose television plotlines are often written at feature-length, extending over three episodes. His multigenerational appeal is at least partly explained by his origins – this is Young Kindaichi, the grandson of Kindaichi Kosuke whose case files spanned novels and movies from 1946 to 1980. Young Kindaichi was seemingly conceived in imitation of *Lupin III* (1971), a modern-day descendant of a famous fictional character, in the assumption that this would avoid some copyright problems. However, as with Lupin, the assumption was much mistaken, leading to a legal protest and an out-of-court settlement between the owners of Young Kindaichi and the estate of his ancestor. ● J.Cl.

*KINDAICHI SHONEN NO JIKENBO ● YOUNG KINDAICHI'S CASE BOOK ● 1997 ● DIR: NISHIO DAISUKE ● SCR: NISHIOKA TAKEYA ET AL ● DES: AKIRA SHINGO, KUMA HIDEMI ● ANI: ARAKI SHINGO ● MUS: WADA KAORU ● PRD: TOEI ANIMATION ● TV SERIES ● EPS: 148*

CHARACTER

# KINOMOTO SAKURA

...inomoto Sakura is not the classic magician of Japanese tradition. She is, rather, ... primary-school girl who finds a mysterious book and, following the advice of a ...ttle lion named Cerberus (or Kero-chan), uses her magical powers to break the ...ook's seal, unintentionally freeing the enchanted tarot cards it contains. Cerberus ... the guardian of the cards and tasks Sakura with finding all the lost cards and ...eeping them safe. ● Very mature for her age, with a sweet appearance and obvious ...ourage, Sakura is another example of the 'magical girl' character, endowed with ...xtraordinary powers that do not reqire a magic wand. More fortunate than other ...imilar characters, the child finds herself having to act in a bright and optimistic ...ituation. CLAMP, an all-female group of designers, created numerous works ...esigned for the adolescent public, positioning themselves, precisely and intuitively, ...n the wake of the *Nakayoshi*, the girls' magazine. With *Card Captor Sakura*, without ...rior planning or detailed design, CLAMP imagined a carefree and showy world ...n which the protagonist is depicted as a miniature angel. The power of magic ...s revealed through the search for knowledge and the idealization of the most ...ultivated feelings: friendship and love. ● The manga remains popular and the anime ...as also generated a television series and two films in the capable hands of the ...Madhouse studio and director Asaka Morio. The theme of collecting cards seems ...o be a reference to a now-popular form of merchandizing. ● M.A.R.

...MAGES FROM THE 1998 TV SERIES
...ARD CAPTOR SAKURA ● TOP: PUBLICITY
...MAGES FOR THE SERIES ● RIGHT: A
...ERIES OF FOUR IMAGES FEATURING THE
...EROINE KINOMOTO SAKURA; WITH THE
...TTLE LION CERBERUS; WITH SHAORAN
...; AND DURING A TRANSFORMATION

K

*CARD CAPTOR SAKURA* ● *1998* ● DIR: ASAKA MORIO, DAICHI AKITARO ● SCR: OKAWA NANASE, KANEKO JIRO ● DES: TAKAHASHI KUMIKO, CLAMP ● ANI: TAKAHASHI KUMIKO ● MUS: NEGISHI TAKAYUKI ● PRD: MADHOUSE ● TV SERIES ● EPS: 70

# KIRA

CHARACTE

DEATH NOTE ● 2006 ● DIR: TOSHIKI INOUE ET AL ● SCR: INOUE TOSHIKI ET AL ● DES: SUGIYAMA SHINJI ● ANI: KITAO MASARU, KAGAMI TAKAHIRO ● MUS: TANIUCHI HIDERI, HIRANO YOSHIHISA ● PRD: MADHOUSE ● TV SERIES ● EPS: 37

ABOVE RIGHT: DEATH GOD RYUKK PEERS OVER THE SHOULDER OF YAGAMI LIGHT, THE TEENAGE ANTI–HERO OF THE 2006 SERIES DEATH NOTE ● ABOVE: LIGHT'S PERFECT FACADE HIDES THE SOUL OF A TRUE FASCIST

Kira does not exist, at least not in the normal sense. Kira is a public figure without a face, the hero of collective fiction, a name given by society to the unknown which it imagines is responsible for the sudden, inexplicable death of numerous criminals. But behind Kira hides a real being, a Japanese schoolboy, the young Yagami Light. At first sight he appears very normal, although very gifted at school. One day, Light finds a mysterious notebook and soon discovers that just writing someone's name in it results in their death within seconds. The well-educated teenager who had an easy childhood is also lonely and reserved; returning home from school and locking himself in his room to ruminate on his hatred of our times. If he used the notebook to eliminate all the (other) killers, wouldn't the world be better off? And wouldn't he somehow become a god? ● Adapted from the manga by Oba Tsugumi and Obata Takeshi, Death Note is a bizarre series with a modern sensitivity. The hero is a monster who seems partially withdrawn from the real world and corrupted by a certain idea of purity. At his side (or floating languidly in the air) is a jaded 'god of death' who observes and chatters to him. Its ugliness is a visual metaphor for Light's restless soul, the projection of his inner demons, his grotesque portrait of a post-modern Dorian Gray. ● Soon on the scene is a rival detective who is also his double (famous but anonymous, brilliant but troubled and indifferent to the rules of the physical world). Kira is a contemporary figure in whom images of the frustrated spectator, the omniscient Internet user and omnipotent game fanatic converge. As well as being an intellectual duel, Death Note is the macabre and fascinating journey to the heart of Kira's madness. ● E.H.

# KIRIGOE MIMA

CHARACTER

RIGHT: SCENES FROM THE 1997 SERIES PERFECT BLUE GIVE A GLIMPSE OF THE PSYCHO–DRAMA EXPERIENCED BY KIRIGOE MIMA

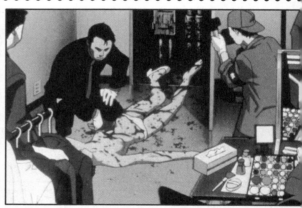

Kirigoe Mima leaves her small village for Tokyo to concentrate on her singing career. As lead vocalist in the pop group Cham, Mima becomes a pop-culture idol worshipped by her fans. Seeking a new direction in her professional life, Mima swaps the reassuring pop stage for the film-set, a decision that will have violent and destabilizing consequences. ● Kon Satoshi began his directorial career with the thriller Perfect Blue, a post-modern work, full of misleading clues and linguistic subtleties. Based on the novel of the same name by Takeuchi Yoshikazu, Perfect Blue explores similar territory to Brian de Palma's Body Double (1984) and Abel Ferrara's Dangerous Game (1993), where reality and fiction merge with disturbing ramifications. The film's editing is highly distinctive, jumbling up the narrative sequence and deliberately mixing delusion with reality. The animation deploys an original style that might at first appear slapdash and repetitive, but which subtly conveys the heroine's deep sense of disorientation. ● Mima's anxiety is projected onto the whole film, which becomes the anguished expression of a fundamentally resilient humanity. Despite malicious intrusions by someone she has trusted, depersonalizing struggles, and dangers and threats from her immediate surroundings, Mima fights to retain her identity and to keep control of her own image. ● C.C.

PERFECT BLUE ● 1997 ● DIR: KON SATOSHI ● SCR: MURAI SADAYUKI ● DES: EGUCHI HISASHI ET AL ● ANI: HAMAZU HIDEKI, SHIRAI HISAO ● MUS: IKUMI MASAHIRO ● PRD: MADHOUSE ● FILM ● DUR: 80 MINS

# KISE KAZUCHIKA

ANIMATOR

Kise Kazuchika (born in 1965) started animating at an early age, making paper-cut cartoons in his teens with fellow fans and future animators Yanagisawa Masahide and Komori Takahiro. Although he set out to study in the Osaka Design School, he quit after only four days to take a job with Anime R, where he learnt key animation under Nakamura Hiromi. His early work included key animation on *Captain Tsubasa* (1981) and *Dirty Pair* (1985) before Kise left the Osaka region for Tokyo in order to work for Production I.G. on the first *Patlabor* film (1989). Although he has credits on games, videos and television shows, his best-known work has been on subsequent Production I.G. feature films. He remains resolutely an animator, staying in the ranks and supervising animation, unlike many other creatives who abandon animation to pursue directing. ● As a key animator on *Roujin-Z* (1991), he collaborated with Kon Satoshi, then merely a set designer, to create untidy, jumbled interiors. He was a key animator on *Ghost in the Shell* (1995), the *Neon Genesis Evangelion* (1995) films and *Blood: The Last Vampire* (2000), and supervised the animation on *Musashi* (2009). Such positions have made him a significant, but often unnoticed, creative force in modern anime. ● Oshii Mamoru once referred to Kise as 'the best basset hound artist in Japan'. Such flippant praise obscures Kise's role in many of the landmark anime of recent years, not to mention his prominent contribution to the realism for which Oshii and Production I.G. often strive, particularly with their digital animation work. He pastiched the look of several sciencie-fiction anime in his character designs for *Last Orders*, a 1997 commercial for Murphy's Irish Stout, featuring several futuristic samurai scrambling to reach a bar before closing time. ● J.Cl.

A SERIES OF IMAGES FROM *GHOST IN THE SHELL* (1995, DIR. OSHII MAMORU, 161 MINS) AND *GHOST IN THE SHELL 2: INNOCENCE* (2004, DIR. OSHII MAMORU, 99 MINS) ● ABOVE LEFT: CYBER-ENHANCED COP BATOU AND HIS PET DOG ● RIGHT: THE LINES BETWEEN HUMAN AND CYBORG ARE DRAWN ON CAPABILITY; NON-ENHANCED HUMANS ARE BECOMING AN UNDERCLASS

SEE ALSO: EVANGELION; I.G.; KEI & YURI; KON SATOSHI; KUSANAGI MOTOKO; OSHII MAMORU; PATLABOR; ROUJIN Z; SAYA; TSUBASA OZORA

K

# KISUGI RUI, HITOMI & AI

'Cat's Eye' is both a bar and the name of crafty gang of art thieves who use the bar as a front for their activities. The gang comprises the three beautiful Kisugi sisters – Rui, Hitomi and Ai. They appear to be carefree and cheeky at first sight, but gradually we discover that their thieving forms part of a precise plan to find their father, the famous painter Michael Heinz, who has disappeared, by reconstructing the clues hidden in his precious paintings. The plan is a difficult one and full of pitfalls. At first, the police are caught off-guard by the thefts, but gradually they become more careful and their investigations more accurate. The sisters' advantage is that Hitomi is engaged to none other than Toshio (Matthew), the detective in charge of arresting them, and from whom they learn in advance the strategies designed to stop the gang. Rui is the expert and mastermind of the operation, Hitomi the most athletic, and Ai the most easygoing. Donning revealing black tracksuits, they move at night, infiltrating museums and buildings protected by agents and armed with security devices. ● Entertaining, fast and light, *Cat's Eye*, in truth, hides little beneath the surface, save a subtle and persistent anxiety. There are moments of surreal hilarity, but, in the end, risk, tension, bitterness and solitude mark the tale and represent the core around which the series is constructed. The style is dry and the rhythm fast, influenced by music, at times rarefied, at others nostalgic. The sisters' accomplice is the night that almost always accompanies and enfolds them as they penetrate the flashing city's most secret corners. ● G.P.

SCENES FROM THE 1983 SERIES CAT'S EYE ● TOP LEFT: THE THREE SISTERS IN ACTION
TOP RIGHT: AI, THE MOST EASYGOING OF THE TRIO ● LEFT: HITOMI, THE MOST ATHLETIC

CAT'S EYE ● 1983 ● DIR: TAKEUCHI YOSHIO, KODAMA KENJI ● SCR: FUJIKAWA KEISUKE ET AL ● DES: SUGINO AKIO, HIRAYAMA SATOSHI ● ANI: HIRAYAMA SATOSHI ● MUS: OTANI KAZUO ● PRD: TMS ● TV SERIES ● EPS: 73

# KITAJIMA MAYA

Kitajima Maya is lithe, gamine and seemingly frail, but has a steely heart. She is determined to be the greatest actress in the world, and to master the ultimate performance technique – acting as if an ethereal mask of glass separates her true self from the audience she bewitches. ● Based on an ongoing 1976 manga series by Suzue Miuchi, the manga *Glass Mask* is virtually contemporary with *Candy Candy* (1976), and adopts many of its tropes. Maya is a wistful, melancholy semi-orphan pining for a lost parent and basking in the attentions of a secret (and incredibly wealthy) admirer. The trials she faces, while described on paper in purely dramatic terms, are much the same as those faced by the protagonists of many sports anime. As in many anime stories, from athletics to ballet, it is not enough to be a 'natural' like Maya's good-natured rival Ayumi. Specialists are discouraged from arrogance, instilled instead with a view of themselves as rough gemstones that need to be honed and polished by relentless, single-minded training. ● Another 'type' from sporting anime, Maya's mentor is a wounded veteran who was never quite able to realize her own potential. A former actress herself, Chigusa Tsukikage now hides hideous scars from a backstage accident, and is determined to push Maya into the most difficult and demanding role – the Crimson Goddess – the role that Chigusa herself never quite mastered. ● If *Glass Mask* seems clichéd, that is often only because it is now encountered alongside its imitators. With over fifty million manga volumes in print, it is one of the best-selling Japanese comics in history and has been adapted into two anime television series, in 1984 and 2005, and a three-part video series in 1998. ● J.Cl.

ABOVE: A PORTRAIT OF KITAJIMA MAYA, THE GREAT DREAMER, FROM THE 1984 SERIES GLASS MASK

GLASS NO KAMEN ● GLASS MASK ● 1984 ● DIR: SUGII GISABURO ● SCR: FUJIKAWA KEISUKE ET AL ● DES: KUNIHO MAKOTO ● ANI: SHIMIZU KEIZO ET AL ● MUS: OTANI KAZUO ● PRD: EIKEN ● TV SERIES ● EPS: 23

# KITAKUBO HIROYUKI

Giving meaning to the difficult profession of an animator requires bringing wide-ranging talents to the role and a decision to leave behind the punishing schedules imposed by animated film. Kitakubo Hiroyuki (born in 1963) was incredibly young when he made his debut on the series, *Lamù* (1981), quickly earning respect and admiration thanks to the skill of his drawing, so much so that in 1985 he began to direct with one of the episodes from the erotic series *Cream Lemon*. ● Kitakubo lived through the boom in the OAV market, contributing with the zeal of someone who wished to impress at any cost: it was as one of the team of authors of the series *Angel Cop* (in the company of Itano Ichiro who arrived from *Macross*) that he won the trust of Otomo Katsuhiro, who put him on the staff of the blockbuster *Akira* (1988) after having seen him direct the short film *A Tale of Two Robots* in *Robot Carnival* (1987). The episode he directed is set in Tokyo in the nineteenth century, prepared to shed its skin to people dressed in western fashions and modern buildings which tower over the traditional wooden houses: here, the unlikely collision occurs between the forebears of two classic robots, built, however, with wood, iron and bamboo. ● If his second test as a director, *Roujin Z* (1991), taken from the Otomo manga, was not up to expectations and a pale copy of the short film, which also featured the theme of change as in the times of *Akira*, the beautiful *Blood The Last Vampire* (2000), the direction of which was assigned to him by Oshii Mamoru, was considerably more successful. *Blood* is a pioneering film through its use of full digital production, swept along at a whirlwind pace and exhibiting excellent animation. ● M.A.R.

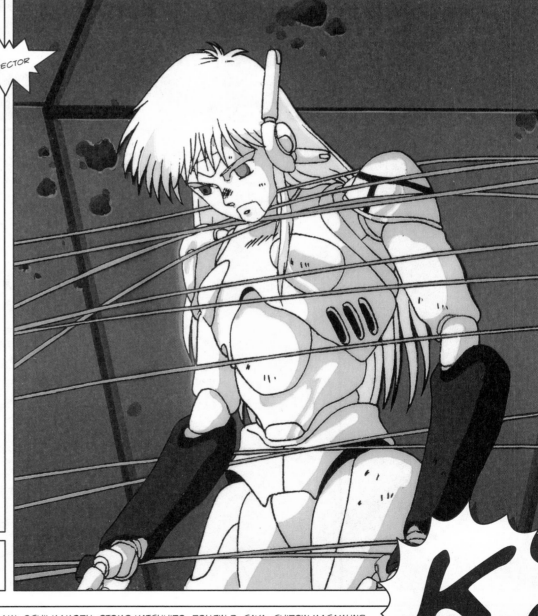

RIGHT: AN IMAGE FROM BLACK MAGIC M-66 (1987, DIR. SHIROW MASAMUNE, KITAKUBO HIROYUKI, 45 MINS) A GREAT COLLABORATION BETWEEN KITAKUBO HIROYUKI AND SHIROW MASAMUNE

SEE ALSO: ITANO ICHIRO; NONOMURA AMI; OSHII MAMORU; OTOMO KATSUHIRO; ROUJIN Z; SAYA; SHIROW MASAMUNE

# KITARO

Blind in one eye and sporting a flowing fringe and traditional Japanese sandals, Kitaro is the last in a long line of ghosts. A monster who grew up in a cemetery, he is accompanied by his father, a talking eyeball with arms and legs. Together, they have adventures in this world and the next, helping the human race and singing cheerful songs with their animal friends. ● Springing from the pencil of Mizuki Shigeru in 1959, the manga *Gegege no Kitaro* is one of the cornerstones of Japanese comic literature, a true masterpiece of horror and humour that still resonates with today's audiences. Used judiciously in animated films and videogames, Kitaro has carved out a place of honour in popular culture. A black-and-white television series by Toei Animation began in 1968, following close behind the horror boom that started a few years earlier with Yokoyama Mitsuteru's manga *Obake no Qtaro* (1965), which provided kids with ghosts and monsters of all kinds. The Toei series was followed by five more series of television programmes, comprising sequels and remakes, as well as several films, converting Mizuki's creation into colour and live action. ● An appealing expression of the traditional *yokai* (a folklore spirit or monster), Kitaro is famous for the shrewdness with which he repairs the damage caused by humans and monsters. He often provides readers with examples of courageous behaviour, usually by children, for use in their daily lives. To date, the classic series in black and white is still the best animated version of the little monster. ● M.A.R.

LEFT: THE LITTLE GHOST KITARO IN SCENES FROM THE 2007 SERIES *GEGEGE NO KITARO*. HIS HAIR, HIS WOODEN SANDALS AND EVEN HIS STRIPED COAT CAN ALL BE USED AS SUPERNATURAL WEAPONS

GEGEGE NO KITARO ● 1968 ● DIR: YAMAGUCHI YASUO ET AL ● SCR: TAKAKU SUSUMU ET AL ● DES: MIZUKI SHIGERU ET AL ● ANI: HOSODA MITSUO ET AL ● MUS: IZUMI TAKU ● PRD: TOEI ANIMATION ● TV SERIES ● EPS: 439

# KITAZUME HIROYUKI

IMAGES OF KITAZUME HIROYUKI'S WORK ON THE GUNDAM SERIES ● BELOW: MOBILE SUIT GUNDAM (1979, DIR. TOMINO YOSHIYUKI, 43 EPS) ● BOTTOM: GUNDAM WING (1995, DIR. IKEDA MASASHI, 49 EPS) ● BOTTOM RIGHT: PUBLICITY IMAGE FOR MOBILE SUIT ZETA GUNDAM (1985, DIR. TOMINO YOSHIYUKI, 50 EPS)

DESIGNER

Kitazume Hiroyuki belongs to a formidable group of young animators and cartoonists, all united by the same overwhelming passion and each creating their own unique and indelible legacy. Kitazume (born in 1961), is cast from the same mould as the celebrated designer Kawamori Shoji and the multi-talented Mikimoto Haruhiko. Like his colleagues he has enjoyed the privilege of working with some of the most enduring figures in anime before withdrawing to a more intimate artistic dimension that has earned him a considerable reputation. ● A talent for sleek and glossy illustrations and a youthful style of drawing are the common threads running through Kitazume's unconventional contribution to the mecha and science-fiction genres. Early in his career, he brought a wealth of bright and colourful work to *Mobile Suit Gundam ZZ* (1986), so much so that he lost sight of the dramatic element of the series and catered mostly for the adolescent sector of its audience rather than the die-hard fans of Tomino Yoshiyiki's historic robot. However, his work as a director in the third chapter of the *Megazone 23* (1989) series sought alternatives to the approach taken by his predecessor Mikimoto Haruhiko and the subjects of the robot-themed *Relic Armor Legaciam* (1987) and *Moldiver* (1993) are all his own. ● Invited to direct a segment of Otomo Katsuhiro's anthology film *Robot Carnival* (1987), Kitazume's offering was the short *Starlight Angel*, which tells the story of a young girl who falls in love with a boy wearing the armour of an awkward robot. The short film has no dialogue and is supported only by a synthpop soundtrack that brings the commonplace story to life and echoes the ideological premise of the whole film. ● M.A.R

SEE ALSO: GUNDAM; MIKIMOTO HARUHIKO; OTOMO KATSUHIRO; TOMINO YOSHIYUKI; YAHAGI SHOGO; YASUHIKO YOSHIKAZU

K

# KITTY

CHARACTER

Kitty the kitten was born in London, where she lives with her family and twin sister Mimmy. She has a passion for reading, music and baking biscuits, and in 1983 she became the US children's ambassador for UNICEF. ● So reads the official biography of the internationally famous character and trademark created by Shimizu Yuko and first propagated by the Japanese Sanrio company in the early seventies. Love her or hate her, Kitty's unmistakable black-dot eyes, yellow nose and red bow have become symbols of rampant consumerism, appearing on a tidalwave of greetings cards, puppets, teacups, handbags and notebooks. The phenomenon is summed up by the Japanese term *kawaii*, meaning 'cute', pronounced with the enraptured squeak of a dreamy-eyed young girl, although the target audience ranges from tiny children to venerable pensioners. ● Although undoubtedly inspired by the welcoming china kittens (*maneki neko*) traditionally placed in the doorways of Japanese shops, there is a contagious kindness behind Kitty's consumerist image, inevitably creating chain reactions of friendship and solidarity. ● Commercial spin-offs also include animated films, in which Kitty and her friends feature in light-hearted adventures. The films, produced by Sanrio, began to appear in 1977 and Kitty has also been featured in numerous TV serials. ● M.A.R.

*HELLO KITTY ● 1974 ● DIR: OGAWA TAMEO ET AL ● SCR: KONPARU TOMORO ● DES: SHIMIZU YUKO ● ANI: AKABORI KANJI ET AL ● MUS: KOJIMA TOYOMI ● PRD: SANRIO ● TV SERIES ● 50 EPS*

*ABOVE RIGHT: THE LITTLE KITTEN IN DIGITAL FORM ● BELOW & RIGHT: KITTY AND HER SISTER MIMMY FROM THE 1974 SERIES HELLO KITTY*

# KNIGHT SABERS

CHARACTERS

In the future metropolis of MegaTokyo, eccentric millionaire Sylia Stingray runs a one-woman vendetta against the corporation that killed her father and co-opted his android creations for evil. Her sole allies are her fellow Knight Sabers, a group of vigilantes clad in robotic hard-suits that conceal their identities and augment their abilities. One member also plays in a rock band, allowing for this superhero anime to generate CD spin-offs. ● In an age where every pop idol seems to have a television show and a number of product endorsements, the Knight Sabers may seem quaintly old-fashioned but at the time of their first appearance, they were a sign of the new purchasing power of the *otaku* generation. Released straight to video in 1987, the first episodes of *Bubblegum Crisis* presented a future cityscape like that of *Blade Runner* (unlike much apocalyptic anime of the early eighties, an earthquake has failed to destroy Tokyo) and shrunk the giant robots of the mecha genre to the size of human bodysuits – perhaps reflecting heightened confidence at the peak of Japan's economic bubble. Tokyo is reborn as a far-future metropolis, and science-fiction heroes are remodelled as heroines, not, as some have mistakenly assumed, as a mark of female empowerment, but because the primarily male audience liked watching girls in action. ● The actresses who voiced the Knight Sabers would later appear in their own live-action concert, spliced together with anime footage for collectors. The Knight Sabers would return in 1998 in a remake that emphasized the fetish nature of their suits and pop performances – Sylia remained the owner of a lingerie shop, and the hard-suits were re-imagined as restrictive costumes resembling something from a bondage catalogue. ● J.Cl.

*BUBBLEGUM CRISIS ● 1987 ● DIR: AKIYAMA KATSUHITO ● SCR: SUZUKI TOSHIMIOHI ET AL ● DES: SONODA KENICHI ● ANI: TANAKA MASAIKO, OKUDA JUN ● MUS: HAIKANOKOJI ● PRD: ANIME INTERNATIONAL COMPANY ● VIDEO SERIES ● EPS: 8*

# KNUTE, DEUNAN

CHARACTER

Deunan Knute is the brainchild of mangaka Shirow Masamune and the female protagonist of *Appleseed*, a franchise that now spans several films, games and television series. Alongside her cyborg companion Briareus, she fights on behalf of the dictator Athena, in defence of a great utopian metropolis. All is not as it seems, however, as the suicide rate slowly begins to rise – people are not happy in their carefully constructed city, and religious and political terrorist factions have emerged to rally against the status quo. As trouble erupts so Deunan and her allies arrive to quash it. ● *Appleseed* lays out many of the themes and modes of characterization that Shirow would later explore more fully in his canonical manga *Ghost in the Shell* (1989), establishing a complex framework in which distinctions between good and bad are progressively blurred. The pro-human independence terrorists are led by a cyborg, and the dictator acts benevolently; this topsy-turvy logic to the world is much like the state of emergency and constant terror refined by Shirow in *Black Magic M-66* (1983). ● In recent years, Aramaki Shinji has directed a new *Appleseed* movie (2004), which uses computer-generated characters to retell the story of Deunan and Briareus. Particularly noteworthy is the experimental visual treatment, which sits somewhere between an anime aesthetic and fully computer-generated imagery in the style of *Final Fantasy: The Spirits Within* (2001). The final outcome is not wholly successful, since the different styles produce differing expectations, but it is a noteworthy experiment nonetheless. ● D.S.

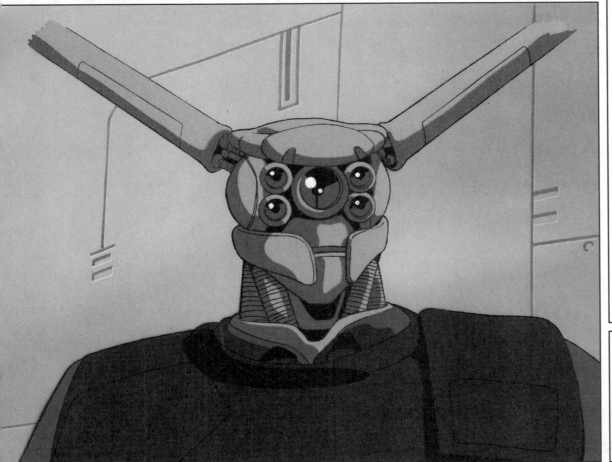

LEFT: DEUNAN KNUTE AND CYBORG BRIAREUS FORM AN UNBEATABLE DUO IN THE 1988 OAV *APPLESEED*

APPLESEED ● 1988 ● DIR & SCR: KATAYAMA KAZUYOSHI ● DES & ANI: HORASAWA YUMIKO ● MUS: YAMANAKA NORIMASA ● PRD: BANDAI VISUAL, GAINAX, TOHOKUSHINSA FILM CORP ● VIDEO ● DUR: 70 MINS

Kobayashi Osamu (born in 1964 in Tokyo) was one of a number of short-film directors working at Studio 4°C, along with Maeda Mahiro (*Blue Submarine No. 6*, 1998) and Yuasa Masaaki (*Mind Game*, 2004). Known for his surreal characterization and the way he represents the city, Kobayashi began his career with a series of experimental animations and continues to express this alternative bent in his more commercial work. ● In his short film *Table and Fishman* (2001), part of the *Digital Juice* series, a man and woman recount how they were cursed and transformed into a small corner table and fish-headed man. This storytelling approach reflects the influence of writers such as Franz Kafka, who also influenced animators like Yamamura Koji and Kato Kunio. ● Kobayashi also bridged the gap between anime and videogame design through his work on the *Grandia* (2000) series and also the random dungeon role-playing game *Evolution* (1999) for the SEGA Dreamcast. In recent years, he has directed two television anime series for Madhouse studios. One of these is the adaptation of Yazawa Ai's fashion manga *Paradise Kiss* (2000). Yazawa's idiosyncratic aesthetic (which combines a quality of pretty, delicate detailing with quirky angular characterization) perfectly complements the style of Kobayashi. He also directed, directed animation and storyboarded an episode of the TV series *Gurren Lagann* (2007, 27 eps). ● D.S.

# KOBAYASHI OSAMU

ANIMATOR

RIGHT & BELOW: SCENES FROM TENGEN TOPPA GURREN LAGANN (*GURREN LAGANN*, 2007, DIR. IMAISHI HIROYAKI, 27 EPS), ON WHICH KOBAYASHI WAS AN EPISODE DIRECTOR AND ANIMATION DIRECTOR

SEE ALSO: GAINAX

# KOMATSUBARA KAZUO

CHARACTER DESIGNER

Komatsubara Kazuo (born in 1943 in Yokohama) tried unsuccessfully to get a job at Mushi Production in 1964, before later trying his luck at Toei Animation, where he was hired as a character designer but only after having taken the training course twice. However, the difficulties of his early career did not stop him from rising to fame through sheer force of will. Subsequently hired by Asahi Film and Hatena Production, Komatsubara refined his brushwork and, in 1969, was among the animation directors who worked on the bloodthirsty *Tiger Mask* (1970). From 1970 onwards, he worked independently and collaborated on a number of anime titles successfully adapted from manga, becoming the trusted artist of two masters who defined the decade: Nagai Go and Matsumoto Leiji. ● Together with Araki Shingo, with whom he shared several stages of a prolific, thirty-year career, Komatsubara is among the principal authors of the graphic and linguistic renaissance of modern anime. With a penchant for technical experimentation, he has, among other things, played with perspective and textured backdrops with the aim of creating a self-contained style of animation adapted to small-screen budgets, although he is equally dynamic in other visual media. In the Eighties, he moved from television into cinema, where he supported Takahata Isao on the independent film project *Goshu the Cellist* (1982) and on the OAV *Devilman* (1987). These projects shook up the OAV sector, which was dominated at the time by poor-quality productions. His story was tragically cut short, however, with his untimely death in the year 2000. His final creation was the design for Tima, a girl robot in *Metropolis* (2001), taken from Tezuka Osamu's manga, which did not make it to the final cut. ● S.G.

LEFT: TETSURO AND MAETEL IN A MELANCHOLY SCENE FROM *GALAXY EXPRESS 999* (1978, DIR. NISHIZAWA NOBUTAKA, 113 EPS) ● KOMATSUBARA KAZUO WAS ANIMATION DIRECTOR FOR THE TV SERIES AND MOVIE

SEE ALSO: ARAKI SHINGO; DATE NAOTO; DEVILMAN; GOSHU; MATSUMOTO LEIJI; NAGAI GO; TAKAHATA ISAO; TEZUKA OSAMU; TOEI ANIMATION

Kon Satoshi was born in 1963 in Kushiro. His reputation has continued to grow in stature ever since his first film, *Perfect Blue* (1997), and he is regarded as one of the most important artists working in Japanese animation. ● Initially a mangaka, Kon published his first book of manga in 1990 (*Kaikisen*). He subsequently collaborated with Otomo Katsuhiro on *Roujin Z* (1991) and worked on the adaptation of his *World Apartment Horror* (1991). After working with Oshii Mamoru on *Patlabor 2: The Movie* (1992) and on the screenplay and sets for the first segment of the anthology film *Memories* (1996), he moved into directing with *Perfect Blue* (1997), a thriller of astonishing realism that dives into the paranoid psyche of a young pop idol ● Originally aimed at the video market, *Perfect Blue* was then shown in cinemas and well received abroad. *Millennium Actress* (2001) is a more complex portrait, structured to jump between several levels of reality as we follow the protagonist's memories of her own life and of the films she has made. Like *Perfect Blue*, this ambitious century-spanning story enjoyed further success abroad. *Tokyo Godfathers* (2003), the story of three homeless people who find a baby on Christmas Eve, was a more populist move that successfully blended comedy and social comment. ● Kon continued his singular career with the strangely satirical series *Paranoia Agent* (2004) and his most important film, *Paprika* (2006), was premiered at the Venice Film Festival. Once again a female protagonist crosses borders – here, those of a dream world – but the psychological element is downplayed in favour of a truly nightmarish vision of bodies and objects ceaselessly decanted into one another and back again. Madhouse may be an old production company established in the early seventies, but – home to Kon since *Perfect Blue* – it could have been created specifically for him. Kon passed away aged 46 in August 2010. ● S.D.

## KON SATOSHI

DIRECTOR

ABOVE: MIMA, FROM *PERFECT BLUE* (1997, DIR. KON SATOSHI, 82 MINS) ● ABOVE LEFT & BELOW: THREE SCENES FROM THE BIZARRE WORLD OF *PAPRIKA* (2006, DIR. KON SATOSHI, 90 MINS), WHERE HEROINE ATSUKO TRANSFORMS INTO DREAM THERAPIST PAPRIKA AND ENTERS PATIENTS' DREAM WORLDS

SEE ALSO: HIRASAWA SUSUMU; KIRIGOE MIMA; MADHOUSE; PAPRIKA; SAGI TSUKIKO; TOKYO GODFATHERS

# KONDO YOSHIFUMI

Kondo Yoshifumi (1950–1998) was born in Niigata and joined the studio A-Pro aged just eighteen, as an animator on sports anime *Star of the Giants* (1968). He subsequently worked on many television serials, including *Lupin III* (1971) under Takahata Isao and Miyazaki Hayao, for whom he worked again on *Panda! Go Panda!* (1972) and for much of the rest of his career. ● Kondo followed Takahata and Miyazaki to Nippon Animation in 1977, working on *Future Boy Conan* (1978) and *Anne of Green Gables* (1979) as a character designer, and then to Telecom in 1980, to work on *Sherlock Hound* (1984), once more as a character designer. However, he resigned in 1985, in what could have been the first manifestation of the tendency to overwork that some have suggested contributed to his early death. ● After working on the ill-fated adaptation of American cartoon-strip *Little Nemo* (1989), Kondo freelanced for the newly-formed Studio Ghibli as a designer and key animator on *Grave of the Fireflies* (1988) and most of Ghibli's best-known eighties productions. Takahata credited him as a major contribution to the success of both *Grave of the Fireflies* and *Only Yesterday* (1991). ● Kondo gained a reputation for remaining calm and quiet at all times; Miyazaki noted, only half in jest, that Kondo was the kind of captain who would refuse to leave a sinking ship. By the time of his first and only film as director, *Mimi o Sumaseba* (*Whisper of the Heart*, 1995), he was widely understood to be the heir apparent at Ghibli, as the older generation approached retirement but he died from an aneurysm in January 1998, the night after Miyazaki had offered him a new job – presumably on *Spirited Away* (2001). A weeping Miyazaki noted at his funeral, 'He was one of the best among the hundreds of animators I ever met'. ● J.Cl.

LEFT: SCENES FROM THE FILM *ONLY YESTERDAY* (1991, DIR. TAKAHATA ISAO, PRD. TOKUMA YASUYOSHI, 199 MINS)

SEE ALSO: ANNE OF GREEN GABLES; CHIHIRO; CONAN; GHIBLI; HOLMES, SHERLOCK; HOSHI HYUMA; LITTLE NEMO; LUPIN III; MIYAZAKI HAYAO; NIPPON ANIMATION; PANDA KOPANDA; SEITA & SETSUKO; OKAJIMA TAEKO; TAKAHATA ISAO

# KOSAKA KITARO

DIRECTOR

Kosaka Kitaro has two great passions: animation and cycling. The interweaving of these two subjects has produced two wonderful medium-length films: *Nasu: Andalusia no Natsu* (*Nasu: Summer in Andalusia*, 2003) and *Nasu: Suitcase no Wataridori* (*Nasu: A Migratory Bird with Suitcase*, 2007). With the exception of the short film *Clover* (1999), these are Kosaka's only directorial works to date. Even so, at forty-seven years old, he is a veteran of the world of Japanese animation. The names of the directors he has worked with, mostly as a key animator, would fill a hall of fame: celebrities such as Oshii Mamoru (*Angel's Egg*, 1985), Otomo Katsuhiro (*Akira*, 1988), Rintaro (*Metropolis*, 2001), Takahata Isao (*Grave of the Fireflies*, 1988, *Pom Poko*, 1994), and, above all, his great teacher: Miyazaki Hayao. ● Were it not for the author of *Princess Mononoke* (1997), for whom he has always harboured boundless admiration and with whom he continues to work freelance, Kosaka would perhaps never have become a film-maker. Through Miyazaki, also a fan of cycling, he discovered Kuroda Io's manga, *Nasu*. Like his great master, Kosaka cleverly manages to evoke emotions, tastes and smells in his work, highlighting places, objects and characters. In the first *Nasu* film, Andalusia is actually a 'character' with almost the same importance as Pepe, the cyclist transported back to his town of birth by one leg of the Vuelta a España race. Kosaka distinguishes himself by skilfully orchestrating different action scenes – focused inside the race, on the track or outside of it – and for being able to successfully implement the basis of animation: the transposition of movement which, in his film, lights up the masterfully produced race, crystallizing time and emotions. ● E.H.

*SEE ALSO: MIYAZAKI HAYAO; OSHII MAMORU; OTOMO KATSUHIRO; RINTARO; TAKAHATA ISAO*

# KOTABE YOICHI

DIRECTOR

Born in 1936 in Taipei, Kotabe Yoichi decided to work in the world of animation after seeing the *Momotaro* series of propaganda films in the forties. His father, an amateur painter, gave him his first drawing lessons and introduced him to the secrets of oil painting. His passion for illustration won him a place at the Tokyo University of Fine Arts and Music, and in 1959, he was offered an opportunity to work for Toei Animation. Here he met the artist Okuyama Reiko – whom he later married – as well as two other young artists, Miyazaki Hayao and Takahata Isao, with whom he has worked on several occasions. ● After a few years of apprenticeship as a storyboard creator and assistant animator, Kotabe made his debut as a director on the series *Little Witch Sally* (1968) and his first major work as animator and character designer for several characters was on *Little Norse Prince* (1968). In 1971, together with Miyazaki and Takahata, he left Toei for TMS to work on an adaptation of *Pippi Longstocking* – a project that was shelved when author Astrid Lindgren refused approval. In the years that followed, Kotabe took on the role of head animator on the popular film *Panda! Go, Panda!* (1972) and continued his collaboration with Miyazaki and Takahata on *Heidi* (1974) and the *Haha wo Tazunete Sanzen Ri* (*3000 Leagues in Search of Mother*, 1976) series as character designer and head animator. He then went on to work as an animator on *Nausicaä of the Valley of the Wind* (1983). Since 1985, Kotabe has worked on some of Nintendo's greatest commercial successes, including the *Super Mario Bros.* and *Pokémon* videogames. ● Most recently, Kotabe and his wife contributed to 2003 anthology film *Winter Days*, along with many other great animators. ● F.L.

*RIGHT: AN IMAGE FROM THE ANTHOLOGY FILM FUYU NO HI (WINTER DAYS, 2003, DIR. KAWAMOTO KIHACHIRO, 40 MINS)*

*SEE ALSO: HEIDI; KAWAMOTO KIHACHIRO; MIYAZAKI HAYAO; NAUSICAÄ; PANDA KOPANDA; POKÉMON; TAKAHATA ISAO; TMS; TOEI ANIMATION*

# KOYAMA TAKAO

SCRIPTWRITER

Koyama Takao (born in 1948 in Tokyo) is one of the most influential scriptwriters in anime, thanks to his seminal television scripts and his mentoring of the next generation of writers. ● While studying literature at Waseda University, Koyama was already working part time in television, writing questions for the programme *Quiz Time Shock*. Joining Tatsunoko Productions after graduation, he was instrumental in authoring the long-running *Time Bokan* anime series, as well as episodes of shows such as *Battle of the Planets* (1978). His later work for other companies includes *City Hunter* (1987), *Urusei Yatsura* (1981) and *Dragon Ball Z* (1989), for which he was once forced to spin an entire twenty-five-minute episode out of a single panel from the original comic. ● Since the late Eighties, Koyama has also taught screenwriting, at first in affiliation with several different institutions but eventually founding his own programme, the Anime Scenario House. The venture was soon renamed 'Brother Noppo', and also functions as a form of writers' agency in the anime business. Alumni of Koyama's training scheme include many of the prominent screenwriters of modern anime, such as Yoshida Reiko, Kawasaki Hiroyuki and Akahori Satoru. ● The sheer ubiquity of Koyama's protégés has led some to criticize the creation of an anime 'monoculture', encouraging supposedly different shows to adopt similar narrative structures. However, one might argue that Koyama merely helps his pupils learn how to survive in the fickle and commercialized world of television scriptwriting. Koyama himself is vocally critical of the formulaic nature of modern anime. His most acclaimed pupil is probably Nobumoto Keiko, the writer of *Macross Plus* (1994) and *Cowboy Bebop* (1998), itself conceived in reaction to many anime stereotypes. ● J.Cl.

RIGHT: A PUBLICITY IMAGE FOR **BATTLE OF THE PLANETS** (1972, DIR. TORIUMI JINZO ET AL, 205 EPS) AND A SCENE FROM THE SAME SERIES (ABOVE) ● BELOW: SPACESHIPS FROM THE SERIES **TIME BOKAN** (1975, DIR. SASAGAWA HIROSHI ET AL, 61 EPS)

SEE ALSO: AKAHORI SATORU; CITY HUNTER; GOKU; MACROSS; NOBUMOTO KEIKO; SPIEGEL, SPIKE; TATSUNOKO; TIME BOKAN; URUSEI YATSURA

K

# KURI YOJI

ABOVE: A TYPICAL EXAMPLE OF THE WORK OF KURI YOJI, IRREVERANT AND STRIKING

In the world of Japanese animation, Kuri Yoji (born in 1928) is a one-off. A versatile artist, he started out as a cartoonist specializing in black humour before achieving distinction as a painter, sculptor and performance artist, famous for his collaborations with Yoko Ono. But Kuri is also a pioneer of independent animated film-making in Japan, founding his own studio, Kuri Jikken Manga Kobo, in 1961 and joining with Yanagihara Ryohei and Manabe Hiroshi to form the iconoclastic and influential Animation Sannin No Kai (Animation Group of Three). ● Whereas others in Japan readily accepted the influence of mainstream American cartoons, Kuri preferred to go his own way, adopting surrealist ideas and drawing inspiration from the animation techniques of Norman McLaren or the visions of Hieronymus Bosch and cultivating a spirit of mischief, like a Japanese version of French illustrator Roland Topor. ● Consisting of numerous short features which combine bold experimentation with scandalous ideas, Kuri's animated work can not but provoke a reaction. In the biting but exuberant *Human Zoo* (1963) or *The Man Next Door* (1967), sadistic gags contrast with a childish style of drawing. The bold caricaturist – cynical torturer of his own characters – has invented an ironically bloodthirsty form of Pop Art. Social conventions such as the couple, utopias and even the human body are rocked to their foundations and join in Kuri's dance, swept away in a stylized but cathartic nightmare. Kuri tirelessly scratches away at the veneer of civilization to reveal the barbarism beneath. Having won prizes in various international festivals and exhibited in galleries worldwide, this totally uninhibited artist now devotes most of his time to painting. ● E.H.

SEE ALSO: KAWAMOTO KIHACHIRO; MOCHINAGA TADAHITO; OFUJI NOBURO; TEZUKA OSAMU

CHARACTERS

# KURO & SHIRO

Kuro and Shiro (Black and White) are two street urchins at the centre of the 2006 feature film *Tekkonkinkreet* by Michael Arias, the first non-Japanese director to make a major-budget anime feature film. Based on the manga *Black and White* by Matsumoto Taiyo, the two wayward street kids are feared by their contemporaries and adversaries of the local yakuza. Calling themselves the 'Cats' of their home town, Treasure City, they are the perfect emblems of a new generation of hero. ● Soot-covered factories on the skyline, uncultivated land, deserted playing fields and alleys filled with rubbish give a peripheral idea of their world, an abandoned place where social rules have been reinvented. In this new order, Shiro (small and cheerful) and Kuro (introverted and belligerent) are the guardians against Snake, an unscrupulous businessman, and his grandiose plans to transform Treasure City into an amusement park. ● A postmodern film in concept and style, *Tekkonkinkreet* is a high-quality work that somehow fails to reach the heights expected of it. Arias' vision of the city and the underworld is fascinating, and the combination of different animation techniques shows the complexity of the main characters' inner world, but a leaden, dialogue-heavy script falls short of Matsumoto's original story. ● C.C.

ABOVE AND LEFT: SCENES FROM THE 2006 POST-MODERN FILM
*TEKKONKINKREET* SHOWING THE BREATH-TAKING ADVENTURES OF
KURO AND SHIRO

TEKKONKINKREET ● 2006 ● DIR: MICHAEL ARIAS ● SCR: ANTHONY WEINTRAUB ● DES: NISHIMI SHOJIRO ● ANI: NISHIMI SHOJIRO ●
MUS: PLAID ● PRD: 4°C ● FILM ● DUR: 111 MINS

# KURODA YOSHIO

DIRECTOR

Kuroda Yoshio (born in 1938 in Tokyo) graduated from the literature department of the prestigious Waseda University. His career spans the entire modern age of television anime, beginning with his first job as a staffer on *Ken the Wolf Boy* in 1963. From then on he continued to work in television, animating in a variety of genres, from the sports anime of *Kick no Oni* (*Kick Fiend*, 1970) to the Wild West adventure of *Koya no Shonen Isamu* (*Cowboy Isamu*, 1973). ● In 1975, he storyboarded and directed the series *Dog of Flanders* (1975) for Nippon Animation, beginning the long and successful run of the 'World Masterpiece Theater'. Initially sponsored by the drinks company Calpis, the WMT series became the annual cash-cow for Nippon Animation – long-running television stories, usually based on children's classics from abroad and taking in stories from Spain, Switzerland, Finland and the USA. Kuroda storyboarded and often directed many of these series, including *Haha wo Tazunete Sanzen Ri* (*From the Apennines to the Andes* or *3000 Leagues in Search of Mother*, 1976, dir. Takahata Isao), *Shokojo Sara* (*A Little Princess*, 1985, dir. Kurokawa Fumio et al) and *Swiss Family Robinson* (1981, dir. Kuroda Yoshio et al). ● Although Kuroda occasionally worked on stories that were not adapted from literature, his non-WMT work, such as Ernest Seaton's *Bannertail the Squirrel*, was often in a similar vein. His work is therefore in a mode of Japanese animation that is crucial to the medium, but entirely at odds with its modern popular incarnation – many of his series were seen on children's television in mainland Europe long before 'anime' became a nineties buzzword. ● He returned to children's classics in 1997 as the director of *Dog of Flanders*, and was also credited as one of six directors on the live-action compilation *Dog Movie* (2004). ● J.Cl.

**SEE ALSO**: PATRASHE; SINDBAD

# KUROSAKI ICHIGO

CHARACTER

Kurosaki Ichigo grows up unaware that his mother's death was caused by the monstrous Grand Fisher, a supernatural soul-destroying creature called a 'hollow'. He discovers the existence of hollows when he encounters the pretty Rukia, a wounded Soul Reaper whose job it is to hunt the hollows down. Taking on Rukia's role while she recuperates, Ichigo also takes on a troubled hollow soul that helps in his fight against the creatures, but constantly tries to take over his mind. ● *Bleach* is one of the success stories of modern anime, consistently appearing in 'top-ten' lists by today's teens, many of whom do not realize the debt it owes to many predecessors. In taking on the powers of a wounded, otherworldly fighter, Ichigo inherits a long tradition of symbiotic heroes dating all the way back to the original *Ultraman* (1966). Similarly, Rukia is another archetype of Japanese science fiction: the mysterious girl, an orphan with magical powers, and a love-interest who must remain unattainable while our hero fulfils his duty. ● *Bleach* cleverly takes its inspirations from the excitement and passions of youth. Ichigo might have an attitude problem, but that is because, like *Devilman* (1972) long before him, the source of his powers threatens to overwhelm his psyche. He might think that everything in the world is ranged against him, but that is because it is. As an archetypal hot-headed anime hero, Ichigo has the perfect opponents to match his belligerence, and has gained an appreciative and admiring audience among modern teenagers. ● J.Cl.

ABOVE: KUROSAKI ICHIGO WITH HIS FEMALE SCHOOLMATES KUCHIKI RUKIA (LEFT) AND INOUE ORIHIME (RIGHT), STARS OF THE 2004 SERIES BLEACH

BLEACH ● 2004 ● DIR: ABE NORIYUKI ● SCR: FURUMURA GENKI ET AL ● DES: KUDO MASASHI ● ANI: KAWAMURA AKIO ET AL ● MUS: SAGISU SHIRO ● PRD: STUDIO PIERROT ● TV SERIES ● EPS: 207

# KUSANAGI MOTOKO

Behind her big, blue eyes and wide, blank stare, cyborg Major Kusanagi Motoko hides a conflicting personality. She is programmed to safeguard public security in her role as a secret agent, yet there seems to be something troubled and confused within her: perhaps the illusion, or a memory, of belonging to fallible humankind and therefore being doomed to die. When the Major is confronted by the ethereal Puppet Master, a hacker who invades the minds of citizens to bend them to his will, these existential preoccupations come to the surface. ● There are two important, contrasting plot elements in *Ghost in the Shell*. One is the vision of a reality in which the corporeal, physical world is taken over by technology; the other is based on typical cop stories (the Japanese title is 'Mobile Armoured Police'). The first narrative strand has philosophical and existential implications: with a 'cyberpunk scenario' as its departure point, *Ghost in the Shell* explores the idea of the end of the individual as a unique identity or, rather, of its rebirth within a new ontological framework. The second strand links this action to a humanistic contest in which the struggle against a common enemy strengthens interpersonal bonds. ● Shirow Masamune's manga created a dystopian universe that is both complex and hyper-technological, tinged at times with religiosity, where various forces challenge the Major and her Section. Oshii Mamoru's film is darker and more disquieting, concentrating on the manga's concluding story about the Puppet Master. It also examines the relationship between Kusanagi and Batou, the massive agent enhanced by cybernetic prosthetics who takes the lead role in *Ghost in the Shell 2: Innocence* (2004). ● C.C.

ABOVE: FOUR IMAGES FROM *GHOST IN THE SHELL 2: INNOCENCE* (2004, OSHII MAMORU, 100 MINS) FEATURING A CYBORG SEX TOY (TOP), KUSANAGI MOTOKO'S LIEUTENANT AND FRIEND BATOU (CENTRE) AND A DRAMATIC URBAN VISTA (ABOVE) ● RIGHT: TWO IMAGES OF MAJOR KUSANAGI EMPHASIZE HER CYBERNETIC ENHANCEMENTS

K

*KOKAKU KIDOTAI* ● *GHOST IN THE SHELL* ● *1995* ● DIR: OSHII MAMORU ● SCR: ITO KAZUNORI ● DES: OKIURA HIROYUKI, KAWAMORI SHOJI ● ANI: OKIURA HIROYUKI ET AL ● MUS: KAWAI KENJI ● PRD: PRODUCTION I.G. ● FILM ● DUR: 82 MINS

# KYOTO ANIMATION

STUDIO

Production company Kyoto Animation began life in 1981 as a small organization specializing in finishing (tracing and painting on cels). The company later opened an image production department and took on subcontract work from other studios, producing in-between animation for projects as diverse as *Cowboy Bebop* (1998) and several *Crayon Shin-chan* movies (2003 onwards). They also painted backgrounds for *Evangelion* (1995). Based far from Tokyo, the centre of the anime industry, the studio made no independent work until 2003. ● Since then, Kyoto Animation has grown rapidly. The two-part OAV *Munto* (2003, dir. Kigami Yoshiji, Aratani Tomoe) was remade for TV and edited for cinema release in 2009. The studio's most famous work is probably TV series *The Melancholy of Haruhi Suzumiya* (*Suzumiya Haruhi no Yuutsu*, 2006, dir. Ishihara Tatsuya), which has become a major international hit, with a feature-length anime in cinemas in 2010. Other major TV series include *Air* (2005, dir. Ishihara Tatsuya et al), *Lucky Star* (2007, dir. Yamamoto Yutaka, Takemoto Yasuhiro) and *K-On!* (2009, dir. Yamada Naoko). ● After years of subcontract work, Kyoto Animation has a well-founded reputation for technical competence, and the high standards of draughtsmanship, colour design and production are a magnet for many aspiring young students of anime who would like to work there. The company also makes net animation and video game opening and ending sequences. ● H.M.

ABOVE: SCENES FROM THE OAV MUNTO (2003, DIR. KIGAMI YOSHIJI, ARAJANI TOMOE, 52 MINS)

SEE ALSO: EIKEN; GALLOP; GROUP TAC; I.G.; MADHOUSE

Lain, an introverted adolescent, receives an email from a classmate telling her that she committed suicide a few days ago. This is the start of a disquieting, labyrinthine narrative in which clues are gradually revealed that will enable Lain to solve the mystery in the initial email. The 'Wired', an information network similar to the Internet, has managed to replicate reality, opening the door to a sort of extra-corporeal immortality and to the possibility of a new, virtual, mysticism. The multifaceted conceit combines echoes of Lewis Carroll's *Alice's Adventures in Wonderland* with conspiracy theory in a wide-ranging story that involves the viewer in the detection of occult clues and the quest for their meaning. ● The age of information produces its own nightmares: in this case, a new information network that calls into question the true basis of reality and the mechanisms that enable the individual to make sense of the world. *Serial Experiments Lain* is ground-breaking, tortuous and devastating. Directed by Nakamura Ryutaro, with graphics by Abe Yoshitoshi and screenplay by Konaka Chiaki, the series explores the depths of newly hatched anxieties, employing a deconstructivist narrative, eloquent and eerie, with its own conception of space (almost always conceived in terms of isolation) and a complex, atmospheric soundtrack. Adopting the themes of 'cyberpunk' and the aesthetic reference of the new Japanese 'cinema of terror', this series proceeds to explore the question of identity in those shadowy zones where the virtual and the material coalesce and reveal the fragility of the collective perception of reality. ● J.Co.

# LAIN

CHARACT

SERIAL EXPERIMENTS LAIN ● 1998 ● DIR: NAKAMURA RYUTARO ET AL ● SCR: KONOKA CHIAKI ● DES: KISHIDA TAKAHIRO ET AL ● ANI: TANAKA YUICHI ● MUS: NAKAIDO REICHI, BOA ● PRD: PIONEER LDC, TRIANGLE STAFF, TV TOKYO ● TV SERIES ● EPS: 13

# LAPUTA

Screened in Japanese cinemas two years after the release of *Nausicaä of the Valley of Wind*, *Laputa: Castle in the Sky* was the first proper feature-length film to come out of Studio Ghibli. The project is rooted in the childhood of director Miyazaki, a great lover of adventure stories, who never forgot the passage in *Gulliver's Travels* where Swift's hero discovers a flying island called Laputa. Although directly influenced by Swift's work, however, the film itself is eminently 'Miyazakian'. ● *Laputa* can be read as the story of two children literally determined to rise above, to leave terra firma behind, defying both gravity and the weight of social opinion. This is certainly the destiny of the young Pazu, whom the viewer first sees working in a mine (inspired by a visit Miyazaki made to Wales). The boy later reaches the surface, and then the skies, after meeting a girl named Sheeta, whose mysterious pendant allows them to levitate. ● A coming-of-age tale and an aerial odyssey produced six years before *Porco Rosso*, Studio Ghibli's other aeronautical escapade, *Laputa* is also a meditation on the ambivalence of human design: the legendary island floating in the skies could prove to be a terrible weapon as well as an artificial paradise. ● Rich in aerobatic chases and races against pirates who prove to be not-so-wicked, and government agents whose aims prove not at all clear-cut, *Laputa* is injected with a taste for discovery and a love of freedom. The film ennobles all kinds of impulses: those of the characters, those of the dreamer and creator of worlds and those of the images themselves, that suddenly come to life. The viewer is entranced and constantly full of wonder, eager not to miss a single second. ● E.H.

SCENES FROM THE 1986 FILM *CASTLE IN THE SKY* ● BELOW: THE FLOATING ISLAND OF LAPUTA ● RIGHT: PAZU AND SHEETA EXPLORE THE ABANDONED ISLAND AND ITS CASTLE

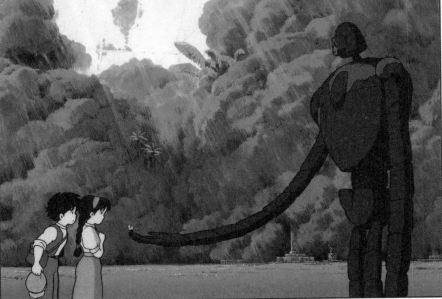

TENKU NO SHIRO LAPUTA ● CASTLE IN THE SKY ● 1986 ● DIR & SCR & DES: MIYAZAKI HAYAO ● ANI: TANNAI TSUKASA ● MUS: HISAISHI JOE ● PRD: TAKAHATA ISAO ET AL, STUDIO GHIBLI ● FILM ● DUR: 124 MINS

L

# LEO
## KIMBA

Leo (Kimba) the white lion wants to bring about his father's utopian dream of a peaceful coexistence between the animal and human worlds. The main character in the first full-colour anime television series, the young lion is another famous creation from Tezuka Osamu. The cub, who first sprang to life in 1950 in the pages of *Manga Shonen*, was arguably Tezuka's most significant contribution to the world of 'funny animals' and illustrates affinities between his work and Disney's. ● It is ironic that the lion, perhaps the most Disney-like character of Tezuka's work, has become the centre of the dispute surrounding *The Lion King* (1994, dir. Roger Allers, Rob Mikoff) and the allegations of plagiarism. The dispute, which led to around a thousand manga and anime professionals drafting a formal petition requesting the Disney company acknowledge the influence of Tezuka's work on *The Lion King*, tarnished the previously friendly relationship between the two studios, particularly since Tezuka had obtained official permission to adapt *Bambi* (1942) to the world of manga and invited Disney professionals to become animators at the Tezuka studio when colour first began to be used. ● Financed partly by the American broadcasting conglomerate NBC and devised initially as an export product, the series *Kimba the White Lion* departed from Tezuka's original manga and took the form of individual episodes, avoiding the period of Kimba's youth and early adulthood. In 1966, the series *Janguru Taitei: Susumu Leo!* (*Jungle Emperor: Onward, Leo!*, dir. Hayashi Shigeyki) related the adventures of an adult Leo at the same time as several episodes of the original series were being edited to become a feature-length film, which would later win a prize at the Venice festival. A remake of the original series in 1986 and other feature-length films in 1991 and 1997 have contributed to the lion's long animated history. ● J.Co.

*SCENES FROM THE 1965 SERIES KIMBA, THE WHITE LION ● ABOVE: LEO (KIMBA) WIH HIS BELOVED LYRE, BABOON COUNSELLOR MANDY, DEER TOMMY AND PARROT COCO ● RIGHT: IMAGES FROM THE SERIES*

*JANGURU TAITEI ● KIMBA, THE WHITE LION ● 1965 ● DIR: YAMAMOTO EIICHI ET AL ● SCR: TSUJI MASAKI ET AL ● DES: TEZUKA OSAMU ● ANI: KATSUI CHIKAO, SAITO HIROSHI ● MUS: TOMITA ISAO ● PRD: MUSHI PRODUCTION ● TV SERIES ● EPS: 52*

# LHADATT, SHIROTSUGU

CHARACTER

Even as a child, Shirotsugu Lhadatt knew what he wanted to do with his life: he wanted to become a pilot. All grown up, he enrolls in the Royal Space Force, an organization that is regarded as something of a joke and a waste of money following its lengthy failed efforts to put a man in space. Shirotsugu, lazy and disillusioned with life, wants to be that man. ● The first feature film produced by Gainax, *The Wings of Honneamise* could be considered an animation manifesto. The design and style of the backgrounds, the varied tone, and the historical and political implications of the plot were hugely influential on later anime. The realism of the visual description is accompanied at times by surreal touches and a general atmosphere of decadence. The past, as imagined by director Yamaga Hiroyuki, has the features of a near future, a reality where cities have exploded into a jumble of streets and people, and religion coexists with the obsessive presence of the media. ● Shirotsugu is a perfect representative of this schizophrenic reality: he is not only a young man inspired by a sincere spiritual quest, but also a weak man who drinks and chases women. In short, he is a son of the twentieth century, with all its paradoxes. ● Like its protagonist, *Wings of Honneamise* is an unbalanced yet original film, engaging and sincere. It is the result of an experiment led by Yamagata and developed by a pool of leading artists, most notably Anno Hideaki as animator, Sadamoto Yoshiyuki as character designer, Sakamoto Ryuichi as soundtrack writer and Itano Ichiro and Maeda Mahiro as animators. ● C.C.

LEFT: PUBLICITY IMAGE FOR THE 1987 FILM *THE WINGS OF HONNEAMISE*, FEATURING THE DISILLUSIONED PROTAGONIST SHIROTSUGU

ORITSU UCHUGUN: ONEAMISU NO TSUBASA ● THE WINGS OF HONNEAMISE ● 1987 ● DIR: YAMAGA HIROYUKI ● SCR: YAMAGA HIROYUKI, ONOGI HIROSHI ● DES: SADAMOTO YOSHIYUKI ● ANI: ANNO HIDEAKI ET AL ● MUS: SAKAMOTO RYUCHI ET AL ● PRD: GAINAX ● FILM ● DUR: 125 MINS

# LIMIT-CHAN

CHARACTER

Cybernella is the prettiest girl in school and always the first to rush to someone's aid. Her friends, Jun and Tomi, adore her and often stay at her home. But she also has a secret: after she was involved in a plane crash, her scientist father took the dying girl to his laboratory where he transformed her into a cyborg. Since then, Cybernella can run as fast as a rocket and lift weights that would be impossible for an ordinary human being — all she has to do is touch the brooch she wears on her chest as if it were a control. She is grateful for the new life that science has made possible, but her dual nature gets her down: in one episode, she says 'I'm not human or a robot either: I'm a strange thing called Cybernella.' On top of that, she must be careful not to go too far with her superhero feats because even her strengthened body could break down. ● Most female anime heroes of the early Seventies were young witches who used magic words and spells, with or without a wand, and formed part of the successful majokko or 'Magical Girl' category. Toei Animation, on the other hand, invented a character who was magical on her own terms. The *Limit-chan* series utilizes the timeworn character of the cyborg, but it also hints at a level of self-awareness and thematic maturity through politically correct messages addressed to the audience. The bully or tough guy of the cartoon, for example, is often a figure of fun and the protagonist's good deeds are depicted as the actions of an angel made of nuts and bolts. ● M.A.R.

MIRACLE SHOJO LIMIT-CHAN ● LIMIT THE MIRACLE GIRL ● 1973 ● DIR: TAMIYA TAKESHI ● SCR: YUKIMURO SHUNICHI ET AL ● DES & ANI: KOMATSUBARA KAZUO ● MUS: KIKUCHI SHUNSUKE, IWATANI TOKIKO● PRD: TOEI ANIMATION ● TV SERIES ● EPS: 25

---

N.D.P. présente

LITTLE NEMO

Les aventures au pays de Slumberland

Un film de Masami HATA & William HURTZ
D' après la bande dessinée de Winsor Mc CAY

Scénario de Chris COLOMBUS & Richard OUTTEN
Histoire de Jean MOBIUS GIRAUD & Yatuka FUJIOKA
Adaptation cinématographique de Ray BRADBURY
Musique de Thomas CHASE & Steve RUCKER
Et la participation de l' ORCHESTRE SYMPHONIQUE DE LONDRES
Chansons de Richard M. SHERMAN & Robert B. SHERMAN
La chanson du générique est chantée par Mélissa MANCHESTER
Voix de la version originale Mickey ROONEY,René AUBERJONOIS & Gabriel DAMON
A TOKYO MOVIE SHINSHA CO, LTD PRODUCTION
Co-producteur Barry GLASSER, Shunzo KATO, Fiji KATAYAMA
Producteur associé Koji TAKEUCHI
Produit par Yutaka FUJIOKA

INFOS et jeux
36 68 03 70        1992 / TMS TOUS DROITS RESERVES        DOLBY STEREO

# LITTLE NEMO

CHARACTER

Little Nemo was created in America, in 1905, from the sophiscticated pen of Winsor McCay, who drew the stories in the Sunday edition of the *New York Herald*. Nemo is a dishevelled child, a dreamer who goes on extraordinary, imaginary adventures. ● The film begins with the arrival of a clown at Nemo's house who asks him to go with him into Slumberland where a princess wants him as a playmate. Once there, little Nemo makes new friends but soon he has to fight to free the princess's father, who has been abducted by the evil King Nightmare. TMS had been thinking of making this film for a number of years. Miyazaki himself was diverted from his commitments on the *Sherlock Hound* series (1984, dir. Miyazaki Hayao, Mikuruya Kyosuke) and began work on the film together with Takahata. ● Two pilots were made, the first by Kondo Yoshifumi in 1984 and the other by Dezaki Osamu in 1987 but it was only in 1989 that Fujioka Yutaka, one of Japan's most enlightened producers, succeeded in giving the script to director Chris Columbus, Jean Giraud (the French comic-book illustrator better known as 'Moebius') and science-fiction author Ray Bradbury, who held the ambiguous claim to 'screen concept' and who exited the project at an early stage. Also involved in the project were the famous animators and Disney employees Frank Thomas, Roger Allers and Ollie Johnston, whilst the music was written by the Sherman brothers. *Little Nemo: Adventures in Slumberland* was released in the USA in 1992, but, despite the high quality of names involved, the result of this strange alliance between Japan and Hollywood was confused and fell short of expectations. ● F.L.

LEFT: THE FRENCH LANGUAGE POSTER FOR THE 1989 FILM ABOUT A YOUNG CHILD'S ADVENTURES IN SLUMBERLAND, LITTLE NEMO

---

LITTLE NEMO: ADVENTURES IN SLUMBERLAND ● 1989 ● DIR: HATA MASAMI, WILLIAM HURTZ ● SCR: CHRIS COLUMBUS ET AL ● DES: JEAN GIRAUD ET AL ● ANI: OTSUKA YASUO ET AL ● MUS: RICHARD & ROBERT SHERMAN ● PRD: TMS ● FILM ● DUR: 84 MINS

# LUFFY, MONKEY D

After eating a piece of magical fruit, aspiring pirate Monkey D. Luffy discovers that he is almost invincibly strong (his inability to float in water is his Achilles heel). Luffy is the protagonist of Oda Eiichiro's epic manga *One Piece* (1997), the tale of a rag-tag cohort of pirates, who sail the oceans in search of the eponymous mythic treasure 'One Piece'. ● The serial manga began life as a short one-page submission entitled *Romance Dawn*, which would later become the title of the series' first chapter. Oda began his manga career at a remarkably young age, submitting a competition entry to the famous Tezuka awards at seventeen and achieving second place, which secured him a role as an assistant at *Shonen Jump* magazine where he would create the aforementioned *Romance Dawn* at only nineteen years old. In many respects, the precocious narrative of Luffy corresponds to that of his creator, both beginning their adventure at seventeen, and seeking fame and fortune in a fast-paced adult world. ● Oda cites Toriyama Akira's *Dragon Ball Z* (1984) manga as his main influence, which can be felt in the epic storyline, ensemble cast and spectacular battles that he carried over into *One Piece*. The deferral of plot conclusion – where situations are left open ended to allow for the return, resurrection and recombination of characters and ideas – is central to the narrative of *Dragon Ball Z*, and it is with this device that Oda continues to tackle the epic story of *One Piece*. ● D.S.

ONE PIECE ● 1999 ● DIR: SHIMIZU ATSUJI ET AL ● SCR: UESAKA HIROHIKO ET AL ● DES: KOIZUMI NOBURO, HISADA KAZUYA ● ANI: KAWAMURA ATSURO ET AL ● MUS: TANAKA KOHEI ● PRD: TOEI ● TV SERIES ● EPS: 393

# LUPIN III

A phenomenon for over forty years, Lupin III is more than just a character. Created in 1967 by 'Monkey Punch' (the pen name of director and designer Kato Kazuhiko) and animated four years later, this gentleman thief with a passion for disguises, jewellery and beautiful women has a worldwide fanbase. ● His success can be attributed to the clever mix of adventure, humour (albeit sometimes childish) and mystery in the stories, but above all to the extremely dynamic graphics that Monkey Punch designed to accompany his protagonist. The real highlights of the series are the chase sequences, carried out using every possible kind of transport, from cars, helicopters and planes to bicycles, trains and parachutes. The competition between Lupin and obstinate Inspector Zenigata, the incarnation of the stereotypical Japanese official, forms a vital part of every episode and allows for an effective balance between recurring themes and new elements. ● Together with his business partners Jigen, the infallible gunslinger with an everlasting cigarette in his mouth, Goemon, the silent samurai, and the beautiful but selfish Fujiko, Lupin is part of a team in which a number of national characteristics are parodied, thereby transcending the cultural forms normally observed in anime. ● Lupin III has been the subject of several television series, as well as an OAV examining the subject of animation. His character has also inspired numerous videogames and feature films. Among the latter, it is impossible to forget *The Castle of Cagliostro* (1979), directed by Miyazaki Hayao, a ground-breaking work celebrated for the elegance of its design (especially the background scenes of Cagliostro's home) and the complexity of the plot. Lupin III is an archetype of the romantic and unselfish thief, and has entertained generations of readers and viewers. ● C.C.

LEFT & BELOW: TWO IMAGES OF MONKEY PUNCH'S GENTLEMAN THIEF LUPIN III FROM THE 1971 SERIES

RUPAN SANSEI ● LUPIN III ● 1971 ● DIR: OSUMI MASAAKI, MIYAZAKI HAYAO, TAKAHATA ISAO ● SCR: YAMAZAKI TADAAKI ET AL ● DES: MONKEY PUNCH ● ANI: OTSUKA YASUO ET AL ● MUS: YAMASHITA TAKEO, ONO YUJI ● PRD: TMS ● TV SERIES ● EPS: 23

# MACH GO GO GO
## SPEED RACER

Somewhere in the fertile imagination of Yoshida Tatsuo, the pop glamour of Elvis Presley's *Viva Las Vegas* jumpsuit crashed into the sophisticated, futuristic gadgetry of James Bond's Aston Martin. Out of the collision was born *Speed Racer* (1966), a manga depicting a wildly fantastic and excessively imaginative world of car-racing, which inspired a popular animated television series just one year after its creation (it was also among the first anime programmes to enjoy success on the western market). Yoshida built on the premise of his earlier manga *Pilot Ace* to create a strikingly unsophisticated conceit, pitting the Mifune family – comprising a racing-driver son, a mechanic and former wrestling champion father, a mother and a younger son with his pet monkey for comic contrast – against a series of antagonists who ranged from caricatured noir figures to eccentric characters bordering on the fantastical. The recurring presence of the enigmatic Racer X added an evocative, darker sub-plot to this typical family portrait: he is finally revealed to be the family's prodigal son. ● *Speed Racer* was adapted for animation in what was to be the second series produced by Tatsunoko, the company founded by the Yoshida brothers (Tatsuo, Kenji and Toyoharu) to create anime from existing manga. Influenced by serialized films, the episodes of *Speed Racer* usually ended in a cliffhanger that would leave the protagonist and his Mach 5, a meteor of a vehicle equipped with studded wheels, robots and other devices, in terrible peril. In 1997, Tatsunoko produced a new version which updated the look of the original and ran for thirty-four episodes. The Wachowski brothers made a live-action cinema adaptation in 2008. ● J.Co.

*LEFT & BELOW: IMAGES FROM THE 1967 SERIES **SPEED RACER** SHOW THE WORLD OF MOTOR-RACING ACCORDING TO YOSHIDA TATSUO*

MACH GO GO GO ● SPEED RACER ● 1967 ● DIR: YOSHIDA TATSUO ET AL ● SCR: TORIUMI JINZO ET AL ● DES: KURI IPPEI, SASAGAWA HIROSHI ● ANI: SUDA MASAMI, SAIJO TAKASHI ● MUS: KOSHIBE NOBUYOSHI, OSHIMA MICHIRU ● PRD: TATSUNOKO ● TV SERIES ● EPS: 52

At the end of the twentieth century, a huge alien spaceship crashes to Earth. Over the next ten years, scientists work on rebuilding it. The warlike former owners of the ship, the giant Zentraedi, attack Earth in an effort to reclaim it. By accident, the spaceship is again catapulted to the boundaries of the solar system and, along with it, the city of Macross, which had been gradually built up around the crash site over the years. So begins the return journey to Earth and the war against the Zentraedi. Notable in the earthly ranks are pilot Roy Fokker, officer Hayase Misa, daring Ichijyo Hikaru and Chinese singer Lynn Minmay. Meanwhile, the Zentraedi have become intent on establishing themselves on Earth. ● The saga of *Macross* (known in the USA as the *Robotech* franchise) includes three ingredients well known to anime fans: variable fighter robots, sentimental trials and tribulations in a love triangle, and music. This last ingredient is at the story's heart. Whereas in *Mobile Suit Gundam* (1979, dir. Tomino Yoshiyuki), an entire fleet of spaceships was destroyed by the wily powers of a single female figure, here a mere song is enough to stop the alien invasion! This romantic notion has transformed the character of Lynn Minmay into the first virtual idol in Japan. ● *Macross* is often associated with the name of animator Kawamori Shoji, but he is only one of the many talented artists who worked on it. The mecha design of its robot Valkyries (precursors of the *Transformers*) has played a fundamental role in the artist's success and that of the series. A number of spin-off sequels have been made (including manga and videogame versions), none as good as the original. The exception is *Macross Plus* (1994, dir. Kawamori Shoji), which modernizes the ingredients of the original plot both musically and graphically, turning towards cyberpunk. ● S.G.

## MACROSS

*TV SERIES*

ABOVE LEFT: SCENES FROM THE 1982 TV SERIES *MACROSS*: HAYASE MISA AND ICHIJO HIKARU ARE INVOLVED IN A LOVE TRIANGLE WITH SINGER LYNN MINMAY (TOP); PILOT ICHIJO HIKARU AND LYNN MINMAY (CENTRE); LYNN MINMAY (BOTTOM) ● TOP: THE SDF-1 FROM THE 1984 FILM *MACROSS: DO YOU REMEMBER LOVE?* (DIR. SHOJI KAWAMORI, NOBORU ISHIGURO) ● ABOVE: ISAMU, ONE OF THE PILOTS OF THE 1994 OAV SERIES *MACROSS PLUS*, A SPIN-OFF FROM THE FAMOUS ORIGINAL SERIES DEDICATED TO THE FLYING FORTRESS

CHOJIKU YOSAI MACROSS ● MACROSS ● 1982 ● DIR: ISHIGURO NOBORU ET AL ● SCR: MATSUZAKI KENICHI ET AL ● DES: MIKIMOTO HARUHIKO ET AL ● ANI: ISHIGURO NOBORU ET AL ● MUS: HANEDA KENTARO ● PRD: STUDIO NUE, TATSUNOKO ● TV SERIES ● EPS: 36

# MADHOUSE

STUDIO

Madhouse was founded in October 1972 by staff from Mushi Production including Dezaki Osamu, Maruyama Masao, Rintaro and Kawajiri Yoshiaki. Their first major production, in 1973, was the TV series and movie *Ace o Nerae!* (*Aim for the Ace*, dir. Dezaki Osamu) ● They also worked on movies and TV series for other production houses, including *Barefoot Gen* (*Hadashi no Gen*, 1983, dir. Mori Masaki). In 1987, Kawajiri directed *Yoju Toshi* (*Wicked City*), the first in a series of distinctive action-oriented adventures with an emphasis on horror and elements of cyberpunk style.
● Diversity is one of Madhouse's strengths. Besides Kawajiri titles such as the OAV series *Cyber City Oedo 808* (1990), or the movie *Ninja Scroll* (*Jubei Ninpocho*, 1993), they produced Asaka Morio's two *Cardcaptor Sakura* movies (1999, 2000) and football TV series *Captain Tsubasa: Road to 2002* (2001, dir. Imagake Isamu, Sugii Gisaburo).
● The late director Kon Satoshi made his feature films *Perfect Blue* (1998), *Millennium Actress* (2002), *Tokyo Godfathers* (2003) and *Paprika* (2006) at Madhouse, as well as TV series *Paranoia Agent* (*Moso Dairinin*, 2004). Hosoda Mamoru made *The Girl Who Leapt Through Time* (*Toki o kakeru shojo*) there in 2006. Madhouse worked with Tezuka Productions on *Metropolis* (2001, dir. Rintaro). Rintaro also directed the company's first CG anime feature, *Yona Yona Penguin*, in 2009. Madhouse makes anime for all ages and tastes in its own unique style. ● H.M.

TWO MADHOUSE PRODUCTIONS ● TOP: A PUBLICITY IMAGE FOR CYBER CITY OEDO 808 (1990, DIR. KAWAJIRI YOSHIAKI, 3 EPS) ● RIGHT: GEN FROM BAREFOOT GEN (1983, DIR. MORI MASAKI, 83 MINS)

SEE ALSO: DEZAKI OSAMU; GHIBLI; HOSODA MAMORU; JUBEI; KANNO MAKOTO; KAWAJIRI YOSHIAKI; KIRIGOE MIMA; KON SATOSHI; PAPRIKA; RINTARO; TIMA; TOKYO GODFATHERS

# MAEDA MAHIRO

One of the premiere creative talents working in the anime industry today, Maeda Mahiro (born in 1963 in Tottori) is best known for his work as designer of the 'Angels' in Anno Hideaki's mecha masterpiece *Neon Genesis Evangelion* (1995). At the time of release, the sleek organic form and geometries of the 'Angels' were highly original. Maeda had earnt his spurs working as an inbetweener and animator for Studio Ghibli and, later, for Gainax on the space movie *Wings of Honneamise* (1987, dir. Yamaga Hiroyuki). ● As a director in his own right Maeda was responsible for *Ao no Roku-go* (*Blue Submarine No. 6*, 1998), an adventure based on the sixties comic by Ozawa Satoru, that exhibits Maeda's trademark inventiveness in character design and animation. ● Maeda's designs combine delicate curved forms with sharp angles and points. His design aesthetic is uniquely animation-orientated, as the addition of motion combines with the quality of the shape and form to create a sensuous overall image. ● Maeda's work reached a large international audience in Quentin Tarantino's two-part martial arts epic *Kill Bill* (2003), when he provided keyframe animation for the animated segments that develop the backstory of assassin O-Ren Ishii. His trademark movement animation style, with its fluid squash-and-stretch and intense detail, is also discernible in his contribution to the short film collection *The Animatrix* (2003). ● D.S.

SCENES FROM *BLUE SUBMARINE NO. 6* (1998, DIR. MAEDA MAHIRO, 4 EPS) ● ABOVE RIGHT: HAYAMI TETSUO BATTLES A HUMAN–SHARK HYBRID ● RIGHT: KINO MAYUMI AND ANTI–HERO HAYAMI TETSUO ● BELOW: THE BLUE SUBMARINE NO. 6

SEE ALSO: 4°C; ANIMATRIX; FINAL FANTASY; LHADATT, SHIROTSUGU

# MAEDA MINORU

An eclectic artist of undeniable ability, Maeda Minoru (born in 1954) has worked on numerous productions since starting, at a very young age, with Studio Junio and later Group TAC. He has also collaborated with Toei Animation, where professional requirements kept him locked into less-than-challenging assignments, as with *Dr Slump* (1981) or *Dragon Ball Z* (1989), where Maeda worked on character design or supervized animation. These were productions aimed at television, where Maeda's best prospect was simply to devise the action scenes as well as possible – which is exactly what he did in the case of *Dragon Ball*, where the duels and battles are the central focus. ● Perhaps the most important feature of Maeda's professional career is the artistic link connecting him to the director Sugii Gisaburo and his colleague Maeda Tsuneo (both associated with Group TAC), with whom he worked as head animator and character designer on adaptations of manga by Adachi Mitsuru. These works initially adhered faithfully to the original design, as in *Nine* (1980, dir. Sugii Gisaburo, Tsuruta Hideaki) or *Hiatari Ryoko* (*Ryoko, A New Day* or *Sunny Ryoko*, 1987, dir. Tokita Hiroko et al), which Maeda endowed with a powerful, formal elegance before later finding a more modern appeal in the films *Touch: Are kara, Kimi wa* (*Touch: Miss Lonely Yesterday*, 1998, dir. Sugii Gisaburo) and *Touch: Cross Road – Kaze no Yukue* (2001, dir. Sugii Gisaburo). In these, he brought to life a number of new adventures not present in Adachi's original manga. He was also responsible for character design on the fantasy film *Kaze o Mita Shonen* (*The Boy Who Saw the Wind*, 2000, dir. Omori Kazuki, Shinohara Toshiya). ● D.S.

SEE ALSO: ANIMATRIX; ANNO HIDEAKI; EVANGELION; GAINAX; GHIBLI; LHADATT, SHIROTSUGU

# MAETEL

CHARACTER

With her distinctive black hat, slender black-clad figure and black cape, Maetel is one of the most aristocratic and enigmatic creations in anime history. Along with her companion Tetsuro, a cheeky and determined little boy, she undertakes a long interstellar journey onboard the space train *Galaxy Express 999*. Tetsuro is desperate to acquire the mechanized body of a cyborg that will give him superhuman strength and immortality. Over the course of the story, he loses his illusions and discovers that both his dream and the woman who accompanies him, whose face is so like that of his dead mother, are not what he thought they were. ● Author Matsumoto Leiji is a master at creating melancholy characters whose fates are pre-ordained and *Galaxy Express* is no exception. Goodbyes are said over and over again, ending in the final parting between the blonde princess Maetel, victim of an inescapable destiny, and the young wanderer, who returns to Earth without the new body he wanted. Unexpected meetings and other adventures enliven the various stages of the train journey across the galaxy, while the film's meaning is masked behind inscrutable faces, emerging only in introspective glimpses that punctuate the narrative. ● *Galaxy Express 999* was a successful manga (running from 1977–81) and inspired a TV series (1978–81) as well as two full-length animation feature films (1979 and 1981), both directed by Rintaro, whose interpretation stayed truest to the spirit of the original. These were followed by Uda Konosuke's shorter, fifty-four-minute film of 1998. Maetel was the main character in two other productions, the OAV *Maetel Legend* (2000, dir. Yokota Kazuyoshi) and the series *Space Symphonie Maetel* (2004, dir. Masaki Shin'ichi), which updated the fascinating character. ● C.C.

RIGHT & BELOW: IN *GALAXY EXPRESS 999*, MAETEL AND TETSURO CROSS THE GALAXY BY TRAIN ● THE TV SERIES (1978) AND FILM (1979) WERE CREATED BY MATSUMOTO LEIJI

GINGA TETSUDO 999 ● GALAXY EXPRESS 999 ● 1979 ● DIR: RINTARO ● SCR: ICHIKAWA KON, ISHIMORI SHIRO ● DES: MATSUMOTO LEIJI ● ANI: KOMATSUBARA KAZUO ● MUS: AOKI NOZOMI, TAKEKAWA YUKIHIDE ● PRD: TOEI ANIMATION ● FILM ● DUR: 130 MINS

# MAISON IKKOKU

MAISON IKKOKU ● 1986 ● DIR: YAMAZAKI KAZUO ET AL ● SCR: TSUCHIYA
TOKIKO ET AL ● DES: MORIYAMA YUJI TAKADA AKEMI ● ANI: KAWANAMI
MASAARI ET AL ● MUS: SUGIYAMA TAKUO ● PRD: DEEN ● TV SERIES ●
EPS: 96

SCENES FROM THE 1986 SERIES MAISON IKKOKU ● BELOW LEFT: KYOKO,
THE FOXY HEROINE OF THE SERIES ● BELOW RIGHT: THE YOUNG KYOKO AND
THE STUDENT YUSAKU GODAI

Home to penniless student Yusaku Godai and a host of original characters, Maison Ikkoku is no ordinary boarding-house. Guests include a scantily clad bar hostess, a plump woman rather fond of a drink and her son, and a mysterious, quiet man in a suit. ● Adapted from one of Takahashi Rumiko's best-known manga, the television series *Maison Ikkoku* opens with the introduction of Kyoko, the new boarding-house manager. Only in her twenties and trying to put her life back together after the death of her husband, Kyoko's arrival radically alters the balance of this little community. For Yusaku, it's love at first sight, but it will be no easy task to win Kyoko over, not only because somebody or something always comes between them whenever he tries to tell her how he feels, but also because Yusaku has to fight a constant battle against his own shyness and chronic clumsiness. ● There are two contradictory movements at work here (one straightforward, the other labyrinthine), giving the series a varied rhythm. Yusaku's individual desire – to win Kyoko's heart – is expressed within the framework of an ensemble dynamic that leans heavily towards buffoonery. An inventive exploration of the narrative potential of a given place and group of people, *Maison Ikkoku* is also a subtle investigation of different forms of comedy, ranging from romantic to pure burlesque. As it alternates between farcical outbursts and dreamy harmony, the series remains firmly anchored in reality and offers its audience an enriching journey through everyday Japanese life. ● E.H.

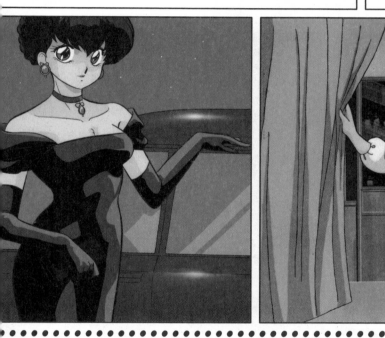

---

Three of the great names of Japanese animation collaborated on the experimental feature-length film *Neo Tokyo*, each one making a distinct episode. Each author was free to experiment with the narrative solutions of their choice. ● Rintaro – also executive producer of the entire project – crafted *Labyrinth Labrynthos* (*Labyrinth*), a piece that provides a framing device for the work as a whole, a modern Alice's journey through a visionary dream world characterized by surrealist allusions. This piece is a short anti-narrative created out of childhood dreams from a time when the director was obsessed with the labyrinth as a device. ● Kawajiri Yoshiaki then takes up the thread with his *Hashiru Otoko* (*Running Man*), telling the tale of a racing driver's last desperate race, in which he destroys his own body in order to break through its limitations. Kawajiri returned to this idea in *World Record* (part of *Animatrix*, 2003), in which he shaped a sombre world indebted to famous cinematic works such as *Rollerball* (1975), dominated by the sensationalism of spectacle, where the visionary quality of the climax seems both cathartic and deadly. ● The concluding section falls to Otomo Katsuhiro, who establishes an ironic and grotesque tone in *The Order to Stop Construction*, which recounts the odyssey of a young engineer sent to supervise work on a completely automated building site in the heart of the Amazon. This entertaining re-reading of Joseph Conrad's *Heart of Darkness* becomes a subtle satire on the obsessive nature of modern man and his mania for technology. ● Made in 1983, the film was not screened until the 1987 Tokyo Science Fiction Film Festival and was, subsequently, badly let down by inadequate distribution, until it finally found an outlet on home video. ● D.D.G.

# MANIE MANIE MEIKYU MONOGATARI

FILM

MANIE MANIE MEIKYU MONOGATARI ● NEO TOKYO ● 1983 ● DIR & SCR & DES: RINTARO, KAWAJIRI YOSHIAKI, OTOMO KATSUHIRO ●
ANI: NAKAMURA TAKASHI ET AL ● MUS: YOSHINO MICKY ● PRD: MADHOUSE ● FILM ● DUR: 50 MINS

# MARIO

CHARACTER

The acrobatic antics of Mario, a plump Italian plumber, have entertained the world for over twenty years. Undoutedly one of the kings of the Japanese graphic culture, a survey from 1990 revealed that his celebrity had surpassed that of Walt Disney's Mickey Mouse among American children. Like the popular mouse, Mario stands out more for his distinctive features (the nose, the cap, the jumps) than for his part in any plot. Like Mickey, Miyamoto Shigeru's creation takes on a universal appeal due to his imperfections, but also his lack of reference to time and place. ● His image has endured throughout the decades, but Mario has only rarely crossed out of the world of videogames. Although Hollywood tried, with little success, to transform him into a film star in 1993 (after an animated television series in 1989), the only true Japanese anime is a medium-length film produced in 1986 and a short video series in 1989. In *Super Mario Brothers* Mario and his brother Luigi find themselves catapulted into the Mushroom Kingdom, where they experience a series of surreal adventures modelled on the game. This was a legitimate spin-off, but the franchise was short-lived. ● However, this has had no effect on the resounding success of the acrobatic plumber, particularly in games, from *Donkey Kong* (1981) to *Super Mario Galaxy* (2007). Dynamic and suited to comedic content, the sporty, cheeky Mario is the Charlie Chaplin of videogames, and the glorious heir to the success of traditional animation. ● E.H.

RIGHT: MARIO, THE WORLD'S MOST FAMOUS PLUMBER ENGAGED IN HIS COMICAL VIDEOGAME ADVENTURES

SUPER MARIO BROTHERS: PEACH-HIME KYUSHUTSU DAI SAKUSEN! ● SUPER MARIO BROTHERS ● 1986 ● DIR: HATA MASAMI ● SCR: TAKAHASHI HIDEO ● DES: NINTENDO ET AL ● ANI: MATSUIYAMA MAYA ● MUS: TEZUKA TAKASHI ● PRD: SUZUKI MASAKATSU & HATANO TSUNEMASA ● FILM ● DUR: 60 MINS

# MARUKO-CHAN

CHARAC

She is an untidy, insolent dreamer, a fervent reader of manga and always ready to challenge the authority of her parents or the domestic status quo. Young Maruko, third-year elementary student in a highly idealized district of Shizuoka City during the Seventies, is a loveable figure and was probably used by Usui Yoshito as the basis for his famous manga character little Shin-Chan. Maruko herself is based on the experiences of her creator, Sakura Momoko, who was born in Shizuoka, the youngest child of a middle-class family, and who became the subject of a long-running anime series entitled *Sazae-san* (1969), centred around the everyday lives of a family from the Tokyo suburbs. ● Characterized by an expressive yet synthetic style, the manga series *Chibi Maruko-chan* first appeared in 1986 in the children's magazine *Ribon*. In January 1990, Fuji TV began transmitting an anime series based on the manga, thereby breaking with the dominant trend in the audiovisual industry, which until that moment had never made a series specifically for pre-adolescent girls. The series was a success thanks to its edgy heroine and her capacity to confront with humour the change in values that took place in the Seventies and which challenged the traditional concepts of family authority. ● In 1993, Sakura decided to end the series, which had reached a record 39.9 per cent of television audiences and led to two successful feature-length films in 1990 and 1992, as well as a broad range of merchandise. However, this 'ending' proved to be a false alarm, since Sakura became involved in a second series, the first episode of which was released on 18 January 1995. The series is still on air and a live-action adaptation of *Chibi Maruko-chan* was commissioned for television in 2006. ● J.Co.

CHIBI MARUKO-CHAN ● 1990 ● DIR: SHIBAYAMA TSUTOMU ● SCR: SAKURA MOMOKO ● DES: SHIGETA YUJI ● ANI: YAMADA MICHISHIRO ET AL ● MUS: NAKAMURA NOBOYUKI, BB QUEENS ● PRD: NIPPON ANIMATION ● TV SERIES ● EPS: 846

# MASAKI TENCHI

CHARACTER

Masaki Tenchi is a normal seventeen-year-old Japanese boy; fresh-faced with a long black pigtail, he is often to be found helping out his grandfather, a Shinto priest. His peaceful existence is upset by the arrival of a lively (and sometimes vicious) entourage of women who descend from space: a delegation of enchanting princesses, girls with super-powers and assorted relations, who would throw the masculine pride of so many cartoon characters into confusion. Tenchi, on the contrary, has the patience of a saint. ● Tenchi, whose name in Japanese means 'heaven' and 'earth', becomes the sole focus of interest, not only for the ladies who crave his heart, but also for the viewer as his adventures lead him through space and time in a number of convoluted situations. ● From a production viewpoint, Tenchi is a lucky charm for AIC studio, which, in conjunction with Pioneer distribution, created an unstoppable machine capable of churning out OAVs, films and television series, as well as a manga by Okuda Hitoshi. A truly multifaceted, creative universe ranges from the *Tenchi Muyo!* (*No Need for Tenchi*, 1992) series to films such as *Tenchi in Love* (1996), in which designers and directors worked together with mixed results, both in terms of animation quality and originality of the proposed storylines. Occasionally, the saga has been entirely relaunched, reprising the narrative from various angles. ● Tenchi's science-fiction adventures include the obligatory nod to comedy and romance, with situations and gags familiar to fans of *Urusei Yatsura* (1981), in which a boy from Earth meets and falls in love with an alien girl, with the catastrophic consequences you might imagine. ● M.A.R.

TENCHI MUYO! ● NO NEED FOR TENCHI ● 1992 ●
DIR: HAYASHI HIROKI ET AL ● SCR: HASEGAWA
NAOKO ● DES & ANI: KAJISHIMA MASAKI ● MUS:
NAGAOKA SEIKO ● PRD: AIC ● VIDEO SERIES ●
EPS: 7

# MASAOKA KENZO

DIRECTOR

The grandfather of anime, a lover of music and art with the face of a dreamer, Masaoka Kenzo was an artist who knew how to seize the moment and he discovered the enchantment of the animated image. Every veteran refers to him when speaking of animation's noble heritage. ● Masaoka (born in 1898 in Osaka) devoted his life to art, from his student days in Kyoto to his time teaching his followers later in life. His first jobs at Makino Production as an assistant director or assistant set designer in the Twenties did not satisfy this turbulent character for long, and he soon chose the difficult path of independence and founded his own studio in 1925. He then went to Nikkatsu and to Shochiku studios, a transitional period during which he found in animation the ideal medium to give a new dimension to his artistic credo. ● Masaoka revolutionized the art of animation, doggedly completing the film *Saragushima* (*Monkey Island*, 1930) while at Nikkatsu studio. When Shochiku went over to sound in 1931, he directed the first cartoon 'talkie' – the short *Chikara to Onna no Yo no Naka* (*The World of Power and Women*), working alongside one of the best talents of the day, the animator Seo Mitsuyo. This was the beginning of a brilliant career that showcased not only Masaoka's sarcastic sense of humour but also his immense technical skill and visionary approach to animation as his work often disregards the propagandistic climate imposed by the government before and during the war to give free rein to fantasy and imagination. ● His masterpiece is *Kumo To Tulip* (*Spider and Tulip*, 1942), in which a singing spider tries to lure a ladybird into his web: the storm scene from this exhibits consummate skill and is still, deservedly, well known even today. Masaoka eventually abandoned the cinema for reasons of health and died in Osaka in 1988. ● M.A.R.

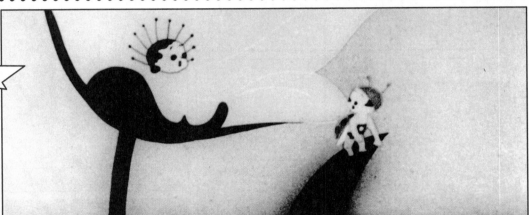

RIGHT: THE SINGER SPIDER AND CHARMING BUG IN MASAOKA'S
MASTERPIECE KUMO TO TULIP (1942, DIR. MASAOKA KENZO, 16 MINS)

M

SEE ALSO: MOCHINAGA TADAHITO; MOMOTARO; OFUJI NOBURO; YABUSHITA TAIJI

# MASHIMO KOICHI

DIRECTOR

Mashimo Koichi (born in 1952 in Tokyo) is best known not for any particular franchise, but for his attitude to the development of anime directors. After a near-fatal skiing accident in the Eighties, Mashimo developed the concept of an atelier studio for animators, or an 'animation-hospital', where artists could develop a sense of their own aesthetic and style, away from the commercial pressures of the conventional studio environment. His concept has parallels with the Japanese contemporary artist Murakami Takashi's Geisai college studio. In the Nineties, Mashimo outlined the concept for his studio to the President of Production I.G., Mitsuhisa Ishikawa, who was enthralled by the idea and agreed to fund it immediately. In 1997, Studio Bee Train opened its doors with its original ambition intact, to develop and nurture the work of aspiring anime artists. In 2006, Bee Train chose to become independent from Production I.G. ● Mashimo's work within the Bee Train studio context has primarily been to develop the work of other artists but, as the studio's main director, much of its output is shaped by him. His trilogy of films *Noir* (2001), *Madlax* (2004) and *El Cazador de la Bruja* (2007) are collectively known as the 'girls with guns' series and each features strong female protagonists and supporting characters. As a result, Mashimo has been positioned by critics as one of the leading auteurs within the genre where strong protagonists and narratives featuring intense emotional interactions between women play a central role. ● D.S.

*SEE ALSO: I.G.*

- - - - - - - - - - - - - - - - - - - - - - - - - - - - - - - - - - - - - - - - - - - - - - - - - - - - - - - - - - - - -

# MATSUMOTO LEIJI

DIRECTOR

In the epilogue to his very sombre manga *Barbara* (1974), the great Tezuka Osamu features one of his draughtsmen colleagues, a *mangaka* who assisted him for a short time in the mid-Fifties and for whom he had deep (reciprocated) admiration – being invited to meet Tezuka's provocative heroine. Twenty-nine years later, the French electro group Daft Punk produced an animated feature film to accompany their album *Discovery*, with its eighties disco-pop resonances. The same draughtsman was to design this anime, called *Interstella 5555: The 5tory of the 5ecret 5tar 5ystem* (2001, dir. Takenouchi Kazuhisa et al), showcasing his inimitable graphic style. ● The man in question is a living legend of manga and Japanese animation. Born Matsumoto Akira in 1938 and renaming himself Leiji (or 'warrior zero') in 1965, he has authored a considerable body of work: *Sexaroïd* (1968), *L'Oiseau bleu* (*Mêterurinku No Aoi Tori: Chiruchiru Michiru No Bôken Ryokô*, 1980) and *Gun Frontier* (1972) being just a few examples. A lover of adventure and flying machines, Matsumoto is also passionate on the subject of World War II, a conflict in which his father, an air force officer, lost his life. Some of Matsumoto's manga on this topic were adapted for the screen under the title *The Cockpit* (1993, dir. Kawajiri Yoshiaki et al). ● After his success as a *mangaka*, Matsumoto Leiji launched into animation in 1974, generating large numbers of cinema and television adaptations of his works. He withdrew from animation after the mid-Eighties, notably because of problems with the rights to his designs, but today he is involved in an increasing number of projects, one of them involving publishing manga on the Internet. This is in addition to keeping his most famous, continuously developing creations in public view. The father of some eminently romantic figures, willowy Queen Emeraldas and the dark space-pirate Harlock among them, has certainly not uttered his last word. ● E.H.

*SERIES BASED ON MATSUMOTO LEIJI'S MANGA ● ABOVE LEFT: THE CAST OF SPACE PIRATE CAPTAIN HARLOCK (1978, DIR. RINTARO, FUKUSHIMA KAZUMI, 42 EPS) ● ABOVE RIGHT & RIGHT: MAETEL AND TETSURO ON BOARD THE GALAXY EXPRESS 999 (1978, DIR. NISHIZAWA NOBUTAKA ET AL, 113 EPS)*

*SEE ALSO: DANGUARD ACE; HARLOCK; INTERSTELLA 5555; ISHINOMORI SHOTARO; MAETEL; TEZUKA OSAMU*

# MAYA

From her very first appearance it is clear that Maya is an unusual bee. With her thick blonde hair, stubborn character and tendency to talk too much and ask questions all the time, Maya exhibits charm and *joie de vivre*, curiosity and tenacity. Having been entrusted to the care of the grown-up bee Cassandra, with whom she makes her first short explorations inside and outside the hive, Maya then decides to leave her small world and savour life in the surrounding forest – a harmonious environment, albeit one full of surprises and dangers. ● Maya's faithful friend Willy is always by her side; lazy, funny and certainly less brave than his fellow traveller. Together, the two of them discover the world of other insects and see life in the forest, a setting depicted with light-hearted irony. They make many friends, from the wise grasshopper Flip to the cross spider Thecla, from the mouse Alexander to Max the worm. ● *Maya the Bee* was a series made especially for children. Co-produced by the Japanese company Nippon Animation and the Austro-German company Apollo Film, the series was based on the short stories of German writer Waldemar Bonsels, *The Adventures of Maya the Bee* and *Heaven Folk*. ● Its educational content is derived from descriptions of the world Maya inhabits; plants, flowers and the exemplary balance of nature are clearly reflected in the fluid drawings and bright colours. The forest is described with realistic attention to detail, while the characters are brought to life each with individual features that differentiate them from one another and identify them as belonging to different species. ● G.P.

*LEFT & ABOVE: MAYA THE BEE AND HER INSECT FRIENDS FROM THE FOREST, ALL CHARACTERS FROM THE 1975 SERIES MAYA THE BEE*

MITSUBACHI MAYA NO BOKEN ● MAYA THE BEE ● 1975 ● DIR: SAITO HIROSHI, ENDO SEIJI, KAMINASHI MITSUO ● SCR: SASA HIKARU, KANAZAWA HITOSHI ● DES: SHIRAUME SUSAMU ● ANI: NOBE TOSHIO, OGAWA TAKAO ● MUS: OGAKI TAKESHI ● PRD: APOLLO FILM, NIPPON ANIMATION ● TV SERIES ● EPS: 55

# MAZINGER Z

A robot of gigantic proportions, a cross between medieval armoured knight and evocation of Lucifer, *Mazinger Z* laid the foundations of the mecha genre. Constructed by Professor Kabuto Juzo from an imaginary alloy – Chogokin Z – to counter the megalomaniacal plans of the diabolical Dr Hell, Mazinger Z is piloted by its creator's grandson, Kabuto Koji, in a succession of battles against evil mechanical monsters. Kabuto, an impetuous teenager, controls the robot from within a flying vehicle that attaches to the giant's head. ● A great icon of seventies pop culture, *Mazinger Z* introduced the mecha concept to the western imagination and brought substantial innovation to the basic model established by *Tetsujin 28-go* (*Gigantor*, 1963). The symbiosis between man and machine – with the giant robot designed as a hyperbolic second skin for its human pilot – and the concept of cybernetic beings, the sum of different parts, find their initial model in Nagai's creation, an idea that would later reach its culmination in *Transformers*. ● Born almost simultaneously in the pages of *Shonen Jump* magazine and on Fuji TV in 1972, *Mazinger Z* combines an eccentric sense of humour, a taste for the bizarre (see, for example, the evil hermaphrodite, Baron Ashura), frequent recourse to melodramatic explosions and an overly sexualized style as demonstrated by the breast-missiles of Aphrodite A (the first female robot in anime). ● J.Co.

SCENES FROM THE FIRST TWO SERIES OF **MAZINGER Z**, BEGUN IN 1972 ● ABOVE RIGHT: GREAT MAZINGER, FROM THE SECOND TV SERIES ● RIGHT: THE SCIENTIST KABUTO JUZO ● BELOW: THE TWO DANGEROUS ENEMIES OF MAZINGER Z, BARON ASHURA (LEFT) AND DR HELL (RIGHT)

MAZINGER Z ● 1972 ● DIR: SERIKAWA YUGO ET AL ● SCR: TAKAHISA SUSUMU ET AL ● DES: NAGAI GO ● ANI: UEMURA KOJI ET AL ● MUS: WATANABE HIROAKI ● PRD: TOEI ANIMATION ● TV SERIES ● EPS: 92

# MELMO

CHARACTER

What a strange character Melmo is! Her huge eyes make her visually typical of *shojo* manga and, as we might expect from one of Tezuka Osamu's characters, she is resourceful, full of life and has a burning curiosity about all things. But it is hard to find anything linking her and the well-behaved world of children's cartoons. Melmo, extremely vivacious and with a lack of awareness that sometimes catapults her into a big mess, is the antithesis of the classic children's character. Orphaned at nine years old when her mother dies in an accident, the young Melmo is left to look after her brothers. From heaven her mother, worried that her young daughter is unable to look after the family, gives her a candy jar containing red and blue sweets, which miraculously allow her to grow older or younger. In the hands of the little heroine, however, a bonbon often leads to trouble. ● Melmo is the leading character of a famous manga by Tezuka, adapted into an animated series in 1971, during the great creator's darkest period. The anime was intended as part of a larger artistic project: a trilogy on sex education directed at young people, this being a concern already present in other works. In this case, however, Melmo created many difficulties for her author and the cartoon, aired in Japan and Italy, attracted controversy and complaints from outraged parents. This controversy destabilizes the almost Disney-like aura attributed to Tezuka by western critics. ● M.A.R.

FUSHIGI NA MELMO ● MARVELLOUS MELMO ● 1971 ● DIR & SCR: TEZUKA OSAMU ET AL ● DES: TEZUKA OSAMU ● ANI: YAMAMOTO SHIGERU, OKADA TOSHIYASU ● MUS: UNO SEIICHIRO ● PRD: MUSHI PRODUCTION ● TV SERIES ● EPS: 26

# MEMOLE

Little Memole, a lovely inhabitant of the planet Rilulu, can fit in the palm of a hand. She arrives on Earth by chance, on board a spaceship carrying 245 fellow travellers, and her curiosity and bravery help her make the most important discovery of her life. After hearing an unfamiliar tune, Memole ventures out into the human world and discovers the big house where Marielle – a weak little girl suffering from a serious illness – lives. Memole watches her secretly through the window and thinks about her often. Indeed, she is driven to return to that house several times. One day, by chance, one of her tears touches Marielle's lips and suddenly the girl seems to get well and gain strength. They become close friends and their friendship increases with each adventure. ● The anime *Little Memole* is a tale of partnership and bravery. Rather than being a story about growing up, the series is an exploration of life's wonders though the two main characters: Marielle, a little girl who has just discovered life thanks to her sudden cure, and wise, generous Memole, full of enthusiasm to learn everything she can about her new surroundings. The style supports the deliciously didactic function of the series, using delicate colours, simple lines and repetitive backgrounds full of gentle poetry. Everything exists in an exemplary, simple balance, as in a fairytale, shrouded in sweet, melancholic nostalgia. Following the great success of the series, Toei Animation also made the special *Tongari Boushi no Memoru: Marielle no Housekibako* (*Memole in the Pointed Hat: Marielle's Jewelbox*, 1985), a sixteen-minute film directed by Nakura Yasuhiro. ● G.P.

RIGHT: MEMOLE AND HER COLOURFUL FRIENDS FROM PLANET RILULU, STARS OF THE 1984 SERIES MEMOLE AND HER POINTED HAT

TONGARI NO BOSHI MEMORU ● MEMOLE AND HER POINTED HAT ● AKA LITTLE MEMOLE ● 1984 ● DIR: KASAI OSAMU ET AL ● SCR: YUKIMURO SHUNICHI ET AL ● DES: SUZUKI GINICHIRO ● ANI: OWASHI HIDETOSHI ET AL ● MUS: AOKI NOZOMI ● PRD: TOEI ANIMATION ● TV SERIES ● EPS: 50

*Memories* is the most famous of the episodic feature films involving Otomo Katsuhiro. In the first part, *Magnetic Rose*, directed by Morimoto Koji, a group of astronauts come upon an asteroid where stands an old opera house that belonged to a famous opera singer many years before. The theatre's computer restages, in the form of disturbing holograms, the memories and desires of its former owner. In *Stink Bomb*, Okamura Tensai's contribution, the atmosphere is one of devilish fun, as we observe the misadventures of a young employee of a pharmaceutical company who, having swallowed a pill to cure a minor cold, becomes a human 'stink bomb', sowing panic in the streets of Tokyo. The final part, *Cannon Fodder*, is set in a post-punk-styled city in which the entire apathetic population has only a single objective: to shoot with huge guns at an invisible enemy located beyond the clouds. ● Otomo's long-awaited return to directing after the colossal success of *Akira* (1988), *Memories* is still considered to be one of the most technically brilliant moments in Japanese animation. *Magnetic Rose* offers a taste of the poetry of dreams and hallucinations and was scripted by screenwriter Kon Satoshi. *Stink Bomb*, on the other hand, is a return to the anti-militaristic satire already explored in *Roujin Z* (1991, dir. Kitakubo Hiroyuki), a film describing a robotic prototype that disastrously escapes from the hands of the army. However, the most interesting episode is directed by Otomo himself; *Cannon Fodder* is a jewel of twenty-three minutes that fascinates with its atypical aesthetics and language. Developed as a single sequence with an opaque graphic style echoing Moebius' European comics, the piece explores, with dry narration, Otomo's rejection of obtuse totalitarian and warmongering regimes, as is summarized in the question the child protagonist asks his father in the final scene, 'But who are we fighting against?' ● S.G.

# MEMORIES

FILM

ABOVE: ONE OF THE ASTRONAUTS IN *MAGNETIC ROSE* (DIR. MORIMOTO KOJI), THE FIRST PART OF THE ANTHOLOGY FILM, *MEMORIES* (1995), DIRECTED BY OTOMO KATSUHIRO

*MEMORIES* ● 1995 ● DIR: MORIMOTO KOJI, OKAMURA TENSAI, OTOMO KATSUHIRO ● SCR: OTOMO KATSUTURO, KON SATOSHI ● DES: INOUE TOSHIYUKI ET AL ● ANI: KAWAJIRI YOSHIAKI ● MUS: ISHINO TAKUYA ET AL ● PRD: MADHOUSE ● FILM ● DUR: 115 MINS

# MIDO MIKO

CHARACTER

The manga and anime series *La Blue Girl*, written by Maeda Toshio, is best known for its erotic horror visuals. Like many of his other works, including most notably *Urotsukidoji* (*Legend of the Overfiend*, 1987), *La Blue Girl* features tentacle rape scenes, the invention of which Maeda would likely claim as his own, and public outcry over such explicit sex anime has often cast a shadow over the huge success of the franchise. ● The story follows the exploits of Mido Miko, an apprentice ninja and future leader of her clan, the Miroku. Using the power of a special talisman, the Miroku clan exert control over a race of bestial demons, the Shikima, and contain their violence. However, when thieves steal this talisman, chaos ensues and Mido Miko must subdue the sex-crazed ranks of the Shikima by force. Sex serves a number of mediating functions in the world of *La Blue Girl*: sex magic enables, for example, the movement of characters to and from the world of the Shikima. It also served to make the series one of the signature censorship cases of the Nineties. ● Outside of Japan, *La Blue Girl* courted controversy for its erotic scenes and was heavily censored for European and American territories. Most famously, it was banned outright for sale on video in the United Kingdom. Along with *Urotsukidoji*, *La Blue Girl*'s unapologetic sexuality arrived at a time when anime and manga were first penetrating mainstream markets. Many of the press controversies over the adult nature of anime cite *La Blue Girl* and fail to recognize how its quirky humour and visual puns act as a foil to the sexual scenarios. ● D.S.

*INJU GAKUEN* ● *LA BLUE GIRL* ● 1992 ● DIR: KAN FUKUMOTO ● SCR: ICHIRYU MEGUMI ● DES: YOSHIMOTO KINJI ● ANI: BIBANBA MIKI, SHIN RIN ● MUS: TAKAHAMA TERUO ● PRD: DAIEI ● VIDEO SERIES ● EPS: 4

---

# MIKIMOTO HARUHIKO

CHARA DESI

Character designer, illustrator and mangaka Mikimoto Haruhiko (born in 1959 in Tokyo) is a constant presence in the animation business. His unmistakable style is at the centre of all his artistic work, from his illustrations for publishers such as Kadokawa Shoten, to his character designs for animation and videogames. Well known for his work on series such as *Macross* (1982, dir. Ishiguro Noburo) and *Mobile Suit Gundam* (1979, dir. Tomino Yoshiyuki), he is also the creator of more pragmatic and reserved characters than those usually found in manga and anime. A dreamer who combines a passion for drawing with extreme perfectionism, Mikimoto – a member of the same generation as Kawamori Shoji and Yuki Nobuteru – makes inspired stylistic choices. His signature devices (girls to fall in love with, graceful pop starlets and expressive eyes) and use of sensual, adult themes create an updated, youthful example of the melodramatic seventies epic. ● Mikimoto is also always ready to stretch the boundaries of any narrative genre, as in movies with ecological themes such as *Tottoi* (*The Secret of the Seal*, 1992, dir. Ishiguro Noboru) and *Coo: Tooi Umi Kara Kita Coo* (*Coo of the Far Seas*, 1993, dir. Imazawa Tetsu). ● M.A.R.

LEFT: MIKIMOTO HARUHIKO'S ILLUSTRATION OF CHRISTINA MCKENZIE AND OTHER CHARACTERS HE CREATED FOR *MOBILE SUIT GUNDAM 0080: WAR IN THE POCKET* (1989, DIR. TAKAYAMA FUMIHIKO, OAV SERIES) ● BELOW: MIKIMOTO'S CHARACTER LYNN MINMAY, SINGING STAR OF *MACROSS* (1982, DIR. ISHIGURO NOBURO ET AL)

SEE ALSO: GUNDAM; HARA KEIICHI; KAWAMORI SHOJI; KITAZUME HIROYUKI; MACROSS

# MINASE TAKI

CHARACTER

With his scrubbed face and innocent gaze, Minase Taki appears to be the perfect schoolboy, but things are rarely what they seem in the anime world. Like the character Light in *Death Note* (2006), Minase reveals his hidden side after he finds a strange book. ● Minase begins practising black magic from the book and finds that its extreme sexual effects can benefit him and some of his friends, but it is not long before he is caught up in the satanic plotting of Dr Kitami Reika, the black-hearted evil genius of the series. She has a range of secret aphrodisiac spells and is endowed with a clitoris that can morph into an impressive penis. Kitami easily seduces the schoolboys, coupling with them in every conceivable way. ● *Bible Black* is one of the most popular of the new-generation *hentai*, but Hamuo's anime does not offer any great technical surprises. The artwork is precise but conventional and his use of music to heighten the atmosphere at moments of climax is predictable but effective. Jutting breasts, voluptuous bodies and phalluses of awesome dimensions complete the familiar repertoire. ● The narrative structure is more complex, played out on two different temporal planes, allowing the characters a certain amount of free will, and the plot hinges on this struggle against a predestined damnation. The anime avoids any overtly sadomasochistic content and instead dwells upon a cliché of this genre: sex as a manifestation of power over others. This time, however, a woman appropriates the active role, which is rare in pornography. ● C.C.

*BIBLE BLACK* ● 2001 ● DIR: HAMUO ET AL ● SCR: MUTO YASUYUKI ● DES: YOSHITEN ● ANI: YOSHITEN, YAMAGUCHI WATARU ● MUS: MORIHIDE ● PRD: MILKY ● VIDEO SERIES ● EPS: 6

*Mind Game* is an adaptation of a manga by Robin Nishi and the brainchild of director Yuasa Maasaki. The film, produced by Studio 4°C, tells the story of a reclusive young man, Nishi, who has fallen deeply in love with his childhood companion Myon. When they meet in a local café, two *yakuza* thugs arrive, a scuffle ensues and Nishi is brutally murdered. The action then shifts to the afterlife, where Nishi negotiates a return to his body and a reversal of time. He returns just before his death and, through a swift manoeuvre, grabs a gun and kills the gangster who was to kill him. Nishi, Myon and her sister steal the *yakuzas*' Cadillac and go on the run, Nishi high on the adrenaline of dying, beating God, and becoming the hero. A sudden twist of the wheel sees them drive off the edge of the highway into the sea and, at that very moment, a huge whale rises out of the water to swallow them and their car in one gulp. In the belly of this whale, they meet an old man and, in the process of becoming reconciled to their fate, confront their own personalities and inner demons. ● An avant-garde directorial approach was needed to best explore the surreal world of the original manga and *Mind Game* is distinguished by its shifting visual style, which could be described as having a 'collage' aesthetic. Photographic elements intermingle with traditional anime methods and direct animation; keyframed sequences combine with straight-ahead animation – the overall effect is a constantly shifting and emotionally resonant world of subjective views and twisting bodies. This aesthetic marries well with the changing narrative expectations that emerge in Nishi's manga. ● D.S.

# MIND GAME

FILM

ABOVE: IMAGE FROM THE SURREAL WORLD OF *MIND GAME*, THE 2004 FILM BY YUASA MASAAKI

*MIND GAME* ● 2004 ● DIR & SCR: YUASA MASAAKI ● DES: SUEYOSHI YUICHIRO ● ANI: SUEYOSHI YUICHIRO ET AL ● MUS: YAMAMOTO SEIJI, KANNO YOKU ● PRD: STUDIO 4°C ● FILM ● DUR: 103 MINS

# MITAMURA YAKKO

CHARACTER

Two chance meetings on a rainy day change the life of young Yakko forever. Daughter of chef Mitamura Shige, Yakko is a kind, modest and considerate girl who adores working alongside her grumpy father and has a soft spot for musician Satomi. But everything changes when she meets little Hashizo Kato – who is lost and upset – and his pet cat. Yakko helps him, takes him home and feeds him while learning all about his life. He's an orphan who was raised by his brother, Kato Go, the lead-singer of a pop group. By chance, Yakko meets Kato Go that same day. The story thereafter follows the lives of these two new friends, in a story of friendship that later turns into love. ● Produced by Toei Animation, television series *Ai Shite Night* (*Love in Rock'n'Roll*) has an earnest and at times naive storyline, clearly intended for a young audience. It contains all the classic ingredients: an innocently beautiful girl, a father who is strict but deeply fond of his daughter and two young friends vying for the attention and love of the leading character. All the conventions of teenage fiction are adhered to – including amusing scenes connected to the supporting characters and a predictable but essential happy ending. The series is animated in a basic and raw style, with the focus placed on the characters and plot. It's a coming-of-age story, following the journey from adolescence to adulthood, and this tone reflects the extreme simplicity of the manga it was inspired by. Of particular note is the portrayal of the early eighties Japanese pop scene; for his depiction of Go's band, Beehive, author Tada Kaoru looked to successful Japanese bands such as The Stalin, Novela, Primadonna and 44 Magnum for inspiration. ● G.P.

RIGHT: SCENES FROM THE 1983 FILM AI SHITE NIGHT, FEATURING YAKKO, HASHIZO AND JULIANO THE CAT

AI SHITE NIGHT ● AKA: LOVE IN ROCK'N'ROLL ● 1983 ● DIR: KASAI OSAMU ET AL ● SCR: MAJIMA MITSURU ET AL ● DES & ANI: YAMAGUCHI YASUHIRO ET AL ●
MUS: AOKI NOZOMI ● PRD: TOEI ANIMATION ● TV SERIES ● EPS: 42

# MIYAZAKI HAYAO

DIRECTOR

Miyazaki Hayao (born in 1941 in Tokyo) is one of the most important figures in the history of anime. A manga writer, cartoonist, director (he won the Golden Bear at the 2002 Berlin Film Festival and an Oscar with *Spirited Away*), scriptwriter and producer, Miyazaki is an extraordinarily complex character. From his father, an aeronautical engineer, he inherited a passion for all things mechanical, especially cars and planes. Films such as *My Neighbour Totoro*, however, where Miyazaki arguably deals with his mother's long-term illness, also exhibit emotional sensibility and complexity. ● Despite gaining a degree in Political Science and Economics, in 1963 Miyazaki succumbed to his passion for drawing and joined Toei Animation as an animator. He debuted as a director in 1978 with television series *Future Boy Conan* and in film with *The Castle of Cagliostro* (1979). His golden moment came when, along with Takahata Isao, he established the independent Studio Ghibli – referring to the World War II Italian scouting planes, a symbol of longed-for artistic freedom. ● The first film produced by the studio was *Laputa: Castle in the Sky* (1986), the year after the studio's founding. Its success owes itself to various factors: a respect for, and almost maniacal attention to detail and poetry and a heart-rending tenderness of the characters; a very personal reconciliation of Japanese and western culture and design resulting in a new visual world; and above all, moral rectitude, a reluctance to distinguish clearly between good and evil, which leaves the viewer with a fresh view of the world. ● F.L.

SCENES SHOWING THE MANY UNIQUE CHARACTERS OF MIYAZAKI HAYAO ● TOP LEFT: THE AVIATORS PORCO ROSSO AND DONALD CURTIS (*PORCO ROSSO*, 1992, DIR. MIYAZAKI HAYAO, PRD. SUZUKI TOSHIO ET AL, 93 MINS) ● TOP RIGHT: KIKI AND TONBO (*KIKI'S DELIVERY SERVICE*, 1989, DIR. MIYAZAKI HAYAO, PRD. SUZUKI TOSHIO ET AL, 102 MINS) ● ABOVE LEFT: HEEN (THE DOG), MARKL AND TURNIPHEAD (*HOWL'S MOVING CASTLE*, 2004, DIR. MIYAZAKI HAYAO, PRD. SUZUKI TOSHIO ET AL, 119 MINS) ● ABOVE RIGHT: PONYO AND SOSUKE (*PONYO ON THE CLIFF BY THE SEA*, 2008, DIR. MIYAZAKI HAYAO, PRD. SUZUKI TOSHIO ET AL, 100 MINS) ● RIGHT (TOP): CHIHIRO AND KAMAJI (*SPIRITED AWAY*, 2001, DIR. MIYAZAKI HAYAO, PRD. SUZUKI TOSHIO ET AL, 125 MINS) ● RIGHT: SOPHIE AND HOWL (*HOWL'S MOVING CASTLE*)

M

SEE ALSO: CHIHIRO; CONAN; HOLMES, SHERLOCK; HOWL'S MOVING CASTLE; KIKI; LAPUTA; LUPIN III; NAUSICAÄ; PONYO; PORCO ROSSO; SAN; TOTORO

# MIYU

CHARACTER

Cruel and wilful but beautiful and always well dressed, Miyu adds an unsettling gothic note to the streets of Kyoto, clad in creepily outdated fashions from the pre-war era. Like Japanese tradition itself, she is ever-present in the modern world and yet often dark, inscrutable and at odds with modernity. ● Anne Rice's novel *Interview With the Vampire* was translated into Japanese as *Daybreak's Vampire* in 1979 and it remains as popular in Japanese as in English and has inspired many imitators. Kakinouchi Narumi's 1988 manga owes a clear debt to Rice's character Claudia in its character Miyu, a much older vampire trapped in the body of a little girl. The story was adapted into anime by Kakinouchi's husband Hirano Toshiki, first on video, then as a television series. ● Miyu, whose name means 'evening beauty', has retained many of her childish ways in adulthood. She can be capricious and cruel and justifies her predation by only taking blood from those who offer it willingly. Indeed, much of her vampirism flies in the face of European tradition – she is not harmed by crucifixes or garlic, and can see her reflection in mirrors. Instead, her adventures feminize and reverse many of the traditions of western vampire lore, as she preys upon or obsesses over male love objects. ● Miyu is a mainstream incarnation of a creation from Japanese erotica – the 'Lolita', who combines youthful looks with adult sophistication. But by defiantly reasserting Japan's past within its present, she is also the forerunner of every temple girl and shrine maiden in modern anime. ● J.Cl.

IMAGES FROM THE 1988 VIDEO SERIES *VAMPIRE PRINCESS MIYU* ●
TOP LEFT: A SKETCH BY THE CREATOR KAKINOUCHI NARUMI ● TOP RIGHT:
THE FEMALE VAMPIRE, MIYU ● RIGHT: AN INTENSE CLOSE-UP OF MIYU'S
COMPANION LARVA

KYUKETSUKI MIYU ● VAMPIRE PRINCESS MIYU ● 1988 ● DIR: HIRANO TOSHIHIRO
● SCR: AIKAWA NOBORU, HAYAMI YUI ● DES: KAKINOUCHI NARUMI ET AL ●
ANI: NISHII MASAHIRO ● MUS: KAWAI KENJI ● PRD: AIC ● VIDEO SERIES ●
EPS: 4

# MOCHINAGA TADAHITO

DIRECTOR

Mochinaga Tadahito (1919–1999) is one of the most fascinating figures in the history of Japanese animation, whose influence spans six decades. After graduating from the Japan School of the Arts, he worked under Seo Mitsuyo on several anime during World War II. During this period, Mochinaga built anime's first multiplane camera, to allow for several cels to be shot at once, and provided key animation on the propaganda cartoon *Momotaro's Sea Eagles* (1943). ● After losing his home in a bombing raid, he moved to Japanese-occupied Manchuria, to work in a local film studio. Marooned at the end of the war, however, he then adopted the Chinese name Fang Ming and was instrumental in establishing the Shanghai Animation Studio – still one of the top production houses in China. ● Returning to Japan in 1953, Mochinaga worked largely in stop-motion animation and in advertising, where he produced the award-winning series of adverts *Beer Through the Ages* (1956). After his *Little Black Sambo* (1956) won Best Children's Film at the Vancouver Film Festival, he founded MOM Films, which produced several American stop-motion television movies for the Rankin/Bass production company, including *Rudolph the Red-Nosed Reindeer* (1964). ● In later life, Mochinaga returned to China, where he taught at the Beijing Film Academy and worked as a news producer for China Broadcasting. His last film, *Boy and the Badger*, was released in 1992. ● J.Cl.

SEE ALSO: HAKUJADEN; KAWAMOTO KIHACHIRO; MOMOTARO; OFUJI NOBURO; YABUSHITA TAIJI

# MOCHIZUKI TOMOMI

DIRECTOR

Mochizuki Tomomi (born in 1958 in Hokkaido) signed up for the local anime club when he was studying at Waseda University in Tokyo. He joined the anime company Asia-do straight out of college, working first as a production manager on the modern-day magic serial *Tokimeki Tonight* (1982). ● His directorial debut was the first episode of *Twilight Q* (1987), intended as a showcase for new directors in the style of the US series *Twilight Zone*. The series, however, was a commercial flop, and the only directors represented were Mochizuki and the then-unknown Oshii Mamoru. Mochizuki's later work is characterized by a focus on feminine themes – school stories, girls' sports and romance – including Hikari no Densetsu (*Legend of Light*, 1986) and *Kimagure Orange Road* (1986). Aged thirty-four, Mochizuki wrote, directed and storyboarded the series *Koko Wa Greenwood* (*Here is Greenwood*, 1991), widely regarded as his masterpiece. When he was offered the director's job on *Umi ga Kikoeru* (*Ocean Waves*, 1993), he was unable to resist the temptation to adapt a much-loved book. The first Studio Ghibli production not to be directed by Miyazaki Hayao or Takahata Isao, *Ocean Waves* was a television movie left to young staffers to make quickly, cheaply and with quality. Mochizuki's work was acclaimed but ran over budget and the combined stress and over-work left him briefly hospitalized. ● Mochizuki continues to multitask in the anime world under the pseudonym Sakamoto Go, and writes scripts for many of the anime that he continues to direct. ● J.Cl.

SEE ALSO: KEI & YURI; KASUGA KYOSUKE; MAISON IKKOKU; SAOTOME RANMA

# MOMOTARO

CHARACTER

The Momotaro of legend was the epitome of Japanese boyhood – a bold, adventurous child who befriends a group of domestic animals and leads them in an attack on demonic adversaries. In World War II, he was used as an icon of the Japanese navy in the first feature-length anime, a propaganda film released in the closing stages of the war. ● Podgy, strident and creepily resolute, this infamous incarnation of the folk-tale Momotaro was intended to instil a dramatic, martial spirit into Japanese children. Instead, he survives today as an unsettling image of 1945 Japan – single-minded, fearless and devoted to the defeat of the horned 'demons' who have invaded the South Pacific islands that Japan claimed as her own. He is also strangely lifeless, thanks to the breakneck pace and limited conditions under which director Seo Mitsuyo was forced to work. With materials in short supply, Seo was forced to scour his artwork with acid to reuse the cels up to four times, giving later scenes in the film a murky, bleak quality, scratched and faded, as if dying before our eyes. ● Momotaro was lucky to survive the war. Occupying American forces tried to destroy all copies, and a lone print resurfaced in the corner of an archive in 1983. We are fortunate to gain this glimpse of a bygone age, as Momotaro and his animal friends embark on training exercises, watch a shadow-play about the evils of western imperialism, and then liberate the grateful creatures of a Pacific island from evil demons – voiced, in a chilling English-language scene, by unidentified prisoners of war. The Pacific saved from invaders, Momotaro and his friends prepare for their next mission, practising parachute landings onto a target shaped like the USA. ● J.Cl.

ABOVE: SCENES FROM THE 1945 FILM MOMOTARO'S DIVINE SEA WARRIORS SHOWING THE MILITARY ADVENTURES OF MOMOTARO THE SOLDIER, A LEGEND REVIVED FOR PATRIOTIC PURPOSES

MOMOTARO UMI NO SHINPEI ● MOMOTARO'S DIVINE SEA WARRIORS ● 1945 ● DIR: SEO MITSUYO ● SCR: KUMAKI KIICHIRO ●
DES: SEO MITSUYO ● ANI: SEO MITSUYO, TAKAGI ICHIRO ● MUS: KOSEKI YUJI ● PRD: SHOCHIKU ● FILM ● DUR: 74 MINS

M

Mori Yasugi (born in 1925 in Tottori) grew up in Taiwan but returned to Japan where he graduated as an architect in Tokyo. A handful of dazzling American short films inspired him to devote himself to animation and he began his career at the Nippon Doga (or Japan Animation) studio. He was true pioneer in an industry still in its infancy and even today he exerts a great influence on the work of such masters as Miyazaki Hayao. Mori worked with the future director of *Princess Mononoke* (1997, dir. Miyazaki Hayao) when he was an animator and character designer at Toei Animation. ● His animated output is distinguished by the naturalism of the characters' fluid body movements. The most famous of his titles are *Hakujaden* (*Legend of the White Snake*, released in the USA as *Panda and the Magic Serpent*, 1958, dir. Yabushita Taiji); *Wankapu Oji no Orochi Taiji* (*Little Prince and Eight-Headed Dragon*, 1963, dir. Serikawa Yugo), where, for the first time in the history of Japanese animation, he took the role of sole director of animation; *Puss 'n' Boots* (1969, dir. Yabuki Kimio); and especially *Little Norse Prince* (1968, dir. Takahata Isao). ● His contribution to the golden age of Japanese animated films ended in 1973 when Mori moved to Nippon Animation. There, he focused primarily on television series and again worked with Miyazaki and Takahata. His efforts are evident in *Heidi* (1974, dir. Takahata Isao), *Dog of Flanders* (1975, dir. Kuroda Yoshio) and, later, in *Future Boy Conan* (1978, dir. Miyazaki Hayao et al), where Miyazaki asked him to assume the role of animation supervisor. Mori is also celebrated for his work as an illustrator of children's books. ● D.D.G.

# MORI YASUJI

ANIMATI
DIRECT

ABOVE: ANIMAL CHARACTERS FROM *LEGEND OF THE WHITE SNAKE* (1958, DIR. YABUSHITA TAIJI, 78 MINS), A FILM THAT MORI WORKED ON AS AN ANIMATOR

SEE ALSO: CONAN; GHIBLI; HAKUJADEN; HEIDI; HOLS; MIYAZAKI HAYAO; NIPPON ANIMATION; PERO; TAKAHATA ISAO; TOEI ANIMATION

Morimoto Koji is a virtuoso animator, a collaborator of some of the greatest anime masters and an independent visionary. In 1986, he co-founded Studio 4°C with producer Tanaka Eiko and her colleague, animator Sato Toshiharu, in order to encourage anime directors' artistic freedom. ● Inclined to elegance, harmony and attention to the smallest detail he became a key animator on *Space Adventure Cobra* (1982, dir. Dezaki Osamu et al), *Macross* (1982, dir. Ishiguro Noburo) and *Dirty Pair* (1985, dir. Yatabe Katsuyoshi et al) before meeting mangaka Otomo Katsuhiro. After working as an animation director on the film adaptation of Katsuhiro's *Akira* (1988) together with Nakamura Takashi, Morimoto turned to directing. He took part in two famous anthology films – *Robot Carnival* (1987) and *Memories* (1996); his contribution to the first was a robot version of the Frankenstein myth while his work for the second redefines the space-opera genre. In 1991, Morimoto completed his first feature film, *Tobe! Kujira no peek* (known in English as *Fly Peek!* or *Peek the Baby Whale*, among other titles), which remains his only work of this length. ● Morimoto works constantly and has collaborated on a wide range of shorts. A great music-lover, making music videos for acts including Ishii Ken, Utada Hikaru and The Bluetones, has been a major aspect of his work. He also contributed to the anthology *Animatrix* (2003), for which he made the ghostly *Beyond* and has made a series of exceptionally innovative shorts, including *Eternal Family* (1997), a singular work using shapes, spaces and perspectives enriched to explore the possibilities offered by computer graphics. His *Onkyo Seimeitai Noiseman* (*Noiseman*, 1997) is a symphony overflowing with sound and colour, somewhere between naive and abstract; half oppressive, half enchanting. In 2005 Morimoto announced his second feature-length film; *Genius Party Beyond – Dimension Bomb Part B* was released in 2008. ● E.H.

# MORIMOTO KOJI

DIRECTOR

ABOVE: SCENE FROM THE FILM *GENIUS PARTY BEYOND – DIMENSION BOMB PART B* (2008, DIR. MORIMOTO KOJI)

167

SEE ALSO: .HACK; 4°C; ANIMATRIX; DUKE TOGO; KEI & YURI; MEMORIES; ROUJIN Z

# MORIYAMA YUJI

Moriyama Yuji (born in 1960) left high school to work in a newspaper advertising department, before joining the anime company Studio Musashi. Drifting through jobs at several small studios, he worked as an animator on shows such as *Planet Robo Danguard Ace* (1977, dir. Katsumata Tomoharu) and *Galaxy Express 999* (1978, dir. Nishizawa Nobutaka et al) before going freelance in the Eighties, storyboarding episodes of *Urusei Yatsura* (1981, dir. Oshii Mamoru et al). He met director Oshii Mamoru on this production and the duo began working together on a manga serial for *Animage* magazine, written by Oshii and drawn by Moriyama. ● With the ending of *Urusei Yatsura*, Moriyama became a character designer on another show based on the work of Takahashi Rumiko (*Urusei Yatsura* was the first), *Maison Ikkoku* (1980, dir. Yamazaki Kazuo et al). Moriyama was also well placed at the beginning of the video age to become one of the new format's greatest exponents, working on many of the seminal works of the period, sometimes in an uncredited role (anonymously providing layouts for *Black Magic M-66*, 1987, dir. Shirow Masamune, Kitakubo Hiroyuki) or under a pseudonym. He played a key role in toning down the erotic content of a *Cream Lemon* (1987, dir. various) episode sufficiently enough for it to gain mainstream appeal as *Project A-Ko* (1986, dir. Nishijima Katsuhiko, Moriyama Yuji), which spawned several sequels and was a popular anime export. ● With practical experience in most areas of anime production, Moriyama is one of a dying breed of anime creators who have genuinely worked their way up through the ranks. His modern work includes contributions (credited to an alias) to the interactive *Phantom* series, and work as a key animator on the *Neon Genesis Evangelion* (1997, dir. Anno Hideaki) movies. He was one of the founding members of Studio Min, a small animation outfit that often works in tandem with Chaos Project and Studio Pierrot. ● J.Cl.

ABOVE: LHADATT SHIROTSUGU AND RIQUINNI, THE LEAD CHARACTERS OF *THE WINGS OF HONNEAMISE* (1987, DIR. YAMAGA HIROYUKI, 120 MINS), ON WHICH MORIYAMA WORKED AS AN ANIMATOR

SEE ALSO: DANGUARD ACE; EVANGELION; MAETEL; MAISON IKKOKU; OSHII MAMORU; NONOMURA AMI; PIERROT; TAKAHASHI RUMIKO; URUSEI YATSURA

---

Motohashi (born in 1953) first found work in the Japanese animation business as a low-ranking animator on *UFO Robot Grendizer Raids* (1975, dir. Katsumata Tomohari et al). As an employee of Araki Productions and Studio Z5, he came to play an instrumental part in many of the works sub-contracted to these animation studios from Tokyo Movie Shinsha. An avowed fan of manga creator Yokoyama Mitsuteru, Motohashi seized opportunities to work on adaptations of his work, starting with the 1980 colour remake of *Tetsujin 28-go* (also known as *Gigantor*, 1963, dir. Imazawa Tetsuo). ● He spent much of the Eighties as a keyframe animator, at first on television robot shows before escaping into arenas more suited to his talents. He was a sketch artist on the surreal *Urusei Yatsura* movie *Only You* (1983, dir. Oshii Mamoru), and began to take character design positions in the Nineties on shows ranging from the urban *Megumi no Daigo* (*Firefighter Daigo*, 2000, dir. Nishizawa Akira) to the rural fantasies of *Inuyasha* (2000, dir. Ikeda Masashi, Nishimi Akira). His modern output is characterized by a long stint on the annual *Detective Conan* movies and also enjoys a continuing relationship with the gaming industry, contributing to anime adaptations of software such as *Tokimeki Memorial* and *Graduation*. ● Today, he is based at Xebec M2, a subsidiary of the Xebec studio in Tokyo's Nerima ward, and continues to have strong links to TMS. He often works in collaboration with director Kamegaki Hajime, to the extent that the pair are sometimes jokingly credited as Kamemoto Hidekazu – a combination of characters from both their names. In 2005, he debuted as a producer with the television series *Petopeto-san* (dir. Nishimori Akira et al). ● J.Cl.

# MOTOHASHI HIDEYUKI

---

SEE ALSO: CONAN; TETSUJIN 28-GO; TMS; UFO ROBOT GRENDIZER RAIDS; URUSEI YATSURA; YOKOYAMA MITSUTERU

# MUGEN & JIN

CHARACTERS

SAMURAI CHAMPLOO ● 2004 ● DIR: WATANABE SHINICHIRO ● SCR: SATO DAI ET AL ● DES: NAKAZAWA KAZUTO, MAEDA MAHIRO ● ANI: NAKAZAWA KAZUTO ET AL ● MUS: FAT JON, NUJABES, FORCE OF NATURE, TSUCHIE ● PRD: MANGLOBE ● TV SERIES ● EPS: 26

Sparks fly when opposites attract, which is certainly true of Mugen and Jin, protagonists of *Samurai Champloo*, a historical series set during the Edo period. ● Mugen is a pirate who has abandoned his seafaring ways. Brazen and quarrelsome, he dislikes being labelled and refuses to look anyone in the eye. He is unbeatable in a swordfight, and mixes breakdance and capoeira moves with jumps and stunts in combat, using his sandals to parry the blows of the enemy. Jin is a *ronin*, a masterless samurai, and unlike Mugen, is thoughtful and silent, knows how to dominate his instincts and has a more composed and traditional character. He believes in the samurai code of *bushido*, although his past is tainted by the sinister murder of his own master. The two meet in a tavern and, because of Mugen's impulsiveness, they cross swords before they have even been introduced. Their duel is put on hold when they are imprisoned by the arrogant local magistrate and are saved by the young airhead Fuu who, in exchange, asks them to accompany her on a long journey in search of her samurai father. ● In the wake of live-action swordfighting movies *Zipang* (1990) and *Zatoichi* (2003), Watanabe continues his irreverent review of the samurai mythos, once again pushing back the limits of accepted styles. Dark glasses and earrings, rap music and hip-hop, graffiti and baseball invade the Edo period in *Samurai Champloo* with hilarious and unexpected results. The direction is virtuoso but never forced, with a prevalence of wide-angle and tilted shots (which enhance Mugen's acrobatics) and a syncopated editing style that intertwines parallel events with scenes changing to the sound of a vinyl scratch. ● S.G.

# MURAI SADAYUKI

SCRIPTWRITER

Murai Sadayuki (born in 1964 in Nara) emerged as a screenwriter in 1993 with the screenplay *Tobenai Otome no Jugyochu*, which won the Fuji TV Young Scenario prize. This led to work with a number of major directors in both animation and live action. With his experiments in narrative, Murai belongs to a new wave in animation alongside the likes of Konaka Chiaki and Hayama Yuji. He analyzes the feelings, doubts and thoughts of Japanese adolescents in depth, often in fantasy or horror scenarios. He scripted *Steamboy* (2004) and the live-action movie version of *Mushishi* (2006) for Otomo Katsuhiro and worked on the psycho-thriller *Perfect Blue* (1996) and the 'waking dream' *Sennen Joyu* (*Millennium Actress*, 2001) for the director Kon Satoshi. These last two films have fragmentary, sometimes hallucinatory editing and explore the blurring of reality and fiction. Similarly, the cryptic series *Boogiepop wa Warawanai* (*Boogiepop Phantom*, 2000), for which Murai wrote a number of episodes, tells the story of the same event seen from different points of view. ● With the series *Kino no Tabi: The Beautiful World* (*Kino's Journey*, 2003), Murai turned to a simpler set-up in the form of self-contained episodes with brilliantly unusual plots where the protagonist undertakes a voyage of discovery through utopian cities with strong metaphorical connotations. Together with his friend Konaka Chiaki, Murai co-wrote scripts for a series of live-action films and *Kazuo Umezu's Horror Theater* (1995) and scripted two works by Konaka Kazuya: the female-led fantasy *The Dimension Travellers* (1998) and the series *Ultraman Nexus* (2004), in which the superhero theme is given new depth. Murai also updated the character of *Astro Boy* for the new 2003 anime series, and has written a number of articles and essays about screenwriting. ● S.G.

RIGHT: THE FRENCH LANGUAGE POSTER FOR THE FILM *PERFECT BLUE* (1996, DIR. KON SATOSHI, 82 MINS)

SEE ALSO: ATOM; GINKO; KIRIGOE MIMA; KON SATOSHI; OTOMO KATSUHIRO; STEAMBOY

M

# MUSHI

STUDIO

Often referred to as 'Mushi Pro', the studio was founded by Tezuka Osamu in 1961. Tezuka worked with Toei Animation on several projects before setting up his own studio in a purpose-built complex next to his home. The studio's first project was a short feature film, *Tales of a Street Corner* (*Aru Machikado no Monogatari*, 1962, dir. Yamamoto Eiichi, Sakamoto Yusaku). Encouraged by positive reactions, Mushi Pro started work on Japan's first weekly serial anime, *Astro Boy* (*Tetsuwan Atom*, 1963, dir. Tezuka Osamu) television series, in 1961. To meet the tight schedule and save costs, Mushi Pro developed anime production methods that are still routinely followed today, such as the 'bank system' in which cels and backgrounds are filed for repeated use, and the standardized colour and line charts that Tezuka developed for his manga work. Their influence on the history of Japanese animation is immense. ● At first, Mushi Pro concentrated on making anime versions of manga created by Tezuka. They also produced three ground-breaking theatrical features aimed at an adult audience: *Senya Ichiya Monogatari* (*One Thousand and One Nights*, 1969, dir. Yamamoto Eiichi), *Cleopatra* (*Cleopatra: Queen of Sex*, 1970, dir. Yamamoto Eiichi, Tezuka Osamu) and *Kanashimi no Belladonna* (*The Tragedy of Belladonna*, 1973, dir. Yamamoto Eiichi). ● Tezuka Osamu had resigned from Mushi Pro by the time the third movie was in production. Amid management disputes and serious financial problems, Mushi Pro declared bankruptcy in November 1973. Former Mushi staff went on to other studios. Many still have influential roles in the anime industry. ● H.M.

TWO ADVENTUROUS PROJECTS BY MUSHI FOUNDER TEZUKA OSAMU ● ABOVE: *CLEOPATRA: QUEEN OF SEX* (1970, DIR. YAMAMOTO EIICHI, TEZUKA OSAMU, 112 MINS) ● RIGHT: *SENYA ICHIYA MONOGATARI* (1969, DIR. YAMAMOTO EIICHI, 128 MINS)

SEE ALSO: ATOM; BELLADONNA; CLEOPATRA; RIBBON NO KISHI; TEZUKA OSAMU; YAMAMOTO EIICHI

# NADIA

With skin as smooth as ebony, round eyes, black hair and a precious stone around her neck, Nadia is a young acrobat travelling in Paris. There she meets Jean, a brilliant inventor, and with him begins the long journey to unravel the mystery of the stone. Their expedition is punctuated by encounters with a number of famous characters they meet along the way, the most important being the perplexing Captain Nemo and a bunch of ramshackle opponents who are so evil, they seem to have spilt over from a Tatsunoko production. ● *The Secret of Blue Water* – designed by a young Anno Hideaki as an adaptation of two masterpieces by Jules Verne, *The Mysterious Island* and *20,000 Leagues Under the Sea* – is a good example of the cultural amalgamation that characterizes the new anime scene. ● The two protagonists make an exceptional couple. Nadia is a committed and introverted ecologist who wears the secret of her origins around her neck, while Jean is a demonstrative and extroverted young man who is fascinated by adventures and by flying machines. Through them, the series describes a bygone world at the end of the nineteenth century, when technology was in its infancy and the possibilities for progress seemed endless, contrasted with the modern world that appears to be a real threat to human civilization. These narrative elements recall Miyazaki's *Castle in the Sky* (1986). The film's light touch in terms of design is also echoed here by Sadamoto Yoshiyuki. The use of soft colours in the layout is masterful, especially the range of blues and greens. The experience of this world is finally filtered by Anno, who uses irony to counteract the inherent pathos within the character of Nadia. ● C.C.

*FUSHIGI NO UMI NO NADIA* ● *THE SECRET OF BLUE WATER* ● 1990 ● DIR: ANNO HIDEAKI ET AL ● SCR: OKADA TOSHIO ET AL ● DES: SADAMOTO YOSHIYUKI ● ANI: NAKAZAWA KAZUTO ET AL ● MUS: SAGISU SHIRO ● PRD: GAINAX ● TV SERIES ● EPS: 39

LEFT: A PUBLICITY IMAGE FOR THE GROUND-BREAKING SERIES THE SECRET OF BLUE WATER

Although he died of hepatitis in 1980, Nagahama Tadao's influence as a director who tried to assert his own vision on the anime world is still felt today. Born in 1936 in Kagoshima, Nagahama was not a gifted draughtsman and relied on skilled animators to portray his visions, which covered every genre from sports stories to children's cartoons. ● With a degree in dramatic art from the Nihon University, Nagahama began his career as puppet director on a very successful television series called *Madcap Island* (1964). In 1968, he directed *Star of the Giants*, the story of a young baseball player who wants to follow the career of his baseball-champion father based on a manga by Kawasaki Noboru. In 1971, he directed *Obake no Qtaro* (*Qtaro the Ghost*), and in the same decade his name was associated with one of the greatest television successes, *The Rose of Versailles*. ● He should also be remembered as director of the so-called 'Romantic robot trilogy', comprising *Cho Denji Robo Combattler V* (1976), *Cho Denji Machine Voltes V* (*Voltus*, 1977) and *Tosho Daimos* (*Starbirds*, 1978). After working closely with Tomino Yoshiyuki and remembering his dramatic art studies, Nagahama tried to go beyond the stereotypes of the robot series, seeking to introduce a psychological introspection into a decidedly light genre that was entirely new for the time. Nagahama was also an experienced musician, and he made many soundtracks under the pseudonym of Aoi Akira. ● F.L.

# NAGAHAMA TADAO

SEE ALSO: HOSHI HYUMA; JARJAYES, OSCAR FRANÇOIS DE; SUNRISE; TOEI ANIMATION

# NAGAI GO

MANGAKA

For European audiences, Nagai Go (born in 1945 in Wajima City) is best known as the creator of *UFO Robot Grendizer Raids* (1975, dir. Katsumata Tomoharu et al), *Mazinger Z* (1972, dir. Serikawa Yugo et al) and *Great Mazinger* (1974, dir. Akihi Masayuk et al), the giant robots whose animated adventures in the Seventies played a large part in making manga popular outside Japan. However the work of this mangaka and screenwriter was not confined to futuristic conflicts between multicoloured mecha but also covered a wide range of styles and genres. Nevertheless, many of his most famous creations have an element in common: the manifest will to break free of the conventional standards of the day at the cost of shocking a proportion of his readers or viewers. ● From the end of the Sixties, even before the creation of the violent *Mazinger* and *UFO Robot Grendizer Raids*, Nagai Go was a pioneer of erotic manga with his school comedy *Harenchi Gakuen* (1972) to which the magazine *Shonen Jump*, launched in 1968, owes a significant part of its success. The manga opened the way to many authors whose inspiration was even more transgressive. ● Nagai used his new popularity to found the Dynamic Productions animation studio, which became Dynamic Planning in 1974, under his own management. Flanked by talented collaborators, the best known of whom are probably Ishikawa Ken and Ota Gosaku, Nagai turned out great quantities of manga year upon year, many of which were immediately adapted for television: the half-human, half-demon hero *Devilman* (1972, dir. Akehi Masayuki, Katsumata Tomoharu); the young adventurer endowed with superhuman powers *Cutey Honey* (1973, dir. Katsumata Tomoharu et al); the violent and bloody *Violence Jack* (1973, dir. Okuda Seiji et al); *Getta Robot* (1974, dir. Katsumata Tomoharu et al); and the manga *Dynamic Heroes* (2005). In a career spanning over forty years, Nagai the mangaka has left a controversial but indelible mark on the world of manga and Japanese animation. ● E.H.

ABOVE: CLOSE-UP OF DR HELL, THE EVIL VILLAIN OF *MAZINGER Z* (1972, DIR. SERIKAWA YUGO ET AL, 92 EPS)

SEE ALSO: CUTEY HONEY; DEVILMAN; GETTA ROBOT; JEEG, THE STEEL ROBOT; MAZINGER Z; UFO ROBOT GRENDIZER RAIDS

# NAKAMURA TAKASHI

DIRECTOR

RIGHT: PUBLICITY IMAGE FOR THE SERIES GOLDEN WARRIOR GOLD LIGHTAN (1981, DIR. MASHIMO KOICHI, NISHIKUBO MIZUHO, 52 EPS), ON WHICH NAKAMURA WORKED AS AN ANIMATOR

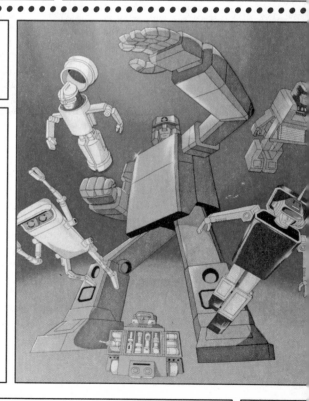

Nakamura Takashi (born in 1955 in Yamanashi) is another promising collaborator of Otomo Katsuhiro's to turn to directing. An artist distinguished by his simple design style and his keen interest in children's literature, Nakamura emerged as a skilled and dynamic animator. ● He learnt principally from two masters. Miyazaki Hayao – with whom he collaborated as key animator on *Nausicaä of the Valley of Wind* (1984) – is without doubt the artist who has most influenced him spiritually and Otomo, whom he came to know at the time of *Genma Taisen* (*Harmagedon*, 1983, dir. Rintaro), introduced him to directing with the short film *Niwatori Otoko to Akia Kubi* (*Chicken Man and Red Neck*, also titled *Nightmare*), a segment of the portmanteau movie *Robot Carnival* (1987), and they worked together again during the laborious production of *Akira* in 1988. ● The road to artistic independence began in 1989 when Nakamura directed the series *Peter Pan no Boken* (*Adventures of Peter Pan*) for Nippon Animation, and applied his personal style of design to the characters. The sense of wonder was enhanced and became a constant in his feature-length debut, *Totsuzen! Neko no Kuni Banipal Witt* (*Catnapped!*, 1995), a multicoloured voyage beyond the real world in which the protagonists are transformed into cats amidst scenes of action and humour. *Parumu no Ki* (*A Tree of Palme*, 2001), loosely inspired by the Pinocchio story, is a sumptuous and elephantine fantasy that Nakamura created and imbued with the pictorial atmosphere of Jean Giraud and of René Laloux' film *Fantastic Planet* (1973). ● When he made the series *Fantastic Children* (2004), using his own subject matter, Nakamura was still thinking of a younger audience, although the sober graphics represent a deliberate intent to focus attention on the mystery of the storyline. ● M.A.R.

SEE ALSO: AKIRA; MIYAZAKI HAYAO; NAUSICAÄ; NIPPON ANIMATION; OTOMO KATSUHIRO

# NAKAZAWA KAZUTO

**DIRECTOR**

Illustrator, director and animator Nakazawa Kazuto, born in 1968 in Niigata and a graduate of the Toei Animation Institute, is considered to be among the most spirited artists working in the field. To describe him as eclectic is almost to denigrate a very solid career. The earliest works ascribed to him might appear traditional, but there are glimpses of his irrepressible inner world characterized by the power of the wind (a recurring theme in his work), dynamism of movement and refinement of detail. Nakazawa can show his mastery in only a few seconds of animation, in a brilliantly executed character design or in the animators' tour de force – the opening and closing sequences of an anime, such as *Record of Lodoss War* (1998) or the recent *Blood+* (2005). ● His directorial talents flourished when he worked with Studio °4C, where he made *Comedy* (2000), one of the episodes comprising the series *Sweat Punch* that were later compiled in the DVD magazine for unconventional animation *Grasshoppa!* Despite its title, the episode directed by Nakazawa is a gothic tale: the adventure of a girl who seeks the aid of a demon to defend her village against invaders. Nakazawa's story opens to Schubert's *Ave Maria*, expresses some profound truths and silvers his protagonists' faces with moonlight. His style here is already much like that of his later projects, television series *Samurai Champloo* (2004) and *Ergo Proxy* (2006). ● Nakazawa remained faithful to shorts in his *Yurururu*, a fragment only a minute long in the *AniKuri* series (2007) broadcast on NHK, in which his pencil quickly fills a blank page with life and colour. Sought after by studios such as Manglobe and Production I.G., Nakazawa directed a new short, *Moondrive* (2008), as part of the anthology *Genius Party Beyond*. ● M.A.R.

SEE ALSO: 4°C; I.G.; MAEDA MAHIRO; MUGEN & JIN; OSHII MAMORU; ROUIJIN Z

---

# NAKURA YASUHIRO

**ANIMATOR**

Born in 1959 in Shizuoka, Nakura Yasuhiro began his anime career as an inbetweener at Toei, working on the series *Galaxy Express 999* (1978, dir. Nishizawa Nobutaka) and *Cyborg 009* (1980, dir. Serikawa Yugo). His remarkable draughtsmanship helped him become a key animator on *Honey Honey* (1981, dir. Shirato Takeshi et al), *Acrobunch* (1982, dir. Asumura Masakazu, Hisaoka Satoshi) and *The Ugly Duckling* (1982), and to begin production on *Red Riding Hood* (1982). ● 1984 saw his big break when he directed the successful television series *Tongari Boshi no Memoru* based on his own manga. When her spaceship breaks down, a little alien girl called Memole is stranded on Earth and has to explore the planet. The drawings for this cartoon are wonderfully warm, like those of a picture book, and the success of the series led to Nakamura becoming animator for two major films, *Tenshi no Tamago* (*Angel's Egg*, 1985) by Oshii Mamoru and *Castle in the Sky* (1986) by Miyazaki Hayao. ● With the series *Tale of Genji* (1987), Nakura returned to his role as producer and animator and the following year saw the release of one of his most distinctive projects, *The Wildcat and the Acorns* (1988), an adaptation of a poem by Miyazawa Kenji. ● His collaborations with Rintaro and again with Oshii, however, took a completely different turn. He worked as chief animator, key animator and character designer on Rintaro's monumental and complex *Metropolis* (2001) and then as key animator for Oshii on *Ghost in the Shell 2: Innocence* (2004), although for Hosoda Mamoru's *The Girl who Leapt through Time* (2006), Nakura returned to a style of drawing and colour that is closer to that of his picture books. ● F.L.

RIGHT: THE FRENCH LANGUAGE POSTER FOR THE FEATURE FILM *METROPOLIS* (2001, DIR. RINTARO, 107 MINS)

SEE ALSO: CYBORG 009; GENJI HIKARU; HOSODA MAMORU; KUSANAGI MOTOKO; LAPUTA; MAETEL; MEMOLE; MIYAZAKI HAYAO; RINTARO; TIMA; TOEI ANIMATION

**N**

# NANA

*TV SERIES*

*Nana*, a manga by Yazawa Ai, is one of the key titles responsible for bringing the *shojo* genre to a high level of maturity and realism, updating the folk-story atmospheres and anachronistic personalities of past decades. ● A girl-next-door and a streetwise kid, both called Nana, are united in destiny by a train journey that symbolically takes them to a new life. The story charts the sentimental ups and downs of the two main characters and deals with problems of an existential nature interwoven with the more practical difficulties of city life. ● Set in a kind of modern Tokyo, the television series, directed by Asaka Morio, brings together the pop elements of Iwai Shunji's live-action movie *Love Letter* (1995) with music that belongs to bygone years. It reveals love in its more realistic aspects, shunning stereotypes but sometimes overdoing the trivial psychoanalysis typical of adolescent serials. Osaki Nana is a silent and thoughtful rocker, seemingly tough in character, marked by her childhood as an orphan and with an adolescence sullied by malicious gossip. Throughout the story, a man called Ren, the guitar player in the band Trapnest, pursues her. The talkative Komatsu Nana (known as Hachi) is, on the other hand, cheerful and carefree. She has a decidedly less troubled past but, endowed with a certain basic naivety, she easily gets into trouble with boys, even getting pregnant during a secret relationship with Takumi, Trapnest's lead singer. The two girls, who are close friends, never really get into conflict, but help each other out. There are numerous secondary characters around them, notably the problematic Shin, who dabbles in the world of prostitution. ● Madhouse's excellent animation is notable for its backgrounds, rich in tones, while the direction uses many of the devices of the original manga. Brief interjections of the 'super-deformed' style are used to reinforce the artistic style of the eighties design. ● S.G.

ABOVE: THE CAST OF THE MANGA AND 2006 TV SERIES NANA ● RIGHT: THE TALKATIVE AND CHEERFUL KOMATSU NANA, FROM THE MANGA

NANA ● 2006 ● DIR: ASAKA MORIO ● SCR: KONPARU TOMOKO ET AL ● DES: HAMADA KUNIHIKO ● ANI: HANADA KUNIHIKO ET AL ● MUS: HASEGAWA TOMOKI ●
PRD: MADHOUSE ● TV SERIES ● EPS: 47

# NARUTO

Naruto Uzumaki is a twelve-year-old boy with a piercing gaze and scruffy blond hair. He has an outgoing personality and a habit of getting into trouble. His orange-coloured overalls and headband are marked with the symbol of the spiral, the emblem of his hometown, Leaf Village. ● The horizontal marks on his cheeks, like stylized whiskers, hint that he is the host of the dreaded Nine-Tailed Fox demon. This powerful demon attacked Leaf Village when Naruto was born. The village's ninja leader imprisoned it inside Naruto's body, and the villagers feared and hated him as if he were the demon. ● Ostracized by his community without knowing why, Naruto has become a show-off in order to draw attention to himself. His aim is to become the strongest ninja in Leaf Village. ● Created in 1997 by mangaka Kishimoto Masashi, and first published in legendary magazine *Shonen Jump* in 1999, *Naruto* recalls the narrative of *Dragon Ball*, another *Shonen Jump* hit. Like Goku in *Dragon Ball*, Naruto also wants to develop his abilities through increasingly difficult challenges that will enable him to reach higher levels of knowledge. During the course of the anime series, begun in 2002, it is noticeable how the main character grows both physically and mentally. In 2007, at the start of series two, entitled *Naruto: Shippuden*, he is now sixteen. ● Empathy for the character is also accentuated by the producer Date Hayato through frequent point-of-view shots. The international success of *Naruto* can be attributed to the simplicity and modernity of the design used by the Studio Pierrot, who have refined the graphic style of the manga, while retaining important details, such as the intricate backgrounds and youth fashion trends in the clothes. ● L.D.C.

ABOVE: PUBLICITY IMAGE FOR THE 2002 SERIES *NARUTO* ● LEFT: NARUTO AND HIS MASTER HATAKE KAKASHI

NARUTO ● 2002 ● DIR: DATE HAYATO ET AL ● SCR: SUMIZAWA KATSUYAJI ET AL ● DES: SUZUKI HIROFUMI ET AL ● ANI: MATSUMOTO ATSUHO ET AL ● MUS: MASUDA TOSHIO, MUSASHI PROJECT ● PRD: STUDIO PIERROT ● TV SERIES ● EPS: 220

# NAUSICAÄ

In 1983, film-maker Miyazaki Hayao adapted his own manga (which he had begun writing in 1982 although he did not complete it until 1994) to make *Nausicaä of the Valley of Wind*. The story of young princess Nausicaä is set a thousand years after the Seven Days of Fire, a great conflagration that the ravaged Earth, destroying human civilization. The remaining human settlements are separated from each other by the fetid and poisonous Sea of Corruption (variously translated in English as the Sea of Decomposition and Toxic Jungle). Nausicaä becomes involved in a war over the weapons that caused the apocalypse, and eventually restores peace to the Earth through compassionate sacrifice. ● This philosophical and ecological epic was unprecedentedly ambitious for an anime at the time of its making. As with Miyazaki's later films, *Nausicaä* displays the director's remarkable ability to combine breadth of vision with painstaking detail. The scene where Nausicaä shelters under the lens of a dead insect's eye against the backdrop of a vast wilderness is one of many examples of this delicacy. ● Still, it is in the skies that Miyazaki is most at home (see also *Porco Rosso* and *Castle in the Sky*). The flying sequences are stunning and the Valley of the Wind is the ideal setting for Nausicaä's 'mehve' glider, on which she flies or drifts at will, while the symphonic music of Hisaishi Joe, working with Miyazaki for the first time, adds another layer of depth to the picture. ● *Nausicaä of the Valley of Wind* was the initial masterpiece that convinced Miyazaki and his producer Takahata Isao to found the Ghibli studio (*Nausicaä* itself was produced by Topcraft). A far inferior version of the film, cut by thirty-two minutes, was screened in the United States under the title *Warriors of the Wind*. ● S.D.

LEFT & BELOW: *SCENES FROM THE 1983 FILM* NAUSICAÄ, *THE STORY OF A YOUNG PRINCESS DESTINED TO BRING PEACE TO PLANET EARTH*

*KAZE NO TANI NO NAUSHIKA* ● *NAUSICAÄ OF THE VALLEY OF WIND* ● 1983 ● DIR & SCR & DES: MIYAZAKI HAYAO ● ANI: KOMATSUBARA KAZUO ET AL ●
MUS: HISAISHI JOE ● PRD: TAKAHATA ISAO ET AL, TOPCRAFT ● FILM ● DUR: 116 MINS

176

Motohashi Koichi founded Nippon Animation in June 1975. Its first production established the speciality for which it is best known. *Flanders no Inu* (*A Dog of Flanders*, 1975, dir. Kuroda Yoshio) was the first of twenty-five anime TV series retelling classic European and American novels. Often known to fans as the World Masterpiece Theater, this influential concept helped to broaden the field of anime beyond science fiction and simple comedy. ● Series such as *Haha o Tazunete Sanzen Ri* (*From the Apennines to the Andes* or *3,000 Leagues in Search of Mother*, 1976, dir. Takahata Isao), *Akage no Anne* (*Anne of Green Gables*, 1979, dir. Takahata Isao, Koshi Shigeo), and *Mirai Shonen Conan* (*Future Boy Conan*, 1978, dir. Miyazaki Hayao et al) helped relatively unknown directors such as Miyazaki and Takahata to reach a wider audience. ● The studio has always actively sought international opportunities, beginning with TV series *Mitsubachi Maya no Boken* (*Maya The Bee*, 1975, dir. Saito Hiroshi et al) co-produced with Germany's Kirch Media Group. BRB International of Spain co-produced *Wanwan Sanjushi* (*Dogtanian and the Three Muskehounds*, dir. Saito Hidetaka et al) in 1981 and *Anime 80 Sekai Isshu* (*Around the World with Willy Fog*, dir. Kurokawa Fumio) in 1983. Other partners include Russian, Chinese and Italian companies. ● The studio has animated many novels that are now beloved classics in Japan, such as *Makiba no shojo Katri* (*Katri, Girl of the Meadows*, 1984, dir. Saito Hiroshi), based on Auni Nuolivaara's Finnish novel. Nippon Animation also makes films and OAVs. ● H.M.

# NIPPON ANIMATION

STUDIO

SCENES FROM THE WORK OF NIPPON ANIMATION ●
ABOVE LEFT, TOP RIGHT & CENTRE RIGHT:
SCENES FROM THE TV SERIES *FUTURE BOY
CONAN* (1978, DIR. MIYAZAKI HAYAO, 26
EPS) ● ABOVE RIGHT: ANNE SHIRLEY,
THE YOUNG HEROINE OF
*ANNE OF GREEN GABLES* (1979,
DIR. TAKAHATA ISAO, 50 EPS)

SEE ALSO: ANNE OF GREEN GABLES; CONAN; MIYAZAKI HAYAO; MUSHI; TAKAHATA ISAO; TOEI ANIMATION

# NISHIKUBO MIZUHO

Nishikubo Mizuho (also known as Toshihiko) was born in 1953 and is married to anime voice actor Mizutani Yoko. He worked as a director and animation director with TMS, where he was unit director for Dezaki Osamu on several episodes of *The Rose of Versailles* (1979, dir. Dezaki Osamu) – contributing to the unique and memorable Impressionist-style of the series – and the second series of *Tomorrow's Joe* (1980, dir. Dezaki Osamu et al). He directed the series *Mori no Youki na Kobito-tachi: Berufi to Rirubitto* (*The Littl' Bits*, 1980) for Tatsunoko before going to Kitty Films to direct the first series based on an Adachi Mitsuru manga, *Miyuki* (1983).
● With the television series *Akai Kodan Zillion* (*Red Photon Zillion*, 1987, dir. Hamazaki Hiroshi, Kobayashi Tetsuya), Nishikubo moved into science fiction, storyboarding and supervising animation. In 1992, he made an anime version of *Video Girl Ai*, the manga chiefly responsible for 'modernizing' the *shojo* genre in the early Nineties, emphasizing the virtual nature of its female protagonist. When Production I.G. launched, he became the principal collaborator of director Oshii Mamoru, for whom he was animation director on *Patlabor 2: The Movie* (1993) and *Ghost in the Shell* (1995). Nishikubo also directed sequences for *Ghost in the Shell 2: Innocence* (2004).
● Together with colleagues Okiura Hiroyuki, Kise Kazuchika and Nishio Tetsuya, Nishikubo is among the main promoters of the realistic, detailed style that has made Production I.G. a ground-breaking animation studio. His work shows in accurate detail and in character design rich in lines and shading, quite different from the classic manga model. Returning towards directing with the series *Otogi Zoshi* (2004), he confirmed his attitude to the refinement of the style, demanding much of his animators. In 2006 Nishikubo directed his first feature-length film using computer graphics, *Atagoal wa Neko no Mori* (*Atagoal: Cat's Magical Forest*), taken from the eponymous manga with its bungling cat protagonist. His latest project is an animated film about the samurai Miyamoto Musashi, scripted and produced by his friend Oshii. ● S.G.

LEFT: ARTWORK OF OSCAR FRANÇOIS DE JARJAYES BY IKEDA RIYOKO, FROM *THE ROSE OF VERSAILLES* (1979, DIR: NAGAHAMA TADAO, DEZAKI OSAMU, 41 EPS)

SEE ALSO: AMANO AI; DEZAKI OSAMU; I.G.; JARJAYES, OSCAR FRANÇOIS DE; KISE KAZUCHIKA; KUSANAGI MOTOKO; OSHII MAMORU; PATLABOR; TATSUNOKO; YABUKI JOE

---

Nishizaki Yoshinobu's name is indelibly linked to *Space Battleship Yamato* (*Star Blazers*, 1974, dir. Ishiguro Noboru et al), the series that created the first anime boom throughout Japan in the Seventies. Born in 1934 and a graduate of Nihon University, Nishizaki began his career in the music industry, setting up a jazz club and becoming a musical producer. He moved into cinema, again as a producer, where he met Tezuka Osamu. He became Tezuka's general manager and produced a free adaptation of the mythological cartoon *Umi no Triton* (*Triton of the Sea*, 1972, dir. Tomino Yoshiyuki) with him. ● The following year, Nishizaki set about the work that would make him famous, not only dealing with production but also having a hand in the script and sometimes the direction. For the drawing, however, Matsumoto Leiji – almost unknown at the time – was called in. Despite its excellent quality, the first series of *Yamato* failed to become popular with television audiences but Nishizaki was not to be deterred. He presented the series again as a 130-minute feature film and, when refused distribution, he hired a cinema to show it to the public. The success of the film was so great that in the next few years a further two series and five films went into production, although it is well-known that Nishizaki and Matsumoto soon went their separate ways, citing strong artistic differences. After trying to repeat his success with the series *Uchu Kubo Blue Noah* (*Blue Noah*, 1979, Takahashi Kazunori et al), a marine version of his famous spaceship, Nishizaki returned to the music world until his recording label failed in 1997. Recently, after recovering the intellectual (but not graphic) property rights to his most famous work, he has said that he would like to make one last film in the *Yamato* saga. ● S.G.

# NISHIZAKI YOSHINOBU

SEE ALSO: ISHIGURO NOBURO; MATSUMOTO LEIJI; TOMINO YOSHIYUKI; YAMATO

# NOBUMOTO KEIKO

SCRIPTWRITER

If Japanese anime has developed greatly over the last twenty years, it is in part thanks to the greater narrative freedom and innovative spirit of the storylines, and it is in this arena that Nobumoto Keiko (born in 1964 in Hokkaido) has made a distinctive contribution. Nobumoto won a major new scriptwriters' competition organized by Fuji TV in 1989 and in the following years, she divided her time between work for animation and live-action cinema (such as the surreal horror film *World Apartment Horror*, 1991, directed by Otomo Katsuhiro). ● Her collaboration with Watanabe Shinichiro on the OAV *Macross Plus* (1994), *Cowboy Bebop* (1998) and *Cowboy Bebop: The Film* (2001) led to a wonderful combination of atmospheric film noir and the Western, whilst portraying a decidedly present-day future and accompanied by an interesting jazz soundtrack. ● Since then, Nobumoto has continued to write for television, and in 2003 she created the huge popular success *Wolf's Rain*. Directed by Okamura Tensai with character design by Kawamoto Toshihiro, the series follows the journey of four lone wolves and once again creates a distinctive view of the near future. Nobumoto's next big hit was *Tokyo Godfathers* (2003, dir. Kon Satoshi), in which three tramps find an abandoned baby while rummaging through the refuse of the capital on Christmas Eve. ● F.L.

SEE ALSO: MACROSS; OTOMO KATSUHIRO; SPIEGEL, SPIKE; TOKYO GODFATHERS

RIGHT: POPULAR HERO SPIKE SPIEGEL IN TWO SCENES FROM *COWBOY BEBOP* (1998, DIR. WATANABE SHINICHIRO, 26 EPS)

---

Shinosuke, known as 'Shin-chan', is the eldest son of the Nohara family. He represents the graphic simplification of an archetype whose potential has rarely been exploited with such creative freedom as in this series by Usui Yoshito: childhood as a land of disobedience, of continual games and of perpetual confrontation with the adult world and authority. ● Shin-chan is a difficult child: insolent, rude, immodest, scatological and filled with an insatiable curiosity about everything relating to adult sexuality. A father with a tenuous grip on his authority, a mother who continues to struggle with her unruly offspring, a little sister and Shiro, the dog, complete this portrait of a typical middle-class family. ● The comical daily exploits of the Nohara family originated in 1990 in the pages of the *Weekly Manga Action* magazine and came to anime two years later. The dry narrative and Usui Yoshtio's synthetic, almost careless, drawings, force the reader to accept some aesthetic imperfections, but also suggest irresistible spontaneity in the form of childish doodles, thus transforming *Crayon Shin-chan* (1992) – especially in its early years – into a work that coherently encompasses its tiny hero's point of view. In 1993, Shin-chan was the lead character in his first feature film – *Crayon Shin-chan: Action Kamen vs Haigure Mao* – the beginning of a saga that has now produced sixteen titles. The development of the television series itself sees a departure from the original manga and launches the characters into adventures which echo the mythology of various film genres and which, at times – as in *Crayon Shin-chan: Arashi o Yobu Moretsu! Otona Teikoku no Gyakushu* (2001), an incisive commentary on parental immaturity – give the adult viewer unexpected surprises. ● J.Co.

# NOHARA SHINOSUKE
## SHIN-CHAN

CHARACTER

CRAYON SHINCHAN ● CRAYON SHIN-CHAN ● 1992 ● DIR: HONGO MITSURO ● SCR: HONMA MITSURU ET AL ● DES: YUASA MASAAKI ● ANI: MORI SHIZUKA, HARA KATSUE ● MUS: ARAKAWA TOSHIYUKI ● PRD: SHINEI DOGA ● TV SERIES ● EPS: 600

# NONOMURA AMI

CHARACTER

Nonomura Ami is a passionate, enthusiastic eleven-year-old girl who seduces her elder brother Hiroshi. Separated from him after the incident, she fantasizes about a reunion amid a picaresque series of sexual encounters with other men. She is reunited with Hiroshi briefly when, as an adult pop star, she performs in London. ● Although the first ever straight-to-video anime was famously the science-fiction story *Dallos* (1983), it is less widely known that the next five video releases were all soft-core pornography, including *Be My Baby*, the first instalment of the *Cream Lemon* anime series, and the first in the series to feature Nonomura Ami. Video allowed viewers to watch films in the privacy of their own homes for the first time, and anime was quick to exploit hidden passions and secret desires. Video cassettes were expensive and sold chiefly to rental stores from which consumers could rent a tape for a single night. With live-action competition already strong in most genres, anime porn producers focused on niche markets that the mainstream could not, or would not, serve. The nature of anime production made even fantasy or science-fiction pornography no more expensive than the ubiquitous lovers-in-a-hotel-room set-up/format. It also made it possible to show images that would be illegal in the real world. ● Ami would return in several sequels to *Be My Baby*, attesting to the young character's popularity, although the nature of these anime and their famous *hentai* predecessor *Lolita Anime* (1984), is a contentious issue. Japanese tradition holds that no real person is being harmed in these images and therefore they are harmless fantasies. International lawyers and pressure groups disagree, however, and see *Cream Lemon* and its successors as dangerous paedophile propaganda, likely to be used to groom susceptible children for abuse. ● J.Cl.

CREAM LEMON ● 1984 ● DIR: MIYAZAKI KAZUYA ET AL ● SCR: UNCREDITED ● DES: NITTA MASAKO ET AL ● ANI: TAJIMA HIROSHI ET AL ● MUS: UNCREDITED ● PRD: FAIRY DUST ● VIDEO SERIES ● EPS: 36

# OFUJI NOBURO

DIRECTOR

Ofuji Shinshichiro (1900–1961), who worked under the pseudonym Ofuji Noburo, was one of the pioneers of Japanese animation, creating landmark works in new technologies and garnering anime its first moments of foreign attention. ● The seventh of eight children raised in a poor family in Tokyo's Asakusa district, Ofuji was orphaned in 1907 and raised by an elder sister. He started work as an apprentice at Junichi Kouichi's Sumikazu Eiga studio in 1918. Working before the advent of the animation cel, his early works relied on paper cutouts to form characters and backgrounds. Ofuji was an early innovator in animation, perfecting the use of silhouettes in *Whale* (1927), experimenting with the possibilities of soundtracks in *Black Cat* (1928) and using early colour processes in the unreleased *Golden Flower* (1929). ● During World War II, Ofuji's sole movie credit was on *Hawai-Marei-Oki Kaisen* (*The War at Sea from Hawaii to Malaya*, 1943), a live-action propaganda film that encouraged viewers to enlist as pilots in the navy, recreating Japanese victories using special-effects footage. In the post-war period, he spearheaded Japanese animation's rehabilitation in the international community, picking up a prize at the 1956 Venice Film Festival for *Yurei Sen* (*The Ghost Ship*). ● His last work was animating cellophane as part of the award-winning Asahi Beer advertisement *Beer Through the Ages* (1956). He died in 1961, before the popular manga and television series *Astro Boy* changed the way Japanese animation was perceived outside its home country. In the year after his death, his name was attached to the prestigious Noboru Ofuji Prize for excellence in animation. In the intervening forty-seven years, the award has become a benchmark of quality in the animation world, with notable recipients including Tezuka Osamu, Kawamoto Kihachiro, Otomo Katsuhiro and Yamamura Koji. ● J.Cl.

LEFT: KURONYAGO, THE LITTLE BLACK CAT STARRING IN HARUNO UTA (SPRING SONG, 1931, DIR. OFUJI NOBURO, 3 MINS), ONE OF OFUJI'S EARLY FILMS

SEE ALSO: KAWAMOTO KIHACHIRO; MASAOKA KENZO; MOCHINAGA TADAHITO; MOMOTARO; TEZUKA OSAMU

High-school student Hiromi joins the girls' tennis club and develops a crush on Reika, a natural leader who is envied and feared by all. Hiromi is also trained by coach Jin, who urges her to make tennis the focus of her life. Neglected by her coach, Reika becomes jealous of Hiromi and an intense rivalry develops between the two girls. ● Created by mangaka Yamamoto Sumika, Oka Hiromi can be regarded as the female counterpart of the boxing hero of *Tomorrow's Joe* (1970). In their rivalry with a 'frenemy', both are driven to improve their sporting prowess (reaching levels of sacrifice and self-harm comparable to the nihilism of the samurai), and both star in animated cartoons made by the talented duo of director Dezaki Osamu and character designer Sugino Akio. Even more than in the anime version of *Joe*, the atmosphere here is one of sublimation: slow-motion sequences and a good dose of narcissism ensure that every gesture becomes a cathartic moment, be it a passing shot or a dramatic entry by the vain Reika. ● In the first series the drawing is sketchy and the backdrops hazy watercolours, in keeping with the romantic/western aesthetic of first-generation *shojo* manga and the approach of artists such as Ikeda Riyoko. The graphic style subsequently becomes grittier, the long-limbed bodies more heavily shaded and the atmosphere more dramatic. As in all of Dezaki's major works, the subject of illness breaks into the story. Jin dies just as Hiromi reaches the peak of success, thus preventing a happy ending. He is replaced in his role of mentor by Katsura, a Buddhist monk, anticipating the life choice made by Yamamoto herself, who long ago withdrew into spiritual retreat on a mountain. ● S.G.

# OKA HIROMI

CHARACTER

ACE O NERAE ● AIM FOR THE ACE! ● 1973 ● DIR: DEZAKI OSAMU, HATA MASAMI ● SCR: OKAMURA KAZUO ● DES: SUGINO AKIO ● ANI: KAWAJIRI YOSHIAKI ET AL ● MUS: MISAWA AKIRA ● PRD: TMS ● TV SERIES ● EPS: 25

# OKAJIMA TAEKO

CHARACTER

Taeko is twenty-seven and works for a large company in Tokyo. When summer comes, she decides to take a holiday that is primarily a journey through time, back to the places where she spent her childhood and adolescence – a trip full of memories destined to surface slowly and to sweep her up in a profound embrace. This nostalgic odyssey is set in opposition to modern urban life, the past against the present. Takahata Isao adapted the story from a manga of the same name by Okamoto Hotaru and Tone Yuko and created a kind of symphony of delicate feelings, not only conscious memory, but also the intangible, complex sentiments that surround the main character. ● If there was ever a film that has managed to deliver the sweet thrill of nostalgia, it is *Only Yesterday*, whose title already suggests how memories slip between our thoughts and come to dictate the way we live. Like petals which allow the wind to carry them in small evolutions before hitting the ground, Taeko seems to be transported by the events and memories she encounters: childhood, the loves of her adolescence and small wounds which silently survive in her mind. ● The enchanted landscape of *Only Yesterday* transforms Taeko, forcing her to take a step forward in life. The story covers nearly two decades, between 1966 and 1982, continuously alternating between past and present, between full, bright colours and subtle tones that gently fade into the background. The animation has a quiet beauty, which the viewer comes to appreciate as they lose themselves in the richness of the characters' faces and the intensity of their expressions. ● G.P.

SCENES FROM THE 1991 FILM *ONLY YESTERDAY* ● ABOVE: TAEKO AND HER MOTHER ● ABOVE LEFT: TAEKO MEETS ORGANIC FARMER TOSHIO AND BEGINS TO QUESTION HER URBAN LIFESTYLE ● LEFT: MEMORIES OF TAEKO'S CHILDHOOD HAUNT HER JOURNEY BACK TO TOKYO

OMOHIDE PORO PORO ● ONLY YESTERDAY ● 1991 ● DIR: TAKAHATA ISAO ● SCR: TAKAHATA ISAO ● DES: KONDO YOSHIFUMI, SATO YOSHIHARU ● ANI: KONDO YOSHIFUMI ● MUS: HISAISHI JOE ● PRD: TOKUMA YASUYOSHI, STUDIO GHIBLI ● FILM ● DUR: 118 MINS

# OKAWARA KUNIO

MECHA DESIGNER

Okawara Kunio (born in 1947) was the first person to be formally acknowledged as a professional mecha designer, although he had initially set out to study textile design and worked in fashion. Dissatisfied with the industry, he took a chance opportunity to join the Tatsunoko Production Company. ● In 1977, while working on the *Yattaman* series (1977, Sasagawa Hiroshi et al), he met Tomino Yoshiyuki and the two began a collaboration that was to continue for many years. They both moved to Nippon Sunrise, where Okawara provided the design work for *Daitarn 3* (1978, dir. Tomino Yoshiyuki et al) and *Muteki Choujin Zanbot 3* (*Zambot 3,* 1977, dir. Tomino Yoshiyuki et al). From the outset, Okawara's work managed the maximum expressive effect from the minimum number of lines, making it easier to create industrial productions of his designs. Nonetheless, his aesthetic taste is clearly seen and his mechanical giants stand out from the 'cylindrical' model of Nagai Go's robots. Okawara's machines are squarer in design, harking back to ancient samurai armour. In addition, Okawara would make sponsors wooden models of his machines instead of drawings to give a better idea of the result he aimed to achieve. ● His next step was *Mobile Suit Gundam* (1979, dir. Tomino Yoshiyuki et al), a series rich in fighting machines that showcased Okawara's innovative work to the best possible advantage. His defining stylistic trait is a meticulous concern for detail that emphasizes the realism of his figures – as in the Gundam's noted calf-muscle – while also reflecting traditional Japanese costumes, rendering his figures at once elegant and highly striking. ● D.D.G.

ABOVE: GUNDAM AGAINST ENEMIES IN A PROMOTIONAL IMAGE ILLUSTRATED BY THE MECHA DESIGNER OKAWARA KUNIO

SEE ALSO: GATCHAMAN; GUNDAM; NAGAI GO; SUNRISE; TATSUNOKO; TOMINO YOSHIYUKI

# OKAZAKI MINORU

DIRECTOR

Okazaki Minoru (born in 1942) left his native Osaka at the age of twenty with the hope of securing a job in the live-action film industry in Tokyo. Instead, he found work with the animation studio Hatena Pro, where he was soon assigned to drawing storyboards on the new production of *Astro Boy* (1963, dir. Tecuka Osamu). ● Okazaki soon moved from storyboarding into directing, mainly in television. His résumé includes many famous shows from the Sixties and Seventies, including *The Rose of Versailles* (1979, dir. Nagahama Tadao et al), *Tiger Mask* (1969, dir. Tamiya Takeshi et al) and *Dororo* (1969, dir. Sugii Gisaburo et al). Okazaki became a significant member of Studio Junio in the Eighties, presiding over a period in which the company employed a remarkable 120 staffers, producing twenty television episodes in a single month. Much of the company's output was for Toei Animation and Tokyo Movie Shinsha. ● Okazaki directed many episodes of the eighties hit *Dr Slump* (1982), as well as the movie spin-off which provided his first feature credit. However, his output remains largely confined to the world of television anime, which he continues to storyboard and direct, such as the television special *Dracula: Sovereign of the Damned* (1980), based on the Marvel comic. ● In 1986, he directed the TV hit *Dragon Ball* with Nishio Daisuke, setting the anime template for Toriyama Akira's manga, and followed with *Dragon Ball GT* in 1996. In 1998, he joined forces with Wagatsuma Hiroshi and Maeda Minoru to found Synergy Japan, a 'new' animation company largely comprising former staffers from Toei Animation. Synergy was one of many contributors to famous anime at the turn of the century, including the *Cowboy Bebop* movie (2001, dir. Watanabe Shinichiro). However, by 2005, the company was better known as Synergy SP, associated with the ShoPro subsidiary of the Shogakukan publishing corporation. Synergy's first anime was the adaptation of *Hayate the Combat Butler* (2007, dir. Kawaguchi Keiichiro). ● J.Cl.

ABOVE: DORORO'S TRAVELLING COMPANION, HYAKKIMARU, IN A FIGHT SCENE FROM *DORORO* (1969, DIR. SUGII GISABURO ET AL, 26 EPS), ON WHICH OKAZAKI MINORU WORKED ● LEFT: A SEQUENCE OF SCENES FROM *DRAGON BALL Z* (1989, DIR. NISHIO DAISUKE, 102 EPS) AND *DRAGON BALL GT* (1996, DIR. OKAZAKI MINORU ET AL, 64 EPS)

SEE ALSO: ARALE; GOKU; KITARO; LUPIN III; TORIYAMA AKIRA

# OKIURA HIROYUKI

DIRECTOR

In the credit sequence for Watanabe Shinichiro's *Cowboy Bebop: Knocking on Heaven's Door* (2001, dir. Watanabe Shinichiro), a stylish succession of black-and-white urban images reinforces the 'cool' aesthetic central to the imaginary world of *Cowboy Bebop*. The images are ultra-realistic, appearing on screen with a fluidity that calls the idea of anime's expressive limitations into question. The sequence is a brilliant manifestation of the talents belonging to animator Okiura Hiroyuki (born in 1966 in Katano), who was invited by Watanabe to work on the film. Okiura previously directed the feature film *Jin-Roh: The Wolf Brigade* (1998), in which his perfectionism was used to create a dark fantasy with shades of Oshii Mamoru's apocalyptic oeuvre. ● Okiura has left his own stylish mark – characterized by obsessive perfectionism, a flair for realism and attention to detail – on a large number of modern anime classics including *Akira* (1988, dir. Otomo Katsuhiro), *Roujin Z* (1991, dir. Kitakubo Hiroyuki), *Magnetic Rose* (the first section of Otomo Katsuhiro's *Memories*, 1995, directed by Morimoto Koji), *Ghost in the Shell* (1995, dir. Oshii Mamoru), *Ghost in the Shell 2: Innocence* (2004, dir. Oshii Mamoru) and Rintaro's *Metropolis* (2001), not to mention *Paprika* (2006, dir. Kon Satoshi) and the series *Paranoia Agent* (2004, dir. Kon Satoshi) by Kon Satoshi. It's no coincidence that Okiura's career has been associated with people interested in the expressive revival of anime, such as Otomo, Kon and Oshii. Indeed, it was Oshii who recommended that Okiura would be the perfect director for *Jin-Roh*, the last and the only instalment of the film saga dreamt up by the director to be animated. ● J.Co.

LEFT: *SCENES FROM THE FILM* JIN–ROH: THE WOLF BRIGADE *(1999, DIR. OKIURA HIROYUKI, 98 MINS), THE ONLY FILM DIRECTED BY OKIURA HIROYUKI*

SEE ALSO: AKIRA; JIN–ROH; KON SATOSHI; OSHII MAMORU; OTOMO KATSUHIRO

# OSHII MAMORU

A great visionary, dealing in forms, worlds and themes that have echoed through every animated medium from cartoons to videogames, Oshii Mamoru numbers among the greatest animated film-makers in the world. His oeuvre has influenced a generation of disciples, both at Production I.G. and around the world, particularly in the USA, where he has worked on a number of James Cameron and Wachowski brothers' films. Since 2001, he has also collaborated with sound designer Tom Myers at Skywalker Sound. ● A lover of film, Oshii began his career as an animator and directed episodes of the television series *Nils no Fushigi na Tabi* (*Nils' Mysterious Journey* or *The Wonderful Adventures of Nils*, 1980) and *Urusei Yatsura* (1981), before moving into movies with the film version of the latter series *Only You* (1983). The experimental nature of the second film in the *Urusei Yatsura* series, *Beautiful Dreamer* (1984), revealed Oshii's new ambitions for Japanese animation. The *Mobile Police Patlabor* (1989) franchise was a huge success in the mecha genre and perfectly illustrated Oshii's philosophy of the mechanical supremacy. In his pioneering cyberpunk film *Ghost in the Shell* (1995), he transformed the body of cyborg Kusanagi into a vessel of the divine. Nine years later, Kusanugi reappeared as a tribute to Surrealist Hans Bellmer in the sequel *Ghost in the Shell 2: Innocence*, the first Japanese animated work shown at the Cannes Film Festival. ● An animator who, unusually, does not draw himself, Oshii has also made live-action films, the most accomplished of which is still the Polish-language film *Avalon* (2001). ● S.S.

LEFT: PUBLICITY POSTER FOR *GHOST IN THE SHELL 2: INNOCENCE* (2000, DIR. OSHII MAMORU, 100 MINS) ● BELOW: THREE SCENES FROM *JIN-ROH: THE WOLF BRIGADE* (1999, DIR. OKIURA HIROYUKI, 98 MINS), A PROJECT CREATED BY OSHII MAMORU

SEE ALSO: DALLOS; KUSANAGI MOTOKO; JIN-ROH; KANNANI YUICHI; PATLABOR; SAYA; URUSEI YATSURA

# OTAKU NO VIDEO

*Otaku* are fans obsessed with anime, manga and science fiction. They collect anything and everything connected with their passion and dress up as their favourite characters at the drop of a hat. In two medium-length videos made in 1991, the Gainax studio took an entertaining voyage to the heart of the *otaku* phenomenon by following the story of young Kubo who, after meeting an old school friend and suffering a bitter disappointment in love, decides to become the greatest of all *otaku* – the 'ota-king'. ● The story begins in 1982 and covers the entire decade and the next, with an epilogue extending to 2035. But *Otaku no Video* is not just an artful animation, studded with references to the gems of the genre: the story is interspersed with unflattering, spoof live-action interviews with several *otaku*. One accumulates videos he doesn't even have time to watch, another is a 'cosplay' fanatic, while a third reveals his obsession with the heroine of an erotic videogame. These scenes are used as a counterpoint to the animated story, which enthusiastically proclaims its characters' intention to abandon any kind of social life. The phenomenon of *otaku* is depicted as an unbalanced lifestyle, certainly, but one that is turning into a collective happening. ● Exploring this ultra-modern tendency to monomania with a sense of irony, from within rather than from without, has made *Otaku no Video* a success. Its heroes set out to sell their own brand of Grand Prix (GP) characters, then try their hand at animation and create *Giant X*. Similarities to the story of the Gainax studio – whose founders had opened a shop selling spin-off products under the name General Products (hence GP) – may not necessarily be coincidental. ● E.H.

BELOW & TOP RIGHT: SCENES OF THE OBSESSED ANIME FANS (OTAKU) FEATURED IN GAINAX'S OAV SERIES OTAKU NO VIDEO ● RIGHT: A PUBLICITY IMAGE FOR THE SERIES

OTAKU NO VIDEO ● 1991 ● DIR: MORI TAKESHI ● SCR: OKADA TOSHIO ● DES: SONODA KENICHI ● ANI: MATSUBARA HIDENORI ● MUS: TANAKA KOHEI ● PRD: GAINAX ● VIDEO SERIES ● EPS: 2

# OTOMO KATSUHIRO

DIRECTOR

ABOVE: THE ORPHAN ROCK (LEFT) AND THE POWERFUL DUKE RED (RIGHT) FROM *METROPOLIS* (2001, DIR. RINTARO, 107 MINS) ● BELOW: SCENE FROM *AKIRA* (1988, DIR. OTOMO KATSUHIRO, 124 MINS)

The origins of Otomo Katsuhiro's work (born in 1954 in Hasama) lie somewhere between experimentation and tradition. He took his first steps as a draftsman in 1973, drawing on classical texts such as *Hansel and Gretel*, *The Wizard of Oz* and *Robinson Crusoe*, which he adapted as unusual and highly personal parodies. His ability to condense scenes allowed him to develop a dynamic and incisive style, seen in the background designs of his work and in the definition of his characters' faces. ● Among his most important output is the manga *Fireball*, which was an immediate success when it was published in 1979. The characteristics of this piece would later become his trademarks: a taste for depicting architecture, simple brushstrokes and a dynamic pace, added to recurring themes, such as the telekinetic powers of his protagonists and his strong focus on technology. One only has to look at *Rojin Z* (1991, dir. Kitakubo Hiroyuki) and *Metropolis* (2001, dir. Rintaro), films on which he was the screenwriter, to appreciate the passionate physicality with which Otomo describes the machines that are both 'inside' and all around humankind. ● In 1982, Otomo started work on his manga *Akira*, considered to be his first great masterpiece, which he would later adapt as a landmark feature film in 1988. He also worked as a character designer for director Rintaro on the film *Genma Taisen* (*Harmagedon*, 1983), and directed the third part of the anthology film *Neo Tokyo* in 1987. However, despite his great success, he retreated from the anime world and made the live-action film *World Apartment Horror* in 1991, only returning to directing animation for an episode of the film *Memories* (1995) and the monumental *Steamboy* (2004). He also directed *Bugmaster*, the popular live-action adaption of *Mushishi* in 2006. ● G.P.

*SEE ALSO: AKIRA; GINKO; MANIE MANIE; MEMORIES; RINTARO; STEAMBOY; TIMA*

# OTSUKA YASUO

ANIMATOR

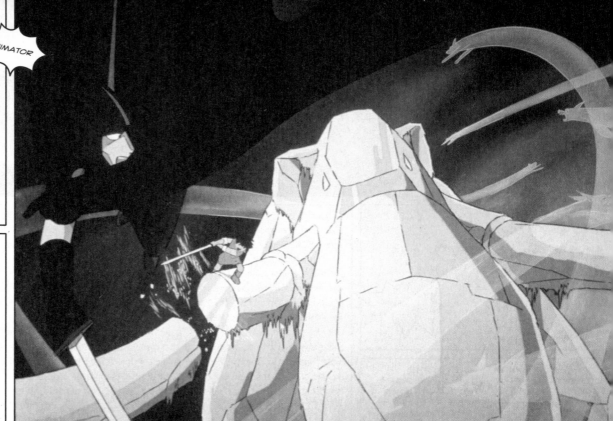

Known mainly by enthusiasts for the substantial contribution he made to the *Lupin III* (1971) series and films, Otsuka Yasuo (born in 1931) has witnessed the story of Japanese animation from its birth, in black and white, right up to the introduction of the television series. He also helped to lay the foundations of Toei Animation in the early Fifties before leaving them to devote himself to an artistic project less susceptible to the demands of a major studio. Today, he devotes himself to teaching students at Telecom Animation Studio. The anime industry owes Otsuka a great deal for having the foresight to foster talents such as Takahata Isao, Kotabe Yoichi and, last but not least, a young Miyazaki Hayao. ● Otsuka is a tireless worker, a designer in love with perfection and the quality of every single scene: see, for example, the movement of the waves in *Sindbad the Sailor* (1962, dir. Yabushita Taiji, Kuroda Yoshio). He also supported bold and innovative film projects, such as Takahata's *Little Norse Prince* (1968, dir. Takahata Isao). As an animator, he has always surprised his audience with his whimsical but carefully conceived characters, while as a character designer he lets a biting irony emerge, as we see in *Lupin III* (1971, dir. Osumi Masaaki et al), in which he preserved the adult component of the original manga character. His great desire is to laugh with the audience, as seen in scenes immortalizing his beloved Fiat 500 driven at crazy speeds in the most exciting chase scenes in the history of anime. ● M.A.R

ABOVE & RIGHT: SCENES FROM ONE OF OTSUKA YAZUO'S EARLY COLLABORATIONS, *LITTLE NORSE PRINCE* (1968, DIR. TAKAHATA ISAO, 82 MINS)

SEE ALSO: HOLS; KOTABE YOICHI; LUPIN III; MIYAZAKI HAYAO; SINDBAD; TAKAHATA ISAO; TOEI ANIMATION

# OTSUKI TOSHIMICHI

PRODUCER

Otsuki Toshimichi was born in 1961 in Ibaraki. His route into anime was radically different from most. As a student he worked part time at *Animage* magazine, before finding work after graduation with King Records, the largest record company in Japan not to be owned by a foreign conglomerate. ● Otsuki's work was at the popular end of music publishing – his early projects at King included producing CD soundtrack collections for the *Certain Death* and *Godzilla* movie series, under the subsidiary label Starchild. Then, after a mass exodus of Starchild staff to form the anime company Youmex, Otsuki became Starchild's manager by default – he was literally the last man standing. ● Otsuki began to focus on new niches in the fan market – he commissioned 'image albums' as spin-off soundtracks for manga that had never been (and would never be) adapted into films. He was instrumental in pushing many anime voice actresses into singing careers and thus helped foster voice actor fandom and merchandizing. ● Otsuki began to commit Starchild's money to front-end investment in anime itself, often as a means of securing the music rights and spin-offs. His name, and Starchild's, began to turn up on production credits for many eighties video series and key television anime of the Nineties, including *Neon Genesis Evangelion* (1995, dir. Anno Hideaki), *Slayers* (1995, dir. Watanabe Takashi et al) and *Revolutionary Girl Utena* (1997, dir. Ikuhara Kunihiko et al). He remains a potent force in modern anime, both initiating productions and encouraging a style that will lend itself to musical spin-offs. ● J.Cl.

ABOVE: PUBLICITY IMAGE FEATURING THE CHARACTERS FROM *NEON GENESIS EVANGELION* (1995, DIR. ANNO HIDEAKI, 26 EPS)

SEE ALSO: ANNO HIDEAKI; EVANGELION; GAINAX; HANEDA KENTARO; KIKUCHI SHUNSUKE; TETSUJIN-28 GO; TENJO UTENA

---

*Panda Kopanda* (*Panda! Go Panda!*), is a cross between a cinema and a television outing for director Takahata Isao (who had not worked in cinema since the fiasco of *Little Norse Prince* in 1968) and is a good example of the double medium-length film. The film was created in 1972 by Miyazaki Hayao for Tokyo Movie Shinsha in response to public enthusiasm for the pandas housed at the Ueno Zoo in Tokyo and was followed in 1973 by the sequel *Panda! Go Panda!: Rainy Day Circus*. ● The anime tells of the extraordinary adventures of young Mimi-chan, while her grandmother is away visiting in another city. When a big panda and his lively cub turn up at the door of her house, the unlikely trio form a family unit and try just about everything to avoid attracting the curiosity of their neighbours. ● Some critics consider the panda, the lead character of the film, to be the ancestor of the giant spirit Totoro, a graceful member of Miyazaki's gallery. Here, however, the project's strength appears to lie in its apparent *nakama*, a Japanese word that means 'team spirit', which was the conceptual and pragmatic engine of Toei Animation animators in the Sixties. The structure of this double film is an effective example of this teamwork: Miyazaki Hayao was responsible for layout and the script, the animator Otsuka Yasuo put all his energies into the humorous action scenes, whilst Takahata Isao oversaw production and aesthetics. ● The film reveals Miyazaki's interest in pedagogy – little Mimi fends for herself without a father figure to guide her – and heralded his imminent professional move to Nippon Animation studio where he worked on *Heidi* (1974, dir. Takamata Isao) and other literary classics. ● M.A.R.

# PANDA KOPANDA
## PANDA! GO PANDA!

FILM

*PANDA KOPANDA* ● *PANDA! GO PANDA!* ● 1972/1973 ● DIR: TAKAHATA ISAO ● SCR & DES: MIYAZAKI HAYAO ● ANI: OTSUKA YASUO ET AL ● MUS: SATO TERUHIKO ● PRD: TMS ● DUR: 30 MINS + 38 MINS

# PAPRIKA

The DC Mini is a device invented by Professor Tokita to allow therapists to enter patients' dreams and explore their unconscious minds. However, when the machine is stolen, it soon becomes clear that even without a connection, and even without subjects being asleep, the device lets the user enter people's dreams and even blend them together. Psychotherapist Chiba Atsuko must use her alter ego, the dream persona Paprika, to stop the criminals merging dreams and reality. ● What interests director Kon Satoshi is not so much the dream scenes themselves as the passage from one dream to another – falling, intruding and experiencing interference as the intoxicating experience of transition brings anguish in its wake. 'Dreams mix with dreams in a whirlwind of dreams,' notes one of characters. *Paprika*'s strength lies in never losing the viewer's attention when confusion threatens: constant metamorphosis (characters become giants, swap one body for another or split into two) ceaselessly brings our attention back to the theme of 'passage' of bodies within the dream. All the dreams are also regularly brought together in a grand parade scene that rattles along, sweeping up animals and household goods alike in a concrete and ironic comment on the total disarray of dreams. ● Paprika holds the key to these dreams. Guardian of the dream world, she is the one who finally 'swallows up' the dreams and restores order from chaos. Ravishingly coiffed, Paprika is also the embodiment of the perfect female figure in animation. She features in erotic fantasies, but these are only developed in strange scenes where her bodily existence is denied, whether by having her dive into another's body or having a man slip his hand under her skin. Pure dream drawing, *Paprika* spices up the lives of its viewers. ● S.D.

IMAGES FROM THE 2006 FILM *PAPRIKA* ● ABOVE: CENTRAL CHARACTER CHIBA ATSUKO AS HER ALTER EGO PAPRIKA ● ABOVE RIGHT: TWO IMAGES OF CHIBA AT WORK WITH PROFESSOR TOKITA ● RIGHT: DETAIL FROM A PUBLICITY IMAGE

*PAPRIKA* ● 2006 ● DIR: KON SATOSHI ● SCR: KON SATOSHI, MAKAMI SEISHI ● DES & ANI: ANDO MASASHI ● MUS: HIRASAWA SUSUMII ● PRD: MADHOUSE ● FILM ● DUR: 90 MINS

# PATLABOR

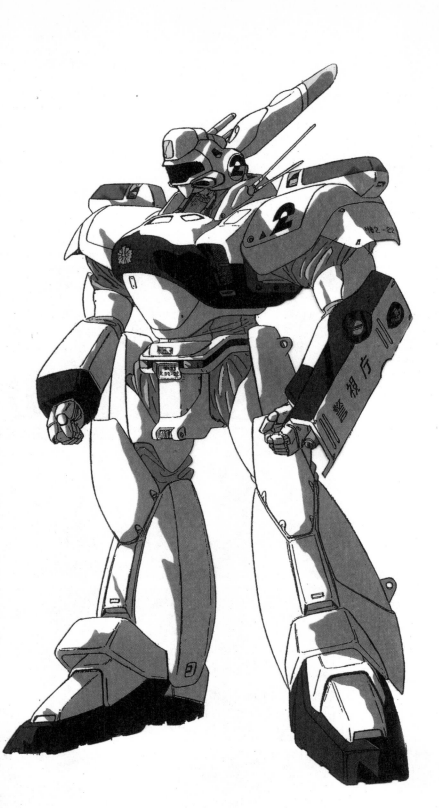

*Mobile Police Patlabor* is set in nineties Japan, where ten-metre-high robots called 'labors' have been put into service in all aspects of public life. There is even a special police department using Patlabors (a shortened form of the 'Patrol' labor vehicles it employs) dedicated to law enforcement. Its most famous division is the Second Platoon, under the command of Goto Kiichi, in which officers from different social backgrounds and their Patlabors are led by the young Izumi Noa to confront eco-terrorists and horrible genetic mutations as well as petty and major criminals. ● *Patlabor* is a highly representative Japanese multimedia product. Created in 1988 by Headgear (five artists and writers led by the brilliant director Oshii Mamoru), it deals with a fairly traditional area of the anime industry, the mecha genre, spawning a manga drawn by Yuki Masami, two OAV series, a television series and three films, as well as countless novels, videogames and parodies. However, unlike other examples of the genre, *Patlabor* has a substantial basis in reality, since the labors do not fly and need ordinary maintenance. The stories told are often related to the world today: from pollution to the threat of terrorism and the dominance of technology to global political instability. The human side of the characters is highlighted by stories of everyday life, with nostalgic and occasionally ironic references to 'the past'. A high-quality franchise, *Patlabor* is undoutedly enriched by the skill of Oshii, who directed *Patlabor the Movie* (1989) and *Patlabor 2: The Movie* (1993), a technical masterpiece depicting a journey of almost prophetic paranoia through modern times. ● M.A.R.

THE 1989 SERIES *PATLABOR*, CREATED BY THE HEADGEAR COLLECTIVE, IS AN OUTSTANDING EXAMPLE OF THE JAPANESE MULTIMEDIA PRODUCT ● ABOVE: A DRAWING FOR PATLABOR ● RIGHT: A DETAIL FROM THE SERIES

KIDO KEISATSU PATLABOR ● PATLABOR ● 1989 ● DIR: YOSHINAGA NAOYUKI ● SCR: ITO KAZUNORI ET AL ● DES: TAKADA AKEMI ● ANI: TAKAGI HIROKI ET AL ● MUS: KAWAI KENJI ● PRD: HEADGEAR, SUNRISE ● VIDEO SERIES ● EPS: 7

# PATRASHE

CHARACTER

*FURANDASU NO INU • DOG OF FLANDERS • 1975 • DIR: KURODA YOSHIO • SCR: NAKANISHI RYUZO ET AL • DES: MORI YASUJI • ANI: SAKAI TOSYUKAZU, TAKAHASHI SHINYA • MUS: WATANABE TAKEO • PRD: NIPPON ANIMATION • TV SERIES • EPS: 52*

When the orphan Nello finds an injured dog on the streets of Antwerp in Flanders, he lovingly takes care of it and names him Patrashe (or Patraasche). From that moment on, the grateful animal starts to help him with his job, pulling the milk cart from his grandfather's house to the city. Nello also forms a firm friendship with a girl called Aloise, despite her father's opposition. The boy has a great talent for art and admires Rubens, longing to see the master's paintings on display in the city cathedral but can't afford the entrance fee. He pins his hopes for a better life on a drawing competition in Antwerp, but loses out to another entrant. After his grandfather's premature death in a fire, desperate and homeless, Nello takes refuge with Patrashe in Antwerp's cathedral to escape the terrible winter. There, he succeeds in seeing Rubens' famous works at last. The next morning, he is found frozen to death, arms around his faithful dog. ● *Dog of Flanders* marked the official opening of the 'World Masterpiece Theatre' series of stories drawn from classics of children's literature. The western settings, depicting early nineteenth-century Europe, immediately captured the attention of Japanese children, as did the fact that the protagonists in the stories were free of the ties of school. These children are often orphans however, and suffer tragedy just around the corner. ● From an aesthetic point of view, the WMT anime present a more sober style of character design and the use of stylistic elements more typical of television anime is visibly reduced. This choice may have been dictated by the very nature of these subjects, which were also fully intended for export at a time in the Seventies before the anime boom. ● S.G.

# PERO

CHARACTER

Banished from the cat kingdom for having spared the life of a mouse, Pero, a gallant, brazen swindler, leaves the imaginary world of Charles Perrault's eighteenth-century fairy tale to become the lead character in a whimsical adaptation of his story in the Toei Animation film *Puss'n'Boots* (1969), directed by Yabuki Kimio. The enormous popularity of the film caused Pero to become the company's mascot and the film was followed by two very different sequels. With the comic counterpoint of a trio of feline assassins, characterized by their clumsiness, and a group of rats which become accomplices to the main character, the film recreated – from the screenplay written by Inoue Hisashi – the plot of the original story and replaced the ogre's character with that of Beelzebub, King of the Underworld. The fast-paced and incredibly imaginative final climax in the 'Castle of Evil' provides a taste of the talent of young Miyazaki Hayao, who worked as an animator and storyboard artist under the supervision of his mentor, Mori Yasuji. ● In 1972, *The Return of Pero*, directed by Katsumata Tomoharu, introduced Pero, together with a new human friend (Jimmy), to the backdrop of a Western. The film combines a number of situations typical of the genre and draws on popular spaghetti Westerns by Sergio Leone which were as authentically American as samurai cinema in Japan. Four years later, *Puss'n'Boots Travels Around the World* (1976) by Shidara Hiroshi completed the trilogy, turning a somewhat depersonalized Pero into a heroic character in a fast-paced version of Jules Verne's *Around the World in Eighty Days*. ● J.Co.

BELOW & RIGHT: PERO, THE WELL-SHOD CAT, IN A VARIETY OF SCENES ILLUSTRATING HIS ILLUSTRIOUS ADVENTURES, FROM THE 1969 FILM *PUSS 'N' BOOTS*

*PUSS'N'BOOTS • 1969 • DIR: YABUKI KIMIO • SCR: INONE HISASHI, YAMAMOTO MORIHISA • DES: OTSUKA YASUO • ANI: MORI YASUJI ET AL • MUS: UNO SEIICHIRO • PRD: TOEI ANIMATION • FILM • DUR: 80 MINS*

魔法のスター
マジカルエミ

Studio Pierrot was founded in May 1979 and has earned a reputation as one of the leading animation producers in Japan. Its wide-ranging catalogue includes science fiction, comedy, educational material, action and adventure, but it is probably best known for its 'Magical Girl' series. Building on the themes of Sixties classics such as *Sally The Witch* (*Mahotsukai Sally*, 1966, dir. Katsuta Toshio), Pierrot's shows stressed the inner conflict that resulted from suddenly acquiring unexpected and magical powers; this created irresistible parables of growing up that little girls could strongly relate to. Kobayashi Osamu's series *Maho no Tenshi Creamy Mami* (*Magical Angel Creamy Mami*, 1983) and Anno Takashi's *Maho no Star Magical Emi* (*Magic Star Magical Emi*, 1985) established a winning formula. ● The studio's first major hit came in October 1981 with the TV series *Urusei Yatsura*, based on Takahashi Rumiko's hit manga and directed by Oshii Mamoru. Another important title was the first ever OAV, *Dallos* (1983) also directed by Oshii. ● More recently, Pierrot has had success with TV series based on popular manga, including *Yu Yu Hakusho* (*Ghost Files*, 1992, dir. Abe Noriyuki), *Fushigi Yuugi* (*The Mysterious Play*, 1996, dir. Kamegaki Hajime at al), *CLAMP Gakuen Tanteidan* (*CLAMP School Detectives*, 1997, dir. Nabeshima Osamu), *Naruto* (2002, dir. Date Hayato et al) and *Bleach* (2004, dir. Abe Noriyuki). ● H.M.

*LEFT: PUBLICITY POSTER FOR MAHO NO STAR MAGICAL EMI (MAGICAL EMI, 1985, DIR. FURUKAWA NOBUYASU ET AL, 38 EPS), ONE OF THE STUDIO'S TRADEMARK 'LITTLE WITCH' PRODUCTIONS*

*SEE ALSO: CREAMY MAMI; DALLOS; KUROSAKI ICHIGO; NARUTO; TAKAHASHI RUMIKO; TOEI ANIMATION; URUSEI YATSURA*

A group of aliens come to Earth from a distant planet where technology is advanced and the words 'hate' or 'war' do not exist. The only defect of the alien society is an exaggerated thriftiness. Arriving after an intergalactic journey, the aliens quickly realize that they need to fill their pockets with money to enjoy most of the fun attractions available to human beings. They are, therefore, forced to engage in the most unlikely types of work, failing amongst other things to understand a single word of the local language, whilst their slim bodies, large heads and small black eyes – similar in appearance to the spirits of the forest in *Princess Mononoke* (1997) – only serve to highlight the PiNMeN's 'alien' status. In their efforts to understand human life, we see them lining up as bowling pins and scattered by bowling balls, diligently mimicking domino tiles or laundry pegs, and even acting as parts of a vending machine. ● PiNMeN are also 'aliens' in the diverse world of anime. They were produced for a television series consisting of twenty episodes broadcast between 2002 and 2005 on Animax, Sony's satellite channel. Each individual episode lasts less than five minutes and the scenes were produced by Studio Pierrot and Trilogy. ● Written and directed by Ikeda Bak (born in 1964 in Kagoshima), *PiNMeN* was produced entirely on computer, with methods and shots borrowed from video clips and the quirky madness of some short story authors. Less extravagant than the works of Morimoto but undeniably cute, this series is ideal web entertainment. ● M.A.R.

# PINMEN

CHARACTER

**193**

*PINMEN ● 2002/2005 ● DIR: IKEDA BAK ● SCR & DES & ANI: IKEDA BAK ● MUS: HOMO SAPIENS SAPIENS ● PRD: STUDIO PIERROT, TRILOGY FUTURE STUDIO ● VIDEO SERIES ● EPS: 20*

CHARACTERS

# POKÉMON

Pokémon (an abbreviation of 'Pocket Monster') are fighting creatures captured and raised by expert trainers in special portable spheres. On his tenth birthday, lively Ash Ketchum (Satoshi in the Japanese series) visits Professor Okido to receive his first Pokémon. But Ash oversleeps and by the time he gets there, all the best Pokémon have gone. He is given an amiable Pikachu, a yellow and black mouse capable of emitting strong electric shocks. The two soon become good friends and begin a long journey that will turn Ash into the greatest Pokémon trainer in Japan! ● Just one year after the Tamagotchi phenomenon, which also relied on children's passion for cyber-pets, *Pokémon* was the most prolific merchandizing success of the Nineties. Created in 1995 (two years before the anime series was broadcast) by Tajiri Satoshi, Pikachu and friends were stars of a videogame phenomenon where the cry of 'Gotta catch 'em all!' urges children to collect as many as they can. ● This idea was simple and successful and has created a market of unexpected proportions, giving birth to a new breed of interactive entertainment that has in turn led to famous imitations of the original series such as *Yu-gi-oh!* (1998) and *Digimon* (1999). This phenomenon marks an era of more openly commercial, globalized and child-friendly animation. The *Pokémon* series follow each other with similar, uncomplicated plots, and will continue as long as interest in the multimedia phenomenon remains high, since the franchise can be reinvented indefinitely because of the mutant-like replication of characters and objects. Like the gaming industry that created them, the Pokémon are constantly evolving. To date, over 600 TV episodes, and 20 movies, specials and OAVs have appeared. ● S.G.

IMAGES FROM THE FIRST *POKÉMON* MOVIE (1998)● ABOVE LEFT: PIKACHU AND HIS TRAINER SATOSHI ● RIGHT: SCENES SHOWING PIKACHU, SATOSHI AND FRIENDS WITH OTHER POCKET MONSTERS

*POKÉMON* ● 1997 ● DIR: HIROAKA MASAMASA, YUYAMA KUNIHIKO ● SCR: TOMIOKA ATSUHIRO ET AL ● DES: TAJIRI SATOSHI ● ANI: YAMADA SHUNYA ● MUS: MIYAZAKI SHINJI ● PRD: OLM ANIMATION STUDIO ● TV SERIES ● EPS: 276

# POM POKO

FILM

ABOVE & BELOW: SCENES SHOWING THE FRIENDLY TANUKI FROM TAKAHATA ISAO'S 1994 ECO-FAIRYTALE *POM POKO*

The third anime made by Takahata Isao for Studio Ghibli, *Pom Poko* (1994) has little in common with the serious themes of *Grave of the Fireflies* (1988) or the nostalgia of *Only Yesterday* (1991). This lively and hugely popular ecological fable tells the story of a village of *tanuki* (Japanese raccoon-dogs) fighting for their survival when human construction projects threaten their environment. ● *Tanukis* are eccentric imps from the panoply of Japanese folklore characters. Capable of shape-shifting into any form, they have large bellies that they use to drum on (making their 'pom poko' noise) and monstrous extendable testicles. They make irresistibly sympathetic characters, as they are at once talkative, lazy, bellicose, clumsy and greedy. ● At first, they wage a comical war against the humans, but the avalanche of gags in the first hour gives way to a disillusioned admission of defeat as it becomes clear that the pom pokos' brash resistance is doomed to failure. The nocturnal parade, when the *tanukis* use every trick they know to frighten the humans away, is immediately forgotten by a blasé child. The pessimistic aspect of the film, set alongside the ecological fable, explores the humans' loss of imagination: they are no longer even capable of feeling wonder. ● *Pom Poko* goes beyond an overt division of animals on one side and humans on the other, as deforestation forces the *tanukis* to try to fit in to city life, which the cunning creatures do with some success. Taking human form, they try to assimilate, even though they are tempted to run away at every turn. Yet they must adapt and forget the rural paradise from which they have been driven. The message is a moving one: within every suit-and-tie-wearing salary slave, there hides a sleeping tanuki. ● S.D.

HEISEI TANUKI GASSEN PONPOKO ● POM POKO ● 1994 ● DIR & SCR: TAKAHATA ISAO ● DES: KAGAWA MEGUMI, OTSUKA SHINJI ● ANI: OTSUKA SHINJI ● MUS: HISAISHI JOE ● PRD: SUZUKI TOSHIO ET AL, STUDIO GHIBLI ● FILM ● DUR: 119 MINS

CHARACTER

# PONYO

The latest creature from Miyazaki Hayao's imagination (drawing on Hans Christian Andersen's *The Little Mermaid*) is the captivating fish-girl Ponyo. She flees the depths of the ocean and her arrogant creator – the sorcerer Fujimoto, who has abandoned humanity to live in the sea – in search of the thrill of adventure. Ponyo's meeting with the little boy Sosuke proves the start of a unique, mutually protective friendship. While Fujimoto calls on the forces of the sea to recapture his creation, child and mermaid journey together to rediscover solidarity and a sense of belonging. ● Executed with a wonderful grace and luminosity, *Ponyo on the Cliff by the Sea* has great thematic depth and a remarkable lightness of touch. Using few narrative elements, the film describes a simple yet fascinating universe that seems to be drawn from a child's imagination. Behind this make-believe world – the house on the sea cliff, the village with its seashore nursing home, Sosuke's father's ship on the far-off horizon – are many issues often found at the heart of Miyazaki's creations: care for the environment, respect for the elderly, the vision of family as an open social structure and the importance of female figures. At the centre of the tale is the idea of guardianship: while Fujimoto guards Ponyo like a precious possession, Sosuke protects her like a parent teaching, her how to live in the world. ● Drawn with joyously childlike line art and soft colours, the film is further enlivened by Hisaishi Joe's wonderful score, which culminates in a breathtaking melody (when the film was shown at the Venice Festival, audiences left the cinema with a smile and the Ponyo theme tune on their lips). ● C.C.

SCENES FROM THE 2008 FILM *PONYO ON THE CLIFF BY THE SEA* ● ABOVE LEFT: THE YOUNG BOY SOSUKE ● ABOVE CENTRE: PONYO AND SOSUKE WITH HIS MOTHER, LISA ● TOP RIGHT: SOSUKE BY THE SEA ● RIGHT CENTRE (TOP): PONYO THE FISH–GIRL ● RIGHT CENTRE (BOTTOM): FUJIMOTO THE WIZARD ● RIGHT: PONYO'S MOTHER, SEA GODDESS GRANMAMARE

*GAKE NO UE NO PONYO* ● *PONYO ON THE CLIFF BY THE SEA* ● 2008 ● DIR & SCR: MIYAZAKI HAYAO ● DES: YOSHIDA NOBORU ● ANI: KONDO KATSUYA ● MUS: HISAISHI JOE ● PRD: SUZUKI TOSHIO ET AL, STUDIO GHIBLI ● FILM ● DUR: 100 MINS

# PORCO ROSSO

Miyazaki Hayao's sixth film, *Porco Rosso*, is very different to the great epics *Nausicaä of the Valley of Wind* (1984) and *Princess Mononoke* (1997) or the children's tales *My Neighbour Totoro* (1988) and *Ponyo on the Cliff by the Sea* (2008). This comedy found success with an often clownish humour and a truculent protagonist sporting a pig's head. ● Marco is a former flying ace from World War I who has turned his hand to hunting pirates in the Adriatic. A curse left him with a pig's head amid perfectly human humans but nobody seems to care, and the only thing about him that attracts remark is his skill as a pilot. He teams up with Fio, an expert female mechanic, and competes against his rival Curtis, whom he finally beats at the end of a long battle that begins in the sky and ends up – hand to hand – in the sea. ● A very simple screenplay gives pride of place to comical situations such as the pilot's first appearance, sleeping in the afternoon sun to the sound of the French revolutionary song 'Le temps de cerises', or the final epic fight that leaves both combatants covered in bruises. The meditative, gliding flights of *Nausicaä* give way to the energy of the war film, and blue gives way to red as the predominant colour. ● This film is the only instance of Miyazaki depicting a specific historical and geographical location – the Mediterranean in the inter-war years – and certain details (particularly with regard to aviation) are unexpectedly realistic. ● The eponymous protagonist, comically named 'Red Pig' in Italian, is overwhelming in his presence. He sports a snout and big, floppy ears, but at the same time, a moustache, tie and sunglasses. A stylish pig, a dandy and a formidable fighter, Porco Rosso remains one of Miyazaki's most popular characters. ● S.D.

SCENES FROM THE 1992 FILM *PORCO ROSSO* FEATURING ITS ECCENTRIC PORCINE HERO ● ABOVE LEFT: PORCO ROSSO WITH AMERICAN FLYING ACE CURTIS ● CENTRE LEFT: IN THE AIR ● BELOW LEFT: WITH PLANE MAKER PICCOLO ● BELOW: FLEEING THE FASCISTS

KURENAI NO BUTA ● PORCO ROSSO ● 1992 ● DIR & SCR: MIYAZAKI HAYAO ● DES: MIYAZAKI HAYAO ET AL ● ANI: KAGAWA MEGUMI ET AL ● MUS: HISAISHI JOE ● PRD: SUZUKI TOSHIO ET AL, STUDIO GHIBLI ● FILM ● DUR: 93 MINS

# PRODUCTION REED

STUDIO

Production Reed was known as Ashi Production until November 2007. Founded in December 1975 by Sato Toshihiko, the company started as a subcontractor for Nippon Animation, before making TV series *Maho no Princess Minky Momo* (*Magical Princess Minky Momo*, also known as *Gigi and the Fountain of Youth*, 1982, dir. Yuyama Kunihiko et al). A precursor of similar works from other studios, *Minky Momo* typified Eighties anime for girls, with its emphasis on the contrast between the sudden fulfillment of all the heroine's dreams and the inner conflicts this brought about. The studio made three further 'Magical Girl' series. ● Reed has also created or worked on many science fiction and adventure series, including *Uchu Senshi Baldios* (*Space Warrior Baldios*, 1981, dir. Hirokawa Kazuyuki), *Choujuu Kishin Dancougar* (*Super-Bestial Machine God Dancougar*, 1985, dir. Habara Nobuyoshi, Okura Seiji), *Sonic Soldier Borgman* (1988, dir. Negishi Hiroshi et al), *Macross 7* (1994, dir. Amino Tetsuro) and *Kaiketsu Zorro* (*Zorro the Magnificent*, 1996, dir. Minoguchi Katsumi et al). ● Most of Reed's work in animation is for a television audience, with few OAVs or movies. They are often original stories rather than manga adaptations – with exceptions such as 2009's *Tsubasa: Shunraiki* (*Tsubasa: Spring Thunder*, dir. Tada Shunsuke) based on CLAMP's manga. ● H.M.

IMAGES FROM TWO SERIES PRODUCED BY ASHI PRO, PREDECESSOR OF PRODUCTION REED ● TOP: SCENE FROM *MAHO NO PRINCESS MINKY MOMO* (*FAIRY PRINCESS MINKY MOMO*, 1982, DIR. YUYAMA KUNIHIKO ET AL, 61 EPS) ● ABOVE & LEFT: SCENE FROM *UCHU SENSHI BALDIOS* (*SPACE WARRIOR BALDIOS*, 1980, DIR. HIROKAWA KAZUYUKI ET AL, 31 EPS) AND A POSTER FOR THE SERIES

SEE ALSO: MACROSS; MIYU; PIERROT; TETSUJIN 28-GO

# RAKKA

CHARACTER

Written by Abe Yoshitoshi, the creator of *Serial Experiments Lain* (1998), *Haibane Renmei* (*League of Ashen Wings: Charcoal Feathers Federation*) has an unusual conceit: describing the lives of angels, or 'Haibane', mysteriously confined in the walled city of Guri. The Haibane emerge from cocoons and live together in this blue-grey purgatory before taking flight for a future destination never elucidated in the series. ● The first episode made a strong impression: little Rakka, newly fallen from the sky, grows wings that tear their way out of her back, opening out from two humps in a gory image with monstrous erotic connotations. The rest of the series avoids such violence, except in one traumatic episode when Rakka lacerates her black-flecked wings with scissors. ● The little Haibane constantly question the reason for their own existence and wonder what they are doing 'there' in a melancholy discourse running throughout the series. The middle segment expands the legend of the grey wings, which describes how, before moulding man, God created angels with grey wings; he then thought better of it, put these creations away in a corner of his mind and forgot about them. God forgot these lost children because they each have a sin that has to be forgiven. Rakka, for example, only finds peace by burying someone who had tried to save her but of whose help she was unaware. The older character Reki, a cigarette always in her mouth, obstinately refuses to acknowledge her errors. The unique nature of *Charcoal Feather Federation* lies in this strange mixture of Christian morality and Japanese horror. ● The series' metaphysical dimension is accompanied by a mischievous description of the angels' social life. They are drawn with clever detail, giving an air of realism to a story that leaves a great many questions unanswered in terms of narrative. ● S.D.

HAIBANE RENMEI ● 2002 ● DIR: ABE YOSHITOSHI, OKORO TOMOKAZU ● SCR: ABE YOSHITOSHI ● DES: TARADA AKIRA ● ANI: UJIE AKIO ET AL ● MUS: OTANI KO ● PRD: RADIX ● TV SERIES ● EPS: 13

---

ascal is a lovable raccoon from the American writer Sterling North's autobiographical novel, *Rascal: A Memoir f a Better Era* (1963). He is also one of the most pampered characters of the 'World Masterpiece Theatre' ranchise, based on a series of children's novels and produced by Nippon Animation. ● When his mother is killed y a hunter, Rascal is saved by the young Robby North and his friend Oscar in the Wisconsin woods. Since he cub is too small to fend for itself Robby decides to look after it at home and the raccoon soon becomes fully fledged member of the North family. ● Rascal is a well-loved character in Japan (more popular even than lickey Mouse) and the promoter's commercial flair has spawned an astonishing number of products: from DVDs istributed by Bandai Visual to teddy bears, teacups, books, soaps and shampoos. A literary creation and *kawaii* cute') icon, Rascal arrived on television in a beautifully animated series directed by Endo Seiji and Koshi Shigeo, wo veterans who share the general directorship of fifty-two episodes (some featuring Miyazaki Hayao as an nimator). Endo's direction is recognizable for his realistic, simple design where more attention is paid to Robby's pbringing and his life with Rascal than on stylistic detail, a decision that highlights the importance of values and motions and sometimes criticizes the harshness of adults (such as the whippings given by Oscar's father). ● M.A.R.

# RASCAL

CHARACTER

ARAIGUMA RASCAL ● RASCAL: A MEMOIR OF A BETTER ERA ● 1977 ● DIR: ENDO SEIJI, KOSHI SHIGEO ● SCR: MIYAZAKI AKIRA ● DES: ENDO SEIJI ● ANI: OKUDA SEIJI ET AL ● MUS: WATANABE TAKEO ● PRD: NIPPON ANIMATION ● TV SERIES ● EPS: 52

---

# REMY
## REMÌ

CHARACTER

emì is an eight-year-old boy who grows up in poverty in the French village of Chavanon, with a mother and father whom he believed to be his real parents. His discovery that he s a foundling, abandoned in Paris as a baby, marks the beginning of his new, tormented life. When his adoptive father loses his job, he sells the little boy to Vitalis, an itinerant artist who performs on the streets with his dogs Capi, Zerbino and Dolce, and the monkey oli Coeur. Remì's life passes quietly with the small company, who are always moving from ne city to another, but things change when Vitalis is imprisoned. Remì is forced to grow p quickly and must learn to live alone. ● He is helped along the way by a number of haracters. He meets Mrs Milligan and her son Arthur as they travel on their luxury yacht nd gets taken in by the Aquin family, where he makes friends with little Lisa. In Paris he neets Matthias, a street boy destined to become his most faithful friend and he finally ncovers his true identity when he discovers that he is Mrs Milligan's first born son. ● aken from the French novel *Sans Famille* (1878) by Hector Malot, *Nobody's Boy* is almost melodrama, with its strongly emotional tones and its ability to express the most intense eelings with light touches. The series describes the desperate search for a place to stay nd a sense of belonging, in which pain, joy, loneliness and despair are always carried to heir extreme consequences. The graphic treatment that characterizes the series was reated by Dezaki Osamu, the designs by Sugino Akio and the richness of scenery by obayashi Shichiro. ● G.P.

IGHT: CLOSE UP OF REMÌ, THE TRAGIC HERO OF THE 1977 SERIES *NOBODY'S BOY*

IE NAKI KO ● NOBODY'S BOY ● 1977 ● DIR: DEZAKI OSAMU ● SCR: YAMAZAKI HARUYA, ITO TSUNEHISA ● DES: SUGINO AKIO ● ANI: UNCREDITED ● MUS: WATANABE TAKEO ● PRD: TMS ● TV SERIES ● EPS: 51

# RIBBON NO KISHI
## PRINCESS KNIGHT

Large dark eyes, a curl of black hair on her forehead and a large hat are the distinctive features of the graceful and sensual 'knight with the fringe', known in the West as Princess Knight. This character, born a woman but forced to dress as a man, is the founding archetype of *shojo* (girls') manga and its long series of tragic heroines, from Lady Oscar to Utena. When Tezuka Osamu first published *Princess Knight* manga in 1953, he was inspired by the intrigues in Shakespearean drama and by Takarazuka theatre, a musical where characters were interpreted exclusively by women. *Princess Knight* was the first post-war comic aimed at a predominantly female readership. ● Tezuka made two other versions of the story, in 1958 and 1963, which vary in style, design and plot development, before he adapted them for animation at Mushi Production in 1967. The television series, most faithful to the third version of the manga, extends the princesses adventures in to some fifty-two episodes. The stylized setting and fantasy elements of the manga are translated to medieval Europe in the animated version, filtered through Hollywood-style sources, including *Snow White* and *Robin Hood*, thereby paying tribute to Tezuka's own sources of inspiration. The author's smooth and stylish design is faithfully adapted in the anime and is further enriched by a palette of pop and expressionist colours. ● The protagonist Sapphire, heir to the throne of Silverland, is born with two souls, one male and one female, because of a joke played upon her by spiteful angel Tink. To ascend the throne and stop it from falling into the hands of the perfidious Duke Duralumin, Sapphire is forced to dress as a man, renouncing love and fighting against injustice. ● L.D.C.

SCENES FROM THE 1967 SERIES *PRINCESS KNIGHT* ● LEFT: SAPPHIRE MEETS HER PRINCE AND FALLS IN LOVE ● BELOW: SAPPHIRE ON HORSEBACK AND WITH TINK (LEFT)

RIBBON NO KISHI ● PRINCESS KNIGHT ● 1967 ● DIR: TEZUKA OSAMU ET AL ● SCR: TEZUKA OSAMU, TSUJI MASAKI ● DES: NAKAMURA KAZUKO ET AL ● ANI: UEGUCHI TERUTO ● MUS: TOMITA ISAO ● PRD: MUSHI PRODUCTION ● TV SERIES ● EPS: 52

# RINTARO

DIRECTOR

Rintaro is the pseudonym used by Hayashi Shigeyuki, living legend of Japanese cinema who has witnessed all the main stages in modern anime during a career spanning more than fifty years. Rintaro worked as character designer in the full-length film *Legend of the White Snake* (1958, dir. Yabushita Taiji) and as an animator on *Astro Boy* (1963), directed by Tezuka Osamu, with whom he later collaborated on many films. A versatile animator and art director, he made a number of television series in the Sixties and Seventies, first with Mushi Production and then with Madhouse, which he founded in 1972 together with his friends Dezaki Osamu, Kawajiri Yoshiaki and Maruyama Masao. He first rose to fame when he worked with Matsumoto Leiji on *Space Pirate Captain Harlock* (1978) and *Galaxy Express 999* (1979), before directing powerful works for Kadokawa Haruki such as *Genma Taisen* (*Harmagedon*, 1983), *The Dagger of Kamui* (1985) and the dreamlike *Neo Tokyo* (1983), in which he was supported by rising star Otomo Katsuhiro. In the latter two titles Rintaro shows a passion for experimentation far from the aesthetic clichés found in more commercial anime, borrowing form and suggestion from Japanese Noh theatre and silent film, and using psychedelic images with strong contrasts. In *X: 1999* (*X: The Movie*, 1997), he returned to a more classic directing style, which did not prevent him from successfully creating a dark atmosphere, echoed in the most recent Captain Harlock revival *The Endless Odyssey* (2002). His masterpiece is *Metropolis* (2001), based on the manga of the same name by Tezuka, in which he makes extensive use of mechanical movement, often to dizzying effect, using designs that recall silent films. He has also worked as artistic supervisor and storyboarder on many Madhouse projects. ● S.G.

SEE ALSO: HARLOCK; JIRO; MAETEL; MANIE MANIE; TEITO MONOGATARI; TIMA

# ROBOT COMMUNICATIONS

STUDIO

Founded in 1986, production company Robot Communications was originally an advertising firm, with an animation division specializing in inserts for TV commercials and movie special effects. Its work on live-action film *Always Sanchome no Yuhi* (*Always Sunset on Third Street*, 2005, dir. Yamazaki Takashi) won a following among film buffs thanks to its expressive camera work and evocative use of computer graphics that brought Fifties Tokyo to life. ● Rather than following the usual path of making weekly TV series for a half-hour broadcast slot, the company has expanded its animation activity by producing short films such as the five-minute *Stray Sheep* (1995, dir. Nomura Tatsutoshi). It also continues its other business activities, producing visual content for TV commercials, movies and computer graphics, designing and managing websites, music software production, character creation, graphic design and mobile phone technologies. ● Robot has taken an unusual route into the anime business; by using the technology and expertise needed for its commercial work to enable and encourage its creative staff – thus minimizing production costs and nurturing independent productions by individual authors – it has been able to create innovative animation. The studio's efforts were rewarded with an Oscar for Best Short Animated Film at the 2009 Academy Awards for *Tsumiki no ie* (*House of Small Cubes*, 2008), directed by Kato Kunio. Kato's next work for Robot was *The Diary of Tortov Riddle* (2003). ● H.M.

BELOW: EVOCATIVE IMAGES FROM THE OSCAR–WINNING SHORT FILM *THE HOUSE OF SMALL CUBES* (2008, DIR. KATO KUNIO, 12 MINS)

*SEE ALSO: TSUMIKI NO IE*

# ROUJIN Z  FILM

No longer able to look after himself, the elderly Mr Takizawa is chosen by the Ministry of Health as a guinea pig to test 'Project Z', a modern, all-purpose robotic bed that will care for the patient's every need. Sensing the lack of human warmth in this project, Haruko, a young volunteer nurse, breaks into the medical centre and finds that the bed shows worrying signs of self-awareness, and does not intend to stay put. Bed and patient live in symbiosis, becoming a kind of cyborg known as 'Roujin Z'. ● *Roujin Z* is one of several nineties anime conceived by Otomo Katsuhiro, who in this case left the directing to his trusted assistant Kitakubo Hiroyuki while taking care of the mechanics design and screenplay. The film takes up some of the themes explored in the better-known *Akira* (1988), though it differs in terms of budget and atmosphere, with more emphasis on social satire. Again, abuse of technology is perceived as resulting in disaster and it is young people (a group of university students) who oppose the government, which, along with the army and the scientific establishment, is pursuing military ambitions in the guise of a social project. ● Otomo does not conceal his passion for the 'metal man' figure, and his obsession with mutation is presented in a farcical way: the bed takes over all the pieces of apparatus it comes across. Even the scenes of destruction are not drawn with his trademark tangled tubes. The testing of the Z, with poor Mr Takiwaza attached to it, is possibly a tribute to the famous mechanical meal sequence in Chaplin's *Modern Times* (1936, dir. Charles Chaplin). ● S.G.

ROUJIN Z ● 1994 ● DIR: KITAKUBO HIROYUKI ● SCR: OTOMO KATSUHIRO ● DES: EGUCHI HISASHI ● ANI: KON SATOSHI ● MUS: ITAKURA BUN ● PRD: MOVIC, STUDIO A.P.P.P. ● FILM ● DUR: 80 MINS

# RYU

CHARACTER

In a prehistoric setting where men and dinosaurs live side by side, Ryu is a fair-skinned boy who is a victim of prejudice in a land of darker-skinned people. When Kitty, the ape who brought him up, is killed Ryu undertakes a mission to find his real mother. Followed on his odyssey by his faithful companions Ran, Don and Kiba. ● An orphan on a sentimental journey can be found in several series of the era and is a common theme in anime (*Maya the Bee*, 1970, dir. Saito Hiroshi, *Nobody's Boy*, 1970, dir. Serikawa Yugo), but in this instance it is combined with the issue of racism – a subject also explored in *UFO Robot Grendizer Raids* (1975, dir. Katsumata Tomoharu et al) and *Koya no Shonen Isamu* (*Cowboy Isamu* or *Wilderness Boy Isamu*, 1973, dir. Takahata Isao et al). At the heart of the story is a multicultural vision that breaks with the typical conservatism of Japanese tradition, metaphorically symbolized by the one-eyed dinosaur, Tyrannus. ● Based on a manga by Ishinomori Shotaro, *Ryu the Cave Boy* is notable for its original style that brought brutal fights, mutual oppression, hunting and violent clashes between man and nature back into fashion. Almost incongruous in a decade where the heroes looked decidedly to the future, the animated series (made by Toei and enhanced by Komatsubara Kazuo's excellent design and Urata Mataharu's picturesque backdrops) intentionally abandoned all science-fiction references found in the original manga. *Ryu the Cave Boy* can also be considered part of the post-catastrophe genre, with particular references to the film classic *Planet of the Apes* (1968, dir. Franklin J. Schaffner). ● D.D.G.

RIGHT: RYU, CAVE GIRL RAN AND LITTLE DON IN SCENES FROM THE 1971 TV SERIES, RYU THE CAVE BOY, PRODUCED BY TOEI

GENSHI SHONEN RYU ● RYU THE CAVE BOY ● 1971 ● DIR: AKIHI MASAYUKI ● SCR: KONDO TADASHI ET AL ● DES: KOMATSUBARA KAZUO ● ANI: URATA MATAHARU ET AL ● MUS: WATANABE TAKEO ● PRD: TOEI ANIMATION ● TV SERIES ● EPS: 22

R

# SAGI TSUKIKO

CHARACTER

Sagi Tsukiko is a young designer working in Tokyo. She is the creator of the pink dog Maromi, a wildly popular mascot character in the same vein as Hello Kitty. When Sagi is beaten up in the street, all she can remember of her attacker is that he was a young kid wearing a baseball cap and gold rollerblades. Two detectives take up the case and begin to look for the attacker known as Shonen Bat (literally Bat Boy, or L'il Slugger in western translations), who strikes again several times, bringing considerable fear to the city. Gradually, the heart of the story emerges from the boy's disturbed psyche. The popular success of the mascot Maromi was based on the false sense of well-being and affectionate warmth it gave its owner and Shonen Bat acts as a kind of 'negative' to Maromi, leading the detectives to wonder if he was one of Sagi's inventions. ● In *Paranoia Agent*, a mini masterpiece in urban film noir and post-modern reconstruction, Kon Satoshi engages in a sociological analysis of Japanese society. The series suggests that city-dwellers, in the grip of a consumerist frenzy, need to escape from their precarious and frenetic existence, which leads to a confusion of fantasy and reality. ● The study of the psyche is of great interest to Kon, in particular the states of change and split reality that are studied again in *Paprika* (2006, dir. Kon Satoshi). *Paranoia Agent* is filled with numerous allusions to Japanese culture, both traditional and pop. It also contains more obscure references, such as the names of characters that allude to phases of the moon and the animal world. ● F.L.

*MOSO DAIRININ ● PARANOIA AGENT ● 2004 ● DIR: KON SATOSHI ● SCR: MINAKAHI SEISHI, YOSHINO TOMOMI ● DES: ANDO MASASHI ● ANI: ASAKI AKIKO ET AL ● MUS: HIRASAWA SUSUMU ● PRD: MADHOUSE ● TV SERIES ● EPS: 13*

# SAILOR MOON

CHARACTER

With her hair tied back in two pigtails, huge eyes and dressed in a sailor-suit school uniform, Sailor Moon, the magical incarnation of schoolgirl Tsukino Usagi, was the iconic 'magical girl' of the Nineties. Created by Takeuchi Naoko, the series took the genre another step forward along the road from comedy to fantasy. Usagi (called Serena in the US translation) forms a magic team or 'sentai' with some fellow girls (an idea possibly inspired by Asamiya Kia's science-fiction manga *Silent Möbius*, 1991) to fight against villainous creatures from other worlds. ● The series is closer to *Cutey Honey* (1973, dir. Katsumata Tomoharu et al) than *Creamy Mami* (1983, dir. Kobayashi Osamu et al), but the latter also contributed to establishing Sailor Moon as an idol for modern youth. The fairytale often merges the boundaries between dreams and reality and its various representations. The magical name Sailor Moon derives from a television heroine loved by Usagi and by her little brother Shingo. Sailor Moon also has to conceal her past life as a princess and falls in love with a mysterious warrior who appears in evening dress to rescue her from trouble. Indeed, the heroine is not very heroic, but capricious, childish and often ignorant of how to use her powers. Thus, she gets into situations with her friends ranging from complicity to angry confrontation; behaviour which helped the audience to identify with her. ● The most original invention lies in the series' style, which draws on some common devices of manga language. There are lots of 'speech bubbles' and enormous 'sweat drops' on the back of the neck, denoting embarrassment, and graphic signs are used to restore the characters' mood, confirming again the metanarrative nature of the production. ● D.D.G.

*IMAGES FROM THE 1992 SERIES SAILOR MOON ● ABOVE LEFT: PRINCESS SERENITY'S LOVE, PRINCE ENDYMION ● ABOVE RIGHT: SAILOR CHIBI CHIBI MOON ● RIGHT: PRINCESS SERENITY, USAGI'S ALTER EGO*

*SAILOR MOON ● 1992 ● DIR: SATO JUNICHI ET AL ● SCR: TOMITA SUKEHIRO ET AL ● DES & ANI: TADANO KAZUKO ET AL ● MUS: ARISAWA TAKANORI, KOMORO TETSUYA ● PRD: TOEI ANIMATION ● TV SERIES ● EPS: 46*

# SAINT SEIYA

Created by Masami Kurumada, the manga *Saint Seiya* is a fascinating exercise in cultural syncretism that mixes eastern and western mythology and religion. The story revolves around a group of boys following the cult of the goddess Athena, who are trained to use their own internal energy (the 'Cosmo') as a weapon against enemies of ever-higher rank: the author has plotted a very precise hierarchy with the protagonists, as Bronze Saints, followed by Silver and Gold Saints and ending with the Greek gods. Overcoming their own limits and acquiring senses known only to the chosen few are vital for the Saints to fulfil their mission and complete the typical story-arc of training. ● The story mixes sources from Christian, Chinese, Greek and Norse mythology and refers to biblical archetypes, such as a patriarch who sires a multitude of children to give new life to the myth of the Saints of Athena. To this is added the warriors' journey through the Temple of Athena and a picturesque Hell where Dantesque figures combine characteristics also typical of Buddhism and Judaism. This symbolism is also seen in the constellations that inspire each of the five Saints: Pegasus, Andromeda, Phoenix, Cygnus and Dragon. ● The television series' elegant design work, by Araki Shingo, emphasizes the characters' androgynous appeal and the fight scenes have an anti-realistic style that uses kinetic lines and spectacular blows to reproduce cosmic explosions. Curiously, the main section of the manga – the fight between the Saints and the god Hades – was left out of the original television series and was only animated in recent years. ● D.D.G.

LEFT: A PUBLICITY IMAGE FOR THE 1986 SERIES SAINT SEIYA (CLOCKWISE FROM LEFT: ANDROMEDA SHUN, DRAGON SHIRYU, CYGUNS HYOGA AND PEGASUS SEIYA) ● BELOW: TWO SCENES FROM THE SERIES: GRAND POPE SHION, POSESSED BY THE EVIL SAGA (LEFT) AND ANDROMEDA SHUN (RIGHT)

SAINT SEIYA ● 1986 ● DIR: MORISHITA KOZO, KIKUCHI KAZUHITO, KOYAMA TAKAO ET AL ● DES: ARAKI SHINGO ET AL ●
ANI: ARAKI SHINGO, AOKI TETSURO ● MUS: YOKOYAMA SEIJI ● PRD: TOEI ANIMATION ● TV SERIES ● EPS: 114

# SAIYUKI ALAKAZAM THE GREAT

FILM

SAIYUKI ● ALAKAZAM THE GREAT ● 1960 ● DIR: YABUSHITA TAIJI, SHIRAKAWA DAISAKU ● SCR: KONTAIBO GORO ET AL ● DES: TEZUKA OSAMU ● ANI: MORI YASUJI, OKUBARA AKIRA ● MUS: HATTORI RYOICHI ● PRD: TOEI ANIMATION ● FILM ● DUR: 88 MINS

The protagonist of Yabushita Taiji and Shirakawa Daisaku's film *Saiyuki* (1960) is Son Goku, the daring, dynamic and ambitious monkey king, one of many anime figures that claim descent (to varying degrees) from the hero of Wu Cheng-En's sixteenth-century Chinese story *Xiyouji* (*Journey to the West*). The hero of *Saiyuki* is a cinematic version of the Son Goku in manga *My Monkey King* (1952), created by Tezuka Osamu after seeing *Tie shan gongzhu* (*Princess Iron Fan*, 1941), Asia's first feature-length animated film, made in China by the brothers Wan Guchan and Wan Laiming. Tezuka worked as a consultant on the film adaptation of his manga and helped to promote it (although he did not direct, as the production company sought to suggest). This proved decisive in stimulating his interest in the medium and ultimately transformed him into a driving force behind the development of the language of anime. ● In *Saiyuki*, Son Goku proclaims himself the king of the monkeys and learns the secrets of magic from the Emperor of Heaven, but he dares to defy the gods and is condemned to accompany the son of Buddha on his journey to India. ● *Saiyuki* was one of the first Japanese feature-length animated films to be exported to the US market under the title *Alakazam The Great*, but despite a soundtrack by Les Baxter and dubbing by stellar voiceover actors, including Jonathan Winters, Dodie Stevens, Arnold Stang, Sterling Holloway and Frankie Avalon (Saiyuki's singing voice) for the songs, the attempt to westernize the film proved unsuccessful. ● J.Co.

# SAKAMOTO RYUICHI

COMPOSER

In 1987, noted pianist Sakamoto Ryuichi, following a series of prestigious partnerships with artists and performers such as David Sylvian, David Byrne, Nam June Paik and Iggy Pop, wrote the original music for two films: Bernardo Bertolucci's *The Last Emperor* and *The Wings of Honneamise* by Yamaga Hiroyuki. For the first of these, he won an Academy Award, paving the way for mainstream recognition of his film music, while the second failed to live up to box-office expectations. The lack of popular response to the complex *Wings of Honneamise* perhaps goes some way towards explaining why it continues to remain the celebrated Japanese composer's sole contact with animation thus far; his refined and elusive scores are a poor match for the commercial soul of the animated film. Nonetheless, Sakamoto's syncretism and eclectic style have made him an enormously successful composer for film and the score he wrote for *Honneamise* (along with Nomi Yuji and Ueno Koji) is an excellent example of his work. Mixing very different sounds and melodies (accentuating Oriental tradition with electronic material), Sakamoto creates a sonic world that echoes the visual universe imagined by Yamaga: Oriental in character, but clearly influenced by the Soviet Union and the USA. If the film is conceived as a sort of farewell to the Cold War, the music underlines its melancholy tone and the existential despondency inherent in its leading character, the astronaut Shirotsugu. ● Developing a limited number of melodic ideas and featuring several superbly-paced episodes, the music occasionally recalls *Blade Runner* (1982, dir. Ridley Scott), from which Sakamoto quoted passages. The soundtrack is a fascinating one-off experiment, a creative model in music, which ends up enriching and deepening each shot. ● C.C.

ABOVE: THE YOUNG SPACE PILOT SHIROTSUGU FROM *THE WINGS OF HONNEAMISE* (1987, DIR. YAMAGA HIROYUKI, 120 MINS)

SEE ALSO: GAINAX; LHADATT, SHIROTSUGU; YAMAGA HIROYUKI

# SALLY

CHARACTER

MAHOTSUKAI SALLY ● SALLY THE WITCH ● 1966 ●
DIR: KASAI OSAMU ET AL ● SCR: SARAI AKIYOSHI
ET AL ● DES: HANE YOSHIYUKI ● ANI: KASAI
TAKASHI ET AL ● MUS: KOBAYASHI YASEI ● PRD:
TOEI ANIMATION ● TV SERIES ● EPS: 109

Created by Yokoyama Mitsuteru for a short manga, Sally is the forerunner of the *majokko* genre and the best known of the first generation of 'magical girls'. The Toei Animation series *Sally the Witch* was initially broadcast in black and white, before turning to colour after the seventeenth episode. ● Sally is a young witch sent to Earth by her parents to learn to act responsibly. Her interactions with the characters she meets take the form of simple adventures, told in self-contained episodes, that allow her to gain experience and reflect on the mechanisms that regulate society. ● The series is a light, subtle analysis of the problems associated with social interactions and with growing up, still a long way from the magical girls who transform themselves in a blaze of colour and perform spectacular feats. Although Sally tries to keep her powers hidden from the people of Earth, her magic metaphorically expresses an adolescent desire for freedom and frustration with the restrictions imposed on her. This formula made it easy for audiences to identify with her and ensured the series' success. The same model was later adopted by other successful series, such as *The Secrets of Akkochan*, (1969, dir. Ikeda Hiroshi et al), *Meggu, The Little Witch*, (1974, dir. Araki Shingo, Serikawa Yugo) and *Lalabel, The Magical Girl* (1980, dir. Shidara Hiroshi et al). ● The design is crucial in creating distinctive characters (influenced by Yokoyama's manga), with a focus on the immediacy of their physical traits and on the backgrounds and settings, as well as the magic effects. There is also a sequel to *Sally the Witch*, made twenty years later in 1989, that tells the story of Sally's return to Earth. ● D.D.G.

Undoubtedly one of Miyazaki Hayao's most highly regarded films, *Princess Mononoke* (1997) beat all box-office records in Japan but was not released in the USA until 1999 and 2000 in France. ● The young warrior Ashitaka is infected with an incurable disease during a fight with a giant demonic boar. He sets out in search of the sickened land from which the demon has come, meeting the teenage girl San along the way. San lives wild with the wolf goddess Moro, and Ashitaka finds himself caught up in a war between human beings and the Forest. ● Full of ideas and vitality, and packed with amazing images, *Princess Mononoke* is an extraordinary film. Miyazaki pushes epic form, visual lyricism and philosophical allegory to their limits, while carefully developing each character and the relationship between his two main protagonists. ● Some of Miyazaki's visual metaphors and sound effects are truly brilliant: the Spirit of the Forest is a 'night-walker', a giant who walks above the trees at night and is transformed into a benevolent-looking reindeer when he comes into silent contact with ordinary mortals; the kodamas, diminutive, sprites of Japanese mythology living in the trees, rattle when they turn their heads; and the feral child San, her face painted red as she savagely licks the blood of her victim. ● This philosophical tale plumbs the depths of sadness, its emotional power amplified by the music of Hisaishi Joe. The traumatic images of the Spirit of the Forest being decapitated and the kodamas falling from the trees, indicate that Miyazaki's funeral lament for the natural world is far more than a moral tale for children. As expressed by the image of the hero's infected arm, the film is utterly pessimistic as to the ability of humans to live in harmony with nature again. ● S.D.

# SAN

CHARACTER

IMAGES FROM THE 1997 FILM *PRINCESS MONONOKE* ● ABOVE LEFT & CENTRE: THE WARRIOR ASHITAKA ● ABOVE RIGHT: SAN WITH THE GODDESS MORO ● RIGHT: SAN READY FOR BATTLE

MONONOKE HIME ● *PRINCESS MONONOKE* ● 1997 ● DIR & SCR & DES: MIYAZAKI HAYAO ● ANI: ANDO MASAHI ET AL ●
MUS: HISAISHI JOE ● PRD: SUZUKI TOSHIO ET AL, STUDIO GHIBLI ● FILM ● DUR: 135 MINS

# SANPEI THE FISHERMAN

TV SERIES

With his sincere face and dazzling smile, Sanpei the Fisherman is always ready to embark on a new challenge, facing any situation with all of his strength and without fear. Dressed in a hat and traditional straw sandals, the young Nihira Sanpei is a sunny and positive figure, who uses his passion for fishing to shape a philosophy for life. Hailing from the same remote mountain village in the north-east of Japan as his creator, Yaguchi Takao, the character of Sanpei first appeared on the pages of *Shonen Magazine* in 1973 and was adapted for television by Nippon Animation in 1980. ● The series presents fishing as a combative sport for the first time, full of scene-grabbing shots, skilled opponents and different fish in each new episode. The heady pace of the action is skilfully emphasized with freeze-frame scenes and special effects created by Okabe Eiji, a trusted director from Nippon Animation. The script, however, focuses on the psychology of the characters involved. In each episode, Sanpei encounters a new enemy, allowing him to learn new techniques and grow spiritually. ● Each episode usually begins with a challenge that Sanpei does not know how to accomplish, then, through introspective analysis and dialogue with other expert fishermen, he goes into action, capturing his prey. Every test is a personal challenge and, however difficult it may seem at first, Sanpei always manages to overcome the odds. ● L.D.C.

LEFT: SANPEI, THE YOUNG AND PROACTIVE HERO OF THE SERIES SANPEI THE FISHERMAN (1980), IS ALWAYS BUSY WITH NEW CHALLENGES THAT TEACH HIM NEW FISHING TECHNIQUES

TSURIKICHI SANPEI ● SANPEI THE FISHERMAN ● 1980 ● DIR: OKABE EIJI, NITTA YOSHIMICHI ● SCR: UMADORI MICHIRU ET AL ● DES: YAGUCHI TAKAO ● ANI: OKASEKO KAZUYUKI ET AL ● MUS: SONE TATSUAKI, YAMAMOTO HIDEYUKI ● PRD: NIPPON ANIMATION ● TV SERIES ● EPS: 109

# SAOTOME RANMA

CHARACTER

Saotome Ranma's misadventures begin when he and his father, Genma, a martial arts expert, decide to take a swim in the damned springs of Jusenkyo in China. Under the spell of the springs, Ranma is cursed to eternally transform into a girl when drenched in cold water and return to being a boy upon contact with hot water. His father is also affected, turning into a giant panda. The situation is deeply worrying for Ranma, but provides great humour for the audience, as the young boy breaks male and female hearts alike, prompting jealousy amongst the other characters. The boy/girl's adventures explore the trials and tribulations of everyday teenage life, featuring encounters with similarly magical strangers and Ranma's growing relationship with his fiancée Akane. ● *Ranma 1/2* addresses the theme of sexual ambiguity in an original and amusing way and its popularity has given rise to seven series, eleven OAVs and three movies. The successful story is based on the eponymous *Ranma Nibun no Ichi*, a manga by Takahashi Rumiko, published by Shogakukan from 1987. Both manga and anime pay tribute to *The Rose of Versailles* (1979), created by Ikeda Riyoko, another much-loved work renowned for the sexual ambiguity of its protagonist. ● F.L.

FAR RIGHT: PUBLICITY IMAGE FOR THE 1989 SERIES RANMA 1/2 SHOWS RANMA FIGHTING AKANE, AS HIS FATHER (IN PANDA FORM) AND HERS LOOK ON ● RIGHT: RANMA AND AKANE

RANMA 1/2 ● 1989 ● DIR: MOCHIZUKI TOMOMITSU ET AL ● SCR: YAWAGAWA SHIGERU ET AL ● DES: NAKAJIMA ATSUKO ● ANI: MOCHIZUKI TOMOMI ET AL ● MUS: MORI EIJI, KAWA KENJI ● PRD: DEEN, KITTY FILMS ● TV SERIES ● EPS: 161

Born in 1936, Sasagawa Hiroshi is a pioneer in television animation. He joined Tatsunoko in 1965 and was immediately involved as director and scriptwriter on *Echu Esu* (*Space Ace*, 1965), the company's first television series. His name was subsequently associated with almost all the company's major productions: he directed *Mach Go Go Go* (1967) and *Poru no Mirakuru Daisakusen* (*Paul's Miracle War*, 1967), was responsible for some episodes of *Gatchaman* (1974) and wrote the scripts for *Casshan: Robot Hunter* (1973, dir. Sasagawa Hiroshi). Sasagawa emerged from this experience as a solid professional, able to cope with the frantic pace of industrial production and cover a range of genres and narrative styles. He successfully combines irony, a great sense of adventure and a touch of melancholy, conveying the sense of someone with a clear idea of the product's overall purpose. With designer Yoshida Tatsuo and director Kuri Ippei, Sasagawa was one of the three artists who built the studio's reputation. ● In 1982, after working on some fifty series, Sasagawa decided to leave Tatsunoko and continue his career as director with the Shinei Doga studio, where he was responsible for the series *Ninja Hattori-kun* (*Hattori the Ninja*, 1981). Other works he has created for different studios include the film *Maken Liner-001 Henshin Seyo* (1972), for Toei, and the series *Tokimeki Tonight* (1980). Despite the passing years, he continued to direct new projects which repeated the successes of the past until the late Nineties. A good example is the series *New Mach Go Go* (*Speed Racer X*, 1997), a remake of *Speed Racer*. Most recently, in 2008, one of his animations featured as a cameo in the new series of *Yattaman*, another of his successful creations. ● D.D.G.

IMAGES FROM THE WORKS OF SASAGAWA HIROSHI ● ABOVE LEFT: THE *GATCHAMAN* TEAM (1974, DIR. TORIUMI JINZO ET AL, 105 EPS) ● ABOVE: THE MONSTER GUZURA (1967, *GUZURA THE AMICABLE MONSTER*, DIR. SASAGAWA HIROSHI, 52 EPS) ● LEFT: PROMOTIONAL ART FOR *SPACE ACE* (*UCHU ACE*, 1965, DIR. SASAGAWA HIROSHI ET AL, 52 EPS)

SEE ALSO: GATCHAMAN; MACH GO GO GO; TATSUNOKO; TIME BOKAN; YATTAMAN; YOSHIDA TATSUO

# SAYA

CHARACTER

Saya, a vampire turned vampire killer, is the last of her kind. Monstrous Chiropteran vampires, hulking beasts with a hunger for human blood, are stalking a remote US army base. Sent to destroy them, Saya gets to work, systematically disassembling them with elegant flourishes of her sword. These bat men heal incredibly quickly, only dying from substantial blood loss. The dark, gothic mood of *Blood: The Last Vampire* and its existential themes mark it out as part of the new wave of millennial anime, alongside *Ghost in the Shell* (1995, dir. Oshii Mamoro), that make a claim for new depths in anime characterization. ● *Blood: The Last Vampire* is distinguished by both its incredible animation and, in particular, its short fifty-minute duration. The animation of action sequences featuring Saya and the silent exploits of her enemies are incredible, demonstrating a cinematographic style and attitude to movement quite unique at the time. Also, the use of a tertiary colour palette of greys, browns and oranges conveys the clear influence of Oshii Mamoru (Oshii penned the original concept, which later formed the basis of a manga). ● Saya inevitably invites comparisons with another female vampire hunter, Buffy, and this is indeed a tenable comparison, since the film was one of the first anime to be directed and produced entirely in English with Japanese subtitles as producers Aniplex and Production I.G. were keen to make a new title that addressed the burgeoning overseas market. The short length of *Blood* has been a source of criticism for many commentators but it can be compared to the classic horror movies by British director James Whale, such as *Frankenstein* (1931), which ran for only sixty minutes. ● D.S.

BLOOD: THE LAST VAMPIRE ● 2000 ● DIR: KITAKUBO HIROYUKI ● SCR: KAMIYAMA KENJI ● DES: TERADA KATSUYA ● ANI: TAKAGI SHINJI ● MUS: IKE YOSHIHIRO ● PRD: I.G. PRODUCTION ● FILM ● DUR: 50 MINS

IMAGES FROM THE 2000 FILM BLOOD: THE LAST VAMPIRE ● TOP LEFT: SAYA THE VAMPIRE HUNTER WITH HER TRUSTY SWORD ● TOP RIGHT: A CHARACTER SKETCH OF DAVID, SAYA'S HANDLER ● ABOVE: A CLOSE-UP OF SAYA

# SAZAE-SAN

TV SERIES

Isono Sazae has been a twenty-something housewife for the last sixty-three years, originating in a 1946 comic strip by Hasegawa Mariko (1920–1992) in the *Asahi Shinbun* newspaper. Although her clothes sometimes change with the times, her hair retains an austere forties style and her adventures rarely transcend the everyday concerns of a mid-twentieth-century homemaker living with her salaryman husband, three children and a cat that is afraid of mice. ● Sazae's story began in a post-war Japan under American occupation, but has remained a constant presence through the Fifties reconstruction, sixties boom, seventies recession, eighties bubble and nineties economic slump. Her life is a catalogue of minor embarrassments, small victories over her neighbours and petty marital stresses. However, sheer endurance has made her an iconic figure, with an old-fashioned lifestyle that is often as alien to modern Japanese as the samurai age was to her original contemporaries. ● Although the comic ended with Hasegawa's retirement in 1974, Sazae-san remains a recognizable figure to the Japanese, thanks to radio and television adaptations and an anime series starting in 1968 which, at forty-one years and over 2,000 episodes, is the longest-running cartoon in the world. Watched by the general public, not just anime fans, *Sazae-san* is also the highest-rated anime series on television, despite a tone and style that have forever kept it from foreign viewers. ● Sazae-san's nostalgic appeal has allowed it to outlive not only its creator and many modern mores (her family is huge by contemporary standards), but also the technology that originally made it. It was reported by the *Asahi Shinbun* in 2007 to be the last remaining anime series made by old-fashioned cel animation. ● J.Cl.

SAZAE-SAN ● 1969 ● DIR: KOBAYASHI KAZUO ET AL ● SCR: TSUJI MASAKI ET AL ● DES: OSUMI TOSHIYUKI ● ANI: UNCREDITED ● MUS: KOHIBE NOBUYOSHI ● PRD: STUDIO EIKEN ● TV SERIES ● EPS: OVER 2000

# SEITA & SETSUKO

CHARACTERS

Seita and Setsuko are two small children, brother and sister, living in a Japan that has been brutalized by war. They are among the most tragic and touching figures in the whole of modern cinema; their suffering, described with scrupulous restraint, is a descent into the kind of hell of which nobody should remain ignorant. ● On 21 September 1945, Seita's life comes to an end near Kobe station. The boy is fourteen and has seen both his mother and sister die. In the company of his spirit, we go backwards in time to a point several months earlier during the terrible firebombing of Kobe. The city is in flames; the young boy becomes separated from his mother and has to take care of his little sister. Abandoned, Seita and Setsuko struggle to survive. Despite sometimes breaking the law and transgressing the bounds of moral behaviour, they never lose their desire to find poetry in what remains of their lives. For example, Setsuko, already undernourished and suffering, buries the fireflies the children use to light their shelter, which have died the previous evening. ● Based on the short novel by Nosaka Akiyuki, this film by Takahata Isao is extremely powerful, with its unique imagery, achingly beautiful poetry and a pathos which never descends into melodrama. *Grave of the Fireflies* is a very dense film, which is exceptionally realistic in its approach and is a cry of protest against all war on behalf of its victims. These orphans are the model for Takahata's imaginative gallery of young people without a family. ● C.C.

SCENES FROM THE 1988 FILM *GRAVE OF THE FIREFLIES* ● ABOVE LEFT: SEITA AND SETSUKO WITH THEIR STRICT AUNT ● ABOVE: LITTLE SETSUKO; ● LEFT: SEITA AND SETSUKO SURROUNDED BY FIREFLIES

HOTARU NO HAKA ● GRAVE OF THE FIREFLIES ● 1988 ● DIR & SCR: TAKAHATA ISAO ● DES: KONDO YOSHIFRUMI ● ANI: KOYAMA NOBUO ● MUS: MAMIYA YOSHIO ● PRD: HARA TOHRU ET AL, SHINCHOSHA, STUDIO GHIBLI ● FILM ● DUR: 85 MINS

The childish soul of sixties anime can be traced to the career of a director who was able not only to accept the content imposed on him by Okawa Hiroshi, tycoon of Toei Animation from 1958 to 1971, but also to deftly deflect any hint of servility towards the famous major with his artistic charm. This characteristic crossed over into the films he directed and was often mistaken for naivety. ● Born in 1931, Serikawa Yugo is, together with Taiji Yabushita, the father of the modern Japanese animated feature-length film. Like Taiji's *Legend of the White Snake* (1958), exclusively designed for a young public, Serikawa was extremely fond of characters drawn from fairytales or children's manga. He tried to put Okawa's dictates into practice, opposing bellicose and egocentric American cinema with the power of his gentle poetry. The box-office failure of films such as *The Orphan Brother* (1961) and *Little Prince and Eight-Headed Dragon* (1963) – technically interesting and innovative for their time – demonstrate Okawa's obsession as a producer, and attest to Serikawa's malleability. ● Considered by western critics as the prince of animation in this period, the director crossed over to television anime after too many overly sentimental and, in truth, a little pedantic, films, such as *Nobody's Boy* (1970), from the novel by Hector Malot. For Toei Animation, Serikawa directed classics such as *Sally, The Witch* (1969), *Science Fiction Saiyuki Starzinger* (1978) and most famously *Mazinger Z* (1972). All these were made with the usual rigorous attention to detail and renowned expertise, which lets the animator's talent shine through. ● M.A.R.

## SERIKAWA YUGO

DIRECTO

SERIKAWA DIRECTED A FEW EPISODES OF THE SERIES JEEG, THE STEEL ROBOT (1975, DIR. NITTA YOSHIO ET AL, 46 EPS) ● ABOVE: A CLOSE-UP OF HIMIKA THE EVIL QUEEN AND ENEMY OF THE JEEG ROBOT.

SEE ALSO: CYBORG 009; HAKUJADEN; JEEG, THE STEEL ROBOT; MAZINGER Z; TOEI ANIMATION; YABUSHITA TAIJI

# SHIN-EI ANIMATION

STUDIO

This production house, founded in September 1976, grew out of A Production (A Pro), which had been created in 1965 by Kusube Daikichiro. A Pro, whose staff included Miyazaki Hayao and Takahata Isao, had been working closely with Tokyo Movie on TV series such as *Lupin III* (1971). After its reorganization as Shin-ei (or 'New A') Animation, the studio was kept busy with sub-contract work for studios including Nippon Animation and Group TAC, but they later became known for adapting the manga of successful creator duo Fujiko Fujio. While making TV anime series, Shin-ei also edited some of these works into feature-length compilations for theatrical release, especially during holiday periods. ● Examples of the studio's work include the second *Doraemon* TV series (1979, dir. Shibayama Tsutomu), the first having been produced at Tokyo Movie; *Ninja Hattori-kun* (*Hattori the Ninja*, 1981, dir. Sasagawa Hiroshi, Ikeno Fumio), *Pro Golfer Saru* (1982, dir. Fukutomi Hiroshi et al) and *Esper Mami* (1987, dir. Par Kyon Sun et al). *Crayon Shin-chan* (1992, dir. Honma Mitsuru) was a success for Shin-ei, as was the feature film *Kappa no Coo to Natsuyasumi* (*Summer Days with Coo*, 2007, dir. Hara Keiichi). ● H.M.

IMAGES FROM THE WORK OF SHIN-EI ANIMATION ● LEFT: TWO SCENES FROM *LUPIN III* (1971, DIR. OSUMI MASAKII, 23 EPS) FEATURING LUPIN, FUJIKO AND DETECTIVE ZENIGATA (ABOVE) AND THE MASTER CRIMINAL (BELOW) ● ABOVE: SCENES FROM *DORAEMON* (1973, DIR. ONUKI NOBUO ET AL, OVER 2000 EPS)

SEE ALSO: DORAEMON; HARA KEIICHI; LUPIN III; MIYAZAKI HAYAO; NOHARA SHINOSUKE; TAKAHATA ISAO

# SHINKAI MAKOTO

*DIRECTOR*

Shinkai Makoto (born in 1973) has prodigiously broken new ground in the world of animation and anime, proving that an animator working alone can achieve the style and quality of serial productions. After studying literature in the mid-Nineties, Shinkai began working as graphic designer for the Falcom videogame company, where he produced some short animated clips using computer graphics.
In his free time, working with just a PC, he completed his first five-minute short, *Kanojo to Kanojo no neko* (*She and Her Cat*, 1999), the story of a lonely girl and her cat, told from the animal's point of view. Shinkai's delicate minimalist style immediately caught the eye of the anime industry and won him several awards. He then chose the path of total independence, devoting himself full time to his new project: a short twenty-five minute film entitled *Hoshi no Koe* (*Voices of a Distant Star*, 2002), for which he won a number of international prizes at art and animation festivals. The character design, clean but faithful to the anime canon, the almost photographic detail of the backdrops and the dreamlike, high-tech imagery gave no indication that this was a home-made production. ● With support from the independent CoMix Wave Films studio, Shinkai then undertook his first full-length feature, releasing *Kumo no Mukou, Yakusoku no Basho* (*The Place Promised in Our Early Days*) in 2004. The film garnered praise and awards worldwide, from Canada to Korea. The sensitivity and elegance of his style reached new heights in the moving *Byousoku 5cm* (*5 Centimeters Per Second*, 2007), a film in three parts about waning love and friendship. ● L.D.C.

ABOVE & RIGHT: FOUR SCENES FROM *5 CENTIMETERS PER SECOND* (2007, DIR. SHINKAI MAKOTO, 62 MINS), A ROMANTIC STORY ABOUT THE SEASONS OF LOVE

SEE ALSO: KAWAMOTO KIHACHIRO; KURI YOJI; TSUJI NAOYUKI; TSUMIKI NO IE

## SHIRATO SANPEI

MANGAKA

The son of a renowned left-wing artist, Shirato Sanpei (born in 1932 in Tokyo) was one of the last of the *kamishibai* painters, making panels of artwork for Japanese 'magic lantern' shows. A narrator, or *benshi*, would tell a lively story to a crowd while pushing pictures in and out of a lit frame. Soon after Shirato's first *kamishibai* work *Mister Tomochan* (1951) was completed, the advent of television destroyed the medium, leading Shirato to transfer his skills into manga. His early work included adaptations of the animal stories of Ernest Seton and works for girls, but it was as the creator of *Ninja Bugeicho* (1959) that he became best known. ● Ninja are largely a creation of the twentieth century – black-clad assassins dressed like the 'invisible' stagehands of the kabuki theatre. With the samurai aristocracy blamed for dragging Japan into World War II, ninja formed a new, proletarian archetype – honest, impoverished yet cunning peasants, literally unseen in historical fiction that had previously concentrated on the ruling class. Despite minimal direct involvement, Shirato is also occasionally credited for the scripts and designs for several anime adaptations of his works, including *Shonen Sarutobi Sasuke* (*Magic Boy*, 1959, dir. Yabushita Taiji, Okuwara Akira), *Shonen Ninja Kaze no Fujimaru* (*Ninja the Wonderboy*, 1964, dir. Shirakawa Daisaku et al) and *Ninpu Kamui Gaiden* (*The Legend of Kamui*, 1969, dir. Watanabe Yonehiko et al). ● In 1967, the director Oshima Nagisa adapted *Ninja Bugeicho* into a cinema feature in the *kamishibai* style – an 'anime' without animation, comprising still images from the manga accompanied by a voiceover. Oshima's movie forms the main bridge between the *kamishibai* era and post-war 'visual novels' – narrated progressions of still images stored in a digital format. Shorn of their political motivations, Shirato's action-adventure ninja stories have had many subsequent imitators in the boys' market, most recently the best-selling *Naruto* (2002, dir. Date Hayato et al). ● J.Cl.

SEE ALSO: JIRO; NARUTO; YABUSHITA TAIJI

Shirato Takeshi is one of the most frequently mentioned names in guides to anime and his importance should not be underestimated. It is easy for some animators to become completely enmeshed in a popular series or character, but although Shirato worked on the successful film version of *Gegege no Kitaro* (1985, dir. Shirato Takeshi) and the wrestling superhero phenomenon *Kinnikuman: Ultimate Muscle* (*Muscleman*, 1983, dir. Yamakichi Yasuo et al), he has also permitted himself authorial digressions under the name of the Taiga Pro studio. ● His résumé includes periods of work on prestigious television and cinema productions, either as an animator, for example on *Jeeg, The Steel Robot* (1975), or storyboard artist. A tireless worker, his long career has seen him move enthusiastically from *Mazinger Z Vs Devilman* (1973, dir. Shirato Takeshi et al) and *UFO Robot Grendizer Raids* (1975, dir. Katsumata Tomoharu et al) to the OAV *Yamato 2520* (1994, dir. Nishizaki Yoshinobu et al). Even when directing a series, he has been known to produce storyboards for other productions, such as the *Cooking Papa* (1992, dir. Tsunoda Toshitaka) anime based on the manga by Ueyama Tochi. ● It was the science-fiction movie *Odin* (1985), however, that brought Shirato international attention. Ten years later, he joined the staff working on the film *Lupin III: Farewell to Nostradamus* (1995, dir. Ito Toshiya, Shirato Takeshi). Another noteworthy work was his television series *Seton Doubutsuki* (*Seton's Animal Tales*, 1989, dir. Shirato Takeshi), whose refined design and unique narrative language told the life story of naturalist Ernest Thompson Seton, already familiar to the Japanese audience thanks to a number of animal series made by Nippon Animation in the Seventies. ● M.A.R

## SHIRATO TAKESHI

DIRECTOR

ABOVE: MIWA AT THE CONTROLS OF HER SPACESHIP IN *JEEG, THE STEEL ROBOT* (1975, DIR. AKEHI MASAYUKI ET AL, 46 EPS), ON WHICH SHIRATO TAKESHI WAS ONE OF THE KEY ANIMATORS

SEE ALSO: JEEG, THE STEEL ROBOT; KITARO; LUPIN III; NAGAI GO; NIPPON ANIMATION; UFO ROBOT GRENDIZER RAIDS

# SHIROW MASAMUNE

SEE ALSO: KNUTE, DEUNAN; KUSANAGI
MOTOKO; OSHII MAMORU

MANGAKA

BELOW: DETAIL FROM *APPLESEED* (2004,
DIR. ARAMAKI SHINJI, 105 MINS), ONE
OF SHIROW MASAMUNE'S BEST KNOWN
CREATIONS

Shirow Masamune is the *nom de plume* of acclaimed mangaka Ota Masanori. Creator of *Ghost in the Shell* (1989), an internationally recognized masterpiece in science-fiction storytelling, he began his career by writing and illustrating *Black Magic M-66* (1987), the success of which raised his profile and led to the development of his other manga *Dominion Tank Police* (1988) and *Appleseed* (1988). ● Throughout all of Shirow's work is the recurring image of a similar action heroine, athletic and deadly, with short hair and a serious demeanour. As with Oshii Mamoru's recurring plotlines, Shirow's heroines comprise a collective singular archetypal heroine, even in his erotic work, Shirow contrasts the serious and technological with the organic and sensuous. Indeed, the relationship between Shirow and his work itself could be compared to the myth of Pygmalion and Galatea. This comparison is not lost on Shirow and he seems to retell the story in each of his narratives, articulating the love between characters in terms of the statue and its maker. Briareus and Deunan in *Appleseed*, as cyborg man and human woman, are an exploration of the impossibility of such relationships. The physical gulf between machine and creator becomes an existential chasm in *Ghost in the Shell*, where the focus becomes the life of the robot-woman Major Kusanagi Motoko, and the effort of those around to understand and appreciate her. ● Shirow's interest in myth is reflected in the punk-rock fantasy *Orion* (1991). A heady mix of fantasy and science fiction, *Orion* gives perhaps the best indication of Shirow's process and imagination, as it sets out complex scientific and mythological themes and references, creating a world of information and excess through which the central characters must carve a heroic path. ● D.S.

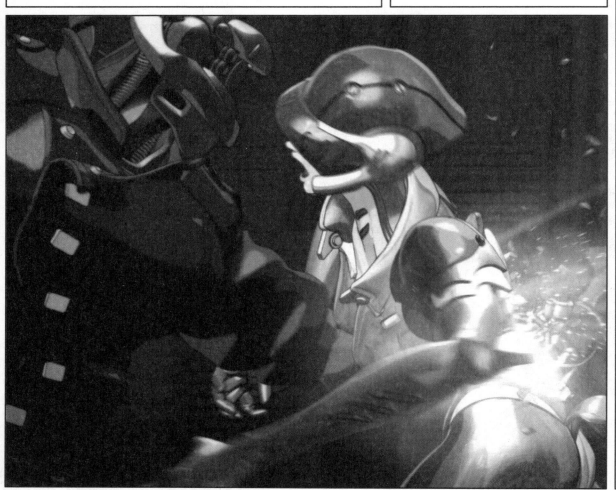

# SINDBAD

CHARACTER

The archetypal adventurer Sindbad is the lead character in a fascinating saga chronicling his seven fantastic voyages. The legend of Sindbad has plausible origins in the Sassanid Empire and was later to be included by Sir Richard Burton in the sixth volume of his English translation of *The Thousand and One Nights*. In this tale, Sindbad is a Persian sailor from Basra, who wins fame and fortune at the time of the Abbasid Caliphate – ideal material to fire the imagination of film-makers willing to test the boundaries of adventure-fantasy. ● Sindbad came to anime at the hands of Kuroda Masao and the pioneer Yabushita Taiji. In *Sindbad the Sailor* (1962), Sindbad appears as a young man in search of adventure – albeit with a somewhat foolish expression. Accompanied by his friend Ali (a child who fulfils the role of comic counterpoint), he stows away on a boat after hearing the tale of an ancient castaway on a magical island whose treasures are guarded by monsters. Early American animators, such as Ub Iwerks and the Fleischer brothers, had already produced an animated version of Sindbad's character but Yabushita and Kuroda's film, with a screenplay by Tezuka Osamu and Kita Morio, tentatively reclaims the status of an epic adventure. Imbued with a sense of wonder, the film reaches its climax in the final scenes, with the island guarded by airborne medusas and presided over by the effigy of a mythological bird. In 1975, Nippon Animation dedicated a fifty-two-episode television series, *Sindbad no Boken* (*Arabian Nights: Sindbad's Adventure*), to the character, which also features other well-known tales and imaginary characters from *One Thousand and One Nights*. ● J.Co.

*SINDBAD THE SAILOR* ● 1962 ● DIR: YABUSHITA TAIJI, KURODA MASAO ● SCR: TEZUKA OSAMU, KITA MORIO ● DES: OTSUKA YASUO ● ANI: YAMAMOTO SANAE ●
MUS: TOMITA ISAO, YONEYAMA MASAO ● PRD: TOEI ANIMATION ● FILM ● DUR: 81 MINS

# SONODA HIDEKI

SCRIPTWRITER

ABOVE: THE CAST OF COLOURFUL CHARACTERS FROM THE SERIES CYBOT ROBOTCHI (1982, DIR. OKASEKO KAZUYUKI, 39 EPS)

SEE ALSO: AKIRA; ARALE; AYUHARA KOZUE; GUNDAM; POKÉMON; TETSUJIN 28-GO; TORIYAMA AKIRA; TSUBASA OZORA

Like many professionals writing for anime, Sonoda Hideki has found himself working – often for Ashi Productions – along two lines at once. On the one hand, he has contributed to group-written, pretension-free television screenplays with only limited forays into originality, such as the volleyball-themed *Attacker You!* (1984, dir. Okaseko Kazuyuki) or the football story *Captain Tsubasa* (1983, dir. Mitsunobu Hiroe et al), whilst on the other he hand, he has fostered projects that express his predilection for fantasy and science fiction, including the OAV *Princess Minerva* (1995, dir. Yamaguchi Mihiro). This more personal work is usually aimed at an enthusiastic *otaku* audience. ● Sonoda has also frequently worked in the robot genre (as almost all anime screenwriters inevitably do), making a number of contributions to *Mobile Suit Victory Gundam* (1993) and the series *Tetsujin 28-go FX* (1993, dir. Imazawa Tetsuo), both of which revisit anime classics. On certain occasions, Sonoda even ventured into parody, as in the television series *Cybot Robotchi* (*Robby the Rascal*, 1982, dir. Okaseko Kazuyuki), which includes humorous touches in the style of Toriyama Akira's *Dr Slump* (1981, dir. Okazaki Minoru et al). For cinematic projects, he has explored horror, as in *Ai City* (*Love City*, 1986, dir. Mashimo Koichi), and fantasy, where he struck gold on the successful *Pokémon* film series. ● M.A.R.

# SORI FUMIHIKO

DIRECTOR

Sori Fumihiko (born in 1964) is one of the new generation of Japanese film-makers whose career path is radically different from that of old-school animators before the Nineties. Whereas earlier animators might have risen through the ranks as sketch artists, storyboarders and inbetweeners, Sori did not start his career in conventional animation at all. His first work was not even in Japan, since the earliest entry on his résumé comes in 1996 when, as a foreign exchange student at the University of Southern California, he worked on special effects at James Cameron's visual effects company Digital Domain. ● After working on James Cameron's *Titanic* (1992), Sori returned to Japan where he spent several years at TBS producing computer graphics for notable live-action television shows, such as *Beautiful Life* (2000), *Stand Up* (2003) and *Unsolved Cases* (*Keizoku*, 1999). In 2002, he demonstrated a masterful grasp of effects work in his live-action movie debut *Ping Pong*, a tale of table tennis aficionados, for which Sori added digital ping-pong balls in order to make his actors look like world champions. ● It was only after almost a decade spent using digital animation in special effects that Sori turned his hand to animation itself as a medium, first as the producer of the 2004 *Appleseed* (dir. Aramaki Shinji), and then as the director of the acclaimed *Vexille* (2007). Both films were less 'animated' than they were movies made entirely using special effects, such as motion-capture, used in much the same way as Disney once used rotoscoping, to turn live actors into the foundation for peerless animation. ● Sori's most recent film, *Ichi* (2008, dir. Sori Fumihiko), is a return to live action, a remake of the blind assassin film *Zatoichi* (2003, dir. Kitano Takeshi). ● J.Cl.

SEE ALSO: ITANO ICHIRO; KAWAMORI SHOJI; KNUTE, DEUNAN; MORIMOTO KOJI; SHINKAI MAKOTO

# SPANK

CHARACTER

Morimura Aiko is fourteen and has recently moved to a pleasant seaside town to stay with her uncle, a painter. Surrounded by a rich world of characters and situations, she is joined by Spank, a gentle and amusing white dog with large black eyes. Spank and Aiko share a pain that will not go away. The girl's father, like the young dog's owner, disappeared at sea on a stormy day and now Aiko and Spank both spend hours staring at the horizon waiting for their return. ● Spank, who never leaves his young mistress's side, colours every story in this series with his charm and overwhelms everyone with his enthusiasm. His friends are the harbour cat Torakiki, the dog Barone and the exquisite female cat Micia, with whom Spank is hopelessly in love. The irresistible adventures of this happy band are intertwined with those of Aiko and her new school friends, forming a detailed story of friendship and growing up, refined in subject matter and elegant in form. ● Each character's personality contributes to stories set at home, at school, by the harbour and at the beach. There is the governess Saki, kind and efficient, who faints at the sight of Spank; Serino, a rich and spoilt girl; the musician Rio; and the cheeky Seya. There are the minor crises of teenagers and their sudden adolescent joys. At the end of every day, Aiko writes a letter to her mother, a fashion designer living in Paris, telling her about the sea, the cry of the seagulls and her daily discoveries. ● G.P.

*SCENES FROM THE 1981 TV SERIES HELLO SPANK ● ABOVE LEFT: SPANK TUCKED UP WITH HIS OWNER AIKO ● LEFT: WITH BARONE THE DOG ● BELOW: WITH TORAKIKI THE CAT*

*OHAYO! SPANK ● HELLO SPANK ● 1981 ● DIR: YOSHIDA SHIGETSUGU ET AL ● SCR: KANEKO SATOSHI, SAKURAI MASAARI ● DES: TARANISHI SHIZUE, KOBAYASHI YUKARI ● ANI: KASAI TAKAO ● MUS: MAIKANO KOJI ● PRD: TMS ● TV SERIES ● EPS: 63*

CHARACTER

# SPIEGEL, SPIKE

Like his predecessor, the master thief Lupin III, Spike Spiegel has an adventurous nature and an indolent, 'couldn't-care-less' attitude. The bounty hunter, born on Mars in 2044, is an anti-hero who stays just inside the law. However, he does not hesitate to side with the weak, even if there is no reward in it. A touch anarchic, he hates kids, animals and women with attitude (or so he says). For three years, Spike and fellow bounty hunter Jet Black have toured the solar system rounding up bad guys in the spaceship Bebop, when circumstances force them to team up, somewhat reluctantly, with a female computer genius called Ed, the mysterious gambler Faye and a Welsh corgi called Ein. ● A fan of Bruce Lee and jazz, Spike was once an assassin for the Red Dragon, a Martian mob syndicate. Now, his survival instinct keeps him at a discreet distance from them. The past, however, returns to torment him in the guise of Vicious, a one-time friend, whom Spike is eventually forced to confront in a bloody shoot-out. A tragic hero, he also loses his beloved Julia, having found her again after searching for years, and dies with a scornful smile as a faraway star is extinguished in outer space. ● As the title suggests, *Cowboy Bebop* plays with cinematographic and musical genres, quoting and combining them. It presses the pedal of improvization, while maintaining an essential coherence and freshness unequalled in the anime world, adding a dash of sober irony. Reminiscent of the recent *Evangelion* (1995, dir. Anno Hideaki), this series is recognized for its directness. In these times of long crazy sagas, its strength is the independence and unique character of each episode. ● S.G.

*ABOVE & RIGHT: ACTION SCENES FROM THE SERIES COWBOY BEBOP (1998), SHOWING THE BOUNTY–HUNTER SPIKE SPIEGEL AT WORK*

*COWBOY BEBOP ● 1998 ● DIR: WATANABE SHINICHIRO ● SCR: NOBUMOTO KEIKO ET AL ● DES: KAWAMOTO TOSHIHIRO, YAMANO KIMITOSHI ● ANI: OGAMI YOICHI ● MUS: KANNO YUKO ● PRD: SUNRISE ● TV SERIES ● EPS: 26*

S

# STEAMBOY

 FILM

The concept of a mechanical man can be found in a great many late-nineteenth-century tales, in response to the spread of the strange machines and mechanization of the Industrial Revolution. In nineteenth-century Manchester, James 'Ray' Steam, budding inventor and son and grandson of great engineers, is both a product of his times and a critical conscience of technological advancements. Perfectly at ease with machines of every kind, he is much like any Japanese anime hero: the same innocent-looking face, the same bright eyes, the same iron will. What makes him unique, however, is the vibrant combination of contradictory aspects in his nature. Although he is the child of a society in the full flush of progress, convinced of his ability to change the world and himself, Ray Steam – unlike his father, disfigured in the course of an experiment – is a child in the truest and most old-fashioned sense, who loves to feel the wind in his hair. ● Conceived and directed by Otomo Katsuhiro, the film required ten years in production and a budget that reached $22 million. In 2004, *Steamboy* was screened at the Venice Film Festival to a cool critical reception. The use of light, colours and backgrounds and the discontinuous, fragmented narrative are a far cry from the universe of Otomo's *Akira* (1988). What interests Otomo is civil and political discourse; Ray Steam, like Tetsuo in *Akira*, is a rebel through and through, the prototype of a man fighting against the times he lives in and their vision of absolute, all-consuming progress. ● C.C.

*SCENES FROM THE 2004 FILM STEAMBOY ● ABOVE RIGHT: STEAMBOY'S OPPONENTS IN THEIR INFERNAL MACHINES ● RIGHT AND BELOW RIGHT: STEAMBOY AND THE ENTERPRISING SCARLETT O'HARA ● BELOW: STEAMBOY IN FLIGHT*

*STEAMBOY ● 2004 ● DIR: OTOMO KATSUHIRO ● SCR: OTOMO KATSUHIRO, MURAI SADAYUKI ● DES: OTOMO KATSUHIRO ● ANI: TAKAGI SHINJI ET AL ● MUS: STEVE JABLONSKY ● PRD: SUNRISE ● FILM ● DUR: 126 MINS*

# SUGII GISABURO

Sugii Gisaburo (born in 1940 in Numazu) is one of the great veterans of Japanese animation. Having begun his career as an inbetweener at Toei Animation in the late Fifties, Sugii moved to Mushi Production in 1962, recently founded by his friend Tezuka Osamu. Here, he helped to make *Astro Boy* (1963), the first Japanese animated television series, as director of animation and then as general director of many episodes. With a sense of humour and great versatility, Sugii directed many comedy and adventure series for Tezuka, such as *Goku no Daiboken* (1964) and *Dororo* (1969), but in 1969, he became associated with the small firm Group TAC, for which he made his first full-length feature, *Jack and the Beanstalk* (1974). In the Eighties, he animated the sports mangas of Adachi Mitsuru, including three specials of *Nine* (1983), then the famous television series *Touch* (1985) and *Hiatari Ryoko* (1987). ● Sugii continued to experiment with different genres, trying his hand at high-school romance in the series *Glass Mask* (1984), derived from Miuchi Suzue's manga, then transposed Miyazawa Kenji's novel *Night on the Galactic Railroad* (1985) and the historical novel *The Tale of Genji* (1987) into highly poetic animated films. ● In 1994, he sparked a whole new trend with an anime based on the *Street Fighter II* videogame. After renewing his partnership with Tezuka Pro and animating the dramatic series *A Tree in the Sun* (2000), he brought a charming children's story by Kimura Yuuichi to the silver screen in 2005 with the poetic feature film *Stormy Night*. ● L.D.C.

ABOVE: A SCENE FROM MUSHI PRODUCTION'S *THE TRAGEDY OF BELLADONNA* (1973, DIR. YAMAMOTO EIICHI, 89 MINS) ON WHICH SUGII GISABURO WORKED AS AN ANIMATOR

SEE ALSO: BELLADONNA; CLEOPATRA; DORORO; HAKUJADEN; KITAJIMA MAYA; MUSHI; TEZUKA OSAMU

# SUGINO AKIO

A director and character designer, Sugino Akio was the right hand of animator Dezaki Osamu at Mushi Production in the early Seventies. Sugino (born in 1944 in Sapporo) was one of the first generation of artists to use a new style called *gekiga* ('dramatic pictures') to pave the way for manga aimed at a grown-up audience. He worked as a mangaka in the early Sixties contributing to magazines such as *Machi* and *Kage*, before joining Mushi Productions as an animator on the recommendation of his colleague Moribi Murano in 1964. He worked as an artist on a number of projects including *Senya Ichiya Monogatari* (*One Thousand and One Nights*, 1969, dir. Yamamoto Eiichi, Tezuka Osamu). ● The television adaptation of the boxing-themed manga *Tomorrow's Joe* (1971, dir. Dezaki Osamu et al) marked his professional debut as an animation director and character designer. It was also the first time he worked with Dezaki, with whom he developed an incredibly close professional relationship, which survived the closure of the Mushi studio in 1972 and continues to this day. Both were involved in the foundation of the Madhouse studio, with animators Rintaro and Kawajiri Yoshiaki, and established themselves as an independent creative unit when they set up the Tokyo Movie Animation Company. The film version of sporty *shojo* manga *Aim for the Ace!* (1973) by Yamamoto Sumika was Sugino's first work as a director for the big screen. Equally at home in fantasy and the neo-noir (such as *Golgo 13*, 1983, dir. Dezaki Osamu) Sugino has most recently been working with Dezaki on a television adaptation of the eleventh-century Japanese literary classic *The Tale of Genji*. ● J.Co.

ABOVE: ALADDIN IS CARRIED AWAY BY A BAND OF ENTHUSIASTIC WOMEN. SUGINO AKIO WAS ONE OF THE MANY ARTISTS INVOLVED IN THE MAKING OF *SENYA ICHIYA MONOGATARI* (ONE THOUSAND AND ONE NIGHTS, 1969, DIR. YAMAMOTO EIICHI, TEZUKA OSAMU, 25 MINS)

SEE ALSO: DEZAKI OSAMU; KAWAJIRI YOSHIAKI; MADHOUSE; MUSHI; RINTARO; TEZUKA OSAMU; YABUKI JOE

# SUNRISE

STUDIO

Sunrise Studio Ltd was founded in September 1972 by former Mushi Pro employees. In 1977, after five years of working with other companies on titles such as *Yusha Raideen* (Brave Raideen, 1975, dir. Tomino Yoshiyuki, Nagahama Tadao) and *Cho Denji Robo Combattler V* (1976, dir. Nagahama Tadao), the studio began to focus on its own titles. It marked this change with a new name: Nippon Sunrise, Inc. The studio was established alongside Nippon Sunrise in 1987. ● Its early robot shows included Tomino Yoshiyuki's *Muteki Chojin Zambot 3* (1977) and *Muteki Kojin Daitarn 3* (1978) but its first major hit was Tomino's *Mobile Suit Gundam* (1979). Although the first series was cut short due to poor viewing figures, it built considerable fan loyalty. Like US TV show *Star Trek*, or Japan's *Uchu Senkan Yamato* (Star Blazers, 1974, dir. Matsumoto Leiji) it was given a new lease of life by fan devotion. ● More Gundam TV series, OAVs, movies, games and toys were produced from 1980 onwards, with constantly changing settings and stars, making it one of Japan's best-loved animated series and a huge influence on popular culture. ● Much of Sunrise's output is TV series, but it has also made feature films and OAVs. Sunrise's shows are created for animation, although they may have their own spin-off manga later, and the studio has made great contributions to animation as an independent medium. ● Among its many works are the television series *Sokihei Votoms* (Armored Trooper Votoms, 1983, dir. Takahashi Ryosuke et al), *Cowboy Bebop* (1998, dir. Watanabe Shinichiro), *Inu Yasha* (2000, dir. Ikeda Masashi, Nishimori Akira) and *Code Geass: Hangyaku no Lelouch* (Code Geass: Lelouch of the Rebellion, 2006, dir. Taniguchi Goro). ● H.M.

IMAGES FROM THREE WORKS PRODUCED BY SUNRISE ● ABOVE: *MOBILE SUIT GUNDAM* (1979, DIR. TOMINO YOSHIYUKI, 43 EPS) ● ABOVE RIGHT: *CODE GEASS: LELOUCH OF THE REBELLION* (2006, DIR. TANIGUCHI GORO, 25 EPS) ● RIGHT: *COWBOY BEBOP: THE MOVIE* (2001, DIR. WATANABE SHINICHIRO, 120 MINS)

SEE ALSO: CHIRICO CUVIE; CITY HUNTER; GUNDAM; KEI & YURI; SPIEGEL, SPIKE; TOMINO YOSHIYUKI; YASUHIKO YOSHIKAZU

# SUPER SENTAI

CHARACTERS

SUPER SENTAI • 1975 • PRD: TOEI • EPS: 1629

The *Super Sentai* franchise, originating in 1975, is representative of a widespread style in Japanese television, a sub-section *tokusatsu* (shows based on special effects). The combatants are an action squad, whose members (usually five characters, distinguished by the colour of their suits) use martial arts against a paranormal enemy force guided by a power-hungry tyrant. The episodes follow a fairly standard and predictable scheme, revolving around battles between different monsters, often with grossly exaggerated proportions, and a robot controlled by the heroes. ● The series incorporates two threads of *tokusatsu*: the superhero or masked hero, in this case multiplying the number, and *kaiju* ('giant monsters'), where actors wearing huge foam-rubber costumes play monsters. The franchise, a relation of anime, also shows a clear love of the mecha genre. *Super Sentai* borrows some common techniques from animation, such as an abundance of slow motion, zoom-ins and textured backdrops (bordering on the kitsch) and emphasizes the ritualistic and repetitive nature of sequences where the heroes change into their costumes. Such series are aimed at a very young audience and the drama is drastically altered in deference to audience and budget considerations. Special effects, set and choreography (with some use of sparks and mini-explosions) are designed with the aim of minimizing expenditure but, thanks to the frenetic pace, they are effective for a television audience. *Dinosaur Team Jyuranger/Kyoryu Sentai jyuranger* (1992) was distributed in the West in a reworked version under the name of Power Rangers, where the scenes in which Japanese actors appear have been substituted with new edits featuring American teenagers. The masked scenes were not changed, since the masked costumes used in the original do not show the actors' faces. ● S.G.

ABOVE: PUBLICITY IMAGE CREATED TO CELEBRATE THE TWENTY-FIFTH ANNIVERSARY OF THE 1975 TV SERIES SUPER SENTAI

# SUZUKI TOSHIO

PRODUCER

IMAGES FROM THE WORK OF PRODUCER SUZUKI TOSHIO ● BELOW LEFT: SOPHIE AND MARKL FROM *HOWL'S MOVING CASTLE* (2004, DIR. MIYAZAKI HAYAO, PRD. SUZUKI TOSHIO ET AL, 118 MINS) ● BELOW RIGHT: PONYO AND SOSUKE FROM *PONYO ON THE CLIFF BY THE SEA* (2008, DIR. MIYAZAKI HAYAO, PRD. SUZUKI TOSHIO ET AL, 101 MINS)

Suzuki Toshio (born in 1948 in Nagoya) graduated with a degree in literature and began his career at the publishers Tokuma Shoten where he wrote for the magazine *Asahi Geino*. In 1978, he became editor of *Animage* and asked Miyazaki to create the manga *Nausicaä of the Valley of Wind*. Thus began his friendship with the director, which became, over time, a close professional relationship. In 1988, he worked on the production of *Grave of the Fireflies*, made by Takahata from a tale by Nosaka Akiyuki that Suzuki loved when he was studying literature. In 1989, Suzuki officially became a producer for Studio Ghibli, where he contributed to the studio's signature style of stunning visuals and brilliantly realized characters. The studio was experiencing such a difficult period that, as Miyazaki said, 'if Suzuki had not been there, there wouldn't even have been a Studio Ghibli'. ● After *Kiki's Delivery Service* (1989, dir. Miyazaki Hayao), adapted from another book much loved by Suzuki, his name came to be linked with the studio's major successes. Under his leadership, the studio began to diversify, creating commissioned works, advertisements and music videos, such as *On Your Mark*, Miyazaki's video for Japanese pop duo Chage and Aska. At the same time, Suzuki paid great attention to marketing, now one of the key elements of the studio's operations. Distribution continued to be a sensitive issue for the studio, with Suzuki reportedly sending producer Harvey Weinstein a sword with a message attached saying 'No Cuts!' in response to Buena Vista's intention to edit Ghibli films for American release. His contribution to the conflict between Studio Ghibli and Disney has helped safeguard the integrity of the studio's films and their image. ● F.L.

SEE ALSO: GHIBLI; KIKI; MIYAZAKI HAYAO; NAUSICAÄ; SEITA & SETSUKO; TOTORO

# TAKADA AKEMI

DESIGNER

Takada Akemi (born in 1952 in Tokyo) began to redesign anime characters and manga in her late teens, without preference for a particular genre. Among those she found most interesting were the works of Hagio Moto, the godfather of *shojo* manga, which inevitably brought her to a more elegant type of character design, capable of captivating both women and men. ● In 1977, she was employed by Tatsunoko Productions, where she worked on famous series such as the superhero anime *Gatchaman* (1972, dir. Toriumi Jinzo et al). Three years later she left the firm to become a freelance designer, and worked on the series *Urusei Yatsura* (1981, dir. Oshii Mamoru et al). Her most important undertaking, however, which earnt her a great reputation, was as character designer for 'magical girl' series *Creamy Mami* (1983). Since the series was not based on an existing manga, Takada was free to create her own original characters, using pastel colours and soft contours to give them an understated sensuality. ● Despite being best known for work related to magic and fantasy, Takada has said she prefers stories with human protagonists, which is perhaps why she chose to work on *Maison Ikkoku* (1986, dir. Yamazaki Kazuo et al), which sees a return to characters originally created by mangaka Takahashi Rumiko. The fairy-tale, poetic style of Takada's drawings brought added value to an already enormously successful series. In 1987, she founded the creative group Headgear, along with other colleagues, where she worked on the popular series *Patlabor* (1988, dir. Oshii Mamoru et al). She continues to work on series such as *Ranma ½* (1989, dir. Shibayama Tsutomu et al) and *Fancy Lala* (1998, dir. Omori Masahiro et al), and has also branched out into books, CD covers and even a line of jewellery, a natural progression for someone whose artistic vision is geared to elegance and beauty. ● D.D.G.

IMAGES FROM TWO SERIES WORKED ON BY TAKADA AKEMI ● ABOVE: CLOSE UP OF AKANE FROM *RANMA ½* (1989, DIR. SHIBAYAMA TSUTOMU ET AL, 161 EPS) ● RIGHT: LUM FROM *URUSEI YATSURA* (1981, DIR. OSHII MAMORU ET AL, 218 EPS)

SEE ALSO: CREAMY MAMI; GATCHAMAN; ITO KAZUNORI; MAISON IKKOKU; OSHII MAMORU; PATLABOR; SAOTOME RANMA; TATSUNOKO; URUSEI YATSURA

MANGAKA

# TAKAHASHI RUMIKO

ABOVE & RIGHT: SCENES FROM INU YASHA (2000, DIR. IKEDA MASASHI, NISHIMORI AKIRA, 167 EPS)

The 'princess of manga', Takahashi Rumiko (born in 1957 in Niigata), was twenty-two when she created the series *Urusei Yatsura* (1979). The comic immediately established two fundamental attributes of her aesthetic: a tendency to create extended narratives with very long plotlines, and an attention to the relationship between the sexes in a society changing despite the weight of tradition. ● Adopting a farcical tone, *Urusei Yatsura* shows the feeble student Moroboshi Ataru grappling with Lum, the beautiful representative of the mythological Oni people. Traditional power relationships are reversed: the woman is the more powerful and strong-minded of the two, while the man is incapable of accepting his own responsibilities. Gags are scattered liberally throughout a crazily paced narrative that becomes an acute critique of society's basic institutions. Concisely drawn, the character design – soft bodies and big eyes with vertical pupils – has become the artist's trademark. ● Takahashi's second success came in 1980 with *Maison Ikkoku*, inspired by her own university years spent sharing a room. The student Godai Yusaku is struggling with his intrusive housemates and his love for the manager, the widow Kyoko. This time the irony is tempered in a melancholy, romantic tale that reflects on the situation of young people struggling with the world of work and the need to build solid relationships. ● *Ranma ½* (1987) hides its reflections on identity and sex within a martial arts story, as the young Saotome Ranma turns into a woman on contact with cold water. Finally, *Inu Yasha* (1996) shows the difficult relationship of a male demon and a modern young woman in a feudal Japanese setting. ● D.D.G.

T

SEE ALSO: MAISON IKKOKU; MORIYAMA YUJI; OSHII MAMORU; SAOTOME RANMA; URUSEI YATSURA

# TAKAHASHI RYOSUKE

DIRECTOR

It is easy to think that Sunrise is entirely defined by the success of *Mobile Suit Gundam* (1979) and its creator, Tomino Yoshiyuki. However the contribution made by Takahashi Ryosuke, one of the studio's most respected directors, should not be overlooked. Born in 1943, some critics had relegated him to the status of anime veteran, but his recent television work, such as *Flag* (2006), is a timely reminder that his generation of animators still has much to offer. ● After his debut at Mushi Production, Takahashi was employed by Sunrise where, under the influence of Tomino, a new kind of mecha and science-fiction genre was being created. Adventure titles such as *Taiyo no Kiba Dougram (Fang of the Sun Dougram*, 1981) and *Aoki Ryusei SPT Layzner (Blue Comet SPT Lazner*, 1985) hail from this intense period and reveal Takahashi's dedication to quality animation. ● Takahashi has been hailed by many fans as the godfather of the 'real robot' genre in which robots are created by plausible scientists and powered by conventional methods, while realistic plotlines reach beyond simple constructs of heroes beating villains. Steel and mechanics are undoubtedly at the centre of Takahashi's world, but events are portrayed with a powerful dose of naturalism and narrated through a jaundiced eye. In his most successful anime, *Armored Trooper Votoms* (1983), such cynicism casts dark shadows on the nature of all animated science fiction. More recent series (such as *Gasaraki*, 1998, created in response to the popularity of *Neon Genesis Evangelion*, 1995, dir. Anno Hideaki), are also directed with his trademark energy and intensity. ● M.A.R.

TWO IMAGES FROM THE WORK OF DIRECTOR TAKAHASHI RYOSUKE ● RIGHT: MERCENARY HERO AKIZUKI YOJIRO WITH HIS MAJICAL SWORD THAT ALWAYS LEADS HIM IN THE DIRECTION OF TROUBLE, *BAKUMATSU KIKANSETSU ROHANIHOHETO* (2006, DIR. OHASHI YOSHIMITSU, TAKAHASHI RYOSUKE, 26 EPS) ● BELOW: THE SCOPE DOG MOBILE SUIT IN ACTION IN *ARMOURED TROOPER VOTOMS* (1983, DIR. TAKAHASHI RYOSUKE ET AL)

SEE ALSO: KAIEDA SHIRO; CYBORG 009; CHIRICO CUVIE

DIRECTOR

# TAKAHATA ISAO

Takahata Isao (born in 1935 in Ise) is one of the world's most celebrated anime directors and co-founder of Studio Ghibli. From an early age, Takahata showed an interest in art and he began his career as an assistant director at Toei Doga in 1959. Here, during meetings with the designers' union, he met Miyazaki Hayao, with whom he established a long professional relationship. ● Takahata's first feature film as director was *Little Norse Prince* (1968), which deals with a child's journey through a world subdued by adult rules, exploring the marvels of nature and providing a glimpse of the poetry in everyday life. Takahata returned to these themes in the animated series *Heidi* (1974) – where the naturalist concerns become even more evident and the tone is overtly optimistic – and in *Future Boy Conan* (1978, dir. Miyazaki Hayao, Takahata Isao), made by his friend Miyazaki, for which he directed some episodes. ● In narrative terms, these works are the exact opposite of what remains his most famous work, the yearning and dramatic *Grave of the Fireflies* (1988), where the dream of a life in harmony with nature comes up against the harsh realities of war: scenes of devastation and bloodied bodies are deftly combined with a sensitive handling of his protagonist's state of mind. Three years earlier, Takahata helped his friend Miyazaki to make *Nausicaä of the Valley of Wind* (1985, dir. Miyazaki Hayao) which proved to be the catalyst for the creation of Studio Ghibli. With this prestigious studio, Takahata went on to make *Only Yesterday* (1991), *Pom Poko* (1994) and *My Neighbours the Yamadas* (1999). ● D.D.G.

IMAGES FROM TWO FILMS DIRECTED BY TAKAHATA ISAO ● ABOVE & RIGHT: SCENES FROM POM POKO (1994, DIR. TAKAHATA ISAO, PRD. SUZUKI TOSHIO ET AL, 119 MINS) SHOWING TAKAHATA'S STYLE WHICH FLITS BETWEEN FANTASY AND REALISM ● BELOW LEFT: FRENCH LANGUAGE DVD COVER FOR LITTLE NORSE PRINCE (1968, DIR. TAKAHATA ISAO, PRD. OKAWA HIROSHI, 82 MINS) ● BELOW CENTRE & RIGHT: TWO SCENES FROM LITTLE NORSE PRINCE FEATURING THE YOUNG FISHERMAN'S SON, HOLS

UN FILM DE
ISAO TAKAHATA
ANIME PAR
HAYAO MIYAZAKI
(LE TOMBEAU DES LUCIOLES)
(LE VOYAGE DE CHIHIRO)

# HORUS
## PRINCE DU SOLEIL

T

SEE ALSO: ANNE OF GREEN GABLES; GHIBLI; GOSHU; HEIDI; HOLS; MIYAZAKI HAYAO; OTSUKA YASUO; PANDA KOPANDA; POM POKO; SEITA & SETSUKO; YAMADAS

# TAKEUCHI NAOKO

ABOVE: CLOSE UP OF THE RED-HAIRED QUEEN BERYL OF THE TV SERIES SAILOR MOON (1992, DIR. SATO JUNICHI ET AL, 46 EPS)

Takeuchi Naoko (born in 1967 in Kofu) made her debut at just twenty years old, when publisher Kodansha agreed to print her short story *Love Call* in its *Nakayoshi* magazine. This was a defining point in her career and all her subsequent works were published by Kodansha. ● Takeuchi's early work was characterized by the staples of *shojo* (girls') manga, where physical characteristics are rendered without much attention to detail and the narrative focuses on romance, relationships and states of mind. Takeuchi continued to produce short love stories of this kind until she achieved great success with *Sailor Moon* in 1992. The original storyline described the adventures of a lone female warrior from the moon, but the publisher later convinced her to create a magic team of female heroes, an idea which was indebted to the earlier manga *Silent Möbius* (1991) by Asamiya Kia, an author with whom Takeuchi would later work. ● *Sailor Moon* revolutionized the traditional concepts of *shojo* manga, focusing on fantasy and sentimental action, closer to the standards of the *tokusatsu* or 'special effects' genre, with an abundance of monsters and secret powers. Additionally, Takeuchi brought further depth to the story by drawing on her own personal experiences and giving the characters names belonging to her family members. ● Takeuchi's subsequent work continued to explore this dimension of hybrid *shojo*-fantasy-action until 1999 when, following her marriage to colleague Yoshihiro Togashi, she stopped work for four years. In 2005, she collaborated as scriptwriter with her husband on the illustrated book *Obonu to Chibonu*. ● D.D.G.

SEE ALSO: SAILOR MOON

# TATSUNOKO

STUDIO

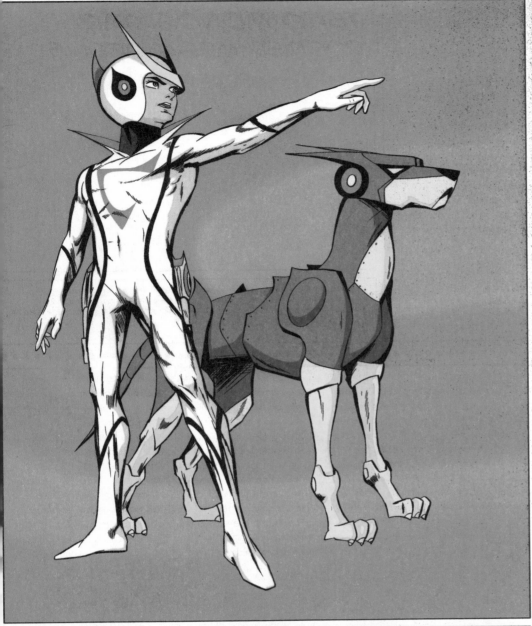

Yoshida Tatsuo and his brothers Kenji and Toyoharu founded Tatsunoko in 1962, intending to create their own manga. As children, they were inspired by superhero comic-books given to them by American soldiers but as adults, seeing the boom in TV animation following *Tetsuwan Atom* (*Astro Boy*, 1963, dir. Tezuka Osamu), they decided to make anime instead. ● In May 1965, Tatsunoko's first series, *Uchu no Ace* (*Space Ace*, 1965, dir. Sasagawa Hiroshi et al) was aired. The character design was by Kuri Ippei, the pen name adopted by Toyoharu for the rest of his professional life. The inspiration of superhero comics is obvious but the show had its own charm and was a considerable success. ● Tatsunoko's main focus is on TV anime; its only manga adaptations have been those of its founder. ● When devising a new show concept, the studio team starts with characters; once they are defined and designed, the story and setting then follow. This enables Tatsunoko to create innovative characters with a wide appeal. Despite the variety of its output – ranging from science fiction and mecha to action, comedy and fantasy – Tatsunoko productions are always original. ● Some of its best-known TV series are *Mach Go Go Go* (1967, dir. Yoshida Tatsuo et al), *Gatchaman* (1972, dir. Toriumi Jinzo et al), *Jinzo Ningen Casshern* (*Casshan: Robot Hunter*, 1973, dir. Sasagawa Hiroshi), *Uchu no Kishi Tekkaman* (*Space Knight Tekkaman*, 1975, dir. Sasagawa Hiroshi), *Time Bokan* (1975, dir. Sasagawa Hiroshi et al), *Mirai Keisatsu Urashiman* (*Future Cop Urashiman*, 1983, dir. Mashimo Koichi et al) and *Akai Kodan Zillion* (*Red Photon Zillion*, 1987, dir. Hamazaki Hiroshi, Kobayashi Tetsuya). ● H.M.

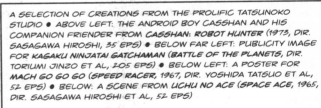

*A SELECTION OF CREATIONS FROM THE PROLIFIC TATSUNOKO STUDIO ● ABOVE LEFT: THE ANDROID BOY CASSHAN AND HIS COMPANION FRIENDER FROM CASSHAN: ROBOT HUNTER (1973, DIR. SASAGAWA HIROSHI, 35 EPS) ● BELOW FAR LEFT: PUBLICITY IMAGE FOR KAGAKU NINJATAI GATCHAMAN (BATTLE OF THE PLANETS, DIR. TORIUMI JINZO ET AL, 205 EPS) ● BELOW LEFT: A POSTER FOR MACH GO GO GO (SPEED RACER, 1967, DIR. YOSHIDA TATSUO ET AL, 52 EPS) ● BELOW: A SCENE FROM UCHU NO ACE (SPACE ACE, 1965, DIR. SASAGAWA HIROSHI ET AL, 52 EPS)*

*SEE ALSO: ATOM; CASSHAN; GATCHAMAN; MACH GO GO GO; MUSHI; TIME BOKAN*

*T*

# TEITO MONOGATARI
## DOOMED MEGALOPOLIS

The malevolent spirit Kato Yasunori has emerged to spread his shadow over the city of Tokyo. In the wake of modernization, this demon from antiquity threatens to derail the plans of city officials. Embroiled in a complex spiritual struggle with the Onmyoji priest Hirai Yamumasa, Kato seeks to resurrect and appease the spirit of Taira no Masakado, an ancient demigod who rests under the city. ● After Hirai is defeated, a mysterious woman, the priestess Keiko Meiko, emerges from the ensemble cast to challenge Kato's tyranny. She has been summoned by Masakado, the very spirit Kato had attempted to channel. In their penultimate struggle, the forces of darkness and light neutralize one another, and Keiko, as the spirit of mercy, finally ends Kato's reign of terror. ● Rintaro's four-part OAV *Teito Monogatari* (*Doomed Megalopolis*) played a central role in the wave of anime imported to the UK and Europe in the Nineties. Distinguished by its high production quality and mature and complex narrative, the series' incredible special-effects sequences highlighted to early audiences the potential to challenge and subvert assumptions about anime as an economic, simplified and unsubtle form. In one sequence, shifting black forms transform from viscous blobs to crows and back, and intense magical combat is delivered at a nerve-shredding pace, making *Doomed Megalopolis* a highlight amid the otherwise patchy quality of early anime exports. ● D.S.

*VIDEO SERIES*

TEITO MONOGATARI ● DOOMED MEGALOPOLIS ● 1991 ● DIR: RINTARO ET AL ● SCR: ENDO AKINORI, CHIAKI TAKAICHI ● DES: MASAYUKI ● ANI: TANAKA SHINJI ET AL ● MUS: TOYAMA KAZZ ● PRD: MADHOUSE ● EPS: 4

# TENJO UTENA

*CHARACTER*

Utena Tenjo is not of this world, nor does she belong to the world of conventional fairytales. Her life was marred by a solitary childhood and, it is suggested, complicity in the death of both her parents. Then, following a chaste kiss at her parents' graveside, a mysterious prince puts a ring on her finger with the seal of a rose and promises to meet her again. Once grown-up, Utena decides not to wait and proclaims herself a prince. With her pink hair and watery blue eyes, she wears a male uniform as a sign of absolute devotion to her love, as she transfers to Ohtori Academy. After crossing swords with one of the good-looking boys at the school (a member of student council) and battling for possession of his girlfriend, she wins control over the disquieting Anthy Himemiya, a student known as the 'Rose Bride'. ● An immaculately conceived creature from the imagination of director Ikuhara Kunihiko, with the support of the Be-Papas group, Utena is the lead character of a *shojo* manga by Saito Chiho. The television anime *Revolutionary Girl Utena* tells a different story from the film, *The Adolescence of Utena* (1999). ● A successor to *Sailor Moon* (1992, dir. Sato Junichi et al), the series is a world apart from typical *shojo* culture, with its intriguing heroine a victim of Ikuhara's unpredictable imagination. She is similar to the protagonists of *Rose of Versailles* (1979, dir. Nagahama Tadao et al) and *Princess Knight* (1967), a woman able to renounce her masculinity, but in love with princely attitudes – a pop icon called to shake up an entire system of codes and rules. Even her language springs from Ikuhara's contaminated readings and visions, such as when he tells Utena to feel '*run-run*' in homage to the lead character of *Hana no Ko Lunlun* (*Flower Angel*, 1979, dir. Endo Yuji). ● M.A.R.

SHOJO KAKUMEI UTENA ● REVOLUTIONARY GIRL UTENA ● 1997 ● DIR: IKUHARA KUNIHIKO ET AL ● SCR: ENOKIDO YOJI ET AL ● DES: SAITO SHIHO, HSEGAWA SHINYA ● ANI: HASE GAWA SHINYA ET AL ● PRD: J.C. STAFF ● TV SERIES ● EPS: 39

With bobbed hair and figure-hugging dresses, Terai Yuki was billed as a star of the future. According to press releases, she had travelled back in time from the year 2017. Pursuing a career as a singer and actress in the early twenty-first century, she was real enough to have a height (5'5") and dress measurements (34/24/34"). In fact, she was an animated character without an anime show, created by Kutsugi Kenichi for a manga in 1997, given a promotional website in 1998 and developed using early 3D computer graphics software in 1999. ● What pop-music impresario would be able to resist the idea of an idol who would never grow old, never switch labels and never fail to appear on time? In a society with a constant appetite for starlets, it was only a matter of time before someone created a 'virtual idol', existing only in a computer. The first, with a short-lived pop career, was Date Kyoko, who released a single called 'Love Communication' in 1997. Soon afterwards, Terai Yuki appeared in several short films broadcast on Fuji TV, each designed for release in the new DVD format. Presented as fragments from unfinished works in progress, pop videos or trailers for non-existent films, *Yuki Terai: Secrets* (2000, dir. Kutsugi Kenichi) presented its star as a virtual idol – a rival for the fictional Sharon Apple, the computer-generated star of *Macross Plus* (1994, dir. Kawamori Shoji). ● Terai Yuki released two CDs and starred in a television commercial and a PlayStation game. Although she failed to truly compete with real-world stars, she is likely to be remembered as an early example of a computer-based phenomenon whose time is yet to come. ● J.Cl.

# TERAI YUKI
## YUKI TERAI

*CHARACTER*

YUKI TERA: SECRET FILMS ● YUKI TERAI – SECRETS ● 2000 ● DIR: KUTSUGI KENICHI ● SCR, DES, ANI, MUS: UNCREDITED ● PRD: FROG ENTERTAINMENT, FUJI TV ● OAV ● DUR: 79 MINS

# TETSUJIN 28-GO
## GIGANTOR

ROBOT

The first giant robot to appear in manga and anime, Gigantor looks like a huge iron cylinder. First appearing in 1956 in a manga by Yokoyama Mitsuteru, the robot was created during World War II by a Japanese inventor as a secret weapon that would win the war in the Pacific. However, before the weapon could be used, Allied forces destroyed the laboratory, killing the robot's creators. With Japan defeated and forced to accept American occupation, control of the iron giant has been left in the hands of young Shotaro, the son of the scientist who invented it. Together, they face countless dangers, doing battle with monsters and other robots. ● Yokoyama's icon of science-fiction fantasy captured the spirit of its time and all Yokoyama had learnt from Tezuka Osamu's manga. His robot is not only the forerunner of many giants to come, but it is also accompanied by considerable psychological baggage. In the anime series, the relationship between the two protagonists generates inner conflicts, while the boy's symbiosis with the metal man was to launch a whole new genre. The 1963 adaptation kept to the original design concept, the black-and-white treatment providing a degree of continuity with Yokoyama's manga. A colour remake, directed by Imazawa Tetsuo in 1980, depicted Shotaro as stopping at nothing to defeat the alien invaders, true to the contemporary superhero tradition. But Imagawa Yasuhiro's 2004 anime was to be the real blockbuster; reverting to the post-war setting of the original manga, the film's high-quality animation transformed the material into an exceptional aesthetic achievement. ● M.A.R.

LEFT: A SCENE FROM THE 1980 TELEVISION SERIES *NEW IRONMAN 28* (*SHIN TETSUJIN 28-GO, NEW GIGANTOR*, 1980, DIR. IMAZAWA TETSUO, 51 EPS)

TETSUJIN 28-GO ● GIGANTOR ● 1963 ● DIR. WATANABE YONEHIKO ET AL ● SCR: OKAMOTO YOSHIKAZU ● DES: YUKOYAMA MITSUTERU ● ANI: WAKABAYASHI TADAO, NOBARA KAZUO ● MUS: ARASHINO HIDEHIKO ● PRD: FUJI TV, TELE CARTOON JAPAN ● TV SERIES ● EPS: 83

# TEZUKA OSAMU

MANGAKA

It may seem like an exaggeration to define Tezuka Osamu (born in 1928 in Osaka) as the *Manga no Kami-sama* (god of manga), but his importance in the consolidation of the art form makes him worthy of the title. Influenced by Disney and the Fleischer brothers, Tezuka created the very aesthetic of Japanese animation, in terms of both character design and the expressive potential of the medium, ignoring economic limitations in order to develop a visual vocabulary of inexhaustible effectiveness. ● As a child, Tezuka was a passionate entomologist, devoted to the pursuit of female company and possessed by an insatiable appetite for culture. He developed an early passion for design and made a precocious professional debut at the age of seventeen with *Machan no Nikkicho* (*Diary of Ma-chan*, 1946), a basic manga narrated in episodes, documenting the everyday misadventures of a child in post-war Japan. He studied medicine at Osaka University but decided not to practise so that he could dedicate his life to manga after the exceptional success of *Shin Takarajima* (1947) – a liberal interpretation of *Treasure Island* by Stevenson – appeared to guarantee him a rosy future. ● In 1956, his dynamic layouts and use of cinematic sources brought him to an inevitable professional evolution, when he began to work in Toei Animation, before founding his own production house, Mushi, at the beginning of the Sixties. Upon his death, on 9 February 1989, he left an immeasurable legacy, in the form of 500 volumes of manga and a body of animation work whose influence endures to this day. The creator of *Astro Boy*, was the first manga author to be honoured in a retrospective exhibition at the National Museum for Modern Art in Tokyo in 1990 and, in 1994, a museum was dedicated to his work in Takarazuka. ● J.Co.

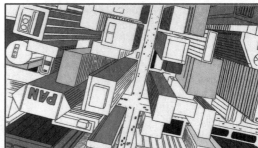

EXAMPLES OF TEZUKA OSAMU'S TALENT ● TOP: A CLOSE UP OF LEO FROM *KIMBA THE WHITE LION* (1965, DIR. YAMAMOTO EIICHI, 52 EPS) ● ABOVE: *ONBORO FILM* (BROKEN DOWN FILM, 1985, DIR. TEZUKA OSAMU, 5 MINS) ● ABOVE RIGHT: SCENE FROM THE SHORT FILM *JUMPING* (1984, DIR. TEZUKA OSAMU, 6 MINS) ● RIGHT: *MORI NO DENSETSU* (LEGEND OF THE FOREST, 1988, DIR TEZUKA OSAMU, 29 MINS)

T

SEE ALSO: ATOM; BIBLE STORIES; CLEOPATRA; DORORO; HI NO TORI 2772; LEO; MUSHI; RIBBON NO KISHI; TIMA

# TEZUKA PRODUCTION

STUDIO

Tezuka Productions was founded in January 1968 by Tezuka Osamu, originally to produce manga. Tezuka had already established Mushi Production to make animation in 1961, but after Mushi went bankrupt in 1973, Tezuka Productions expanded to include animation. ● The studio made TV series such as *Fushigina Melmo* (*Marvelous Melmo*, 1971, dir. Nagaki Tsunehito) and TV specials including *Kaitei Cho Tokkyu Marine Express* (*Undersea Super Train: Marine Express*, 1979, dirs Tezuka Osamu, Dezaki Tetsu). The feature film *Hi No Tori 2772* (*Phoenix 2772* aka *Space Firebird*, dir. Sugiyama Suguru) was a success at the box office in 1980 and won several international awards. ● Tezuka also created personal animation at Tezuka Pro. He made experimental short anime, such as *Jumping* (1984, dir. Tezuka Osamu et al) and *Onboro Film* (*Broken Down Film*, 1985, dir. Tezuka Osamu). He also made animated versions of his 'Lion Books' comics, including *Run wa Kaze no Naka* (*Lunn Flies Into The Wind*, 1985, dir. Tezuka Osamu). ● Tezuka died in 1989 and Tezuka Production manages his copyrights and licenses. Animated adaptations of Tezuka manga made after his death include a new 'Jungle Taitei' series (*Kimba the White Lion*, 1989, dir. Yamamoto Eiichi et al), *Mitsume ga Toru* (*The Three-Eyed One*, 1990, dir. Ueda Hirohito et al), a new TV version of *Astro Boy* (2003, dir. Konaka Kazuya), and the CGI film *Astro Boy* in 2009 (dir. David Bowers). While Tezuka's legendary manga *Metropolis* was animated by Rintaro in 2001. ● H.M.

THREE SERIES FROM TEZUKA PRODCUCTIONS ● ABOVE RIGHT: THE SURGEON *BLACK JACK* (1993, DIR. DEZAKI OSAMU, 10 EPS) ● BELOW RIGHT: PUBLICITY IMAGE FOR *MARINE EXPRESS* (1979, DIR. TEZUKA OSAMU, DEZAKI TETSU, 91 MINS) ● BELOW: SCENE FROM *RUN WA KAZE NO NAKA* (*LUNN FLIES INTO THE WIND*, 1985, DIR. TEZUKA OSAMU, 24 MINS)

SEE ALSO: ATOM; BELLADONNA; BIBLE STORIES; BLACK JACK; CLEOPATRA; DORORO; HI NO TORI 2772; LEO; MELMO; RIBBON NO KISHI; TIMA

# TIMA

A creation of Tezuka Osamu, Tima is a little girl with exceptional powers: at first unaware of her robotic nature, she soon has to decide her own destiny, as well as a wider collective, in the futuristic city of Metropolis. The brilliant designer Tezuka created a whole universe around her, inspired by his memories of old American films – faces and characters, biblical references and the anxieties of a nation that had just been through a war. Conceived as a reaction – or homage – to Fritz Lang's *Metropolis* (1926), Tezuka created the story when he was only fifteen years old. He then reworked this story into a manga that was printed in 1949 as the second chapter in his science-fiction trilogy. ● With Otomo Katsuhiro as screenwriter and Rintaro as director, the artwork of *Metropolis* (2001) remains faithful to Tezuka's manga, resulting in retro stylization, with thirties jazz music on the soundtrack. The story starts with the visit of a boy, Kenichi, and his uncle, Detective Ban, to a city organized on different levels, an inspired visual representation of the caste system. The pair are in pursuit of a renegade scientist but they soon realize that their real enemy, covertly wielding power in the city, is the power-mad industrialist Duke Red, who plans to use the mysterious Tima to control the city from atop his robotic skyscraper, the 'Ziggurat'. ● The film has far wider references than its obvious themes of betrayal and the central father–son relationship and introduces a succession of fascinating characters, among them the implacable young sharpshooter Rock and the robot Pero, Detective Ban's very humanized helper. Rintaro's film is a great spectacle of light and colour, where even the robots are made to seem warm and involving, endowed with the full range of human emotions. ● C.C.

*FOUR IMAGES FROM RINTARO'S 2002 FILM METROPOLIS ● ABOVE LEFT: ROCK BETWEEN TWO CITY GUARDS ● CENTRE LEFT: TIMA THE BABY ROBOT ● LEFT: INVESTIGATOR PERO ● BELOW: TIMA, THE YOUNG GIRL WITH EXTRAORDINARY ABILITIES*

METROPOLIS ● 2002 ● DIR: RINTARO ● SCR: OTOMO KATSUHIRO ● DES & ANI: NAKURA YASUHIRO ● MUS: HONDA TOSHIYUKI ● PRD: MADHOUSE, TEZUKA PRODUCTION ● FILM ● DUR: 109 MINS

*T*

# TIME BOKAN

The name *Time Bokan* has come to define an entire range of anime produced by the Tatsunoko studio. Conceived by the studio founder, Yoshida Tatsuo, the first series contains the core narrative from which the next eight series stem. An inventor creates a time machine, the Time Bokan, but disappears on its maiden voyage. Tanpei, a thirteen-year-old mechanical genius, his ten-year-old companion Junko and C-Robot, their robot sidekick, embark on a quest to find the missing inventor. Along the way, they use the time machine to help those in difficulty, but are opposed by a dark, sensual lady and her two clumsy helpers. The contrast between the cheerful altruism of the young protagonists and the insatiable greed of the evil trio of adults creates a curious mixture of adventure and comedy. ● Other series produced by the studio at this time were more adult and tragic in nature, but with the *Time Bokan* world, Tatsunoko introduced a crazy parody of the world of superheroes, in which characters always perform the same role and merely change their names and their clothing from one series to another. Time travel works as a pretext to use the same gag in different environments, in the style of the famous comic anime *Doraemon* (1973, dir. Onuki Nobuo et al). Director Sasagawa Hiroshi exploits the cyclical repetition of every episode in order to increase its comic effect. The successful character designs, which contrast the heroes' sensitive features with the grotesqueness of the wicked and funny characters, is the work of illustrator Amano Yoshitaka, in a style totally new for him. ● L.D.C.

LEFT: SCENE FROM THE 1975 TV SERIES *TIME BOKAN*, TATSUNOKO'S PARODY OF THE SUPERHERO UNIVERSE

*TIME BOKAN* ● 1975 ● DIR: SASAGAWA HIROSHI ET AL ● SCR: TORIUMI JINZO ET AL ● DES: YOSHIDA TATSUO ET AL ● ANI: TANAKA EIJI ET AL ● MUS: YAMAMOTO MASAYUKI, JINBO MASAAKI ● PRD: TATSUNOKO ● TV SERIES ● EPS: 65

# TMS ENTERTAINMENT

TMS Entertainment, originally founded in 1946, has undergone several changes of name and ownership, but has continued to make good-quality animated entertainment for a wide range of audiences. ● The broadcast of Tezuka Osamu's *Astro Boy* in 1963 created a TV animation boom and Fujioka Yutaka created Tokyo Movie, later part of TMS, to help meet the demand. Instead of simply making more sci-fi shows, Fujioka explored other subjects, such as sport, everyday life and humour. ● Three of the company's early sports series were *Kyojin no Hoshi* (*Star of the Giants*, 1968, dir. Nagahama Tadao et al), *Attack Number 1* (1969, dir. Okabe Eiji et al) and *Ace o Nerae!* (*Aim for the Ace!*, 1973) directed by Dezaki Osamu, who worked on many Tokyo Movie anime. ● Other prominent titles include the television series *Obake no Q-Taro* (*Q-Taro the Ghost*, 1965, dirs Okabe Eiji, Nagahama Tadao), *Tensai Bakabon* (*Genius Bakabon*, 1971, dir. Saito Hiroshi), *Lupin III* (1971, dir. Osumi Masaaki et al), *Takarajima* (*Treasure Island*, 1978, dir. Dezaki Osamu), *Versailles no Bara* (*The Rose of Versailles*, 1979, dir. Aagahama Tadao et al), *Rokushin Gattai Godmars* (*Godmars*, 1981, dir. Imazawa Tetsuo et al), *Sore Ike! Anpanman* (*Anpanman*, 1988, dir. Nagaoka Akinori) and *Meitantei Conan* (*Case Closed*, 1996, dir. Kodama Kenji, Yamamoto Yasuichiro). The studio's movies include *Panda Kopanda* (1972, dir. Takahata Isao), *Ie Naki Ko* (*Nobody's Boy*, 1980, dir. Dezaki Osamu) and Otomo Katsuhiro's *Akira* (1988). TMS also made the first 26 episodes of the 1969 Moomin TV series, completed by Mushi. ● H.M

RIGHT: SCENE FROM THE POPULAR TMS SERIES *MOOMINS* (1969, DIR. OSUMI MASAAKI ET AL, 65 EPS) BASED ON TOVE JANSSON'S MOOMIN STORIES

SEE ALSO: AKIRA; CONAN; DEZAKI OSAMU; HOSHI HYUMA; JARJAYES, OSCAR FRANÇOIS DE; LUPIN III; OKA HIROMI; OTOMO KATSUHIRO; PANDA KOPANDA

# TOEI ANIMATION

This animation production company was founded in July 1956 as the successor to Nihon Doga (founded in January 1948), one of several long-established Japanese studios, some of which were active before World War II. At the time it was founded, Japanese animation companies were still small and, in its early days, Toei produced live-action films. The company's ambition, however, was to make full-length animated cartoons to rival Disney's and Toei Doga (restructured in 1998 as Toei Animation) was formed especially for this purpose. The new company's first full-length film was *Hakujaden* (1958, dir. Yabushita Taiji), based on a Chinese legend. From then on, they produced one feature-length film each year. These films eventually formed the basis of Toei's connection with Studio Ghibli. ● Toei Animation also made a number of television series rivalling Tezuka's Mushi Production and has a long history, with many of the most famous artists and directors in the industry learnt their craft working for the studio, among them Miyazaki Hayao, Takahata Isao, Otsuka Yasuo, Katsumata Tomoharu, Kotabe Yoichi and Hosoda Mamoru. The studio's signature full-length films include: *Wanpaku Oji no Orochi Taiji* (*Little Prince and the Eight-Headed Dragon*, 1963, dir. Serikawa Yugo); *Little Norse Prince* (1968, dir. Takahata Isao), *Puss 'n' Boots* (1969, dir. Yabuki Kimio), *Dobutsu Takarajima* (*Animal Treasure Island*, 1971, dir. Ikeda Hiroshi) and *Tatsunoko Taro* (*Taro the Dragon Boy*, 1979, dir. Uruyama Kirio). Among the television series which Toei Animation have produced are *Sally, The Witch* (1966, dir. Kasai Osamu), *Cyborg 009* (1968, dir. Serikawa Yugo et al), *Mazinger Z* (1972, dir. Serikawa Yugo et al), *UFO Robot Grendizer Raids* (1975, dir. Katsumata Tomoharu), *Candy Candy* (1976, dir. Serikawa Yugo), *Galaxy Express 999* (1978, dir. Nishizawa Nobutaka et al), *Dragon ball* (1986, dir. Okazaki Minoru et al), *Saint Seiya* (1986, dir. Kikuch Kazuhito, Morishita Koji), *Sailor Moon* (1992, dir. Junichi Sato et al) and *One Piece* (1999, dir. Taniguchi Goro, Uta Kannosuke). ● T.N.

SCENES FROM TWO SUCCESSFUL TOEI ANIMATION SERIES ● ABOVE RIGHT: *CYBORG 009* (1979, DIR. SERIKAWA YUGO ET AL, 50 EPS) ● RIGHT: *SPACE PIRATE CAPTAIN HARLOCK* (1978, DIR. RINTARO, FUKUSHIMA KAZUMI, 42 EPS)

235

SEE ALSO: CANDY CANDY; CYBORG 009; DANGUARD ACE; DIGIMON; GHIBLI; GOKU; HAKUJADEN; HARLOCK; HOLS; HOSODA MAMORU; HOKUTO NO KEN; KATSUMATA TOMOHARU; KITARO; KOTABE YOICHI; LUFFY; MAETEL; MITAMURA YAKKO; PERO; RYU; SAILOR MOON; SALLY; TAKAHATA ISAO; UFO ROBOT GRENDIZER RAIDS

# TOKYO GODFATHERS

Transsexual Hana, alcoholic Gin and Miyuki, a teenager on the run from home, are the unlikely godfathers to whom Kon Satoshi entrusts his personal story of Christmas. Keeping them together is a newborn baby found by chance on the streets of Tokyo: one of them wants to take it to the police, one wants nothing to do with it and one wants to keep it. In the week between Christmas and New Year, between disputes and making up, mishaps and surprises, the little girl becomes the source of a journey, not only through the city, but also through the pasts of the three characters. ● Kon's third feature, *Tokyo Godfathers*, confirms his talent and originality; by taking on a story both comic and melodramatic, the director demonstrates his ability to produce a lighter film with multiple characters. Having paid homage to the art of Hitchcock and Welles in earlier works, here Kon tackles another myth of American cinema, the atypical John Ford Western *The Three Godfathers* (1948). However, this Hollywood story of three outlaws struggling with a newborn is only one of the elements inspiring this animation. ● The theme of identity emerges in *Tokyo Godfathers* but is explored in triplicate. As part of a surreal but effective family, Hana, Gin and Miyuki are forced to question themselves according to their relationship to other people and their roles are redefined time and time again. The combination of three characters shrugs off the negative connotations so often associated with the family in Japanese animation. Free of a need to leave the unit and the impulse to break out of the family, the three paradoxically represent the ideal environment in which to raise a child. Perhaps they are a model for the twenty-first century. ● C.C.

LEFT: SCENES FROM THE 2003 FILM *TOKYO GODFATHERS* FEATURING THE UNORTHODOX GODFATHERS HANA, GIN AND MIYUKI, AND THEIR INFANT CHARGE

TOKYO GODFATHERS ● 2003 ● DIR: KON SATOSHI ● SCR: NOBUMOTO KEIKO, KON SATOSHI ● DES: KONISHI KENICHI, KON SATOSHI ● ANI: KONISHI KENICHI ● MUS: SUZUKI KEIICHI ● PRD: MADHOUSE ● FILM ● DUR: 92 MINS

# TOMINO YOSHIYUKI

DIRECTOR

After studying directing and screenwriting, Tomino Yoshiyuki (born in 1947 in Odawa) looked for a job in animation and, though no draughtsman, he found a place as a writer on the historic *Astro Boy* (1963, dir. Tezuka Osamu et al) and also directed many episodes. When Mushi Production closed down, he set up as a freelance director and storyboarder and was invited by the volcanic producer Nishizaki Yoshinobu to direct the mythological series *Umi no Triton* (*Triton of the Sea*, 1972), which broke new ground in anime by making no clear distinction between 'goodies' and 'baddies'. A science-fiction buff, influenced by the American cult film *Destination Moon* (1950), Tomino also planned and directed three robot series for Sunrise studio which diverged from the fashionable model of the time: the ironic *Super Machine Daitarn 3* (1977), the dramatic *Unchallengeable Zambot 3* (1978) and the realistic *Mobile Suit Gundam* (1979). The last of these three came to be recognized as a turning point in the mecha genre, introducing a new realism to the form and having much in common with two other contemporary cult productions: *Future Boy Conan* (1978, dir. Takahata Isao) and *The Rose of Versailles* (1979, dir. Nagahama Tadao et al). ● Inspired by a Robert Heinlein novel and a near contemporary of *Star Wars* (1977, dir. George Lucas), *Gundam* turned out to be one of the most long-lived sagas in the history of animation, attracting a vast fanbase. Tomino personally directed a number of sequels for television, cinema and OAV, and also wrote several novels that fit into the original 'Universal Century' timeline. ● There are many productions for which Tomino is acknowledged as having provided the original concept, but in which he was not involved in the story or animation. Though officially freelance, Tomino is closely associated with Sunrise, which only rarely allows him roles other than the franchising of *Gundam*. The most famous is *Brain Powered* (1998), a post-*Evangelion* fantasy with a more positive outcome than *Gundam* and his other anime. ● S.G.

IMAGES FROM SERIES DIRECTED BY TOMINO YOSHIYUKI ● RIGHT: TWO DEPICTIONS OF THE MIGHTY *MOBILE SUIT GUNDAM* (1979, DIR. TOMINO YOSHIYUKI, 43 EPS) ● BELOW: *ZAMBOT 3* THE ROBOT HERO OF THE EPONYMOUS SERIES (1978, DIR. TOMINO YOSHIYUKI ET AL, 23 EPS)

SEE ALSO: ATOM; DAITARN 3; GUNDAM; IDEON; SUNRISE; TEZUKA OSAMU; YASUHIKO YOSHIKAZU

T

Created by Maria Perego, Topo Gigio, often translated as 'Louie the Mouse', enjoyed extraordinary success in Italy. After his debut in the *Canzonissima* variety show in 1959, the puppet became a central character of children's afternoon television, and later a star of the *Zecchino d'Oro* children's festival. He also found fame in Japan and, in 1967, Ichikawa Kon brought the puppet to the world of animation in the film *Toppo Jijo no Botan Senso* (*Topo Gigio and the Missile War*). Although the film was not a great success, Nippon Animation decided to make a television series in 1988, in which Topo Gigio arrives in the twentieth century from the future. After a breakdown on his spaceship, Topo Gigio is hurled from the year 2395 to a current-day Santa Catalina City, where he discovers that, unlike his own era where men and mice have gained equal status in society, he is now in an era where mice are hunted down by men. Luckily for him, he meets nine-year-old Gina, who protects him from danger and above all, from Megalo, a cat resembling the popular anime character Doraemon. Thanks to Gina, Topo Gigio also meets Mimi, a female mouse. ● The first series consists of twenty-one episodes and is followed by a second thirteen-episode series, entitled *Yume miru Toppo Jijo* (*Dreaming Topo Gigio*). ● F.L.

# TOPO GIGIO

CHARACT

*TOPO GIGIO* ● 1988 ● DIR: KOSHI SHIGEO, ISHIGURO NOBORU, KITAGAWA MASAHITO, OMACHI CHIYU ● SCR: ISHIGURO NOBORU, TADAOKI CHIYA ● DES: SHIRAUME SUSUMU ● ANI: IGUCHI TADAICHI, ISHINO HIROKAZU ● MUS: KOSHIBE NOBUYOSHI ● PRD: NIPPON ANIMATION, TV ASAHI ● TV SERIES ● EPS: 34

# TORIYAMA AKIRA

MANGAKA

THREE ANIME SERIES BASED ON TORIYAMA AKIRA'S MANGA ● BELOW & RIGHT: A SEQUENCE OF SCENES FROM *DRAGON BALL Z* (1989, DIR. NISHIO DAISUKE, 102 EPS) AND *DRAGON BALL GT* (1996, DIR. OKAZAKI MINORU ET AL, 64 EPS)

Toriyama Akira (born in 1955 in Nagoya) is a designer who uses clear and fluid lines and easily manages the transition from the comic to the epic. He is also the creator of one of the most celebrated manga and anime of the mid-Eighties, the popular – and sometimes controversial – saga of *Dragon Ball* (1986), in which science fiction is interwoven with Chinese folklore and the story of the Monkey King as described in the classic sixteenth-century text *Xiyouji* (*Journey to the West*, 1590). Toriyama was inspired by one of his earlier works, *Dragonboy* (1983), a manga about martial arts influenced by the films of Jackie Chan and, in particular, *Jui Kuen* (*Drunken Master*, 1973). ● Another of Toriyama's manga creations, which took on a cult status thanks to its television adaptation, is *Dr Slump*, a surreal comic series published weekly in *Shonen Jump* from 1980 to 1984. ● On founding his own Bird studios, Toriyama continued to create pages of short, one-shot manga but did not get involved in long-running franchises such as *Dragon Ball*. In recent years he has achieved most recognition for his character design work on videogame series such as *Dragon Quest* (1986) and its spin-offs including *Dragon Quest Monsters* (2002), where a unique balance of gentle characterization and potentially epic scale finds fertile ground for development. *Chrono Trigger* (1995), *Tobal No. 1* (1996), *Tobal 2* (1997) and *Blue Dragon* (2006) – the latter adapted to anime by Studio Pierrot with Toriyama's direct involvement and considered to be his farewell to the animation world – are other role-playing games illustrating the author's distinctive personal style. ● J.Co.

*SEE ALSO*: ARALE; GOKU; OKAZAKI MINORU

# TOTORO

CHARACTER

Totoro is perhaps the most enigmatic and iconic of all Miyazaki Hayao's fantasy characters and certainly contends for top spot among Japanese animation's most famous creatures. An imaginary combination of owl and bear, the giant Totoro invites us to reconnect with our childhoods through Satsuki and Mei, the protagonists of the 1988 feature film *My Neighbour Totoro*, as the audience is projected into the forests of post-war Japan, viewing them from a child's perspective. ● *My Neighbour Totoro* (1988) is certainly one of the most important anime films, if only for the simple reason that it presented the world with a vision that competed with the Disney product on its own terms, but outside of the Hollywood model. Through the work of Miyazaki Hayao and the Ghibli studio, anime shifted from its position in a dialectic with North American animation, in which anime stood for violence and adult themes, to become a national film practice that was no longer reliant on such content. Through the critical acclaim afforded to *My Neighbour Totoro* worldwide, public opinion on anime was changed forever. ● *My Neighbour Totoro* was the first film to demonstrate on a world stage the incredible quality of animation and storytelling coming out of Studio Ghibli. The background painting by Oga Kazuo, which took its inspiration from both western and Japanese painting traditions, was combined with the incredible keyframe animation of Miyazaki himself and orchestral compositions by Hisaishi Joe. A simple story of courage and imagination, *My Neighbour Totoro* is the definitive children's anime, and Miyazaki Hayao's most simple and effective film to date. ● D.S.

SCENES FROM THE 1988 FILM *MY NEIGHBOUR TOTORO* ● ABOVE RIGHT: THE GIANT CREATURE TOTORO WITH SATSUKI AND LITTLE MEI ● RIGHT: THE TWO CHILDREN WITH THEIR FATHER ● BELOW: WAITING FOR A BUS IN THE RAIN

TONARI NO TOTORO ● MY NEIGHBOUR TOTORO ● 1988 ● DIR & SCR & DES: MIYAZAKI HAYAO ● ANI: SATO YOSHIHARU ● MUS: HISAISHI JOE ● PRD: HARU TOHRU ET AL, STUDIO GHIBLI ● FILM ● DUR: 86 MINS

T

# TSUBASA OZORA

CHARACTER

For Tsubasa (known as Oliver or Holly in parts of Europe), football is a matter of bravery, selflessness and imagination. On the field, the young champion is identified by his athletic prowess, the combination of strength and intelligence that never fails to surprise his opponents, and also the way he spurs on his teammates to do their best. A metaphor for growth and coexistence, each match plays out like a game of chess: for every move there is an opposing one and pace varies throughout play. The anime ends up reversing the concept of football as a team sport and turns it into a collection of individuals. ● Tsubasa is a twenty-first-century footballer, midway between Ronaldinho, with his fair play and eternal smile, and Cristiano Ronaldo, with his ability to place the ball. He is highly skilled at scoring penalties, possesses expert dribbling and shooting technique and also has a deep-seated spirit of sacrifice, a player who scores but acknowledges the worth of his colleagues at the same time. ● Devised by mangaka Takahashi Yoichi, who developed his passion for football watching the World Cup in 1978, Tsubasa first appeared in a one-off story in the magazine *Shonen Jump*. From there, the young champion's rise from the dusty playing fields of Japanese high schools to competing with Brazilian professionals has moved beyond the page and even the screen. As in other sports series, the central elements of the franchise's success are pathos and suspense. Episodes also follow a well-established and effective pattern, making Tsubasa one of the most popular heroes with western audiences. ● C.C.

IMAGES FROM THE 1983 SERIES CAPTAIN TSUBASA ●
ABOVE LEFT: CAPTAIN TSUBASA ● LEFT: TSUBASA AND KOYAMA ●
BELOW: TSUBASA IN TRAINING

CAPTAIN TSUBASA ● 1983 ● DIR: IMAKAKE ISAMU ET AL ● SCR: SONODA HIDEKI ET AL ● DES: OKASAKO NOBUHIRO ● ANI: SUZUKI DAIJI ET AL ●
MUS: TOBISAWA HIROMOTO ● PRD: GROUP TAC, TOEI ANIMATION ● TV SERIES ● EPS: 128

# TSUJI MASAKI

SCRIPTWRITER

Tsuji Masaki (born in 1932 in Nagoya) is a scriptwriter, scenarist and mystery writer for the anime industry, active for over forty years. He is perhaps best known for his subtle comedies, domestic dramas and detective stories. Prolific in the Sixties and Seventies, he worked for a number of different companies, including Toei Animation, Mushi Production and Tokyo Movie Shinsha. ● It will come as no surprise, given his sensitive ability to convey subtle emotional drama even through outright slapstick, that he worked on anime adaptations of much of Takahashi Rumiko's work, most notably *Urusei Yatsura* (1981, dir. Oshii Mamoru et al). Tsuji also worked on many anime adaptations of Tezuka Osamu's manga, always remaining true to the source material but also, where possible, incorporating some of his own trademark flair and feel for comedy and suspense. ● In 2007, Tsuji Masaki received the Special Achievement prize at the Japan Media Arts Plaza for his life-long work in anime scriptwriting. On receiving the award he remarked, 'It is nice to live a long life, isn't it? Neither money nor glory were in my mind. Because I liked animation, I went on writing frantically just thinking, if only I could create even slightly more amusing ones.' ● D.S.

SCENES FROM TWO FAMOUS TEZUKA OSAMU CREATIONS MADE IN COLLABORATION WITH TSUJI MASAKI ● ABOVE: *PRINCESS KNIGHT* (1967, DIR. TEZUKA OSAMU ET AL, 52 EPS) ● LEFT: *KIMBA THE WHITE LION* (1965, DIR. YAMAMOTO EIICHI ET AL, 52 EPS)

SEE ALSO: LEO; MUSHI; RIBBON NO KISHI; TAKAHASHI RUMIKO; TMS; TOEI ANIMATION; URUSEI YATSURA

There is now an abundance of Japanese animated one-reelers, short films often distributed via the experimental circuit or screened by contemporary art centres. The Imageforum collective, the focus for alternative films in Tokyo since 1977, has published a compilation entitled *Thinking and Drawing: Japanese Art Animation of the New Millennium* (2005) and produced *Tokyo Loop* (2007), an omnibus of short features about Tokyo commissioned from sixteen artists, illustrators and animators. ● The most unusual film-maker of this generation is undoubtedly Tsuji Naoyuki (1972). He lives in Yokohama, where he makes 16mm short films. His first efforts (1992–4) featured animated puppets and plasticine figures. Since 1995, his technique has not changed: he draws with charcoal, then erases his work with a view to drawing over it again, leaving a grey afterimage on the page with the effect of jerky, slowed-down movement. ● His first major work, *Yami wo Mitsumeru Hane* (*A Feather Stares at the Dark*, 2004), creates a fabulous, imaginative world, often sexually charged, in which his figures (angels, children, demons) are born and undergo changes, accompanied by the simple but intoxicating guitar music of Takanashi Makiko. ● Tsuji then made three short films featuring clouds, combined in *Trilogy about Clouds* (2005), where his vaporous drawing technique is particularly well suited to the subject. In *Children of Shadows* (2007), he returned to the narrative vein of *A Feather Stares at the Dark*, drawing inspiration from Grimms' fairy tales, in particular *Hansel and Gretel*. Finally, his short but beautiful *The Place Where We Were* (2008) deals with the subject of childbirth. ● He has twice been selected for the Directors' Fortnight in Cannes (2004 and 2005) and his work was featured at the Rotterdam Festival in 2007. ● S.D.

# TSUJI NAOYUKI
DIRECTOR

SEE ALSO: KAWAMOTO KIHACHIRO; KURI YOJI; SHINKAI MAKOTO; TSUMIKI NO IE

# TSUKUDA MIINA
CHARACTER

In a not-too-distant future, the sports of Earth have become a hugely desirable commodity throughout the universe and alien races tussle to see the latest athletic spectacles, often resulting in bullying attacks on sports stadiums when favourite teams are defeated. In an effort to stop these outbreaks, a group of female fighters called Rabbit Force are dispatched to stop and apprehend any troublemakers. ● At the same time, young Tsukuda Miina, a clumsy and dreamy teenager, is trying to juggle her life as a high-school student with her new job as a television presenter. Despite a disastrous first day as a sports commentator, Miina soon proves herself to be a hugely capable and ambitious young woman. However, when aliens begin to attack the Earth during an interview with a sporting star, Miina finds she has special abilities and fights off the invader. Later, at a secret moon base, she becomes an official member of Rabbit Force. A transformation sequence ensues that recalls the memorable costume changes of Nagai Go's *Cutey Honey* (1973, dir. Katsumata Tomoharu) and magical girl anime such as CLAMP's *Card Captor Sakura* (1996, dir. Daichi Aktaro). ● *Getsumen To Heiki Miina* is part of the tradition of surreal and satirical comedy that is at the heart of contemporary anime, building on works such as *Urusei Yatsura* (1981, dir. Oshii Mamoru), *Project A-Ko* (1986, dir. Nishijima Katsuhiko, Moriyama Yuji) and *Keroro Gunsou* (*Sergeant Frog*, 1999, dir. Yamamoto Yusuke, Sato Junichi). The series subverts the tropes of 'magical girl' anime and conflates it with the high-velocity action of *Super Sentai* aesthetics, parodying the worlds evoked by *Sailor Moon* (1992, dir. Sato Júnichi et al) and *Project A-ko*, the latter is recalled with spectacular effect during the combat set pieces that characterize each episode. ● The series began as a fictional series within the live-action television show *Densha Otoko* (2005, Takeuchi Hideki et al), though the anime differs in storyline and art style from its live-action namesake. The image of the super-powered bunny girl recalls the protagonist of Gainax's breakthrough *Daicon IV* (1983, Yamaga Hiroyuki), and this in turn reveals the references to *Otaku* that figure strongly in the show's world. ● D.S.

GETSUMEN TO HEIKI MIINA ● LUNAR RABBIT WEAPON MIINA ● 2007 ● DIR: KAWAGUCHI KEIICHIRO ● SCR: TAKEGAMI JUNKI ● DES: KUMAZEN TAKASHI ● ANI: SAKAGAMI TAKAHIKO ● MUS: YAMASHITA KOSUKE ● PRD: STUDIO GONZO ● TV SERIES ● EPS: 13

# TSUMIKI NO IE
FILM

LEFT: TWO SCENES FROM THE MELANCHOLY SHORT FILM *THE HOUSE OF SMALL CUBES*, 2008, DIRECTED BY KATO KUNIO

*Tsumiki no Ie* (*The House of Small Cubes*) is a twelve-minute animated film by Japanese director Kato Kunio. It was premiered in 2008, and in June of that year, it won the Cristal Award at the Annecy International Animated Film Festival. In Japan, the film and its author came to general public attention in when it became the first Japanese work to win the Academy Award for Best Short Animated Film in 2009. ● Director Kato uses coloured pencil drawings as the basis for his animation. His theme is the meaning and value of life. The hero is an old man who lives in a house which has had more and more storeys added to keep pace with the constantly rising sea level outside. The film contains nothing new technically and thematically, but the power of the composition is outstanding. ● Kato Kunio (born in 1977 in Kagoshima) graduated from Tama University of Arts. He began making animation while still a student and joined the Robot Communications advertising production company after graduation. There, he worked on animated material for television and websites, while producing short animated films independently. His works prior to *Tsumiki no Ie* include *The Apple Incident* (2001) and *Aru Tabibito no Nikki* (*The Diary of Tortov Riddle*, 2003). ● In Japan, where there are few sources of funding and cinema festivals for short aniamtions and independent productions, Kato has joined the great Yamamura Koji as one of the directors whose works are now most eagerly anticipated. ● H.M.

TSUMIKI NO IE ● THE HOUSE OF SMALL CUBES ● 2008 ● DIR: KATO KUNIO ● PRD: ROBOT COMMUNICATIONS ● FILM ● DUR: 12 MINS

242

The most famous twins in manga could not be more fatally different. Kazuya Uesugi is top of the class, adored by little girls, studious and a champion in any sport ● Tatsuya, on the other hand, is the exact opposite, lazy, indolent and invisible in the eyes of his female companions. However, what unites them is their friendship – and love – for their neighbour and fellow classmate, Minami, the school's prized pupil and thus Kazuya's ideal candidate for a companion. Fate has it that the boy dies in an accident and suddenly the idle twin discovers he is living the glorious life of his brother, from student league baseball to Minami's heart, which has already been conquered. ● Tatsuya and Kazuya are the protagonists of Adachi Mitsuru's comic masterpiece, *Touch*, a roman-fleuve consisting of twenty-six volumes, firmly clinging to the broad shoulders of the sports genre, which in Japan is usually successful and much appreciated. The solid format of manga and Adachi's narrative, a poet and singer for adolescents, are perfect to fuse in animated films. The usual interpreter of his comics is Sugii Gisaburo, the veteran director, and author of the television series *Touch* (1985) and the films *Miss Lonely Yesterday* (1998) and *Touch: Cross Road* (2001), which tell the story of Tatsuya five years after high school. ● Above all, the 1985 television anime provides the greatest satisfaction. The portrait of Japanese youth is built on values and feelings that are reflected in the twins and Minami, as if they emanated from a microcosm in which the power of friendship must be absolutely preserved. It is also said that the preparation for mourning and the scene showing the two youngsters in tears after Kazuya's funeral is a masterpiece of dramatic construction. ● M.A.R.

# UESUGI TATSUYA & KAZUYA

CHARACTERS

TOUCH ● 1985 ● DIR: SUGII GISABURO ● SCR: TAKAHOSHI YUMIKO ET AL ● DES: MAEDA MINGRU, KOBAYASHI ● ANI: MAEDA MINORU ET AL ● MUS: SERIZAWA HIROAKI ● PRD: GROUP TAC ● TV SERIES ● EPS: 101

# UFO ROBOT GRENDIZER RAIDS

TV SERIES

Grendizer is an extraordinarily advanced robot. Built from an indestructible alloy called 'gren', he is thirty metres tall, weighs twenty-eight tonnes and can reach speeds of 770 kilometres per hour. He literally fell to Earth, driven from the planet Fleed after being set on fire by the forces of Vega, a ruthless warlord. Inside this fighting robot lives Prince Duke Fleed, who was rescued by Doctor Procton, director of the Institute of Space Research, and kept in hiding from Vega under the name of Actarus. When a militia from Vega begins to threaten the Earth, Actarus calls upon his loyal robot and together they take up the battle against evil to save the planet from destruction. ● Grendizer and Duke Fleed/Actarus share the same destiny and story. While Grendizer has sophisticated weapons and superior strength, Actarus, with his noble spirit, is his ideal pilot. In their courageous struggle against enemy forces, this young and generous man of extraordinary sensitivity tirelessly defends peace and justice. Actarus is the incarnation of the anti-militarist philosophy of his creator Nagai Go (the author of the original manga) who, taking advantage of interest in UFOs in the mid-Seventies, was inspired by the flying saucers that were sighted all over the world to devise his original creation. ● *UFO Robot Grendizer Raids* is the final chapter in an anime trilogy that begins with *Mazinger Z* (1972, dir. Serikawa Yugo et al) and *Great Mazinger* (1974, dir. Serikawa Yugo et al). The series was welcomed with unanticipated enthusiasm in Europe and parts of the Arabic-speaking world, and enjoyed much more success than it had in Japan. ● G.P.

RIGHT: ACTARUS, PILOT AND MIND OF THE ROBOT GRENDIZER, FROM THE 1975 TV SERIES UFO ROBOT GRENDIZER RAIDS

UFO ROBOT GRENDIZER RAIDS ● UFO ROBO GRENDIZER ● 1975 ● DIR: KASAI OSAMU, AKEHI MASAYUKI ET AL ● SCR: UEHARA SHOZO ET AL ● DES: YAMASHITA TOSHINARI, SAYAMA YOSHINORI ● ANI: YAMASHITA TOSHINARI ● MUS: KIKUCHI SHUNSUKE ● PRD: DYNAMIC, TOEI ANIMATION ● TV SERIES ● EPS: 74

4

# UROTSUKIDOJI

VIDEO SERIES

*Urotsukidoji*, although released at the end of the Eighties, is as typical of the Nineties as grunge music and 'cyberpunk', as the lustful tentacled demons emerging from the mind of author Maeda Toshio became yet another example of subculture making its way into the mainstream. ● Urotsukidoji's plot involves the reconciliation of three realms, a variation on the famous tale of the Chinese Three Kingdoms. Two parallel worlds adjoin that of the human race: the realm of the Makai demons, and the domain of the Jujinkai, half-human-half-beasts. Every 3,000 years, a super-being, the 'Overfiend', arises to bring about a balance between the three. For over 300 years Jujinkai Amano Jiyaku has sought the host for the next reincarnation and finds him in Japan: he is Tatsuo Nagumo, a high-school student. ● Such fantasy plotlines have served countless anime titles, where otherworldly beings watch over a chosen one. This time, the demons disagree. They fear that the boy Nagumo will only bring chaos and destruction to all and, on crossing over to the human world to dispatch him, they also decide to go on a 'raping' rampage. ● While Takayama's direction does not age well, *Urotsukidoji* should be remembered for its stunning sound design and appropriation of devices from *ukiyo-e* – from Hokusai to Utamaro – and pink cinema, that enabled Maeda to bypass censors and depict creatures whose numerous tentacles penetrate every orifice of underaged schoolgirls and their more lascivious teachers. 'Tentacle porn', as the genre was later defined, became an iconic form of depravity, in the tradition of Japanese erotic-grotesque, though not as dark as *muzan-e* – a violently erotic variant of *ukiyo-e* – from artists like Suehiro Maruo. ● S.S.

UROTSUKIDOJI ● LEGEND OF THE OVERFIEND ● 1987 ● DIR: TAKAYAMA HIDEKI ● SCR: AIKAWA NOBORU ET AL ● DES: SEKIME RIKIZO ET AL ● ANI: YANASAWA TETSUYA ● MUS: AMANO MASAMICHI ● PRD: WEST CAPE PRODUCTIONS ● EPS: 16

# URUSEI YATSURA

TV SERIES

*Urusei Yatsura* plays a crucial role in the development of anime fandom in the West. Beyond the sensationalism of anime erotica and the boys' club of giant robots, *Urusei Yatsura* was one of the first franchises to present a world rich in Japanese mythology and folklore with an unapologetic and contemporary twist. These exotic details made the television show, manga and movies a favourite with nascent *otaku*, who delighted in the obscurity and spectacle of each episode. ● The protagonists are teenager Moroboshi Ataru and space-alien Princess Lum, and the image of Lum was perhaps the definitive icon of Japanese anime, certainly in the West, throughout the Eighties. The pair meet though a chance encounter in the first episode, as Ataru stumbles across the invading forces of Lum's otherworldly empire. Chosen through an apparently 'random' computer system, Ataru is challenged to a game of tag against the beautiful bikini-babe Lum, daughter of the invading king. Through a succession of chance exchanges that see Ataru winning the game of tag and ending up betrothed to Lum, the series charts the surreal relationship between lascivious Ataru, jealous Lum and an eccentric mix of ensemble characters. ● Aside from introducing a generation of budding anime and manga fans to the complexity and imagination of Japanese mythology, it is important to note the importance of *Urusei Yatsura* in establishing anime comedy. The loaded pauses, surreal slapstick and comedy of errors that Ataru and Lum inflict upon one another weave a rich social picture contrary to the ostensibly violent and serious view of anime driven by other franchises. The incredible sensation of fun that exudes from *Urusei Yatsura* is timeless. ● D.S.

LEFT: THE ALIEN PRINCESS LUM, IN HER TIGER–STRIPED FUR BIKINI, FROM THE 1981 TV SERIES URUSEI YATSURA

URUSEI YATSURA ● 1981 ● DIR: OSHII MAMORU ET AL ● SCR: HOSHIYAMA HIROYUKI ET AL ● DES: TAKADA AKEMI ET AL ● ANI: AOSHIMA KATSUMI ET AL ● MUS: KAZATO SHINSUKE ET AL ● PRD: STUDIO DEEN, STUDIO PIERROT ● EPS: 195

Before Hollywood appropriated vampires for action blockbusters such as *Blade* (1998) and *Underworld* (2003), these descendants of Dracula had already been brought back to life in Japan by Kikuchi Hideyuki during the Eighties. This popular horror and science-fiction author created a series of novels about the activities of D, a 'knight-errant' who roams a post-nuclear world astride his cybernetic horse. The first novel was turned into a mediocre movie, full of slow-motion action and textured backgrounds, while the third novel was brought to the screen in a lavish co-production faithfully reproducing Amano Yoshitaka's original illustrations. ● D belongs to the same lone hero tradition as Clint Eastwood's gunslingers and Mel Gibson's *Mad Max* (1979). Taciturn, introverted and at war with himself, D is set apart because he is a half-human, half-vampire hybrid, but it is to him that humans turn when they are in trouble. His past is shrouded in mystery and he has sworn revenge against vampires, even though his father was a powerful member of the race of 'Noble' vampires, now in decline, which survive in the legendary City of the Night. ● D possesses the physical strength of a vampire but, unlike them, he can go out during the daytime. He is a superb swordsman and can see through the disguises behind which vampires often hide in order to gain human beings' trust. A 'symbiote' with the form of a human face lives in his left hand and helps him by sucking in the aura of vampires. ● S.G.

## VAMPIRE HUNTER D

CHARACTER

ABOVE: THREE SCENES FROM ASHIDA TOYOO'S CULT 2001 MOVIE *VAMPIRE HUNTER D*

*VAMPIRE HUNTER D* ● 1985 ● DIR: ASHIDA TOYOO ● SCR: HIRANO YASUSHI ● DES: AMANO YOSHITAKA ● ANI: MATSUSHITA HIROMI ● MUS: KOMURO TETSUYA ● PRD: ASHI PRODUCTION ● FILM ● DUR: 75 MINS

## VASH THE STAMPEDE

CHARACTER

*TRIGUN* ● 1998 ● DIR: NISHIMURA SATOSHI ● SCR: KURODA YOSUKE ● DES: YOSHIMATSU TAKAHIRO ● ANI: OHASHI YOSHIMITSU ● MUS: IMAHORI TSUNEO ● PRD: MADHOUSE ● TV SERIES ● EPS: 26

The gunslinger known as Vash the Stampede wanders planet Gunsmoke with a bounty of sixty billion 'double dollars' on his head. Wherever Vash goes, trouble follows, even though the young man in the red raincoat, goggles and spiky blond hair is on the side of justice and goes to great lengths to help others. Were it not for his occasional entertaining outbursts and his passion for women and sweets, he could pass for a distant, futuristic nephew of western cinema's lonely heroes. ● Created in 1995 by Nightow Yasuhiro, a designer often employed in the anime industry, the manga is divided into two series, *Trigun* (1995) and the more recent *Trigun Maximun* (2004), showcasing a graphic style that, whilst not always pleasing, indulges the endless obsession of certain mangaka with grimaces and deformed faces. One might call this a graphic transliteration of the 'comic'. ● Madhouse was responsible for the successful adaptation of this publication to the small screen. The resulting television series, broadcast in 1998, was directed by Nishimura Satoshi and is greatly admired by young audiences, mainly thanks to the lead character, a dispenser of delightful and thrilling justice. Tackling elements of science fiction and 'cyberpunk' within the series, with *Trigun* Madhouse studio confirmed the skills of its workforce and cemented its distinctive reputation. ● M.A.R.

Watanabe Shinichi (born in 1964 in Yokoyama) belongs to the generation who grew up during the anime boom years of the Seventies. The saga of *Lupin III* (1971) shaped his mischievous, inclusive and easygoing style of comedy and he used himself as the model for Nabeshin, an afro-haired alter ego with the power to change the plot of the anime he appears in, Shinichi's best-known and most absurd series *Excel Saga* (1999). Watanabe entered the anime industry at the end of the Eighties and began to make a name for himself as a storyboarder and episode director on the sports-themed series *Goal Field Hunter* (Goal FH, 1994). ● In 1997, he directed his first comedy series, *Hare Tokidoki Buta* (Tokyo Pig), starring a child and his magic piglet. He became famous with the series *Excel Saga,* which took television comedy to new and demented extremes: combining the *manzai* tradition of fast-talking stand-up with the distortion of cartoons, it opens the way to a new genre. Each episode sends up a specific genre – from the *sentai* 'task-force' style squadrons to *kawaii* (cute) culture with its ultra-sweet little animals. Visually, Watanabe takes all the characteristics of classic anime to extremes, with an overabundance of expressionistic graphic backgrounds and distorted inserts. The bizarre zaniness of the series extended to the spin-off *Puni Puni Poemi* (2001), which was followed by other comic series with uninhibited female protagonists such as *Tenchi Muyo! GXP* (2002). With *Nerima Daikon Brothers* (2006) Watanabe turned his comedic talents towards musicals and made fun of the Japanese passion for karaoke through the bewildering adventures of a trio of blues-crazy Japanese turnip farmers. *Excel Saga's* Nabeshin intervenes in this series too, by providing the protagonists with gadgets that always have disastrous side-effects. ● L.D.C.

## WATANABE SHINICHI

DIRECTOR

SEE ALSO: ISHII KATSUHITO; KEI & YURI; LUPIN III; MASAKI TENCHI; TSUKUDA MINA; URUSEI YATSURA

# WATANABE SHINICHIRO

A leading name on the current anime scene and unexpectedly discovered by fans after directing *Cowboy Bebop* (1998), Watanabe (born in 1965 in Kyoto) devoted little time to his first job as designer, instead he focused almost immediately on directing and distinguishing himself as an assistant director and storyboard artist on several series produced by Sunrise. In 1994, along with the veteran Kawamori Shoji, he co-directed *Macross Plus* (1994), an OAV in four episodes that intelligently recreated the world of *Super Dimensional Fortress Macross*. This led to a friendship and an artistic association with the scriptwriter Nobumoto Keiko and musician Kanno Yoko, the team that made *Cowboy Bebop*. ● The Bebop TV is striking for its freshness and high technical quality. Watanabe is a director with a flamboyant style who likes to play with film vocabulary, moving between different styles without ever becoming excessive. Following director Anno Hideaki, he abandons many of the typical stylistic features of anime, such as old-fashioned grainy backdrops, insisting on a more realistic style of drawing and employs narrative methods closer to those of live cinema. He pays great attention to music (rarely is a piece used repeatedly) and to editing (flashbacks are short and ambiguous, but immediately suggestive). The more recent *Samurai Champloo* (2004) also demonstrates his eclectic sense, blending *jidaigeki* (period drama) with references to hip-hop culture. America has rewarded him, not only by helping to produce the feature-length film version of *Cowboy Bebop* (2001) and making him guest of honour at the 'Big Apple Anime Fest' in 2002, but also by including his two shorts on the American produced project *Animatrix* (2003). ● S.G.

LEFT: CHARACTERS FROM *COWBOY BEBOP* (1998, WATANABE SHINICHIRO, 26 EPS), THE FIRST SERIES TO SHOWCASE WATANABE SHINICHIRO'S TALENT AS A DIRECTOR

SEE ALSO: ANIMATRIX; APPLE, SHARON; MUGEN & JIN; SPIEGEL; SPIKE; SUNRISE

---

Brawling and restless in sixties Tokyo, Joe, the eponymous hero of *Tomorrow's Joe*, meets Tange Danpei, a boxing coach fallen on hard times, who sees in him the 'makings of a champion' and is determined to turn him into a professional. However, the boy soon ends up in trouble, attempting to extort money from a rich heiress called Shiraki Yoko. Joe is sent to a young offenders' institution, where he meets and is encouraged by the professional boxer Rikiishi Toru. ● Dezaki Osamu faithfully adapts the epic manga by Chiba Tetsuya and Takamori Asao with a fresh approach for the time (shots are twisted and low-angled, like scenes flashing past in a car). His evocative reconstruction of the surroundings uses mostly opaque, if not exactly 'dirty', colours, producing effects similar to a charcoal drawing. With above-average workmanship for the period (particularly considering that drawings were hardly ever reused), the series laid the foundations for the sporting-nihilist genre and owes much of its success to the tireless artwork of Araki Shingo. Outstripping the manga's narrative, the anime had to stop at its seventy-ninth episode and wait for ten years to elapse before it reached the famous tragic death of the main character in the corner of the ring. Joe's non-conformism and his desire for social advancement made him a cult symbol for Japanese teenagers who lived through a period of social unrest and protest. The series was so popular that, on Rikiishi's death, a fictitious funeral was organized and attended by hundreds of the character's fans. ● S.G.

# YABUKI JOE

CHARACTER

---

*ASHITA NO JOE* ● *TOMORROW'S JOE* ● 1970 ● DIR: DEZAKI OSAMU ET AL ● SCR: YUKIMURO SHUNICHI ET AL ● DES & ANI: SUGINO AKIO ET AL ● MUS: YAGI TADAO ● PRD: MUSHI PRODUCTION ● TV SERIES ● EPS: 79

# YABUKI KIMIO

DIRECTOR

Yabuki Kimio was a key figure during the early years of Toei Animation. As an animator with a particular penchant for romantic wanderings and unbridled fantasy, he made the link between the emerging identity of anime and the European fairytale tradition, which had for some time been feeding the imagination of the western animation coming out of the Disney studios. *Puss'n' Boots* (1969), the film which brought both the Toei characters and the genius of the young animator Miyazaki Hayao to the public eye, is one of the most famous works of his career, together with the delicate *Swan Lake* (1981). This was made to celebrate the studio's twenty-fifth anniversary, where Yabuki continued to work as an independent director, although he had left the staff in 1973. ● Yabuki also helped direct *Little Prince and Eight-Headed Dragon* (1963) by Serikawa Yugo, and then worked as a director in the studio's television department, on the series *Ken, the Wolf Boy* (1963) and *A Little Ninja Fujimaru* (1964), later debuting as a director of full-length films with *Tales from Hans Christian Anderson* (1968), an adaptation of several autobiographical tales by the Danish writer. ● Television work such as *Dororon Enmakun* (1973), inspired by the manga by Nagai Go, *Ikkyu-san* (1975) and *The Pumpkin Wine* (1982) were forays into his adolescent romanticism in the style of the manga by Miura Mitsuru. These he alternated with feature-length film-making, namely magical fantasy in the western tradition, including *Twelve Months* (1980) and *Rainbow Brite and the Star Stealer* (1985), a controversial co-production between Japan and the USA, which Kabuki worked on with the French illustrator Bernard Deyriès, and intended to create a mythology around the character of Rainbow Brite, originally designed as a Hallmark greeting card illustration. ● J.Co.

ABOVE: ORIGINAL POSTER FOR YABUKI'S FILM *PUSS 'N' BOOTS* (1969, DIR. YABUKI KIMIO, 80 MINS). THE CAT PERO WAS TO BECOME THE BELOVED MASCOT OF TOEI ANIMATION

SEE ALSO: HAKUCHO NO MIZUUMI; KEN, THE WOLF BOY; NAGAI GO; PERO; TOEI ANIMATION

# YABUSHITA TAIJI

ABOVE: SCENE FROM THE FILM HAKUJADEN (LEGEND OF THE WHITE SNAKE, 1958, DIR. YABUSHITA TAIJI, 78 MINS), RELEASED IN THE USA AS PANDA AND THE MAGIC SERPENT. INSPIRED BY CHINESE LEGENDS, THE FILM FEATURES ANIMATION BY THE GREAT YASUJI MORI

SEE ALSO: HAKUJADEN; MASAOKA KENZO; MOCHINAGA TADAHITO; MOMOTARO; OFUJI NOBURO; TOEI ANIMATION

Yabushita Taiji (1903–1986) was a crucial connection between the pre- and post-war anime eras: a figure from the early days of cinematography who drifted into anime production. Graduating in photography from the Tokyo School of Arts in 1925, he worked briefly for the Shochiku studio before moving to the Ministry of Education, where he shot several silent films, including a documentary about the round-the-world maiden flight of the first Zeppelin. In the post-war period, when Japanese cinemas were swamped by high-quality Disney features that had been denied them by the wartime censors, he moved into animation at Nippon Doga, working on Masaoka Kenzo's *Tora-chan to Hanayome* (*Tora's Bride*, 1948), one of the first, stumbling attempts to revitalize Japan's animation industry. ● Yabushita was instrumental in anime's recovery in the Fifties. In 1958, after Nippon Doga's take-over by Toei Animation, he was ideally placed to oversee production on the full-length, full-colour anime film *Legend of the White Snake* (released in the USA as *Panda and the Magic Serpent*, 1958, dir. Yabushita Taiji, Okabe Kazuhiko), which went on to win a special award at the Venice Children's Film Festival in 1959, and was the first colour anime to receive a US release in 1961. ● Yabushita was central in several anime features of the Sixties, producing a small but influential group of Toei children's works that included *Anju to Zushio-Maru* (*The Orphan Brother*, 1961, dir. Yabushita Taiji, Serikawa Yugo) and *Shonen Jack to Mahotsukai* (*Jack and the Witch*, 1967, dir. Yabushita Taiji). He served as a mentor and inspiration to many of the next generation of creators, not only as their boss, but also as a lecturer in animation at Tokyo Designer Gakuin from 1970, and published several influential textbooks. ● J.Cl.

Like Truman Burbank of *The Truman Show* (1998), Yahagi Shogo is caught up in a world that doesn't exist in a real sense, but instead as a simulation maintained to pacify and control the population. Oblivious to this great conspiracy, our hero comes across a cutting-edge new motorcycle, the 'Bahamut', and is immediately assailed by shadowy agents. Escaping, he begins to realize that this is no ordinary bike and that its futuristic technologies have the potential to unpick the fabric of the virtual reality constructed by an unseen conspiracy of forces. The story continues apace as we follow Yahagi fleeing from various assailants, while at the same time coming to understand the potential of his vehicle, which can transform into a mechanical warrior. Armed with his machine, the star-crossed hero is thrust into the heart of the conspiracy, meeting virtual idols, steroid-pumped soldiers and armies of clones. ● In subsequent series and additional parts, this story scales up by greater and greater degrees, away from the city streets and into the corporate headquarters and remote penthouses of the metropolis. With a narrative tackling apocalyptic themes of civil unrest and environmental destruction, while maintaining the trope of the false world and duped citizens, *Megazone 23* (1985) has been compared to *The Matrix* trilogy (1999, 2003, 2003, dir. Wachowski Brothers). The concept of a highly evolved technological culture staging an earlier everyday society within a virtual reality is explored in both works. Yahagi Shogo, with his reluctant heroism and impassive nature, is certainly recalled in the performance of Keanu Reeves as Neo, and the shifting territories of the *Matrix* films parallel the various locations of the classic *Megazone 23*. ● D.S.

# YAHAGI SHOGO

MEGAZONE TSU SAN ● MEGAZONE 23 ● 1985 ● DIR: ISHIGURO NOBORU ● SCR: HISHIYAMA HIROYUKI, EMU ARII ● DES & ANI: HIRANO TOSHIHIRO ET AL ●
MUS: SAGISU SHIRO ● PRD: AIC ● VIDEO SERIES ● EPS: 4

# YAMADAS

CHARACTERS

*My Neighbours the Yamadas* is the first film by Studio Ghibli to use computer-generated animation and the latest film directed by the master Takahata Isao. In Japan, Yamada is a fairly common family name. At the outset, the film appears to create a portrait of a typical family struggling with traditional everyday problems: the main characters are a father who works to keep the family afloat, a wife who stays at home and two children, a boy and a girl, as well as a dog called Pochi. ● The subject of the film stems from a manga of the same name by Isaichi Ishii. Like the original's vignettes, Takahata's film is made up of short episodes, announced by a simple title and completed by a *haiku*. Known for his strict realism, Takahata finds a freer style in his latest work. The monotony of everyday life is relieved by caricature and by scenes in which the director lets his characters float in fantasy. In order to reinforce this style, Takahata tried out a new technique, in which he managed to introduce cultural and graphic references that he had been thinking about for some time. The film's design is reminiscent of watercolour sketches, with brief definition and coloured spots in pastel tones, later processed and animated by computer in order to restore an unexpected fluidity of movements. For this technique, Takahata was inspired by *ukiyo-e* artists from the Edo period. ● F.L.

ABOVE & RIGHT: THE EVERYDAY FAMILY THE YAMADAS CAUGHT IN A VARIETY OF MUNDANE AND FANTASTIC SITUATIONS IN TAKAHATA ISAO'S 1999 FILM *MY NEIGHBOURS THE YAMADAS*

*HOHOKEKYO TONARI NO YAMADA-KUN* ● *MY NEIGHBOURS THE YAMADAS* ● 1999 ● DIR & SCR: TAKAHATA ISAO ● DES: ISHII HISAICHI ● ANI: KONISHI KENICHI ● MUS: YANO AKIKO ● PRD: UJIIE SEIICHIRO, SHOJI TAKASHI ET AL, STUDIO GHIBLI ● FILM ● DUR: 104 MINS

Y

Yamaga Hiroyuki (born in 1962 in Niigata) studied at the Osaka College of Art, where he shared an apartment with two other aspiring animators, Anno Hideaki and Akai Takami. With them, he made the opening animations for *Daicon III* at the twentieth science-fiction convention in Osaka in 1981. Following the success of this short animation, Yamaga was asked to assist with the *Macross* television series (1982), where he was a pupil of veteran animator Ishiguro Noboru. From this moment on, Yamaga became the group's focal point, and in 1983 he directed the opening animations for *Daicon IV*. Backed by Bandai, he founded the Gainax studio with his colleagues in 1984, where he wrote the screenplay for and directed the first Gainax project, the ambitious feature-length film *The Wings of Honneamise* (1987). The studio's second outing was the OAV series *Top o Nerae! Gunbuster* (*Gunbuster*, 1988). Yamaga's attempts to compromise between commercial and intellectual demands – creating curvaceous young girls and giant robots in a more complex narrative universe – received public and critical acclaim. ● While writing the screenplay for external projects such as the OAV *Mobile Suit Gundam 0080: War in the Pocket* (1989) at Gainax, Yamaga concentrated more and more on production. In 2001, he returned to directing with the television series *Mahoromatic* and the delirious series *Magical Shopping Arcade Abenobashi* (2002), which blends crazy humour and exaggerated dialogue in a touching reflection on growing up. ● L.D.C.

# YAMAGA HIROYUKI

ABOVE: LHADATT SHIROTSUGU IN THE ROYAL SPACE FORCE IN YAMAGA HIROYUKI'S FIRST FILM *THE WINGS OF HONNEAMISE* (1987, DIR. YAMAGA HIROYUKI, 120 MINS)

SEE ALSO: ANNO HIDEAKI; DAICON III & IV; GAINAX; GUNDAM; ISHIGURO NOBORU; LHADATT, SHIROTSUGU

# YAMAMOTO EIICHI

DIRECTOR

SEE ALSO: ATOM; BELLADONNA; CLEOPATRA; LEO; MUSHI; TEZUKA OSAMU; TOEI ANIMATION

SCENES FROM FILMS DIRECTED BY YAMAMOTO EIICHI FOR MUSHI PRODUCTIONS ● BELOW: *THE TRAGEDY OF BELLADONNA* (1973, DIR: YAMAMOTO EIICHI, 89 MINS) ● BELOW RIGHT: *CLEOPATRA: QUEEN OF SEX* (1970, DIR. TEZUKA OSAMU, YAMAMOTO EIICHI, 112 MINS)

*The Tragedy of Belladonna* (1973) by Yamamoto Eiichi (born in 1940 in Kyoto) is probably the most innovative and radical manifesto expressed by anime to differentiate it from the indistinguishable look of western animation. Using mesmerizing choreography and combining static images with fluid movements based on the sophisticated illustrations of Kuni Fukai, it echoes the art of Gustav Klimt and Aubrey Beardsley. Unfortunately, this ambitious experiment, which was based on the character of Joan of Arc, came too early and its failure contributed to the closure of the Mushi Production studio. The film was the last in the Animerama trilogy – the first instalment was *Senya Ichiya Monogatari* (A Thousand and One Nights, 1969), followed by *Cleopatra* (1970), also directed by Yamamoto – whose goal was to make an unprecedented move towards adult anime. While the first two films in the trilogy included elements of eroticism in their visual language and had traditional narrative styles reminiscent of Tezuka, *Belladonna* was unashamed in its desire to shock. Yamamoto would return to this approach years later with his screenplay for the exquisite erotic film *Koushoku Ichidai Otoko* (The Sensualist, 1991, dir. Abe Yukio).
● Yamamoto began his career as an animator at Yokoyama Ryuichi's Otogi Pro studio, before anime had fully defined its own code and language. In 1961, he joined Tezuka's animation studio, where he worked as a producer, scriptwriter and director for some of the studio's most iconic figures – *Astro Boy* (1963) and *Kimba the White Lion* (1965) – with occasional forays into daring experiments such as the astonishing medium-length film *Aru Machikado no Monogatari* (Stories from a Street Corner, 1962). After Mushi Production closed, Yamamoto went to work for Toei Animation, where he took over the reins of the series *Star Blazers* (1974), amongst other titles, and directed the realist melodrama *Oshin* (1984) as well as the space-opera *Odin: Koshi Hansen Starlight* (1985), before retiring in 1991. ● J.Co.

# YAMASHITA IKUTO

MECHA DESIGNER

Yamashita Ikuto (born in 1965 in Gifu) is renowned for his contribution to mecha design, the giant fighting robot icons of Japanese animation. Apart from his striking original work on *Sento Yosei Yukikaze* (Yukikaze, 2002, dir. Okura Masahiko), he has contributed to Gainax productions including *Fushigi no Umi no Nadia* (The Secret of Blue Water, 1990, dir. Anno Hideaki) and the landmark television series *Shinseiki Evangelion* (Neon Genesis Evangelion, 1995, dir. Anno Hideaki.) ● His mecha designs employ a complex, sinuous shape echoing human physical anatomy, while at the same time reflecting cutting-edge technologies, car design and even lizard and dinosaur anatomy. In this, Yamashita shifts away from the 'kabuto' styling of blocky, samurai armour-inspired mecha, found in manga such as Tetsujin 28-go (1956). ● Maeda Mahiro's Angel designs in Evangelion are the perfect counterpoint to Yamashita's mecha. Both are stunning and elegant but also deadly, reflecting not only the murderous beauty of nature, but also futuristic technologies and alien science. These two creative visions combine with Anno Hideaki's conceptual framework to create one of the most memorable and important anime of the past twenty years. ● D.S.

SEE ALSO: ANNO HIDEAKI; EVANGELION; GAINAX; MAEDA MAHIRO; NADIA; TETSUJIN 28-GO

YAMATO

SPACESHIP

*Star Blazers*, perhaps the best known of all anime science-fiction epics, began in 1974 with the voyage of the battleship *Yamato* (a name taken from a real ship that was sunk in 1945 but restored to life once more in the pages of the manga that turned the ship into an enduring myth and popular icon). Formerly a warship, the *Yamato* becomes the bearer of life and hope for a planet Earth weakened by radioactive bombardment inflicted by the alien Gamilas. Its crew have to face a year-long voyage (measured by an implacable countdown), while at the same time, their interwoven relationships make the manga (and its associated television series) a forerunner of the space-opera genre whose origin is more usually traced back to the *Gundam* (1979, dir. Tomino Yoshiyuki) and *Macross* (1982, dir. Ishiguro Noboru et al) sagas. The ecological subtext and message of universal fellowship implicit in the help given by the ethereal Starsha from the planet Iscandar (*Yamato*'s destination) reveal a certain underlying idealism, though the series is distinguished by a mainly epic approach which is not the case of later science-fiction milestones *Captain Harlock* (1978, dir. Rintaro, Fukushima Kazumi), *Galaxy Express 999* (1978, dir. Nishizawa Nobutaka et al) and *Queen Millennia* (1981). More than in these series, *Yamato* reveals a taste for historically inspired war stories carefully depicting military life in accordance with a model that might even suggest vague parallels with *Star Trek*. ● The first broadcasts did not enjoy the success they deserved, but thanks to the versions made for the cinema *Yamato* generated numerous sequels and became a symbol of space adventure remembered even today as one of the first forays into animation aimed at a more adult audience. The animated series was also successful in the West, where it was renamed *Star Blazers*, while the ship was rebaptized the *Argo* in obvious reference to Jason and the Argonauts' mythological expedition. ● D.D.G.

ABOVE: THE SPACE BATTLESHIP YAMATO BRINGING HOPE TO THE PEOPLE OF EARTH IN THE 1974 TV SERIES STAR BLAZERS

UCHU SENKAN YAMATO ● STAR BLAZERS ● 1974 ● DIR: ISHIGURO NOBORU ET AL ● SCR: FUJIKAWA KEISUKE ET AL ● DES: MATSUMOTO LEIJI ET AL ●
ANI: ASHIDA TOYUO ET AL ● MUS: MIYAGAWA HIROSHI, HANEDA KENTARO ● PRD: ACADEMY PRODUCTION ● TV SERIES ● EPS: 26

Yasuhiko Yoshikazu is not the type to allow himself to be restrained by an artistic straitjacket. Born in 1947 in Hokkaido, he joined Tezuka Osamu's Mushi Production company as a very young man. Together with Tomino Yoshiyuki, he created one of the unforgettable legends of anime: *Mobile Suit Gundam* (1979). However, like others of his generation, Yoshikazu refused to live in the past, seeking instead to find the best setting for his creative flair – not an easy prospect, since the golden age he experienced at the Sunrise studio and his successful partnership with Tomino brought about extraordinary works such as *Yuusha Raideen (Brave Raideen*, 1975), *Muteki Choujin Zanbot 3 (Zanbot 3*, 1977), and *Cho Denji Robo Combattler V (Super Electromagnetic Robo Combattler V*, 1976). This was followed by an unsuccessful interval as director and scriptwriter of big-budget films that were not easily accessible for the mainstream Japanese audience. ● Yashuhiko blamed himself for their failure, along with the convolutions of the anime cinema machine. However, these films were a continuation of his science fiction and super-robot work for television in the Seventies. The films combine splendid character designs – also seen in his historical manga – and an impressive quality of animation made with meticulous care. If the lively *Crusher Joe* (1983, dir. Yasuhiko Yoshikazu, Takizawa Toshifumi) could be compared with the mad fictitious science fiction of Takachiho Haruka, in *Arion* (1986) Yoshikazu looked again to Greek mythology for introspective means of escape, and this failed to appeal to his fans' uninformed taste. In *Venus Wars* (1989), taken from one of his manga, his interpretation is weighed down by the scriptwriting, having been unable to find more effective narrative alternatives. ● M.A.R.

# YASUHIKO YOSHIKAZU

CHARACTER DESIGNER

ABOVE: CHARACTERS DESIGNED BY YASUHIKO YOSHIKAZU FROM THE LEGENDARY *MOBILE SUIT GUNDAM* (1979, DIR. TOMINO YOSHIYUKI, 43 EPS) (FROM LEFT TO RIGHT: FRAU BOW, BRIGHT NOA, SAYLA MASS, HARO THE ROBOT, MIRAI YASHIMA, KAI SHIDEN, HAYATO KOBAYASHI AND RYU JOSE)

SEE ALSO: GUNDAM; MUSHI; TEZUKA OSAMU; SUNRISE; TOMINO YOSHIYUKI

Yattaman, a heroic threesome fighting evil, consists of young Ganchan, creator of hyper-tech toys for his father's shop, his beautiful friend Aichan and their versatile little robot, Omocchama, who looks like a die. The evil in question is the bizarre Drombo Gang, led by the uninhibited Miss Doronyo and her two ungainly sidekicks, Boyakki and Tonzula, who perform the wishes of the mysterious Dr Dokrobei. The doctor is hunting for a magic stone, fragments of which are scattered around the world. The two groups clash repeatedly, taking the field with robots and armoured vehicles with all kinds of weird and wonderful functions. Ganchan fights only with a *kendama* (a hammer-like object with ball connected to it by a string), while it is Omocchama's job to feed their powerful robot Yatta-can, which gives birth to large numbers of identical little robots designed to attack the enemy. ● The Drombo Gang are constantly making a hash of things: Miss Doronyo always ends up in just her bra, and the doctor punishes them with cynical cruelty. ● Although there is no time travel involved, *Yattaman* is part of the *Time Bokan* series, maintaining its satirical edge and easygoing atmosphere, with practically the same storyline in each episode. Vital ingredients include trips to exotic or fabulous destinations, cuddly mecha robots (the antithesis of their aggressive Nagaian counterparts), comic musical interludes and a concluding skull-shaped atomic cloud. The accent is on freewheeling madcap comedy. The plots and characters have only the most tenuous link with reality, not least the very loose premise on which the rivalry between the two groups is based. *Yattaman* has become a cult anime, in Japan and abroad, no longer imitating but inspiring imitation. In 2008, director Miike Takashi made an entertaining live-action version. ● S.G.

CHARACTER

# *YATTAMAN*
## YATTERMAN

ABOVE: GANCHAN, HIS BEAUTIFUL FRIEND AICHAN AND THEIR PROBLEM-SOLVING ROBOT, OMOCCHAMA, FROM THE 1977 TV SERIES TIME BOKAN SERIES: YATTAMAN

TIME BOKAN SERIES: YATTAMAN ● 1977 ● DIR: KURI IPPEI, SASAGAWA HIROSHI ● SCR: SAKAI AKIYOSHI, TORIUMI JINZO ● DES: AMANO YOSHITAKA ● ANI: ASHIDA TOYOO, UTAGAWA KAZUHIKO ● MUS: JINBO MASAAKI, YAMAMOTO MASAYUKI ● PRD: TATSUNOKO ● TV SERIES ● EPS: 108

# YOKOYAMA MITSUTERU

MANGAKA

SEE ALSO: ATOM; SALLY; TETSUJIN 28-GO; TEZUKA OSAMU; TIMA

Thanks to a highly varied output, Yokoyama Mitsuteru stands out as an innovator and creator of genres amongst manga's famous names. Born in 1934 in Kobe, he chose to devote himself to manga because of his love for the works of Tezuka Osamu (*Metropolis* in particular) and made his professional debut in 1951 with *Otonashi no Ken*. Five years later, the Iron Man of *Tetsujin-28 Go!* (*Gigantor*) was born and with it the mecha genre saw the light, appearing on television in 1963 in a pioneering rendition of Yokoyama's work in the new serial animation format. ● In 1966, it was the 'magical girl' genre's turn, with *Little Witch Sally*, a single volume with scenes bordering on horror that generated a long animated series among the first to experience the transition to colour (the initial episodes are in black and white). *Babel II* is well known in the field of science fiction and portrays themes of James Bond-style adventure, regarded for its daring concepts, such as genetic manipulation, psychic powers and creatures from other worlds. The protagonist is a teenager who receives a gift from an extraterrestrial, in the form of extrasensory powers, which he uses in the service of justice to combat an *esper* bent on conquering the world. ● Stylistically, Yokoyama clearly pays homage to the rounded design and typical caricature of the master Tezuka, combining a fast-paced narrative with frequent action scenes of great dramatic impact. During the Seventies and Eighties he worked on *Sangokushi*, a colossal work based on the Chinese history *Chronicles of the Three Kingdoms* and with the Nineties revival, his *Giant Robo* experienced its second flush of youth. He died in 2004 when a lit cigarette started a fire while he was sleeping. ● D.D.G.

Born in 1932, Yoshida Tatsuo taught himself to draw and worked as an illustrator on a number of newspapers after World War II. He moved to Tokyo in 1962, and founded the Tatsunoko animation studio, which, under his supervision, came to be one of the most interesting and original studios of the Sixties, in terms of its storylines and its visual style, characterized by rounded design, vivid colours and the ability to merge the languages of the genre. His co-founders were Yoshida Kenji and Yoshida Toyoharu, the latter of whom would go on to sign off on many productions under the pseudonym Kuri Ippei. ● Aware of the importance of the new television market, Yoshida focused his efforts over the same period on distinguishing his work from that of Toei Animation, which was particularly active in the field of cinema. His first success came with the *Mach Go! Go! Go!* series (1967, dir. Yoshida Tatsuo et al), which went down particularly well in America, where it was renamed *Speed Racer*. In 1972, a lucky year for him, he won the Shogakukan Manga Award for creating *Maya the Bee* (1975), a famous series that mixed adventure with drama. At the same time, the launch of the *Gatchaman* (*Battle of the Planets*, 1974, dir. Toriumi Jinzo et al) television series, also blessed with success, confirmed the status of the superhero genre, perfected in the following years with the trilogy consisting of *Casshan* (1973, dir. Sasagawa Hiroshi), *Hurricane Polymar* (1974, dir. Toriumi Eiko et al) and *Uchu no Kishi Tekkaman* (*Tekkaman*, 1975, dir. Sasagawa Hiroshi et al). His love of a humour-filled story gave rise, in 1974, to the well-received series *Time Bokan* (1975, dir. Sasagawa Hiroshi et al), which features a delicious parody of the popular science fiction of the time. Unfortunately, this charismatic leader's career was ended in the late Seventies, when he died of liver cancer. ● D.D.G.

# YOSHIDA TATSUO

DIRECTOR

ABOVE: DETAIL FROM THE SERIES *ANIMENTARI KETSUDAN* (*ANIMENTARY: THE DECISION*, 1971, DIR. KUROKAWA FUMIO ET AL, 26 EPS)

SEE ALSO: CASSHAN; GATCHAMAN; MACH GO GO GO; TATSUNOKO; TIME BOKAN; YATTAMAN

# YUASA MASAAKI

DIRECTOR

Yuasa Masaaki (born in 1965 in Fukuoka) is without doubt one of the most exciting and original anime directors to emerge in recent years. His presence within a production is immediately felt; the unruly and eccentric visual style that he brings is worlds apart from the standardized anime aesthetic. Yuasa's design is entirely about the virtues of animation; fluid, plasmatic forms stretch and twist, the emphasis constantly on movement. When he does arrive at a moment of stillness, the composition is never sedate and he shows the subject from a highly original angle, emphasizing an inner aspect of the character or scene. ● Through films like *Mind Game* (2004), and his television series *Kemonozume* (2006) and *Kaiba* (2008), Masaaki has established himself as one of the leading figures in contemporary anime direction. The peculiarity of his style allows him to broach new subject matter, and to satirically reflect on the conventions of established anime. In *Kemonozume*, he collapses romance saga conventions with *shonen* swords and sorcery to explore themes of masculinity and pride; in *Kaiba*, he explores cute commodification through Tezuka-inspired characters caught up in a dark trade in body parts. Yuasa Masaaki bridges the gap between the independent film-making of Kato Kunio and Yamamura Koji, and the impact of his work is creating space for new practitioners to work in the otherwise highly conformist anime industry. ● D.S.

# YUKIMURO SHUNICHI

SCRIPTWRITER

It's almost impossible to remember all the titles for which Yukimuro Shunichi, one of the cornerstones of Japanese entertainment, has written screenplays. Like his late colleague Toriumi Jinzo, the wonderful Tatsunoko studio employee, Yukimuro belongs to the old school: he does not market videogames and sees writing as an inviolable and prestigious sanctuary, and a literary honour. ● Born in Chiba in 1941, Yukimuro quickly discovered the pleasures of creating stories for anime. Professionally, he is a free spirit and does not write for a single client but has frequently worked for Toei Animation, Tokyo Movie Shinsha and Nippon Animation. By the Sixties, he was well known for his screenplays for *Sally the Witch* (1966) and *GeGeGe no Kitaro* (1968). ● Yukimuro is also an exceptional example of the profession at a time when artists compared themselves with other artists: a line of conduct now devoid of egocentric writers and their boundless desire to hybridize with other media. Among his most famous titles are *Kimba the White Lion* (1965), *Sazae-san* (1969), the beautiful *Ore wa Teppei* (*My Name is Teppei*, 1977), *Candy Candy* (1976) and *Little Memole* (1984). He also became famous for creating the famous manga *Hello Spank* (1979) together with designer Takanashi Shizuo. ● M.A.R.

SCENES FROM TWO OF YUKIMURO SHUNICHI'S SCREENPLAYS ● ABOVE RIGHT: THE LIVE-ACTION SERIES *VAMPIRE* (1968, DIR. YAMADA TSUTOMU, MABUNE TEI, 26 EPS) ● RIGHT: TWO SCENES FROM *KIMBA THE WHITE LION* (1965, YAMAMOTO EIICHI ET AL, 52 EPS)

SEE ALSO: CANDY CANDY; GETTA ROBOT; KITARO; SALLY; SPANK; TOEI ANIMATION

# YUYAMA KUNIHIKO

DIRECTOR

In the early Nineties, Yuyama Kunihiko appeared in the pages of *Animage* magazine in a solitary black-and-white snapshot, sporting a bushy mop of hair and his trademark Elvis Costello glasses. Then a conscientious television director he certainly could not have foreseen the huge success he would achieve with the series *Pokémon* (1997). ● Fond of the fantasy genre and spectacular science fiction, but not of exaggerated narrative, the young Yuyama came to the public's attention with the classic *Kujira no Hosefiina* (*Josephina the Whale*, 1979), a poetic series of simple but evocative visuals. He then turned from fantasy characters, such as *Maho no Princess Minky Momo* (*Fairy Princess Minky Momo*, 1982) and the sexy Yokho from *Genmu Senki Leda* (*Leda: The Fantastic Adventure Of Yohko*, 1985), to the robotic *Sengoku Majin GoShogun* (*Macron One*, 1981), which presents a less gloomy vision of science fiction than past models. Yuyama heightens dramatic development by revealing the characters' psychies, including those of the enemy. ● Without exception, his direction demonstrates an undeniable passion for storytelling. In addition to television series, Yuyama has directed several successful films which have broken box-office records with the help of veteran Kotabe Yoichi. ● M.A.R.

LEFT: POSTER FOR MAHO NO PRINCESS MINKY MOMO (FAIRY PRINCESS MINKY MOMO, 1982, DIR. YUYAMA KUNIHIKO ET AL, 61 EPS), FOR WHICH YUYAMA DIRECTED EPISODES AND TWO VIDEO FEATURES

Y

SEE ALSO: MAETEL; POKÉMON

# ESSAYS

FROM DOGA EIGA TO ANIME...260
CHILDISH PERCEPTIONS...261
ERO-ANIME: MANGA COMES ALIVE...262
TAKING A LONGER AND DEEPER LOOK...263
HOW MANGA REINVENTED COMICS...264
COMPUTER GRAPHICS OR BACK TO GOOD
OLD ORIGINALS?...265
'THE POWER OF GOD'...266
ENTERTAINMENT FOR THE EYES...267
MANN(G)A FROM HEAVEN...268
RELATIONSHIPS BETWEEN MANGA AND ANIME...269
VIDEOGAMES + MANGA + ANIME...270
TROUBLES OF THE HUMAN HEART...271
FROM CITY TO NETWORK...272

# FROM DOGA EIGA TO ANIME
## A HISTORY OF JAPANESE ANIMATION

# MARIA ROBERTA NOVIELLI

A *nime*, the term now used to describe Japanese animation, has its roots in an artform that originated over three centuries ago, when street performers breathed life into some of Japan's favourite tales for audiences in the principal cities. The popular nature of this tradition was its great strength: untrammelled by convention, freely available and dangerously ubiquitous. When the advent of the cinema began to draw the attention of the general public away from the itinerant story-tellers, animated films (still referred to by the old name of *doga eiga*) enjoyed immediate popular success – no doubt because they were seen as preserving the older tradition and continued to convey the comforting values of the past. ● The production of animated films received a considerable boost from the screening of *Fantasmagorie* by Emile Cohl in 1909, the first work of its kind. In just a few years, native Japanese productions multiplied, cementing the reputation of those now recognized as the pioneers of the genre: Shimokawa Hekoten, who worked as a cartoonist on several daily newspapers, noted for his blackboard drawing technique; Kouchi Junichi a technical pioneer of silhouette animation (who was also an active propagandist when the military came to power in the Twenties); Kitayama Seitaro, one of the first to blend aspects of native culture with Western stylistic and thematic influences; finally, there was Ofuji Nobuhiro, creator of the *chiyogami* technique, who cut elegant and sophisticated silhouettes from very thin paper and superimposed them on glass panels to produce both fanciful and ethereal images. Used to tell stories steeped in Japanese cultural tradition, Ofuji's figures, particularly their lack of facial features and expression, seemed to convey the inner fragility of a people overwhelmed by their country's headlong plunge into militarism. ● In the Twenties, despite a proliferation of small production houses, the animated film industry gradually came under the control of the military regime. After the invasion of Manchuria in 1931, the military effort was stepped up and animated cartoons, and indeed films generally, were made to serve the ends of propaganda, becoming out-and-out manifestos of martial virtues. An outstanding example is director Seo Mitsuyo's *Momotaro's Divine Sea Warriors* (1945), in which a winsome selection of pure and industrious animals, accompanied by a rousing musical score, exalt the spirit of abnegation embraced by the Japanese population during those years. ● In the immediate post-war period, Japan's animation companies were at first slow in identifying a rewarding market. Nevertheless, within a decade the fledgling production houses had grown into a large-scale film industry. ● The first important new

> THE ADVENT OF CINEMA BEGAN TO DRAW THE ATTENTION OF THE GENERAL PUBLIC AWAY FROM ITINERANT STORY-TELLERS, AND ANIMATED FILMS ENJOYED IMMEDIATE POPULAR SUCCESS

developments occurred in 1960, a year of political turmoil that saw student protests against renewal of the security treaty between the United States and Japan. In the cinema, it was marked by the emergence of works by such committed directors as Oshima Nagisa, Yoshida Kiju and Imamura Shohei, while in the world of animation the unease of the young was interpreted by a number of young directors. At the forefront was the so-called 'Group of Three' animators (*Animeshon sannin no kai*): Yanagihara Ryohei, Kuri Yoji and Manabe Hiroshi. In their films, the angst of the younger generation is conveyed by social satire, the solidity and psychological depth of their characters, and the use of often abstract and deliberately irreverent images. In particular, Kuri Yoji sought to win back cultural territory, caustically highlighting the massive changes that Japanese society had undergone, the new role of women, the changing dynamics of marriage and family life, and the upsurge of violence among the young and their alienation from their parents' values. ● During the same period, another cartoonist and film director, Tezuka Osamu, gave life and movement to the pictures of the manga comic, launching anime as we know it today. The animation of popular manga characters was the decisive step towards the legitimation of anime as a children's product and its widespread dissemination, first at home, then abroad. But, in Japan, the comic strip was still preferred to its animated version because it could be enjoyed privately. This obstacle was finally overcome in 1984, with the release of OAVs (Original Animation Videos), aimed mainly at an adult audience. But neither should we overlook the massive influence of directors such as Miyazaki Hayao and Takahata Isao, who in these years won immense followings. ● Deserving of separate treatment is the work of the young authors of the Eighties, all of whom have become famous in the West. To them we owe a new development in the story of animation: a blending of media, to the point of creating a new art form. This amalgam provided a very direct interpretation of the effects of the 'bubble economy' on society: life as an illusion, the concept of a kind of physical invulnerability, a gradual detachment from reality. A leading exponent of this trend is the director Oshii Mamoru, director of the first anime for OAV (*Dallos*, 1983). To the merger of anime and manga, he added the thematic element of science fiction, already extremely popular in animation, thanks largely to the robotic works of Nagai Go. He also drew on the style of contemporary videogames and increasingly included real figures in imaginary contexts. The effect is one of an symbiotic relationship between man and machine, a metaphor for the enforced assimilation of the individual into a totally organized society, resulting in a growing inability to communicate. During the same period, Otomo Katsuhiro produced his masterpiece *Akira* (1988), an even more apocalyptic vision of humanity and a cry of anguish at man's corruption and need for purification.

# CHILDISH PERCEPTIONS
## THOUGHTS ON THE JAPANESE GENIUS FOR ANIMATION

## STÉPHANE DELORME

I f the Japanese have a genius for animation, it relates primarily to childhood perceptions and how, through the miraculous use of detail, they can 'render' the feelings of a child. The lazy term for this phenomenon is *kawaii* (sweet/cute), a convenient word to summarize the complex of minute perceptions that anime seeks to create with infinite care and subtlety. ● Miyazaki Hayao is the master of such perceptions, which in his case take three main forms. First is the way he renders touch. The suction-pad sound effects (heard when little Mei clings to her Totoro or as Ponyo breaks the surface securely attached to her jellyfish) show that impressions of touch are primarily connected with fantasy sound effects. He makes us experience what the animated character is feeling: drawings on paper must have a physical rendering. ● The second technique is disproportion. There is always a moment when the drawing swells and intensifies, reducing human beings to the status of figurines. Giants undoubtedly have allegorical significance, personifying nature's predominance over mankind – the Forest Spirit walking in the treetops in *Princess Mononoke* (1999); the Eternal Sea becoming a Thousand-and-One-Nights princess in *Ponyo on the Cliff by the Sea* (2008) – but they first signify an overturning of the adult view of the world, in which a 'grown-up' is someone with no one greater to refer to. ● For children, the giant is embodied in two contradictory ways: as a mighty companion (such as Totoro, or No Face the masked creature who follows Chihiro in *Spirited Away*, 2001) or as a dislocated colossus unable to support his own greatness. In *Nausicaä* (1983), the awakened giant visibly dissolves, even though he continues to hurl balls of fire; while in *Mononoke*, when the Forest Spirit sticks out his gigantic neck and is hit by a deadly bullet, we are shocked and scandalized to see his body disintegrate. ● Finally, Miyazaki conveys a typically childish relationship with the multitude, the crowd, the pack, epitomized by the world of little-eyed balls (*Totoro*), eyed waves (*Ponyo*), or kodamas turning their heads with a rattling noise (*Mononoke*). Again, this is how a child perceives the world, making no distinction between the animal, vegetable and mineral realms, animistic in outlook before he learns discernment. ● Another way to convey childish perceptions is to bring the child face to

> IF THE ISSUE OF TRAUMA COMES ACROSS SO STRONGLY IN THE ANIME, IT IS BECAUSE TRAUMA IS ESSENTIALLY A CHILDHOOD PHENOMENON, AND IT IS THE ESSENTIALLY CHILDISH WORLD OF THE COMIC STRIP THAT DESCRIBES ITS MAGNITUDE.

face with something incommensurable. How does a child come to terms with something beyond his comprehension? How does he perceive something horrific? The question is posed by Takahata Isao in *Grave of the Fireflies* (1998) and Mori Masaki in *Barefoot Gen*. ● In *Barefoot Gen* (1983), the explosion of the bomb dropped on Hiroshima is shown through the eyes of a child. Strictly speaking, Gen does not see anything, but the unprecedented image that appears on screen is of a broken, dismembered, melting doll, its eyes falling from their sockets. This is extreme violence, but without a single drop of blood being shed. It was believed that no one would ever dare to depict the moment of the explosion, and strangely it was this naive, crude, sketchy drawing that successfully represented the unrepresentable. The great disparity between the unnameable historical horror witnessed by the child and the simple, atrophied image used to convey it, produces a special kind of sadness. ● More generally, if the issue of trauma comes across so strongly in the anime, it is because trauma is essentially a childhood phenomenon, and it is the essentially childish world of the comic strip that describes its magnitude. In Chigira Koichi's *Brave Story* (2006), little Wataru escapes into a dream world when his father leaves his mother. The world of wonders in which he finds himself (called 'Vision') is one vast dream for lost children. His friend Mitsuru, his dark double, also has to cope with an overwhelming family trauma, but to hide his suffering he erects an ice palace around himself. The remarkable series *Haibane Renmai* (2002) describes the self-sufficient lifestyle of a mysteriously assembled band of angel-children, all with a childhood trauma to come to terms with or be forgiven for. For these haloed angels or the courageous little warriors of *Brave Story*, it is less a question of lending greater psychological substance to beings drawn on paper (who frankly do not need it) than of placing the animated character on the edge of a metaphysical void. ● For the drama of children undergoing trauma, which they perceive as enormous and insurmountable, is always ultimately the drama of time, the fact that the past cannot be put to rights. A number of anime focus on the phenomenon of time as it swamps, drowns, overwhelms children whose short lives have not prepared them to confront this demon. The childish regret of not being able to go back in time is also found in adults returning to the places of their childhood (Takahata's *Only Yesterday*, 1991). It gives rise to all kinds of eccentricities, as in *The Girl who Leapt Through Time* (2006), which describes the childish fantasy of wanting to reshape the past, though even there trauma lies in wait. ● One step further and childish perceptions become the delusions of schizophrenics, twisted visions of the world with no backbone. This results in the mad girl of *Serial Experiments Lain* (1998) or Satoshi Kon's monstrous *Paprika* (2006), which create childish worlds of pure desire, pure caprice, where the infinite potential of the wonderful turns to nightmare. *Paprika* is the hellish reversal of Miyazaki's paradise: perceptions of touch give way to the ghoulish interpenetration and dissolution of people's bodies; giants are able to swallow the world itself; the animistic sense of a world throbbing with life is replaced by a clanking parade of consumer objects. In opposition to this brilliantly imagined disintegration stands the warrior boy of *Brave Story*, an anime which teaches the child to be courageous, grow up, get things in proportion and leave childish perceptions behind.

# ERO—ANIME: MANGA COMES ALIVE

## STEPHEN SARRAZIN

In light of how pervasive erotic animation is in contemporary Japan, we can only wonder at the speed and urgency with which it made its way into the core of its pop culture. Although Japan did not shy away from graphic representations of sexuality, notably during the Edo period, much changed after the country opened itself to the West, bringing with it an entirely new set of moral codes and precepts. (And this was only exacerbated during the post -war American occupation of the country.) While undercover publications of 'naughty' drawings and pictures circulated discreetly, Tezuka Osamu was perhaps unknowingly opening Pandora's box with his curvaceous young women who never seemed to grow out of adolescence. Later on, Tezuka would be the first mainstream manga and anime artist to introduce sex in his work, producing *Senya Ichiya Monogatari* (*One Thousand and One Nights*, 1969), and directing *Cleopatra* (1970).
● The Sixties saw the launch of a new manga aesthetic in the pages of *Garo* and *Com*, while the Seventies introduced key figures who radicalized the use of eroticism in manga, such as Nagai Go, who would go on to create *Cutey Honey* in 1973, and *hentai* (pornographic) godfather Ishii Takashi, who appeared in 1971, whose depictions of sexuality were far more adult oriented. This 'independence' of style motivated a group of artists and supporters to establish the first Comic Market, in 1975, as a way to promote new fanzines, new artists and new writers, and introduced several creators of popular boy-love series. ● Yet much of this content targeted an audience made up of straight university students and young businessmen. ● *Shojo* manga, initially influenced by the charm of Tezuka's world, also came to life in the Seventies, with women artists emphasizing the detailed cuteness of Tezuka's slim, wide-eyed heroines. This mix marked a significant turning point that would lead to the 'lolicon' market frenzy of the Eighties, during which time taboos were falling left and right, compelling the government to come up with new means of censorship and a few arrests. ● 'Lolicon', as depicted in the pages of the first magazine devoted to it, *Lemon People* (1982), opened the door to increasingly explicit representations of minors involved in all manner of sexual acts with other minors as well as with adults. The most successful writer of the time, Uchiyama Aki, introduced one of the key Tokyo Loli icons: the soiled panties. Uchiyama avoided the usual sex fare and focused on images of very young girls in toilets. Lolicon would also launch the first series of truly erotic video anime, *Cream Lemon* (1987). It remains to this day one of the dominant forms of ero-anime. Even Miyazaki Hayao's beloved character Nausicaä is shown flying without panties. ● Another major genre finds its origins in *Urusei Yatsura* (1978), in *Weekly Shonen Sunday*, with its harem fantasies and alien girls wearing odd costumes. This would inspire such creators as Anno Hideaki, Yamaga Hiroyuki and Akai Takami, who together formed the Gainax company,

to combine science-fiction, anime and lolicon for an anime piece they put together for the opening of *Daicon III* (1983), a mix of giant robots, *kaijyu*, ultraman lore and one small schoolgirl, for a celebrated science-fiction fair in Japan. This produced an era of alien lovefests and man—machine cyber-couplings. Other outside influences, such as horror cinema, blended in and created an entire sub-genre of obsessed and demon-possessed teenagers who found their own harems in their local high schools, as in Maeda Toshio's *Legend of the Overfiend* (1987). More recent versions of this have seen the return of the 'convent/boarding school' theme, with either teachers or students conspiring in S&M and dark magic covenants, as in Muto Yasuyuki's *Bible Black* (2001). ● Indeed, its focus on the notion of youth has come to define much of contemporary Japanese eroticism. Though few countries can claim to have as varied an output of erotic content as Japan, from the truly joyous and passionate to the brutal and unimaginably demeaning, the object of desire may be allowed to possess all the attributes of adulthood, but the viewer must never doubt that he/she is (way) under twenty. ● However, there came a time in the late Eighties and early Nineties when adults returned to the foreground with the *bishojo* (beautiful woman) style finally taking over lolicon. Magazines such as *Penguin Club* and *Hot Milk* helped to introduce penchants for elegance, new wave and auteurism among anime directors, comedy, and *oppai* (large breasts) and lactating animation, later a staple in Murakami Takashi's artwork. ● This was largely brought about by the public upheaval surrounding the arrest of child murderer Miyazaki Tsutomu, in whose home were found extreme lolicon manga and anime. Miyazaki came to symbolize the dark side of what is referred to as *hentai*, and which now apparently encompasses, outside Japan, all of its erotic anime. By the mid-Nineties, the Japanese government was finally applying 'adult content' notices on ero-manga and anime products, as well as requiring shops to provide distinct areas for such goods. ● The last decade saw a new, revamped version of lolicon content, moulded by the countless fashion and social trends that Japan goes through at groundbreaking speed, from the *ageha* (Barbie) style doe-eyed eroticism of the 109 Gals to *Xena*-inspired buxom warriors of *Queen's Blade*. ● These trends have become more territorial, introducing in the process a clearer lustful geography within Tokyo, from Shibuya to the Akihabara mecca. More surprisingly, a new loli writer brought unexpected credibility to the genre by establishing a firm and devoted female fan base. The works of Machida Hiraku reinvented the Lolita, gave her back a sense of despair and shadow, and made eroticism bleak and unavoidable yet glorious, a cross between Roman porno master Tanaka Noboru and manga's overcast prince, Tsuge Yoshiharu, proving that, as the first decade of the twenty-first century comes to end, forty years after *One Thousand and One Nights*, there are few boundaries over which Japan's erotic imagination is unwilling to spill.

> 'LOLICON' OPENED THE DOOR TO INCREASINGLY EXPLICIT REPRESENTATIONS OF MINORS INVOLVED IN ALL MANNER OF SEXUAL ACTS WITH OTHER MINORS AS WELL AS WITH ADULTS.

# TAKING A LONGER AND DEEPER LOOK
## TIME AS AN ARTIFICIAL CREATION

### GRAZIA PAGANELLI

I t can be said that time and space have the same density in Japanese animation. Or rather, time manipulates the space, organizes the narrative elements, modulates and channels the viewer's attention, creates a rhythm and constructs an aura around the characters. ● Strangely, this came about largely as a matter of financial necessity. To restrain rising production costs, the number of drawings was reduced: from fifteen frames per second (the normal standard in Western animation) to as little as five in some cases, inevitably detracting from the film's fluidity of movement and sense of continuity. Though unintentional, this process became formalized and, as a distinctive aspect of the genre, gave rise to a new cinematic 'language', with all the attendant cultural, stylistic and expressive implications. ● In Japanese animation, time therefore tends to 'expand', particular moments are intensified, heightening their pathos and tension. Time stands still, for example, during the volleyball matches in series such as *Attack Number One* (1969), as a crucial action is transformed into a frozen moment by visual repetition of the same detail, progressively enlarged. A close up of the eyes of the heroine, as she prepares to smash, interrupts the flow of the match. Still images follow one another in rapid succession: hands, the net, an opponent's expression, the petrified crowd. ● In this, we recognize the fixed dynamics of manga, but in anime the value of this immobility is turned on its head. It is not so much a matter of accumulation of action, but of concentration of emotions. It is emotion that disrupts the pace and strongly influences the dynamic and narrative structure of the scene. All this is heightened by the soundtrack, sometimes featuring a musical motif (which can be repetitive to the point of obsession) and sometimes pure silence. The momentary absence of sound, or indeed the repeated micro-theme, gives time a canvas on which to lay out all the waiting and expectation required to amplify our perceptions. ● Space, then, helps to transform time into a malleable material. The set expands and distances are magnified. The characters suddenly find themselves moving in immense open spaces, while the eye is focused increasingly on minute details and gestures. Whether it is a football match or a clash between good and evil, the impression created is one of alienation, as if all certainty of the outcome has been lost. The viewer feels time literally stands still, heightening the extraordinary events taking place before their eyes. ● Again, repetition plays a strategic role: repeating

**THE IMPRESSION CREATED IS ONE OF ALIENATION, AS IF ALL CERTAINTY OF THE OUTCOME HAS BEEN LOST. THE VIEWER FEELS TIME LITERALLY STANDS STILL, HEIGHTENING THE EXTRAORDINARY EVENTS TAKING PLACE BEFORE THEIR EYES.**

the same images serves to maintain and prolong the temporal tension in an exaggerated fashion. The eye stops moving and bores in deeper. We are invited to look longer and deeper in order to feel and perceive all the sensations that accumulate (and indeed multiply) in a given situation. In such moments, there is an interaction between film and viewer. The audience enters into the film and finds a virtual space of their own. A moment's pause provides a breathing space in which the work can be contemplated as it deserves. There are many situations where, for example, time seems to be stretched out as a stratagem to encourage reflection. ● This is true not only for stories of boys and girls, men and women wrestling with their feelings and the problems of life (or competing on the sports field), but also for robots and adventurers, engaging in tragic endeavours with the noble purpose of saving humanity. In *Candy Candy* (1976) there is a long farewell between Candy and her lover Terrence on the stairs of a hospital, where the thoughts and feelings of two lives meet and mingle. Similarly there is a scene in *Ghost in the Shell* (1995) where Major Kusanagi swims in the deep sea and is carried to the surface by the current, while a red sunset lights up the sky and stretches out the scene. These are two very different examples of the same technical procedure, illustrating just how malleable time can be in the world of animation. ● In the first case, time stands still as the conflicts established throughout the narrative come together and are resolved; in the second, the situation is more fluid and less easy to define: it is the passage of time that is emphasized, simple and linear, especially in the relationship between viewer and character. The change of landscape, as the minutes (or possibly hours) pass, is a key moment in the economy of the film, a gathering point for ideas and energies, again emphasizing the rarefaction of the narrative. ● There are, however, situations in which time's fixity is countered and radicalized, with the graphics speeding up the movement. Pushed beyond the limits of vision, speed transforms things and creates non-existent lines. The lines created by the racing cars in *Mach Go Go Go* (*Speed Racer*, 1967), for example, defy realism and are drawn in an extremely stylized form. They might seem stationary, but the continuous roar of engines assures us of their frenzy. They might seem unreal, but the story and the characters, the immediate iconographic conventions, tell us this is all true. ● In such cases, time takes on an even greater duality, as if it could be expressed on two contrasting levels: speed and slowness, acceleration and immobility, where the breathing space is accompanied, paradoxically, by the visual exaltation of movement, where the kinetic lines of light and colour intervene. Here, then, is the visual artifice that is a metaphor and summary of every animated work.

# HOW MANGA REINVENTED COMICS

## PAUL GRAVETT

With so much of anime deriving from manga, one of anime's roles outside Japan has been as an ambassador for Japanese comics. Broadly, Japanese animation has proven far easier to export to the West, after some relatively straightforward dubbing, than the long, black-and-white, 'back-to-front' comics which demand text translations and either 'flopping' or reverse-reading. So for example, *Astro Boy* in Tezuka Osamu's cartoons zoomed onto America's TV screens within eight months or so of his Japanese debut on New Year's Day 1963, whereas his manga origins starting in 1951 had to wait until 2002 to appear in English. Despite cultural references and stylistic traits, anime was broadly not so different from drawn animation enjoyed worldwide. In contrast, manga was long perceived as so 'alien' to American comics that nobody touched it and *Astro Boy* had to make do with flawed US imitations from publishers Gold Key (1965) and Now Comics (1987–9).
● One major factor which has made manga distinct from other comic traditions is its arsenal of narrative devices and techniques which cumulative generations of mangaka or comic authors have refined or introduced to expand the expressive capabilities of the medium. Initially, from the early twentieth century, Japanese cartoonists had adopted or adapted western formats and conventions, starting with American newspapers' broadsheet full-pages or 'Sunday funnies' and four-panel horizontal daily comic strips, read vertically in Japan, then expanding to multi-page tales inspired partly by American comic books. What enabled the mangaka to diverge from their peers abroad, however, were the opportunities to unfold much longer stories than anything in either standard American titles or Franco-Belgian *bande dessinée* (BD) albums. ● Significantly, Osaka-based publishers had devised the *akahon* or red book – compact, cheap novelty hardbacks for kids usually with only three full-width panels per page. For *New Treasure Island* (*Shin takarajima*) in 1947, Tezuka, eighteen at the time, had wanted to enlarge Sakai Shichima's synopsis into a 250-page epic but Sakai pruned it back to 192 pages, still a remarkable page-count at the time. When their collaboration sold 400,000 copies, it became the model for other *akahon* publishers and launched Tezuka's solo career. The advent of thick weekly manga magazines brought another outlet for lengthier projects in their *furoku* or extra supplements. Here mangaka could break free from short episodes set strictly to some ten to fifteen pages which always had to end on a cliffhanger, and elaborate stories of sixty pages or more. Finally, their periodical serials were reduced from roughly American comic book size into handy paperbacks of around 200 pages, which could run to numerous volumes. ● Deadline pressures on mangaka to deliver yet another instalment to a magazine encouraged many to 'decompress' their plotting and let the visual take precedence over the verbal. Their ability to devote more pictures to a scene allowed them to portray more of its moment-to-moment actuality and find ways to convey motion and emotion. The goal became to immerse the reader in the protagonist's experiences and feelings, to create a sense of presence and involvement, of stepping inside the body, head and heart of the protagonist, of being there and participating rather than merely observing – above all to make you feel. ● Part of that immediacy comes from mangaka's chance to show, rather than just tell. For years, many western mainstream comics were originated or dominated by writers and editors, the 'word people', for whom the artist played a subsidiary role as mere illustrator of their finely hewn texts and dialogues. No wonder a wordless panel, let alone a sequence or page, in these was a rarity. Mangaka, on the other hand, understood and could exploit the power of silent imagery to convey mood, nature, weather, landscape or the intensity of movement or passion.
● Mangaka also knew that the only way to surprise a comic reader is by the turn of a page. The smaller dimensions of a manga book commonly meant fewer panels per page than their western equivalents, so they could stretch out their story across more pages, thereby increasing the number of page turns and heightening the propulsion driving the reader onwards through the story. The unit of a comic was no longer the single panel, strip or page but very much the whole two-page spread. More pages also permitted a greater use of such widescreen vistas, seldom seen before in comic books or BD albums, aside from Jack Kirby or Philippe Druillet. In contrast, Umezu Kazuo in *The Drifting Classroom* devotes three spreads in succession to punch home the horror of a headteacher's gory wound. Adding to this impact is the way such images often 'bleed' or spread off the outer edges of the printed page. This breaking free beyond the neat confines of the panel border suggests that the moment itself has become larger, longer-lasting, resonant, as if its time and space are expanding. Whether for technical or aesthetic reasons, such bleed effects were rare in western comics, although more recently they have become more common. ● This is just one example of how manga is impacting on comic creators worldwide. There is an abundance of other techniques ready to be absorbed into their work: the way a black background behind panels indicates a flashback; the range of abstract 'auras' to manifest mental states in *shojo* or girls' manga; their insertion of a character's asides in smaller lettering as commentary on a scene; the fluid portrayals of the same character as realistic, cartoonish or super-deformed within the same page; and the striking effectiveness of emptying a panel of all imagery except for a phrase or thought in text form. No longer alien, these and other unique solutions developed by mangaka will continue to enrich the comic medium as it evolves and mutates through the new millennium.

> THE GOAL BECAME TO IMMERSE THE READER IN THE PROTAGONIST'S EXPERIENCES, TO CREATE A SENSE OF INVOLVEMENT, OF STEPPING INSIDE THE BODY, OF BEING THERE AND PARTICIPATING RATHER THAN MERELY OBSERVING

# COMPUTER GRAPHICS OR BACK TO GOOD OLD ORIGINALS?
## THE EVOLUTION OF ANIMATED FILMS

## GIANNI RONDOLINO

A s Bernard Génin pointed out, 'the biggest event of the Nineties was John Lasseter's *Toy Story* (1995), the first feature film in the history of cinema to use only computer-generated imagery' (cf. *Le cinéma d'animation*, Paris 2003; Turin 2005). This was an extraordinary event for many reasons, but really just the final step in a technical and artistic journey which had begun thirty or so years earlier, when computer animated films were born: from the very first experiments with computer techniques to the innovative work of Peter Foldes or the Whitney brothers. In any case, the use of computers in film has changed not only the technical aspect of cinema, but also its visual, artistic and dramatic elements. In fact, the possibilities offered by new technology have proved a major contribution to special effects, which aren't just about science fiction – they are actually used in any kind of film which involves any particularly complicated situation. So we can safely say that contemporary cinema is (or may well become) to a great extent computer animation, if, by computer animation, we mean the techniques used which create the film image by image. ● If we take *Toy Story* as a watershed moment between *before* and *after*, between what we can define as traditional animation and contemporary films, which are often computerized, it isn't hard to retrace the story by looking at the technical aspects, to describe the 'evolution of animated films'. In other words, is it right to say that this kind of cinema really has evolved in recent decades, undergoing an actual transformation? Or has it essentially remained the same, now using techniques that new technology has just updated, simplified, made more fluid, with greater potential for expression? ● Obviously this is a rhetorical question. It seems to me that retracing the history of animation and comparing yesterday's films with today's, with individual and country-specific styles, two-dimensional drawings and three-dimensional objects, it's possible to embark on a journey step by step, following the basic principle which constitutes the very essence of film – a way of producing and reproducing movement. So, the camera, which records reality, breaking it down into static shots and putting them all back together during the projection stage, is also able to create virtual movement using static images created specifically for that purpose. So there's no need for natural movement, as it can be recreated ready for the screen: drawings and objects which are static before they are caught on camera, come alive and move on the screen, putting an end to the idea – tested by Émile Reynaud, even before the Lumière brothers invented cinema – of drawing directly onto the film, without even using a camera. ● But this doesn't mean that computers have contributed nothing new to animated films – quite the opposite in fact. It's just that it's appropriate

WHEN A WHOLE NEW WORLD APPEARS ON THE SCREEN BEFORE US DOES IT REALLY MATTER WHETHER IT IS ALL CONJURED UP BY HAND, OR WITH SOPHISTICATED COMPUTER TECHNOLOGY?

to see it as a natural development, technically fascinating and paving the way for other dramatic possibilities for animated films. The fascination comes from these very 'unreal' images, which don't actually have to bear much resemblance to reality itself. It's a whole new world which appears on the screen before us like a dream, often straying far, far away from the laws of nature, inventing fantastical new places and incredible characters, telling enchanting stories. Whether this is all conjured up by hand, with the saintly patience of old-fashioned animators, or with sophisticated computer technology, it doesn't really matter – not to modern anonymous viewers anyway, whose everyday world is filled with the very same technology. ● In the same way, the extensively discussed differences between Japanese animation, developed since the Sixties, and its western, mainly American equivalent, do not really mean very much. In other words, apart from the obvious differences in form and content, and the technical issues which appear to set simplified, hastily put-together animation (so-called *limited animation*) against a more elaborate, rich style (*full animation*), the basic problem remains the same. It all comes down to an animated film which depicts a fictitious, invented, fantastical reality, aimed at an audience which appreciates the extreme escapism from the mundane, banal, often repetitive reality. In any case, it is interesting to see how, over the decades, Japanese television series have seen an endless number of new fantastical or poetic elements, unlike their American counterparts. From a technical point of view as well, with or without computer technology, they have seemed more varied, stimulating, with remarkable results. And so we could start a whole new chapter in the story of animated films, which would have to go back to our initial question: has there been an evolution or not? ● Extending the discussion to include the big screen as well as television series, we can see that there is now a wide range of different techniques, from traditional drawing to CGI. There are computer animated films (*Toy Story* or *Final Fantasy*, 2001) and traditional ones; there's John Lasseter (and his disciples) and Miyazaki Hayao (and his disciples). Indeed, with the latter, and his flowing, charming style, which is both simple and poetic, we are reminded that what counts, more than the techniques used, is the idea of conveying a 'vision of the world'. He takes us back to our childhood or, if you prefer, to the kind of films that can most conveniently be described as Disney-like, and that, over time, have become decadent and generic. It's almost as though we're going back to our roots, rediscovering the subtle fascination of a craftsman's technique, which computers threatened to destroy once and for all.

# 'THE POWER OF GOD'
## THE LIFE AND TIMES OF THE SUPER ROBOT

## FABRIZIO MODINA

Nearly half a century after they first burst onto our TV screens, it's almost impossible to separate the images of giant robots from the same concept in Japanese animation. More than just *shojo*, more than extreme sporting phenomena, more than nonsensical comedy and fantastical eroticism, these creatures were soon a part of the very fabric of the nation, becoming an unrivalled icon which was exported around the world. A fusion of literary references, mythology and tradition, Super Robots combine elements of the country's past with a celebration of a modern Japan where technology is so advanced that, to the rest of the world, it seems positively futuristic. At first glance, these steel creatures resemble revamped samurai armour, while their souls glow with values inherited from legendary warriors, inspired by a love for their homeland and a commitment to order and justice for which they would face up to any sacrifice under the sun. And yet in spite of the enormity of these giants and their range of weapons which are capable of wiping out whole planets, they are still reliant on the driving force of a human being's hand which is responsible for their artificial identity. This kind of *deus ex machina* can be justified by the pilot's gradual assumption of responsibility – a long internal journey towards maturity and a full understanding of the thin line between good and evil which is often highlighted by the disastrous consequences of the abuse of science. 1963 saw the birth of the first Super Robot in *Tetsujin 28-Go*, the creation of mangaka Yokoyama Mitsuteru, who was inspired by the legend of the Golem of Prague and Mary Shelley's *Frankenstein*. He imagined what would become of his country if a flying mechanical soldier, more than ten metres tall, could be enlisted during the Second World War. But with the premature defeat of Japan, the prototype was destined to become a relic until Kaneda Shotaro, the deceased creator's son, decided to use him to defend the nation from would-be criminal organisations, manoeuvring him externally with an elaborate remote control. ● Nine years later, *Mazinger Z* (1972) by Nagai Go arrived on our screens, breathing life into a phenomenon unlike any that had come before, defining fundamental principles which were destined to become law: the internal control unit which requires greater involvement from the pilot, formidable weapons which can be activated by voice recognition (such as the famous rocket punch), comedy sidekicks and of course an ultra-efficient secret base. The emergence of *Mazinger Z* from its hangar beneath a swimming pool creates an unprecedented moment, a kind of ritualistic event which thrilled almost every single child and teenager in Japan. The pilot, Kabuto Koji, is a reckless and rebellious high-school student who

**SUPER ROBOTS COMBINE ELEMENTS OF THE COUNTRY'S PAST WITH A CELEBRATION OF A MODERN JAPAN WHERE TECHNOLOGY IS SO ADVANCED THAT, TO THE REST OF THE WORLD, IT SEEMS POSITIVELY FUTURISTIC**

embodies the illicit dreams of his repressed peers who witness his exploits from the other side of the screen. ● The metal merchandizing created for *Mazinger Z* flew off the shelves as fast as it could be restocked, creating one of the most influential marketing successes in the nation's history. The *Mazinger Z* phenomenon was so great that it generated a sequel, *Great Mazinger*, and a spin-off, *UFO Robot Grendizer Raids* (1975), which would export 'Super Robot mania', under the name of *Goldorak* and *Goldrake*, to conquer the world, starting with France and Italy. It was this period that saw huge offensives of extraterrestrials, or monsters emerging from underground, a parade of freaks and fantasies more striking than the protagonists themselves, but sadly wiped out by their own repetitive attempts. ● Between 1974 and 1975, the two main strands connected to transformations appeared: *gattai*, which were the combination of several different elements to create a single robot (*Getta Robot*, 1974) and *henkei*, which could change shape, turning from anthropomorphic forms into vehicles or spaceships (*Yusha Raideen*, 1975). *Cho Denji Robo Combattler V* (1976) took mecha design one complicated step further, with an elaborate system of *gattai*, bringing together five different vehicles in an exhilarating animated sequence which was so detailed that sponsors could easily convert the images into hugely successful toys. ● In 1979, director Tomino Yoshiyuki came up with the work that would mark the transition from children's TV series to a more experimental genre intended for an older audience: *Mobile Suit Gundam*. Misunderstood at the time because of its innovative script, which steered clear of alien invasions, describing instead an incredibly realistic civil war which had broken out between Earth and its space colonies, *Gundam* would later be reassessed, emerging as a national hero and enjoying an enduring appeal. ● *Gundam* paved the way for the new generation of 'Real Robots', intricate metal soldiers which designers strived to make more and more realistic. The best representatives of the genre are the Valkyries of *Macross*, 1982's highly original space opera, which saw military pilot Ichijo Hikaru thrust into a galactic conflict. The Valkyries could quickly transform into a jet, a robot or a hybrid of the two and could be reproduced anonymously en masse. Their spatial acrobatics took on more of a background role, leaving the pilots firmly in the limelight. ● Overshadowed by other genres in the second half of the Eighties and much of the Nineties, Super Robots were back with a vengeance in *Neon Genesis Evangelion*, a dark, disturbing anime which came out in 1995, mixing religion, esotericism and technology. Once and for all, it defined the target audience of the robot genre as a more adult one, with more demanding tastes. The Eva exiles take the symbiosis between robots and pilots to extremes, transforming the latter into the disembodied conscience cast adrift in the artificial body of his host. The creative crisis which began in the Nineties and which is still underway saw a trend for revivals, encouraging new generations to experience the great classics of the past, updated for modern viewers and given graphical makeovers which are certainly breathtaking, but somehow lacking in the spirit that immortalized the Super Robots of the Seventies and Eighties.

# ENTERTAINMENT FOR THE EYES
## MANGA AND AN EDUCATION OF VIOLENCE

## GIONA A. NAZZARO

**PERHAPS MORE THAN THE BAD INFLUENCE OF THE VIOLENCE PORTRAYED, CENSORS WOULD DO WELL TO WARN OF THE LATENT THREAT THAT THESE CARTOONS POSE TO CUSTOMARY FORMS OF PERCEPTION**

owards the end of the Seventies, when Italy was being overwhelmed by the phenomenon of Japanese cartoons, parents and teachers joined forces to denounce the unprecedented level of violence they contained. At first glance, they didn't seem to compare with their US counterparts – at least in qualitative terms – especially the productions of Warner and Disney. This did nothing to diminish either their commercial success or their ability to capture the imagination of children and teenagers – with the black-and-white adventures of *UFO Robot Grendizer Raids* (1975) and *Jeeg, The Steel Robot* (1975).

This impressive achievement, backed up by the vast array of merchandise to satisfy children's and teenagers' burgeoning consumer instincts – from chewing gum, school diaries, notebooks and rucksacks, to T-shirts and snacks – has, without much reasoned analysis, been attributed to the violence contained in the vicious and epic battles which set giant robots against monsters from outer-space. ● In fact, the issue of the violence inherent in Japanese animation confronts the very principle of characterization and reality. Violence is a symptom, the sign of an acceleration – as demonstrated by the futurists. If we look back to the first image in *Grendizer*, we see the epiphany of one two-dimensional world which has been extinguished and another which is totally interactive, on the verge of appearing in the lines of a mecha drawing, inevitably assumed to be a first collective step towards the Land of the Rising Sun. The clash of two worlds was bound to be a violent one. Perhaps more than the bad influence of the violence portrayed, censors would do well to warn of the latent threat that these cartoons pose to customary forms of perception. Nagai Go's creation, which appeared in Italy on Rai Due in April 1978, introduced itself as fast and violent; the violence is not an ingredient, but rather a symptom and a sign. ● Science fiction, a genre not particularly common in Italy, has become a common language, thanks to the series format and narrative structure which are repeated relentlessly from one episode to the next with the occasional and inevitable exception of the obligatory monster or robot. Even the process of the most minimal series structure is in fact the sign of the mass-produced violence which stole the attention and the intelligence of the viewers of the late Seventies, and meant that coming out of the Eighties, cartoons were a bit less overwhelmed and a bit more structured. Continuing this analysis, we see how the crossover with Japanese cartoons has always boldly flown the flag of violence, triumphantly traumatic, in worlds which are always changing and expanding. So manga can be seen as a recreational activity based around a cultural oxymoron. Even today, now that the language of anime and manga has been absorbed by western culture, the speed of the story-telling continues to be a crucial prerequisite to the Japanese cartoon industry. Marvel's heroes are steeped in metatextual navel-gazing, anchored in unwavering continuity, always speaking more, perhaps too much, before the fighting begins. In contrast, manga heroes get straight to the battle – less philosophizing, more action. It is significant that the aspect that is most striking to younger readers is the artwork, the line of the pencil in the background, seemingly incomplete, hardly alluded to, but making the shapes appear empty, or, on the contrary, grotesquely excessive and deformed when conveying sentiments such as anger or pain. This strategy allows manga authors to condense the text of the narrative significantly. The lines and the curves are all that are needed to understand manga. In fact, it's not the narrative itself which is fast, but rather the revelation and succession of events. Take, for example, the work of Oda Eiichiro in *One Piece* (1997), one of the best-loved and most widely distributed manga. To the uninitiated, it seems to be a frenzy of images, a confusing show of onomatopoeia, with moving lines everywhere you look, far-reaching perspectives and magnified close-ups, grotesque figures almost impossible to appreciate for a more traditional viewer. But in fact these are the very elements which delight manga readers, especially younger fans, and bring the stories to life. Given the mass consumption element of manga's communication strategy, a quick glance at the pages of Arakawa Hiromu's *Fullmetal Alchemist* (2001) makes it clear that – although less chaotic than Oda's designs – there is the same formal and cultural syncretism and use of graphic violence, which is extreme but seems reduced in a context fed by references to steampunk literature and traditional alchemy. Kishimoto Masashi, author of *Naruto* (1999), as well as Toriyama Akira, creator of the *Dragonball* (1984) series and Kurumada Masami, who was behind *Saint Seiya* (1986), follow the same format of an incredibly physical conflict in which bloodshed is inevitable, decorative and plentiful. Even though moral recommendations stipulate that the protagonists of these cartoons which are so eagerly devoured by teenagers from around the world are grown-ups, it is actually their childlike looks that make the reading experience so gratifying and satisfying as a sensorial and sensual experience. ● Manga accelerate, provoke and live out the physical risk on behalf of the readers who identify themselves with the heroes – take Kurumada's Seiya, for example – in a process which, whilst seeming to bring to mind a mirroring effect, describes the story of stepping over a shadowy line that allows us to come out of ourselves. We are no longer 'we'. Perhaps Japanese comics are nothing but a tool to help us learn how to lose ourselves. And if this is the case, why are we so fascinated with the violence of this process?

# MANN(G)A FROM HEAVEN

## MICHEL ROUDEVITCH

**A**nimated cartoons from the Far East – almost always in the form of repetitive television series, from the saccharine tear-jerker *Candy Candy* (1976) to intergalactic adventures such as *UFO Robot Grendizer Raids* (1975) – have been accused of all the evils detected in young people's programmes. But the critics forget that many bad habits and stereotypes, born of an emphasis on quantity, were developed in the West as early as the Fifties. With the advent of television, Californian companies, abandoning programmes from quality studios, opted for locally developed sub-products turned out on the cheap on the other side of the world and destined for worldwide distribution. For instance, with the warm approval of the moguls at MGM in the late Fifties, the Hanna-Barbera duo, creators of *Tom and Jerry*, gave up crafting quality by the metre and launched into quantity by the kilometre. ● While not rebelling againt the standards of limited animation (though preceded in this respect by their American occupiers), many Japanese animators yielded to the economic imperatives and practised sub-contracting, before venturing out on their own and taking the road of 'Japanization'. Tezuka Osamu, the most famous of the mangaka – and the most productive – came to terms with these constraints without sacrificing his mastery of all genres. Stimulated rather than put off by the sub-standard techniques, many talented artists made their mark in unconventional ways. These ranged from the phantasmagoria of Ofuji Nobuhiro to the corrosive haiku of Kuri Yoji (who was also a painter and sculptor), from the satirical vein of Kinoshita to the puppets of Kawamoto Kihachiro, who rediscovered the magic of *No* masks, and indeed of *bunraku* dolls. It was Kawamoto who conceived and orchestrated the production of *Winter Days* (2003), a collective work by thirty-seven animators from both East and West, inspired by the eponymous collection of poems by Basho Matsuo, the great master of the haiku. All these directors expressed themselves in the short-film genre, while Yabushita Taiji's *Hakujaden* (*Legend of the White Snake*, 1958), the very first feature-length colour film produced in Japan, was a popular success and even distributed in the United States. Its timeless charm (featuring a snake-princess from China), confirmed many in their vocations, including a seventeen-year-old adolescent named Miyazaki Hayao.

## THE ART OF MIYAZAKI HAYAO AND OTHER LONG-STANDING AUTHORS

A complete artist, combining the skills of scriptwriter, graphic designer, animator and producer, Miyazaki Hayao is notable not only for the credibility of even his most fantastic visions fuelled by childhood memories, further reading of documentary sources and in-depth investigations in the field, but also for his great humanity and felicity of expression, using a rich palette ranging from the magic of the Adriatic to the twilights and early mornings of the Rising Sun, a thematic range combining Swift and Verne with heroic

> STIMULATED RATHER THAN PUT OFF BY THE SUB-STANDARD TECHNIQUES, MANY TALENTED ARTISTS MADE THEIR MARK IN UNCONVENTIONAL WAYS

fantasy. Born during World War II (the 'war to end all wars' for the Japanese) to a family involved in the aeronautics business, he soon started drawing flying machines. He made his mark at the Toei studio, where he formed a bond with the scriptwriter and producer Takahata Isao. The pair worked together on a number of series and began experimenting with full-length features. Encouraged by the success of their screen adaptation of a comic strip of his own invention (*Nausicaä of the Valley of the Wind*), in 1984 Miyazaki joined forces with Takahata to found the Ghibli studio. There followed a series of masterpieces which they took turns to direct. All of Miyazaki's productions have been triumphs: from *Laputa: Castle in the Sky* (1986) to *Ponyo on the Cliff by the Sea* (2008). ● Takahata must take the credit for a fine adaptation of an autobiographical story by Nosaka Akiyuki, *Grave of the Fireflies* (1988). It is a beautiful and moving film – without a happy ending, which enhances the story's authenticity. Takahata claims to have lived a very similar adventure in his youth. In the same year, mangaka Otomo Katsuhiro captured people's imaginations in bringing a superb and no less harrowing adaptation of his cult comic strip to the big screen. In the wake of *Akira* (1988), a new wave of brilliant adult productions began to appear, apocalyptic in tone and for the most part extremely violent, featuring urban warfare, often in interaction with American blockbusters.

## POKÉMOMANIA, PANACEA OR PANDEMIC?

'There is no doubt that Japan produces the largest number of animated cartoons, but most of these are narrative and commercial. It is important that animated films be seen as an art form', declared pioneer Tezuka, two years before his death in 1989. ● In the Nineties, with the help of Pikachu and his gang (and the Nintendo company), videogames mobilising cohorts of winsome creatures began to proliferate. The fluffy Pocket Monsters invaded and took over through a plethora of magazines and multimedia games. ● An initial animated TV series (104 episodes) became the favourite programme of children in Japan, the USA, Canada and Australia, and production began on a further 104 episodes. ● And what shall we say of the almighty *Transformers*, given such a boost by Steven Spielberg? Of course, it is part of an endless war between robots (titanic extraterrestrials fighting over our planet), drawn from a Japanese series; a manga fantasy dating from the end of the last century, which has spawned an armada of Hasbro action toys, not to mention videogames! But it is at least as much – and maybe more, despite a large degree of human figuration – an animated film, given the multitude of destructive robots. Where does biology end and cybernetics begin? At this stage of confusion/dereliction, spectacular though it may be, it is above all a matter of business. Cinema, too, is an industry, said André Malraux, author of *La Condition humaine*, which has also been adapted for the small screen.

# RELATIONSHIPS BETWEEN MANGA AND ANIME

## PHILIP BROPHY

## HANDMADE IN JAPAN

An especially endearing aspect of anime is how flat its images appear before us. They seem to be in denial of their impulse to 'animate'. It's a graphic hand-drawn, super-flatness that communicates with great depth – one that, ironically, formally and materially views its surface as a universe for its encoding and layering. The absence of any photographic aura globally scars animation and anime equally, segregating them somewhat from cinema and leading them to be slightly stigmatized and perceived as 'not-cinema'. In itself, this is not a problem, although becoming conscious of how deeply ingrained this differentiation is aids the viewer in comprehending the 'animatic grain' of anime. ● Photography brought to life the Renaissance dream of light, depth and perspective. This 'hands-free mechanical-eye' feat has since magically cast cinema as being beyond rendering, leaving animation gripped by a manually mediated appearance. Impinged by late-nineteenth-century orthodoxy, photography, cinema and 'cinegraphic' CGI live the dream of looking out of the window to the world, while comics and animation look like they are still contemplating themselves on the drawing board. While Western photography and cinematography have progressed through either embracing or contesting the camera's predisposition towards actuality and 'realism', anime maps alternative dimensions of 'unreality' on its plane of materiality, intensifying the graphic and nullifying the photographic. The power of the pen and the boldness of the brush guide anime as a motion medium born of manga, where the act of drawing by hand is viewed as a powerful mode of narration. ● Beyond manga, Japanese culture is abundant in ways that the handmade and hand-operated is acknowledged. Manual dexterity and physical manipulation are evidence of an interface between human creativity, technological application and material connection. Accordingly, the hand is technological and the machine is organic, feverishly interchangeable. As ritualized in the way that department stores wrap their parcels delicately by hand, manual dexterity, physical touch and material tactility are cosmologically aligned with the everyday, no matter how technologically advanced its exchanges. ● As such, an asynchronism in sensibility forges a rift between anime and the recent rise of CGI in American animation and live-action: anime's handmade production simulates machine-made manifestations, while Hollywood's computer-generated production insinuates human-generated manifestations. Even if computers are employed in anime (as they increasingly are), they will appear hand-drawn, to express the Japanese sense of physicality. Conversely, Hollywood's CGI spectacles archaically transform the cinema into a Sistine Chapel, claiming closeness to the godly touch of unmediated perfection in life-likeness.

> CINEMA AND 'CINEGRAPHIC' CGI LIVE THE DREAM OF LOOKING OUT OF THE WINDOW TO THE WORLD, WHILE COMICS AND ANIMATION LOOK LIKE THEY ARE STILL CONTEMPLATING THEMSELVES ON THE DRAWING BOARD

## CALLIGRAPHIC MOMENTUM

Anime employs a concept of linear energy, where a causal vein of energy is contracted from one point to the next in either dispersive wave form or directed beam form. While Occidental thought will readily exemplify this by analogue systems like electricity (where man tames nature through 'inventive containment', then allows energy to territorially pass along a controlled line), Oriental thought provides a more immediate and corporeal model: chi, the energy that exists in anyone and anything. It can be hidden, exposed, tapped, exercised, abused. From the many martial arts through to disciplines like t'ai chi, one channels energy as a linear flow coursing through the body. This type of transference of invisible chi occurs in a range of energy manifestations in physical reality: from the stature of one's standing body, to the slice of the samurai sword, to the brush stroke in calligraphy. All are marked embodiments of channelled energy. Each example – the shape of the body, the slice of the sword, the calligraphic character – is a visual mark which is held in place by the latent dynamics of an invisible energy controlled by the body. ● The calligraphic momentum of anime is a particularly self-reflexive condition. If we take calligraphy to be not only the traditional art of expressive brushwork but also the ways in which chi leaves its mark on anyone and anything, anime is the graphing and encoding of how things exist in the most fundamental sense. While the history of western art – both the art itself and the ways in which it 'sees' non-western art – is a para-evolutionary charting of progressive visualisation according to optical paradigms of 'how things look', anime is a dynamic graphing of the same but with attention paid to 'how things are'. Across six centuries of Japanese visual art, the brush has been used less as a tool and more as a 'musculatory extension' of the body/arm/hand. It is the instrument for channelling energy so that any act of depiction is more properly the recording of energy that simulated an actioning of its form. This advanced philosophical awareness through manual dexterity underpins the bulk of Japan's traditional practices – so much so that the representational and the ideogramatic are reversed. The ideogram idealizes the energy of a thing due to its calligraphic inscripture, leaving the representation to be merely the surface effect of that energy's documentation. ● This supplanting of the representation with the ideogram is at the heart of how anime's sense of motion differs from western animation derived equally from Leonardo's vanishing perspective and Muybridge's photographical analyses. Anime literally animates brushstrokes rather than not things: this is its core relationship with manga. Anime's formal characteristics are based less on watching things move and more on observing the frequency, range and ratio of their momentum. The resulting 'calligraphic momentum' never closely matches how things move or appear in the real world, yet anime is remarkable in its evocation of movement itself. Spiralling colons of billowing smoke, lapping waves of agitated water, shimmering fields of windblown pampas grass, even passing through a fluoro-lit underground freeway tunnel – these are among the many poetic moments of motion in anime.

# VIDEOGAMES + MANGA + ANIME
## THE INCREASING CONVERGENCE OF MEDIA

### DAVID SURMAN

A longside manga and anime, videogames play a major role in the media output of Japan, and these three form the core of what Douglas McRay has termed the country's 'gross national cool' – the cultural and commercial spell Japanese popular media seem to have cast over so many audiences the world over. Japanese developers have played a major role in the design and implementation of games from their inception in the Sixties through to the present day. The 'console wars' period of games design, from the late Eighties through to the turn of the millennium, was dominated by the creative output and technological innovation of the Japanese. As anime fandom developed, so too did a newly burgeoning culture of videogames, in which the 'Japaneseness' was not hidden or neutralized but rather extolled as a commercial virtue.

● The development of contemporary videogames from the launch of the PlayStation in 1995 onwards corresponds to changes in the worlds of manga and anime media. A new generation of artists and designers working across these three platforms seemed collectively to express an understanding of the growing convergence of the media. Kojima Hideo's *Metal Gear Solid* (1998) for PlayStation, Anno Hideaki's anime series *Neon Genesis Evangelion* (1995) and Shirow Masamune's manga *Ghost in the Shell* (1991) each share an intense preoccupation with themes of identity and technology, and in particular identity through technology. To understand the Japanese videogame, we should therefore take time to understand the developments taking place in manga and anime, and vice versa. Shirow's heroine Kusanagi Motoko is like a cat with nine lives, able to find new bodies and return from defeat, but she is also like the game character, continuing after game over, switching out broken parts and opting for upgrades, hacking in to find strategic advantages on the chess board of combat. ● Spend even a brief time playing and you will see how the contemporary videogame relies heavily on the early influence of manga and anime. Through the huge impact of feature films like Otomo Katsuhiro's *Akira* (1988), games designers were able to imagine new configurations of player and world. We can see the mark of North American cinema on videogames because western audiences are so literate in its conventions, and with a new literacy in anime and manga a new history emerges, of games made in the wake of anime classics. The cyberpunk and fantasy themes of many manga and anime were substantially developed by videogames, since the principles of interactivity and multipath and counterfactual narratives so central to cyberpunk were integral to the gaming apparatus. So in certain instances, games explore territory where anime and manga fear to tread. Recent beat-'em-up versions of classic *shonen* narratives *Dragon Ball Z* and *Naruto* actually add a dimension that exceeds the original manga and anime versions. While most adaptations take for granted a degree of loss of brand integrity, these recent fighting games seem to understand the referent texts at a very fundamental level, providing action that allows players to get directly hands-on with the characters of the series,

> AS ANIME FANDOM DEVELOPED, SO TOO DID A NEWLY BURGEONING CULTURE OF VIDEOGAMES, IN WHICH THE 'JAPANESENESS' WAS NOT HIDDEN OR NEUTRALIZED BUT RATHER EXTOLLED AS A COMMERCIAL VIRTUE

understanding their movement, special attacks and fighting style with a new level of fidelity. ● There are many correspondences between serial manga, television anime and roleplaying videogames. Each in their own way takes a considerable amount of time to develop its characters and narrative, with a typical roleplay genre videogame taking in excess of sixty hours to complete. In the Japanese home of the Nineties, the games console (invariably a Super Famicom or SEGA Genesis) would sit comfortably alongside shelves of manga and VHS anime. Across these media would be a spread of common characters, franchises and genres, and fandom for one type of media would naturally elicit interest in the other. Increasingly, to fully appreciate manga and anime, one would have to, by extension, take an active interest in the world of videogames. Nowadays we take for granted the convergence of these various media types, and many franchises like the *.hack* world actively rely on all three media types to propagate their storylines. The ensemble cast of the contemporary roleplay game mirrors that of film and comic book; as in the internationally successful *Final Fantasy* games, these characters follow archetypal patterns laid out in the genre terms of anime and manga – the magical girl, the stubborn boy, the quiet hero, the decadent prince. These games can be seen as the incorporation of interaction into anime, which might seem conceptually simplistic, until you consider the stellar success and widespread influence of the franchise. Videogames need storytellers, and the horizontal movement of creative talent from the manga and anime industries into games is closely guarded in Japanese development culture. The myth of a perfectly interactive anime is too seductive to ignore, and the ambition to create it drives the practice of a great many studios.

● Reciprocally, videogames have substantially influenced manga and anime storylines and characterization. With the generation of directors and artists for whom games have become a core reference point, there have been natural shifts in the attitude and values of the characters they create. Characters are increasingly defined not by the impact of their actions within the plot, but rather by the qualities of who (or what) they are, physically or otherwise. This emphasis on affordances (which constantly asks, 'what is the character capable of doing?') reflects the gameworld mechanics of using 'object a' on 'object b', trial and error and physical properties. General cultural shifts that have come out of the changing world of gaming and the Internet have similarly been figured into Japanese popular media more generally. In narratives like *Serial Experiments Lain* (1998), *Denno Coil* (2008) and *Real Drive* (2008), the playworld of the virtual is set up as the status quo; the influence of games design is represented as so ubiquitous and totalising that it isn't questioned. More often than not, anime and manga set out a play world for characters to interact within, and into this space the viewer can project their imagination. Even the more morose plots are set against a backdrop of serious play, as in the narrative of CLAMP's *X* series (1992, 1996, 2000) where characters fight in deadly arenas that float invisibly above the everyday city. Through to the bitter end, Kaneda's grudge battle against Tetsuo is framed as play, and in this it is indebted to the capability of games, as much as *Akira* is itself an inspiration to games designers.

# TROUBLES OF THE HUMAN HEART
## THE INFINITE FORMS OF THE JAPANESE ANIMATED LANDSCAPE

## DANIELE DOTTORINI

I n the world of animation, images keep returning. To state this is not to assert that images are repeated, and that therefore they are copies of one another. Animation is a place where graphic art redevelops, recaptures and re-appropriates the forms, contours and signs of an imaginary world that has a vast iconography, constantly amalgamating and transforming them and finding new ways of expressing them. Animation is suspended between the need to imitate nature through drawing and to transfigure it by means of its own power of abstraction (suspended between its existence in cinematic form and, at the same time, pure movement of line and colour). It can be seen as a unique moment in the history of representational art and an extraordinary comment on those images that nature itself has produced over the course of time. To say that images return, then, means that the anime, as well as being the place where images draw upon a vast pictorial heritage, is, simultaneously, the result of reconfigurations that are original. ● Japanese animation has taken just such an explosion of forms and recurrent images to its extreme limits, fashioning it into a mode of expression that is all its own, especially when dealing with the image and power of landscape: this is where the multiplicity of expressive forms and styles in Japanese cartoon film shows evidence of a mobile and changing world, able to move between abstraction and hyperrealism. Far from being a mere backdrop to the characters' actions, the landscape of Japanese animation is a living element that is important for expression and is capable of determining the styles and forms of the anime. ● The image, first and foremost, evokes other images. That is, the landscape can bring into play various forms of pictorial imagination, amalgamating them with the iconography peculiar to Japanese culture, as in the early scenes of *Princess Mononoke* (1999) by Miyazaki Hayao (or those in the manga *Mushishi* by Urushibara Yuki, or in its live-action interpretation *Bugmaster*, 2005, by Otomo Katsuhiro). Images like those in *Mononoke* reveal a mountainous landscape seen from above, immersed in a sea of fog and, shortly afterwards, a broad and gentle hilly landscape; there is a transformation, a shifting double vision. In the first block of pictures it is a Romantic view, reminiscent of nineteenth-century English and German painting (the first shot directly recalling pictures by Caspar David Friedrich, for example *The Wanderer above the Sea of Mist*, 1818). The other view, seen in the second block, belongs to the tradition of modern and contemporary landscape painting (Italian, English

and Flemish). The image redevelops the western pictorial tradition, but into this are absorbed ways of seeing, signs, and imaginative, spiritual and cultural forms that are typically Japanese. East and West become fused with one another, or rather they amalgamate, giving way, in the landscape, not to a neutral backdrop to the action, but to an entity that is alive and full of expression. ● The picture of the landscape is thus a hybrid, as in the aforementioned style of Otomo in *Cannon Fodder*, an episode of the film *Memories* (1995), in which the scenario is made up of images, forms and styles taken directly from German and Soviet silent films of the Twenties, almost as if to underline the power of animated pictures to actually re-invent cinema. The same process forms the basis of Tezuka Osamu's project in the film *Metropolis* (2001) directed by Rintaro, an original re-working – partly, if not mainly, visual – of Fritz Lang's 1926 masterpiece of the same name. Thus cinematic images return in a new form and, as a consequence, become something different. ● But the way landscape is viewed always distorts and determines the ambience. It therefore plays a role in the emotional and psychological changes that the characters undergo; we have only to think of the *shojo* anime, such as *Candy Candy* (1976) or *Lady Oscar* (1979), in which the landscape alters stylistically, from the point of view of colour, light and form, according to the characters' state of mind, or it constitutes the neutral background to real or psychological battles, as in the robots of Nagai Go – from the saga of *Mazinger* (1972) to *UFO Robot Grendizer Raids* (1975) or in anime like *Casshan* (1973) and *Hokuto no Ken* (*Fist of the North Star*, 1984). Many anime are characterized by what is really a common obsession in contemporary Japan: a world devastated by nuclear conflict. And the post-atomic setting of these films is one of their most troubling aspects: the landscapes of *Hokuto no Ken* and *Casshan* portray a world devoid of life, with nothing but dry and barren rock, in unnatural and strident colours which deeply reflect the melancholic and desperate atmosphere of the two series, as well as showing the potential for landscape to be a spatial expression of feeling writ large. ● But over and above the natural landscape in its multiple forms, there is the cityscape, which is the other great medium of expression in contemporary animation. Urban spaces are extremely important among the various landscapes that play a role in anime, whether it is the artificial and alienating city of Oshii Mamoru's films – from *Patlabor II* (1992) to *Ghost in the Shell* (1995) to *The Sky Crawlers* (2008) – in which the urban landscape is the theatre of the tragic events that befall the protagonists, forming an indifferent human setting for those tragedies; or whether it is like the visionary and dreamlike city of Kon Satoshi's films – from *Perfect Blue* (1997) to *Paprika* (2006). The wild and devouring city, abandoned and dying, or the one which is ordered and indifferent, both play a large part in the science-fiction productions of Japanese animation films and are troubling symbols of modernity. ● The world of anime is thus a complex one, in which landscape plays a fundamental role of representing anxieties and changes in the protagonists' state of mind – we only have to think of recent series such as *Soul Taker* (2001) by Shinbo Akiyuki, in which the colours and shapes of the landscape change in relation to the events experienced by the characters. In order to do this, the landscape portrayed has also to be the place where the recollection of images, their ability to 'return' as memory and allusion to other images (no matter whether these occur in films, pictures or photographs), is brought into play, and taken up in an endless spiral, as homage or violation or even, simply, as a form which belongs to the particular language of film animation.

> JAPANESE ANIMATION HAS TAKEN AN EXPLOSION OF FORMS AND RECURRENT IMAGES TO ITS EXTREME LIMITS, FASHIONING IT INTO A MODE OF EXPRESSION THAT IS ALL ITS OWN

# FROM CITY TO NETWORK

## CARLO CHATRIAN

O riginally, the city was a place identifying a culture and a people. Being a citizen meant representing the civilization that a community expressed in its common life. Early settlements tended to define their boundaries with extreme precision, more for cultural than for military reasons, to distinguish them from an undifferentiated – if not hostile – 'elsewhere'. But as settlements grew and communications improved over the centuries, this concept was gradually emptied of meaning and the city became a mere agglomeration. ● When cinema was born, the city was an organized space, a centre of economic power and, probably, the place where most of the audience lived and worked. It was therefore the first environment represented by film-makers, who initially wanted the settings of their stories to be recognizable. Animated films, on the other hand, free of any claim to realism, could from the beginning appeal to the spectator's imagination, playing on a period's inner concerns and interests. The city was therefore eclipsed by the countryside or a fantasy world of the kind we find in the very first animated film, Georges Méliès's *A Trip to the Moon* (1902). The 'trip' described in such films takes place in its own world, totally unconnected with daily life, in which the city was assuming an ever more important role. This has been true of Disney, but also of the Japanese cinema, from its origins to the successful films of the Ghibli studio, which in their own sensitive way perpetuate the fantastical element inherent in the very concept of animation. ● There was a change of perspective when makers of animated films began using their unique medium to reflect the present or speculate on the future and, in so doing, descended from abstraction to the political sphere. This shift occurred in Japan before anywhere else and was most evident in productions using *limited animation*, which seemed to reduce the fluidity that we regard as natural. Representations of the city – understood as an agglomeration of persons – were symptomatic in this respect. While the scenario of the *Atlas UFO Robot* series (1975) was still deliberately vague, the *Gundam* saga (1979) created a more modern setting in which humanity is no longer an indistinct backdrop but assumes dramatically present outlines – hence the need to describe places and living conditions in greater detail. There is a recurrent image in robot series which clearly demonstrates this fear of coming to terms with reality: the aseptic bedroom in which citizens take refuge. These places gradually broaden out and take on the shape of colonies – real settlements in miniature. ● It would, however, be misleading to look for steady development in one direction: the history of animation – and particularly TV series – is often a case of two steps forwards and one back. This is due in large part to the availability of an inexhaustible mine of ideas on which film-makers can draw:

the manga. An original medium resulting from the ongoing interplay of western influences and native Japanese story-telling, the manga immediately became a vehicle for social criticism and representation. When Tezuka published his *Metropolis* in 1949, taking a single image from Fritz Lang's film and imagining a city haunted by the threat of catastrophe, the manga was already analysing and critically reflecting on pre-existing materials. This comic strip rich in implications and narrative ideas was to serve as a matrix for many future animated films. It was no accident that no one dared transform it into an anime until 2001. ● The term 'metropolis' literally means 'mother city', and a mother is the only figure lacking in the comic. The imaginary cities of Japanese animation are heirs to this concept: the city will not be a place of birth – except of the kind forced by technology – but of bewilderment, deception and loss of identity. Lacking a centre and abandoned to itself, the city glimpsed in Japanese animated films – whether *Ai City* (1986) or *Perfect Blue* (1997) – has no social venues, or such venues are merely bland places, settings for sporting, melodramatic or erotic enterprises – for instance schools or emergency hospitals. ● From *Ghost in the Shell* (1995) onwards, the contemporary anime seems to shun topographical references. The immaterial dimension introduced by computer games renders superfluous the image of the city as a place of meeting or conflict. The case of a character such as Saeba Ryo in *City Hunter* (1987) is emblematic of a vision anchored to a now redundant model: Hojo Tsukasa's series harks back to a metropolis on the American model, dominated by tall skyscrapers. But in contemporary animation, streets and bars have been superseded by anonymous districts on the periphery, secondary streets or multi-lane ring roads, places of transit more suggestive of a network – the image that has replaced the concept of the city in the collective imagination. ● From this point of view, the aseptic style of a series such as *Gantz* (2004) typifies the relational emptiness of the modern city. Once a temple of community, the city has become a place of isolation – an aseptic space in which identity is no longer mirrored but dissolves in a horizon of indifference. Populated by aliens, robots and humans, the night-time streets of the series directed by Itano Ichiro are the theatre for a struggle for domination and survival more reminiscent of a concentration camp. Although the concept was already there in *Akira* (1988), in that film the expressive use of colour put the accent on the baroque dimension of passion and resistance. ● *Akira* is in some respects a turning point: on the one hand, it anticipates terrible despairing visions, like those proposed by Oshi; on the other, it alludes to more utopian and humanistic positions, of the kind promoted by Kon in *Tokyo Godfathers* (2003) or Arias in *Tekkonkinkreet* (2006). In both films, though the city has degenerated into a megalopolis, there are allusions to the nourishing function it performed in its early days. The anonymous, desolate nocturnal streets are inhabited by people with an almost anachronistic sense of belonging that is truly reassuring.

> THE IMAGINARY CITIES OF JAPANESE ANIMATION WILL NOT BE A PLACE OF BIRTH – EXCEPT OF THE KIND FORCED BY TECHNOLOGY – BUT OF BEWILDERMENT, DECEPTION AND LOSS OF IDENTITY.

GLOSSARY...274

INDEX OF TITLES...279

INDEX OF DIRECTORS
& CREATORS...285

INDEX OF CHARACTERS...289

BIBLIOGRAPHY...292

# GLOSSARY

Words with their own entry in the glossary are marked with an *

## 3D-CG

Abbreviation of three-dimensional computer graphics, created on a computer with rendering software.

## ACTION FIGURE

Miniature, articulated reproduction of a character, in plastic or resin.

## ANIMATION

Any work using the stop motion (or frame-by-frame) technique. Animation films differ from live action films in that the movement is artificially recreated and does not occur naturally.

## ANIME

Contraction of the English word animation*. In Japan it refers to any kind of animated work (Japanese or otherwise), while in the West the term is used specifically to mean to animated cartoons from Japan.

## ANIME COMICS

Manga produced from anime photogrammes.

## ANIPARO

Contraction of anime parody, for example THE CRAZY WORLD OF GO NAGAI (1990).

## BACKGROUND

The background scenery for a scene, drawn on sheets of paper which are usually bigger than the cels* which contain the character designs. Abstract backgrounds with a graphic motif are very common and serve to metaphorically accentuate a character's state of mind.

## BANK SYSTEM

This expression refers to the practice, common in televised anime, of using an animated sequence (or part of one, for example a background) in a number of episodes, without having to design it from scratch each time. The bank system was tested to success by Tezuka Osamu in 1963 for ASTROBOY.

## BGM

Abbreviation of background music.

## BISHOJO/ BISHONEN

Literally 'beautiful girl/boy'. This term is often used to refer to characters in homosexual manga or anime.

## BOSOZOKU

Literally 'tribe of exaggerated speed'. They are motorcyclists who hurtle through the night in large and rowdy gangs. In the world of anime the most famous bosozoku are those from AKIRA (1988).

## BUNKO

Pocket-sized tankobon*.

## BUNRAKU

Puppet theatre created in the twentieth century.

## BUSHIDO

Literally 'the way of the samurai'. Describes the samurai code of honour (bushi).

## CEL

A transparent acetate sheet, on which is drawn or copied a single movement from an animated sequence. The designs are first created on paper, where they can be corrected and refined, and then the finished versions are copied onto acetate.

## CG

Abbreviation of computer graphics.

## -CHAN

Suffix added to the names of babies, children and young women, used as a diminutive or a pet name.

## CHANBARA

'Swashbuckling' film (or anime), or an opera in the feudal style, containing many combats.

## CHARACTER DESIGNER

The person responsible for the graphic design of the characters in an anime, or who adapts characters from an already existing manga. They produce a model sheet* for each character.

## CHIBI

LITERALLY 'SMALL'. DESCRIBES YOUNG ANIMALS OR SMALL, TENDERHEARTED CHARACTERS WHO ARE TYPICALLY KAWAII*.

## COLOURATION

ALSO CALLED 'PAINT'. PHASE DURING THE MAKING OF AN ANIME, IN WHICH THE CEL* IS COLOURED BY THE DESIGNERS RESPONSIBLE. THE COLOURS ARE PLACED ON THE OPPOSITE SIDE OF THE CEL, WHICH CONTAIN SHAPES TRACED IN INDIAN INK.

## COSPLAY

POPULAR HOBBY IN JAPAN WHICH CONSISTS OF WEARING A COSTUME REPRESENTING A FAMOUS CHARACTER. THE FAVOURITE SUBJECTS FOR COSPLAYERS ARE CHARACTERS FROM MANGA ANIME, AND GAMES.

## DIRECT ANIMATION

ALSO KNOWN AS ANIMATION WITHOUT CAMERA OR DRAWN-ON FILM ANIMATION: THE ANIMATION IS DRAWN DIRECTLY ONTO THE FILM STOCK, RATHER THAN BEING PHOTOGRAPHED FRAME BY FRAME.

## DOJINSHI

AMATEUR MANGA WHICH OFTEN BORROWS THE MOST FAMOUS CHARACTERS FROM OFFICIAL MANGA AND INVENTS NEW STORIES ABOUT THEM, NOT AS WRITTEN BY THE ORIGINAL AUTHOR.

## DRAMA

A FICTION SERIES USING ACTORS, USUALLY SENTIMENTAL IN NATURE, AND OFTEN INSPIRED BY A MANGA*. IN CONTRAST TO ANIME SERIES, MANY DRAMAS ARE SHOWN ON A DAILY AS WELL AS ON A WEEKLY BASIS.

## ESP

ABBREVIATION OF EXTRA SENSORY PERCEPTION, SUCH AS TELEKINESIS OR TELEPORTATION. AMONG THE MOST FAMOUS CHARACTERS IN ANIME WITH ESP POWERS ARE THOSE FROM AKIRA (1988).

## EYE-CATCH

IN A TV SERIES, THIS IS THE BRIEF ANIMATED INTERVAL, USUALLY A JINGLE OF THE TITLE, OR THE SERIES LOGO, DIVIDING AN EPISODE IN HALF BY ANNOUNCING THE ADVERTISEMENT BREAK.

## FRAME

THIS TERM DESCRIBES BOTH A SINGLE IMAGE FROM A FILM (OR VIDEO), AND A SINGLE IMAGE FROM AN ANIMATION SEQUENCE. A FRAME CAN CONTAIN SEVERAL ANIMATION CELS SUPERIMPOSED IN DIFFERENT LAYERS.

## FULL ANIMATION

AN EXTREMELY FLUID AND COMPLETE ANIMATION, USING 24 DIFFERENT FRAMES FOR EVERY SECOND OF FILM TO CREATE THE ILLUSION OF SMOOTH MOVEMENT.

## GEKIGA

LITERALLY 'DRAMATIC IMAGES'. THIS TERM, INVENTED BY TATSUMI YOSHIHIRO, DEFINES A TYPE OF DRAMATIC MANGA INTENDED FOR AN ADULT AUDIENCE.

## HANYO

CREATURE BORN FROM THE UNION OF A YOKAI AND A HUMAN BEING, OFTEN DISMISSED AS A HALF-BREED. THE MOST FAMOUS HANYO IN ANIME IS THE PROTAGONIST OF INUYASHA (2000).

## HENSHIN

LITERALLY 'TRANSFORMATION'. DESCRIBES THE PROCESS OF MUTATION OR CHANGING OF COSTUME TYPICAL OF MANY CHARACTERS FROM MANGA AND ANIME. THIS TRANSFORMATION IS USUALLY UNIQUE AND RITUALISTIC AND IS PLAYED OUT IDENTICALLY IN EACH EPISODE. HENSHIN SEQUENCES ARE FOUND IN SAILOR MOON (1992) AND SAINT SEIYA (1986) AND IN ALL THE EPISODES OF POWER RANGERS*.

## HENTAI

LITERALLY MEANING 'PERVERTED', THE TERM REFERS TO PORNOGRAPHIC MANGA OR ANIME. JAPANESE CENSORSHIP OFTEN REQUIRES DETAILS IN SEXUAL SCENES TO BE DIGITALLY CAMOUFLAGED.

## HEROIC FANTASY

AN EPIC FANTASY SET IN THE MIDDLE AGES, IN WHICH COMBAT WITH FIREARMS IS REPLACED BY HAND TO HAND COMBAT. THERE ARE NO SUPERNATURAL OR MAGIC ELEMENTS.

## IDOL

YOUNG JAPANESE POP SINGER. WITH THEIR SONGS AND CHILD-LIKE DEMEANOUR, THE IDOLS HAVE BECOME THE SPOKESPEOPLE FOR THE KAWAII* AESTHETIC.

## INBETWEENS

ALSO KNOWN AS INTERLAY OR DOGA, THIS IS REALLY AN ANIMATION FRAME WHICH IS PLACED BETWEEN TWO KEYFRAMES*. THE INBETWEENS ARE PRODUCED BY INBETWEENERS, WORK USUALLY TAKEN ON BY ANIMATORS AS THEIR FIRST WORKING EXPERIENCE.

## JOSEI MANGA

MANGA CREATED FOR AN AUDIENCE OF OLDER WOMEN.

## KABUKI

TRADITIONAL THEATRE FOUNDED IN THE 16TH CENTURY. KABUKI ACTORS ARE ALWAYS MALE.

**KAIJU EIGA**

MONSTERS FILM, FOR EXAMPLE *GODZILLA* (1954).

**KAKIOROSHI**

MANGA PUBLISHED DIRECTLY IN TANKOBON*.

**KANA**

WRITTEN SYMBOL FROM THE JAPANESE LANGUAGE. IT IS USED IN DIFFERENT PARTS OF SPEECH AS A PREFIX OR VERB CONJUGATION. KANA IS INCLUDED IN TWO OTHER TERMS: HIRAGANA AND KATAKANA. THE LATTER IS USED ABOVE ALL TO TRANSLITERATE FOREIGN TERMS.

**KANJI**

JAPANESE IDEOGRAM. IT CAN BE USED IN ALL PARTS OF THE SENTENCE, USED AS A NOUN, ADJECTIVE AND VERB. KANJI CAN ON OCCASION BE SUBSTITUTED BY KANA*.

**KATANA**

TYPICAL SAMURAI SWORD.

**KAWAII**

LITERALLY 'CUTE'. A FASHION OR AESTHETIC HIGHLY POPULAR IN JAPAN, FROM THE 1980S ONWARDS, WHICH REVERES ANYTHING CUTE OR HELPLESS, WHICH AROUSES TENDERNESS OR TAKES ONE BACK TO THE INNOCENCE OF CHILDHOOD.

**KEYFRAME**

ALSO KNOWN AS A GENGA. THIS IS THE FRAME WHICH OPENS OR CLOSES A SEGMENT OF ANIMATION, AND GENERALLY INCLUDES THE START OR END OF A COMPLETE MOVEMENT BY ONE OR MORE CHARACTERS. THE KEYFRAMES ARE PRODUCED BY THE PRINCIPAL ANIMATORS.

**KODOMO MANGA**

MANGA CREATED FOR AN AUDIENCE OF CHILDREN AGED BETWEEN SIX AND ELEVEN YEARS OLD.

**KOHAI**

TERM USED TO REFER TO A WORK OR STUDY COMPANION YOUNGER THAN ONESELF.

**–KUN**

SUFFIX USED WHEN SPEAKING TO CHILDREN OR INFERIORS. FOR EXAMPLE SHINJI–KUN.

**LAYER**

A LAYER OF ANIMATION. A NUMBER OF CELS ARE PLACED ON TOP OF EACH OTHER IN DIFFERENT LAYERS AND CAN BE PRINTED IN A SINGLE FRAME IN A FILM, TO CREATE A COMPLEX, MULTI-LAYERED SCENE. THE PAPER BACKGROUNDS ARE ALWAYS PLACED AT THE VERY BOTTOM OF THE LAYERS.

**LIMITED ANIMATION**

TYPE OF ANIMATION USING FEWER THAN 24 FRAMES PER SECOND (AS IN FULL ANIMATION). DEVELOPED IN BOTH THE WEST AND IN JAPAN TO LOWER COSTS AND SPEED UP PRODUCTION.

**LOLI**

CONTRACTION OF LOLITA (FROM THE BOOK BY NABOKOV). A SUB-GENRE OF HENTAI* FEATURING YOUNG ADOLESCENT PROTAGONISTS.

**MAH–JONG MANGA**

MANGA BASED ON THE POPULAR GAME OF THE SAME NAME.

**MAJOKKO**

LITERALLY 'LITTLE ENCHANTRESS'. A SUB-GENRE OF SHOJO MANGA* IN WHICH MAGIC AND FANTASY ELEMENTS ABOUND AS IN, FOR EXAMPLE, THE ENCHANTING *CREAMY MAMI* (1983).

**MANGA**

LITERALLY 'IMPROMPTU DESIGN', THE TERM DESCRIBES A COMIC STRIP, AND HAS BEEN ATTRIBUTED TO THE FAMOUS PAINTER HOKUSAI, BECAUSE OF HIS COLLECTION OF BOOKS OF SKETCHES AND CARICATURES: DESIGNS WHICH SUGGEST THE IDEA OF MOVEMENT THROUGH A SERIES OF ACTIONS OR POSES FEATURING THE SAME CHARACTER.

**MANGA CD**

MUSIC CD INSPIRED BY MANGA.

**MANGAKA**

MANGA CREATOR.

**MANHUA**

CHINESE COMICS.

**MANHWA**

KOREAN COMICS.

**MECHA (MEKA)**

CONTRACTION OF MECHANICAL. IN MANGA AND ANIME IT DESCRIBES ANY MECHANICAL INSTRUMENT, INCLUDING VEHICLES, WEAPONS AND ROBOTS.

**MECHA DESIGNER**

THE DESIGNER WHO DEFINES THE GRAPHIC APPEARANCE OF MECHA*.

**MEITANTEI MANGA**

MANGA ABOUT THE POLICE OR IN THE STYLE OF A DETECTIVE STORY AS, FOR EXAMPLE, *DETECTIVE CONAN* (1996).

## MERCHANDIZING

TOYS, ACTION-FIGURES*, GADGETS, AND OTHER CONSUMER PRODUCTS (INCLUDING COSTUMES) RELATED TO AN ANIME BRAND.

## NINJA

FEUDAL SPY OR HIRED KILLER, WHO USES MARTIAL ARTS AND ILLUSION TECHNIQUES.

## ONI

DEMON FROM JAPANESE FOLKLORE, GENERALLY DEPICTED AS A HUMANOID WITH HORNS, WHO CAN BREATHE FIRE OUT OF HIS MOUTH. IN THE WEST IT IS COMPARABLE WITH THE FIGURE OF THE OGRE.

## POWER RANGERS

TELEVISION FILM BASED ON THE ACROBATIC FIGHTS OF A TEAM OF TEENAGE HEROES.

## MODEL SHEET

ALSO KNOWN AS SETTEI. A SERIES OF DESIGNS WHICH REPRESENT A CHARACTER FROM AN ANIME IN ITS MOST COMMON POSES, ACCOMPANIED BY DETAILED INSTRUCTIONS ON COLOUR AND THE ANATOMIC PROPORTIONS OF THE FIGURE. THE MODEL SHEET IS THE FIRST POINT OF REFERENCE FOR ALL ANIMATORS INVOLVED IN CHARACTER ANIMATION.

## NOH

CLASSIC THEATRE FOUNDED IN THE 14TH CENTURY, CHARACTERIZED BY THE ACTORS' SLOWNESS OF MOVEMENT AND THE USE OF MASKS.

## OST

ABBREVIATION OF ORIGINAL SOUNDTRACK. A SOUNDTRACK FOR AN ANIME, DISTRIBUTED ON CD. THIS IS ONE OF THE MOST IMPORTANT ELEMENTS OF ANIME MERCHANDIZING*.

## RADIODRAMA

A DRAMA BROADCAST ON THE RADIO.

## OAV/OVA

ORIGINAL VIDEO ANIME, ANIME CREATED DIRECTLY FOR THE HOME VIDEO MARKET. THE FIRST OVA WAS DALLOS (1983).

## RENDERING

THE PROCESS WHICH TRANSFORMS THE MATHEMATICAL COORDINATES OF A THREE-DIMENSIONAL IMAGE INTO ITS PHOTO-REALISTIC EQUIVALENT, VIA THE APPLICATION OF TEXTURE, LIGHT AND SHADOW. THIS PROCESS IS THE BASIS OF ALL THREE-DIMENSIONAL COMPUTERIZED ANIMATION.

## MONO NO AWARE

LITERALLY 'EMPATHY TOWARD THINGS'. A TERM WHICH DESCRIBES A CONSCIOUSNESS OF THE PRECARIOUS NATURE OF THINGS AND THE SLIGHT SENSE OF REGRET WHICH ACCOMPANIES THEIR PASSING.

## OMAKE

BONUS PART OF AN ANIME DISTRIBUTED FOR THE DVD MARKET. OMAKE OFTEN HAVE HUMOROUS TRAITS, VIA THEIR USE OF SD*.

## OTAKU

LITERALLY 'YOUR HOUSE'. IN THE WEST THIS TERM DESCRIBES A FAN OF MANGA AND ANIME. IN JAPAN THE TERM HAS A RATHER NEGATIVE MEANING, SINCE IT REFERS TO AN INDIVIDUAL WHO IS INCAPABLE OF FORMING RELATIONSHIPS WITH OTHERS.

## RONIN

LITERALLY 'MAN WAVE'. A SAMURAI WITHOUT A PATRON OR A NOMADIC SAMURAI.

## MULTIPLANE CAMERA

THE TOOL WHICH IN ANIMATION PROCESSES SUBSTITUTES THE CLASSIC CINECAMERA USED IN LIVE CINEMA. IT IS A VERTICAL FRAME WITH A NUMBER OF LAYERS, EACH ONE ABLE TO CONTAIN A LAYER* OF ANIMATION. BY REGULATING THE DISTANCE BETWEEN THESE LAYERS AND SHOOTING THEM ALL FROM ABOVE, IT IS POSSIBLE TO PLAY WITH THE DEPTH OF THE SHOT AND THE FOCUS, THEREBY CREATING COMPLEX SCENOGRAPHIC COMPOSITIONS.

## ONA

ABBREVIATION OF ORIGINAL NET ANIME, AN ANIME CREATED SPECIFICALLY FOR THE INTERNET.

## ONESAMA

TITLE USED TO REFER TO ONE'S OWN OLDER SISTER OR A WOMAN OLDER THAN ONESELF BUT STILL YOUNG, AND PARTICULARLY WORTHY OF RESPECT.

## PENCIL TEST

PHASE IN THE CREATION OF AN ANIME* IN WHICH A RAPID PREVIEW OF A SEQUENCE IS SHOWN, IN ORDER TO IDENTIFY POSSIBLE DEFECTS. THE VARIANT OF THIS, THE LINE TEST, IS CARRIED OUT BEFORE THE DESIGNS HAVE BEEN COLOURED.

## ROTOSCOPE

THIS IS THE TOOL WHICH ALLOWS FOR THE DESIGN OF AN ANIMATED SEQUENCE, BY TRACING IMAGES ONTO PREVIOUSLY RECORDED LIVE-ACTION MATERIAL. IT IS OFTEN USED AS A SHORT-CUT TO CREATE A FLUID ANIMATION WITH PHOTO-REALISTIC TENDENCIES.

## SAKKAN

CONTRACTION OF SAKUGA KANTOKU, AN ANIMATION DIRECTOR. THIS PERSON IS RESPONSIBLE FOR SUPERVISING, CORRECTING AND MAKING UNIFORM ALL THE DESIGNS OF THE ANIMATORS, IN LINE WITH THE MODEL SHEET* CREATED BY THE CHARACTER DESIGNER*.

## -SAN

SUFFIX INDICATING MR, MISS, MRS, OR MS FOR EXAMPLE, TANAKA-SAN.

## SD

ABBREVIATION OF SUPER DEFORMED, THE DIMINUTIVE, SQUASHED-DOWN VERSION OF A CHARACTER FROM MANGA OR ANIME. THE SD STYLE IS FULL OF COMEDY AND DEMENTED CHARACTERS.

## SEIYU

VOICE ARTIST. UNLIKE THE PRACTICE IN THE US, JAPANESE DUBBING IS CARRIED OUT ONCE THE ANIMATION IS COMPLETE.

## SEINEN MANGA

MANGA CREATED FOR AN OLDER AUDIENCE. SEINEN DEAL WITH COMPLEX ISSUES, AND USE A REFINED GRAPHIC STYLE.

## SENPAI

TERM USED TO REFER TO AN OLDER PERSON, WORTHY OF RESPECT.

## SENSEI

TEACHER, PROFESSOR.

## SEPPUKU

LITERALLY 'CUT IN THE BELLY', THIS IS THE RITUAL SUICIDE PRACTISED BY SAMURAI IN PARTICULAR CASES OF FAILURE.

## SHINJU

DOUBLE SUICIDE, FOR LOVE. AT THE CENTRE OF MANY DRAMATIC WORKS FROM THE PAST.

## SHOJO AI

LITERALLY 'FEMALE LOVE'. SEE YURI*.

## SHOJO MANGA

MANGA CREATED FOR GIRLS BETWEEN THE AGES OF 6 AND 18.

## SHONEN AI

LITERALLY 'MALE LOVE'. SEE YAOI*.

## SHONEN MANGA

MANGA CREATED FOR MALE ADOLESCENTS.

## SPACE-OPERA

A SAGA SET IN SPACE, IN THE HYPOTHETICAL SETTING OF A GALACTIC EMPIRE. AS IN, FOR EXAMPLE, YAMATO (1977), GUNDAM (1979) AND COBRA (1982).

## SPIN-OFF

AN ANIMATED SERIES OR MANGA WHICH EMERGED OUT OF A PRECEDING SERIES AND DEVELOPS THE STORY OF A MINOR CHARACTER OR REVISITS ELEMENTS OF THE PLOT OR SETTING.

## SPOKON

A MANGA OR ANIME SET IN THE WORLD OF SPORT WITH ATHLETIC PROTAGONISTS, FOR EXAMPLE: STAR OF THE GIANTS (1969).

## STORYBOARD

ALSO KNOWN AS E-KONTE, MEANING LITERALLY 'CONTINUITY IMAGES'. THIS IS THE FIRST GRAPHIC REPRESENTATION OF A FILM USING A STYLE SIMILAR TO THAT OF A MANGA, IN WHICH THE SUCCESSION OF SQUARE FRAMES IS REPRODUCED, WITH INSTRUCTIONS FOR THE MOVEMENT OF ANIMATION EQUIPMENT.

## STRAIGHT AHEAD ANIMATION

DRAWING A SCENE FRAME BY FRAME FROM BEGINNING TO END, INSTEAD OF DRAWING KEY FRAMES AND THEN GOING BACK TO FILL IN THE GAPS LATER.

## TANKOBAN

A VOLUME WITH A PAPERBACK COVER OF AROUND 200 PAGES, IN WHICH THE EPISODES FROM A POPULAR MANGA SERIES ARE COLLECTED.

## YAOI

MALE HOMOSEXUAL MANGA WITH FREQUENT SEX SCENES.

## YOKAI

SPECTRE FROM JAPANESE FOLKLORE. GENERALLY, YOKAI ARE BENIGN AND PROTECT NATURE. THEY HAVE THEIR OWN SHAPES AND NAMES WHICH DISTINGUISH THEM FROM EACH OTHER. THE ANIME WHICH HAS MADE THEM FAMOUS IS GEGEGE NO KITARO (1969).

## YON-KOMA

THE JAPANESE VERSION OF THE WESTERN COMIC STRIP: USUALLY FOUR IRONIC VIGNETTES READ VERTICALLY.

## YURI

FEMALE HOMOSEXUAL MANGA.

# INDEX OF TITLES

BOLD TYPE REFERS TO INDIVIDUAL FILM, OAV, TV SERIES AND GAME ENTRIES IN THE BOOK.

THIS INDEX FEATURES TITLES IN ENGLISH, FRENCH (FR), ITALIAN (IT), JAPANESE (JP) AND SPANISH (SP).

**.HACK**...*008*
**.HACK//LEGEND OF THE TWILIGHT**...*008*
**.HACK//SIGN**...*008*
.HACK//SIGN: ATRAPADOS EN LA RED (SP) see .HACK// SIGN
1001 NIGHTS (JP) see SEN'YA ICHIYA MONOGATARI
5 CENTIMETERS PER SECOND...*214*
8 MAN...*053*

AA! MEGAMISAMA! (JP) see OH MY GODDESS!
**ABENOBASHI MAGICAL SHOPPING MALL**...*060*
ABENOBASHI MAHO SHOTENGAI (JP) see ABENOBASHI MAGICAL SHOPPING MALL
ACE O NERAE! (JP) see AIM FOR THE ACE!
ADDIO GIUSEPPINA (IT) see JOSEFINA THE WHALE
ADIOS JOSEFINA, ADIOS (SP) see JOSEFINA THE WHALE
ADORABILE LILY, L' (IT) see AKAZUKIN CHACHA
**ADVENTURES AT TONDERA HOUSE**...*026*
ADVENTURES OF SINDBAD see SINDBAD NO BOKEN
AI CITY (JP)...*217*
AI NO KUSABI (JP)...*012*
AI SHITE NIGHT (JP)...*162*
**AIM FOR THE ACE!**...*180, 221, 234*
AIM FOR THE TOP! GUNBUSTER see GUNBUSTER
AKAGE NO AN (JP) see ANNE OF GREEN GABLES
AKAHORI GEDOU HOUR RABUGE...*010*
AKAI KODAN ZILLION (JP) see ZILLION
AKAZUKIN CHACHA (JP)...*061*
**AKIRA**...*011, 061, 134, 220, 234*

ALAKAZAM THE GREAT see SAIYUKI
ALBATOR (FR) see CAPTAIN HARLOCK
ALITA, ANGEL DE COMBATE (SP) see BATTLE ANGEL
ALPS NO SHOJO HEIDI (JP) see HEIDI, GIRL OF THE ALPS
ANA DE LAS TEJAS VERDES (SP) see ANNE OF GREEN GABLES
**ANGEL'S EGG**...*013, 046*
ANIMAL TREASURE ISLAND...*235*
**ANIMATRIX**...*014*
ANIME HACHIJUNIKAN SEKAI ISSHU (JP) see AROUND THE WORLD WITH WILLY FOG
ANIME OYAKO GEKIJO (JP) see SUPERBOOK: VIDEO BIBLE
ANIMENTARY KETSUDAN (JP) ...*255*
ANJU TO ZUSHIO-MARU (JP) ...*248*
ANNA DA CAPELLI ROSSI (IT) see ANNE OF GREEN GABLES
ANNE AUX CHEVEUX ROUX (SP) see ANNE OF GREEN GABLES
**ANNE OF GREEN GABLES**...*015, 094*
ANPANMAN...*234*
AO NO ROKUGO (JP) see BLUE SUBMARINE NO. 6
AOKI RYUSEI SPT LAYZNER (JP) see LAYZNER
APE MAGIA, L' (IT) see HUTCH THE HONEYBEE
APPLESEED...*019, 129, 216, 217*
ARABIAN NIGHTS SINDBAD NO BOKEN (JP) see SINDBAD NO BOKEN
ARABIAN NIGHTS: SINDBAD'S ADVENTURE see SINDBAD NO BOKEN
ARAIGUMA RASCAL (JP) see RASCAL THE RACCOON
ARION...*253*
**ARMORED CORE**...*020*
ARMORED TROOPER VOTOMS see VOTOMS
AROUND THE WORLD WITH WILLY FOG...*057*
ARU MACHIKADO NO MONOGATARI (JP) see STORIES FROM A STREET CORNER
ASHITA NO JOE (JP)...*110, 221, 246*
ASHITA NO NADJA (JP)...*090*
ASTRO BOY...*019, 022, 027, 039, 097, 169, 229, 232, 251*
ATLAS UFO ROBOT (IT) see UFO ROBOT GRENDIZER RAIDS
ATOM see ASTRO BOY
ATTACK NUMBER ONE...*023, 039*
ATTACKER YOU!...*217*

AVENTURAS DE CANDY; LAS (SP) see CANDY CANDY
AVENTURAS DE DUKE FLINT, LAS (SP) see UFO ROBOT GRENDIZER RAIDS
AVENTURAS DE FLY, LAS (SP) see DRAGON QUEST
AVENTURAS DE GIGI, LAS (SP) see MINKY MOMO

BABEL II...*018*
BAKABON...*234*
BAKUMATSU KIKANSETSU ROHANIHOHETO (JP)...*226*
BAKURETSU HUNTERS see SORCEROR HUNTERS
BALENA GIUSEPPINA, LA (IT) see JOSEFINA THE WHALE
BAREFOOT GEN...*064*
BASTARD!!...*012*
BATAILLE DES PLANETES, LA (FR) see GATCHAMAN
BATMAN: GOTHAM KNIGHT...*021*
BATTLE ANGEL...*061*
BATTLE OF THE PLANETS see GATCHAMAN
BATTLE ROYALE...*013*
BERSERK...*073, 084*
BESAME LICIA (SP) see AI SHITE NIGHT
**BIBLE STORIES**...*026*
BISHOJO SENSHI SAILOR MOON (JP) see SAILOR MOON
**BLACK JACK**...*027, 048, 232*
BLACK MAGIC M-66...*125, 216*
BLADE RUNNER...*011*
BLASSREITER...*100*
BLEACH...*009, 138*
BLOOD: THE LAST VAMPIRE...*092, 123, 125, 210*
BLUE COMET SPT LAYZNER see LAYZNER
BLUE DRAGON...*238*
BLUE SUBMARINE NO. 6...*069, 130, 149*
BOLA DE DRAGON (SP) see DRAGON BALL
BORGMAN...*198*
BORROWER ARRIETTY, THE...*066*
BRAIN POWERD...*237*
BRAVE RAIDEEN see RAIDEEN
BROCHE ENCANTADO, EL (SP) see CREAMY MAMI
BROKEN DOWN FILM see ONBORO FILM
BUBBLEGUM CRISIS...*012, 019, 061, 128*
BUDDHA...*026*
BYOUSOKU 5 CM (JP) see 5 CENTIMETERS PER SECOND

CABALLEROS DEL ZODIACO, LOS (SP) see SAINT SEIYA
CALIMERO Y PRISCILLA (SP) see CALIMERO
**CALIMERO**...*029*
CAMPIONES: OLIVER E BENJY (SP) see CAPTAIN TSUBASA
**CANDY CANDY**...*029, 125, 235, 256*
CANDY (FR) see CANDY CANDY
CAPITAN RAIMAR (SP) see CAPTAIN HARLOCK
CAPTAIN HARLOCK...*075, 077, 097, 235, 252*
CAPTAIN TSUBASA...*217, 240*
CARD CAPTOR SAKURA...*035, 121, 242*
CASE CLOSED...*234*
CASSHAN: ROBOT HUNTER...*030, 104, 120, 209, 225, 229*
CASSHERN SINS...*020*
CASTILLO EN EL CIELO (SP) see CASTLE IN THE SKY
CASTLE IN THE SKY...*056, 066, 085, 141*
CASTLEVANIA: CURSE OF DARKNESS...*019*
CAT RETURNS, THE...*066, 078*
**CAT SOUP**...*030*
CAT'S EYE...*086, 124, 130*
CAVALIERI DELLO ZODIACO, I (IT) see SAINT SEIYA
CAVALLIERI DEL DRAGO, I (IT) see DRAGON QUEST
CAZADOR (SP) see CITY HUNTER
CHATEAU DANS LE CIEL, LE (FR) see CASTLE IN THE SKY
CHE CAMPIONI HOLLY E BENJY (IT) see CAPTAIN TSUBASA
CHE HA BISOGNO DI TENCHI? (IT) see TENCHI MUYO!
CHERRY MIEL (FR) see CUTEY HONEY
CHEVALIERS DU ZODIAQUE, LES (FR) see SAINT SEIYA
CHIBI MARUKO-CHAN (JP)...*152*
CHICA INFERNA (SP) see HELL GIRL
CHIE THE BRAT...*036*
CHICA MARIONETA J (SP) see SABER MARIONETTE J
CHILD'S TOY...*061*
CHINMOKU NO KANTAI (JP) see SILENT SERVICE
CHO DENJI ROBO COMBATTLER V (JP) see COMBATTLER V
CHOBITS...*061*
CHOJIN DENSETSU UROTSUKIDOJI (JP) see UROTSUKIDOJI
CHOPPY AND THE PRINCESS see PRINCESS KNIGHT
CHRONIQUE DE LA GUERRE DE LODOSS (FR) see RECORD OF LODOSS WAR
CHRONO CRUSADE...*033*
CHRONO TRIGGER...*238*

CIELI DI ESCAFLOWNE, I (IT) see ESCAFLOWNE

CITY HUNTER...034, 086

CLEOPATRA: QUEEN OF SEX...024, 036, 079, 251

COBRA see SPACE ADVENTURE COBRA

CODE GEASS HANGYAKU NO LELOUCH (JP) see CODE GEASS: LELOUCH OF THE REBELLION

CODE GEASS: LELOUCH OF THE REBELLION...035, 222

COMANDO G (SP) see GATCHAMAN

COMBATTLER V...253

CONAN EL NINO DEL FUTURO (SP) see FUTURE BOY CONAN

CONAN IL RAGAZZO DEL FUTURO (IT) see FUTURE BOY CONAN

CONAN LE FILS DU FUTURE (FR) see FUTURE BOY CONAN

CONTES DE TERREMER, LES (FR) see TALES FROM EARTHSEA

CORAZZATA SPAZIALE YAMATO, LA (IT) see YAMATO

COWBOY BEBOP...014, 036, 112, 179, 219, 222, 246

CRAYON SHIN-CHAN (JP)...076, 179, 213, 219

CREAM LEMON...180

CREAMY MAMI...038, 039

CREAMY, MERVEILLEUSE CREAMY (FR) see CREAMY MAMI

CRONICA DELLA GUERRA LODOSS (IT) see RECORD OF LODOSS WAR

CROSS GAME...009

CRUSHER JOE...253

CUENTOS DE TERRAMAR (SP) see TALES FROM EARTHSEA

CUTEY HONEY...016, 018, 039, 051, 058, 114, 242

CYBER CITY OEDO 808...148

CYBERFORMULA GPX...222

CYBERNELLA (IT) see LIMIT THE MIRACLE GIRL

CYBORG 009...040, 099, 235

CYBOT ROBOTCHI...217

DAGGER OF KAMUI...106, 207

DAICON III & IV...041, 242

DAITARN 3...042, 237

DALLOS...043

DAN ET DANY (FR) see DIRTY PAIR

DANGUARD ACE...044, 100, 120

DARKER THAN BLACK...028

DEATH NOTE...122

DENEI SHOJO AI (JP) see VIDEO GIRL AI

DENSETSU KYOJIN IDEON (JP) see IDEON

DETECTIVE CONAN see CASE CLOSED

DEVILMAN...035, 039, 047, 051, 114, 131, 215

DISTRITO COMMERCIAL MAGICO ABENOBASHI (SP) SEE ABENOBASHI MAGICAL SHOPPING MALL

DIGIMON...049, 090

DIRTY PAIR, THE...118

DOBUTSU TAKARAJIMA (JP) see ANIMAL TREASURE ISLAND

DOG OF FLANDERS, A...192

DOLCE CANDY (IT) see CANDY CANDY

DOMINION TANK POLICE...216

DOOMED MEGALOPOLIS see TEITO MONOGATARI

DORAEMON...050, 076, 234

DORAEMON EL GATO COSMICO (SP) see DORAEMON

DORORO...050

DORORON ENMA-KUN (JP)...247

DOUGRAM...226

DR SLUMP...018, 217, 238

DR. SLUMP ET LA PETITE ARALE (FR) see DR. SLUMP

DR. SLUMP: LAS TRAVESURAS DE ARALE (SP) see DR. SLUMP

DRAGON BALL...049, 068, 120, 175, 235, 238

DRAGON QUEST...050, 238

DRAGON BALL Z...010, 183

DUKE FLEED (SP) see UFO ROBOT GRENDIZER RAIDS

EMBRASSE-MOI LUCILE (FR) see AI SHITE NIGHT

ENCANTEVOLE CREAMY, L' (IT) see CREAMY MAMI

ESCAFLOWNE...112, 116, 113

ESPER MAMI...076, 213

ESTRELLAS LUMINOSAS (SP) see YAMATO

EUREKA 7...028

EVANGELION...016, 030, 054, 060, 093, 113, 219, 226, 237, 251

EX-DRIVER...059

EXCEL SAGA...056, 245

EXTRA...008

EYESHIELD 21...061

FAIRY PRINCESS MINKY MOMO see MINKY MOMO

FANCY LALA...224

FANG OF THE SUN DOUGRAM see DOUGRAM

FANG OF THE SUN DOUGRAM see TAIYO NO KIBA DOUGRAM

FEDELE PATRASHE, IL (IT) see DOG OF FLANDERS

FILLE DES ENFERS, LA (FR) see HELL GIRL

FINAL FANTASY...013, 055

FIST OF THE NORTH STAR...021, 087

FLAG...226

FLANDERS NO INU (JP) see DOG OF FLANDERS

FLASH KICKER see CAPTAIN TSUBASA

FLCL...056

FLY (FR) see DRAGON QUEST

FLYING HOUSE, THE see ADVENTURES AT TONDERA HOUSE

FRUITS BASKET...046

FULGUTOR (FR) see GOSHOGUN

FULLMETAL ALCHEMIST...019, 028, 053

FUMOON...232

FURI KURI (JP) see FLCL

FUSHIGI NO UMI NO NADIA (JP) see SECRET OF BLUE WATER

FUSHIGINA MELMO (JP)...157

FUTURE BOY CONAN...037, 080, 227, 237

FUTURE COP URASHIMAN see URASHIMAN

GAKE NO UE NO PONYO (JP) see PONYO

GALAXY EXPRESS 999...077, 131, 150, 235, 252

GALAXY FRAULEIN YUNA...010

GALL FORCE...012

GANTZ...062, 069

GASARAKI...226

GATCHAMAN...013, 063, 209, 224, 229, 255

GAUCHE THE CELLIST...070, 131

GEDO SENKI (JP) see TALES FROM EARTHSEA

GEGEGE NO KITARO (JP)...126, 215, 256

GENIUS BAKABON see BAKABON

GENIUS PARTY...008

GENIUS PARTY BEYOND...008, 112

GENMU SENKO LEDA (JP)...257

GENSHI SHONEN RYU (JP) see RYU THE CAVE BOY

GETSUMEN TO HEIKI MIINA (JP) see LUNAR RABBIT WEAPON MIINA

GETTA ROBOT (JP)...051, 065

GETTER ROBO see GETTA ROBOT

GHOST IN THE SHELL...071, 092, 101, 123, 139, 216

GIANT ROBO...013

GIGANTOR see TETSUJIN 28-GO

GINGA TETSUDO 999 (JP) see GALAXY EXPRESS 999

GIRL WHO LEAPT THROUGH TIME, THE...090, 111

GLASS MASK see GLASS NO KAMEN

GLASS NO KAMEN (JP)...125, 221

GOAL FH see GOAL FIELD HUNTER

GOAL FIELD HUNTER...245

GOLDORAK (FR) see UFO ROBOT GRENDIZER RAIDS

GOLEADORES (SP) see GOAL FIELD HUNTER

GOLGO 13...048, 051, 221

GOSHOGUN...257

GOSHU LE VIOLLONCELLISTE (FR) see GAUCHE THE CELLIST

GOTRINITON (IT) see GOSHOGUN

GRANDE AVVENTURA DEL PRINCIPE VALIANT, LA (IT) see LITTLE NORSE PRINCE

GRANDE SOGNO DE MAYA, IL (IT) see GLASS NO KAMEN

GRANDES AVENTURAS DE LA CASA TONDERA, LAS (SP) see ADVENTURES AT TONDERA HOUSE

GRAVE OF THE FIREFLIES...066, 133, 144, 211, 227

GREAT DETECTIVE CONAN see CASE CLOSED

GREAT DETECTIVE HOLMES see SHERLOCK HOUND

GRENDIZER see UFO ROBOT GRENDIZER RAIDS

GTO: GREAT TEACHER ONIZUKA...072

GUERRA ENTRE PLANETAS (SP) see GATCHAMAN

GUERRERO SAMURAI, EL (SP) see RURONI KENSHIN

GUNBUSTER...016, 056, 251

GUNDAM...019, 020, 073, 093, 127, 217, 222, 226, 237, 250, 253

GUNNM (JP) see BATTLE ANGEL

GURREN LAGAN...060, 130

GUZURA THE AMICABLE MONSTER...209

HACOU L'ABEILLE (FR) see HUTCH THE HONEYBEE

HADASHI NO GEN (JP) see BAREFOOT GEN

HAIBANE RENMEI (JP)...199

HAKUCHO NO MIZUUMI (JP)...074

HAKUJADEN (JP)...074, 207, 212

HAKUJADEN LA LEGENDE DU SERPENT BLANC (FR) see HAKUJADEN

HARBOUR LIGHT MONOGATARI FASHION LALA (JP) see FANCY LALA

HARE TOKIDOKI BUTA (JP)...245

HATTORI THE NINJA see NINJA HATTORI-KUN

HEIDI, GIRL OF THE ALPS...015, 081, 189, 227

HEISEI TANUKI GASSEN POMPOKO (JP) see POM POKO
HELL GIRL...046
HELLO KITTY...128
HELLO SPANK see OHAYO! SPANK
HERMIT VILLAGE see SENNIN BUNRAKU
HI NO TORI 2772 (JP)...027, 082, 232
HIATARI RYOKO (JP)...009, 221
HIDAMARI NO KI (JP) 221
HIMITSU NO AKKO-CHAN (JP) see SECRET AKKO-CHAN
HIS & HER CIRCUMSTANCES...016, 056, 060
HOHOKEKYO TONARI NO YAMADA-KUN (JP) see MY NEIGHBOURS THE YAMADAS
HOKUTO NO KEN (JP)...087
HOMBRE DE ACERO, EL (SP) see TETSUJIN 28-GO
HONNEAMISE NO TSUBASA (JP) see WINGS OF HONNEAMISE
HORUS LE PRINCE DU SOLEIL (FR) see LITTLE NORSE PRINCE
HORUS PRINCE OF THE SUN see LITTLE NORSE PRINCE
HOSHI NO KOE (JP) see VOICES OF A DISTANT STAR
HOTARU NO HAKA (JP) see GRAVE OF THE FIREFLIES
HOUSE OF SMALL CUBES see TSUMIKI NO IE
HOWL'S MOVING CASTLE...066, 090, 091, 223
HOWL NO UGOKU SHIRO (JP) see HOWL'S MOVING CASTLE
HUMANOID MONSTER BEM...026
HURRICANE POLYMAR...255
HUTCH THE HONEYBEE...229

IDEON...093
IE NAKI KO (JP)...199
IKKYU-SAN (JP)...247
IL ETAIT UNE FOIS...GIGI! (FR) see MINKY MOMO
IMBATTIBILE DAITARN 3 (IT) see DAITARN 3
IN PRINCIPIO – STORIE DALLA BIBBIA (IT) see BIBLE STORIES
IN THE BEGINNING: BIBLE STORIES see BIBLE STORIES
INITIAL D...096, 105
INTERSTELLA 5555...097, 106
INU YASHA (JP)...222
IRON-ARM ATOM see ASTRO BOY
IRONMAN NO. 28 see TETSUJIN 28-GO

JACK AND THE WITCH...248
JARINKO CHIE (JP) see CHIE THE BRAT
JEEG, THE STEEL ROBOT...104, 113, 215
JIGOKU SHOJO (JP) see HELL GIRL
JIN-ROH...092, 105, 114
JINZO NINGEN CASSHARN (JP) see CASSHAN: ROBOT HUNTER
JOJO NO KIMIYONA BOKEN (JP) see JOJO'S BIZARRE ADVENTURE
JOJO'S BIZARRE ADVENTURE...107
JOSÉ MIEL (SP) see HUTCH THE HONEYBEE
JOSEFINA THE WHALE...267
JUBEI NINPOCHO (JP) see NINJA SCROLL
JUMPING...231
JUNGLE EMPEROR see KIMBA THE WHITE LION
JUNGLE TAITEI (JP) see KIMBA THE WHITE LION

(K)

KABOCHA WINE, THE (JP) see PUMPKIN WINE
KAGAUKI NINJATAI GATCHAMAN (JP) see GATCHAMAN
KAIBA...062, 256
KAIBUTSU-KUN (JP)...108
KAITEI CHO TOKKYU MARINE EXPRESS (JP)...232
KAMUI NO KEN (JP) see DAGGER OF KAMUI
KANASHIMI NO BELLADONNA (JP) see TRAGEDY OF BELLADONNA
KANOJO TO KANOJO NO NEKO (JP) see SHE AND HER CAT
KAPPA NO COO TO NATSUYASUMI (JP) see SUMMER DAYS WITH COO
KARESHI KANOJO NO JIJO (JP) see HIS & HER CIRCUMSTANCES
KARIGURASHINO ARIETTY (JP) see BORROWER ARRIETY
KATE & JULIE (IT) see DIRTY PAIR
KAZE NO TANI NO NAUSICAA (JP) see NAUSICAÄ OF THE VALLEY OF WINDS
KEI & YURI see DIRTY PAIR
KEMONOZUME...256
KEN IL GUERRIERO (IT) see FIST OF THE NORTH STAR
KEN LE SURVIVANT (FR) see FIST OF THE NORTH STAR
KEN PEPITO, EL NINO LOBO (SP) see KEN THE WOLF BOY
KEN THE WOLF BOY...118
KENSHIN LE VAGABOND (FR) see RURONI KENSHIN

KIDO KEISATSU PATLABOR (JP) see PATLABOR
KIDO SENKAN NADESICO (JP) see MARTIAN SUCCESSOR NADESICO
KIDO SENSHI GUNDAM (JP) see GUNDAM
KIE LA PETITE PESTE (FR) see JARINKO CHIE
KIKI'S DELIVERY SERVICE...066, 119
KIMAGURE ORANGE ROAD...071, 114
KIMBA THE WHITE LION...142, 231, 232, 241, 251, 256
KINDAICHI FILES see YOUNG KINDAICHI'S CASEBOOK
KINDAICHI SHNEN NO JIKENBO (JP) see YOUNG KINDAICHI'S CASEBOOK
KING ARTHUR...114, 120
KING OF GAMES see YU-GI-OH!
KINNUKIMAN: ULTIMATE MUSCLE...215
KISS ME, LICIA (IT) see AI SHITE NIGHT
KNIGHTS OF THE ZODIAC see SAINT SEIYA
KODOMO NO OMOCHA (JP) see CHILD'S TOY
KOKAKOU KIDOTAI (JP) see GHOST IN THE SHELL
KOKYOSHIHEN EUREKA 7 (JP) see EUREKA 7
KONCHU MONOGATARI MISHAGINO HUTCH (JP) see HUTCH THE HONEYBEE
KONCHU MONOGATARI SHIN MINASHIGO HUTCH (JP) see HUTCH THE HONEYBEE
KOSHOKU ICHIDAI OTOKO (JP) see SENSUALIST, THE
KOTETSU JEEG (JP) see JEEG, THE STEEL ROBOT
KUJIRA NO HOSEFINA (JP) see JOSEFINA THE WHALE
KUMO NO MUKOU, YAKUSO NO BASHO (JP) see PLACE PROMISED IN OUR EARLY DAYS, THE
KUMO TO TULIP (JP) see SPIDER AND THE TULIP
KYASHAN IL MITO (IT) see CASSHAN: ROBOT HUNTER
KYOJIN NO HOSHI (JP) see STAR OF THE GIANTS
KYUKETSUKI MIYU (JP) see VAMPIRE PRINCESS MIYU

LA CASA VOLADORA (SP) see ADVENTURES AT TONDERA HOUSE
LA PRINCESA SALLY (SP) see SALLY THE WITCH
LABYRINTH TALES see MANIE MANIE MEIKYU MONOGATARI

LAPUTA – IL CASTELLO NEL CIELO (IT) see CASTLE IN THE SKY
LAURA OU LA PASSION DU THEATRE (FR) see GLASS NO KAMEN
LAYZNER...226
LEDA: FANTASTIC ADVENTURES OF YOHKO see GENMU SENKO LEDA
LEGEND OF KAMUI see NINPU KAMUI GAIDEN
LEGEND OF THE FOREST see MORI NO DENSETSU
LEGEND OF THE OVERFIEND see UROTSUKIDOJI
LEGEND OF THE WHITE SNAKE see HAKUJADEN
LEGGENDA DEL SERPENTE BIANCO, LA (IT) see HAKUJADEN
LEO THE LION see KIMBA THE WHITE LION
LEYENDA DE KIMBA, EL LEON BLANCO, LA (SP) see KIMBA THE WHITE LION
LIME WARS...010
LIMIT THE MIRACLE GIRL...144
LITTILE NINJA FUJIMARU...215, 247
LITTLE MEMOLE...158, 256
LITTLE NEMO...088, 133, 134, 144
LITTLE NORSE PRINCE...089, 134, 188, 227, 235
LITTLE WITCH MEG...018
LITTLE WITCH SALLY see SALLY THE WITCH
LODOSS TO SENKI (JP) see RECORD OF LODOSS WAR
LOVE & POP...016
LOVE CITY see AI CITY
LOVE IN ROCK'N'ROLL see AI SHITE NIGHT
LOVE LETTER...174
LUCILE AMOUR ET ROCK'N'ROLL (FR) see AI SHITE NIGHT
LUNAR RABBIT WEAPON MIINA...242
LUNN FLIES INTO THE WIND see RUN WA KAZE NO NAKA
LUPIN III...048, 056, 097, 120, 145, 188, 213, 215, 234

MACH GO GO GO...146, 209, 229, 255
MACRON ONE see GOSHOGUN
MACROSS...017, 075, 097, 100, 116, 147, 151, 198
MACROSS PLUS...017, 036
MAGIC BOY see SHONEN SARUTOBI SASUKE
MAGIC KNIGHT RAYEARTH...035
MAGICAL ANGEL CREAMY MAMI see CREAMY MAMI
MAGICAL EMI...038
MAGICAL PRINCESS MINKY MOMO see MINKY MOMO

MAGICAL SHOPPING ARCADE ABENOBASHI...010, 251
MAHO NO PRINCESS MINKY MOMO (JP) see MINKY MOMO
MAHO NO STAGE FANCY LALA (JP) see FANCY LALA
MAHO NO STAR MAGICAL EMI (JP) see MAGICAL EMI
MAHO NO TENSHI CREAMY MAMI (JP) see CREAMY MAMI
MAHOROMATIC...251
MAHOTSUKAI SALLY THE WITCH see SALLY THE WITCH
MAISON IKKOKU...046, 101, 151, 225
MAJO NO TAKKYUBIN (JP) see KIKI'S DELIVERY SERVICE
MAJOKKO MEG-CHAN (JP) see MEG THE LITTLE WITCH
MALICIEUSE KIKI (FR) see ESPER MAMI
MANIE MANIE...151
MANIE MANIE MEIKYU MONOGATARI (JP) see MANIE MANIE
MARIA NOS MIRA (SP) see MARIA WATCHES OVER US
MARIA WATCHES OVER US ...046
MARIA-SAMA GA MITERU (JP) see MARIA WATCHES OVER US
MARINE EXPRESS see KAITEI CHO TOKKYU MARINE EXPRESS
MARTIAN SUCCESSOR NADESICO...030
MARTINA E IL CAMPANELLO MISTERIOSO (IT) see ESPER MAMI
MARVELLOUS MELMO see FUSHIGINA MELMO
MAYA THE BEE...155, 255
MAZINGER Z...039, 051, 104, 114, 156, 161, 212, 215, 235
MEG LA SORCIERE (FR) see MEG THE LITTLE WITCH
MEG THE LITTLE WITCH...018
MEGALOPOLIS (IT) see TEITO MONOGATARI
MEGAZONE 23...019, 248
MEITANTEI CONAN (JP) see CASE CLOSED
MEITANTEI HOLMES (JP) see SHERLOCK HOUND
MEMOLE AND HER POINTED HAT see LITTLE MEMOLE
MEMORIES...008, 132, 159
METROPOLIS...131, 134, 233, 268
MIGHTY ATOM see ASTRO BOY
MILLENIUM ACTRESS...132
MIMI O SUMASEBA (JP) see WHISPER OF THE HEART
MIND GAME...008, 130, 161
MINIFEE (FR) see SALLY THE WITCH
MINKY MOMO...257
MIRACLE SHOJO LIMIT-CHAN (JP) see LIMIT THE MIRACLE GIRL
MIRAI KEISATSU URASHIMAN (JP) see URASHIMAN
MIRAI SHONEN CONAN (JP) see FUTURE BOY CONAN
MISTERIO DE LA PIEDRA AZUL, EL (SP) see SECRET OF BLUE WATER
MISTERO DELLA PIETRA AZZURRA, IL (IT) see SECRET OF BLUE WATER

MITSUBACHI MAYA NO BOKEN (JP) see MAYA THE BEE
MITSUME GA TORU (JP)...232
MIYUKI...009
MOBILE POLICE PATLABOR see PATLABOR
MOBILE SUIT GUNDAM see GUNDAM
MOMOTARO UMI NO SHINPEI (JP) see MOMOTARO'S DIVINE SEA WARRIORS
MOMOTARO'S DIVINE SEA WARRIORS...165
MONCOLLE KNIGHTS...010, 046
MONONOKE HIME (JP) see PRINCESS MONONOKE
MOOMINS...234
MORI NO DENSETSU...116, 231
MORIYAMA YUJI...168
MOSO DAIRININ (JP) see PARANOIA AGENT
MOUSE...010
MUNDO MAGICO DE GIGI, EL (SP) see MINKY MOMO
MUNTO...140
MURASAKI SHIKIBU GENJI MONOGATARI (JP) see TALE OF GENJI
MUSCLEMAN see KINNIKUMAN
MUSHISHI...067, 097
MUTEKI CHOJIN ZAMBOT 3 (JP) see ZAMBOT 3
MUTEKI KOJIN DAITARN 3 (JP) see DAITARN 3
MY NAME IS TEPPEI...256
MY NEIGHBOUR TOTORO...066, 085, 189, 239
MY NEIGHBOURS THE YAMADAS...066, 227, 249
MY PATRAASCHE see DOG OF FLANDERS

NADIA ET LE SECRET DE L'EAU BLEUE (FR) see SECRET OF BLUE WATER
NANA...174
NARUTO...175
NAUSICAÄ OF THE VALLEY OF WINDS...066, 085, 134, 176, 227
NAVE ESPACIAL (SP) see YAMATO
NEKO NO ONEGAESHI (JP) see THE CAT RETURNS
NEKOJIRO-SOU (JP) see CAT SOUP
NEON GENESIS EVANGELION see EVANGELION
SHINSEIKI EVANGELION (JP) see EVANGELION
NERIMA DAIKON BROTHERS...245
NICKY LARSON (FR) see CITY HUNTER
NIGHT FOR LOVE see AI SHITE NIGHT
NIGHT SHIFT NURSES...084
NINE...009, 221
NINJA BUGEICHO (JP)...024
NINJA HATTORI-KUN (JP)...094, 209

NINJA SCROLL...107
NINJA THE WONDERBOY see LITTLE NINJA FUJIMARU
NINPU KAMUI GAIDEN (JP)...215
NO NEED FOR TENCHI see TENCHI MUYO!
NOBODY'S BOY see IE NAKI KO
NOLAN (FR) see RYU THE CAVE BOY
NORAKURO-KUN (JP)...009

OBAKE NO QTARO (JP) see QTARO THE GHOST
OCCHI DI GATTO (IT) see CAT'S EYE
ODIN KOSHI HANSEN STARLIGHT (JP) see ODIN PHOTON SPACE SAILOR STARLIGHT
ODIN PHOTON SPACE SAILOR STARLIGHT...215, 251
OEUF DE L'ANGE, L' (FR) see ANGEL'S EGG
OH! MI DIOSA (SP) see OH MY GODDESS!
OH MY GODDESS!...025, 059
OHAYO! SPANK...218
OJOS DE GATO (SP) see CAT'S EYE
OMAKI SHONEN KEN (JP) see KEN THE WOLF BOY
OLIVE ET TOM, CHAMPIONS DE FOOT (FR) see CAPTAIN TSUBASA
OMOIDE POROPORO (JP) see ONLY YESTERDAY
ON YOUR MARK...223
ONBORO FILM (JP)...232
ONE PIECE...049, 090, 145, 235
ONE THOUSAND AND ONE NIGHTS...024
ONLY YESTERDAY...066, 181, 227
ORA GUZURA DA DO (JP) see GUZURA THE AMICABLE MONSTER
ORE WA TEPPEI (JP) see MY NAME IS TEPPEI
ORION...216
ORITSU UCHUGUN HONNEAMISE NO TSUBASA (JP) see WINGS OF HONNEAMISE
ORPHAN BROTHERS, THE see ANJU TO ZUSHIO-MARU
OTAKU NO VIDEO (JP)...060, 186

PANDA AND THE MAGIC SERPENT see HAKUJADEN
PANDA KOPANDA (JP)...133, 134, 189, 234
PAPRIKA...084, 132, 190
PARANOIA AGENT...084, 132, 204
PATLABOR...046, 092, 101, 102, 132, 123, 191
PAUL LE PECHEUR (FR) see SANPEI THE FISHERMAN

PAUL NO MIRACLE DAISAKUSEN (JP) see PAUL'S MIRACLE WAR
PAUL'S MIRACLE WAR...209
PEACH-HIME KYUUSHUTSU DAISAKUSEN (JP) see SUPER MARIO BROTHERS: GREAT MISSION TO RESCUE PRINCESS PEACH
PERFECT BLUE...122, 132, 169
PERRO DE FLANDES, EL (SP) see DOG OF FLANDERS
PESCA A LA TUA CARTA SAKURA (IT) see CARD CAPTOR SAKURA
PHOENIX 2772 see HI NO TORI 2772
PICCOLA MAGA MEG, LA (IT) see MEG THE LITTLE WITCH
PINMEN...193
PIRATA ESPACIAL CAPITAN HARLOCK, EL (SP) see CAPTAIN HARLOCK
PLACE PROMISED IN OUR EARLY DAYS, THE...214
PLANET ROBOT DANGUARD ACE see DANGUARD ACE
POKÉMON...194
POLI ROCKERO (SP) see URASHIMAN
POM POKO...066, 134, 195, 227
PONYO...066, 085, 196, 223
PORCO ROSSO...066, 197
PRINCESS ARMY...010
PRINCESS KNIGHT...079, 095, 200, 241
PRINCESS MINERVA...217
PRINCESS MONONOKE...066, 085, 134, 207
PRINCESS NINE...013
PRINCIPE DE LA ESPADA DEL SOL, EL (SP) see LITTLE NORSE PRINCE
PRISONER, THE...054
PRO GOLFER SARU...213
PROFESSIONAL, THE see GOLGO 13
PUMPKIN WINE, THE...025, 247
PUNI PUNI POEMI...245
PUSS'N'BOOTS...192, 235, 247

QTARO THE GHOST...234
QUEEN MILLENIA...058, 252
QUEEN OF A THOUSAND YEARS see QUEEN MILLENIA

RACCONTI DI TERRAMARE (IT) see TALES FROM EARTHSEA
RAHXEPHON...028
RAIDEEN...253

RANMA 1/2...046, 115, 208, 224, 225
RASCAL THE RACCOON...094, 199
RAVE MASTER...046
RECORD OF LODOSS WAR...061, 102
REDLINE...098
REY ARTURO, EL (SP) see KING ARTHUR
RED PHOTON ZILLION see ZILLION
REGRESO DEL GATO, EL (SP) see CAT RETURNS, THE
REMI EL NINO SIN HOGAR (SP) see IE NAKI KO
REMI LE SUE AVVENTURE (IT) see IE NAKI KO
REMI SANS FAMILLE (FR) see IE NAKI KO
RETOUR DE LÉO, LE (FR) see KIMBA THE WHITE LION
REVOLUTIONARY GIRL UTENA...095, 230
RIBBON NO KISHI (JP)...200 see also PRINCESS KNIGHT
RINGU...012
ROBBY THE RASCAL see CYBOT ROBOTCHI
ROBOCITO (SP) see CYBOT ROBOTCHI
ROBOTTINO (IT) see CYBOT ROBOTCHI
ROBOT CARNIVAL...125, 127
ROBOT PLANETARIO DANGUARD ACE (IT) see DANGUARD ACE
ROKUMON NO MONCOLLE KNIGHT (JP) see MONCOLLE KNIGHTS
ROSE OF VERSAILLES...048, 065, 094, 095, 103, 208, 234, 237
ROUGH...009
ROUJIN Z...123, 125, 203
ROYAL SPACE FORCE: WINGS OF HONNEAMISE see WINGS OF HONNEAMISE
ROYAUME DES CHATS, LE (FR) see CAT RETURNS, THE
RUN WA KAZE NO NAKA...232
RURONI KENSHIN...061, 083
RYO, UN RAGAZZO CONTRO UN IMPERIO (IT) see URASHIMAN
RYU IL RAGAZZO DELL CAVERNE (IT) see RYU THE CAVE BOY
RYU THE CAVE BOY...099, 203

SABER MARIONETTE J...010
SAILOR MOON...039, 095, 204, 219, 228, 230, 235, 242
SAINT SEIYA...082, 205, 235
SAIYUKI...206
SAKURA TAISEN (JP) see SAKURA WARS
SAKURA WARS...010, 020
SAKURA, CAZADORA DE CARTAS (SP) see CARD CAPTOR SAKURA

SAKURA, CHASSEUSE DES CARTES (FR) see CARD CAPTOR SAKURA
SALLY LA MAGA (IT) see SALLY THE WITCH
SALLY THE WITCH...207, 235, 256
SAMURAI CHAMPLOO...169, 246
SANPEI THE FISHERMAN...208
SAZAE-SAN...053, 210, 256
SCIENCE NINJA TEAM GATCHAMAN see GATCHAMAN
SECRET AKKO-CHAN...038
SECRET OF BLUE WATER, THE...016, 171, 251
SEITOSHI SEIYA (JP) see SAINT SEIYA
SEN TO CHIHIRO GA KAMIKAKUSHI (JP) see SPIRITED AWAY
SENGOKU MAJIN GOSHOGUN (JP) see GOSHOGUN
SENNEN JO-O (JP) see QUEEN MILLENIA
SENNIN BUNRAKU (JP)...053
SENSUALIST, THE...251
SENYA ICHIYA MONOGATARI...024, 036, 221, 251
SERIAL EXPERIMENTS LAIN...140
SERO HIKO NO GOSHU (JP) see GAUCHE THE CELLIST
SETON DOBUTSUKI (JP) see SETON'S ANIMAL TALES
SETON'S ANIMAL TALES...138, 215
SHE AND HER CAT...214
SHERLOCK HOUND...075, 080, 088
SHIKI-JITSU (JP)...016
SHINSEIKI EVANGELION (JP) see EVANGELION
SHOJO KAKUMEI UTENA (JP) see REVOLUTIONARY GIRL UTENA
SHONEN JACK TO MAHOTSUKAI (JP) see JACK AND THE WITCH
SHONEN NINJA KAZE NO FUJIMARU (JP) see LITTLE NINJA FUJIMARU
SHONEN SARUTOBI SASUKE (JP)...215
SIGNÉ CAT'S EYE (FR) see CAT'S EYE
SILENT MÖBIUS...120, 228
SILENT SERVICE, THE...109
SIN: THE MOVIE...013
SINDBAD NO BOKEN (JP)...216
SINDBAD THE SAILOR see SINDBAD NO BOKEN
SKY CRAWLERS, THE...092, 110
SINDBAD IL MARINAIO (IT) see SINDBAD NO BOKEN
SINBAD LE MARIN (FR) see SINDBAD NO BOKEN
SOKIHEI VOTOMS (JP) see VOTOMS
SOL BIANCA...012
SONIC UNLEASHED...019
SORCEROR HUNTERS...010, 115
SORE IKE! ANPANMAN (JP) see ANPANMAN
SOUL EATER...028
SPACE ACE see UCHU ACE
SPACE ADVENTURE COBRA...036, 048, 075

SPACE BATTLESHIP YAMATO see YAMATO
SPACE BETWEEN, THE see AI NO KUSABI
SPACE FIREBIRD see HI NO TORI 2772
SPACE PIRATE CAPTAIN HARLOCK see CAPTAIN HARLOCK
SPACE ROBOT (IT) see GETTA ROBOT
SPACE RUNAWAY IDEON see IDEON
SPADA DEI KAMUI, LA (IT) see DAGGER OF KAMUI
SPEED RACER see MACH GO GO GO
SPIDER AND THE TULIP, THE...153
SPIRITED AWAY...031, 085
SPIRITO NEL GUSCIO, LO (IT) see GHOST IN THE SHELL
SPOOKY KITARO see GEGEGE NO KITARO
STAR BLAZERS see YAMATO
STAR OF THE GIANTS...090, 133, 234
STARVENGERS see GETTA ROBOT
STEAMBOY...220
STORIES FROM A STREET CORNER...251
STRANGER MUKOH HADEN (JP) see SWORD OF THE STRANGER
STRATOS 4...013
STREET FIGHTER II: THE ANIMATED MOVIE...033, 221
SUMMER DAYS WITH COO...069, 076, 213
SUMMER WARS...090
SUN FANG DOUGRAM see DOUGRAM
SUPER AGENTE COBRA (SP) see SPACE ADVENTURE COBRA
SUPER ATRAGON...013
SUPER DURAND (FR) see URASHIMAN
SUPER ELECTROMAGNETIC ROBOT COMBATTLER V see COMBATTLER V
SUPER MARIO BROTHERS: GREAT MISSION TO RESCUE PRINCESS PEACH...079, 152
SUPERBOOK: VIDEO BIBLE...026
SWAN LAKE see HAKUHO NO MIZUUMI
SWORD OF THE STRANGER...028

TAIHO SHICHAUZO (JP) see YOU'RE UNDER ARREST!
TAIYO NO KIBA DOUGRAM (JP) see DOUGRAM
TAIYO NO KO HOLS (JP) see LITTLE NORSE PRINCE
TALE OF GENJI...065, 072,
TALES FROM EARTHSEA...021, 066
TARO THE DRAGON BOY see TATSUNOKO TARO

TATSUNOKO TARO...235
TEITO MONOGATARI...230
TEKKAMAN THE SPACE KNIGHT see UCHU NO KISHI TEKKAMAN
TEKKONKINKREET...008, 137
TENCHI MUYO! (JP)...153, 245
TENGEN TOPPA GURREN LAGAN (JP) see GURREN LAGAN
TENKU NO ESCAFLOWNE (JP) see ESCAFLOWNE
TENKU NO SHIRO LAPUTA (JP) see CASTLE IN THE SKY
TENSAI BAKABON (JP) see BAKABON
TENSHI NO TAMAGO (JP) see ANGEL'S EGG
TETSUJIN 28-GO...053, 217, 231, 251, 255
TETSUWAN ATOM (JP) see ASTRO BOY
TEZUKA OSAMU NO KYUYAKU SEISHU MONOGATARI (JP) see BIBLE STORIES
THREE-EYED ONE see MITSUME GA TORU
TIGER MASK...044, 047, 110, 120, 131
TIME BOKAN...013, 042, 234, 254
TIME FIGHTERS see TIME BOKAN
TIME KYOSHITSU TONDERA HOUSE NO DAIBOKEN (JP) see ADVENTURES AT TONDERA HOUSE
TOBOR THE EIGHTH MAN see 8 MAN
TOKO O KAKERU SHOJO (JP) see GIRL WHO LEAPT THROUGH TIME
TOKYO GODFATHERS...132, 236
TOKYO PIG see HARE TOKIDOKI BUTA
TOMORROW'S JOE see ASHITA NO JOE
TOMORROW'S NADJA see ASHITA NO NADJA
TONARI NO TOTORO (JP) see MY NEIGHBOUR TOTORO
TONGARIBOSHI MEMORU (JP) see LITTLE MEMOLE
TOP O NERAE! GUNBUSTER (JP) see GUNBUSTER
TOPO GIGIO...238
TOUCH...009, 072, 221, 243
TRAGEDY OF BELLADONNA...024, 221, 251
TRANZOR Z see MAZINGER Z
TREE IN THE SUN see HIDAMARI NO KI
TREN DEL ESPACIO, EL (SP) see GALAXY EXPRESS 999
TREN GALACTICO (SP) see GALAXY EXPRESS 999
TRIGUN...245
TSUBASA: RESERVOIR CHRONICLE (JP) see TSUBASA CHRONICLE
TSUBASA CHRONICLE...035
TSUMIKI NO IE (JP)...242
TSURIKICHI SANPEI (JP) see SANPEI THE FISHERMAN

UCHU ACE (JP)...209, 229
UCHU KAIZOKU CAPTAIN HARLOCK
   (JP) see CAPTAIN HARLOCK
UCHU NO KISHI TEKKAMAN
   (JP)...104, 255
UCHU SENKAN YAMATO (JP) see
   YAMATO
UFO ROBOT GOLDRAKE (IT) see
   UFO ROBOT GRENDIZER RAIDS
**UFO ROBOT GRENDIZER
   RAIDS**...018, 051, 114, 235, **243**
UNA GIUNGLA DI AVVENTURE PER
   KIMBA (IT) see KIMBA THE WHITE
   LION
URASHIMAN...229
*UROTSUKIDOJI* (JP)...013, **244**
*URUSEI YATSURA* (JP)...012,
   025, 101, 225, 241, 242, **244**
UTSUNOMIKO...058

VIAJE A LA ULTIMA GALAXIA (SP)
   see YAMATO
VAMPIRE...256
VAMPIRE HUNTER D...013, 021,
   245
VAMPIRE PRINCESS MIYU...083,
   115, 164
VERSAILLES NO BARA (JP) see
   ROSE OF VERSAILLES
VEXILLE...030, 217
VIAJES DE SIMBAD, LOS (SP) see
   SINDBAD NO BOKEN
VIDEO GIRL AI...012, 061, 071,
VIERGE MARIE VOUS REGARDE,
   LA (FR) see MARIA WATCHES
   OVER US
VIRGEN MARIA NOS OBSERVA, LA
   (SP) see MARIA WATCHES OVER US
VISION D'ESCAFLOWNE (FR) see
   ESCAFLOWNE
VOICES OF A DISTANT STAR...214
VOIX DES ETOILES, LA (FR) see
   VOICES OF A DISTANT STAR
VOTOMS...032, 226

WAKUSEI ROBO DANGUARD ACE (JP)
   see DANGUARD ACE
WHITE SNAKE LEGEND see
   HAKUJADEN
WHISPER OF THE HEART...133
WINGS OF HONNEAMISE...143, 250
WOLF'S RAIN...019

X...035

YAKIN BYOUTOU (JP) see NIGHT
   SHIFT NURSES
YAMATO...021, 097, 178, 215, 252
YAMATO, LE CUIRASSÉ DE
   L'ESPACE (FR) see YAMATO
YATTAMAN...042, 254
YELLOW SUBMARINE...024
YOKAI NINGEN BEM (JP) see
   HUMANOID MONSTER BEN
YOU'RE UNDER ARREST!...046, 059
YOUNG KINDAICHI'S
   CASEBOOK...120
YU-GI-OH! (JP)...061
YU YU HAKUSHO: GHOST
   FILES...009
YUKI TERAI: SECRETS...230
YUME MIRU TOPO GIGIO (JP) see
   TOPO GIGIO
YUSHA RAIDEEN (JP) see RAIDEEN

ZAMBOT 3...042, 222, 237, 253
ZERO Y LE DRAGON (SP) see
   DRAGON BALL
ZILLION...071, 229

# INDEX OF DIRECTORS AND CREATORS

BOLD TYPE REFERS TO INDIVIDUAL ENTRIES IN THE BOOK.

**4°C (STUDIO)...008**
ANIMATRIX...014
KURO & SHIRO...137
MEMORIES...159
MIND GAME...161
MORIMOTO KOJI...167
NAKAZAWA KAZUTO...173

**ABE NORIYUKI...009**
GTO...072
KUROSAKI ICHIGO...138
**ADACHI MITSURU...009**
GROUP TAC...072
MAEDA MINORU...149
NISHIKUBO MIZUHO...178
SUGII GISABURO...221
UESUGI, TATSUYA & KAZUYA...243
**AKAHORI SATORU...010**
AMANO AI...012
GAINAX...060
GOKU...068
KAWAI KENJI...115
KOYAMA TAKAO...135
**AKIYAMA KATSUHITO...012**
KNIGHT SABERS...128
**AMANO MASAMICHI...013**
HANEDA KENTARO...075
HISAISHI JOE...085
KANNO YOKO...112
KAWAI KENJI...115
KIKUCHI SHUNSUKE...120
SAKAMOTO RYUICHI
**AMANO YOSHITAKA...013**
ASHIDA TOYOO...021
FINAL FANTASY...055
GATCHAMAN...063
TIME BOKAN...234
VAMPIRE HUNTER D...245
YATTAMAN...254
**ANNO HIDEAKI...016**
DAICON II & IV...041
EVANGELION...054
GAINAX...060
IDEON...093
LHADATT, SHIROTSUGU...143
NADIA...171
OTSUKI TOSHIMICHI...189
SPIEGEL, SPIKE...219
YAMAGA HIROYUKI...250
YAMASHITA IKUTO...251
**ARAKI SHINGO...018**
AYUHARA KOZUE...023
CUTEY HONEY...039
DANGUARD ACE...044
HIMENO MICHI...082
JARJAYES, OSCAR FRANÇOIS DE...103

KINDAICHI HAJIME...120
MOTOHASHI HIDEYUKI...168
MUSHI...170
SAINT SEIYA...205
SALLY...207
**ARAMAKI SHINJI...019**
ELRIC, EDWARD...053
GUNDAM...073
KNUTE, DEUNAN...129
SHIROW MASAMUNE...216
SORI FUMIHIKO...217
**ASHIDA TOYOO...021**
HOKUTO NO KEN...087
MUSHI...170
VAMPIRE HUNTER D...245
YAMATO...252
YATTAMAN...254

**BONES (STUDIO)...028**
ELRIC, EDWARD...053
SPIEGEL, SPIKE...219

**CLAMP...035**
DEVILMAN...047
KINOMOTO SAKURA...121
NAGAI GO...172

**DEEN (STUDIO)...046**
HIMURA KENSHIN...083
MAISON IKKOKU...151
OSHII MAMORU...185
SAOTOME RANMA...208
URUSEI YATSURA...244
**DEZAKI OSAMU...048**
BIBLE STORIES...026
BLACK JACK...027
CANDY CANDY...029
COBRA...036
DUKE TOGO...051
GENJI HIKARU...065
JARJAYES, OSCAR FRANÇOIS DE...103
LITTLE NEMO...144
MORIMOTO KOJI...167
MUSHI...170
NISHIKUBO MIZUHO...178
OKA HIROMI...180
REMY...199
RINTARO...201
SUGINO AKIO...221
TEZUKA OSAMU...231
TEZUKA PRODUCTION...232
YABUKI JOE...246

**DYNAMIC PRODUCTION (STUDIO)...051**
CUTEY HONEY...039
DEVILMAN...047
GETTA ROBOT...065
MAZINGER Z...156
NAGAI GO...172
UFO ROBOT GRENDIZER RAIDS...243

**EIKEN (STUDIO)...053**
KYOTO ANIMATION...140
SAZAE-SAN...210

**FUJIKAWA KEISUKE...058**
CUTEY HONEY...039
JEEG, THE STEEL ROBOT...104
KISUGI...124
MAETEL...150
MAZINGER Z...156
UFO ROBOT GRENDIZER RAIDS...243
YAMATO...252
**FUJISHIMA KOSUKE...059**
BELLDANDY...025

**GAINAX (STUDIO)...060**
AKAHORI SATORU...010
ANNO HIDEAKI...016
DAICON III & IV...041
EVANGELION...054
FLCL...056
KNUTE, DEUNAN...129
KOBAYASHI OSAMU...130
LHADATT, SHIROTSUGU...143
MAEDA MAHIRO...149
NADIA...171
OTAKU NO VIDEO...186
YAMAGA HIROYUKI...250
**GALLOP (STUDIO)...061**
HIMURA KENSHIN...083
INITIAL D...096
**GHIBLI (STUDIO)...066**
TALES FROM EARTHSEA...021
CHIHIRO...031
HARU...078
KIKI...119
KONDO YOSHIFUMI...133
LAPUTA...141
MIYAZAKI HAYAO...163
OKAJIMA TAEKO...181
POM POKO...195
PONYO...196
PORCO ROSSO...197
SAN...207
SEITA & SETSUKO...211
SUZUKI TOSHIO...223
TAKAHATA ISAO...227
TOEI...235
TOTORO...238
YAMADAS...249

**GONZO (STUDIO)...069**
CHRISTOPHER, ROSETTE...033
GANTZ...062
TSUKUDA MIINA...242
**GOTO TAKAYUKI...071**
AMANO AI...012
**GROUP TAC (STUDIO)...072**
GENJI HIKARU...065
SUGII GISABURO...221
TSUBASA OZORA...240
UESUGI, TATSUYA & KAZUYA...243

**HANEDA KENTARO...075**
COBRA...036
HOLMES, SHERLOCK...088
MACROSS...147
YAMATO...252
**HARA KEIICHI...076**
DORAEMON...050
NOHARA SHINOSUKE...179
**HATA MASAMI...079**
LITTLE NEMO...144
MARIO...152
**HAYAKAWA KEIJI...080**
**HIMENO MICHI...082**
ARAKI SHINGO...018
JARJAYES, OSCAR FRANÇOIS DE...103
**HIRANO TOSHIHIRO...083**
KAWAI KENJI...115
MIYU...164
YAHAGI SHOGO...248
**HIRASAWA SUSUMU...084**
GUTS...073
PAPRIKA...190
**HISAISHI JOE...085**
CHIHIRO...031
KIKI...119
HOWL'S MOVING CASTLE...091
LAPUTA...141
MIYAZAKI HAYAO...163
NAUSICAÄ...176
OKAJIMA TAEKO...181
POM POKO...195
PONYO...196
PORCO ROSSO...197
SAN...207
TOTORO...238
**HOJO TSUKASA...086**
CITY HUNTER...034
HOKUTO NO KEN...087
KISUGI...124
**HOSODA MAMORU...090**
DIGIMON...049
HOWL'S MOVING CASTLE...091
KANNO MAKOTO...111
LUFFY, MONKEY D....145
MADHOUSE...148
MIYAZAKI HAYAO...163
NAKURA YASUHIRO...173
TOEI...235

**I.G. (STUDIO)...092**
AMANO AI...012

FLCL...056
ITO KAZUNORI...101
JIN-ROH...105
KANNAMI YUICHI...110
KISE KAZUCHIKA...123
KUSANAGI MOTOKO...139
MADHOUSE...148
MASHIMO KOICHI...154
NAKAZAWA KAZUTO...173
NISHIKUBO MIZUHO...178
OKIURA HIROYUKI
OSHII MAMORU...185
SAYA...210

**IKEDA RIYOKO...094**
ARAKI SHINGO...018
CLAMP...035
HIMENO MICHI...082
JARJAYES, OSCAR FRANÇOIS
DE...103
SAOTOME RANMA...208

**IKUHARA KUNIHIKO...095**
BELLADONNA...024
IKEDA RIYOKO...094
JARJAYES, OSCAR FRANÇOIS
DE...103
RIBBON NO KISHI...200
TENJO UTENA...230

**ISHIGURO NOBORU...097**
BEM...026
GINKO...067
MACROSS...147
MIKIMOTO HARUHIKO...160
MORIMOTO KOJI...167
TOPO GIGIO...238
YAHAGI SHOGO...248
YAMAGA HIROYUKI...250
YAMATO...252

**ISHII KATSUHITO...098**
I.G....092
MADHOUSE...148

**ISHINOMORI SHOTARO...099**
CYBORG 009...040
RYU...203

**ITANO ICHIRO...100**
DANGUARD ACE...044
GANTZ...062
GONZO...069
GUNDAM...073
LHADATT, SHIROTSUGU...143
MACROSS...147

**ITO KAZUNORI...101**
.HACK...008
I.G....092
KUSANAGI MOTOKO...139
OSHII MAMORU...185
PATLABOR...191
TAKADA AKEMI...224

**IZUBUCHI YUTAKA...102**
GUNDAM...073
KAWAMORI SHOJI...116
MIKIMOTO HARUHIKO...160
OSHII MAMORU...185

**KAJIWARA IKKI...110**
DATE NAOTO...045
HOSHI HYUMA...090
LUPIN III...145
YABUKI JOE...246

**KANNO YOKO...112**
APPLE, SHARON...017
HANEDA KENTARO...075
KANZAKI HITOMI...113
MACROSS...147
MIND GAME...161
OSHII MAMORU...185
SPIEGEL, SPIKE...219
WATANABE SHINICHIRO...246

**KATSUMATA TOMOHARU...114**
CUTEY HONEY...039
DANGUARD ACE...044
DEVILMAN...047
FUJIKAWA KEISUKE...058
GETTA ROBOT...065
HARLOCK...077
KITARO...126
MATSUMOTO LEIJI
MORIYAMA YUJI...168
MOTOHASHI HIDEYUKI...168
NAGAI GO...172
PERO...192
RYU...203
SHIRATO TAKESHI...215
TOEI...235
UFO ROBOT GRENDIZER RAIDS...243

**KAWAI KENJI...115**
AKAHORI SATORU...010
KANNAMI YUICHI...110
KUSANAGI MOTOKO...139
MIYU...164
OSHII MAMORU...185
PATLABOR...191
SAOTOME RANMA...208

**KAWAJIRI YOSHIAKI...116**
ANIMATRIX...014
CONAN...037
JUBEI...107
MADHOUSE...148
MANIE MANIE...151
MATSUMOTO LEIJI...154
MUSHI...170
OKA HIROMI...180
RINTARO...201
SUGINO AKIO...221
VAMPIRE HUNTER D...245

**KAWAMORI SHOJI...116**
APPLE, SHARON...017
GUNDAM...073
IZUBUCHI YUTAKA...102
KANZAKI HITOMI...113
MACROSS...147
MATSUMOTO LEIJI
MIKIMOTO HARUHIKO...160
YUKI TERAI...230
WATANABE SHINICHIRO...246

**KAWAMOTO KIHACHIRO...117**
KOTABE YOICHI...134
MOCHINAGA TADAHITO...164
OFUJI NOBORU...180

**KIKUCHI MICHITAKA...127**

**KIKUCHI SHUNSUKE...120**
CASSHAN...030
DANGUARD ACE...044
DATE NAOTO...045
DORAEMON...050
FOG, WILLY...057
GETTA ROBOT...065
GOKU...068
HANEDA KENTARO...075
LIMIT-CHAN...144
UFO ROBOT GRENDIZER RAIDS...243

**KISE KAZUCHIKA...123**
EVANGELION...054

I.G....092
KEI & YURI...118
KON SATOSHI...132
KUSANAGI MOTOKO...139
NISHIKUBO MIZUHO...178
OSHII MAMORU...185
TSUBASA OZORA...240

**KITAKUBO HIROYUKI...125**
ITANO ICHIRO...100
NONOMURA AMI...180
OKIURA HIROYUKI...184
OSHII MAMORU...185
OTOMO KATSUHIRO...187
ROUJIN Z...203
SAYA...203

**KITAZUME HIROYUKI...127**
GUNDAM...073
MIKIMOTO HARUHIKO...160
OTOMO KATSUHIRO...187

**KOBAYASHI OSAMU...130**
GAINAX...060
MADHOUSE...148
MAEDA MAHIRO...149

**KOMATSUBARA KAZUO...131**
ARAKI SHINGO...018
DATE NAOTO...045
DEVILMAN...047
GETTA ROBOT...065
GOSHU...070
HARLOCK...077
LIMIT-CHAN...144
NAGAI GO...172
NAUSICAÄ...176
RYU...203

**KON SATOSHI...132**
HIRASAWA SUSUMU...084
KIRIGOE MIMA...122
KISE KAZUCHIKA...123
MADHOUSE...148
MEMORIES...159
MURAI SADAYUKI...169
NOBUMOTO KEIKO...179
OKIURA HIROYUKI...184
OTOMO KATSUHIRO...187
PAPRIKA...190
ROUJIN Z...203
SAGI TSUKIKO...204
TOKYO GODFATHERS...236

**KONDO YOSHIFUMI...133**
ANNE OF GREEN GABLES...015
CHIHIRO...031
CONAN...037
HOLMES, SHERLOCK...088
HOSHI HYUMA...090
KIKI...119
LITTLE NEMO...144
LUPIN III...145
MIYAZAKI HAYAO...163
NIPPON ANIMATION...177
OKAJIMA TAEKO...181
SEITA & SETSUKO...211

**KOSAKA KITARO...134**

**KOTABE YOICHI...134**
HEIDI...081
TOEI...235

**KOYAMA TAKAO...135**

**KURI YOJI...136**
KAWAMOTO KIHACHIRO 117
MOCHINAGA TADAHITO...164
OFUJI NOBORU...180

**KURODA YOSHIO...138**
PATRASHE...192

**KYOTO ANIMATION (STUDIO)...140**

KOSAKA KITARO...134
LAPUTA...141
LITTLE NEMO...144
LUPIN III...145
NADIA...171
NAKAMURA TAKASHI...172
NAKURA YASUHIRO...173
NAUSICAÄ...176
NIPPON ANIMATION...177
OTSUKA YASUO...188
PANDA KOPANDA...189
PERO...192
PONYO...196
PORCO ROSSO...197
SAN...207
SUZUKI TOSHIO...223
TAKAHATA ISAO...227
TOTORO...238
YABUKI KIMIO...247

MOCHINAGA TADAHITO...164
HAKUJADEN...074
KAWAMOTO KIHACHIRO 117
YURI KOJI...136
MASAOKA KENZO...153
MOMOTARO...165
OFUJI NOBURO...180

MOCHIZUKI TOMOMI...165
CREAMY MAMI...038
SAOTOME RANMA...208

MORI YASUJI...166
HAKUJADEN...074
PATRASHE...192
PERO...192
SAIYUKI...206

MORIMOTO KOJI...167
4°C...008
ANIMATRIX...014
MEMORIES...159

MORIYAMA YUJI...168

MOTOHASHI HIDEYUKI...168

MURAI SADAYUKI...169
KIRIGOE MIMA...122
STEAMBOY...220

MUSHI (STUDIO)...170
ASHIDA TOYOO...021
ATOM...022
BIBLE STORIES...026
BLACK JACK...027
CLEOPATRA...036
GROUP TAC...072
LEO...142
MELMO...157
PRINCESS KNIGHT...200
RINTARO...201
SUGINO AKIO...221
SUNRISE...222
TATSUNOKO...229
TEZUKA OSAMU...231
TEZUKA PRODUCTION...232
TOEI...235
YABUKI JOE...246
YASUHIKO YOSHIKAZU...253

NAGAHAMA TADAO...171
DEZAKI OSAMU...048

HOSHI HYUMA...090
JARJAYES, OSCAR FRANÇOIS DE...103
NISHIKUBO MIZUHO...178
OKAZAKI MINORU...183
TOMINO YOSHIYUKI...237

NAGAI GO...172
ANNO HIDEAKI...016
CLAMP...035
CUTEY HONEY...039
DEVILMAN...047
DYNAMIC PRODUCTION...051
FUJISAWA KEISUKE...058
GETTA ROBOT...065
JEEG, THE STEEL ROBOT...104
KATSUMATA TOMOHARU...114
KOMATSUBARA KAZUO...131
MAZINGER Z...156
OKAWARA KUNIO...182
YABUKI KIMIO...247

NAKAMURA TAKASHI...172
AKIRA...011
MORIMOTO KOJI...167

NAKAZAWA KAZUTO...173
MUGEN & JIN...169
NADIA...171

NAKURA YASUHIRO...173

NIPPON ANIMATION...177
ANNE OF GREEN GABLES...015
CONAN...037
KURODA YOSHIO...138
MARUKO-CHAN...152
MAYA THE BEE...155
MORI YASUJI...166
NAKAMURA TAKASHI...172
PANDA KOPANDA...189
PRODUCTION REED...198
SANPEI THE FISHERMAN...208
SHIRATO TAKESHI...215
TOPO GIGIO...238
YABUSHITA TAIJI...248
YUKIMURO SHUNICHI 256

NISHIKUBO MIZUHO...178

NISHIZAKI YOSHINOBU...178
MATSUMOTO LEIJI...154
SHIRATO TAKESHI...215
TOMINO YOSHIYUKI...237

NOBUMOTO KEIKO...179
KOYAMA TAKAO...135
MACROSS...147
SPIEGEL, SPIKE...219
TOKYO GODFATHERS...236
WATANABE SHINICHIRO...246

OFUJI NOBURO...180
KAWAMOTO KIHACHIRO 117
YURI KOJI...136
MASAOKA KENZO...153

OKAWARA KUNIO...182
DAITARN 3...042
GUNDAM...073

OKAZAKI MINORU...183
ARALE...018
GOKU...068

OKIURA HIROYUKI...184
JIN-ROH...105
KUSANAGI MOTOKO...139
NISHIKUBO MIZUHO...178
OSHII MAMORU...185

OSHII MAMORU...185
DALLOS...043
DEEN...046
ITO KAZUNORI...101
IZUBUCHI YUTAKA...102
JIN-ROH...105
KAWAI KENJI...115
KISE KAZUCHIKA...123
KITAZUME HIROYUKI...127
KOSAKA KITARO...134
MORIYAMA YUJI...168
MOTOHASHI HIDEYUKI...168
NAKURA YASUHIRO...173
NISHIKUBO MIZUHO...178
OKIURA HIROYUKI...184
PATLABOR...191
TAKADA AKEMI...224
TSUJI MASAKI...241
URUSEI YATSURA...244

OTOMO KATSUHIRO...187
AKIRA...011
GINKO...067
KISE KAZUCHIKA...123
KITAKUBO HIROYUKI...125
KITAZUME HIROYUKI...127
KON SATOSHI...132
KOSAKA KITARO...134
MANIE MANIE...151
MEMORIES...159
MORIMOTO KOJI...167
MURAI SADAYUKI...169
NAKAMURA TAKASHI...172
NOBUMOTO KEIKO...179
OFUJI NOBURO...180
OKIURA HIROYUKI...184
RINTARO...201
ROUJIN Z...203
STEAMBOY...220
TIMA...233

OTSUKA YASUO...188
CONAN...037
HEIDI...081
HOLS...089
LUPIN III...145
MIYAZAKI HAYAO...163
PANDA KOPANDA...189
SINDBAD...216
TAKAHATA ISAO...227
TOEI...235

OTSUKI TOSHIMICHI...189

PIERROT (STUDIO)...193
ABE NORIYUKI...009
CREAMY MAMI...038
DALLOS...043
GTO: GREAT TEACHER ONIZUKA...072
KASUGA KYOSUKE...114
KUROSAKI ICHIGO...138
MORIYAMA YUJI...168
NARUTO...175
PINMEN...193
PRODUCTION REED...198
TORIYAMA AKIRA...238
URUSEI YATSURA...244

PRODUCTION REED (STUDIO)...198

RINTARO...207
HAKUJADEN...207
HARLOCK...097
JIRO...207
KOSAKA KITARO...134
MAETEL...150
MANIE MANIE...151
MUSHI...170
OTOMO KATSUHIRO...187
SUGINO AKIO...221
TEITO MONOGATARI...230
TIMA...233
ACE O NERAE!...221
GOLGO 13...221
ASHITA NO JOE...221
YAMATO...252

SAKAMOTO RYUICHI
LHADATT, SHIROTSUGU...143

SASAGAWA HIROSHI...209
MACH GO GO GO...146
OKAWARA KUNIO...182
GATCHAMAN...209
CASSHAN...209
TATSUNOKO...229
TIME BOKAN...233
YATTAMAN...254

SERIKAWA YUGO...212
CANDY CANDY...029
CYBORG 009...040
HAYAKAWA KEIJI...080
JEEG, THE STEEL ROBOT...104
KATSUMATA TOMOHARU...114
MORI YASUJI...166
NAGAI GO...172
NAKURA YASUHIRO...173
RYU...203
SALLY...207
HAKUJADEN...212
MAZINGER Z...212
SALLY THE WITCH...212
TOEI...235
YABUKI KIMIO...247

SHIN-EI (STUDIO)...213
DORAEMON...050
KAIBUTSU-KUN...108
SASAGAWA HIROSHI...209
LUPIN III...213
NOHARA SHINOSUKE...213
NINJA HATTORI-KUN...213
PRO GOLFER SARU...213
ESPER MAMI...213
KAPPA NO COO TO NATSUYASUMI...213

SHINKAI MAKOTO...214

SHIRATO SANPEI...215

SHIRATO TAKESHI...215

SHIROW MASAMUNE...216
ARAMAKI SHINJI...019
ITO KAZUNORI...101
KNUTE, DEUNAN...129

SONODA HIDEKI...217

SORI FUMIHIKO...217

SUGII GISABURO...221
BELLADONNA...024

CHUN-LI...033
DORORO...050
GENJI HIKARU...065
GROUP TAC...072
KITAJIMA MAYA...125
OKAZAKI MINORU...183
UESUGI, TATSUYA & KAZUYA...243
TOUCH...243
SUGINO AKIO...221
COBRA...036
DEZAKI OSAMU...048
OKA HIROMI...180
SUGIURA KOJI...053
REMY...199
YABUKI JOE...246
SUNRISE (STUDIO)...222
CHIRICO CUVIE...032
CITY HUNTER...034
DAITARN 3...042
DEEN...046
GUNDAM...073
IDEON...093
KAIEDA SHIRO...109
KEI & YURI...118
KITAZUME HIROYUKI...127
NAGAHAMA TADAO...171
OKAWARA KUNIO...182
SPIEGEL, SPIKE...219
TOMINO YOSHIYUKI...237
SUZUKI TOSHIO...223

TAKADA AKEMI...224
CREAMY MAMI...038
ITO KAZUNORI...101
KASUGA KYOSUKE...114
PATLABOR...191
URUSEI YATSURA...244
TAKAHASHI RUMIKO...225
BELLDANDY...025
DEEN...046
KAWAI KENJI...115
MAISON IKKOKU...151
MORIYAMA YUJI...168
SAOTOME RANMA...208
TSUJI MASAKI...241
URUSEI YATSURA...244
TAKAHASHI RYOSUKE...226
CHIRICO CUVIE...032
GUNDAM...073
KAIEDA SHIRO...109
SUNRISE...222
TAKAHATA ISAO...227
ANNE OF GREEN GABLES...015
CONAN...037
GHIBLI...066
GOSHU...070
HAKUJADEN...074
HEIDI...081
HOLS...089
KOMATSUBARA KAZUO...131
KONDO YOSHIFUMI...133
KOSAKA KITARO...134
LUPIN III...145
MIYAZAKI HAYAO...163
MORI YASUJI...166
NAUSICAÄ...176
NIPPON ANIMATION...177
OKAJIMA TAEKO...181
OTSUKA YASUO...188
PANDA KOPANDA...189

POM POKO...195
RYU...203
SEITA & SETSUKO...211
TOEI...235
YAMADAS...249
TAKEUCHI NAOKO...228
SAILOR MOON...228
SILENT MÖBIUS...228
TATSUNOKO (STUDIO)...229
AMANO AI...012
AMANO YOSHITAKA...013
CASSHAN...030
BIBLE STORIES...026
EIKEN...053
GATCHAMAN...063
KOYAMA TAKAO...135
MACH GO GO GO...146
OKAWARA KUNIO...182
SASAGAWA HIROSHI...209
TAKADA AKEMI...224
TIME BOKAN...234
YATTAMAN...254
TEZUKA OSAMU...231
ADACHI MITSURU...009
ARAKI SHINGO...018
ASHIDA TOYOO...021
ATOM...022
BELLADONNA...024
BIBLE STORIES...026
BLACK JACK...027
CLEOPATRA...036
CUTEY HONEY...039
DEZAKI OSAMU...048
DORORO...050
FUJISAWA KEISUKE...058
GROUP TAC...072
HI NO TORI 2772...082
ISHINOMORI SHOTARO...099
KAWAJIRI YOSHIAKI...116
KAWAMOTO KIHACHIRO 117
KOMATSUBARA KAZUO...131
YURI KOJI...136
LEO...142
MATSUMOTO LEIJI...155
MELMO...157
MUSHI...170
NISHIZAKI YOSHINOBU...178
OFUJI NOBURO...180
OKAZAKI MINORU...183
PRINCESS KNIGHT...200
SAIYUKI...206
SINDBAD...216
SUGII GISABURO...221
TETSUJIN 28-GO...231
TEZUKA PRODUCTION...232
TIMA...233
YASUHIKO YOSHIKAZU...253
TEZUKA PRODUCTION...232
TMS ENTERTAINMENT  234
AYUHARA KOZUE...023
COBRA...036
DORAEMON...050
EDOGAWA CONAN...052
HOLMES, SHERLOCK...088
JARJAYES, OSCAR FRANÇOIS
DE...103
KAIBUTSU-KUN...108
KISUGI RUI, HITOMI & AI
LITTLE NEMO...144
LUPIN III...145
OKA HIROMI...180
PANDA KOPANDA...189
REMY...199
SPANK...218

TOEI ANIMATION (STUDIO) ... 235
CALIMERO...029
CANDY CANDY...029
CUTEY HONEY...039
CYBORG 009...040
DANGUARD ACE...044
DATE NAOTO...045
DEVILMAN...047
DIGIMON...049
EIKEN...053
GETTA ROBOT...065
GOKU...068
HAKUJADEN...074
HARLOCK...077
HOKUTO NO KEN...087
HOLS...089
HOSODA MAMORU...090
INTERSTELLA 5555...097
JEEG, THE STEEL ROBOT...104
KEN THE WOLF BOY...118
KIKUCHI SHUNSUKE...120
KINDAICHI HAJIME...120
KITARO...126
KOMATSUBARA KAZUO...131
LIMIT-CHAN...144
LUFFY, MONKEY D....145
MAZINGER Z...156
MEMOLE...158
MITAMURA YAKKO...162
MORI YASUJI...166
OKAZAKI MINORU...183
OTSUKA YASUO...188
PERO...192
RYU...203
SAILOR MOON...204
SAINT SEIYA...205
SAIYUKI...206
SALLY...207
SASAGAWA HIROSHI...209
SERIKAWA YUGO...212
SINDBAD...216
TAKAHATA ISAO...225
TEZUKA OSAMU...231
TSUBASA OZORA...240
YABUSHITA TAIJI...248
TOMINO YOSHIYUKI...237
ARAMAKI SHINJI...019
DAITARN 3...042
GUNDAM...073
IDEON...093
KITAZUME HIROYUKI...127
NAGAHAMA TADAO...171
OKAWARA KUNIO...182
SUNRISE...222
YAMATO...252
YASUHIKO YOSHIKAZU...253
TORIYAMA AKIRA...238
ARALE...018
GOKU...068
LUFFY, MONKEY D....145
OKAZAKI MINORU...183
DRAGONBALL...238
TSUJI MASAKI...241
TSUJI NAOYUKI...242
KAWAMOTO KIHACHIRO 117

WATANABE SHINICHI...245
WATANABE SHINICHIRO...246
ANIMATRIX...014

APPLE, SHARON...017, 036
MUGEN & JIN...169
NOBUMOTO KEIKO...179
OKAZAKI MINORU...183
OKIURA HIROYUKI...184
SPIEGEL, SPIKE...219
SUNRISE...222

YABUKI KIMIO...247
BELLDANDY...025
HAKUCHO NO MIZUUMI...074
KEN THE WOLF BOY...118
PERO...192
YABUSHITA TAIJI...248
HAKUJADEN...074
MASAOKA KENZO...153
MORI YASUJI...166
OTSUKA YASUO...188
RINTARO...201
SAIYUKI...206
SERIKAWA YUGO...212
SINDBAD...216
YAMAGA HIROYUKI...250
ANNO HIDEAKI...016
DAICON III & IV...041
GAINAX...060
LHADATT, SHIROTSUGU...143
MORIYAMA YUJI...168
SAKAMOTO RYUICHI...206
TSUKUDA MIINA...242
YAMAMOTO EIICHI...251
BELLADONNA...024
CLEOPATRA...036
LEO...142
SUGINO AKIO...221
TEZUKA OSAMU...231
TSUJI MASAKI...241
YUKIMURO SHUNICHI 256
YAMASHITA IKUTO...251
MAISON IKKOKU...151
MORIYAMA YUJI...168
YASUHIKO YOSHIKAZU...253
GUNDAM...073
KITAZUME HIROYUKI...127
SUNRISE...222
YOKOYAMA MITSUTERU...255
CREAMY MAMI...038
MOTOHASHI HIDEYUKI...168
YOSHIDA TATSUO...255
MACH GO GO GO...146
SASAGAWA HIROSHI...209
TATSUNOKO...229
TIME BOKAN...234
YUASA MASAAKI...256
CAT SOUP...030
MIND GAME...161
NOHARA SHINOSUKE...179
YUKIMURO SHUNICHI...256
CANDY CANDY...029
LIMIT-CHAN...144
MEMOLE...158
YUYAMA KUNIHIKO...257
PRODUCTION REED...198
MEMOLE...158

# INDEX OF CHARACTERS

**BOLD** TYPE REFERS TO INDIVIDUAL ENTRIES IN THE BOOK. CHARACTER NAMES ARE INDEXED BY FAMILY/ LAST NAME WHERE ONE EXISTS, IE CLOUD STRIFE IS LISTED AS STRIFE, CLOUD.

## A

ACTARUS...243
AGAWA NANAMI...105, 185
AICHAN...254
AKAGI, DR. RITSUKO...054, 189
AKANE...018
**AKIRA...011**
AKIZUKI YOJIRO...226
ALADDIN...170, 221
ALITA see GALLY
**AMANO AI...012**, 071
AMANOJYAKU...244
AMEMIYA KEI...105
ANN see SHIRLEY, ANNE
**ANNE OF GREEN GABLES...015**, 094, 177
ANTONIUS...079, 251
**APPLE, SHARON...017**, 230
**ARALE...018**
**ARREN...021**
ARTHUR, KING...114
ASAKURA JOE...063, 135, 209
ASHITAKA...207
ASHURA, BARON...156
ASTRO BOY see ATOM
ASTRO GIRL...022
**ATOM...022**, 039, 232
AYANAMI REI...054, 189, 251
**AYUHARA KOZUE...023**
AYUKAWA MADOKA...114
AZNABLE, CHAR...127
AZUMA TETSUYA see CASSHAN

BAI-NIANG...074
BAN SHUNSAKU...232
BARON (CAT)...066, 078
BARONE (DOG)...218
BATOU...101, 123, 139, 185
BEEHIVE (BAND)...162
**BELLADONNA...024**, 221, 251
**BELLDANDY...025**, 059
**BEM...026**
BENTEN see YANAGAWA MERRILL
BERA...026
BERO...026
BERYL, QUEEN...228
BETTY BOOP...022
BIDAN, CAMILLE...127

**BLACK JACK...027**, 232
BLACK, JET...112, 219, 246
BLACKSTONE, SHO...097
BOW, FRAU...253
BOWMAN, GULD...017
BOYAKKI...254
BRANDO, DIO...107
BRIAREOS see HECATONCHIRES, BRIAREOS

## C

**CALIMERO...029**
CANDY CANDY see WHITE, CANDICE
CANTI...056
CAPTAIN HARLOCK see HARLOCK
CAPTAIN KAIEDA see KAIEDA, SHIRO
CARD CAPTOR SAKURA see KINOMOTO SAKURA
**CASSHAN...030**, 229
CAT'S EYE see KISUGI
CERBERUS see KERO-CHAN
CHERRY (SABER MARIONETTE)...010
CHIBA MAMORU...095, 204
CHIBA, DR. ATSUKO...190
CHIGUSA TSUKIKAGE...125
**CHIHIRO...031**, 163
**CHIRICO CUVIE...032**
**CHRISTOPHER, ROSETTE...033**
CHRONO...033
**CHUN-LI...033**
CITY HUNTER...034, 086
**CLEOPATRA...036**, 058, 079, 170, 251
COB...021
COBALT see JETTO
**COBRA...036**, 075
COCO (PARROT)...142, 241
**CONAN...037**, 89, 177
COO...076
COSMO YUKI...093
CRAYON SHIN-CHAN see NOHARA SHINNOSUKE
**CREAMY MAMI...038**
CRESCENDOLLS (BAND)...097
CROSSWORD...027
CURTIS, DONALD...163, 197
**CUTEY HONEY...039**, 058
CUTHBERT, MATTHEW & MARILLA...015
CYBERNELLA see LIMIT-CHAN
**CYBORG 009...040**, 099, 235
CYBOT ROBOTCHI...217

DAICON GIRL...041
DAISUKE JIGEN...145, 213

**DAITARN 3** (ROBOT)...042
**DALLOS...049**
DAMON, MARCUS see DIGIMON
DAN, CAPTAIN...044, 120
**DANGUARD ACE** (ROBOT)...**044**, 114, 120
DATE KYOKO...230
**DATE NAOTO...045**, 110
DAVID (BLOOD: THE LAST VAMPIRE)...210
DEEDLIT...102
DETECTIVE CONAN see EDOGAWA CONAN
**DEVILMAN...047**, 051
DIO see BRANDO, DIO
**DIGIMON...049**
DIRTY PAIR see KEI & YURI
DOI SHIZUHA...013
DOKROBEI, DR....254
DON (RYU THE CAVE BOY)...203
**DORAEMON...050**, 076, 213
DORNKIRK, EMPEROR...113
DORONYO, MISS...254
**DORORO...050**
DRACULA...108
**DUKE TOGO...051**
DURALUMIN, DUKE...200
DYSON, ISAMU...017, 147

EBOSHI...207
ED...112, 219, 246
**EDOGAWA CONAN...052**
EIN (DOG)...219
ELRIC, ALPHONSE...028, 053
**ELRIC, EDWARD...053**, 028
ENDO LORNA...059
ENDYMION, PRINCE see CHIBA MAMORU
**EVANGELION** (ROBOT)...**054**, 016, 189

FANEL, FOLKEN...113
FANEL, VAN...112, 113, 116
FERSEN, AXEL VON...094, 103
FIANA...032
FIREBIRD see HI NO TORI
FLOWER, JANE...036
**FOG, WILLY...057**
FOKKER, ROY...147
FRANKEN...108
FRIENDER (ROBOT DOG)...030, 229
FUDO AKIRA...047, 051
FUJIEDA, YOSHINO 'YOSHI' see DIGIMON
FUJIMOTO...196
FUJITSUBO, LADY...065
FUJIWARA TAKUMI...096
FULLMETAL ALCHEMIST see ELRIC, EDWARD
FUSE KAZUKI...092, 105, 184, 185

GABIMARU RIKIYA...148
GABRIEL (BASSET HOUND)...123
**GALLY...061**
GANCHAN...254
**GANTZ...062**
**GATCHAMAN...013**, **063**, 135, 209, 229
GATTLER, GENERAL...198
GAUCHE see GOSHU
GAZULA see GUZURA
**GEN...064**, 148
**GENJI HIKARU...065**
**GETTA ROBO** (ROBOT)...**065**
**GETTER ROBOT** see GETTA ROBO
GIGANTOR see TETSUJIN 28-GO
GILMORE, DR. ISAAC...040, 099
GIN...236
**GINKO...067**
GIULIANO...029
GOGOL see GABIMARU RIKIYA
GOHAN...183, 238
**GOKU...068**, 238
GOLD LIGHTAN (ROBOT)...172
**GOSHU...070**
GOTENKS...183
GOTO KIICHI...191
GRANDIER, ANDRÉ...018, 103
GRANMAMARE...196
GRENDIZER (ROBOT)...243
GRIFFITH...073
GRUNWALD...089, 188
**GTO: GREAT TEACHER ONIZUKA...072**
**GUNDAM** (ROBOT)...019, **073**, 127, 160, 182, 222, 237
GURREN LAGANN (ROBOT)...060, 130
**GUTS...073**
GUZURA...209

## H

HANA...236
HARAN BANJO...042
**HARLOCK...077**, 154, 201
HARO (ROBOT)...253
**HARU...078**
HARUHARA HARUKA...056
HARUKO (ROUJIN Z)...203
HARUNO SAKURA...175
HATAKE KAKASHI...175
HATTER, SOPHIE...091, 163, 223
HAYAKAWA MIDORI...023
HAYAMI TETSUO...149
HAYASE MISA...147
HECATONCHIRES, BRIAREOS...019, 129, 216
HEEN...091, 163
**HEIDI...081**
HEINRICH, ALBERT AKA CYBORG...004 040, 099
HELL, DR....114, 156, 172
HELLO KITTY see KITTY
**HI NO TORI...082**

HIDAKA YUMEMI... 140
HILDA... 089, 227
HIMIKA, QUEEN... 104, 212
**HIMURA KENSHIN...** *083*
HIRAI YAMUMASA... 230
**HIRASAKA RYUJI...** *084*
HIROSHI... 108
HIYAMA HIKARU... 114
**HOKUTO NO KEN...** *087*
HOLMES, SHERLOCK... 052, **088**, 075, 080
**HOLS...** *089*, 188, 227
HONJO MIKASE... 013
HORUS see HOLS
**HOSHI HYUMA...** *090*
HOSHINO TETSURO... 131, 150, 154, 201
HOUND, SHERLOCK see HOLMES, SHERLOCK
**HOWL...** *091*, 163
HUDSON, MRS... 088
HYAKKIMARU... 050, 183
HYOGA, CYGNUS... 082, 205

ICHIJO HIKARU... 147
ICHIMONJI TAKUMA... 044, 120
**IDEON** (ROBOT)... *093*
IKARI GENDO... 054, 189
IKARI SHINJI... 016, 054, 189
IMAMURA SUZUME... 140
IMHOF, KASHA... 093
INGRAM (ROBOT)... 092, 191
INOUE ORIHIME... 138
INU-YASHA... 225
ISHIKAWA GOEMON... 145
ISONO SAZAE see SAZAE-SAN

JAMES RAY STEAM see STEAMBOY
**JARJAYES, OSCAR FRANÇOIS DE...** *103*, 048, 094, 178
JEANNE see BELLADONNA
**JEEG** (ROBOT)... *104*, 215
JETTO... 022
JEWEL PRINCESS... 039
JIJI (CAT)... 119
JIMSY... 037
JIN (SAMURAI CHAMPLOO) see MUGEN & JIN
JINPEI... 063, 209
**JIRO...** *106*
JO (BAKURETSU TENSHI)... 069
JOE (GATCHAMAN) see ASAKURA JOE
JOESTAR, JONATHAN... 107
JOJO see JOESTAR, JONATHAN
JOSE, RYU... 253
**JUBEI...** *107*
JULIA (HOKUTO NO KEN)... 087
JULIANO (CAT)... 162
JUN... 063, 209
JUNKO... 013, 136, 234

KABUTO JUZO... 156
KABUTO KOJI... 156
KADAJ... 055
KAGERO... 107
**KAIBUTSU-KUN...** *108*
**KAIEDA, SHIRO...** *109*
KAMAJI... 031, 163
KAMINA... 060, 130
KANEDA (AKIRA) see KANEDA SHOTARO
KANEDA SHOTARO... 011
**KANNAMI YUICHI...** *110*
**KANNO MAKOTO...** *111*
**KANZAKI HITOMI...** *113*
**KASUGA KYOSUKE...** *114*
KATO GO... 162
KATO HASHIZO... 162
KATO MASARU... 062
KATO YASUNORI... 230
KATSE, BERG... 135
KATSURAGI MISATO... 016, 054, 189
**KEI & YURI...** *118*
KEI (AKIRA)... 187
KEIKO MEIKO... 230
KEN (GATCHAMAN) see WASHIO KEN
**KEN THE WOLF BOY...** *118*
KENICHI... 201
KENSHIN see HIMURA KENSHIN
KENSHIRO see HOKUTO NO KEN
KERO-CHAN... 121
KETCHUM, ASH... 194
**KIKI...** *119*, 163
KIKUHARA KARIN... 013
KILDREN... 110
KIMBA see LEO
**KINDAICHI HAJIME...** *120*
KING (LION)... 171
KINO MAYUMI... 149
**KINOMOTO SAKURA...** *121*, 035
**KIRA...** *122*
**KIRIGOE MIMA...** *122*, 132, 169
KIRINO LISA... 044, 120
KISHIMOTO KEI... 062, 100
**KISUGI (RUI, HITOMI & AI)...** *124*
**KITAJIMA MAYA...** *125*
KITAMI, DR. REIKA... 161
**KITARO...** *126*
**KITTY...** *128*
**KNIGHT SABERS...** *128*
**KNUTE, DEUNAN...** 019, 058, *129*, 216
KOBAYASHI HAYATO... 253
KODAI SUSUMU... 058
**KOMATSU 'HACHI' NANA...** *174*
KOZUKI LUNA... 030
KUBO KEN... 186
KUCHIKI RUKIA... 009, 138
KUDO, SHINICHI AKA JIMMY... 052
KUNISAKI RENA... 008
KUNISAKI SHUGO... 008
**KURO & SHIRO...** *137*
KURONO KEI... 062
KURONYAGO... 180
**KUROSAKI ICHIGO...** *138*, 009
KUSAKABE, MEI... 239
KUSAKABE, PROF.... 239
KUSAKABE, SATSUKI... 239

KUSANAGI MOTOKO... 092, *139*
KUSANAGI SUITO, COMMANDER... 110
**KYOSUKE...** *145*

LA BLUE GIRL see MIDO MIKO
LADY OSCAR see JARJAYES, OSCAR FRANÇOIS DE
**LAIN...** *140*
LAMPEROUGE, LELOUCH... 222
LANA... 037, 080, 177
LANGLEY, ASUKA SORYU... 054, 189
LAPUTA ROBOT... 141
LARVA... 115, 164
LEBANNON... 021
**LEO...** *142*, 231, 232, 241, 256
**LHADATT, SHIROTSUGU...** *143*, 168, 206, 250
LI SYAORAN... 121
LIME (SABER MARIONETTE)... 010
**LIMIT-CHAN...** *144*
**LITTLE NEMO...** *144*
LITTLE NORSE PRINCE see HOLS
LISA (PONYO)... 196
LITTNER, YOKO... 060, 130
LOZ... 055
**LUFFY, MONKEY D....** *145*
LUIGI... 152
LUM... 046, 224, 225, 244
**LUPIN III...** 048, 097, *145*, 213
LUNN... 232
LUPIN, ARSENE see LUPIN III
LYNN MINMAY... 147, 160
LYRE... 142, 256

M-66 (ROBOT)... 125
MCKENZIE, CHRISTINA... 160
**MAETEL...** 131, *150*, 154, 201
MAGICAL EMI... 193
MAIA see MAYA THE BEE
MAKIMURA KAORI... 034, 086
MANDY (MANDRILL/ BABOON)... 142, 241
**MANIE MANIE...** *151*
MARIE ANTOINETTE (DAUPHINE, LATER QUEEN OF FRANCE)... 094, 103
MARIELLE... 158
**MARIO...** *152*
MARK ANTONY (ROMAN GENERAL) see ANTONIUS
MARKL... 091, 163, 223
**MARUKO-CHAN...** *152*
**MASAKI TENCHI...** *153*
MASS, SAYLA... 253
**MAYA THE BEE...** *155*
**MAZINGER Z** (ROBOT)... *156*
MCCOY, DOG... 043
MEG (BAKURETSU TENSHI)... 069
MEG (LITTLE WITCH MEG)... 207

MEGANOIDS... 042
**MELMO...** *157*
**MEMOLE...** *158*
MERLE... 113
**MIDO MIKO...** *160*
MIDORI see HAYAKAWA MIDORI
MIFUNE GO... 146, 229
MIMI (PANDA KOPANDA)... 189
MIMMY... 128
**MINASE TAKI...** *161*
MINE FUJIKO... 145, 213
MINKY MOMO... 198, 257
MISTY MAY... 186
MITAMURA SHIGE... 162
**MITAMURA YAKKO...** *162*
MITSUHASHI TAKASHI... 072
**MIYU...** *164*
MIYUKI... 236
**MOMOTARO...** *165*
MONONOKE HIME see SAN
MOOMIN... 234
MORIMURA AIKO... 218
MORISATO KEIICHI... 025, 059
MORISAWA YU... 038
MORO... 207
MOROBOSHI ATARU... 046, 225, 244
MOTEUCHI YOTA... 012
**MUGEN & JIN...** *169*
MUSTANG, ROY... 053
MYON... 161
MYUNG FANG LONE... 017

NADIA... 171
NADJA... 090
NAGARE RYOMA... 065
NAKAMURA AYAMO... 013
NAKANISHI RYU... 063
NANDABA NAOTO... 056
**NARUTO...** *175*
**NAUSICAÄ...** *176*
NEKO-MUSUME... 126
NIHIRA SANPEI see SANPEI THE FISHERMAN
NISHI... 161
NOA, BRIGHT... 253
NOBI NOBITA... 050, 213
NO-FACE... 031
**NOHARA SHINOSUKE...** *179*, 076
**NONMURA AMI...** *180*
NONOMURA SHUN... 043
NORSTEIN, THOMAS H. see DIGIMON
NYAKO... 030
NYATTA... 030

O'HARA, SCARLETT... 220
OBABA... 176
OCHANOMIZU, PROFESSOR... 021
OEDO, DR.... 044, 120

OKA HIROMI... *180*
OKAJIMA (FAMILY)...066, 133, 181
OKAJIMA TAEKO...066, 133, *181*
OKIDO, PROF...194
OMOCCHAMA (ROBOT)...254
ONIZUKA EIICHI see GTO: GREAT TEACHER ONIZUKA
ONO ICHIKO...140
OSAKI NANA... *174*
OTONASHI KYOKO...151
OVERFIEND...244

PAGOT, MARCO see PORCO ROSSO
PAPRIKA...132, *190*
PARN...102
PATRASHE (DOG)... *192*
PAZU...141
PERO (ROBOT)...233
PERO (CAT)... *192*, 247
PHOENIX see HI NO TORI
PICCOLO (PORCO ROSSO)...197
PICCOLO (DRAGONBALL)...068, 238
PIKACHU...194
PINMEN... *192*
PINOCCHIO...022
PINOKO...027
POKÉMON... *194*
PONYO...066, 085, *196*, 163, 223
PORCO ROSSO... *197*, 088
PRINCESS KNIGHT... *200*, 232, 241
PRINCESS MONONOKE see SAN

RACER X...146
RAKKA... *199*
RAN (RYU THE CAVE BOY)...099, 203
RAOH (HOKUTO NO KEN)...087
RASCAL... *199*
RAY, AMURO...127
RED, DUKE...187
REGAN, MARIN...198
REI (HOKUTO NO KEN)...087
REMI see REMY
REMY... *199*, 048
RENO...055
RIGER ALEX...043
RIGODON...057
RIQUINNI...168
ROCK...173, 187, 232, 233
ROMY, PRINCESS...057
ROSETTE CHRISTOPHER see CHRISTOPHER, ROSETTE
ROUJIN Z... *203*
RUDE...055

RUFFY see LUFFY, MONKEY D.
RUKIA...009
RYU THE CAVE BOY... *099*, 203
RYUK...122
RYUZAKI REIKA... *180*

SADO, DR. ...044
SAEBA RYO see CITY HUNTER
SAGI TSUKIKO... *204*
SAILOR CHIBI CHIBI MOON...204
SAILOR MOON...095, *204*
SAINT SEIYA... *205*
SAKAKINO LISA...059
SAKURAGI HANAMICHI...072
SALLY (LITTLE WITCH SALLY)... *207*
SAMEJIMA MAMIMI...056
SAN... *207*
SANPEI THE FISHERMAN... *208*
SANYO REIKA...042
SAOTOME RANMA...046, *208*
SAPPHIRE, PRINCESS see PRINCESS KNIGHT
SATO MAKO...096
SAYA... *210*
SAZAE-SAN... *210*
SCOOP, FLASH...209, 229
SCOPEDOG (ROBOT)...032, 226
SEITA & SETSUKO... *211*
SEIYA, PEGASUS see SAINT SEIYA
SEN see CHIHIRO
SENGOKU see SHUNSUKE SENGOKU
SERENITY, PRINCESS see TSUKINO USAGI
SHEETA...141
SHERLOCK HOUND see HOLMES, SHERLOCK
SHEZAR, ALLEN...113
SHIBA HIROSHI...104
SHIDEN, KAI...253
SHIKIBU MURASAKI...065
SHIMA TETSUO...011
SHIMAMURA JOE see CYBORG 009
SHIMURA MICHI...146, 229
SHIN-CHAN see NOHARA SHINNOSUKE
SHION, GRAND POPE...205
SHIRLEY, ANNE, see ANNE OF GREEN GABLES
SHIRO (TEKKONKINKREET) see KURO & SHIRO
SHIRYU, DRAGON...205
SHUN, ANDROMEDA...205
SHUNSUKE SENGOKU...148
SIMON...060, 130
SINDBAD... *216*
SKULD...025
SOSUKE...066, 163, 196, 223
SOUND INSECT...167
SPACE FIREBIRD see HI NO TORI
SPANK (DOG)... *218*
SPARROWHAWK...021
SPEED RACER see MIFUNE GO

SPIEGEL, SPIKE...112, 179, *219*, 222, 246
STEAM, JAMES RAY see STEAMBOY
STEAMBOY... *220*
STINGRAY, SYLIA...128
STRIFE, CLOUD...055
SUGANO SOICHI...059
SUPER SENTAI... *223*
SUNAKAKE-BABA...126
SUPPAMAN...018
SYAORAN see LI SYAORAN

TACHIBANA BEAUTY...042
TAIRA NO MASAKADO...230
TAKAHASHI KEISUKE...096
TAMASHIRO MIWA...215
TANAKA...186
TAKAZAWA KIJURO see ROUJIN Z
TANGE DANPEI...246
TANPEI...013, 136, 234
TANUKI (POMPOKO)...066, 195, 227
TANUKI, DR. ...044
TAROZA...106
TATSUNOKO ASARI...209, 229
TATSUNOKO, DR. ...209, 229
TATSUO NAGUMO...244
TENCHI MUYO see MASAKI TENCHI
TENDO AKANE...046, 115, 208, 224
TENJO UTENA... *230*
TENKAI...106
TENMA TOBIO see ATOM
TENMA, DOCTOR...021
TEPPELIN, NIA...060
TERAI YUKI... *230*
TETSUJIN 28-GO... *231*, 255
TETSUO (AKIRA) see SHIMA TETSUO
TETSUWAN ATOM see ATOM
THERRU...021
THUNDER, NINA ANNA...059
TICO (MOUSE)...057
TIMA...173, *233*
TINK...200, 241
TOKITA, PROF. ...190
TOKYO GODFATHERS... *247*
TOMMY (DEER)...142, 241, 256
TOMOE MUSASHI...065
TONBO...119, 163
TONZULA...254
TOPO GIGIO... *238*
TORAKIKI (CAT)...218
TOSHIO...133, 181
TOTORO... *239*
TOYODA AKIRA...232
TRIXIE see SHIMURA MICHI
TSUBASA OZORA... *240*
TSUDA KOSUKE...111
TSUKINO USAGI see SAILOR MOON
TSUKUDA MIINA... *242*
TUEDO KAMEN/MASK see CHIBA MAMORU
TURNIPHEAD...091, 163
TWAIN, MARK (US AUTHOR)...106

UCHIHA SASUKE...175
UCHU ACE...209
UESUGI, TATSUYA & KAZUYA... *243*
URAN see ASTRO GIRL
URD...025
URSULA...119
UZUMAKI NARUTO see NARUTO

VALENTINE, FAYE...112, 219, 246
VALERIANO...029
VAMPIRE HUNTER D... *245*
VAMPIRE PRINCESS MIYU see MIYU
VASH THE STAMPEDE... *245*

WASHIO KEN...063, 135, 209, 229
WATSON, DOCTOR...075, 088
WHITE, CANDICE... *029*
WITCH OF THE WASTE...091
WOLFMAN...108

XU-XIAN...074

YABUKI JOE...246
YAGAMI LIGHT see KIRA
YAHAGI SHOGO... *248*
YAMADAS... *249*
YANAGAWA MERRILL...148
YASHIMA, MIRAI...253
YATTAMAN... *254*
YAZOO...055
YOSHIMURA SATOMI...023
YUKI TERAI see TERAI YUKI
YURI see KEI & YURI
YUSAKU GODAI...151, 225

ZAMBOT 3 (ROBOT)...237
ZENIBA...031
ZENIGATA, INSPECTOR...097, 145, 213
ZENTRAEDI...147

# BIBLIOGRAPHY

JOHN E. INGULSRUD
READING JAPAN COOL:
PATTERNS OF MANGA
LITERACY AND DISCOURSE
(Lexington Books, 2009)

MIYAZAKI HAYAO
THE ART OF HOWL'S
MOVING CASTLE
(Shogakukan Inc, 2008)

THE ART OF MIYAZAKI'S
SPIRITED AWAY
(Shogakukan Inc, 2008)

THE ART OF MY
NEIGHBOR TOTORO
(Shogakukan Inc, 2010)

THE ART OF PONYO
(Simon & Schuster Inc, 2009)

STARTING POINT
1979-1996
(Shogakukan Inc, 2009)

FRED PATTERN
WATCHING ANIME,
READING MANGA
(Stone Bridge Press, 2004)

PHILIP BROPHY
100 ANIME
(BFI Publishing, 2005)

TEZUKA: THE MARVEL
OF MANGA
(NGV, 2006)

BRIGITTE
KOYAMA-RICHARD
ONE THOUSAND YEARS
OF MANGA
(Flammarion, 2008)

GILLES POITRAS
THE ANIME COMPANION:
WHAT'S JAPANESE IN
JAPANESE ANIMATION?
(Stone Bridge Press, 1998)

THOMAS LAMARRE
ANIME MACHINE: A MEDIA
THEORY OF ANIMATION
(University of Minnesota
Press, 2009)

STEVEN T. BROWN
CINEMA ANIME
(Palgrave Macmillan, 2008)

SIMON RICHMOND
THE ROUGH GUIDE
TO ANIME
(Rough Guides, 2009)

FRENCHY LUNNING
MECHADEMIA VOL I:
EMERGING WORLDS
OF ANIME AND MANGA
(University of Minnesota
Press, 2006)

SUSAN J. NAPIER
ANIME FROM AKIRA
TO HOWL'S MOVING
CASTLE: EXPERIENCING
CONTEMPORARY
JAPANESE ANIMATION
(Palgrave MacMillan, 2006)

SANDRA BUCKLEY
ENCYCLOPEDIA
OF CONTEMPORARY
JAPANESE CULTURE
(Routledge, 2001)

BRIAN RUH
STRAY DOG OF ANIME:
THE FILMS OF
MAMORU OSHII
(Palgrave MacMillan, 2004)

JONATHAN
CLEMENTS &
HELEN MCCARTHY
THE ANIME ENCYCLOPEDIA:
JAPANESE ANIMATION
SINCE 1917
(Stone Bridge Press,
2nd edition, 2006)

HELEN MCCARTHY
500 ESSENTIAL
ANIME MOVIES
(Ilex Press, 2008)

THE ART OF OSAMU
TEZUKA, GOD OF MANGA
(Ilex Press, 2009)

HAYAO MIYAZAKI:
MASTER OF
JAPANESE ANIMATION
(Stone Bridge Press, 1999)

- & JONATHAN
CLEMENTS
THE EROTIC ANIME
MOVIE GUIDE
(Titan, 1998)

COLIN ODELL
& MICHELLE LEBLANC
STUDIO GHIBLI: THE FILMS
OF HAYAO MIYAZAKI
AND ISAO TAKAHATA
(Kamera Books, 2009)

FREDERIK L. SCHODT
MANGA! MANGA!
THE WORLD OF
JAPANESE COMICS
(Kodansha, 1983)

DREAMLAND JAPAN:
WRITINGS ON
MODERN MANGA
(Stone Bridge Press, 1996)

JONATHAN CLEMENTS
SCHOOLGIRL MILKY CRISIS:
ADVENTURES IN THE
ANIME AND MANGA TRADE
(Titan, 2009)

ONODA POWER, NATSU
GOD OF COMICS:
OSAMU TEZUKA AND
THE CREATION OF POST-
WORLD WAR II MANGA
(University of Mississippi Press,
2009)

JOSEPH STEIFF
& TRISTAN D. TAMPLIN
ANIME AND PHILOSOPHY
(Open Court, 2010)

HU TZE-YUE
FRAMES OF ANIME: CULTURE
AND IMAGE-BUILDING
(Hong Kong University Press, 2009)

FREDERIC P. MILLER,
AGNES F. VANDOME
& JOHN MCBREWSTER
STUDIO GHIBLI
(Alphascript Publishing, 2010)

ANDREW OSMOND
SATOSHI KON:
THE ILLUSIONIST
(Stone Bridge Press, 2008)

**TOMOHIRO MACHIYAMA & PATRICK MACIAS**
*CRUISING THE ANIME CITY: AN OTAKU GUIDE TO NEO TOKYO*
(Stone Bridge Press, 2004)

**SUGIMOTO YOSHIO**
*THE CAMBRIDGE COMPANION TO MODERN JAPANESE CULTURE*
(Cambridge University Press, 2009)

**JASON S. YADAO**
*THE ROUGH GUIDE TO MANGA*
(Rough Guides, 2009)

# ONLINE RESOURCES

**ANIDO**

English language website of Japanese professional animation association founded 1967. Fascinating and informative.

http://www.anido.com/index-e.html

**ANIMATED DIVOTS**

Information on anime and world animation, bibliography, good list of links (both current and historic) for further research, maintained by American Richard Llewellyn.

http://www.animated-divots.net

**ANIMATION WORLD NETWORK**

US site with animation information from around the world.

http://www.awn.com

**ANIME JUMP**

US anime site, great historical features, convention reports, reviews. Opinionated, well researched and funny.

http://www.animejump.com

**ANIMINT**

Information-packed French website, frequently updated.

http://www.animint.com

**ANIPAGES DAILY**

An animation news, information and history blog from Benjamin Ettinger. Passionate, well informed and well researched, it puts anime into its context in the world animation scene.

http://www.animejump.com

**ENCICLO'ROBO'PEDIA**

Italian site packed with information on giant-robot anime

http://www.encirobot.com

**TEZUKA IN ENGLISH**

Highly informative, intelligently researched website with detailed information on Osamu Tezuka and lists of works available in translation

http://tezukainenglish.com

# ACKNOWLEDGEMENTS & PICTURE CREDITS

The publishers would like to thank Helen McCarthy for her invaluable advice and editorial assistance and also Jonathan Collis.

All works illustrated are copyright the authors.

© Academy Production, Voyager Entertainment: 252; © AIC, Miyu Production Committee: 115t, 164; © Akira Committee Company Ltd: 11tr, br, 187; © Akira Committee Company Ltd/ Cahiers du Cinéma: 11tl; © Akiyoshi Hongo, Toei Animation: 49; © 1988 Akiyuki Nosaka – Shinchosha/Ronald Grant Archive: 211r; © 1988 Akiyuki Nosaka – Shinchosha/The Kobal Collection: 211tl, bl; © Aoyama Gosho/Shogakukan, Yomiuri TV, UNIVERSAL MUSIC, ShoPro, TMS: 52br; © Aoyama Gosho/Shogakukan, Yomiuri TV, UNIVERSAL MUSIC, ShoPro, Toho, TMS: 52tl, tr; © Aoyama Gosho/Shogakukan, YTV, TMS: 52bl; © Arakawa Hiromu/Square Enix, MBS, Bones, ANX, Dentsu: 28, 53; © Artmic, Tatsunoko, Tokyo Kids: 30; © 1990 Bandai Visual: 43; © Bandai Visual, Bee Train, Yomiko Advertising: 8top; © Bandai Visual, Gainax: 143, 168, 206, 250; © 1987 Bandai Visual/Movic/ Shirow Masamune/Seishinsha: 125bottom; © 1982 Big West, Bandai Visual, 147l; © Big West, Macross Plus Project: 17, 147br, 160r; © 1984 Big West, MBS, Shogakukan, Tatsunoko Production Co.: 147tr; © Bird Studio, Shueisha, Toei Animation: 18bottom, 68br, bl; © Bird Studio, Shueisha, FUNimation Entertainment:238bl; © Bird Studio, Shueisha, FUNimation Entertainment/Ronald Grant Archive:183, 238tr, cr, bc, br; © Buronson, Tetsuo Hara/NSP 1983/© Toei Animation 1984: 87; © Capcom, Sony Music Entertainment, Group TAC: 33bottom; © CLAMP, Kodansha: 35tr, br; © CLAMP/Kodansha/'The Movie Tsubasa Chronicle the Princess in Birdcage Kingdom' Committee: 35tl; © 1998–1999 CLAMP.Kodansha.NHK.NEP: 121; © Daft Life Co. Ltd, Toei Animation/Cahiers du Cinéma: 97top; © Daichi Doga, Fuji TV: 26; © Daicon IV Committee: 041; Destination Films/The Kobal Collection: 236; © Discovery/Mink: 84; © 1989 Eiko Kadono – Nibariki – GN: 119, 163tr; © 2001 Filmlink International/ Hideyuki Kikuchi/Asahi Sonorama/Vampire Hunter D Production Committee: 245; © From Software: 20; © Fujiko Pro, Shogakukan, TV Asahi, Shin-ei Animation, ADK: 50top, 76cl, cr, 213tl, tr, br; © Fujiko Studio, Shogakukan, TMS: 108; © Fujishima Kosuke, Kodansha, Aa Megamisama Production Committee: 25, 59tr, trc, trb; © Fujisawa Tooru, KODANSHA, Fuji TV, SME Visual Works, Studio Pierrot: 72; © FUNimation Entertainment/Toei Animation/Ronald Grant Archive: 68tl; Fuyu no hi (Winter Days): 134; © Gainax/KGI: 56; © Gainax, Nakashima Kazuki, Aniplex, KDE-J, TV Tokyo: 60, 130; © Gainax/Project Eva/TV Tokyo/NAS: 16, 54, 189; © Gainax, Toshiba EMI: 186; © 1983 Gen Production: 64, 148b; © Genius Party/© Genius Party Beyond/© 2004 MIND GAME Project/ Studio 4°C: 8bottom; © Genius Party Beyond/Studio 4°C: 167; © Gonzo, Fuji TV, Gospel Bullet, Kadokawa Shoten, Clockwerx Co., Ltd: 33top; © Gonzo KK, Baku-ten Production Committee: 69bl, br; © 2008 Gonzo, Nitroplus, Blassreiter Project: 100t; © 1990 Group SNE/Kadokawa Shoten Publishing Co. Ltd/Marubeni Corporation/Tokyo Broadcasting System: 102; © 1994 Hatake Jimusho – GNH: 66bl, 195, 227t, c; © Headgear, Emotion, TFC: 92, 191; © Hikari Productions/TMS: 231; © 1999 Hisaishi Ishii, Hatake Jimusho, GNHB/Cahiers du Cinéma: 249; © Hojo Tsukasa/Coamix, TMS: 124; © 1991 Hotaru Okamoto – Yuko Tone – GNH: 66cl, 133, 181; © ICHI Co. Ltd: 217; © Igarashi Yumiko/Mizuki Kyoko/Toei Animation: 29bottom; © Ikeda Riyoko, Shueisha: 94top, 178; © Ikeda Riyoko/TMS: 18top, 48br, 103; © Ishii Katsuhito, Aoi Promotion, Grasshoppa: 98; © Ishimori Production Inc., Toei Animation: 40, 99, 203, 235t; © Izumi Todo, Kodansha/© Toei Animation: 90; © Kaiji Kawaguchi/Kodansha.Sunrise: 109; © Kajiwara Ikki/Tsuji Naoko/Kodansha, Toei Animation: 45, 110; © Kakinouchi Narumi, Akita Shoten, AIC: 83; © Kaoru Tada/Minato Production, Toei Animation: 162; © 2004 Katsuhiro Otomo, Mash Room/Steamboy Committee: 220; © Katsura Masakazu/ Shueisha, I & G Tatsunoko, Production I.G.: 12, 71; © Kogure Masao/Summer Days with Coo Committee: 76 br; © Kosuke Fujishima.ExD.Bandai Visual/D.G.A.: 59tl, bl, tc, tcc, tcb; © Kuri Yoji: 136; © Kurumada Masami, Shueisha, Toei Animation: 82bottom, 205; © 2003 Kyoto Animation: 140; © Leiji Matsumoto, Toei Animation: 44, 77, 114tc, 120, 131, 150, 154, 201cr, b, 235b; © Madhouse, Inc.: 106, 107; © 2006 Madhouse, Inc. and Sony Pictures Entertainment (Japan) Inc./Cahiers du Cinéma: 132tl, bl, br, 190; © 1997 Madhouse Inc., © Rex Entertainment Co., Ltd.: 132tr; © 1997 Madhouse Inc., © Rex Entertainment Co., Ltd/Cahiers du Cinéma: 122bottom tr; © 1997 Madhouse Inc., © Rex Entertainment Co., Ltd/F.K.G.B./La Cinémathèque française: 169; © 1997 Madhouse Inc., © Rex Entertainment Co. Ltd/Ronald Grant Archive: 122bottom tl, br; © 1990, 1991 Madhouse/Japan Home Video: 148t; © 1999 Mamoru Oshii/Bandai Visual, Production I.G.: 92crb, 105, 184; © 2002 Masashi Kishimoto/Pierrot: 175; © 1995 Mash Room/Memories Project: 159; © 2006 Matsumoto Taiyo/Shogakukan, Aniplex, Asmik Ace, Beyond C, Dentsu, TOKYO MX/Cahiers du Cinéma: 137; © Mikimoto Haruhiko/Sotsu.Sunrise: 160l; © 2004 MIND GAME Project/Studio 4°C: 161; © Miura Kentaro, Hakusensha, NTV, VAP: 73bottom; © Monkey Punch, TMS: 48tl, tr, 97, 145, 213cl, bl; © Mushi Production: 24, 221top, 251l;